Chil

Writers' & Artists'
YEARBOOK
2005

Reprinted 2004

37 Soho Square, London W1D 3QZ
www.acblack.com

A&C Black uses paper produced with elemental chlorine-free pulp, harvested from managed sustainable forests.

A CIP catalogue record for this book is available from the British Library.

ISBN 0-7136-6903-9

Printed in Great Britain by
William Clowes Ltd, Beccles, Suffolk

Children's Writers' & Artists' YEARBOOK 2005

First Edition

A directory for children's writers and artists containing children's media contacts and practical advice and information

A & C Black · London

Contents

Theatre

Listings

Resources for children's writers

Listings

Societies, prizes and festivals

Listings

Finance for writers and artists

Foreword

Michael Morpurgo is the Children's Laureate for 2003–2005 and has written more than 100 books for children. His many books include *The Butterfly Lion*, *The Wreck of the Zanzibar* and *Why the Whales Came*, which has been adapted to film. He has won numerous awards worldwide including the Whitbread Children's Book of the Year and the Nestlé Smarties Book Prize. His latest novel is *Private Peaceful*.

I've been very lucky. Whilst many struggle to publish their first book, I sent off my first short story and, joy of joys, a publisher said they liked it! They even said they wanted four more! But I had a head start. Let me explain.

I was teaching in a primary school at the time. At the end of each school day I would always read a book to my class of 10 and 11 year-olds. I tried very hard to find books that would resonate for all of them, but was not always successful in this. I found myself one day reading the first chapters of a book I was hopeful would go down well. It didn't. There was that dreaded crescendo of shuffling and whispering and yawning. I persisted but it didn't get any better. I returned home in despair.

To cheer me up, I think, my wife Clare said that maybe next time I should tell them a story of my own, make one up. I'd done this a bit, as most parents do, when our children were very young. 'You were good at it,' she said. Thus fortified, I lay awake all night weaving a tale in my head. Then at 3 o'clock the next day I stood up and declared to my class that we were abandoning the book. Instead I would tell them a story of my own. This was not greeted with overwhelming enthusiasm, I have to say. But I steeled my nerves and launched wholeheartedly into my story. The shuffling stopped. The whispering stopped. No one yawned. I could do this! I could do it!

The trouble was I didn't know quite how to end my story – I still have that problem – so I postponed the ending, and turned my story into a soap, timing it as best I could so that the tension of my tale was at its peak just before the bell went. 'More tomorrow,' I'd say. 'Oh, sir,' they'd moan. I loved that.

A teacher friend got to hear of this – the children had told him about Mr Morpurgo's fantastic story. He said he knew someone who worked as an editor at an educational publishing company, that he happened to know they were looking for short stories for a new series, and that I should write one of my stories out and send it off. So I did, and heigh-ho, I became a professional writer.

As I said, I've been very lucky. I had my fair share of rejection slips later of course. (I think I prefer the disparaging one to the polite ones.) But at least I had that initial acceptance, that acknowledgement that I could do it, which buoyed me up through the difficult years, during which three subsequent novels could find no publisher, and sales and reviews of some others were less than encouraging. There was no *Children's Writers' & Artists' Yearbook* to turn to then. The truth was of course that with every book I was learning my craft, developing technique, and daring to take new risks. I was growing up as a writer, finding my voice. I had other luck too. Aidan Chambers, that legendary editor, wrote me a letter, just a paragraph of which was enough to convince me that an editor who I greatly respected thought I'd written something special. Then later, when my novel *War Horse* just failed to win the Whitbread Prize (I'm good at that), my neighbour and great mentor Ted Hughes took me out for a day, to cheer me up. He told me as we sipped tea in Bideford that I had written a fine book, and then he added: 'What's more important is that you'll write a finer one.' Oh lucky man, oh lucky writer.

After 30 years as a writer and after publishing 100 books (a significant figure to a cricket player who never managed it where it mattered – on the pitch) I've now been given the wonderful opportunity as the Children's Laureate, to encourage others, young and old, to enjoy the best of children's literature. Part of what I do, of what many children's authors do, is to enthuse and enable others to write themselves. Each of us has, of course, a different approach, but I have come to certain general conclusions about my creative process. It cannot be corralled or forced. It cannot be driven by fear of failure. My stories come about organically, from the world I see and have seen around me, from people I meet, places I go, feelings I have. I record. I try each day to write a few lines about some event of the day, an abandoned moustache on a pavement in York, a crushed badger in a ditch, skipping along the lane with my granddaughter. I write only about what I know and care about passionately. I learnt a long time ago, that first the story needs time to be woven in my head – I call it dreamtime. Dreams cannot be rushed. But the moment comes when the dreaming and/or the procrastination has to end, and I have to face the blank page. Then I tell it down, speak it on to the page, letting the story find its voice. More often than not I don't know how my story will end. I try to trust the story, to trust characters to make their own end. I try to stay out of it.

I was talking to a group of schoolchildren the other day. One boy asked me: 'Do your stories come from your emotions, or from your head?' I had to think long and hard. 'From both,' I replied, 'but one after the other. The emotion, the passion drives the story, infuses the characters, sets them on their path, but I then use my head. But not too much. It is a balance.'

The truth is we are all lucky in this world of children's literature. We are doing something we love, otherwise we wouldn't do it. If we are lucky we can even earn a bit of a living from it. Best of all, we can enrich children's lives at the same time. Any book I write, any book you write, may be a catalyst for a child, may turn him into a reader, may turn her into a writer. That's supreme (a recently acquired favourite word of mine), just supreme.

Michael Morpurgo, Children's Laureate
February 2004

Books

Getting started

You just have! By buying or borrowing the *Children's Writers' & Artists' Yearbook* you have taken the first step towards a potential new career in the field of children's publishing. Alison Stanley gives the benefit of her experience for success in this expanding market.

Whether you want to write for magazines, television, write or illustrate books, adapt for radio, get published in the UK or overseas, find an agent, illustrate greetings' cards, attend a festival, course or conference, or surf the children's literature websites, you will find the information on how to do it in this *Yearbook*.

But to help you on your way, here are 10 top tips:

1. Read, read, read

- Read as many children's books as you can – picture books, young fiction, novels, teen reads, non-fiction, the classics, the prize-winners – and find out just what is being published... and what children like to read.
- Look at children's magazines and newspaper supplements as they will give you ideas about current trends.
- Read reviews in national newspapers, read children's literary magazines such as *Books for Keeps* and *Carousel* (see *Magazines about children's literature and education* on page 212).

2. Get out and about

- Visit your local bookshop and browse in the children's section.
- Go to your library and talk to the children's librarian. Children's books are read by children but usually bought by adults – so find out what parents, teachers, librarians and other professionals are recommending for young people.
- If you have children, don't just go by what they are reading, ask their friends too – children have wide reading tastes, just like adults. Ask permission to sit in on their school 'storytime' (or a literacy hour or a guided reading session if educational publishing is what you are interested in).
- Go to a festival! There are many literature festivals held throughout the year and most have children's literary events. All children's literature festivals will have a sprinkling of new and well-known authors and illustrators in attendance, and most authors and illustrators will be accompanied by a representative from their publishing company. So you can see and hear the author/illustrator and even do a bit of networking with the publisher! You will also be guaranteed some fun. Festivals are also a useful way of seeing children's reactions to their favourite authors and books in an informal situation.

3. Watch... and listen

- Familiarise yourself with the children's media: watch children's television and listen to children's radio programmes (see the *Television, film and radio* section beginning on page 217), and check out the websites listed throughout the *Yearbook*. Look at children's character merchandising and greetings cards.

4. Network

- Being an author or illustrator can be a lonely business – don't work in a vacuum. Talk to others of your discipline at festivals, conferences and book groups. Join the Federation of Children's Book Groups (see page 260) where you can network to your heart's content. Find out if there are any writer/illustrator groups in your area. If you are already published, join the Scattered Authors Society (see page 273).

5. Never underestimate the job in hand

- Writing and illustrating for children is not an easy option. Many people think they can dash off a children's story and a few sketchy illustrations and that they will be good enough to publish. But, if you have researched the marketplace you will realise that it is a hugely competitive area and you have to be talented, have something original to say, have an unique style... and know how to persevere in order to get your work published and out to a wider audience.

6. Use your experiences

- Having your own children, or working in a child-related profession is helpful, but shouldn't be relied on to bring you a new career as a children's writer or illustrator. (Never use this line when submitting a manuscript: 'I wrote this story for my children and they enjoyed it so please will you publish it?' Any story you write for your own children, grandchildren, nieces, nephews, etc is likely to be enjoyed by them because children love attention.) Publishers will only want to take on something that has appeal for a wide range of children – both nationally and internationally – never forget that publishing is a business. However, do use your experiences in terms of ideas, especially the more unusual ones, like seeing your first alien fall from the sky!

7. Research catalogues and websites

- Look at publishers' catalogues and websites, not just to find out what they are publishing, but because many of them give guidance for new writers and illustrators. When submitting a manuscript or portfolio to a publisher, it is a good idea to let them know that you know (and admire!) what they already publish. You can then make your case about where your submission will fit in their list. Let them know that you mean business and have researched the marketplace.

8. Submit your material with care

- First decide whether to approach an agent or to go it alone and submit your material direct to a publisher (see *How to get an agent* on page 121, *Do you have to have an agent to succeed?* on page 125 and *Publishing agreements* on page 165 for the pros and cons of each approach.) Check that the agent or publisher you are thinking of approaching accepts (a) unsolicited material, and (b) is interested in the type of work you are doing. For example, don't send your potential prize-winning novel to an educational publisher, and don't send your ideas for a Guided Reading Series at Key Stage 1 to a 'trade' publisher without an educational list. And don't send your illustrations for a children's picture book to an agent who only deals with teenage fiction – there will be zero interest from them and you will be very disappointed.

- Submit your work to the right publisher/agent and the right person within the company. Ring first to find out who the best person for your work might be, whether it be in a publishing company, an agency, a television production company or a children's magazine. Also ask whether they want a synopsis and sample chapters or the complete manuscript or, for artwork, a selection of illustrations or your whole portfolio.
- Presentation is important. For example, no editor will read a handwritten manuscript. It should be typed/word processed, using double spacing with each page clearly numbered. (Should an editor be interested in your work, it will be photocopied for all involved in the acquisition process to read. Photocopiers have a habit of chewing up pages and there's nothing worse than pages being missing at a crucial part of a novel.) If your manuscript is accepted for publication, the editor will want the text electronically.
- For illustrations, select work on a paper that can be easily photocopied – a white/cream background with no unusual textures for your first pitch (such as sandpaper or glass – yes it really has happened!) And remember, publishers' photocopiers are notoriously bad at reproducing colour accurately, so if you are relying on the vibrancy of your colour to wow an art director, bear in mind that by the time they have been photocopied a few times for interested parties to see, the colours will not be the same. If your artwork is computer generated, send hard copies with your disk – it saves time when being shown around.

9. Identify your USP

- Ask yourself what the unique selling point of the material you are submitting for publication is. You may have an original authorial 'voice', you may have a particularly innovative illustration style or technique, or you may have come up with an amazingly brilliant idea for a series. If, after checking out the marketplace, you think you have something truly original to offer, then believe in yourself and be convincing when you offer it for publication.

10. Don't give up!

- Editors receive hundreds of manuscripts, and art directors receive hundreds of illustration samples every day. For a publisher, there are many factors that have to be taken into consideration when evaluating these submissions, the most important of which is 'Can we publish it successfully?' – i.e. 'Will it sell?' Publishing is a big business and it is ever more competitive. Even after an editor or art director has seen and liked your work, there are many other people involved before something is acquired for publication: the marketing manager, the publicist, the rights director, the book club manager, the sales director and, of course, the financial director. You will find this mantra repeated again and again in many of the articles in this book: *Have patience, keep at it*. If you believe in your 'product' eventually someone else will too. And meanwhile, keep perfecting your craft. After all, you are doing it because you enjoy it, aren't you?

Alison Stanley has been a senior commissioning editor of children's fiction at Puffin Books and at HarperCollins Children's Books. She is now selling her USP as a freelance.

See also...

- *A word from J.K. Rowling*, page 67
- *Spotting talent*, page 68
- *Out of the slush pile*, page 72
- *Fiction for 6–9 year-olds*, page 79
- *Writing humour for young children*, page 82
- *Teenage fiction*, page 85
- *What does an editor do?* page 88
- *The amazing picture book story*, page 145

Children's book publishers UK and Ireland

*Member of the Publishers Association or Scottish Publishers Association
†Member of the Irish Book Publishers' Association

Abbey Home Media

435–7 Edgware Road, London W2 1TH
tel 020-7563 3910 *fax* 020-7563 3911
email info@abbeyhomemedia.com
Managing Director James Harding

Activity books, board books, novelty books, picture books, non-fiction, reference books, audiotapes and CDs. Advocates learning through interactive play. Age groups: preschool, 5–10.

Academy of Light Ltd

Unit Ic, Delta Centre, Mount Pleasant, Wembly, Middlesex HA0 1UX
tel 020-8795 2695 *fax* 020-8903 3748
email yubraj@academyoflight.co.uk
website www.academyoflight.co.uk
Managing Director & Chief Editor Dr Yubraj Sharma, *Marketing & Financial Director* Mrs Mita Shah

Spirituality and alternative medicine; children's. Founded 2000.

Allegra Publishing Ltd

122 Trade Tower Plantation Wharf, London SW11 3UF
tel 020-7228 9502 *fax* 020-7228 9511
email info@allegrapublishing.com
website www.allegrapublishing.com
Publisher Felicia Law

Specialises in creating bright and innovative, frequently character-led, children's learning projects which often contain extended add-ons, such as audios, videos, toys and learning tools and games. Board books, novelty books, picture books, pop-up books, how-to books, art, reference books, ELT, science, tapes and CDs. Age groups: preschool, 5–10. Founded 2002.

Andersen Press Ltd*

20 Vauxhall Bridge Road, London SW1V 2SA
tel 020-7840 8703 (editorial) *fax* 020-7233 6263
email andersenpress@randomhouse.co.uk
website www.andersenpress.co.uk
Managing Director/Publisher Klaus Flugge, *Directors* Philip Durrance, Joëlle Flugge (company secretary), Janice Thomson (editorial)

Picture books, and junior (*Tigers* series) and teenage fiction. Recent successes include the *Elmer* series by David McKee an *Doing it* by Melvin Burgess. Other authors include Anne Fine, Michael Foreman, Tony Ross and Jeanne Willis. Illustrators include Ralph Steadman and Max Velthuijs, winner of the the 2004 Hans Christian Andersen Award for Illustration for his *Frog* series.

Submission details For novels, send 3 sample chapters, a synopsis and return postage. Juvenile fiction should be 3000–5000 words long, and older fiction about 15,000–30,000 words. The text for picture books should be under 2000 words long. No poetry or short stories. Do not send MSS via email.

Andromeda Children's Books – see Pinwheel Ltd

Anglia Young Books

148 High Street, Chesterton, Cambridge CB4 1NW
email info@millpublishing.co.uk
websites www.angliayoungbooks.co.uk, www.millpublishing.co.uk
Educational publisher. Historical fiction for use in the KS2 classroom. Also publishes cross-curricular material; the *Write into History* series delivers grammar in the context of historical stories and *Crosslinks* focuses on reading, writing and thinking across the curriculum.Welcomes suggestions from teachers for new resources. Authors and illustrators should send a brief synopsis of their intended title or portfolio. Imprint of Mill Publishing.

Anvil Books/The Children's Press†

45 Palmerston Road, Dublin 6, Republic of Ireland
tel (01) 4973628 *fax* (01) 4968263
Directors Rena Dardis (managing), Margaret Dardis (editorial)

Children's Press: adventure, fiction, ages 9–14. Anvil: Irish history and biography. Only considers MSS by Irish-based authors and of Irish interest. Send synopsis with IRCs (no UK stamps); unsolicited MSS not returned. Founded 1964.

Atlantic Europe Publishing Co. Ltd

Greys Court Farm, Greys Court, Henley-on-Thames, Oxon RG9 4PG
tel (01491) 628188 *fax* (01491) 628189
email info@atlanticeurope.com
Directors Dr B.J. Knapp, D.L.R. McCrae

Educational: children's colour illustrated information books, co-editions and primary school class books covering science, geography, technology, mathematics, history, religious education. Recent successes include the *Curriculum Visions* series and *Science at School* series. Founded 1990.

Submission details Submit via email to authors@atlanticeurope.com with no attachments. No MSS accepted by post. Established teacher authors only.

Autumn Publishing

Appledram Barns, Birdham Road, Chichester, West Sussex PO20 7EQ
tel (01243) 531660 *fax* (01243) 774433
email autumn@autumpublishing.co.uk
website www.autumpublishing.co.uk

Autumn Publishing's philosophy is that children should enjoy learning with its books. Byeway Books is the imprint for all titles. Founded 1976.

Byeway Books (imprint)

Activity books, novelty books and picture books to enable children to learn whilst they play. Also lift-the-flap board books, sticker books, wall charts, colouring books and colourful flash cards designed to help young children have fun while learning the alphabet and counting. Publishes approx. 200 titles each year and has 600 in print. Recent successes include *Help with Homework* range, wall chart range and *Practice Makes Perfect* range.

Submission details No responsibility is accepted for the return of unsolicited MSS.

Award Publications Ltd

1st Floor, 27 Longford Street, London NW1 3DZ
tel 020-7388 7800 *fax* 020-7388 7887
Managing Director Ron Wilkinson

Children's books: full colour picture story books; early learning, information and activity books. No unsolicited material. Founded 1954.

Barefoot Books Ltd

124 Walcot Street, Bath BA1 5BG
tel (01225) 322400 *fax* (01225) 322499
email info@barefootbooks.co.uk
website www.barefootbooks.co.uk
Publisher Tessa Strickland

Children's picture books and audiobooks: myth, legend, fairytale. No unsolicited MSS. Founded 1993.

Barn Owl Books

157 Fortis Green Road, London N10 3LX
email ann.jungmann@pop3.poptel.org.uk
websites barnowlbooks.com, www.franceslincoln.co.uk
Contact Ann Jungman

Specialises in publishing out-of-print children's books from the recent past by authors such as Jacqueline Wilson, Michael Rosen, Joan Aiken, Margaret Mahy, Jeremy Strong, Ann Jungman and illustrator Quentin Blake. Reprints only: no new submissions.

Barrington Stoke*

Sandeman House, Trunk's Close, 55 High Street, Edinburgh EH1 1SR
tel 0131-557 2020 *fax* 0131-557 6060
email anna.gibbons@barringtonstoke.co.uk
website www.barringtonstoke.co.uk
Managing Director Sonia Raphael, *Editorial Manager* Anna Gibbons

Fiction for reluctant readers aged 9–12 and teenage. Publishes approx. 30 titles a year and has over 100 books in print. Recent successes include *Wartman* by Michael Morpurgo, *Living with Vampires* by Jeremy Strong and *Dream On* by Bali Rai.

Submission details No unsolicited MSS. All work is commissioned from well-known authors and adapted for reluctant readers. Founded 1998.

BBC Audiobooks Ltd*

St James House, The Square, Lower Bristol Road, Bath BA2 3BH
tel (01225) 878000 *fax* (01225) 310777
website www.bbcaudiobooks.com
Directors Paul Dempsey (managing), Jan Paterson (publishing), Rachel Stammers (marketing)

Large print books and complete and unabridged audiobooks. Does not publish original books. Children's imprint: Galaxy Children's Large Print. Recent successes include *Midnight* by Jacqueline Wilson, *Artemis Fowl: The Eternity Code* by Eoin Colfer and *Shadowmancer* by G.P. Taylor – all published in audio and large print. Formed in 2002 from the amalgamation of Chivers Press, Cover To Cover and BBC Radio Collection.

BBC Children's Books*

80 Strand, London WC2R 0RL
tel 020-7010 3000 *fax* 020-7010 6060
website www.penguin.co.uk
Directors Sally Floyer (publishing), Mark Young David King, Peter Bowron, Brian Landers, Anthony Forbes Watson (Chairman)

Penguin Books and BBC Worldwide have formed a new global publishing venture. A new company has been formed that will publish 60–80 titles a year under the imprint of BBC Children's Books; this will sit alongside Penguin's existing children's publishing portfolio, which includes *Spot, Peter Rabbit, Ladybird Books* and *Puffin*.

With BBC Worldwide the new company will develop publishing franchises supporting new BBC properties for the global market and explore further publishing opportunities within the extensive BBC children's archive. BBC Worldwide will transfer its existing Children's Books business to the new company, which will be co-owned by Penguin and BBC Worldwide. Division of Penguin Group (UK).

BBC Children's Learning*

White City, 201 Wood Lane, London W12 7ST
tel 020-8433 1676 *fax* 020-8433 1697
websites www.bbcworldwide.com, www.bbcschoolshop.com
email alison.smith@bbc.co.uk
Head of Publishing Susan Ross, *Publishing Director of Children's Books* Sue Tarsky

Educational and textbooks, resources for teachers; electronic, audio and video, CD-Roms and DVDs, activity books, board books, novelty books, painting and colouring books, pop-up books. Publishes for preschool–15+.

Belair – see Folens Publishers

Bite – see Hodder Headline Ltd

A & C Black Publishers Ltd*

37 Soho Square, London W1D 3QZ
tel 020-7758 0200 *fax* 020-7758 0222
email enquiries@acblack.com
website www.acblack.com
Chairman Nigel Newton, *Managing Director* Jill Coleman, *Directors* Colin Adams, Charles Black, Sarah Fecher (children's books), Oscar Heini (production), Paul Langridge (rights), Janet Murphy (Adlard Coles Nautical), Kathy Rooney, Terry Rouelett (distribution), David Wightman (sales), Jonathan Glasspool (reference)

Children's and educational books (including music); ceramics, art and craft, drama, ornithology, reference (*Who's Who, Whitaker's Almanack*), sport, theatre, books for writers. Subsidiary of Bloomsbury Publishing plc. Founded 1807.

A & C Black/Andrew Brodie Publications (imprints)

Director Sarah Fecher, *Commissioning Editors* Mary-Jane Wilkins (non-fiction), David Norris (educational resources)

Fiction for 5–8 and 9–12 year-olds, series fiction, reference, plays, poetry. A & C Black publishes approx. 50 titles each year. Andrew Brodie Publications are a range of educational books for primary and secondary schools and about 20 titles are published each year.

Recent fiction successes include, for 5–8 year-olds: *Duncan & the Pirates* by Peter Utton in the *Chameleons* series; fiction for 7–9 year-olds: *Live the Dream!* by Jenny Oldfield in the *White Wolves* series; fiction for 8–11 year-olds: *Bryony Bell Tops the Bill* by Frankeska G. Ewart in the *Black Cat* series. Recent non-fiction successes include *Science Works* by Jacqui Bailey and Matthew Lilly, *Real Lives* by Sallie Purkis and *Going Up* by Jen Alexander. Recent education successes include *Developing Science* by Christine Moorcroft, *Best Handwriting* by Andrew Brodie and *Foundations Activity Packs.*

Submission details For fiction please enquire about current guidelines before submitting work as the content of each seasonal list varies. Allow 6–8 weeks for a response. No submissions by email. Look at recently published titles and in catalogues to gauge a feel of current publishing interests. Much of the fiction list has been commissioned to appeal to the educational market and to be part of large series, but increasingly fiction books are being presented to appeal to the trade as standalone titles. For education books the focus is on materials related to the National Curriculum.

Blackstaff Press Ltd†

4C Heron Wharf, Sydenham Business Park, Belfast BT3 9LE
tel 028-9045 5006 *fax* 028-9046 6237
email info@blackstaffpress.com
website www.blackstaffpress.com
Managing Editor Patsy Horton

Educational books for primary school children. Also adult fiction, poetry, biography, history, sport, politics, natural history, humour. Founded 1971.

Blackwater Press – see Folens Publishers

Bloomsbury Publishing Plc*

38 Soho Square, London W1D 3HB
tel 020-7494 2111 *fax* 020-7434 0151
website www.bloomsburymagazine.com
Chairman and Chief Executive Nigel Newton, *Directors* Liz Calder (publishing), Alexandra Pringle (publishing), Kathleen Farrar (international), Karen Rinaldi (Bloomsbury USA), Kathy Rooney (reference), David Ward (sales), Minna Fry (marketing), Katie Collins (publicity), Ruth Logan (rights), Penny Edwards (production), Arzu Tahsin (paperbacks), Sarah Odedina (children's), Colin Adams (finance), Will Webb (design), Jill Coleman

Fiction, biography, illustrated, reference, travel, children's, trade paperbacks and mass market paperbacks. Founded 1986.

Bloomsbury Children's Books (imprint)

website www.bloomsbury.com
Ceo Nigel Newton, *Publishing Director* Sarah Odedina, *Commissioning Editors* Ele Fountain, Emma Matthewson

Novelty books, picture books, fiction for ages 5–8 and 9–12, teenage fiction, series fiction and poetry. Publishes approx. 60 titles a year and has over 500 books in print. Recent publications include the *Harry Potter* series by J.K. Rowling, *Pirates!* by Celia Rees and *Mole and the Baby Bird* by Marjorie Newman and Patrick Benson.

Submission details Send a synopsis of the book together with 3 chapters. No unsolicited MSS.

Overseas branches Bloomsbury USA (New York) and Bloomsbury Verlag (Berlin). Founded 1995.

Bookmart Ltd

Blaby Road, Wigston, Leicester LE18 4SE
tel 0116-275 9060 *fax* 0116-275 9090
email books@bookmart.co.uk
website www.bookmart.co.uk
Publishing Director Linda Williams

Colour illustrated titles: children's fiction and non-fiction, poetry, novelty books, pop-up books, activity books. Age groups: preschool, 5–10, 10–15.

Boxer Books Ltd

63 Holywell Hill, St Albans,
Herts. AL1 1HF
tel (01727) 765321
email david@boxerbooks.com
website www.boxerbooks.com
Creative Director David Bennett

Innovative books for babies and toddlers: board books, novelty books, picture books. Age groups: preschool, 5–10.

Brilliant Publications*

1 Church View, Sparrow Hall Farm, Edlesborough, Dunstable LU6 2ES
tel (01525) 229720 *fax* (01525) 229725
email editorial@brilliantpublications.co.uk
website www.brilliantpublications.co.uk
Managing Director Priscilla Hannaford

Resource books for teachers and others concerned with the education of 0–13 year-olds. All areas of the curriculum published. Study catalogue or visit website before sending proposal. Founded 1993.

Brimax – see Autumn Publishing

British Museum Company Ltd*

46 Bloomsbury Street, London WC1B 3QQ
tel 020-7323 1234 *fax* 020-7436 7315
website www.britishmuseumcompany.co.uk
Director of Publishing Alasdair Macleod, *Senior Commissioning Editor* Carolyn Jones

The world's leading museum publisher, with a growing children's list encompassing authoritative illustrated reference and information titles as well as a range of activity and colouring books. Founded 1973.

b small publishing

Pinewood, 3A Coombe Ridings,
Kingston upon Thames, Surrey KT2 7JT
tel 020-8974 6851 *fax* 020-8974 6845
email info@bsmall.co.uk
Publisher Catherine Bruzzone

Activity books and foreign language learning books for 2–12 year-olds. Founded 1990.

Buster Books – see Michael O'Mara Books Ltd

Cambridge University Press*

The Edinburgh Building, Shaftesbury Road, Cambridge CB2 2RU
tel (01223) 325892 *fax* (01223) 325891 (UK and Ireland), *tel* (01223) 312393 *fax* (01223) 315052 (for Continental Europe, Middle East, North Africa & South Asia)
email information@cambridge.org
website www.cambridge.org
Chief Executive of the Press Stephen R.R. Bourne, *Publishing Division Directors* Andrew Brown (Adademic), Andrew Gilfillan (Educational), Colin Hayes (ELT), Conrad Guettler (Journals), Michael Holdsworth (Business), Ian Brodie (Distribution), James Berry (Financial), Nicholas Reckert (International)

For children: curriculum-based education books and software for schools and colleges (primary, secondary and international). Part of the National Grid for Learning. English language teaching for adult and younger learners.

For adults: anthropology and archaeology, art and architecture, astronomy, biological sciences, classical studies, computer science, dictionaries, earth sciences, economics, e-learning products, engineering, film, English language teaching, history, language and literature, law, mathematics, medical sciences, music, philosophy, physical sciences, politics, psychology, reference, technology, social sciences, theology, religion. Journals. The Bible and Prayer Book. Founded 1534.

Campbell Books – see Macmillan Publishers Ltd

Caterpillar Books – see Magi Publications

CGP

Coordination Group Publications,
Kirkby-in-Furness, Cumbria LA17 7WZ
(0870) 7501282 (0870) 7501292
email info@cgpbooks.co.uk
website cgpbooks.co.uk

Educational books centred around the National Curriculum, including revision guides and study books for GCSE, KS3, KS2, KS1 and A level. Subjects include ICT, maths, history, English, science, geography, psychology, business studies, religious studies, child development, design and techology, PE, music, French, German and Spanish.

Submission details Looking for talented teachers to help write new material for A2 Psychology, A2 Sociology and AS/A2Business Studies. Also looking for teachers of Applied ICT. Send an email to caroline.hornby@cgpbooks.co.uk or phone (01229) 715714.

Also on the lookout for top teachers at all levels in all subjects. Potential authors should send an email with their name, subject area and level, plus contact address, ready for when a project comes up in their subject area.

Paul Chapman Publishing Ltd

1 Oliver's Yard, 55 City Road, London EC1Y ISP
tel 020-7324 8500 *fax* 020-7324 8600
website www.paulchapmanpublishing.co.uk
Consultant P.R. Chapman, *Commissioning Editor* Marianne Lagrange

Education. Subsidiary of SAGE Publications Ltd.

The Chicken House*

2 Palmer Street, Frome, Somerset BA11 1DS
tel (01373) 454488 *fax* (01373) 454499
email chickenhouse@doublecluck.com
website www.doublecluck.com
Managing Director & Publisher Barry Cunningham, *Deputy Managing Director* Rachel Hickman, *Publishing Director* David Riley, *Creative Director* Elinor Bagenal

Novelty books, picture books, fiction for ages 5–8 and 9–11 and teenage fiction. Publishes approx. 25 titles a year. Recent successes include *Lucas* by Kevin Brooks, *Inkheart* by Cornelia Funke and *The Sheep Fairy* by David Sym and Ruth Louie Symes.

Submission details Will consider unsolicited MSS. Send synopsis and 2–3 sample chapters. Allow 6–8 weeks for response.

Child's Play (International) Ltd

Ashworth Road, Bridgemead, Swindon, Wilts. SN5 7YD
tel (01793) 616286 *fax* (01793) 512795
email allday@childs-play.com
website www.childs-play.com
Chairman Adriana Twinn, *Publisher* Neil Burden

Children's educational books: board, picture, activity and play books; fiction and non-fiction. Founded 1972.

Chivers Press

St James House, The Square, Windsor Bridge Road, Bath BA2 3AX
tel (01225) 335336 *fax* (01225) 310771
email christine@chivers.co.uk
website www.chivers.co.uk
Publishing Director Jan Paterson, *Contact* Christine Graham

One of the most prolific publishers of large print books and unabridged audiobooks in the world. Has over 3000 titles, encompassing a wide range of bestselling authors and catering for all tastes, including children's titles (*Galaxy Large Print* series). Imprint of BBC Audiobooks Ltd. Founded 1979.

Christian Education

1020 Bristol Road, Selly Oak, Birmingham B29 6LB
tel 0121-472 4242 *fax* 0121-472 7575
email enquiries@christianeducation.org.uk
website www.christianeducation.org.uk

Publications and services for teachers of RE including *RE today* magazine, curriculum booklets, training material for children and youth workers in the Church. Worship resources for use in primary schools. Christian drama and musicals, Activity Club material and Bible reading resources.

Chrysalis Children's Books

The Chrysalis Building, Bramley Road, London W10 6SP
tel 020-7221 2213 *fax* 020-7314 1598
email childrens@chrysalisbooks.co.uk
website www.chrysalisbooks.co.uk
Publisher Sarah Fabiny, *Editorial Manager, Education* Joyce Bentley, *Editorial Manager, Fiction and Preschool* Liz Flanagan, *Editorial Director, Trade Non-fiction* Honor Head

Titles range from illustrated educational books covering all areas of the curriculum to reference and information books for the home and school. Lively information and story books for the under 5 age group; lavishly illustrated, high-quality picture books for older children; educational guides for parents; interactive non-fiction and novelty books. Publishes approx. 300 titles each year and has 1200 in print. Recent successes include *Adventures in Literacy, Fairy Tales and Fantastic Stories* and *The Story of the Little Mole Who Knew it was None of His Business*. Imprints: Belitha Press, Big Fish, David Bennett Books, Learning World, Pavilion Children's Books, Zig Zag.

Submission details Will not consider unsolicited MSS. Submit MSS via an agent. Founded 2003.

Claire Publications

Unit 8, Tey Brook Craft Centre, Great Tey, Colchester, Essex CO6 1JE
tel (01206) 211020 *fax* (01206) 212755
email mail@clairepublications.com
website www.clairepublications.com
Educational publisher of mathematics materials for primary and secondary schools. Also literacy and language materials, including games, puzzles and photocopiable teachers' resources. Supplies training workshops.

James Clarke & Co. Ltd*

PO Box 60, Cambridge CB1 2NT
tel (01223) 350865 *fax* (01223) 366951
email publishing@lutterworth.com
website www.lutterworth.com
Managing Director Adrian Brink

Theology, academic, reference books. Founded 1859.

Lutterworth Press (subsidiary)
The arts, biography, children's books (fiction, non-fiction, picture, rewards), educational, environmental, general, history, leisure, philosophy, science, sociology, theology and religion.

Patrick Hardy Books (imprint)
Children's fiction.

Colourpoint Books*

Colourpoint House, Jubilee Business Park, 21 Jubilee Road, Newtownards, Co. Down, Northern Ireland BT23 4YH
tel (028) 9182 0505 *fax* (028) 9182 1900
email info@colourpoint.co.uk
website www.colourpoint.co.uk
Commissioning Editor Sheila Johnston

Educational textbooks for primary (5–11 year-olds), Key Stage 3 (11–14 year-olds), Key Stage 3 Special Needs (10–14 year-olds), GCSE (14–16 year-olds) and A-Level/undergraduates (age 17+). Subjects include English, geography, history and politics, home economics, ICT, maths and religious education.

Submission details Because Northern Ireland is a small market, Colourpoint concentrates on pupil books which are bought in class set quantities. Potential authors should send some sample pages of their material to show that they can connect with their target age group and not write above or below the ability range, say how long they have been successfully teaching a particular subject and whether they have been involved in writing before. Include return postage. Founded 1993.

Constable & Robinson Ltd*

3 The Lanchesters, 162 Fulham Palace Road, London W6 9ER
tel 020-8741 3663 *fax* 020-8748 7562
email enquiries@constablerobinson.com
website www.constablerobinson.com
Non-Executive Chairman Benjamin Glazebrook, *Managing Director* Nick Robinson, *Directors* Jan Chamier, Nova Jayne Heath, Adrian Andrews

Publishes the *Smarties* series: non-fiction fun for 6–11 year-olds. For adults: biography, current affairs, fiction, general and military history, health, psychology, travel.

Submission details Not commissioning children's books at present.

The Continuum International Publishing Group Ltd

The Tower Building, 11 York Road, London SE1 7NX
tel 020-7922 0880 *fax* 020-7922 0881
email info@continuumbooks.com
website www.continuumbooks.com
Chairman & Ceo Philip J. Sturrock, *Directors* Robin Baird-Smith (publishing: religious and general), Philip Law (editorial: academic, religious, biblical studies and theology), Anthony Haynes (editorial: professional and philosophy), Janet Joyce (publishing: journals and humanities), Frank Roney (finance), Ed Suthon (sales and marketing), Benn Linfield (publishing services)

Serious non-fiction, academic and professional, including scholarly monographs and educational texts and reference works in history, politics and social thought; literature, criticism, performing arts; religion and spirituality; education, psychology, women's studies, business.

Education books include *Getting the Buggers to Write* and *Getting the Buggers to be Creative* by Sue Cowley.

cp publishing

The Children's Project Ltd, PO Box 2, Richmond, Surrey TW10 7FL
email info@childrensproject.co.uk
tel 020-8546 8750 *fax* 020-8974 5849
website www.childrensproject.co.uk
Directors/Co-founders Helen Dorman, Clive Dorman

High-quality visual books that help parents and carers better understand and communicate with their children from birth. The Children's Project is dedicated exclusively to supporting the family and improved outcomes for children. It draws upon the experience and expertise of parents, health professionals and academics to provide up-to-date information in a form that is easily accessible to everyone – parents, carers and practitioners. Founded in 1995; first books published 2000.

Crown House Publishing Ltd

Crown Buildings, Bancyfelin, Carmarthen SA33 5ND
tel (01267) 211345 *fax* (01267) 211882
email books@crownhouse.co.uk
website www.crownhouse.co.uk
Chairman Martin Roberts, *Directors* David Bowman (managing director), Glenys Roberts, David Bowman, Karen Bowman, Caroline Lenton

Publishes a range of teacher resources detailing the latest and best techniques for enhancing learning and teaching ability. List includes accelerated learning, thinking skills, multiple intelligence, emotional intelligence, mindmapping and music. Also publishes titles in the areas of psychotherapy, business training and development, Mind, Body & Spirit. Founded 1998.

Crowswing Books

PO Box 301, King's Lynn, Norfolk PE33 0XW
tel (01553) 840694
email submissions@crowswingbooks.co.uk
website www.crowswingbooks.co.uk
Contact Patricia Cole

Limited edition science fiction, fantasy and horror fiction for children and adults.

Submission details Writers and illustrators should always enquire first with a brief one-page synopsis of the work they have to offer. Writers should submit no more than the first 2 sample chapters. Illustrators should submit a small portfolio of work, 6 pieces max. Include a publication history to date (if any) and a brief biographical paragraph about yourself. A personal response to your work cannot be guaranteed beyond acknowledgement. Include sae or IRC for return of material. Founded 2003.

Dean – see Egmont Books

Dorling Kindersley – see Penguin Group (UK)

Dref Wen

28 Church Road, Whitchurch,
Cardiff CF14 2EA
tel 029-2061 7860 *fax* 029-2061 0507
Directors Roger Boore, Anne Boore, Gwilym Boore, Alun Boore, *Editor* Catrin Hughes

Original, adaptations and translations of foreign and English language full-colour picture story books for children. Also activity books, novelty books, Welsh language fiction for 7–14 year-olds, teenage fiction, reference, religion, audiobooks and poetry. Educational material for primary and secondary schoolchildren in Wales and England, including dictionaries, revision guides and Welsh as a Second Language. Publishes approx. 50 titles a year and has 450 in print. Founded 1970.

Submission details No unsolicited MSS. Phone first.

Dublar Scripts

204 Mercer Way, Romsey, Hants SO51 7QJ
tel (01794) 501377 *fax* (01794) 502538
email scripts@dublar.freeserve.co.uk
website www.dublar.co.uk
Managing Director Robert Heather

Pantomimes. Imprint: Sleepy Hollow Pantomimes. Founded 1994.

The Educational Company of Ireland†

Ballymount Road, Walkinstown, Dublin 12,
Republic of Ireland
tel (01) 4500611 *fax* (01) 4500993
email info@edco.ie
website www.edco.ie
Executive Directors Frank Maguire (chief executive), R. McLoughlin, *Financial Controller* A. Harrold, *Sales and Marketing Manager* M. Harford-Hughes, *Publisher* Frank Fahy

Educational (primary and post-primary) books in the Irish language. Publishes approx. 60–70 titles each year and has 600–700 in print. Ancillary materials include CD-Roms, CDs and audiotapes. Recent successes include *Sunny Street/Streets Ahead* Primary English Languge Programme, *Fonn 1, 2, 3* (Irish language publications for post-primary) and *Geo* (geography publication for post-primary). Trading unit of Smurfit Ireland Ltd. Founded 1910.

Submission details Send an A4 page outlining the selling points and proposal, a draft table of contents and a sample chapter. Allow 3 months for response.

Educational Explorers

PO Box 3391, Winnersh, Wokingham RG41 5ZD
tel 0118-978 9680 *fax* 0118-978 2335
email explorers@cuisenaire.co.uk
website www.cuisenaire.co.uk
Directors M.J. Hollyfield, D.M. Gattegno

Educational. Mathematics: *Numbers in colour with Cuisenaire Rods*; languages: *The Silent Way*; literacy, reading: *Words in Colour*; educational films. No unsolicited material. Founded 1962.

Egmont Books*

239 Kensington High Street, London W8 6SA
tel 020-7761 3500 *fax* 020-7761 3510
email firstname.surname@ecb.egmont.com
website www.egmont.co.uk
Interim Managing Director Robert McMenemy, *Publishing Director* David Riley, *Senior Publishers* Susan Reuben (licensing), Cally Poplak (fiction and picture books), Sue Parish (annuals, Dean and stationery)

Annuals, activity books, novelty books, picture books, fiction for 5–8 and 9–12 year-olds, teenage fiction, series fiction, film/TV tie-ins, home learning, stationery and gift books. Characters include *Thomas the Tank Engine, Barbie, Mr Men, Miffy*, *Postman Pat* and *Action Man*. Recent successes include *A Series of Unfortunate Events* by Lemony Snicket, *The Barbie Annual 2004* and *Thomas the Tank Engine Story Library*. Imprints: Egmont, Dean.

Submission details Will consider unsolicited MSS. For picture books send some sample pages. For longer fiction send the first 3 chapters and a synopsis. Include an sae. No submissions by email. Allow 3–6 months for response. Founded 1878.

Evans Brothers Ltd*

2A Portman Mansions, Chiltern Street,
London W1V 6NR
tel 020-7487 0920 *fax* 020-7487 0921
email sales@evansbooks.co.uk
website www.evansbooks.co.uk
Directors Stephen Pawley (managing), Brian D. Jones (international publishing), A.O. Ojora (Nigeria), *UK Publisher* Su Swallow, *Children's Publisher* Anna McQuinn

Educational books, particularly preschool, school library and teachers' books for the UK, primary and secondary for Africa, the Caribbean and Brazil. Part of the Evans Publishing Group. Founded 1908.

Faber & Faber Ltd*

3 Queen Square, London WC1N 3AU
tel 020-7465 0045 *fax* 020-7465 0034
website www.faber.co.uk
Chief Executive Stephen Page, *Publicity Director* Rachel Alexander, *Marketing Director* Noel Murphy, *Production Director* Nigel Marsh, *Rights Director* Camilla Smallwood, *Children's Director* Suzy Jenvy, *Commissioning Editor* Julia Wells

High-quality general fiction and non-fiction, drama, film, music, poetry. For children: fiction for 5–8 and 9–12 year-olds, teenage fiction, poetry and some non-fiction. Recent successes include *Trouble on Thunder Mountain* by Russell Hoban and Quentin Blake, *Shadowmancer* by G.P. Taylor, and the *Eddie Dickens* series by Philip Ardagh.

Submission details Only accepts submissions through an agent.

C.J. Fallon†

Lucan Road, Palmerstown, Dublin 20, Republic of Ireland
tel (01) 6166400 *fax* (01) 6166499
email editorial@cjfallon.ie
Executive Directors H.J. McNicholas (managing), P. Tolan (financial), N. White (editorial)

Educational text books. Founded 1927.

David Fickling Books – see Random House Group Ltd

First and Best in Education Ltd

Earlstrees Court, Earlstrees Road, Corby, Northants. NN17 4HH
tel (01536) 399004 *fax* (01536) 399012
email info@firstandbest.co.uk
website www.firstandbest.co.uk
Contact Anne Cockburn (editor)

Education-related books (no fiction). Currently actively recruiting new writers for schools; ideas welcome. Sae must accompany submissions. Founded 1992.

Flame Tree Publishing

Crabtree Hall, Crabtree Lane, London SW6 6TY
tel 020-7386 4700 *fax* 020-7386 4701
email info@flametreepublishing.com
website www.flametreepublishing.com
Managing Director Frances Bodiam, *Publisher/Creative Director* Nick Wells

Education (preschool and Key Stages 1 and 2). For adults: music, reference, art, cookery. Part of The Foundry Creative Media Company Ltd. Founded 1992.

Floris Books*

15 Harrison Gardens, Edinburgh EH11 1SH
tel 0131-337 2372 *fax* 0131-347 9919
email floris@florisbooks.co.uk
website www.florisbooks.co.uk
Editors Christopher Moore, Gale Winskill, *Children's Editor* Gale Winskill

Children's activity books, picture books, fiction for 5–8 and 9–12 year-olds and teenage fiction. Publishes approx. 20 titles each year and has 120 in print. Recent successes include *West: The Christmas Owls*. Imprints: Flyways, Kelpies. Also for adults: religion, science, Celtic studies and craft books.

Submission details No unsolicited picture books. Founded 1978.

Flyways (imprint)

Children's fiction paperbacks for the more able reader. Recent successes include *Davidow: Spirit of the Mountain*.

Submission details Will consider unsolicited MSS. Send synopsis and sample chapter.

Flyways – see Floris Books

Folens Publishers*

Apex Business Centre, Boscombe Road, Dunstable LU5 4RL
tel (0870) 609 1237 *fax* (0870) 609 1236
email folens@folens.com
website www.folens.com
Managing Director Malcolm Watson, *Publishing Manager* Peter Burton, *Primary Publisher* Zoe Nichols

Educational (primary, secondary and tertiary) books and learn-at-home books for QCA Schemes of Work, numeracy/literacy frameworks, special needs and exam board-specific publishing. Publishes atlases, dictionaries and revision guides. Subject areas include history, geography, science, maths, French, PSHE, citizenship, English, religious education, physical education and ICT. Recent successes include *GCSE Applied Science*, *Folens History – Invasion, Plague and Murder* and *World of Display – Hands-on Numeracy*. Imprints: Folens, Belair.

Submission details Will consider unsolicited MSS. Send synopsis, rationale and sample section by post or email. Material will be acknowledged on receipt; reply with decision to publish within 1–3 months. Founded 1987.

Folens Publishers

Hibernian Industrial Estate, Greenhills Road, Tallaght, Dublin 24, Republic of Ireland
tel (01) 4137200 *fax* (01) 4137282
website www.folens.ie
Chairman Dirk Folens, *Managing Director* John O'Connor, *Primary Managing and Commissioning Editor* Deirdre Whelan, *Secondary Managing Editor* Margaret Burns

Educational (primary, secondary, comprehensive, technical, in English and Irish). Founded 1956.

Blackwater Press (imprint)†

Fiction for 9–12 year-olds, teenage fiction, picture books and *Brainstorm* series of activity books. Recent successes include *Irish Lengend* series, *Reaching the Heights* by Peter Gunning (novel for 8–12 year-olds) and *Izzy and the Skunk* by Marie-Louise Fitzpatrick (picture book). Also general/adult non-fiction and Irish interest.

Submission details Will consider unsolicited MSS. Send synopsis and first chapter. Allow 6 weeks for response. Founded 1993.

Framework Press Educational Publishers Ltd

Heinemann, Halley Court, Jordan Hill,
Oxford OX2 8EJ
tel (01865) 314194 *fax* (01865) 314116
email nigel.kelly@repp.co.uk
Publisher Nigel Kelly

School management, professional development, raising attainment, PSHE and Citizenship.

David Fulton Publishers Ltd*

Chiswick Centre, 414 Chiswick High Road,
London W4 5TF
tel 020-8996 3610 *fax* 020-8996 3622
email mail@fultonpublishers.co.uk, helen.fairlie@fultonpublishers.co.uk, nina.stibbe@fultonpublishers.co.uk
website www.fultonpublishers.co.uk
Chairman David Fulton, *Publishing Director* Christopher Glennie, *Marketing Director* Rachael Robertson, *Publisher* Helen Fairlie, *Commissioning Editor* Nine Stibbe

Books for the education community: textbooks for ITT students and practical books for teachers in schools. Its publishing meets the needs of the community, focusing on curricular, pedagogical and organisational developments and DfEE/QCA/TTA requirements. Recent successes include *A Handbook for Learning Support Assistants* by Glenys Fox and *A Handbook for Pre-school SEN Provision* by Collette Drifte. Part of Granada Learning.

Submission details Aims to publish books within 4 months of receiving the final MSS. Commissions academics from HEIs to write textbooks. Practitioner texts come from a variety of sources including HEI staff, teachers, LEA trainers and advisers. Founded 1987.

Gairm Publications

29 Waterloo Street, Glasgow G2 6BZ
tel 0141-221 1971 *fax* 0141-221 1971
Editorial Director Derick Thomson

Gaelic and Gaelic-related only: dictionaries, language books, novels, poetry, music, children's books, quarterly magazine, *Gairm*. Founded 1952.

Galaxy Large Print – see Chivers Press

Galore Park Publishing Ltd*

PO Box 96, Cranbrook, Kent TN17 4WS
website www.galorepark.co.uk

Educational: language courses in Latin, Spanish, French, German and English. Also maths and science. Recent success includes the *So you really want to learn Latin* series. Founded 1999.

Geddes & Grosset*

David Dale House,
Lew Lanark ML11 9DJ
tel (01555) 665000 *fax* (01555) 665694
email info@gandg.sol.co.uk
Publishers Ron Grosset, Mike Miller

Popular reference, children's non-fiction and activity books. Founded 1988.

Ginn & Co. – see Harcourt Education Ltd

Glowworm Books Ltd

Broxburn EH52 5LH
tel (01506) 857570 *fax* (01506) 858100
website www.btinternet.com/~amaising.com

The company was formed by the amalgamation of Glowworm Books and The Amaising Publishing House (established in 1988 with the publication of the first 4 titles in its *Maisie* series, written by Aileen Paterson). Recent successes include further books in the *Maisie* series and *The History of Scotland for Children* by Judy Paterson. It has 42 titles in print, written by 10 authors.

Submission details MSS are not accepted without prior arrangement. Founded 1999.

Gomer Press

Llandysul, Ceredigion SA44 4QL
tel (01559) 362371 *fax* (01559) 363758
email gwasg@gomer.co.uk
website www.gomer.co.uk
Directors Jonathan Lewis, John H. Lewis, *Editors* Mairwen Prys Jones, Bethan Mair, Gordon Jones, Ceri Wyn Jones

Literature and non-fiction with a Welsh background or relevance: biography, history, aspects of Welsh culture, children's books. No unsolicited MSS; preliminary enquiry essential. Founded 1892.

W.F. Graham

2 Pondwood Close, Moulton Park,
Northampton NN3 6RT
tel (01604) 645537 *fax* (01604) 648414
email www.wfgraham.co.uk
Activity books including colouring, dot-to-dot, magic painting, puzzle, word search and sticker books. Also picture books and story books.

Granada Learning*

The Chiswick Centre, 414 Chiswick High Road, London W4 5TF
tel 020-8996-3333 *fax* 020-8742-8390
website www.granada-learning.com

Educational multimedia company publishing innovative, curriculum-based resources for the UK and abroad. It has a catalogue of over 800 software and hardware products for preschool children, primary and secondary, through to A level and adult education. Products are developed by teachers and educationalsts. The Granada Learning Group includes ASE, BlackCat (educational software for primary schools), David Fulton Publishers (see separate entry), Granada Learning Software, Granada Learning Professional Development, LearnWise (e-learning products), Leckie & Leckie (see separate entry), Letts Educational (see separate entry), nferNelson (see separate entry), SEMERC (see separate entry) and The Skills Factory.

Gullane Children's Books – see Pinwheel Ltd

Haldane Mason Ltd

PO Box 34196, London NW10 3YB
tel 020-8459 2131 *fax* 020-8728 1216
email info@haldanemason.com
Directors Sydney Francism (editorial), Ron Samuels (art)

High-quality illustrated books: children's (activity books), cookery, alternative health, box sets. Opportunities for freelances. Publishes approx. 8 books each year and has 30 in print. Recent successes include *Big Box of Science Fun*, *Old Macdonald's Farm* and *Discovering Knights & Castles*. Children's imprint: Red Kite Books. Founded 1995.

Submission details Will consider unsolicited MSS. Phone or email first to check interest.

Harcourt Education Ltd*

Halley Court, Jordan Hill, Oxford OX2 8EJ
tel (01865) 310533 *fax* (01865) 314641
email uk.schools@harcourteducation.co.uk
website www.harcourteducation.co.uk
Chief Executive John Philbin

Division of Reed Elsevier (UK) Ltd.

Ginn & Co. (imprint)

fax (01865) 314189
Managing Director Paul Shuter

Textbook/other educational resources for primary schools.

Heinemann Educational (imprint)

website www.heinemann.co.uk
Publishing Director Ravi Mirchandani

Textbooks, literature and other educational resources for all levels.

Rigby Heinemann (imprint)

website www.myprimary.co.uk
fax (01865) 314189
Managing Director Paul Shuter

Textbook/other educational resources for primary schools.

Patrick Hardy Books – see James Clarke & Co. Ltd

HarperCollins Publishers*

77–85 Fulham Palace Road, London W6 8JB
tel 020-8741 7070 *fax* 020-8307 4440
email firstname.surname@harpercollins.co.uk
website www.harpercollins.co.uk
Ceo/Publisher Victoria Barnsley

For adults: fiction (commercial and literary) and non-fiction. Subjects include autobiographies, current affairs, general non-fiction, humour, politics, popular culture, reference (including encyclopedias, bilingual and English dictionaries, guides and handbooks, phrase books, popular reference), science, media-related books, Mind, Body & Spirit, sport, and audio. Imprints include Collins Crime, Collins Dictionaries/COBUILD, Collins/Times Maps and Atlases, Collins Willow, Estates, Fourth Estate, HarperCollins, HarperCollins Entertainment, Thorsons/Element. All fiction and trade non-fiction must be submitted through an agent. Founded 1819.

HarperCollins Audio (imprint)

Publishing Director Rosalie George
Selection of fiction and non-fiction recordings of adult and children's titles by famous name readers.

Estates

Publishing Director David Brawn

Authors include Agatha Christie, J.R.R. Tolkien, C.S. Lewis. Imprint: Tolkien.

HarperCollins Children's (division)

website www.harpercollinschildrensbooks.co.uk
Managing Director Sally Gritten, *Publishing Directors* Gillie Russell (fiction), Venetia Davie (properties), Sue Buswell (picture books), *Design Director* Sophie Stericker

Annuals, activity books, novelty books, picture books, painting and colouring books, pop-up books and book and tape sets. Fiction for 5–8 and 9–12 year-olds, teenage fiction and series fiction; poetry; film/TV tie-ins. Publishes approx. 265 titles each year. Recent successes include *Private Peaceful* by Michael Morpurgo, *Goodbye Mog* by Judith Kerr and *Noddy*. Properties include *Paddington, Narnia, Little Grey Rabbit, Brambly Hedge, Percy the Parkeeper, Animal Stories*. Imprints: HarperCollins Children's Books.

Submission details No unsolicited MSS: only accepts submissions via agents.

Collins Education (division)
website www.collinseducation.com
Managing Director Jim Green, *Director of Educational Publishing* Paul Cherry, *Publishing Manager, Primary Literacy* Jill Cornish, *Publishing Manager, Maths, Science & ICT* Melanie Hoffman, *Publishing Manager, Secondary English & Drama* Isabelle Zahar, *Publishing Manager, Secondary Humanities, Social Science and Vocational* Thomas Allain Chapman

Books, CD-Roms and online material for UK schools and colleges. Commissioned material only.

Letterland (imprint)
Home-learning titles from preschool to further education.

Heinemann Educational – see Harcourt Education Ltd

Hippo – see Scholastic Children's Books

Hit Entertainment plc

Maple House, 149 Tottenham Court Road, London W1T 7NF
tel 020-7554 2500 *fax* 020-7388 9321
email kprice@hitentertainment.com
website www.hitentertainment.com
Head of Publishing Katie Price, *Publishing Executive* Helena Mansell, *Publishing Development Executive* Emma Marks, *Publishing Assistant* Louise Harvey

Children's entertainment company and owner of classic brands such as *Bob the Builder, Pingu, Barney & Friends, Angelina Ballerina, Thomas & Friends, The Wiggles* and *The Rhubbadubbers*. Produces activity books, board books, novelty books, picture books, painting and colouring books, pop-up books. Founded 1989.

Hodder Gibson

2A Christie Street, Paisley PA1 1NB
tel 0141-848 1609 *fax* 0141-889 6315
email hoddergibson@hodder.co.uk
websites www.hodderheadline.co.uk, www.madaboutbooks.com
Managing Director John Mitchell

Educational books specifically for Scotland. No unsolicited MSS. Formed by an amalgamation of Robert Gibson & Sons (Glasgow) and the Scottish branch of Hodder & Stoughton Educational. Part of the Hodder Headline Group.

Hodder Headline Ltd*

338 Euston Road, London NW1 3BH
tel 020-7873 6000 *fax* 020-7873 6024
Chairman Richard Handover, *Group Chief Executive* Tim Hely Hutchinson, *Directors* Martin Neild (managing, Headline), Jamie Hodder-Williams (managing, Hodder & Stoughton General), Charles Nettleton (managing, Hodder & Stoughton Religious and Hodder Children's Books), Malcolm Edwards (managing, Australia and New Zealand), Philip Walters (managing, Hodder Arnold), Colin Fairbain (finance), David Kewley (interim managing, Bookpoint), Mary Tapissier (group personnel/training/admin)

For adults: fiction (commercial and literary) and non-fiction. Subjects include autobiography, biography, food and wine, gardening, history, humour, Mind, Body & Spirit, popular science, religion, self-help, sport, travel and TV tie-ins. Imprints include Coronet, Flame, Headline, Help Yourself, Hodder & Stoughton, Hodder Christian Books, Lir, Mobius, New English Library, Review and Sceptre. Founded 1986.

Hodder Children's Books (division)
Managing Director Charles Nettleton, *Publishing Directors* Anne McNeil (fiction and picture books), Anne Clark (non-fiction and Wayland)

Activity books, novelty books, picture books, fiction for 5–8 and 9–12 year-olds, teenage fiction, series, fiction, film/TV tie-ins, reference, plays, religion, poetry and audio. Recent successes include *The Fire-Eaters* by David Almond, *Felicity Wishes, Snowflakes* and *Sparkledust* by Emma Thomson and *Animal Classification* by Polly Goodman. Publishes approx. 500 titles each year and has about 2000 in print. Imprints: Hodder, Wayland, Bite.

Submission details Will not accept unsolicited MSS.

Hodder Arnold (division)
Directors Philip Walters (managing), Elisabeth Tribe (schools publishing), Katie Roden (consumer education), Georgina Bentliff (health sciences), Mary Attree (journals and reference books), Alyssum Ross (production & design), Catherine Newman (sales & marketing)

Publishes under Hodder & Stoughton Educational, Teach Yourself, Headway. Textbooks for the primary, secondary, tertiary and further education sectors and for self-improvement. Academic and professional books and journals.

Hopscotch Educational Publishing Ltd*

Unit 2, 56 Pickwick Road, Corsham, Wilts. SN13 9BX
tel (01249) 701701 *fax* (01249) 701987
email sales@hopscotchbooks.com
website www.hopscotchbooks.com
Editorial Director Margot O'Keeffe, *Creative Director* Frances Mackay

National Curriculum teaching resources for primary schools. All subjects at all levels. Recent successes include *Accelerated Learning in the Literacy Hour* and *Problem Solving*. Founded 1997.

Horwitz Gardner Ltd

168E High Street, Egham, Surrey TW20 9HP
tel (01784) 477470
email info@horwitzgardner.com
website www.horwitzgardner.com

Specialises in literacy resources, all linked to the UK National Literacy Strategy.

John Hunt Publishing Ltd

46A West Street, New Alresford, Hants SO24 9AU
tel (01962) 736880 *fax* (01962) 736881
email john@johnhunt-publishing.com
Director John Hunt

Children's and adult religious, full colour books for the international market. MSS welcome; send sae. Founded 1989.

Icon Books Ltd*

Grange Road, Duxford, Cambridge CB2 4QF
tel (01763) 208008 *fax* (01763) 208080
email info@iconbooks.co.uk
website www.iconbooks.co.uk
Directors Peter Pugh (managing), Jeremy Cox (creative), Simon Flynn (marketing)

Adult non-fiction: *Introducing* series, literature, history, philosophy, politics, psychology, sociology, cultural studies, religion, science, current affairs, computers, women, anthropology, humour, music, cinema, linguistics, economics. Founded 1991.

Wizard (imprint)

email wizard@iconbooks.co.uk

Activity books, fiction for 5–8 and 9–12 year-olds, teenage fiction, reference and narrative non-fiction. Publishes approx. 15 titles each year and has 25 in print. Recent successes include *Fighting Fantasy Gamebooks* by Steve Jackson and Ian Livingstone, *Big Numbers* by Mary and John Gribbin and *Darkness Visible: Inside the World of Philip Pullman* by Nicholas Tucker.

Submission details Will consider unsolicited MSS.

The Islamic Foundation

Markfield Conference Centre, Ratby Lane, Markfield, Leics. LE67 9SY
tel (01530) 244944 *fax* (01530) 244946
Director General Dr Manazir Ahsan, *Deputy Director* Chowdhury Mueen-Uddin

Books on Islam for adults and children. Founded 1973.

Jolly Learning Ltd

Tailours House, High Road, Chigwell, Essex IG7 6DL
tel 020-8501 0405 *fax* 020-8500 1696
email info@jollylearning.co.uk
website www.jollylearning.co.uk
Director Christopher Jolly, *Commissioning Editor* Amanda Learmonth

Educational: primary and English as a Foreign Lanuage. The company is committed to enabling high standards in the teaching of reading and writing. *Jolly Phonics* provides a foundation for reading and writing. Publishes approx. 25 titles each year and has 200 in print. Recent successes include *Jolly Dictionary*, *Jolly Readers* and *Jolly Phonics Starter Kit*. Imprint: Jolly Phonics.

Submission details Unsolicited MSS are only considered for add-ons to existing products. Founded 1987.

Miles Kelly Publishing

The Bradfield Centre, Great Bardfield, Essex CM7 4SL
tel (01371) 811309 *fax* (01371) 811393
email info@mileskelly.net
website www.mileskelly.net
Directors Kelly Gerard, Jim Miles, Kate Miles

High-quality illustrated non-fiction titles for children and family: activity books, board books, story books, poetry, reference, posters and wallcharts. Age groups: preschool, 5–10, 10–15, 15+. See also page 56. Founded 1996.

Kelpies – see Floris Books

Kingfisher Publications plc

New Penderel House, 283–288 High Holborn, London WC1V 7HZ
tel 020-7903 9999 *fax* 020-7242 4979
email sales@kingfisherpub.co.uk
website www.kingfisher.com

Kingfisher (imprint)

Non-fiction Publishing Director Gill Denton, *Fiction Publishing Director* Anne Marie Ryan

Novelty books, picture books, fiction for 5–8 and 9–12 year-olds, series fiction, reference and poetry. Publishes approx. 50 new non-fiction titles and 25 new fiction titles each year and has about 500 in print. Recent successes include *Kingfisher Young Knowledge* (science for age 5+) and *Kingfisher Knowledge* (general knowledge for age 8+), *The Kingfisher Book of Nursery Tales* by Vivian French and *Small Bad Wolf* by Sean Taylor (from the *I am Reading* series. Imprint of Houghton Mifflin Company in Boston, US.

Submission details Will not consider unsolicited MSS.

Kingscourt*

McGraw-Hill House, Shoppenhangers Road, Maidenhead, Berks. SL6 2QL
tel (01628) 502500 *fax* (01628) 635895
email enquiries@kingscourt.co.uk
website www.kingscourt.co.uk

Editorial Director Melissa Rosati

Educational publisher of resources for Key Stages 1–3, including *Big Books for Shared Reading, Guided Reading, Story Chest, Literacy Links Plus* and *Maths Links Plus*. Resources support National Literacy and Numeracy Strategies, the Scottish Guidelines 5–14, Northern Ireland curriculum and Curriculum 2000 in Wales. Co-sponsors of the National Literacy Association (NLA). Part of the McGraw-Hill Companies. Founded in 1988.

The King's England Press

Cambertown House, Commercial Road, Goldthorpe, Rotherham, South Yorkshire S63 9BL
tel (01226) 270258 *fax* (01709) 897787
email sales@kingsengland.com
websites www.kingsengland.com, www.pottypoets.com

Poetry collections for both adults and children. Successes include *The Spot on My Bum: Horrible Poems for Horrible Children* by Gez Walsh, *Always Eat Your Bogies and Other Rotten Rhymes* by Andrew Collett, *Wang Foo the Kung Fu Shrew and Other Freaky Poems Too* by Chris White and *Vikings Don't Wear Pants* by Roger Stevens and Celia Warren.

Also publishes reprints of Arthur Mee's *King's England* series of 1930s guidebooks, books on folklore, and local and ecclesiastical history. Founded 1989.

Jessica Kingsley Publishers*

116 Pentonville Road, London N1 9JB
tel 020-7833 2307 *fax* 020-7837 2917
email post@jkp.com
website www.jkp.com
Directors Jessica Kingsley (managing), Amy Lankester-Owen (editorial)

Psychology, psychiatry, arts therapies, social work, special needs (especially autism and Asperger Syndrome), education, law, practical theology. Founded 1987.

Ladybird – see Penguin Group (UK)

Learning World – see Chrysalis Children's Books

Leckie & Leckie*

8 Whitehill Terrace, St Andrews, Fife KY16 8RN
tel (01334) 475656 *fax* (01334) 477392
email enquiries@leckieandleckie.co.uk
website www.leckieandleckie.co.uk

Educational resources. Dedicated to the ongoing development of materials specifically for education in Scotland, from Standard Grade, Foundation to Higher Level. Over 50 titles are currently available in Leckie & Leckie's study guide range. Part of Granada Learning.

Letts Educational*

Chiswick Centre, 414 Chiswick High Road, London W4 5TF
tel 020-8996 3333 *fax* 020-8742 8390
email mail@lettsed.co.uk
website www.lettsed.co.uk
Directors Stephen Baker (managing), Wayne Davies (publishing), Andrew Thraves (publishing), Helen Jacobs (publishing), Lee Warren (finance)

Children's activity books, home study publications for 0–18 year-olds and homework and revision books. Also for adults: accountancy and taxation; computer science; economics; industry, business and management; mathematics and statistics; vocational training and careers. Associate and subsidiary companies: Granada Learning, nferNelson, Black Cat, Granada Media, SEMERC. Founded 1979.

Frances Lincoln Ltd

4 Torriano Mews, Torriano Avenue, London NW5 2RZ
tel 020-7284 4009 *fax* 020-7485 0490
email reception@frances-lincoln.com
website www.frances-lincoln.com
Directors John Nicoll (managing), Anne Fraser (editorial, adult books), Janetta Otter-Barry (editorial, children's books)

Illustrated, international co-editions: gardening, architecture, environment, interiors, art, gift, children's books. Founded 1977.

Frances Lincoln Children's Books (imprint)

Novelty books, picture books, fiction for 5–8 year-olds, religion, poetry.

Submission details Submit material through an agent; occasionally considers unsolicited MSS.

Lion Hudson plc*

Mayfield House, 256 Banbury Road, Oxford OX2 7DH
tel (01865) 302750 *fax* (01865) 302757
email enquiries@lionhudson.com
website www.lionhudson.com
Directors Paul Clifford (managing & editorial), Denis Cole, Tony Wales, John O'Nions, Roy McCloughry, Nick Jones, Stephen Price, Rodney Shepherd

Reference, paperbacks, illustrated children's books, educational, gift books, religion and theology; all reflecting a Christian position. No adult fiction.

Lion Children's Books (imprint)

website www.lion-publishing.co.uk

High-quality illustrated books, especially Bible stories and prayer collections, Christmas and Easter books. Also activity books, board books, picture books, non-fiction, fiction, poetry, religion. Lion is the leading UK imprint of children's Bibles.

Submission details Send preliminary letter before submitting MSS. Founded 1971.

Little Tiger Press – see Magi Publications

Livewire – see The Women's Press

Longman – see Pearson Education

Lutterworth Press – see James Clarke & Co. Ltd

Macdonald Young Books – now Hodder Children's Books – see Hodder Headline Ltd

McGraw-Hill Education*

McGraw-Hill House, Shoppenhangers Road, Maidenhead, Berks. SL6 2QL
tel (01628) 502500 *fax* (01628) 635895
20 Canada Square, Canary Wharf, London E14 5LH
tel 020-7176 7000
email emea_queries@mcgraw-hill.com
website www.mcgraw-hill.co.uk
Directors Simon Allen (managing – EMEA), Alan Martin (operations), Rupert Mitchell (professional, Northern Europe), Murray St Leger (higher education sales & marketing, Northern and Central Europe), Melissa Rosati (higher education, editorial)

Higher education: business, economics, computing, maths, humanities, social sciences, world languages. Professional: business, medical, computing, science, technical, medical, general reference.

Macmillan Education Ltd – see Macmillan Publishers Ltd

Macmillan Publishers Ltd*

The Macmillan Building, 4 Crinan Street, London N1 9XW
tel 020-7833 4000 *fax* 020-7843 4640
website www.macmillan.co.uk
Chief Executive Richard Charkin, *Directors* M. Barnard, C.J. Paterson, G.R.U. Todd, D. North, Dr A. Thomas, D.J.G. Knight

For adults: fiction (commercial and literary) and non-fiction. Subjects include academic and professional (textbooks, monographs and journals), autobiography, biography, business, encyclopedias, gardening and cookery, gift books, health and beauty, history, humour, military and war, music, natural history, poetry, philosophy, politics and world affairs, psychology, sport, theatre and film, travel. Imprints include Boxtree, Macmillan, Pan, Picador, Sidgwick & Jackson.

Macmillan Children's Books Ltd (division)

20 New Wharf Road, London N1 9RR
tel 020-7014 6000 *fax* 020-7014 6001
website www.panmacmillan.com
Managing Director & Publisher Kate Wilson, *Publishing Director, Fiction* Sarah Davies, *Publishing Director, Picture Books* Suzanne Carnell, *Publishing Director, Campbell Books* Camilla Reid

Picture books, fiction, poetry, non-fiction, early learning, pop-up, novelty, board books. Publishes approx. 200 titles each year and has 1500 in print. Recent successes include *Snail and Whale* by Julia Donaldson and Alex Scheffler, *Princess Diaries 5* by Meg Cabot, and *Dear Zoo* book and toy pack by Rod Campbell. Imprints: Macmillan Children's Books, Campbell Books, Young Picador.

Submission details Will not consider unsolicited MSS.

Boxtree (imprint)

Senior Editor Ingrid Connell, *Editor* Natalie Jerome

TV and film tie-ins; illustrated and general non-fiction; mass market paperbacks linked to TV, film, rock and sporting events; humour.

Macmillan Education Ltd (division)

Macmillan Oxford, Between Towns Road, Oxford OX4 3PP
tel (01865) 405700 *fax* (01865) 405701
website www.macmillaneducation.com
Chairman Christopher Paterson, *Managing Director* Christopher Harrison, *Publishing Directors* Sue Bale, Alison Hubert, *Finance Director* Paul Emmett, *Production Director* John Peacock, *IT Director* Ian Johnstone

English language teaching materials. School and college textbooks and materials in all subjects for international markets.

Macmillan Heinemann English Language Teaching

Macmillan Oxford, Between Towns Road, Oxford OX4 3PP
tel (01865) 405700 *fax* (01865) 405701
Chairman Christopher Paterson, *Managing Director* Christopher Harrison, *Director, ELT Publishing* Sue Bale

English language teaching materials.

Magi Publications

1 The Coda Centre, 189 Munster Road, London SW6 6AW
tel 020-7385 6333 *fax* 020-7385 7333
website www.littletigerpress.com
Publisher Monty Bhatia, *Editors* Jude Evans

Caterpillar Books (imprint)

email jasher@caterpillarbooks.com
Publisher Jamie Asher

Quality books for preschool children, including pop-ups, board books, cloth books and activity books.

Little Tiger Press (imprint)

email info@littletiger.co.uk

Children's picture books, novelty books, board books, pop-up books and activity books for preschool age to 10 year-olds.

Submission details New material will be considered from authors and illustrators; see website for guidelines. Founded 1987.

Mantra

5 Alexandra Grove, London N12 8NU
tel 020-8445 5123 *fax* 020-8446 7745
email sales@mantrapublishing.com
website www.mantralingua.com
Managing Director M. Chatterji

Children's multicultural picture books; multilingual friezes/posters; dual language books/cassettes; South Asian literature/teenage fiction; CD-Roms and videos. Founded 1984.

Kevin Mayhew Ltd

Buxhall, Stowmarket, Suffolk IP14 3BW
tel (01449) 737978 *fax* (01449) 737834
email info@kevinmayhewltd.com
website www.kevinmayhewltd.com
Directors Kevin Mayhew (chairman), Gordon Carter (managing), *Religious Books Editor* Marian Reid, *Children's Editor* Graham Harris

Christianity: prayer and spirituality, pastoral care, preaching, liturgy worship, children's, youth work, drama, instant art. Music: hymns, organ and choral, contemporary worship, piano and instrumental. Publishes approx. 300 titles each year and has several thousand in print.

Recent children's book successes include *Frogs in Assembly* (primary school, curriculum-based assemblies), *Help! It's Sunday* (all-age services or assemblies) and *X=Life* (exploring Christian life with 11–16 year-olds).

Submission details Will consider unsolicited MSS. Immediate acknowledgement; approx. 2 month assessment period. Founded 1976.

Meadowside Children's Books

185 Fleet Street, London EC4A 2HS
tel 020-7400 1061 *fax* 020-7400 1037
email info@meadowsidebooks.com
website www.meadowsidebooks.com
Publisher Simon Rosenheim, *Art Director* Mark Mills

Picture books, board books, novelty books, pop-up books and sticker books. Founded 2003.

Mentor Books†

43 Furze Road, Sandyford Industrial Estate, Dublin 18, Republic of Ireland
tel (353) 1 295 2112 *fax* (353) 1 295 2114
email all@mentorbooks.ie
website www.mentorbooks.ie
Managing Director Daniel McCarthy, *Managing Editor* Claire Haugh

Fiction for 5–8 and 9–12 year-olds, teenage fiction, series fiction, film/TV tie-ins. Educational (primary and secondary): languages, history, geography, business, maths, science. Also, for adults: fiction, non-fiction, guidebooks, biographies and history. Publishes approx. 60 titles each year and has 300 in print.

Submission details Will not consider unsolicited MSS or even letters from prospective authors. Founded 1980.

The Mercier Press†

Douglas Village, Cork, Republic of Ireland
tel (021) 4899858 *fax* (021) 4899887
email books@mercierpress.ie
website www.mercierpress.ie
Directors G. Eaton (chairman), J.F. Spillane (managing), M.P. Feehan

Books for adults and children. Subjects include Irish literature, folklore, history, politics, humour, education, theology, law, current affairs, health, mind and spirit and general non-fiction. Imprint: Marino Books. Founded 1944.

Mill Publishing

PO Box 120, 4, Balloo Avenue,
County Down BT 19 7BX
tel (0800) 731 2837
email info@millpublishing.co.uk
website www.millpublishing.co.uk

Produces material to meet the needs of the National Curriculum. The Skillbuilder system, in its separate Literacy and Numeracy versions, provides schools with a means of achieving the objectives required by the National Literacy Strategy and National Numeracy Strategy. The *Write into History* series develops key writing skills using the approach set out in *Grammar for Writing*. The *Crosslinks* series covers reading, writing and thinking across the curriculum.

Anglia Young Books (imprint)
See separate entry.

National Association for the Teaching of English (NATE)*

50 Broadfield Road, Sheffield S8 OXJ
tel 0114-255 5419 *fax* 0114-255 5296
email natehq@btconnect.com
website www.nate.org.uk
Chair John Johnson, *Vice-chair* Simon Wrigley, *Company Secretary* Lyn Fairfax, *Development & Communications Officer* Trevor Millum, *Publications Manager* Anne Fairhall, *Publications Co-ordinator* Julie Selwood

Educational (primary, secondary and tertiary): teaching English, drama and media. Publishes approx. 10 titles each year and has 58 in print. Recent publications include *Guided Reading* packs (Key Stage 3 focus), *ICT and Literacy – Ideas and*

Resources for KS1/2 and *Cracking Good Picture Books* (Key Stage 1 focus). Imprint: NATE.

Submission details Submissions should be made via a 'Publication Proposal' form for consideration by the Publications Manager and 3 members of the Editorial Board. Allow 3–6 weeks for response. Will consider unsolicited MSS. Founded 1963.

The National Trust

36 Queen Anne's Gate, London SW1H 9AS
tel 020-7222 9251 *fax* 020-7222 5097
Publisher Margaret Willes

History, cookery, architecture, gardening, guidebooks, children's non-fiction. No unsolicited MSS. Founded 1895.

Neate Publishing*

33 Downside Road, Winchester SO22 5LT
tel (01962) 841479 *fax* (01962) 841743
email sales@neatepublishing.co.uk
website www.neatepublishing.co.uk
Directors Bobbie Neate (managing), Ann Langran, Maggie Threadingham

Non-fiction books, CDs and posters for primary school children. Founded 1999.

Thomas Nelson Ltd – see Nelson Thornes Ltd

Nelson Thornes Ltd*

Delta Place, 27 Bath Road, Cheltenham, Glos. GL53 7TH
tel (01242) 267100 *fax* (01242) 221914
email name@nelsonthornes.com
website www.nelsonthornes.com
Directors Fred Grainger (managing), David Vincent, Adrian Ford

Print and electronic publishers for the educational market: primary, secondary, further education, professional. Part of the Wolters Kluwer Group of Companies.

nferNelson Publishing Co. Ltd*

The Chiswick Centre, 414 Chiswick High Road, London W4 5TF
tel (0845) 6021937 *fax* 020-8996 3660
email information@nfer-nelson.co.uk
website www.nfer-nelson.co.uk
General Manager Tim Cornford

Independent provider of tests, assessments and assessment services for education. Its aim is to help educational professionals to understand and maximise the potential of their pupils and students. Publishes assessments for the 0–19 age group, though the majority of its assessments are aimed at 5–14 year-olds. Testing and assessment services include literacy, numeracy, thinking skills, ability, learning support and online testing. Founded 1981.

Jane Nissen Books

Swan House, Chiswick Mall, London W4 2PS
tel 020-8994 8203 *fax* 020-8742 8198
email niss@easynet.co.uk

Fiction for 5–8 and 9–12 year-olds, teenage fiction and poetry. Publishes approx. 4 titles each year and has 18 in print. Recent successes include *Old Peter's Russian Tales* by Arthur Ransome, *Kings and Queens* by Eleanor and Herbert Farjeon and *Tennis Shoes* by Noel Streatfeild. Seeking to publish more children's 'forgotten' classics.

Submission details Submit MSS via an agent. Founded 2000.

The O'Brien Press Ltd

20 Victoria Road, Rathgar, Dublin 6, Republic of Ireland
tel (01) 492 3333 *fax* (01) 492 2777
email books@obrien.ie
website www.obrien.ie
Directors Michael O'Brien, Ide ní Laoghaire, Ivan O'Brien

For children: fiction for all ages; illustrated fiction series – *Solos* (age 3+), *Pandas* (age 5+), *Flyers* (age 6+) and *Red Flag* (8+); substantial novels (10+) – contemporary, historical, fantasy. Also for adults: biography, politics, local history, true crime, sport, humour, reference. No poetry, adult fiction or academic. Founded 1974.

Submission details Unsolicited MSS (sample chapters only), synopses and ideas for books welcome – submissions will not be returned.

Michael O'Mara Books Ltd

9 Lion Yard, Tremadoc Road, London SW4 7NQ
tel 020-7720 8643 *fax* 020-7627 8953
website www.mombooks.com
Chairman Michael O'Mara, *Managing Director* Lesley O'Mara, *Commissioning Editorial Director* Lindsay Davies

General non-fiction: biography, humour, history, ancient history, anthologies and royal books. Founded 1985.

Buster Books (imprint)

email busterbooks@michaelomarabooks.com
Managing Director Lesley O'Mara, *Managing Editor* Philippa Wingate, *Senior Creative Editor* David Sinden

Novelty and picture books for young children. Publishes approx. 40 titles a year. Recent successes include *Groovy Cheques for a Groovy Chick*, *My First Words* (set of 9 board books in box) and *My First Magic Games* (large format board book).

Submission details Submit novelty and non-fiction (no fiction) with sae. Allow 1–2 months for response.

Orchard Books – see The Watts Publishing Group Ltd

The Orion Publishing Group Ltd*

Orion House, 5 Upper St Martin's Lane, London WC2H 9EA
tel 020-7240 3444 *fax* 020-7240 4822
website www.orionbooks.co.uk
Directors Jean-Louis Lisimachio (chairman), Peter Roche (chief executive)

For adults: fiction and non-fiction and audio. Imprints include Everyman, Gollacz, Orion, Phoenix and Weidenfeld & Nicolson. Founded 1992.

Orion Children's Books (division)

Publisher Fiona Kennedy, *Editorial Manager* Jane Hughes, *Editor* Christine Slenczka

Picture books, fiction for 5–8 and 9–12 year-olds, teenage fiction, series fiction and audio. Publishes approx. 50 titles each year and has about 350 in print. Recent successes include *The Doomspell Trilogy* by Cliff McNish, *The Book of Dead Days* by Marcus Sedgwick and *Horrid Henry* by Francesca Simon. Imprints: Orion Children's Books, Dolphin Paperbacks.

Submission details Will consider unsolicited MSS. Allow 2 months for response. Submissions via agents take priority.

Oxford University Press*

Great Clarendon Street, Oxford OX2 6DP
tel (01865) 556767 *fax* (01865) 556646
email enquiry@oup.com
website www.oup.com
Ceo Henry Reece, *Group Finance Director* Roger Boning, *Academic Division Managing Director* Tim Barton, *UK Children's and Educational Division Managing Director* Kate Harris, *ELT Division Managing Director* Peter Marshall, *Publishing Director Journals* Martin Richardson *UK Personnel Director* John Williams, *Sales Director* Tim Mahar

Anthropology, archaeology, architecture, art, belles-lettres, bibles, bibliography, children's books (fiction, non-fiction, picture), commerce, current affairs, dictionaries, drama, economics, educational (infants, primary, secondary, technical, university), English language teaching, electronic publishing, essays, foreign language learning, general history, hymn and service books, journals, law, maps and atlases, medical, music, oriental, philosophy, political economy, prayer books, reference, science, sociology, theology and religion; educational software; *Grove Dictionaries of Music & Art*. Trade paperbacks published under the imprint of Oxford Paperbacks. Founded 1478.

Children's and Educational Division

Managing Director, Children's and Education Kate Harris; *Children's: Publisher, Fiction and Picture Books* Liz Cross, *Head of Dictionaries and Reference* Vineeta Gupta; *Schoolbooks: Publishing Director* Denise Cripps, *Publisher, English and Geography* Rachel Houghton, *Publisher, Modern Foreign Languages and Classics* Dick Capel-Davies, *Publisher, Science, Maths and Technology* Elspeth Boardley, *Primary Publisher* Jane Harley, *Publisher, Primary Literacy* Fiona Undrill

Picture books, fiction, poetry and dictionaries. Authors include Tim Bowler, Gillian Cross, Julie Hearne and Geraldine McCaughrean.

Parragon

4 Queen Street, Bath BA1 1HE
tel (01225) 478888 *fax* (01225) 478897
email info@parragon.com
Directors Trevor McCurdie, Guy Parr, Catherine Hardy (publishing), *Commissioning Editors* Jane Walker, Catherine Jones

Activity books, novelty books, picture books, fiction for 5–8 year-olds, poetry, reference, religion and audio. Publishes approx. 400 titles each year and has about 4500 in print. Recent successes include *Five Minute Treasury*, *Gold Star Workbooks* and *Princess Sticker and Colouring*. Imprints: Parragon, Bright Sparks.

Submission details Any material submitted cannot be returned. Telephone calls cannot be accepted. Founded 1988.

PCET Publishing

27 Kirchen Road, London W13 OUD
tel 020-8567 9206 *fax* 020-8566 5120
email info@pcet.co.uk
website www.pcet.co.uk

Pictorial Charts Educational Trust (PCET) publishes visual resources for primary and secondary education: wallcharts, photopacks, activity books and other classroom accessories to support the National Curriculum. Also has a charitable arm which provides funding and teaching resources for the developing world.

Pearson Education*

Edinburgh Gate, Harlow, Essex CM20 2JE
tel (01279) 623623 *fax* (01279) 414130
email firstname.lastname@pearsoned-ema.com
website www.pearsoned.co.uk
President, Pearson Education Ltd Rod Bristow

Materials for school pupils, students and practitioners globally.

Longman (imprint)

Edinburgh Gate, Harlow, Essex CM20 2JE
tel (0800) 579579 *fax* (01279) 414130
email schools.enq@pearsoned-ema.com
website www.longman.co.uk

Educational: primary and secondary. Primary: literacy and numeracy. Secondary: English, maths, science, history, geography, modern languages, design and technology, business and economics, psychology and sociology.

Penguin Longman (imprint)
English language teaching.

York Notes (imprint)
Literature guides for students.

Penguin Group (UK)*

80 Strand, London WC2R 0RL
tel 020-7010 3000 *fax* 020-7010 6060
website www.penguin.co.uk
Ceo Anthony Forbes Watson, *Managing Directors* Helen Fraser (Penguin), Andrew Welham (Dorling Kindersley)

Books for adults and children (see below and BBC Children's Books). Adult subjects include biography, fiction, current affairs, fiction, general leisure, health, history, humour, literature, politics, spirituality and relationships, sports, travel and TV/film tie-ins. Adult imprints include Allen Lane, Dorling Kindersley, Hamish Hamilton, Hugo's Language Books, Michael Joseph, Penguin, Penguin Press, Rough Guides, Viking. Owned by Pearson plc.

Puffin (division)
Managing Director Francesca Dow, *Publishing Directors* Rebecca McNally (fiction), Mandy Suhr (picture books)

Children's paperback and hardback books: picture books, board books, novelty books, fiction, poetry, non-fiction, popular culture; and audio. Recent successes include *The English Roses* by Madonna, Eoin Colfer's *Artemis Fowl* series and Jeremy Strong's humorous titles for younger readers. Backlist titles by authors such as Roald Dahl, Gene Kemp, Jill Paton Walsh, Leon Garfield, Mildred D. Taylor, as well as the *Puffin Classics* and *Puffin Modern Classics*. Operates the Puffin Book Club.

Submission details No unsolicited MSS or synopses.

Warne (division)
websites www.funwithspot.com, www.flowerfairies.com, www.peterrabbit.com
Managing Director Sally Floyer, *Publishing Director* Stephanie Barton

Specialises in preschool illustrated developmental books for 0–6, non-fiction 0–8; licensed brands; children's classic publishing and merchandising properties. No unsolicited MSS.

Ladybird (division)
website www.ladybird.co.uk
Managing Director Sally Floyer

Dorling Kindersley (division)
Managing Director Andrew Welham, *Publisher* Christopher Davis, *Adult Publisher* John Roberts, *Children's Publisher* Miriam Farbry, *DK Designs* Sophie Mitchell

Illustrated non-fiction for adults and children: gardening, medical, travel, food and drink, Mind, Body & Spirit, history, reference, pregnancy and childcare, antiques. Age groups: preschool, 5–8, 8+.

Piccadilly Press

5 Castle Road, London NW1 8PR
tel 020-7267 4492 *fax* 020-7267 4493
email books@piccadillypress.co.uk
website www.piccadillypress.co.uk
Managing Director & Publisher Brenda Gardner, *Senior Editor* Yasemin Uçar, *Editorial Assistant* Maddy Clark

Picture books, humorous teenage fiction, series fiction, film/TV tie-ins, parental advice trade paperbacks. Publishes approx. 25–30 titles each year and has 200 in print. Recent successes include *Dancing in My Nuddy-Pants* by Louise Rennison, *Mates Dates* series by Cathy Hopkins and *Wilbie, Footie Mad!* by Sally Chambers.

Submission details Will consider unsolicited MSS. Send synopsis and 3 sample chapters. Allow 6 weeks for response. Looking to publish humorous teenage books which deal with contemporary issues. Founded 1983.

Picthall & Gunzi Ltd

21A Widmore Road, Bromley BR1 1RW
tel 020-8460 4032 *fax* 020-8460 4021
email chez@picthallandgunzi.demon.co.uk
website www.picthallandgunzi.co.uk
Directors Deborah Murrell (joint managing), Chez Picthall (joint managing), Christiane Gunzi (editorial), Dominic Zwemmer (art)

High-quality, illustrated non-fiction for children: activity books, board books, novelty books, encyclopedias, non-fiction. Age groups: preschool, 5–10, 10–15. See also page 57.

Pinwheel Ltd

Winchester House, 259–269 Old Marylebone Road, London NW1 5XJ
tel 020-7616 7200 *fax* 020-7616 7201
email angela.brooksbank@pinwheel.co.uk, shaheen.bilgrami@pinwheel.co.uk
website www.pinwheel.co.uk
Managing Director Andrew Flatt

Children's non-fiction, picture books and novelty titles. Unsolicited MSS will not be returned.

Andromeda Children's Books (imprint)
Publishing/Creative Director Linda Cole
Illustrated non-fiction for children aged 3–12.

Gullane Children's Books (imprint)
Creative Director Paula Burgess

Picture books for children aged 0–8 years old.

Pinwheel Children's Books (imprint)
Publishing/Creative Director Linda Cole
Cloth and novelty books for children aged 0–5.

The Playwrights Publishing Company

70 Nottingham Road, Burton Joyce,
Notts. NG14 5AL
tel 0115-931 3356
email playwrightspublishingco@yahoo.co.uk
website www.geocities.com/playwrightspublishingco
Proprietor Liz Breeze, *Consultant* Tony Breeze

One-act and full-length drama published on the internet: serious work and comedies, for mixed cast, all women or schools. Reading fee unless professionally produced; sae required. Founded 1990.

Point – see Scholastic Children's Books

Poolbeg Group Services Ltd

123 Grange Hill, Baldoyle, Dublin 13,
Republic of Ireland
tel (01) 8321477 *fax* (01) 8321430
email poolbeg@poolbeg.com
website www.poolbeg.com
Directors Kieran Devlin (managing), Paula Campbell (publisher)

Children's and teenage fiction. Authors include Alan Cantrill, Ann Carroll, Lucinda Jacob and Malachy Doyle. Also adult popular fiction, non-fiction, current affairs. Imprint: Poolbeg. Founded 1976.

Portland Press Ltd

59 Portland Place, London W1B 1QW
tel 020-7580 5530 *fax* 020-7323 1136
email editorial@portlandpress.com
website www.portlandpress.com
Directors Rhonda C. Oliver (managing), Chris J. Finch (finance), John Day (IT), Adam Marshall (marketing)

Biochemistry and molecular life science books for graduate, postgraduate and research students. Illustrated science books for children: *Making Sense of Science* series. Founded 1990.

Mathew Price Ltd

The Old Glove Factory, Bristol Road, Sherborne, Dorset DT9 4HP
tel (01935) 816010 *fax* (01935) 816310
email mathewp@mathewprice.com
Chairman Mathew Price

Illustrated fiction and non-fiction children's books for all ages for the UK and international market. Specialist in flap, pop-up, paper-engineered titles as well as conventional books. Founded 1983.

Priddy Books

4 Crinan Street, London N1 9XW
020-7418 5515 *fax* 020-7418 85507
email claire.cartwright@priddybooks.com
website www.priddybooks.com
Publisher Roger Priddy, *Editorial Manager* Jo Douglass, *Design Manager* Robert Tainsh

Specialises in photographic baby/toddler and preschool books: activity books, board books, novelty books, picture books.

Prim-Ed Publishing – UK

4th Floor, Tower Court,
Foleshill Enterprise Park, Couraulds Way,
Coventry CV6 SNX
tel (0870) 0131208 *fax* (0870) 0131 209
website www.prim-ed.com
Contact Seamus McGuiness

Educational publisher specialising in copymasters (photocopiable teaching resources) for primary school and special needs lower secondary pupils. Books written by practising classroom teachers.

Ragged Bears Publishing Ltd

Unit 14A, Bennett's Field Trading Estate,
Southgate Road, Wincanton,
Somerset BA9 9DT
tel (01963) 824184 *fax* (01963) 31147
email info@raggedbears.co.uk
website www.raggedbears.co.uk
Managing Director Henrietta Stickland, *Submissions Editor* Barbara Lamb

Activity books, picture books, novelty books and fiction for 5–8 year-olds. Publishes 5–10 titles each year and has 150 in print. Recent successes include *Big Dig* by Paul Stickland, *Lovely Ruby & The Mermaid* by Nancy Trott and *We're Going on an Aeroplane* by Steve Augarde. *Dinosaur Roar!* has sold over 10 million copies since its publication almost 10 years ago. *Little Robots* by Mike Brownlow is now an animated TV series on Cbeebies.

Submission details Will consider unsolicited MSS. Allow 3–4 months for response. Takes very few unsolicited ideas as the list is small. Include sae for return of MSS; do not send original artwork. Founded 1994.

Random House Group Ltd*

20 Vauxhall Bridge Road, London SW1V 2SA
tel 020-7840 8400 *fax* 020-7233 8791
website www.randomhouse.co.uk
Chairman/Ceo Gail Rebuck, *Directors* Simon Master (deputy chairman), Ian Hudson (managing), Larry Finlay (managing, Transworld), Mark Gardiner (finance), Brian Davies (managing director, overseas operations), Alfred Willmann (group bibliographic), Clare Harington (group communications), Philippa Dickinson (children's)

For adults: fiction (commercial and literary) and non-fiction. Subjects include art, autobiography, belles-lettres, biography, business, cookery, current affairs, diet and fitness, drama, essays, film and TV tie-ins, health and beauty, history, humour, lifestyle, music, parenting, personal development, poetry, politics, philosophy, reference, science, spirituality, sport, translations and travel. Imprints include Arrow Books, Jonathan Cape, Century, Chatto & Windus, Ebury Press, Fodor Guides, Harvill Secker Press, William Heinemann, Hutchinson, Pimlico, Rider, Secker and Warburg, Vermillion and Vintage. Subsidiary of Bertelsmann AG.

Random House Audio Books

tel 020-7840 8419 *fax* 020-7233 6127
Editor Georgia Marnham

Random House Children's Books (division)

61–63 Uxbridge Road, London W5 5SA
tel 020-8579 2652 *fax* 020-8579 5479
Managing Director Philippa Dickinson, *Publishing Director – Fiction* Annie Eaton, *Publishing Director – Picture Books* Caroline Roberts, *Publisher – Doubleday Picture Books* Penny Walker, *Senior Commissioning Editor – Fiction* Alex Antscherl, *Senior Commissioning Editor – Picture Books* Natascha Biebow, *Commissioning Editor – Jonathan Cape Picture Books* Helen Mackenzie-Smith, *Associate Publisher – Jonathan Cape Picture Books* Ian Craig, *Associate Publisher – Jonathan Cape Fiction* Delia Huddy, *Publisher – Jonathan Cape* Tom Maschler, *Publicity Director* Clare Hall-Craggs

Picture books, fiction, poetry, non-fiction and audio cassettes. Authors include Jacqueline Wilson, Anne Fine, Michael Morpurgo, Philip Pullman and Roald Dahl, and illustrators include Quentin Blake, Helen Cooper, Shirley Hughes, John Burningham and Babette Cole.

Imprints: Bodley Head Children's Books, Corgi Children's Books, Doubleday Children's Books, Hutchinson Children's Books, Jonathan Cape Children's Books, Red Fox Children's Books, David Fickling Books. Merged with Transworld Children's books in November 2001; now ranks amongst the top 5 children's publishers in the UK.

David Fickling Books (imprint)

31 Beaumont Street, Oxford OX1 2NP
tel (01865) 339000 *fax* (01865) 339009
email dfickling@randomhouse.co.uk
website davidficklingbooks.co.uk
Publisher David Fickling, *Editor* Bella Pearson

Picture books, fiction for 5–8 and 9–12 year-olds, teenage fiction and poetry. Publishes approx. 12 titles each year. Recent successes include: *The Curious Incident of the Dog in the Night-Time* by Mark Haddon, *Pants* by Giles Andreae and Nick Sharratt and *The Various* by Steve Augarde. Publishes books simultaneously with Random House Inc.

Submission details Will consider unsolicited MSS; allow 3 months for response and include a covering letter and sae. If possible find an agent first. Founded 2000.

Ransom Publishing Ltd

Rose Cottage, Howe Hill, Watlington, Oxon OX49 5HB
tel (01491) 613711 *fax* (01491) 613733
email ransom@ransompublishing.co.uk
website www.ransom.co.uk
Directors Jenny Ertle (managing), Steve Rickard (creative)

Educational (preschool and primary): literacy including special needs. Range of digital content from preschool to secondary for literacy, numeracy, science and goegraphy. Publishes approx. 5–10 titles each year and has about 40 in print. Recent successes include *Learn and Print Educational Pack, Rainbow Readers* and *Living Phonics.* Looking to publish books for older children struggling to learn to read, i.e. Key Stages 2 and 3.

Submission details Will consider unsolicited MSS but prefers a preliminary email. Selects very little as material needs to correspond to Ransom key publishing areas. Founded 1995.

Reader's Digest Children's Publishing Ltd

The Ice House, 124–126 Walcot Street, Bath BA1 5BG
tel (01225) 473200 *fax* (01225) 460942
email jill_eade@readersdigest.co.uk
Publisher Rosanne McManus, *Contact* Jill Eade

Innovative, high-quality books designed to encourage children to use their creativity and imagination. Board, novelty, cinema and TV tie-ins. Licensed characters and brands. Also a wide range of children's religious titles. Imprint: Reader's Digest Young Families. Fully owned subsidiary of Reader's Digest Association Inc. Founded 1981.

Red Bird Publishing

Kiln Farm, East End Green, Brightlingsea, Colchester, Essex CO7 0SX
tel (01206) 303525 *fax* (01206) 304545
email info@red-bird.co.uk
website www.red-bird.co.uk
Publisher Marin Rhodes-Schofield

Innovative children's activity packs and books produced with a mix of techniques and materials such as Glow in the Dark, Mirrors, Stereoscopic 3D, Moiré and other optical illusions. Authors are specialists in their fields. Activity books, novelty books, picture books, painting and colouring books, hobbies, nature and the environment, science, teaching, posters. Age groups: preschool, 5–10, 10–15.

Red Kite Books – see Haldane Mason Ltd

Religious and Moral Education Press (RMEP)

St Mary's Works, St Mary's Plain, Norwich NR3 3BH
tel (01603) 612914 *fax* (01603) 624483
email admin@scm-canterburypress.co.uk
website www.scm-canterburypress.co.uk
Ceo Gordon Knights, *Editorial Director* Mary Mears

Educational books and teachers' resources (primary and secondary): religious education, citizenship, PSHE, assembly resources (collective worship). Publishes approx. 10–20 titles each year and has about 150 in print. Recent successes include *The Riddle of Destiny* (*Biblos* secondary curriculum resources for teaching the Bible), *The Awkward Squad* (from the *Superstars* series) and *Round the Year* (99 stories for the primary school assembly).

Submission details Will consider unsolicited MSS. Send an outline or synopsis to the Editorial Director, indicating how the proposed publication would meet school curriculum requirements. Allow 4–6 weeks for a response. Most RMEP authors are, or have been, school teachers or college lecturers – mostly specialists in religious education. Founded 1980.

Rigby Heinemann – see Harcourt Education Ltd

RoutledgeFalmer – see Taylor and Francis Books Ltd

Saint Andrew Press*

121 George Street, Edinburgh EH2 4YN
tel 0131-240 2253 *fax* 0131-220 3113
email standrewpress@cofscotland.org.uk
website www.standrewpress.com
Head of Publishing Ann Crawford

Publishing house of the Church of Scotland: publishes books that explore Christianity, spirituality, faith and ethical and moral issues, as well as more general works of fiction and non-fiction; children's.

St Pauls

St Pauls Publishing, 187 Battersea Bridge Road, London SW11 3AS
tel 020-7978 4300 *fax* 020-7978 4370
email editions@stpauls.org.uk
website www.stpauls.ie

Theology, ethics, spirituality, biography, education, general books of Roman Catholic and Christian interest. Founded 1948.

Salariya Book Company Ltd

Book House, 25 Marlborough Place, Brighton BN1 1UB
tel (01273) 603306 *fax* (01273) 693857
email salariya@salariya.com
website www.salariya.com
Director David Salariya

Children's non-fiction. Imprint: Book House. Founded 1989.

Schofield & Sims Ltd

Dogley Mill, Fenay Bridge, Huddersfield HD8 0NQ
tel (01484) 607080 *fax* (01484) 606815
email sales@schofieldandsims.co.uk
Chairman C.N. Platts

Educational: nursery, infants, primary; posters. Founded 1901.

Scholastic Children's Books*

Commonwealth House, 1–19 New Oxford Street, London WC1A 1NU
tel 020-7421 9000 *fax* 020-7421 9001
email publicity@scholastic.co.uk
Publisher Richard Scrivener

Activity books, novelty books, picture books, fiction for 5–12 year-olds, teenage fiction, series fiction and film/TV tie-ins. Recent successes include *Predator's Gold* by Philip Reeve; *Poison* by Chris Wooding, *Montmorency* by Eleanor Updale, *Sleeping Beauty* by Adele Geras; *The Wicked History of the World* by Terry Deary and Martin Brown. Imprints include Hippo, Point, Scholastic Fiction, Scholastic Non-fiction, Scholastic Press. Imprint of Scholastic Ltd.

Submission details Will consider unsolicited submissions: send synopsis and sample chapter only.

Scholastic Fiction – see Scholastic Children's Books

Scholastic Ltd*

Villiers House, Clarendon Avenue, Leamington Spa, Warks. CV32 5PR
tel (01926) 887799 *fax* (01926) 883331
website www.scholastic.co.uk
Directors M.R. Robinson (USA), R.M. Spaulding (USA), D.J. Walsh (USA)

Founded 1924.

Children's Division

Publisher Richard Scrivener

See Scholastic Children's Books.

Direct Marketing

Managing Director, Book Fair Division & Book Club Division Miles Stevens-Hoare, *Managing Director, Trade Sales and Marketing* Gavin Lang, *Rights Director* Caroline Hill-Trevor

Children's book clubs and school book fairs. See page 61.

Educational Division
Publishing Director Anne Peel

Publishers of books for teachers (*Bright Ideas* and other series), primary classroom resources and magazines for teachers (*Child Education, Junior Education* and others). Founded 1964.

Scholastic Non-fiction – see Scholastic Children's Books

Scholastic Press – see Scholastic Children's Books

SCP Publishers Ltd*

Unit 6, Newbattle Abbey Business Annexe, Newbattle Road, Dalkeith EH22 3LJ
email info@scottishbooks.com
website www.scottishbooks.com
Directors Brian Pugh, Avril Gray

Scottish Children's Press
tel 0131-660 4757 *fax* 0131-660 4666

'Scottish books for children.' Picture books, fiction for 5–8 and 9–12 year-olds, reference, poetry and cookery. Publishes approx. 3 titles each year and has 32 in print. Recent successes include *Wee Willie Winkie* (nursery rhymes and songs), *Teach the Bairns to Cook/Bake* and *Danger by Gaslight* (fiction for age 8+). Also, for adults: Scottish fiction, Scottish non-fiction and Scots language.

Submission details Will not accept unsolicited MSS. See website or send for submission guidelines. Founded 1992.

Scripture Union

207–209 Queensway, Bletchley, Milton Keynes, Bucks. MK2 2EB
tel (01908) 856000 *fax* (01908) 856111
email postmaster@scriptureunion.org.uk
website www.scriptureunion.org.uk
Publishing Director Malcolm Hall

Christian books and Bible reading materials for people of all ages; educational and worship resources for churches; adult non-fiction; children's fiction and non-fiction (age groups: under 6, 6–7, 8–10 and youth). Publishes approx. 30 titles each year for children/young people and has 200–250 in print. Recent successes include *Fabulous Phoebe* by Kathy Lee, *Friends First* by Claire Pedrick and Andy Morgan and *An Alien at Christmas* by Brian Ogden. Scripture Union works as a charity in over 120 countries and publishes in approx. 20.

Submission details Will consider unsolicited MSS. Send sample and outline to Christina Simms in Publishing Dept. Authors should note that Scripture Union is a ministry as well as a publishing house. All books have an overt Christian or Biblical content. Founded 1867.

SEMERC

The Chiswick Centre, 414 Chiswick High Road, London W4 5TF
tel 020-8996 3333 *fax* 020-8742 8390
website www.semerc.com

'Solutions for inclusion.' Publisher of ICT resources for learners of all ages with special educational needs. Part of Granada Learning.

Short Books Ltd

15 Highbury Terrace, London N5 1UP
tel 020-7226 1607 *fax* 020-7226 4169
email mark@shortbooks.biz
website www.theshortbookco.com
Editorial Directors Rebecca Nicolson, Aurea Carpenter

Children's books: biographies of famous people from the past. Also non-fiction for adults, mainly biography and journalism.

Submission details Children's biographies should be 15,000–20,000 words long. All prospective authors will be informed by email of how their proposal has been received. MSS will not be returned. Founded 2000.

Simon & Schuster*

Africa House, 64–78 Kingsway, London WC2B 6AH
tel 020-7316 1900 *fax* 020-7316 0331/2
website www.simonsays.co.uk
Directors Ian Chapman (managing), Suzanne Baboneau (publishing), Caroline Proud (sales and marketing), Diane Spivey (rights), Ingrid Selberg (children's publishing)

For adults: fiction (commercial and literary) and serious non-fiction. Subjects include biography, current affairs, history and science. Imprints include Free Press, Martin Books, Pocket Books, Scribner and Simon & Schuster Audioworks. No unsolicited MSS. Founded 1986.

Simon & Schuster Children's Publishing
Children's Publishing Director Ingrid Selberg, *Fiction Editorial Director* Venetia Gosling, *Senior Commissioning Editor, Picture Books* Helen Mortimer, *Art Director* Margaret Hope

Activity books, novelty books, picture books, fiction for 5–8 and 9–12 year-olds, teenage fiction, series fiction, film/TV tie-ins. Publishes approx. 180–200 titles each year. Recent successes include *The Spiderwick Chronicles* by Holly Black and Tony Diterlizzi, *Alice's Adventures in Wonderland* (Robert Sabuda, pop-up book) and *Wendy* by Karen Wallace.

Submission details No unsolicited MSS. Will only consider MSS via agents.

Stacey International

128 Kensington Church Street, London W8 4BH
tel 020-7221 7166 *fax* 020-7792 9288
email enquiries@stacey-international.co.uk
website www.stacey-international.co.uk
Chairman Tom Stacey, *Managing Director* Max Scott, *Commissioning Editor* Caroline Singer

Illustrated non-fiction, encyclopedic books on regions and countries, Islamic and Arab subjects, world affairs, art, travel, belles-lettres, children's books (picture books, fiction for 5–8 and 9–12 year-olds and reference). Publishes approx. 3 children's titles each year and has 7 in print. Recent successes include *The Children's Encyclopedia of Arabia*, *The Pearl Diver* and *Elvis the Camel*. Seeking to publish picture books and reference books.

Submission details Will consider unsolicited MSS. Send synopsis. Founded 1973.

Storysack Ltd

Resource House, Kay Street, Bury BL9 6BU
tel 0161-763 6232 *fax* 0161-763 5366
email storysack@cs.com
website www.storysack.co.uk
Children's Editor Neil Griffiths

Storysacks for children aged 3+. Storysacks are cloth bags of resources to encourage children and parents to enjoy reading together. Each sack is based around a picture story book with a supporting fact book on a similar theme, a parent guide, characters and a game. Founded 1999.

Tamarind Ltd

PO Box 52, Northwood, Middlesex HA6 1UN
tel 020-8866 8808 *fax* 020-8866 5627
email info@tamarindbooks.co.uk
website www.tamarindbooks.co.uk
Managing Director Verna Wilkins

'Multicultural children's books for a multicultural world': picture books, fiction for 5–8 year-olds, biographies and posters. Publishes 5 titles each year and has 43 in print. Recent successes include *Princess Katrina and Her Hair Charmer* by Christina Shingler, *Hurricane* by Verna Allette Wilkins and *Black Profiles*.

Submission details Will consider unsolicited MSS with sae. Allow one month for response. Looking for books which give black children a high positive profile. Founded 1987.

Tango Books Ltd

3D West Point, 36–37 Warple Way,
London W3 0RG
tel 020-8996 9970 *fax* 020-8996 9977
email sales@tangobooks.co.uk
Directors Sheri Safran, David Fielder

Children's novelty books, including pop-up, touch-and-feel and cloth books.

Tarquin Publications

Stradbroke, Diss, Norfolk IP21 5JP
tel (01379) 384218 *fax* (01379) 384289
email tarquin-books.demon.co.uk
website www.tarquin-books.demon.co.uk
Partners Gerald Jenkins, Margaret Jenkins

Mathematical models and paper engineering books for intelligent children. Publishes 7–8 titles each year and has 103 in print. Recent successes include *Mathematical Merry-go-round*, *A Handbook of Paper Automata Mechanisms* and *Paper Gliders*.

Submission details Do not send unsolicited MSS. Send a one-page proposal of idea. Founded 1970.

Taylor and Francis Books Ltd*

11 New Fetter Lane, London EC4P 4EE
tel 020-7583 9855 *fax* 020-7842 2298
Moving Sept 04 to 4 Park Road, Milton Park, Abingdon, Oxon OX14 4RN
tel (01235) 828600 *fax* (01235) 828000
email info@tandf.co.uk
websites www.tandf.co.uk, www.tfinforma.com
Managing Director, Taylor & Francis Books Ltd Roger Horton

Academic and reference books. Imprints include BIOS Scientific Publishers, CRC Press, Dunitz, Europa Publications, Fitzroy-Dearborn, Garland Science, Parthenon Press, Pschology Press, Routledge, RoutledgeCurzon, RoutledgeFalmer, Spon Press and Taylor & Francis.

RoutledgeFalmer (imprint)

website www.routledgefalmer.com

Education books for teachers.

The Templar Company plc

Pippbrook Mill, London Road, Dorking,
Surrey RH4 1JE
tel (01306) 876361 *fax* (01306) 889097
email info@templar.co.uk
website www.templarco.co.uk
Managing Director Amanda Wood, *Publishing Manager* Rebecca Elliott, *Creative Director* Fiona MacMillan

High-quality illustrated children's books, including novelty books, picture books, pop-up books, board books, non-fiction and gift titles. See also page 58.

D.C. Thomson & Co. Ltd – Publications

2 Albert Square, Dundee DD1 9QJ
London office 185 Fleet Street,
London EC4A 2HS

Publishers of newspapers and periodicals. Children's books (annuals), based on weekly magazine characters; fiction. For fiction guidelines, send a large sae to Central Fiction Dept.

Time Warner Books UK*

Brettenham House, Lancaster Place,
London WC2E 7EN
tel 020-7911 8000 *fax* 020-7911 8100
Chief Executive David Young, *Directors* Ursula Mackenzie (publisher), Barbara Boote (editorial), Richard Beswick (editorial), Alan Samson (editorial), Peter Cotton (art), Richard Kitson (sales), Nigel Batt (financial), Terry Jackson (marketing), Stephen Roberts (commercial)

Hardback and paperback fiction and general non-fiction. No unsolicited MSS. Founded 1988.

Atom (division)

website www.atombooks.co.uk
Editorial Director Tim Holman, *Editor* Darren Nash

Teen fiction with a fantastical edge. Authors include Gary Kilworth, Patricia McKillip (winner of 2003 World Fantasy Award with *Darkly Faerie*), Catherine Webb and Terry Brooks.

Submission details Will consider unsolicited science fiction and fantasy novels. Submissions should include a full synopsis and no more than 30pp of double-spaced text. No short stories or poetry, and no emailed submissions. If material is to be returned, enclose sae. Address material to Atom Submissions, Time Warner Book Group.

Top That! Publishing plc

Marine House, Tide Mill Way, Woodbridge,
Suffolk IP12 1AP
tel (01394) 386651 *fax* (01394) 386011
email lorraine@topthatpublishing.com
website www.topthatpublishing.com
Directors Barrie Henderson (managing), Simon Couchman (creative), Dave Greggor (sales), Mike Kudar (production), *Managing Editor* Lorraine Johnson

Activity books, novelty books, reference books and CD-Roms. Publishes 150 titles each year and has 300 in print. Recent successes include *Extreme Sports* (*I-Quest* series), *Designer Denim* (*Mini Maestro* series) and *Fun Kit: Energy*. Imprint: Top That! Kids.

Submission details Phone the Editorial Dept before sending MSS to ascertain interest. Founded 1998.

Treehouse Children's Books

2nd Floor Offices, Old Brewhouse,
Lower Charlton Trading Estate, Shepton Mallet,
Somerset BA4 5QE
tel (01749) 330529 *fax* (01749) 330544
email richard.powell4@virgin.net
Editorial Director Richard Powell

Preschool children's books and novelty books. Imprint of Emma Treehouse Ltd (see page 58). Founded 1989.

Trentham Books Ltd

Westview House, 734 London Road, Oakhill,
Stoke-on-Trent ST4 5NP
tel (01782) 745567 *fax* (01782) 745553
email tb@trentham.books.co.uk
website www.trentham-books.co.uk
Editorial office 28 Hillside Gardens,
London N6 5ST
email 020-8348 2174
Directors Dr Gillian Klein (editorial), Barbara Wiggins (executive)

Education (including specialist fields – multi-ethnic issues, equal opportunities, bullying, design and technology, early years), social policy, sociology of education, European education, women's studies. Does not publish books for use by parents or children, or fiction, biography, reminiscences and poetry. Founded 1978.

Trotman & Company Ltd

2 The Green, Richmond, Surrey TW9 1PL
tel 020-8486 1150 *fax* 020-8486 1161
website www.trotmanpublishing.co.uk
Managing Director Toby Trotman, *Editorial Director* Mina Patria, *Commissioning Editor* Rachel Lockhart

Independent advice and guidance on careers and higher education. Founded 1970.

Usborne Publishing Ltd

Usborne House, 83–85 Saffron Hill,
London EC1N 8RT
tel 020-7430 2800 *fax* 020-7430 1562
email mail@usborne.co.uk
website www.usborne.com
Publishing Director Jenny Tyler, *Editorial Director, Fiction* Megan Larkin, *General Manager* Robert Jones

Activity books, novelty books, picture books, fiction for 5–8 and 9–12 year-olds, series fiction, reference, poetry and audio. Reference subjects include practical, computers, craft, natural history, science, languages, history, geography. Publishes 120 titles each year and has about 1000 in print. Recent successes include *That's Not My Dolly* (touchy-feely board book), *Genes and DNA* (internet-linked guide) and *Fairy Things to Make and Do* (activity book). Imprint: Usborne.

Submission details Looking for high-quality imaginative children's fiction. Send non-fiction correspondence to Jenny Tyler and fiction correspondence to Megan Larkin. Founded 1973.

Walker Books Ltd

87 Vauxhall Walk, London SE11 5HJ
tel 020-7793 0909 *fax* 020-7587 1123
email mail@walker.co.uk
website www.walkerbooks.co.uk
Directors David Lloyd (chairman), David Heatherwick

(managing), Mark Briars (finance), Michel Blake (production), Jane Winterbotham (publishing), Henryk Wesolowski (sales & marketing), Gill Evans (publishing), *Publishers* Deidre McDermott, Caroline Royds, Loraine Taylor, Denise Johnstone-Burt

Activity books, novelty books, picture books, fiction for 5–8 and 9–12 year-olds, teenage fiction, series fiction, film/TV tie-ins, plays, poetry and audio. Publishes approx. 300 titles each year and has 2300 in print. Recent successes include *Eaglestrike* by Anthony Horowitz, *Dear Tooth Fairy* by Alan Durant and Vanessa Cabban and *Maisy's Rainbow Dream* by Lucy Cousins. Imprint: Walker Books.

Submission details Will not consider unsolicited MSS. Write to the Editor. Allow 3 months for response. Founded 1980.

Ward Lock Educational Co. Ltd

BIC Ling Kee House, 1 Christopher Road, East Grinstead, West Sussex RH19 3BT
tel (01342) 318980 *fax* (01342) 410980
email wle@lingkee.com
website www.wardlockeducational.com
Directors Au Bak Ling (chairman, Hong Kong), Au King Kwok (Hong Kong), Au Wai Kwok (Hong Kong), Albert Kw Au (Hong Kong), *General Manager* Penny Kitchenham

Primary and secondary pupil materials, Kent Mathematics Project: *KMP BASIC* and *KMP Main* series covering Reception to GCSE, Reading Workshops, *Take Part* series and *Take Part Starters*, teachers' books, music books, *Target* series for the National Curriculum: *Target Science* and *Target Geography*, religious education. Founded 1952.

Warne – see Penguin Group (UK)

The Watts Publishing Group Ltd*

96 Leonard Street, London EC2A 4XD
tel 020-7739 2929 *fax* 020-7739 2318
email gm@wattspub.co.uk
website www.wattspublishing.co.uk
Directors Marlene Johnson (managing), Philippa Stewart (publishing, Franklin Watts), Ann-Janine Murtagh (publishing, Orchard Books), Clare Somerville (sales & marketing), Alan Lee (production), Zosia Knopp (rights)

Novelty books, picture books, fiction for 5–8 and 9–12 year-olds, teenage fiction and poetry. Has approx. 300 titles in print. Imprints: Orchard Books, Franklin Watts, Aladdin/Watts, Cat's Whiskers.

Cat's Whiskers (imprint)

Publishing Director Philippa Stewart

Children's picture books.

Franklin Watts (division)

Publishing Director Philippa Stewart

Children's illustrated non-fiction, reference, education. Imprint: Aladdin/Watts.

Orchard Books (division)

Publishing Director Ann-Janine Murtagh

Children's picture books, fiction, poetry, novelty books, board books. Recent successes include *Clarence Bean, That's Me* by Lauren Child, *The Witch's Children and the Queen* by Ursula Jones and Russell Ayto and *Stargirl* by Jerry Spinelli.

Wizard – see Icon Books Ltd

The Women's Press

Top Floor, 27 Goodge Street, London W1P 2LD
tel 020-7580 7806 *fax* 020-7637 1866
website www.the-womens-press.com
Acting Managing Director Stella Kane

Books by women in the areas of literary and crime fiction, biography and autobiography, health, culture, politics, handbooks, literary criticism, psychology and self-help, the arts. Founded 1978.

Livewire (imprint)

Books for teenagers and young women.

Wordsworth Editions Ltd

8B East Street, Ware, Herts. SG12 9HJ
tel (01920) 465167 *fax* (01920) 462267
email enquiries@wordsworth-editions.com
website www.wordsworth.editions.com
Directors Michael Trayler (managing), Helen Trayler (operations), Dennis Hart (sales)

Reprints of classic books: literary, children's, exploration, military; myth, legend and folklore; poetry; reference. Founded 1987.

Y Lolfa Cyf.

Talybont, Ceredigion SY24 5AP
tel (01970) 832304 *fax* (01970) 832782
email ylolfa@ylolfa.com
website www.ylolfa.com
Director Garmon Gruffudd, *Editor* Lefi Gruffudd

Welsh-language popular fiction and non-fiction, music, children's books (recent successes include *Iawn Boi!* by Caryl Lewis and *Stori Dafydd ap Gwilym* by Gwyn Thomas and Margaret Jones); Welsh-language tutors; Welsh politics in English and a range of Welsh-interest books for the tourist market. Founded 1967.

York Notes – see Pearson Education

Young Picador – see Macmillan Publishers Ltd

Zero to Ten Ltd*

2A Portman Mansions, Chiltern Street, London W1U 6NR
tel 020-7487 0920 *fax* 020-7487 0921

email sales@evansbrothers.co.uk
Publishing Director Su Swallow

Non-fiction for children aged 0–10: board books, toddler books, first story books, etc. Part of the Evans Publishing Group. Founded 1997.

Cherrytree Books (imprint)
UK Publisher Su Swallow

Children's non-fiction illustrated books mainly for schools and libraries.

Zoë Books Ltd

15 Worthy Lane, Winchester, Hants SO23 7AB
tel (01962) 851318
email enquiries@zoebooks.co.uk
website www.zoebooks.co.uk
Directors Imogen Dawson (managing/publishing), C.W. Dawson, J.T. Dawson

Children's information books for schools (primary and secondary) libraries. Has over 100 titles in print. Recent successes include *Postcards From* series, *Clothes and Crafts* series and *World Habitats* series.

Submission details Will not consider unsolicited MSS. No opportunities for freelances. Not looking for new writers. Founded 1990.

ZooBooKoo International Ltd

4 Gurdon Road, Grundisburgh, Woodbridge, Suffolk IP13 6XA
tel (01473) 735346 *fax* (01473) 735346
email sales@zoobookoo.com
website www.zoobookoo.com
Sales Director Karen Wattleworth

Designer/manufacturer of ZooBooKoo Original Cube Books, multi-level educational folding cube books. Titles include: *World Football, Human Body, Magic Maze, Add and Subtract, Planets, Natural Europe* and *Dolphins & Whales.*

Children's book publishers overseas

Listings are given for children's book publishers in Australia (below), Canada (page 34), New Zealand (page 36), South Africa (page 37), the USA (page 38) and Europe (page 48).

AUSTRALIA

**Member of the Australian Publishers Association*

Allen & Unwin Pty Ltd*

83 Alexander Street, Crows Nest, NSW 2065
postal address PO Box 8500, St Leonards, NSW 1590
tel (02) 8425 0100 *fax* (02) 9906 2218
email info@allenandunwin.com
website www.allenandunwin.com
Directors Patrick Gallagher (managing), Paul Donovan (sales & marketing), Peter Eichhorn (finance), *Publishers, Children & Teenagers* Rosalind Price, Erica Wagner

Picture books, fiction for 5–8 and 9–12 year-olds, teenage fiction, series fiction, narrative non-fiction and poetry. Also adult/general trade books, including fiction, academic, especially social science and history. Publishes approx. 40 titles each year and has about 310 in print. Recent successes include *Horrible Harriet* by Leigh Hobbs (picture book), *Think Smart, Hazel Green* by Odo Hirsch (junior fiction) and *How to Make a Bird* by Martine Murray. Imprint: Allen & Unwin.

Submission details Will consider unsolicited MSS (but not picture book texts). Prefers to receive full MSS by post, with a brief synopsis and biography. Allow 3 months for response. Seeking junior fiction, quirkey non-fiction by wise, funny, inventive authors with a dinstinctive voice. Founded 1990

Michelle Anderson Publishing Pty Ltd*

PO Box 6032, Chapel Street North, South Yarra 3141
tel (03) 9826 9028 *fax* (03) 9826 8552
email mapubl@bigpond.net.au
website www.michelleandersonpublishing.com
Directors Michelle Anderson, M. Slamen

Picture books for children aged 3–8. Also for adults: general health and mind/body. Publishes 2 children's titles each year and has 6 in print. Recent successes include *Broken Beaks* (explaining homelessness to children), *What About Me?* (story for siblings of sick children) and *Who Am I?* (yoga for children). Imprint: Michelle Anderson Publishing.

Submission details Will consider unsolicited synopses but not MSS. Allow 3 weeks for response. Founded 2002.

The Australian Council for Educational Research

19 Prospect Hill Road, Private Bag 55, Camberwell, Victoria 3124
tel (03) 9277 5555 *fax* (03) 9277 5500
email info@acer.edu.au
website www.acerpress.com.au

Range of books and kits: for teachers, trainee teachers, parents, psychologists, counsellors, students of education, researchers.

Cygnet – see University of Western Australia Press

Elsevier Australia*

30–52 Smidmore Street, Marrickville, NSW 2204
tel (02) 9517 8999 *fax* (02) 9550 6007

Elsevier Education (division)
Managing Director & Children's Publisher David O'Brien

Curriculum-based textbooks and classroom resources for the states of Australia and across all syllabus areas from kindergarten to Year 12. Imprints: Rigby, Heinemann, CIS, Barrie Publishing, Heinemann Library. Founded 1982.

HarperCollins Publishers (Australia) Pty Limited Group*

25–31 Ryde Road, Pymble, NSW 2073
postal address PO Box 321, Pymble, NSW 2073
tel (02) 9952 5000 *fax* (02) 9952 5555
Managing Director Brian Murray, *Children's Publisher* Lisa Berryman

Literary fiction and non-fiction, popular fiction, children's, reference, biography, autobiography, current affairs, sport, lifestyle, health/self-help, humour, true crime, travel, Australiana, history, business, gift/stationery, religion.

Hodder Headline Australia Pty Ltd*

Level 17, 207 Kent Street, Sydney, NSW 2000
tel (02) 8248 0800 *fax* (02) 2848 0810
email auspub@hha.com.au
website www.hha.com.au
Directors Malcolm Edwards (managing), Lisa Highton, Mary Drum, David Cocking

General, children's. No unsolicited MSS.

Lothian Books*

132 Albert Road, South Melbourne, Victoria 3205
tel 613-9694-4900 *fax* 613-9645-0705
email books@lothian.com.au
website www.lothian.com.au
Directors Peter Lothian (managing), Bruce Hilliard (sales & marketing), *Children's Publisher* Helen Chamberlain, *Children's Book Publicist* Georgina Way

Picture books, fiction for 5–8 and 9–12 year-olds, teenage fiction and series fiction. Publishes approx. 65 titles each year and has 750 in print. Recent successes include *Journey from the Centre of the Earth* by Isobelle Carmody and Marc McBride (picture book), *Nips Go National* by Ruth Starke (junior fiction) and *Julia, My Sister* by Bronwyn Blake (young adult). Imprints: Start-Ups, Takeaways, Lothian Young Adult Fiction, The Quentaris Chronicles. Also for adults: health, gardening, reference, Australian history, business, sport, biography, New Age, humour, Buddhism.

Submission details Will not accept unsolicited MSS. Submit MSS via an agent. List is full until 2006. Founded 1888.

Macmillan Education Australia Pty Ltd*

Melbourne office Locked Bag 1, Prahran, Victoria 3181
tel (03) 9825 1025 *fax* (03) 9825 1010
email mea@macmillan.com.au
Sydney office Level 2, St Martin's Tower, 31 Market Street, Sydney, NSW 2000
tel (02) 9285 9200 *fax* (02) 9285 9290
email measyd@macmillan.com.au
Directors Richard Charkin (chief executive – UK), Ross Gibb (executive chairman), Shane Armstrong (managing), Peter Huntley (sales), Sandra Iversen (primary publishing), Rex Parry (secondary publishing), George Smith (production), *Company Secretary/Financial Controller* Terry White, *Children's Publisher* Sandra Iverson

Educational books.

New Frontier Publishing

6 Merle Street, Epping 2121
tel (2) 987 61050 *fax* (2) 987 64106
Director Ronald Proft

Aims to uplift, educate and inspire through its range of children's books. Activity books, picture books, fiction, dictionaries, textbooks. Caters for 5–10 year-olds.

Pan Macmillan Australia Pty Ltd*

Level 18, 31 Market Street, Sydney, NSW 2000
tel (02) 9285 9100 *fax* (02) 9285 9190
email pansyd@macmillan.com.au
website www.macmillan.com.au
Directors Ross Gibb (chairman), James Fraser (publishing), Roxarne Burns (publishing), Siv Toigo (finance), Peter Phillips (sales), Jeannine Fowler (publicity and marketing)

Commercial and literary fiction; children's fiction, non-fiction and character products; non-fiction; sport.

Pearson Education Australia

95 Coventry Street, South Melbourne 3205
tel (3) 969 70666 *fax* (3) 969 92041
website www.pearsoned.com.au/schools
Publisher Denise Ryan

Fiction, novels, poetry, education, geography, history, science, textbooks, CD-Roms. Age groups: 5–10, 10–15, 15+.

Penguin Group (Australia)*

250 Camberwell Road, Camberwell, Victoria 3124
postal address PO Box 701, Hawthorn, Victoria 3122
tel (03) 9811 2400 *fax* (03) 9811 2620
website www.penguin.com.au
Managing Director Gabrielle Coyne, *Publishing Director* Robert Sessions, *Executive Publisher – Books for Children & Young Adults* Julie Watts, *Publisher – Books for Children & Young Adults* Laura Harris, *Commissioning Editor* Lisa Riley

Picture books, fiction for 5–8 and 9–12 year-olds, teenage fiction, series fiction and film/TV tie-ins. Also for adults: fiction and general non-fiction. Publishes approx. 85 titles each year and has about 500 in print. Recent successes include *Cuthbert's Babies* by Pamela Allen (picture book), *Rascal* books by Paul Jennings (younger readers) and *Saving Francesca* by Melina Marchetta (young adult). Children's imprints: Puffin (paperback). A Pearson company.

Submission details Will consider unsolicited MSS but submit only one MS at a time. Send proposals to The Editor, Books for Children and Young Adults at the postal address (above). Enclose an sae for the return of material. Does not accept proposals by email or fax. Founded 1935.

Prim-Ed Publishing Pty Ltd

4 Bendsten Place, Balcatta, WA 6021
tel 618-9240-9888 *fax* 618-9240-1513
website www.prim-ed.com

Educational publisher specialising in blackline master or copymasters and student workbooks for schools and homeschoolers.

Puffin – see Penguin Group (Australia)

University of Queensland Press*

PO Box 6042, St Lucia, Queensland 4067
tel (07) 3365 2127 *fax* (07) 3365 7579
email uqp@uqp.uq.edu.au
website www.uqp.uq.edu.au
General Manager Greg Bain

Scholarly works, tertiary texts, indigenous Australian writing, Australian fiction, young adult fiction, poetry, history, general interest. Founded 1948.

Random House Australia Pty Ltd*

20 Alfred Street, Milsons Point, NSW 2061
tel (02) 9954 9966 *fax* (02) 9954 4562
email random@randomhouse.com.au
website www.randomhouse.com.au
Managing Director Margaret Seale, *Head of Publishing, Random House* Jane Palfreyman, *Head of Publishing, Bantam Doubleday* Fiona Henderson, *Children's Publisher* Lindsay Knight, *Illustrated Publisher* Steve Barnett, *Sales & Marketing Director* Carol Davidson, *Commercial Manager* Daren Chan, *Rights & Permissions Manager* Nerrilee Weir

General fiction and non-fiction; children's, illustrated. Imprints: Arrow, Avon, Ballantine, Bantam, Black Swan, Broadway, Century, Chatto & Windus, Corgi, Crown, Dell, Doubleday, Ebury, Fodor, Heinemann, Hutchinson, Jonathan Cape, Knopf, Mammoth UK, Minerva, Pantheon, Pavilion, Pimlico, Random House, Red Fox, Rider, Vermillion, Vintage, Virgin. Agencies: BBC Worldwide. Subsidiary of Bertelsmann AG.

Submission details For Random House and Transworld Publishing, unsolicited non-fiction accepted, unbound in hard copy addressed to Submissions Editor. Fiction submissions are only accepted from previously published authors, or authors represented by an agent or accompanied by a report from an accredited assessment service.

Scholastic Australia Pty Ltd*

PO Box 579, Gosford, NSW 2250
tel (02) 4328 3555 *fax* (02) 4323 3827
website www.scholastic.com.au
Managing Director Ken Jolly, *Children's Publishers* Ken Jolly, Andrew Berkhut

Children's fiction/non-fiction; educational materials for elementary schools, teacher reference. Founded 1968.

Thomson Learning Australia*

102 Dodds Street, Southbank, Victoria 3006
tel (03) 9685 4111 *fax* (03) 9685 4199
email customerservice@thomsonlearning.com.au
website www.thomsonlearning.com.au

Educational books.

Trocadero Press

Suite 204, 74 Pitt Street, NSW 2000, Sydney
tel (2) 922 10168 *fax* (2) 922 10169
website www.trocaderopublishing.com
Managing Director Scott Brodie

High-quality colour illustrated non-fiction reference books, as single titles and series. Also entertaining non-fiction colour illustrated trade books. Caters for 10–15 year-olds.

University of Western Australia Press*

UWA, 35 Stirling Hwy, Crawley 6009, Western Australia
tel (618) 6488 3670 *fax* (618) 6488 1027
email uwap@cyllene.uwa.edu.au
website www.uwapress.uwa.edu.au
Director Dr Jenny Gregory

Fiction for 5–8 and 9–12 year-olds and teenage fiction. Also for adults: natural history, history, maritime history, critical studies, women's studies, general non-fiction, contemporary issues. Publishes approx. 6 children's titles each year. Recent successes include *The Legend of Lasseter's Reef* by Mark Greenwood, *Silverskin* by Guundie Kuchling and *Digger* by Liliana Stafford. Children's imprints: Cygnet, Cygnet Young Fiction.

Submission details Will consider unsolicited MSS. Contact UWAP for guidelines. Seeking to publish books with Australian themes, an environmental message and historical topics. Founded 1954.

John Wiley & Sons Australia Ltd

33 Park Road, Milton, Queensland 4064
tel (07) 3859 9755 *fax* (07) 3859 9715
email brisbane@johnwiley.com.au
website www.johnwiley.com.au
Managing Director P. Donoughue

Educational, technical, atlases, professional, reference, trade. Imprints: John Wiley & Sons, Jacaranda, Wright Books. Founded 1954.

CANADA

**Member of the Canadian Publishers' Council*

†Member of the Association of Canadian Publishers

Annick Press Ltd†
15 Patricia Avenue, Toronto, Ontario M2M 1H9
tel 416-221-4802 *fax* 416-221-8400
email annick@annickpress.com
website www.annickpress.com
Co-editors Rick Wilks, Colleen MacMillan

Preschool to young adult fiction and non-fiction. Founded 1975.

Doubleday Canada*
1 Toronto Street, Suite 300, Toronto, Ontario M5C 2V6
tel 416-364-4449 *fax* 416-957-1587
website www.randomhouse.ca
Chairman John Neale, *Publisher* Maya Mavjee

General trade non-fiction: current affairs, politics; fiction; children's illustrated. Division of Random House of Canada Ltd. Founded 1942.

Dundurn Press†
8 Market Street, Suite 200, Toronto, Ontario M5E 1M6
tel 416-214-5544 *fax* 416-214-5556
email info@dundurn.com
website www.dundurn.com
Directors J. Kirk Howard (President), Beth Bruder (Vic-President, sales & marketing), Tony Hawke (editorial)

Serious non-fiction, scholarship, history, biography, art. Part of the Dundurn Group. Founded 1973.

Boardwalk Books (imprint)
Young adult fiction.

Fitzhenry & Whiteside Ltd†
195 Allstate Parkway, Markham, Ontario L3R 4T8
tel 905-477-9700 *fax* 905-477-9179
email godwit@fitzhenry.ca
tel 1-800-387-9776 (toll free) *fax* 1-800-260-9777 (toll free)
Director Sharon Fitzhenry, *Children's Publisher* Gail Winskill

Trade, educational, children's books. Founded 1966.

Gage Learning Corporation
164 Commander Boulevard, Toronto, Ontario M1S 3C7
tel 416-293-8141 *fax* 416-293-9009
website www.gagelearning.com
President Chris Besse

Elementary and secondary school textbooks; professional and reference materials. Founded 1844.

Harcourt Canada Ltd*
55 Horner Avenue, Toronto, Ontario M8Z 4X6
tel 416-255-4491 *fax* 416-255-4046
email firstname_lastname@harcourt.com
website www.harcourtcanada.com
President Wendy Cochran

Educational materials from K–Grade 12, testing and assessment. Imprints: Harcourt Religion (formerly Brown-ROA), Harcourt Brace & Company, Holt, Rinehart and Winston, MeadowBrook Press, The Psychological Corporation, Therapy Skill Builders/ Communications Skill Builders. Founded 1922.

HarperCollins Publishers Ltd*
2 Bloor Street East, 20th Floor, Toronto, Ontario M4W 1A8
tel 416-975-9334 *fax* 416-975-9884
website www.harpercanada.com
President David Kent

Publishers of literary fiction and non-fiction, history, politics, biography, spiritual and children's books. Founded 1989.

Irwin Publishing Ltd
325 Humber College Blvd, Toronto, Ontario M9W 7C3
tel 416-798-0424 *fax* 416-798-1384
email irwin@irwin-pub.com
President Brian O'Donnell, *Chairman* Jack Stoddart

Educational books at the elementary, high school and college levels.

Key Porter Books Ltd†
70 The Esplanade, 3rd Floor, Toronto, Ontario M5E 1R2
tel 416-862-7777 *fax* 416-862-2304
email aporter@keyporter.com
website www.keyporter.com
Publisher/Ceo Anna Porter, *President* Diane Davy, *Children's* Joe Darrell

Fiction, nature, history, Canadian politics, conservation, humour, biography, autobiography, health, children's books. Founded 1981.

Kids Can Press Ltd†
29 Birch Avenue, Toronto, Ontario M4V 1E2
tel 416-925-5437 *fax* 416-960-5437
email info@kidscan.com
Publisher Valerie Hussey, Karen Boersma

Juvenile/young adult books.

McGraw-Hill Ryerson Ltd*
300 Water Street, Whitby, Ontario L1N 9B6
tel 905-430-5000 *fax* 905-430-5020
website www.mcgrawhill.ca

Educational and trade books.

Madison Press

1000 Younge Street, Suite 200, Toronto, Ontario M4W 2K2
tel 416-923-5027 *fax* 416-923-7169
website www.madisonpressbooks.com
Editorail Director Wanda Nowakowska

Picture books, non-fiction, history. Ages groups: 5–10, 10–15.

Napoleon Publishing/Rendez Vous Press*†

178 Willowdale Avenue, Suite 201, Toronto, Ontario M2N 4Y8
tel 416-730-9052 *fax* 416-730-8096
email napoleon.publishing@transmedia95.com
website www.napoleonpublishing.com
Publisher Sylvia McConnell, *Editor* Allister Thompson

Children's books and adult fiction. Founded 1990.

Nelson*

1120 Birchmount Road, Scarbourgh, Ontario M1K 5G4
tel 416-752-9100 *fax* 416-752-9646
President/Ceo George W. Bergquist, *Senior Vice President, Finance/Cfo* Lesley Gouldie, *Senior Vice President, School* Greg Pilon, *Vice President, Higher Education* Ron Kelly, *Vice President, Media Services* Susan Cline, *Vice President, Operations* Ed Berman, *Vice President, Human Resources* Marlene Nyilassy, *Editorial Director, Higher Education* Evelyn Veitch, *Director of Publishing, School* David Steele, *Director of Marketing, Higher Education* James Rozsa, *Director of Sales, School* James Reeve, *Director of Information Systems & Technology* Bruce Sharron

Educational publishing: school (K–12), college and university, career education, measurement and guidance, professional and reference, ESL titles. Founded 1914.

Oxford University Press, Canada*

70 Wynford Drive, Don Mills, Ontario M3C 1J9
tel 416-441-2941 *fax* 416-444-0427
website www.oup.com/ca
President Joanna Gertler

General, educational and academic.

Pearson Education Canada*

26 Prince Andrew Place, Toronto, Ontario M3C 2T8
tel 416-447-5101 *fax* 416-443-0948
website www.pearsoned.ca
President Tony Vander Woude

Academic, technical, educational, children's and adult, trade.

Pippin Publishing Corporation

Suite 232, 85 Ellesmere Road, Toronto, Ontario M1R 4B9
tel 416-510-2918 *fax* 416-510-3359
email jld@pippinpub.com
website www.pippinpub.com
President/Editorial Director Jonathan Lovat Dickson

ESL/EFL, teacher reference, adult basic education, school texts (all subjects), general trade (non-fiction).

Raincoast Books

9050 Shaughnessy Street, Vancouver, BC V6P 6E5
tel 604-323-7100 *fax* 604-323-2600
email publishing@raincoast.com
website www.raincoast.com

Fiction and non-fiction for adults and children. Imprints: Polestar, Press Gang.

Submission details Will not accept unsolicited MSS. No queries via email. Send a query letter via regular mail for the attention of the Editorial Department. Allow 8–16 weeks for reply.

Scholastic Canada Ltd

Scholastic Canada Ltd, 175 Hillmount Road, Markham, Ontario L6C 1Z7
website www.scholastic.com
Art Director Ms Yüksel Hassan

Serves children, parents and teachers through a variety of businesses including Scholastic Book Clubs and Book Fairs, Scholastic Education, Classroom Magazines, Trade, and Les éditions Scholastic. Publishes recreational reading for children and young people from kindergarten to Grade 8 and educational materials in both official languages. Its publishing focus is on books by Canadians. Scholastic Canada Ltd is a wholly owned subsidiary of Scholastic Inc.

Submission details No unsolicited MSS. Fiction – length: picture books (4–8 years) under 1000 words; first chapter books (7–9 years) 7000–10,000 words; junior novels 9–14 years 25,000–40,000 words. Non-fiction subjects: up to 4 years – animals, school, seasons, etc; 5–6 years – biography, Canadiana, history, etc; 7–10 years – adventure, animals, sports, etc; 11–14 years – crafts, friendship, technology, etc.

Artists may submit several photocopied samples of their work and a brief resumé to the art director. Never send originals or anything that cannot be replaced.

Total Publishing

7 Bates Road, Outermont, Quebec H2V 4V7
tel 514-270-6860 *fax* 514-276-2533
website www.total-publishing.com
Contact Stephanie Labbe

Activity books, novelty books, picture books, biography, fairy tales, history. Age groups: preschool, 5–10, 10–15.

Tundra Books Inc.†

481 University Avenue, Suite 900, Toronto, Ontario M5G 2E9
tel 416-598-4786 *fax* 416-598-0247
website www.tundrabooks.com
Children's Publisher Kathy Lowinger

High-quality children's picture books.

Women's Press*

180 Bloor Street West, Suite 801, Toronto, Ontario M5S 2V6
tel 416-929-2774 *fax* 416-929-1926
email info@cspi.org
website www.womenspress.ca
President & Publisher Dr Jack Wayne, *Managing Editor* Althea Prince PhD

The ideas and experiences of women: fiction, creative non-fiction, children's books, plays, biography, autobiography, memoirs, poetry. Owned by Canadian Scholars' Press. Founded 1987.

NEW ZEALAND

**Member of the New Zealand Book Publishers' Association*

David Bateman Ltd*

30 Tarndale Grove, Bush Road, Albany, Auckland
postal address PO Box 100242, North Shore Mail Centre, Auckland 1330
tel (09) 415-7664 *fax* (09) 415-8892
email bateman@bateman.co.nz
website www.bateman.co.nz
Chairman/Publisher David L. Bateman, *Directors* Janet Bateman, Paul Bateman (joint managing), Paul Parkinson (joint managing)

Natural history, gardening, encyclopedias, sport, art, cookery, historical, juvenile, travel, motoring, maritime history, business, art, lifestyle. Founded 1979.

Dunmore Press Ltd*

PO Box 5115, Palmerston North
tel (06) 358-7169 *fax* (06) 357-9242
email books@dunmore.co.nz
website www.dunmore.co.nz
Directors Murray Gatenby, Sharmian Firth

Education, history, sociology, business studies, general non-fiction. Founded 1970.

HarperCollins Publishers (New Zealand) Ltd

3 View Road, Glenfield, Auckland
tel (09) 443-9400 *fax* (09) 443-9403
website www.harpercollins.co.nz
Managing Director Tony Fisk, *Children's Publisher* Lorain Day

General literature, non-fiction, reference, children's.

Mallinson Rendel Publishers Ltd

Level 5, 15 Courtenay Place, PO Box 9409, Wellington
tel (04) 802-5012 *fax* (04) 802-5013
email publisher@mallinsonrendel.co.nz
Publisher & Managing Director Ann Mallinson, *Editor* Carol Dee

Picture books, fiction for 5–8 and 9–12 year-olds and teenage fiction. Publishes approx. 7 titles each year and has 76 in print. Recent successes include *Schnitzel von Krumm Forget-Me-Not* by Lynley Dodd, *Right Where It Hurts* by David Hill and *Henry and the Flea* by Brian Falkner. Imprint: Mallinson Rendel.

Submission details Will accept unsolicited MSS but is only interested in submissions from New Zealand authors. Founded 1980.

Milly Molly Books

752 Gladstone Road, Gisbourne 3815, PO Box 539
tel (06) 8687769 *fax* (06) 8687767
email john@millymolly.com
website www.millymolly.com
Managing Director John Pittar

Picture books, gift books, fiction, education, CD-Roms for preschool children and 5–10 year-olds. Promotes acceptance of diversity and sound values worldwide.

Nelson Price Milburn Ltd

1 Te Puni Street, Petone
postal address PO Box 38-945, Wellington Mail Centre, Wellington
tel (04) 568-7179 *fax* (04) 568-2115
email jacqui.rivera@thomson.com

Children's fiction, primary school texts, especially school readers and maths, secondary educational.

New Zealand Council for Educational Research*

Box 3237, Education House, 178–182 Willis Street, Wellington 1
tel (04) 384-7939 *fax* (04) 384-7933
email info@nzcer.org.nz
website www.nzcer.org.nz
Director Robyn Baker, *Publisher* Bev Webber

Education, including educational policy and institutions, early childhood education, educational achievement tests, Maori education, curriculum and assessment, etc. Founded 1934.

Pearson Education New Zealand Ltd*

Private Bag 102908, North Shore Mail Centre, Glenfield, Auckland 10
tel (09) 444-4968 *fax* (09) 444-4957
email firstname.lastname@pearsoned.co.nz
Managing Director Rosemary Stagg

New Zealand educational books.

Reed Publishing (New Zealand) Ltd*
39 Rawene Road, PO Box 34901, Birkenhead, Auckland 10
tel (09) 480 4950 *fax* (09) 480-4999
Chairman John Philbin, *Managing Director* Alan Smith, *Publishing Manager* Peter Janssen

NZ literature, specialist and general titles, primary, secondary and tertiary textbooks.

RSVP Publishing Company*
PO Box 47166, Ponsonby, Auckland
tel (09) 372-3480 *fax* (09) 372 8480
email rsvppub@iconz.co.nz
website www.rsvp-publishing.co.nz
Managing Director/Publisher Stephen Picard

Fiction, metaphysical, children's. Founded 1990.

Scholastic New Zealand Ltd*
21 Lady Ruby Drive, East Tamaki, Auckland
postal address Private Bag 94407, Greenmount, Auckland
tel (09) 274-8112 *fax* (09) 274-8114
email publishing@scholastic.co.nz
website www.scholastic.co.nz
General Manager David Peagram, *Publishing Manager* Christine Dale, *Senior Editor* Penny Scown

Picture books, fiction for 5–8 and 9–12 year-olds, teenage fiction and series fiction. Publishes approx. 24 titles each year and has over 200 in print. Recent successes include *My Story: Abandon Ship* by Shirley Corlett, *Oliver in the Garden/Oliver's Party* by Margaret Beames and Sue Hitchcock and *A Handfull of Blue* by Vince Ford. Imprints: Scholastic NZ, Blue Balloon.

Submission details Will consider unsolicited MSS. Include an sae for its return. For picture books send copies of illustrations, *not* original artwork. Founded 1962.

Shortland Publications
10 Cawley Street, Ellerslie, Auckland 5
Submissions Louise Williams, Shortland Publications, Private Bag 11904, Ellerslie, Auckland 5
tel (09) 526-6200 *fax* (09) 526-4499
email Louise_Williams@mcgraw-hill.com

International primary reading market: potential authors should familiarise themselves with Shortland products. Looking for fresh ideas. *Cocky Circle* series 24pp read-to books for 2–6 year-olds.

Submission details Currently seeking submissions for emergent/early and fluency reading material (8–24pp): stories need to be simple and to feature supports for the child learning to read, e.g. repetition of vocabulary and sentence structure. Also short fiction (ages 9–12): MSS up to 1500 words long. Stories must lend themselves to a different illustration on each page. Fantasy and humour are always good sellers. All submissions should cater for an international market; include sae. Founded 1984.

Weldon Owen Education
Level 1, 39 Market Place, Auckland 1015
tel (09) 358-0190 *fax* (09) 358-0793
website www.weldonowen.com

Supplementary educational titles for school systems internationally. Produces literacy-teaching programmes for kindergarten through to Grade 6. Also resources for home-schooling. Series include *Wings* (8–10 year-olds), *Infoquest* and *Explorers* for 8–12 year-olds. Founded 2001.

SOUTH AFRICA
**Member of the Publishers' Association of South Africa*

Cambridge University Press**
Dock House, Portswood Ridge,
Victoria & Alfred Waterfront,
Cape Town 8001
tel (021) 419-8414
email information@cup.co.za
website www.cambridge.org
Director Hanri Pieterse

African Branch of CUP, responsible for sub-Saharan Africa and English-speaking Caribbean. Publishes distance learning materials and textbooks for various African countries, as well as primary reading materials in 28 local African languages.

Chart Studio Publishing (Pty) Ltd
Portion 58 Kromdraai, Krugersdorp, Johannesburg 1740
tel (11) 9570151 *fax* (11) 9570313
email chartstudio@chartstudio.com
website www.chartstudio.com

Educational, fun-to-learn products including posters, flip-charts, fun-time fold-out books, flash cards, wooden puzzles, board books. Age groups: preschool, 5–10, 10–15, 15+.

Clever Books Pty Ltd*
PO Box 13816, Hatfield, Pretoria 0028
tel (012) 3423263 *fax* (012) 4302376
email mmcd@cleverbooks.co.za
General Manager Michael McDermott

Educational titles for the RSA market. Founded 1981.

Jacklin Enterprises (Pty) Ltd
PO Box 521, Parklands 2121
tel (011) 265-4200 *fax* (011) 314-2984
email mjacklin@jacklin.co.za
Managing Director M.A.C. Jacklin

Children's fiction and non-fiction; Afrikaans large print books. Subjects include aviation, natural history, romance, general science, technology and transportation. Imprints: Mike Jacklin, Kennis Onbeperk, Daan Retief.

Juta & Company Ltd*

PO Box 14373, Landsdown 7779, Cape Town
tel (021) 797-5101 *fax* (021) 762-0248
email books@juta.co.za
website www.juta.co.za
Ceo Rory Wilson

School, academic, professional, law and electronic. Founded 1853.

Maskew Miller Longman (Pty) Ltd*

Howard Drive, Pinelands 7405, Cape Town
postal address PO Box 396, Cape Town 8000
tel (021) 531-7750 *fax* (021) 531-4877
email administrator@mml.co.za
website www.mml.co.za

Educational and general publishers.

Oxford University Press Southern Africa*

Vasco Boulevard, N1 City, Goodwood, Cape Town 7460
postal address PO Box 12119, N1 City, Cape Town 7463
tel (021) 595-4400 *fax* (021) 595-4430
email oxford.za@oup.com.za
website www.oup.com.za
Managing Director Kate McCallum

Reference books for children and school books: Preschool and Foundation Phase, Intermediate Phase, Senior Phase, dictionaries, thesauruses, atlases and teaching English as a main and as a second language.

Shuter and Shooter Publishers (Pty) Ltd*

230 Church Street, Pietermaritzburg 3201, KwaZulu-Natal
postal address PO Box 109, Pietermaritzburg 3200, KwaZulu-Natal
tel (033) 3946-830/3948-881 *fax* (033) 3427-419
email dryder@shuter.co.za
website www.shuter.co.za
Publishing Director D.F. Ryder

Primary and secondary educational, science, biology, history, maths, geography, English, Afrikaans, biblical studies, music, teacher training, agriculture, accounting, early childhood, dictionaries, African languages. Founded 1925.

USA

**Member of the Association of American Publishers Inc.*

Barron's Educational Series Inc.

250 Wireless Boulevard, Hauppage, NY 11788
tel 631-434-3311 *fax* 631-434-3723
website www.barronseduc.com
Chairman/Ceo Manuel H. Barron,
President/Publisher Ellen Sibley

Test preparation, juvenile, cookbooks, Mind, Body & Spirit, crafts, business, pets, gardening, family and health, art, study guides, school guides. Founded 1941.

Blackbirch Press – see Thomson Gale

Bloomsbury USA

Suite 300, 175 Fifth Avenue, New York, NY 10010
tel 212-674-5151 *fax* 212-780-0115
email bloomsbury.kids@bloomsburyusa.com
website www.bloomsbury.com/usa/childrens
Editorial Director, Children's Books Victoria Wells Arms, *Director of Marketing and Publicity (Children's)* Kate R. Kubert, *Assistant Editor* Julie Romeis

Literary fiction, general non-fiction and children's. Branch of Bloomsbury UK. Founded 1998.

Bloomsbury Children's (USA)

Novelty books, picture books, fiction for 5–8 and 9–12 year-olds, teenage fiction, series fiction and poetry. Publishes 40 titles each year and has 80 in print. Recent successes include *Pirates!* by Celia Rees, *Bill in a China Shop* by Katie McAllaster Weaver and Tim Raglin and *The Alphabet Room* by Sara Pinto.

Submission details Will consider unsolicited MSS with sase. Allow 6 months for response. Founded 2002.

Boyds Mills Press

815 Church Street, Honesdale, PA 18431
tel 570-253-1164 *fax* 570-253-0179
email contact@boydsmillspress.com
website www.boydsmillspress.com
President Clay Winters, *Publisher* Kent L. Brown Jr, *Editorial Director* Larry Rosler, *Art Director* Tim Gillner

Publishes approx. 60 titles each year for children of all ages. Founded 1991.

Boyds Mills Press (imprint)

Activity books, picture books and fiction for 9–12 year-olds. Recent successes include *The President is Shot!* by Harold Holzer, *My Special Day at Third Street School* by Eve Bunting and *Least Things* by Jane Yolen.

Submission details Will consider both unsolicited MSS and queries; send to Jeanna DeLuca,

Manuscript Coordinator. Looking for middle-grade fiction with fresh ideas and subject matter, and young adult novels of real literary merit. Non-fiction should be fun and entertaining as well as informative, and non-fiction MSS should be accompanied by a detailed biography. Interested in imaginative picture books and welcomes submissions from both writers and illustrators. Submit samples as b&w and/or colour copies or transparencies; submissions will not be returned. Include sase with all submissions. Send art samples to Tim Gillner, Art Director.

Calkins Creek Books (imprint)
Editor Carolyn P. Yoder
History.

Wordsong (imprint)
Editor Wendy Murray
Poetry.

Calkins Creek Books – see Boyds Mills Press

Candlewick Press

2067 Massachusetts Avenue, Cambridge, MA 02140
tel 617-661-3330 *fax* 617-661-0565
website www.candlewick.com
Editorial Director/Associate Publisher Liz Bicknell, *Executive Editor* Mary Lee Donovan, *Editorial Director (novelty)* Joan Powers, *Editor-at-Large* Amy Ehrlich

Children's books 6 months–14 years: board books, picture books, novels, non-fiction, novelty books. Submit material through a literary agent. Subsidiary of Walker Books Ltd, UK. Founded 1991.

Carolrhoda Books – see Lerner Publishing Group

Charlesbridge Publishing

85 Main Street, Watertown, MA 02472
tel 617-926-0329 *fax* 617-926-5720
email masabia@charlesbridge.com
website www.charlesbridge.com
President & Publisher Brent Farmer, *Vice President & Associate Publisher* Mary Ann Sabia

Board books, novelty books, picture books and non-fiction for preschool through to age 10. Lively, plot-driven story books plus nursery rhymes, fairy tales and humorous stories for the very young. Non-fiction list specialises in nature, concept and multicultural books.

Chronicle Books

85 Second Street, 6th Floor, San Francisco, CA 94105
tel 415-537-4200 *fax* 415-537-4460
email frontdesk@chroniclebooks.com
website www.chroniclebooks.com
Chairman and Ceo Nion McEvoy, *Publisher* Jack Jensen, *Associate Publishers* Christine Carswell, Debra Laude, Victoria Rock

Activity books, board books, novelty books, picture books and fairy tales for children. Also for adults: cooking, how-to books, nature, art, biographies, fiction, gift. Founded 1967.

Clarion Books – see Houghton Mifflin Company

The Continuum International Publishing Group Inc.

370 Lexington Avenue, New York, NY 10017-6503
tel 212-953-5858 *fax* 212-953-5944
email contin@tiac.net
website www.continuum-books.com
Chairman/Publisher Philip Sturrock

General non-fiction, education, literature, psychology, politics, sociology, literary criticism, religious studies. Founded 1999.

Copper Beach – see Millbrook Press

Cricket Books

Carus Publishing Company, Cricket Magazine Group, P0 Box 300, Peru, IL 61354
email mmiklavcic@caruspub.com

Picture books, chapter books, poetry, non-fiction and novels for children and young adults. Also publishes *Cricket*, the award-winning magazine of outstanding stories and art for 9–14 year-olds (see page 206), and other magazines for young readers. Division of Carus Publishing.

Submission details Primarily interested in chapter books, middle-grade fiction, and young adult novels, as well as exceptional non-fiction for all ages, but will also consider picture books. Send MSS to Submissions Editor, Cricket Books, Carus Publishing Company, 332 South Michigan Avenue, Suite 1100, Chicago, IL 60604, USA.

Marcato Books (imprint)
Exceptional non-fiction and innovative fiction for young readers of all ages, especially teenagers.

DC Comics

1700 Broadway, New York, NY 10019
tel 212-636-5400 *fax* 212-636-5975
website www.dccomics.com

Activity books, board books, novelty books, picture books, painting and colouring books, pop-up books, fiction, fairy tales, art, hobbies, how-to books, leisure, entertainment, film/TV tie-ins, calendars, comics, gift books, periodicals, picture cards, posters, CD-Roms, CD-I, internet for preschool age to 15+.

DC Comics has published and licensed comic

books for over 60 years in all genres for all ages, including super heroes, fantasy, horror, mystery and high-quality graphic stories for mature readers. Imprints: WildStorm, Vertigo. A Warner Bros. Company.

Dial Books for Young Readers – see Penguin Putnam Books for Young Readers

Dominie Press Inc.

1949 Kellogg Avenue, Carlsbad, CA 92008
tel 760-431-8000 *fax* 760-431-8777
website www.dominie.com

Educational children's publisher dedicated to providing the finest learning materials to children of ages 3–16. Subjects include nature and environment, biographies, science, fiction, fairy tales and teaching. High-quality photographic books on animals, insects, amphibians, marine and ocean life, habitats, etc.

Dover Publications Inc.

31 East 2nd Street, Mineola, NY 11501
tel 516-294-7000 *fax* 516-742-5049
website www.doverpublications.com
President, Dover Publications Clarence Strawbridge, *Vice-President, Editorial* Paul Negri, *Key editorial staff* Janet Kopito, Diane T. Rubins

Activity books, novelty books, picture books, fiction for 5–8 and 9–12 year-olds, teenage fiction, series fiction, reference, plays, religion, poetry, audio and CD-Roms. Also adult non-fiction. Publishes approx. 150 children's titles and has over 2500 in print. Recent successes include *How to Draw Aquarium Animals, Korean Girl and Boy Paper Dolls* and *At the Hospital* (colouring book).

Submission details Will consider unsolicited MSS but write for guidelines. Founded 1941.

Dutton Children's Books – see Penguin Putnam Books for Young Readers

Eerdmans Publishing Company

255 Jefferson Avenue SE, Grand Rapids, MI 49503
tel 616-459-4591 *fax* 616-459-6540
website www.eerdmans.com
President William B. Eerdmans

Independent publisher of a wide range of religious books, from academic works in theology, biblical studies, religious history, and reference to popular titles in spirituality, social and cultural criticism and literature. Founded 1911.

Eerdmans Books for Young Readers

Editor-in-Chief Judy Zylstra

Picture books, biographies, novels and Bible stories. In all its books it 'seeks to nurture children's faith in God and help them understand and explore the wonder, joy, and challenges of life'.

Encyclopaedia Britannica Inc.

310 South Michigan Avenue, Chicago, Illinois 60604
fax 312-294-2108
email international@eb.com
website www.britannica.com

Encyclopedias, reference books, almanacs, videos and CD-Roms for adults and children aged 5–15+.

Evan-Moor Educational Publishers

18 Lower Ragsdale Drive, Monterey, CA 93940
tel 831 649 5901 *fax* 831 649 6256
website www.evan-moor.com
President William Evans, *Senior Editor* Marilyn Evans

Educational materials for parents and teachers of children (ages 3–12): activity books, textbooks, how-to books, CD-Roms. Subjects include maths, geography, history, science, reading, writing, social studies, art and craft. Publishes approx. 50 titles each year and has over 450 in print. Founded 1979.

Farrar, Straus and Giroux Inc.

19 Union Square West, New York, NY 10003
tel 212-741-6900 *fax* 212-741-6973
websites www.fsgbooks.com, fsgkidsbooks.com
President/Publisher Jonathan Galassi, *Editor-in-Chief* John Glusman

General publishers. Founded 1945.

Farrar, Straus Giroux Books for Young Readers

Editorial Director Margaret Ferguson, *Publisher, Frances Foster Books* Frances Foster, *Publisher, Melanie Kroupa Books* Melanie Kroupa, *Executive Editors* Wesley Adams, Beverly Reingold, *Editor* Robert Mayes, *Associate Editor* Janine O-Malley

Books for toddlers through to young adults: picture books, fiction for 5–8 and 9–12 year-olds, teenage fiction and poetry (occasionally). Publishes 80 hardcover originals plus 20 paperback reprints each year and has approx. 500 titles in print. Recent successes include *The Tree of Life* by Peter Sís, *The Canning Season* by Polly Horvath and *Buddha Boy* by Kathe Koja. Imprints: Frances Foster Books, Melanie Kroupa Books, Sunburst (paperback).

Submission details Send query letter first but will consider unsolicited MSS. Include a covering letter containing any pertinent information about yourself, your writing, your MSS, etc and a sase for return of MSS. For illustrations, send only 2–3 samples; do *not* send original artwork. Address submissions to Children's Editorial Department. Allow 3 months for response. Looking to publish books of high literary merit.

Walter Foster Publishing Inc.

23062 La Cadena Drive, Laguna Hills, Irvine, CA 92653
tel 949-380-7510 *fax* 949-380-7575
website www.walterfoster.com
Chief Executive Ross Sarracino

'Fostering creativity for more than 80 years.' Instructional art books for children and adults. Also art and activity kits for children.

Free Spirit Publishing

217 Fifth Avenue North, Suite 200, Minneapolis, MN 55401
tel 612 338 2068 *fax* 612 337 5050
email help4kids@freespirit.com
website www.freespirit.com
President Judy Galbraith

Award-winning publisher of non-fiction materials for children and teens, parents, educators, and counsellors. Specialises in SELF-HELP FOR KIDS® and SELF-HELP FOR TEENS® materials which empower young people and promote positive self-esteem through improved social and learning skills.Topics include self-esteem and self-awareness, stress management, school success, creativity, friends and family, peacemaking, social action, and special needs (i.e. gifted and talented, children with learning differences). Publishes approx. 18–22 new products each year, adding to a backlist of over 100 books, audio tapes, and posters. Free Spirit authors are expert educators and mental health professionals who have been honoured nationally for their contributions on behalf of children. Founded 1983.

Front Street Books

862 Haywood Road, Asheville, NC 28806
tel 828-221-2091 *fax* 828-221-2112
email contactus@frontstreetbooks.com
website www.frontstreetbooks.com
President & Publisher Stephen Roxburgh, *Associate Publisher* Nancy Hogan, *Art Director* Helen Robinson, *Editor* Joy Neaves

Independent publisher of books for children and young adults: picture books, fiction (5–8, 9–12, teenage), non-fiction, poetry, anthologies. Recent successes include *Heck Superhero* by Martine Leavitt, *Honeysuckle House* by Andrea Cheng and *The Big House* by Carolyn Coman. Imprints: Front Street, Front Street/Lemni Scaat.

Submission details For fiction, submit 2–3 sample chapters and a plot summary. For picture books, do not send MSS but send a query letter describing your project as fully as possible. For poetry, send up to 25 poems that are representative of your work. For non-fiction send a detailed proposal and sample chapter. Include sase. Allow 3–4 months for response. Founded 1994.

Golden Books for Young Readers

1745 Broadway, NY 10019
tel 212 782 9000
website www.goldenbooks.com
Ceo Peter Olsen

Children's books, educational workbooks and products, electronic books and software, children's videos. Imprint of Random House Inc.

Greenhaven Press – see Thomson Gale

Grolier – see Scholastic Inc.

Grosset & Dunlap – see Penguin Putnam Books for Young Readers

Handprint Books

413 Sixth Avenue, Brooklyn, New York 11215
tel 718-768-3696 *fax* 718-369-0844
email submissions@handprintbooks.com
website www.handprintbooks.com
Publisher Christopher Franceschelli

A range of children's books: picture and story books through to young adult fiction. Imprints: Handprint Books, Ragged Bears, Blue Apple.

Submission details Welcomes submissions of MSS of quality for works ranging from board books to young adult novels. For novels, first query interest on the subject and submit a 7500-word max. sample. Accepts MSS on an e-submission basis only, sent as attachments in a word processing format readily readable on a PC. Artwork should be sent as Jpegs and total size should not exceed 200K and website addresses containing artists' illustrations may be submitted. Submission of the following is discouraged: series fiction, licensed character (or characters whose primary avatar is meant to be as licenses), I-Can-Read- type books, titles intended primarily for mass merchandise outlets.

HarperCollins Publishers*

10 East 53rd Street, New York, NY 10022
tel 212-207-7000 *fax* 212-207-7145
website www.harpercollins.com
HarperCollins SanFrancisco 1160 Battery Street, San Francisco, CA 94111
tel 415-477-4400 *fax* 415-477-4444
President/Ceo Jane Friedman

Adult fiction (commercial and literary) and non-fiction. Subjects include biography, business, cookbooks, educational, history, juvenile, poetry, religious, science, technical and travel. Imprints include Access, Amistad, Avon, Cliff Street Books, Ecco, Eos, Fourth Estate, HarperAudio, Harper Business, HarperCollins, HarperEntertainment, HarperResource, HarperSanFrancisco, HarperTorch, Large Print Editions, William Morrow, William Morrow Cookbooks, Perennial, PerfectBound (e-books), Quill, Rayo and ReganBooks. No unsolicited material; all submissions must come through a literary agent. Founded 1817.

HarperCollins Children's Books Group
1350 6th Avenue, New York, NY 10019
tel 212-261-6500
website www.harperchildrens.com
President & Publisher Susan Katz

Imprints: Greenwillow Books, Joanna Cotler Books, Laura Geringer Books, HarperCollins Children's Books, HarperFestival, HarperTrophy, Avon, HarperTempest.

HarperCollins Children's Books (imprint)
1350 Avenues of the Americas, New York, NY 10019
tel 212-261-6588 *fax* 212-261-6603
website www.harperchildrens.com
President & Publisher Susan Katz, *Editorial Director* Alix Reid

Activity books, board books, novelty books, picture books, pop-up books, nature, environment, non-fiction, calendars, gift books, audio tapes, fiction, poetry, fairy tales for ages 5–15.

Imprints: HarperCollins Hardcover, Harper Trophy Paperbacks, HarperFestival, HarperChildren's Audio.

Holiday House
425 Madison Avenue, New York, NY 10017
tel 212-688-0085
President John Briggs, *Vice-President/Editor-in-Chief* Regina Griffin

General children's books. Send query letter before submitting MSS. Always include sae. No multiple submissions. Founded 1935.

Henry Holt and Company LLC*
115 West 18th Street, New York, NY 10011
tel 212-886-9200 *fax* 212-633-0748
website www.henryholt.com
President/Publisher John Sterling

History, biography, nature, science, self-help, novels, mysteries; books for young readers; trade paperback line, computer books. Founded 1866.

Houghton Mifflin Company*
222 Berkeley Street, Boston, MA 02116
tel 617-351-5000

Fiction and non-fiction – cookbooks, history, political science, biography, nature (Peterson Guides), and gardening guides; reference, both adult and juvenile. No unsolicited MSS. Imprints: Mariner (original and reprint paperbacks); Houghton Mifflin Children's Books; American Heritage® Dictionaries. Founded 1832.

Clarion Books (imprint)
215 Park Avenue South, New York, NY 10003
tel 212-420-5800 *fax* 212-420-5850
Vice-President & Associate Publisher, Clarion Books Dinah Stevenson, *Director, Children's Rights* Rebecca Mancini, *Editor* Jennifer Green

Board books, picture books, biographies, non-fiction, fiction, poetry and fairy tales for ages 5–15.

Hyperion*
77 West 66 Street, New York, NY 10023-6298
tel 212-456-0100 *fax* 212-456-0157
website www.hyperionbooks.com
President Robert Miller, *Vice-President/Publisher* Ellen Archer, *Vice-President/Publisher (Hyperion Books for Children)* Lisa Holton

General fiction and non-fiction, children's books. Division of Buena Vista Publishing, formerly Disney Book Publishing Inc. Founded 1990.

Kar-Ben Publishing – see Lerner Publishing Group

KidHave Press – see Thomson Gale

Kids Story Book LLC
5135 Avenida Encinas, Suite B, Carlsbad, CA 92008
tel 800-849-9960
email info@kidsstorybook.com
website www.kidsstorybook.com
Kids Story Book is a personalised, interactive, animated, audio CD story book that automatically reads the story, written for children aged 3–7.

LernerClassroom – see Lerner Publishing Group

Lerner Publishing Group
241 First Avenue North, Minneapolis, MN 55401-1607
tel 612-332-3344 *fax* 612-332-7615
email info@learnerbooks.com
website www.lernerbooks.com
Publisher Adam Lerner, *Non-fiction Submisions Editor* Jennifer Zimian, *Fiction Submisions Editor* Zelda Wagner

Independent publisher of high-quality children's books for K–12 schools and libraries: picture books, fiction for 5–8 and 9–12 year-olds, teenage fiction, series fiction and non-fiction. Subjects include biography, social studies, science, sports and curriculum. Publishes approx. 200 titles each year and has about 1500 in print. Imprints: Lerner Publications, Carolrhoda Books, First Avenue Editions, Kar-Ben Publishing, LernerSports and LernerClassroom. Founded 1959.

Submission details Only accepts submissions during November; submissions received in any other month will be returned to the sender unopened. A sase, addressed to either Ms Zimian or

Ms Wagner is required; allow 8 months for a response. No telephone calls. For guidelines, address to 'Guideline request' and send a business-sized sase. *For illustrations* Accepts unsolicited artists' samples at all times of the year. Submit slides, Jpeg or PDF files on disk, colour photocopies or tearsheets; do not send original artwork. Include a resumé detailing previous work. Address to the Art Director.

Carolrhoda Books (imprint)

website www.carolrhodabooks.com

Picture books aimed at 5–8 year-olds; longer fiction for age 7+, including chapter books and middle-grade and young adult novels; biographies. Interested in unique, honest stories that stay away from moralising and religious themes; also science fiction/fantasy for young readers. Popular characters include Little Wolf and Harriet. Authors and illustrators include Nancy Carlson and Jan Wahl. Founded 1969.

Submission details All submissions must have a sufficiently posted sase otherwise there will be no response and MSS will not be returned. For non-fiction, send the complete MS with a one-page outline/synopsis and a resumé to Ms Zimian. For picture book submissions send the whole MS to Ms Wagner; dummy books are not necessary. For longer fiction send a brief outline/synopsis and a few sample chapters not exceeding 50pp, to Ms Wagner.

Kar-Ben Publishing (imprint)

6800 Tildenwood Lane, Rockville, MD 20852-4371
tel 301-984-8733 *fax* 301-881-9195
website www.karben.com
Contact Judye Groner, Madeline Wikler

Books on Jewish themes for children and families. Subjects include the High Holidays, Passover, Sukkot and Simchat Torah, Hanukkah, Purim, Selichot, Tu B'Shevat, crafts, cooking, folk tales, and contemporary stories, Jewish calendars, music, and activity books. Founded 1974.

Submission details Welcomes unsolicited MSS and artists' samples at all times of the year. Include a sase for a response and allow 3–5 weeks for a reply. Will consider fiction and non-fiction for preschool through to high school age, including holiday books, life-cycle stories, Bible tales, folk tales, board books and activity books. Illustrators should send colour photocopies or tearsheets, not original artwork.

LernerClassroom (imprint)

website www.lernerclassroom.com

Non-fiction books and teaching guides for grades K-8 in social studies, science, reading/literacy and mathematics. Books are paired with teaching guides that are correlated to national and state standards.

Little, Brown & Company

1271 Avenue of the Americas, New York, NY 10020
tel 212-522-8700 *fax* 212-522-7997
website www.twbookmark.com
Chief Executive Larry Kirshbaum

General literature, fiction, non-fiction, biography, history, trade paperbacks, children's. Art and photography books under the Bulfinch Press imprint. Imprint of AOL Time Warner Book Group.

Books for Young Readers

Executive Director Andrea Spooner, *Vice-President, Associate Publisher and Editor-in-Chief* Megan Tingley, *Editor* Jennifer Hunt

Fiction and non-fiction for all ages including young adult. Subjects include art, biographies, fairy tales, film/TV tie-ins, entertainment, how-to books, pets, sport. Also activity books, board books, novelty books, picture books, pop-up books, poetry, calendars and gift books. Recent successes include *I Know an Old Lady Who Swallowed a Fly* by Mary Ann Hoberman and Nadine Bernard Westcott (ages 0–3), *You Read to Me, I'll Read to You: Very Short Fairy Tales to Read Together* by Mary Ann Hoberman and Michael Emberley (ages 4–8) and *How to Train Your Dragon* by Cressida Cowell ages 8–12.

Lucent Books – see Thomson Gale

McGraw-Hill*

2 Penn Plaza, New York, NY 10121
tel 212-512-2000
website www.books.mcgraw-hill.com
Group Vice-President Theodore Nardin

Professional and reference: engineering, scientific, business, architecture, encyclopedias; college textbooks; high school and vocational textbooks: business, secretarial, career; trade books; training materials for industry. Division of The McGraw-Hill Companies.

Marcato Books – see Cricket Books

Milkweed Editions

1011 Washington Avenue South, Suite 300, Minneapolis, MN 55415
tel 612-332-3192 *fax* 612-215-2550
websites www.milkweed.org, www.worldashome.org
Editor Emile Buchwold

Fiction, poetry, essays, the natural world, children's novels (ages 8–14). Founded 1979.

Millbrook Press

2 Old New Milford Road, PO Box 335, Brookfield, CT 06804
tel 203-740-2220 *fax* 203-740-2526

website www.millbrookpress.com

Educational publisher: preschool to secondary school. Produces curriculum-oriented children's books with a concentration on quality non-fiction for the school and library market.

Submission details The Millbrook Press and Twenty-First Century Books only accepts submissions from literary agents; no unsolicited MSS. Interested in works that have a strong, relevant tie to a school curriculum, such as maths, science, American history, social studies, biography, etc. Proposals aimed at teachers or parents are not appropriate. Does not accept fiction, picture books, activity books, or other novelty submissions. Literary agents should send a sample chapter, query letter and outline, rather than a completed MSS. Include a sase with all submissions and allow at least 6–8 weeks for a response. MSS will be returned if not selected for further review only if a sase for its return is supplied. Founded 1991.

Copper Beach Books (imprint)

Books created by affiliate companies in the UK.

Submission details Does not accept unsolicited MSS or submissions.

Millbrook Press (imprint)

Maths, science, American history, social studies and biography for a younger age bracket.

Twenty-First Century Books (imprint)

Maths, science, American history, social studies and biography for Secondary school age bracket.

Orchard Books

555 Broadway, New York, NY 10012
tel 212-343-6782 *fax* 212-343-4890
website www.scholastic.com
Editorial Director Ken Geist

Books for children and young adults; picture books, fiction. Imprint of Scholastic Inc. Founded 1987.

The Overlook Press*

141 Wooster Street, New York, NY 10012
tel 212-673-2210 *fax* 212-673-2296
website www.overlookpress.com
President and Publisher Peter Mayer, *Associate Publisher* Tracy Carns

Non-fiction, fiction, children's books.

Oxford University Press Inc.*

198 Madison Avenue, New York, NY 10016
tel 212-726-6000 *fax* 212-726-6455
website www.oup-usa.org
President Laura Brown

Children's fiction and non-fiction. Subjects include art, history, literature, music, myths and fairy tales, poetry, reference, science. Also scholarly, professional, reference, bibles, college textbooks, religion, medical, music.

Parragon Publishing

1250 Broadway, 24th Floor, New York, NY 10001
tel 212-629-9773 *fax* 212-629 9756
email usinfo@parragon.com
website www.parragon.com

The world's largest 'value-orientated' publisher of children's titles.

Peachtree Publishers Ltd

1700 Chattahoochee Avenue, Atlanta, GA 30318-2112
tel 404-876-8761 *fax* 404-875-2578
email hello@peachtree-online.com
website www.peachtree-online.com
President and Publisher Margaret Quinlin, *Editorial Director* Kathy Landwehr

Children's picture books, novels and non-fiction books. Adult non-fiction subjects include self-help, parenting, education, health, regional guides. No adult fiction.

Submission details For children's books, send complete MSS; for all others, send query letter with 3 sample chapters and table of contents to Helen Harriss with sase for response and/or return of material. Founded 1977.

Pearson Prentice Hall

One Lake Street, Upper Saddle River, NJ 07458
tel 201-236-7000
email communications@pearsoned.com
website www.phschool.com

Educational secondary publisher of scientifically researched and standards-based instruction materials for today's Grade 6–12 classrooms with a mission is to create exceptional educational tools that ensure student and teacher success in language arts, mathematics, modern and classical languages, science, social studies, career and technology, and advanced placement, electives, and honors. Division of Pearson Education.

Penguin Putnam Books for Young Readers*

345 Hudson Street, New York, NY 10014
tel 212-366-2000 *fax* 212-366-2666
email online@penguinputnam.com
website www.penguinputnam.com
President Douglas Whiteman

Children's picture books, board and novelty books, young adult novels, mass merchandise products. Imprints: Dial Books for Young Readers, Dutton Children's Books, Dutton Interactive, Phyllis Fogelman Books, Grosset & Dunlap, PaperStar, Philomel, Planet Dexter, Platt & Munk, Playskool, Price Stern Sloan, PSS, Puffin Books, G.P. Putnam's Sons, Viking Children's Books, Frederick Warne. Division of Penguin Putnam Inc. Founded 1997.

Dial Books for Young Readers (imprint)
fax 212-414-3394
President/Publisher Nancy Paulsen, *Editorial Director* Laura Hornik, *Vice President/Publisher, Phyllis Fogelman Books* Phyllis Fogelman

Children's fiction and non-fiction, picture books, board books, interactive books, novels.

Dutton Children's Books (imprint)
tel 212-366 2792 *fax* 212-243-6002
President/Publisher Stephanie Lurie, *Editorial Director, Dutton Children's Trade* Donna Brooks

Picture books, young adult novels, non-fiction photographic books. Founded 1852.

Grosset & Dunlap (imprint)
President/Publisher, Grosset & Dunlap Debra Dorfman

Children's picture books, activity books, fiction and non-fiction. Imprints: Grosset & Dunlap, Platt & Munk, Somerville House USA, Planet Dexter. Founded 1898.

Price Stern Sloan (imprint)
Vice President/Publisher Jon Anderson

Children's novelty/lift-flap books, activity books, middle-grade fiction, middle-grade and young adult non-fiction, cutting-edge graphic readers, picture books, books plus. Imprints: Crazy Games, Doodle Art, Planet Dexter, Serendipity, Troubador Press, Wee Sing. Founded 1963.

Puffin Books (imprint)
President & Publisher Tracy Tang, *Executive Editor* Kristin Gilson, *Senior Editor* Sharyn November

Picture books, fiction for 5–8 and 9–12 year-olds, teenage fiction, series fiction and film/TV tie-ins. Publishes approx. 225–275 titles each year. Recent successes include *Rules of the Road* by Joan Bauer, *A Long Way from Chicago* by Richard Peck and *26 Fairmount Avenue* by Tomie dePaola.

Submission details Will consider unsolicited MSS for novels only. Send with sase to Submissions Editor. Seeking to publish mysteries. Founded 1941.

G.P. Putnam's Sons (imprint)
President/Publisher Nancy Paulsen

Children's hardcover and paperback books. Imprints: G.P. Putnam's Sons, Philomel Books, PaperStar. Founded 1838.

Viking Children's Books (imprint)
President Regina Hayes

Fiction, non-fiction, picture books. Founded 1925.

Frederick Warne (imprint)

Original publisher of Beatrix Potter's *Tales of Peter Rabbit*. Founded 1865.

Penguin Putnam Inc.*

375 Hudson Street, New York, NY10014
tel 212-366-2000 *fax* 212-366-2666
email online@penguinputnam.com
website www.penguinputnam.com
President, The Penguin Group David Wan, *Chairman* John McKinson, *Ceo* David Shanks

Publisher of consumer books in both hardcover and paperback for adults and children; also produces maps, calendars, audiobooks and mass merchandise products. Adult imprints: Ace, Ace/Putnam, Allen Lane The Penguin Press, Avery, Berkley Books, BlueHen, Boulevard, DAW, Dutton, Grosset/Putnam, HP Books, Jove, Mentor, Meridian, Onyx, Penguin, Penguin Classics, Penguin Compass, Perigee, Plume, Prime Crime, Price Stern Sloan Inc., Putnam, G.P. Putnam's Sons, Riverhead Books, Roc, Signet, Signet Classics, Jeremy P. Tarcher, Topaz, Viking, Viking Compass, Viking Studio, Marian Wood Books. Children's imprints: Dial Books for Young Readers, Dutton Children's Books, Grosset & Dunlap, PaperStar, Philomel Books, Planet Dexter, Price Stern Sloan Inc., Puffin, G.P. Putnam's Sons, Viking Children's Books, Wee Sing, Frederick Warne. Divisions: Berkley Publishing Group, Dutton, Plume, NAL, Penguin Putnam Books for Young Readers, The Putnam Publishing Group, Viking Penguin.

Price Stern Sloan – see Penguin Putnam Books for Young Readers

Puffin Books – see Penguin Putnam Books for Young Readers

G.P. Putnam's Sons (children's) – see Penguin Putnam Books for Young Readers

Random House/Golden Books Young Readers Group

1745 Broadway, New York, NY 10019
tel 212-782-9000
website www.goldenbooks.com
Ceo Peter Olsen

Children's books, educational workbooks and products, electronic books and software, children's videos.

Random House Inc.*

1540 Broadway, New York, NY 10019
tel 212-782-9000 *fax* 212-302-7985
299 Park Avenue, New York, NY 10170
and 280 Park Avenue, New York, NY 10017
tel 212-572-2600 *fax* 212-572-8700
website www.randomhouse.com
Chairman/Ceo Peter Olson, *President/Coo* Erik Engstrom

Adult general fiction and non-fiction and audio publishing. Imprints include Fodors Travel Publications, Living Language, The Modern Library, Princeton Review, Random House Adult Trade Books, Random House Large Print Publishing, Random House Puzzles and Games, Random House Reference, Random House Value Publishing (Children's Classics, Crescent Books, Derrydale, Gramercy Books, Testament Books, Wings Books) and Villard Books. Subsidiary of Bertelsmann AG.

Random House Children's Media Group (division)
President & Publisher Craig W. Virden

Children's mprints: Crown Books for Young Readers, CTW Publishing, Delacorte Press, Disney Books, Doubleday Books for Young Readers, Dragonfly Books, First Choice Chapter Books, Golden Books for Young Readers (see page 41), Knopf Books for Young Readers, Knopf Paperbacks, Laurel-Leaf, Picture Yearling, Random House Children's Publishing, Skylark, Starfire, Yearling Books.

Roaring Brook Press

2 Old New Milford Road, PO Box 335, Brookfield, CT 06804
tel 203-740-2220 *fax* 203-740-2526
Publisher Simon Broughton, *Publishers* Neil Porter, Deborah Brodie, Lauren Wohl

Picture books, fiction 8–12 and young adults. Publishes about 40 titles a year. Recent successes include *My Friend Rabbit* by Eric Rohmann (Caldecott Medal winner 2003) and *The Man Who Walked Between the Towers* by Mordicai Gerstein (Caldecott Medal winner 2004). Division of Holtzbrink Publishing Holdings Ltd Partnership.

Submission details Does not accept unsolicited MSS or submissions. Founded 2001.

Running Press Book Publishers

125 S 22 St, Philadelphia, PA 19103-4399
tel 215-567-5080 *fax* 215-568 2919
President Stuart Teacher, *Publisher* Carlo DeVito, *Design Director* Bill Jones, *Production Director* Peter Horodowich, *Editorial Director* Jennifer Worick

Art, craft/how-to, general non-fiction, children's books. Imprints: Courage Books, Running Press Miniature Editions. Founded 1972.

Scholastic Education

557 Broadway, New York, NY 10012
tel 212-343-6100
website www.scholastic.com

Educational publisher of research-based core and supplementary instructional materials. A leading provider in reading improvement and professional development products, as well as learning services that address the needs of the developing reader – from grades pre-K to high school.

Publishes 34 curriculum-based classroom magazines used by teachers in grades pre-K–12 as supplementary educational materials to raise awareness about current events in an age-appropriate manner and to help children develop reading skills. Magazines include *Scholastic News®*, *Junior Scholastic®*, *The New York Times Upfront®*, *Science World®*, *Scope®* and others, covering subjects such as English, maths, science, social studies, current events, and foreign languages. The magazine's online companion, *Scholastic News Online* is the leading news source for students and teachers on the internet.

Scholastic Education has also developed technology-based reading assessment and management products to help administrators and educators quickly and accurately assess student reading levels, match students to the appropriate books, predict how well they will do on district and state standardised tests, and inform instruction to improve reading skills.

Its wholly owned operations in Australia, Canada, New Zealand, and the UK have original trade and educational publishing programmes.

Scholastic Library Publishing (division)
90 Sherman Turnpike, Danbury, CT 06816
tel 203-797-3500
website www.scholastic.com

Online and print publisher of reference products. Major reference sets include *Encyclopedia Americana®*, *The New Book of Knowledge®*, *Nueva Enciclopedia Cumbre®*, *Lands and Peoples* and *The New Book of Popular Science.*

Children's Press and Franklin Watts (imprints)
Children's fiction and non-fiction: all subjects and all grades. Has over 2400 titles in print.

Grolier (imprint)
website www.publishing.grolier.com

Children's non-fiction and reference materials in print and online.

Scholastic Inc.*

557 Broadway, New York, NY 10012
tel 212-343-6100 *fax* 212-343-6930
website www.scholastic.com
Chairman/President/Ceo Richard Robinson, *Executive Vice President, Book Group* Barbara Marcus, *Executive Vice President, Scholastic Entertainment* Deborah Forte, *Executive Vice President, Educational Publishing* Julie McGee

Innovative textbooks, magazines, technology and teacher materials for use in both school and the home. Scholastic is a global children's publishing and media company with a corporate mission to instill the love of reading and learning for lifelong pleasure in all children. Founded 1920.

Scholastic Trade Press
557 Broadway, New York, NY 10012
tel 212 343 6100
website www.scholastic.com
Award-winning publisher of original children's books. Publishes over 750 different titles per year including the branding publishing properties *Harry Potter®* and *Captain Underpants®*, the series *Clifford The Big Red Dog®*, *I Spy™*, and Scholastic's *The Magic School Bus®*, as well as licensed properties such as *Barney®*, *Star Wars®* and *Scooby Doo™*. Imprints: Scholastic Press, Arthur A. Levine Books, Cartwheel Books®, Scholastic Paperbacks, Scholastic Reference™, The Blue Sky Press®, The Chicken House™ and Orchard Books®.

Klutz
How-to books packaged with the tools of their trade (from juggling cubes to face paints to yo-yos). Includes an educational product line for pre-K–4 children in maths, reading and general knowledge. Products are designed for doing, not just reading: 'We think people learn best through their hands, nose, feet, mouth and ears. Then their eyes. So we design multi-sensory books'.

Scholastic Press (imprint)
Editorial Director Elizabeth Stabla, *Executive Editors* Tracy Mach, Dianne Hess, *Senior Editor* Lauren Thompson, *Associate Editors* Jennifer Ress, Leslie Budrich

Picture books, fiction for 5–8 and 9–12 year-olds, teenage fiction, poetry, religion and non-fiction for 3 year-olds–teenage. Publishes approx. 35–50 titles each year. Recent successes include *A Corner of the Universe* by Ann M. Martin, *Gregor the Overlander* by Suzanne Collins and *Old Turtle and the Broken Truth* by Douglas Wood and Jon J. Muth.

Submission details Will not consider unsolicited MSS. Send query letter or submit via an agent. Currently considering picture books, non-fiction and fresh, literary middle grade and young adult fiction. Also especially interested in subtly handled treatments of the key relationships in children's lives: unusual approaches to commonly dry subjects, such as biography, history, maths, science, etc. Not interested in board books, flap books or other novelty formats; books intended mainly as resources for teachers and librarians; genre or series fiction such as mystery, fantasy, historical (fiction should stand out first as excellent literature).

Scott Foresman
One Lake Street, Upper Saddle River, NJ 07458
tel 201-236-7000
email communications@pearsoned.com

Elementary educational publisher. Publishes high-quality teacher and student materials in all school disciplines: reading, science, mathematics, language arts, social studies, music, technology, and religion. Imprints: Scott Foresman, Silver Burdett Ginn.

Generations of children learned to read with the company's highly successful *Dick and Jane* series. The company's continued commitment to reading education is best exemplified with the *Scott Foresman Reading* and *Lectura Scott Foresman* programmes, available for K–6 students. Part of Pearson Education. Founded 1896.

Simon & Schuster Children's Publishing Division*
1230 Avenue of the Americas, New York, NY 10020
tel 212-698-7200 *fax* 212-698-2793
President Kristina Peterson

Preschool to young adult, fiction and non-fiction, trade, library and mass market. Imprints: Aladdin Paperbacks, Atheneum Books for Young Readers, Little Simon, Margaret K. McElderry Books, Simon & Schuster Books for Young Readers, Simon Spotlight. Division of Simon & Schuster. Founded 1924.

Sleeping Bear Press – see Thomson Gale

Gareth Stevens Publishing
330 West Olive Street, Suite 100, Milwaukee, WI 53212
tel 414-332-3520 *fax* 414-332-3567
email info@gspub.com
website www.garethstevens.com
Publisher Robert Famighetti, *Art Director* Tammy Guenewald, *Production Director* Jessica Morris, *Creative Director* Mark Sachner

Educational books and high-quality fiction for 4–16 year-olds. Subjects include atlases and reference, arts and crafts, emergent readers, nature, science, social studies, history and Spanish/bilingual. Publishes approx. 300 new titles each year and has over 100 in print. Part of WRC Media Inc. Founded 1983.

Thomson Gale
15822 Bernardo Center Drive, Suite C, San Diego, CA 92127
tel 858-485-7474 *fax* 858-485-9542

Serves information and education needs through its vast content pools, which are used by students and consumers in their libraries, schools and on the internet. Listed below are its children's imprints serving the K–12 market. Part of The Thomson Corporation.

Blackbirch Press (imprint)
Illustrated non-fiction for students in elementary and middle schools.

Greenhaven Press (imprint)
High-quality non-fiction resources for the education community.

KidHave Press (imprint)
Non-fiction references for younger researchers.

Lucent Books (imprint)
Non-fiction resources for upper-elementary to high school students.

Sleeping Bear Press (imprint)
310 North Main, Suite 300, Chelsea, MI 48118
tel 800-487-2323

Illustrated fiction and non-fiction books for younger researchers.

U·X·L (imprint)
Curriculum-driven references for upper-elementary to high school students.

Tor Books
175 Fifth Avenue, 14th Floor, New York, NY 10010
tel 212-388-0100 *fax* 212-388-0191
Fiction: general, historical, western, suspense, mystery, horror, science fiction, fantasy, humour, juvenile, classics (English language); non-fiction: adult and juvenile. Affiliate of Holtzbrinck Publishers. Founded 1980.

Twenty-first Century Books – see Millbrook Press

U·X·L – see Thomson Gale

Viking Children's Books – see Penguin Putnam Books for Young Readers

Walker & Co.
104 Fifth Avenue, New York, NY 10011
tel 212-727-8300 *fax* 212-727-0984
websites www.walkerbooks.com, www.walkeryoungreaders.com
Publisher George Gibson, *Mystery* Michael Seidman, *Juvenile* Emily Easton

Picture books, non-fiction and fiction (middle grade and young adult). Recent successes include *Testing Miss Malarkey* by Judy Finchler and Kevin O'Malley and *Stella the Star* by Mark Shulman and Vincent Nguyen. General publishers for adults: biography, popular science, health, business, mystery, history.

Submission details Particularly interested in picture books, illustrated non-fiction, middle grade and young adult fiction. No series ideas. Send 50–75pp and synopsis for longer works; send the entire MSS for picture books. Include sase for return of material. Founded 1960.

Franklin Watts – see Scholastic Education

Wordsong – see Boyds Mills Press

EUROPE

France

Flammarion
4 rue Casimir Delavigne, 75006 Paris
tel (1) 40 51 31 60 *fax* (1) 46 33 59 45
email jho@flammarion.fr
website www.flammarion.fr

Leading French publisher. Children's imprints include: Albums du Père Castor, Castor Poche, Tribal, Etonnants Classiques, GF – Flammarion. Founded 1875.

Père Castor (imprint)
Children's Publisher Hélène Wadowski

Children's picture books, junior fiction, activity books, board books, how-to books, comics, gift books, fairy tales, dictionaries and records and tapes. Covers preschool, 5–10, 10–15 age groups.

Gallimard Jeunesse
5 rue Sebastien Bottin, 75007 Paris
tel (1) 49 54 42 00 *fax* (1) 45 44 94 03
email enquiries@gallimard-jeunesse.fr
website www.gallimard-jeunesse.fr
Children's Publisher Christine Baker, *Editor, Young Children's Books* Anne de Bouchony

Publisher of high-quality children's fiction and non-fiction including board books, novelty books, picture books, pop-up books. Founded 1911.

Hachette Livre/Gautier-Languereau
43 quai de Grenelle, 75905 Paris Cedex 15
tel (43) 92 33 34 *fax* (43) 92 33 38
Director Frederique de Buron, *Editorial Director* Emmanuelle Massonaud, *Publisher* Emmanuelle Henry, *Artistic Manager* Maryvonne Denizet

Novelty books, picture books and poetry. Publishes approx. 55 titles each year. Recent successes include *Babayaga* by Taï-Marc Le Thanh and Rébecca Dautremer and *Cache-Lune* by Eric Puybaret.

Submission details Will consider unsolicited MSS. Allow 2 months for response. Founded 1992.

Kaléidoscope
Kaléidoscope, 11 Rue de Sèvres, F–75006 Paris
tel (1) 45 44 07 07 *fax* (1) 45 44 53 71
email infos@editions-kaleidoscope.com
website www.editions-kaleidoscope.com
Children's Publisher Isabel Finkenstaedt

Specialises in up-market picture books for 0–6 year-olds. Founded 1988.

Universpoche-Pocket Jeunesse
12 avenue d'Italie, 75013 Paris
tel (44) 16 07 96 *fax* (44) 16 05 20
email cecile.bergand@universpoche.com

website www.universjeunesse.fr
Publishing Director Jean-Claude Dubost, *Literary Director* Natacha Dereintsky

Fiction for 5–8 and 9–12 year-olds, teenage fiction, series, fiction and film/TV tie-ins. Publishes approx. 150–160 titles each year.

Submission details Will consider unsolicited MSS. Allow one month for response.

Germany

Carl Hanser Verlag

Vilshofener Strasse 10, 81679 München
tel (89-99) 830191 *fax* (89-99) 830461
email info@hanser.de
website www.hanser.de
Children's Publisher Friedbert Stohner

High-quality hardcover books for all ages from preschool to young adults. Board books, picture books, cinema and TV tie-ins, fiction and non-fiction Age groups: 5–10, 10–15, 15+. Founded 1928.

Carlsen Verlag

Kinderbucklektorat, Volckersstrasse 14–20, D22765 Hamburg
tel (40) 398040 *fax* (40) 39804390
email erdmut.gross@carlsen.de
website www.carlsen.de
Children's Publisher Kaluas Humann

Children's picture books, board books and novelty books. Illustrated fiction and non-fiction. Teenage fiction and non-fiction. Publishes both German and international authors. Publisher of the *Harry Potter* series. Age groups: preschool, 5–10, 10–15, 15+.

Submission details Unsolicited MSS welcome but must include an sae for its return. Do not follow up by phone or post. For illustrations, submit no more than 3 colour photocopies and unlimited b&w copies. Founded 1953.

Deutscher Taschenbuch Verlag (DTV)

Friedrichstrasse 1/A, D–80801 München
tel (89) 381 67281 *fax* (89) 381 67482
website www.dtvjunior.de
Children's Publisher Anna Schiekel

Fiction and non-fiction for children and teenagers. Authors include Astrid Lindgren, Uwe Timm and Joan Aiken. Founded 1971.

Ravensburger Buchverlage

Marktstrasse 22–26, 88212 Ravensburg
tel (49) 751 860 *fax* (49) 751 861289
email buchverlag@ravensburger.de
website www.ravensburger.de
Directors Renade Hevre, Johannes Hauchstein, *Commmissioning Editors* Sabine Zurn, Dr Elisabeth Blabert, Ulrike Hekger

Activity books, novelty books, picture books, fiction for 5–8 and 9–12 year-olds, teenage fiction, series fiction and educational games and puzzles. Publishes approx. 450 titles each year and has 1500 in print. Founded 1883.

Submission details Will consider unsolicited MSS for fiction only. Allow 2 months for response.

Italy

Edizioni El/Einaudi Ragazzi/Emme Edizioni

Via J. Ressel 5, 34018 San Dorligo della Valle TS
tel (040) 3880311 *fax* (040) 3880330
email edizionel@edizioniel.it
Children's Publisher Orietta Fatucci

Activity books, board books, picture books, pop-up books, non-fiction, novels, poetry, fairy tales, fiction. Age groups: preschool, 5–10, 10–15, 15+. Publishes over 270 new titles per year.

Fabbri

R.C.S. Libri S.pA, Via Mecenate 91, 20138 Milano
tel (02) 50951 *fax* (02) 5065361
website www.rcslibri.it/fabbri

Children's fiction, especially fantasy. Publishes Tolkien, Clive Barker, and Paolini's *Eragon*.

Arnoldo Mondadori Editore S.p.A (Mondadori)

Via Arnoldo Mondadori, 15–37131, Verona
tel (045) 934111 *fax* (045) 934566
website www.mondadori.it
Children's Publisher Margherita Forstan, Fiammette Giorgi

Activity books, board books, novelty books, picture books, painting and colouring books, pop-up books, how-to books, hobbies, leisure, pets, sport, comics, poetry, fairy tales, education, fiction and non-fiction. Age groups: preschool, 5–10, 10–15, 15+. Founded 1907.

Adriano Salani Editore s.r.l.

Corso Italia 13, I–20122 Milano
tel (02) 80206624 *fax* (02) 72018806
email info@salani.it
website www.salani.it
Publisher Grazia Maria Mazzitelli

Picture books, how-to books, comics, gift books, fiction, novels, poetry, fairy tales. Age groups: preschool, 5–10, 10–15, 15.

Spain

Destino Infantil & Juvenil

Avinguda Diagonal 662, 6è, 08034 Barcelona
tel (93) 496 7001 *fax* (93) 496 7041
email destinojoven@edestino.es
website www.edestino.es
Children's Publisher Patrizia Campana, *Children's Editor* Marta Vilagut

Fiction for 6–16 year-olds. Picture books, pop-up books, fiction and some unusual illustrated books. Age groups: preschool, 5–10, 10–15, 15+.

Editorial Crulla

Balmes 245, 4t, 08006 Barcelona
tel (93) 292 21 72 *fax* (93) 238 01 16
email editorial@cruilla.com
website www.cruilla.com
Publishing Director Josep Herrero, *Literary Director* Montse Ingla

Activity books, novelty books, fiction for 5–8 and 9–12 year-olds, teenage fiction and poetry. Publishes approx. 120–130 titles each year. Recent successes include *El Vaizell de Vapor* (series), *Vull Llegir!* and *Molly Moon Stops the World/Molly Moon's Incredible Book of Hypnotism*. Founded 1984.

Random House Mondadori

Travessera de Gracia 47–49, 08021 Barcelona, Spain
tel (34) 93 3660300 *fax* (34) 93 2414823
website www.randomhousemondadori.es

Preschool activity, novelty and picture books through to young adult fiction. Also a packager and printer.

Beasco (division)
Character publishing, including Disney and Fisher-Price.

Lumen (division)
Classics and illustrated books.

Montena (division)
Contemporary literary fiction including fantasy.

Fundación Santa Maria/Ediciones SM

C/Impresores, 15, Urb. Prado des Espino, 28669 Boadilla, Madrid
tel (91) 422 88 00 *fax* (91) 422 61 16
email communicacion@grupo-sm.com
website www.grupo-sm.com
Publishing Director José Luis Cortes Salinas

Activity books, novelty books, picture books, fiction for 5–8 and 9–12 year-olds, teenage fiction, series fiction, reference and religion. Publishes approx. 220 titles each year and has about 100 in print. Recent successes include *El Sindrome de Mozart* by Gonzalo Moure and *Cuentos Para Sentir* by Begoña Ibarrola.

Submission details Will consider unsolicited MSS by post or by email. Include sae for return of MS. Allow 5 months for response. Looking for good quality literature for children and young readers.

Vicens Vives SA

Avenida Sarriá 130–132, 08017 Barcelona
tel (93) 252 3700 *fax* (93) 252 3711
website www.vicensvives.es
Managing Director Roser Espona de Rahola

Activity and novelty books, fiction, art, encyclopedias, dictionaries, education, geography, history, music, science, textbooks, posters. Age groups: preschool, 5–10, 10–15, 15+.

Children's audio publishers

Many of the audio publishers listed below are also publishers of books.

Abbey Home Entertainment plc

435–437 Edgware Road, London W2 1TH
tel 020-7563 3910 *fax* 020-7563 3911
Contact Anne Miles

Specialises in the acquisition, production and distribution of quality audio/visual entertainment for children. Bestselling children's spoken word and music titles are available on CD and cassette in the Tempo range including *Postman Pat, Watership Down, Michael Rosen, Baby Bright, Wide Eye, SuperTed* and *Fun Song Factory*.

Backbone Productions Ltd

PO Box 28409, London N19 4WX
tel 020-7281 0445 *fax* 020-7561 0105
email office@copingwithgrowing.com
website www.copingwithgrowing.com
Managing Director Edward Harris

Therapeutic resources for children.

Barefoot Books Ltd

124 Walcot Street, Bath BA1 5BG
tel (01225) 322400 *fax* (01225) 322499
email info@barefootbooks.co.uk
website www.barefootbooks.co.uk
Publisher Tessa Stickland, *UK Editor* Natasha Carr

Narrative unabridged audiobooks, spoken and sung. Established 1993.

Barrington Stoke

Sandeman House, Trunk's Close, 55 High Street, Edinburgh EH1 1SR
tel 0131-557 2020 *fax* 0131-557 6060
email anna.gibbons@barringtonstoke.co.uk
website www.barringtonstoke.co.uk
Chairman David Croom, *Managing Director* Sonia Raphael, *Editorial Manager* Anna Gibbons

Cassette tapes accompanied by 2 books: *Virtual Friends* and *Virtual Friends Again* by Mary Hoffman, *Problems with a Python* and *Living with Vampires* by Jeremy Strong, *Tod in Biker City* and *Bicycle Blues* by Anthony Masters, *Hat Trick* and *Ghost for Sale* by Terry Deary. Founded 1998.

BBC Audiobooks Ltd

St James House, The Square, Lower Bristol Road, Bath BA2 3BH
tel (01225) 878000 *fax* (01225) 310771
website www.bbcaudiobooks.com
Managing Director Paul Dempsey, *Publishing Director* Jan Paterson, *Marketing Director* Rachel Stammers, *Finance Director* Mike Bowen, *Commissioning Editor* Kate Walsh

Spoken word entertainment that can be enjoyed at convenience. Recent successes include *Midnight* by Jacqueline Wilson, *Artemis Fowl: The Eternity Code* by Coin Colfer and *Shadowmancer* by G.P. Taylor – all published in audio and large print. Children's imprints include: Chivers Children's Audiobooks, BBC Cover to Cover, 'Read-Alongs'. Formed in 2002 from the amalgamation of Chivers Press, Cover To Cover and BBC Radio Collection.

BBC Cover to Cover

St James House, The Square, Lower Bristol Road, Bath BA2 3BH
tel (01225) 878000 *fax* (01225) 310771
website www.bbcaudiobooks.com

Unabridged children's bestselling titles. List includes readings of stories by today's major children's authors, such as Philip Pullman, Eoin Colfer and Jacqueline Wilson. Imprint of BBC Audiobooks Ltd.

Bloomsbury Publishing Plc

38 Soho Square, London W1D 3HB
tel 020-7494 2111 *fax* 020-7734 8656
website www.bloomsbury.com
Contact Arzu Tahsin, Paperback Publishing Director

A broad selection of literary fiction and non-fiction; selected children's fiction and picture book packages.

Bolinda Publishing

2 Ivanhoe Road, London SE5 8DH
tel 020-773 1088
email bolinda@marisa.fsbusines..co.uk
website www.bolinda.com
UK Publisher Marisa McGreevy

CDs and cassettes of children's, teenage and adult fiction titles. UK-based teenage list launched in 2002 with titles including *Troy* by Adele Geras (shortlisted for the Carnegie Medal and the Whitbread Book Awards) and *Thursday's Child* by Sonya Hartnett (winner of *The Guardian* Children's Fiction Prize). UK-based children's and adult lists to be launched in 2004. Publishes 18 titles a year and has 150 titles available. Based in Melbourne, Australia; established in the UK in 2002.

Chivers Children's Audiobooks

St James House, The Square, Lower Bristol Road, Bath BA2 3BH
tel (01225) 878000 *fax* (01225) 310771

website www.bbcaudiobooks.com

Both the adult and children's lists feature current bestselling fiction and popular classics by some of Britain and the USA's best authors, read by some of the world's most celebrated actors. In addition, there is an extensive monthly programme of titles available on CD. Chivers Press pioneered the recording of complete and unabridged books with the first titles being published in 1980 and it now has a backlist in excess of 3000 titles ranged from 2-cassette to 16-cassette formats. Imprint of BBC Audiobooks Ltd.

Cló Iar-Chonnachta Teo.

Indreabhán, Conamara, Co. Galway, Republic of Ireland
tel (091) 593307 *fax* (091) 593362
email cic@iol.ie
website www.cic.ie
Ceo Micheál Ó Conghaile, *General Manager* Deirdre O'Toole

Predominantly Irish-language children's book with accompanying CD/cassette of stories/folklore/poetry. Established 1985.

CSA Word

6A Archway Mews, London SW15 2PE
tel 020-8871 0220 *fax* 020-8877 0712
email info@csaword.co.uk
website www.csaword.co.uk
Managing Director Clive Stanhope, *Audio Director* Victoria Williams

CDs and cassettes of classic children's literature such as *Just William*, *Billy Bunter* and *Black Beauty*; also current literary authors. Publishes 3 titles a year and has 20 titles available. Founded 1991.

Dref Wen

28 Church Road, Whitchurch, Cardiff CF14 2EA
tel 029-2061 7860 *fax* 029-2061 0507
Directors Roger Boore, Anne Boore, Gwilym Boore, Alun Boore

Welsh language audiobooks. Founded 1970.

The Educational Company of Ireland Ltd

Ballymount Road, Walkinstown, Dublin 12, Republic of Ireland
tel (01) 4500611 *fax* (01) 4500993
email info@edco.ie
website www.edco.ie
Executive Directors Frank Maguire (chief executive), R. McLoughlin, *Financial Controller* A. Harrold, *Sales and Marketing Manager* M. Harford-Hughes, *Publisher* Frank Fahy

Irish language CDs and audiotapes. Trading unit of Smurfit Ireland Ltd. Founded 1910.

HarperCollins Audio

77–85 Fulham Palace Road, London W6 8JB
tel 020-8741 7070 *fax* 020-8307 4517
website www.harpercollins.co.uk
Publishing Director Rosalie George

Publishers of a wide range of genres including fiction, non-fiction, poetry, Classics, Shakespeare, comedy, personal development and children's. All works are read by famous actors. Established 1990.

Hodder Headline Audiobooks

338 Euston Road, London NW1 3BH
tel 020-7873 6000 *fax* 020-7873 6024
email rupert.lancaster@hodder.co.uk
Publisher Rupert Lancaster, *Publicity* Lucy Dixon

Publishes outstanding authors from within the Hodder Headline group and from elsewhere. The list is made up of quality non-fiction; fiction, from John le Carré to Louis de Bernieres to Ardal O'Hanlon; WHSmith's Classic Collection; self-help titles from authors such as Susan Jeffers and Richard Carlson; religious titles; children's (i.e. the highly acclaimed dramatised *Winnie the Pooh*); sporting autobiographies including Alex Ferguson, Brian Moore and Dickie Bird; comedy titles such as *Wallace & Gromit* and the *Magic Roundabout Adventures*, bestselling collaborations with Classic FM; Derek Jacobi's acclaimed readings of the *Brother Cadfael* mysteries, and C.S. Forester's *Hornblower* novels read by Ioan Gruffudd. Founded 1994.

Ladybird Books

80 Strand, London WC2R 0RL
tel 020-7010 3000 *fax* 020-7010 6060
Product Manager Emma Williams

Ladybird Books in book-and-tape format for children aged 0–8 years, including titles from the *Animal Funtime* and *Little Stories* series. Imprint of Penguin Audiobooks.

Macmillan Audio Books

20 New Wharf Road, London N1 9RR
tel 020-7014 6000 *fax* 020-7014 6001
email a.muirden@macmillan.co.uk
website www.panmacmillan.co.uk
Audio Publisher Alison Muirden, *Editorial Co-ordinator* Zoe Howes

Children's book and tape packs include *Gruffalo* by Julia Donaldson and Axel Scheffler, and *Room on the Broom* and *Smartest Giant in Town* by Julia Donaldson. Also adult fiction, non-fiction and autobiography. Publishes approx. 5–10 titles each year and has 15 available. Voted Audio Publisher of the Year 2003 at the Spoken Word Awards. Established 1995.

Naxos AudioBooks

18 High Street, Welwyn, Herts. AL6 9EQ
tel (01438) 717808 *fax* (01438) 717809
email naxos_audiobooks@compuserve.com
website www.naxosaudiobooks.com
Managing Director Nicolas Soames

Classic literature, modern fiction, non-fiction, drama and poetry on CD and cassette. Also junior classics and classical music. Founded 1994.

The Orion Publishing Group Ltd

5 Upper St Martin's Lane, London WC2H 9EA
tel 020-7520 4425 *fax* 020-7379 6158
email pandora.white@orionbooks.co.uk
Audio Manager Pandora White

Adult and children's fiction. Established 1998.

Penguin Audiobooks

Penguin Books Ltd, 80 Strand, London WC2R 0RL
tel 020-7010 3000 *fax* 020-7010 6695
email audio@penguin.co.uk
website www.penguin.co.uk/audio
Audio Publisher Jeremy Ettinghausen

The audiobooks list reflects the diversity of the Penguin book range, including classic and contemporary fiction and non-fiction, autobiography, poetry, drama and, in Puffin Audiobooks, the best of contemporary and classic literature for younger listeners. Authors include Nick Hornby, Sue Townsend, Seamus Heaney, Roald Dahl and Eoin Colfer. Readings are by talented and recognisable actors. Over 500 titles are now available. Founded 1993.

Puffin Audiobooks – see Penguin Audiobooks

SmartPass Ltd

15 Park Road, Rottingdean, Brighton BN2 7HL
tel (01273) 300742
email info@smartpass.co.uk
websites www.smartpass.co.uk, www.spaudiobooks.com
Managing Director Phil Viner, *Creative Director* Jools Viner

SmartPass audio guides present English literature texts for Key Stage 3, SATS and GCSE as full-cast dramas with an educational twist. The *PassMaster* comments, explains and explores the novel, play or poetry, as well as its background in history and in society. It includes dramatised debate and discussion to tease out information about themes, the author's biography and study strategies. Publishes approx. 3 titles each year and has 11 available.

SPAudiobooks: the first full-cast unabridged drama has been released, read by the author with fully dramatised dialogue. Established 1991.

Usborne Publishing Ltd

Usborne House, 83-85 Saffron Hill, London EC1N 8RT
tel 020-7430 2800 *fax* 020-7430 1562
email mail@usborne.co.uk
website www.usborne.com
Publishing Director Jenny Tyler, *General Manager* Robert Jones

Walker Books Ltd

87 Vauxhall Walk, London SE11 5HJ
tel 020-7793 0909 *fax* 020-7587 1123
Publisher Loraine Taylor

Audiobooks include bestselling fiction titles such as the *Alex Rider* series, *Judy Moody* and *Confessions of a Teenage Drama Queen*. For younger children, the *Listen and Join In* audio range comprises entertaining story-based activities based on favourite picture books, including *We're Going on a Bear Hunt*, *Guess How Much I Love You* and *Can't You Sleep Little Bear?* See also page 28.

Walking Oliver

The Manning Partnership Ltd, 6 The Old Dairy, Melcombe Road, Bath BA2 3LR
tel (01225) 478444 *fax* (01225) 478440
email sales@manning-partnership.co.uk
website www.manning-partnership.co.uk
Managing Director Garry Manning, *Sales Director* Rober Hibbert

Committed to producing traditional yet innovative music for children that is fun, enriching and of the highest quality. Features world-reknowned tenor Paul Austin Kelly. Established 2003.

Children's book packagers

Many modern illustrated books are created by book packagers, whose special skills are in the areas of book design and graphic content. In-house editors match up the expertise of specialist writers, artists and photographers who usually work on a freelance basis.

Aladdin Books Ltd

28 Percy Street, London W1P 0LD
tel 020-7323 3319 *fax* 020-7323 4829
email aladdin@dircon.co.uk
Directors Charles Nicholas, Bibby Whittaker

Full design and book packaging facility specialising in children's non-fiction and reference. Founded 1980.

The Albion Press Ltd

Spring Hill, Idbury,
Oxon OX7 6RU
tel (01993) 831094 *fax* (01993) 831982
Directors Emma Bradford (managing), Neil Philip (editorial)

Produces quality integrated illustrated titles from the initial idea to the printed copy. Specialises in children's books: poetry, fairy tales, myths, Native Americans. Produces 4 titles each year.

Submission details Will not consider unsolicited MSS. Interested in seeing fine samples of illustrations but no cartoons or technical drawings. Include an sae. Founded 1984.

Andromeda Oxford Ltd

Kimber House, 1 Kimber Road, Abingdon,
Oxon OX14 1SG
tel (01235) 55029611
email mail@andromeda.co.uk
website www.andromeda.co.uk
Directors David Holyoak (managing), Graham Bateman (publishing), Clive Sparling (production), Simon Matthews (finance), Christopher Collier (sales), Linda Cole (creative)

Produces for the international market adult and junior reference books: history, natural history, geography, science, art. Also children's information and activity books. Founded 1986.

Arcturus Publishing Ltd

26–27 Bickels Yard, 151–3 Bermondsey Street,
London SE1 3HA
tel 020-7407 9400 *fax* 020-7407 9444
email roberta.bailey@arcturus publishing.com
Managing Director, Arcturus Children's Publishing Roberta Bailey

Children's non-fiction and school library books, including activity books, pop-up books, reference, education, geography, history and science.

Nicola Baxter

PO Box 215, The Brew House, Framingham Earl Road, Yelverton, Norwich NR14 7UR
tel (01508) 491111 *fax* (01508) 491100
email nb@nicolabaxter.com
website www.nicolabaxter.com
Manager, Commissioning Editor & Author Nicola Baxter

Full packaging service for children's books, from concept to film or any part of the process in between. Produces both fiction and non-fiction titles in a wide range of formats, from board books to encyclopedias and also novelty books. Opportunities for freelances. Founded 1990.

Bender Richardson White

PO Box 266, Uxbridge, Middlesex UB9 5NX
tel (01895) 832444 *fax* (01895) 835213
email brw@brw.co.uk
Directors Lionel Bender (editorial), Kim Richardson (sales & production), Ben White (design)

Design, editorial and production of activity books, non-fiction and reference books. Specialises in non-fiction: natural history, science, history and educational. Packages approx. 60–70 titles each year.

Submission details Writers should send a letter and synopsis of their proposal. Opportunities for freelances. Founded 1990.

The Book Guild Ltd

Temple House, 25 High Street, Lewes,
East Sussex BN7 2LU
tel (01273) 472534 *fax* (01273) 476472
email info@bookguild.co.uk
website www.bookguild.co.uk
Directors G.M. Nissen CBE (chairman), Carol Biss (managing), Anthony Nissen, Jane Nissen, David Ross, Paul White (financial), Janet Wrench (production)

Fiction for 5–8 and 9–12 year-olds. Produces approx. 10 children's titles each year. Offers a range of publishing options: a comprehensive package for authors incorporating editorial, design, production, marketing, publicity and distribution; editorial and production only for authors requiring private editions; or a complete service for companies and organisations requiring books for internal or promotional purposes – from brief to finished book.

Submission details Write for submission information. Founded 1982.

Book Street Ltd

Foresters Hall, 25–27 Westow Street, London SE19 3RY
tel 020-8771 5115 *fax* 020-8771 9994
email graham@popking.demon.co.uk

Designers and packagers of large format children's books for the international market.

Bookwork Ltd

Unit 17, Piccadilly Mill, Lower Street, Stroud, Glos. GL5 2HT
tel (01453) 752521 *fax* (01453) 751544
email bookwork@compuserve.com
Directors Louise Pritchard (editorial), Alan Plank (production), Jill Plank (design), *Editor* Annabel Blackledge

Creates innovative books for children of all ages: activity books, board books, picture books, how-to books, reference books. Also supplies a full editorial and design service to other publishers. Imprint: Pangolin.

Brainwaves Ltd

31 Chart Lane, Reigate, Surrey RH2 7DY
tel (01737) 224444 *fax* (01737) 225777
Editorial Director Keith Faulkner

Packager of activity books, board books, novelty books, picture books, pop-up books and gift books.

Breslich & Foss Ltd

2A Union Court, 20–22 Union Road, London SW4 6JP
tel 020-7819 3990 *fax* 020-7819 3998
Directors Paula G. Breslich, K.B. Dunning

Books produced from MS to bound copy stage from in-house ideas. Specialising in crafts, interiors, health, children's classics and fairy tales. Founded 1978.

John Brown Junior

The New Boathouse, 136–142 Bramley Road, London W10 6SR
tel 020-7565 3000 *fax* 020-7565 3060
email info@jbjunior.com
website www.jbjunior.com
Directors Andrew Jarvis (managing), Sara Lynn (creative)

Creative development and packaging of children's products including books, magazines, partworks, CD-Roms and websites.

Brown Wells & Jacobs Ltd

Foresters Hall, 25–27 Westow Street, London SE19 3RY
tel 020-8771 5115 *fax* 020-8771 9994
email graham@popking.demon.co.uk
website www.bwj.org
Director Graham Brown

Design, editorial, illustration and production of high-quality non-fiction illustrated children's books. Specialities include pop-up and novelty books. Packages approx. 30–40 titles each year.

Submission details Opportunities for freelances. Founded 1979.

Cambridge Publishing Management Ltd

149B Histon Road, Cambridge CB4 3JD
tel (01223) 367288 *fax* (01223) 368237
email initial.surname@cambridgepm.co.uk
website www.cambridgepm.co.uk
Managing Director Jackie Dobbyne, *Publishing Director* Julia Morris

Creative editorial and book production company specialising in complete project management of education, ELT, travel and illustrated non-fiction titles, from MS to delivery of final files on disk. Opportunities for freelances. Founded 1999.

Cowley Robinson Publishing Ltd

8 Belmont, Bath BA1 5DZ
tel (01225) 339999 *fax* (01225) 339995
website www.cowleyrobinson.com
Directors Lee Robinson (chairman), Stewart Cowley (publishing), Rob Kendrew (production)

Children's international co-editions. Novelty format creation. Licence and character publishing developments. Information and early learning. Founded 1998.

Creations For Children International

Steenweg op Deinze 150, 9810 Nazareth, Belgium
tel (9) 2446090 *fax* (9) 2446099
email info@c4ci.com, jan.meeuws@c4ci.com
website www.c4ci.com
Directors Marc Barbier (business & sales), Marc Janbloet (book publishing & sales), *Production Manager* Joost Demuynck, *Chief Editor* Mr Jan Meeuws

Packagers of high-quality mass market children's illustrated books, including fairy tale and classic adventure story books. Activity books, board books, novelty books, picture books, painting and colouring books, pop-up books.

Design Eye Ltd

4th Floor, The Fitzpatrick Building, 188-194 York Way, London N7 9QP
tel 020-7700 7654 *fax* 020-7700 3890
Managing Director Jeffrey Nobbs

Packager and publisher of interactive kit books for adults and children: arts and crafts, science, history and fiction. Opportunities for freelances. Member of the Quarto Group. Founded 1988.

Elm Grove Books Ltd

Elm Grove, Henstridge,
Somerset BA8 0TQ
tel (01963) 362498 *fax* (01963) 362982
email elmgrovebooks@aol.com
Directors Hugh Elwes, Susie Elwes

Packager of children's books. Opportunities for freelances. Founded 1993.

Graham-Cameron Publishing & Illustration

The Studio, 23 Holt Road, Sheringham,
Norfolk NR26 8NB
tel (01263) 821333 *fax* (01263) 821334
email forename@graham-cameron.com
website www.graham-cameron-illustration.com
and 59 Redvers Road, Brighton BN2 4BF
tel (01273) 385890
Directors Mike Graham-Cameron (managing), Helen Graham-Cameron (art), Duncan Graham-Cameron (marketing)

Offers illustration and editorial services for picture books and educational materials. Handles activity books, picture books, fiction for 5–8 and 9–12 year-olds, non-fiction, reference and poetry. Illustration agency with 37 artists.

Submission details Send an outline and the first 3 pages. Founded 1984.

Gusto

Head office Karenslyst Alle 18E, 0278 Oslo, Norway
tel (47) 22434005 *fax* (47) 85034316
email james@gusto.tv
UK office Ask House, Northgate Avenue, Bury St. Edmunds IP32 6BB
tel (01284) 768278
email james@gusto.tv
website www.gusto.tv
Directors Jessica Taylor (editorial), James Tavendale (publishing & sales), Jan Chr. Danielsen (art)

Packager of gift books, children's books, cookbooks and handbooks. Children's books include *Jeff the Chef*, *Funnymals* and *Men at Work*. Board books, novelty books, picture books and how-to books. Based in the UK, Norway and Italy. Established in 2000 as SmallWorld Publishing; renamed Gusto in 2004.

Haldane Mason Ltd

PO Box 34196,
London NW10 3YB
tel 020-8459 2131 *fax* 020-8728 1216
email info@haldane.masoncom
Directors Ron Samuel, Sydney Francis

Packager of books on alternative health and children's non-fiction. Opportunities for freelances. Founded 1995.

Hardlines Ltd

Park Street, Charlbury, Oxon OX7 3PS
tel (01608) 811255 *fax* (01608) 811442
email info@hardlines.co.uk
website www.hardlines.co.uk
Managing Director R. Hickey, *Directors* P. Wilkinson, G. Walker

Primary, secondary academic education (geography, science, modern languages) and co-editions (travel guides, gardening, cookery). Multimedia (CD-Rom programming and animations). Opportunities for freelances. Founded 1985.

Hawcock Books

Grafton House, High Street, Norton St Philip,
Nr Bath BA2 7LG
tel (01373) 834055 *fax* (01373) 834622
email popupbooks@aol.com Hawcock
website www.hawcockbooks.co.uk

Company devoted to the design and production of highly creative and original pop-up art and 3D paper-engineered concepts. Most of its experience is in developing, providing editorial for, printing and manufacturing pop-up books and novelty items for the publishing industry. Also undertakes demanding commissions from the advertising world for model-making, point-of-sale and all printed 3D aspects of major campaigns.

Inky Press

The Old Candlemakers, West Street, Lewes,
East Sussex BN7 2NZ
tel (01273) 487440 *fax* (01273) 487441
email surname@ivypress.co.uk
Directors Peter Bridgewater (creative), Sheila Mortimer (editorial), Jenny Manstead (sales), *Publisher* Tony Potter

A new packager of interactive and design-driven picture books for children up to the age of 10. Opportunities for freelances. Part of the Ivy Publishing Group.

Miles Kelly Packaging

The Bradfield Centre, Great Bardfield, Essex CM7 4SL
tel (01371) 811309 *fax* (01371) 811393
email info@mileskelly.net
website www.mileskelly.net
Directors Kelly Gerard, Jim Miles, Kate Miles

Offers a complete packaging service from conception through to finished copies of high-quality illustrated non-fiction titles for children and family. See also page 16. Founded 1996.

Lion Hudson International Co-Editions

Concorde House, Grenville Place, London NW7 3SA
tel 020-8959 3668 *fax* 020-8959 3678
email coed@angushudson.com
website www.angushudson.com

Managing Director Nicholas Jones

Adult and children's Christian books including international co-editions. Publishing imprints: Candle Books, Monarch Books. Founded 1971 as Angus Hudson; merged with Lion Publishing 2004.

Marshall Cavendish Partworks Ltd

119 Wardour Street, London W1F 0UW
tel 020-7734 6710 *fax* 020-7734 6221
website www.marshallcavendish.co.uk
Group Editor Rebecca Fry

Cookery, crafts, gardening, do-it-yourself, history, children's interests, general illustrated non-fiction. Founded 1969.

Marshall Editions Ltd

The Old Brewery, 6 Blundell Street, London N7 9BH
tel 020-7700 6700 *fax* 020-7700 4191
email info@marshalleditions.com
Publisher Hilary Arnold

Highly illustrated non-fiction for adults and children, including history, health, gardening, home design, pets, natural history, popular science.

Monkey Puzzle Media Ltd

Gissing's Farm, Fressingfield, Eye, Suffolk IP21 5SH
tel (01379) 588044 *fax* (01379) 588055
email rgc@ndirect.co.uk
Director Roger Goddard-Coote

Offers a full packaging service from concept or commission through to delivery of repro-ready disks or film. Specialises in children's non-fiction and reference. Produces approx. 60 titles each year.

Submission details Will consider unsolicited MSS and copies of illustrations with an sae. Founded 1998.

Orpheus Books Ltd

2 Church Green, Witney, Oxon OX28 4AW
tel (01993) 774949 *fax* (01993) 700330
email info@orpheusbooks.com
website www.orpheusbooks.com
Executive Director Nicholas Harris (editorial, design and marketing)

Produces children's non-fiction books for the international co-editions market: activity books, novelty books, non-fiction and reference. Produces approx. 8–20 titles each year.

Submission details Welcomes samples from illustrators and CVs from writers. Founded 1993.

Picthall & Gunzi Ltd

21A Widmore Road, Bromley, Kent BR1 1RW
tel 020-8460 4032 *fax* 020-8460 4021
email chez@picthallandgunzi.demon.co.uk
website www.picthallandgunzi.co.uk
Directors Deborah Murrell (joint managing), Chez Picthall (joint managing), Christiane Gunzi (editorial), Dominic Zwemmer (art)

Offers a complete package, from concept through to publication, producing high-quality, illustrated non-fiction books for children: activity books, board books, novelty books, encyclopedias, non-fiction.

Pinwheel Ltd

Winchester House, 259–269 Old Marylebone Road, London NW1 5XJ
tel 020-7616 7200 *fax* 020-7616 7201
website www.pinwheel.co.uk
Directors Andrew Flatt (managing), Linda Cole (publishing), Paula Burgess (creative)

Packages unique and innovative children's books for the international market, across 3 imprints (see page 22).

Playne Books Ltd

Park Court Barn, Trefin, Haverfordwest, Pembrokeshire SA62 5AU
tel (01348) 837073 *fax* (01348) 837063
email playne.books@virgin.net
Design and Production David Playne, *Editor* Gill Davies

Specialises in highly illustrated adult non-fiction and books for very young children. All stages of production undertaken from initial concept (editorial, design and manufacture) to delivery of completed books. Include sae for return of work. Founded 1987.

Tony Potter Publishing Ltd

1 Stairbridge Court, Bolney Grange Business Park, Stairbridge Lane, Bolney, West Sussex RH17 5PA
tel (01444) 232889 *fax* (01444) 232142
email sheilamortimer@zoo.co.uk
website www.tonypotter.com
Directors Tony Potter (managing), Christine Potter, Sheila Mortimer

Creates custom children's book and own brand innovative paper-based products for children and adults. Also creates high-quality children's titles as a packager and occasionally publishes under its own imprint: Tony Potter Publishing. Opportunities for freelance designers. Founded 1997.

Mathew Price Ltd

The Old Glove Factory, Bristol Road, Sherborne, Dorset DT9 4HP
tel (01935) 816010 *fax* (01935) 816310
email mathewp@mathewprice.com

Packager of novelty books, picture books, fiction for 5–8 year-olds and non-fiction. Produces approx. 35 titles each year.

Submission details Include sae with MS. Founded 1983.

The Puzzle House

Ivy Cottage, Battlesea Green, Stradbroke, Suffolk IP21 5NE
tel (01379) 384656 *fax* (01379) 384656
email puzzlehouse@btinternet.com
website www.thepuzzlehouse.co.uk
Partners Roy Preston and Sue Preston

Editorial service creating crossword, quizz, puzzle and activity material for all ages. Founded 1988.

Quarto Children's Books Ltd

3rd Floor, The Fitzpatrick Building, 188-194 York Way, London N7 9QP
tel 020-7607 3322 *fax* 020-7700 2951
Editorial Director Beck Ward, *Managing Director* Clyde Hunter

Highly illustrated children's non-fiction and fiction.

Apple Press (imprint)

Leisure, domestic and craft pursuits; cookery, gardening, sport, transport, children's.

Tangerine Designs Ltd

2 High Street, Freshford, Bath BA2 7WE
tel (01225) 722382 *fax* (01225) 722856
email tangerinedesigns@aol.com
Managing Director Christine Swift

Packagers and co-edition publishers of children's books including novelty books and licensed titles. New licensed character properties available in 2004. Submissions only accepted if sae is enclosed. Founded 2000.

Tango Books Ltd

29 Chiswick Green Studios, Evershed Walk, London W4 5BW
tel 020-8996 9970 *fax* 020-8996 9977
email sheri@tangobooks.co.uk
website www.tangobooks.co.uk
Directors Sheri Safran, David Fielder, *Submissions* Edith Fricker (*tel* 020-8996 9973 *email* edith@tangobooks.co.uk)

Creates and produces international co-productions of children's novelty books only (touch-and-feel, flaps, pop-ups, foils, etc). No flat picture books. Produces mainly for the 0–6 age group but some for up to age 12. Books are highly visual with lots of illustrations and minimal text, except for non-fiction where there is scope for longer texts. Publishes in the UK under Tango.

Submission details The max. word count for ages 0–6 is 750 words. Text should be for novelty format (repetition works well). No particularly British themes or characters. No poetry. Artwork: modern style, fresh and fun. Likes collage, bright and bold styles, pen and ink coloured in. Less keen on watercolour unless very special. Send submissions with sae for their return. Allow one month for reply. Founded 1983.

The Templar Company plc

Pippbrook Mill, London Road, Dorking, Surrey RH4 1JE
tel (01306) 876361 *fax* (01306) 889097
email info@templar.co.uk
website www.templar.co.uk
Directors Amanda Wood, Ruth Huddleston, Elaine Hunt

Children's gift, novelty, picture and illustrated information books; most titles aimed at international co-edition market. Established links with major co-publishers in USA, Australia and throughout Europe. Imprints: Templar Publishing, Amazing Baby.

TKC Design

105 Sladedale Road, London SE18 1PX
tel/fax 020-8855 7602 *mobile* (07973) 828923
email TracyCarrington@tkcdesign@aol.com
Contact Tracy Carrington

Packager for the international children's market in the 0–11 age group (fiction and non-fiction). Also promotional and marketing design for print. Offers a complete service from origination to print-ready disks. Also offers the creation of branding styles and design for new and existing licensed characters; concept development; project management including scheduling, budgeting and setting up teams for large-scale, multi-component projects; creative original and innovative design. Has a bank of experienced freelancers/consultants (authors, illustrators, designers and editorial services). Founded 2004.

Toucan Books Ltd

3rd Floor, 89 Charterhouse Street, London EC1M 6HR
tel 020-7250 3388 *fax* 020-7250 3123
Directors Robert Sackville West, Ellen Dupont

International co-editions; editorial, design and production services. Founded 1985.

Emma Treehouse Ltd

Little Orchard House, Mill Lane, Beckington, Somerset BA11 6SN
tel (01373) 831215 *fax* (01373) 831216
email info@emmatreehouse.com
website www.emmatreehouse.com
Directors David Bailey, Richard Powell (creative & editorial)

Specialist creator of novelty books for children aged 0–7: bath books, books with a sound concept, cloth books, novelty books, flap books, touch-and-feel books. Packager and co-edition publisher with international recognition for its innovative and often unique concepts. The company has produced over 25 million books, translated into 33 different languages. Opportunities for freelance artists. Founded 1992

Tucker Slingsby Ltd

Roebuck House, 288 Upper Richmond Road West, London SW14 7JG
tel 020-8876 6310 *fax* 020-8876 4104
email firstname@tuckerslingsby.co.uk
Directors Janet Slingsby, Del Tucker

Highly illustrated adult and children's books and magazines from concept to delivery of film, disk or finished copies. Produces for preschool to teenage: annuals, activity books, novelty books, picture books, film/TV tie-ins, non-fiction, religion and reference. Produces approx. 100 titles each year.

Submission details Opportunities for freelances and picture book artists. Submit by post. Founded 1992.

Ventura Publishing Ltd

80 Strand, London WC2R 0RL
tel 020-7010 3000 *fax* 020-7010 6707
email funwithspot@penguin.co.uk
website www.funwithspot.com
Managing Director Sally Floyer

Specialises in production of the *Spot* books by Eric Hill.

David West Children's Books

7 Princeton Court, 55 Felsham Road, London SW15 1AZ
tel 020-8780 3836 *fax* 020-8780 9313
email dww@btinternet.com
website www.davidwestchildrensbooks.com
Proprietor David West, Partner Lynn Lockett

Packagers of children's illustrated reference books. Specialises in science, art, geography, history, sport and flight. Produces 40 titles each year. Opportunities for freelances. Founded 1986.

Working Partners Ltd

1 Albion Place, London W6 0QT
tel 020-8748 7477 *fax* 020-8748 7450
email enquiries@workingpartnersltd.co.uk
website www.workingpartnersltd.co.uk
Chairman Ben Baglio, *Managing Director* Chris Snowdon, *Creative Director* Rod Ritchie, *Editorial Director* Deborah Smith

Children's and young adult fiction – series, trilogies, single titles. Founded 1995.

Children's book clubs

Not all the companies listed here are 'clubs' in the true sense: some are mail order operations and others sell their books via book fairs.

Baker Books

Manfield Park, Cranleigh, Surrey GU6 8NU
tel (01483) 267888 *fax* (01483) 267409
email bakerbooks@dial.pipex.com
website www.bakerbooks.co.uk

School book clubs for children aged 3–13. Operates in the UK and reaches English medium schools overseas.

BFC Books for Children

Greater London House, Hampstead Road, London NW1 7TZ
Customer services tel (0870) 165 0292
fax (0870) 165 0222
website www.booksforchildren.co.uk

Offers a wide range of books, tapes, toys and CD-Roms for babies through to teenagers. Books include fiction, non-fiction and national curriculum-related material. Membership gives access to Books for Children website, and 4-weekly colour magazines offering books for sale. Conditions of membership: 6 books in first year must be ordered through the website or magazine. Part of the BCA Group.

Bibliophile

5 Thomas Road, London E14 7BN
tel 020-7515 9222 *fax* 020-7538 4115
email order@bibliophilebooks.com
website www.bibliophilebooks.com
Secretary Annie Quigley

To promote value-for-money reading. Upmarket literature and classical music on CD available from mail order catalogue (10 p.a.). Over 3000 titles covering art and fiction to travel, history and children's books. Founded 1978.

The Book People Ltd

Catteshall Manor, Catteshall Lane, Godalming, Surrey GU7 1UU
tel (01483) 861144 *fax* (01483) 861256
website www.thebookpeople.co.uk

Popular general fiction and non-fiction, including children's and travel. Monthly.

Disney Book Club

Customer services Grolier Ltd, PO Box 49, Norwich NR5 9PP
tel (01603) 726 900
email customerservices@grolier.co.uk
website www.disneybookclub.co.uk

Offers books based on Disney characters, Disney storybooks, yearbooks, calendars and supplements. Six free books on joining. New books sent every 4 weeks. Membership may be cancelled after acceptance of 3 shipments.

The Poetry Book Society

Book House, 45 East Hill, London SW18 2QZ
tel 020-8870 8403 *fax* 020-8870 0865
email info@poetrybooks.co.uk
website www.poetrybooks.co.uk

Quarterly. See page 115.

Primary Books

The Old Dairy Manor Farm, High Street Gratety, Andover, Hants. SP11 8JS
tel (01264) 889000 *fax* (01264) 889900
email theoffice@primarybooks.co.uk
website www.primarybooks.co.uk

Operates through local franchises which organise book fair events in schools, and offer advice to teachers and parents on book selection.

Puffin Book Club

Penguin Books, 80 The Strand, London WC2R 0BR
Customer services Edinburgh Gate, Harlow, Essex CM20 2JE
Freephone tel (0500) 454 444 (UK), (1) 800 340 131 (ROI) *fax* 020-7010 6667, (01279) 621 102
email pbccustomerservice@penguin.co.uk
website www.puffinbookclub.co.uk

A schools-based club from Puffin Books giving access to a range of discounted books for 5 age ranges: Junior for 0–5, Xtra for 5–7, Zone for 7–9, Word for 9–11, Max for 11+. The club offers selections from Puffin, Penguin, Dorling Kindersley and Ladybird as well as bestsellers from other publishers. The *Puffin Book Club* magazine features books on offer as well as editorial features, activities and competitions.

Red House

PO Box 142, Bangor LL57 4ZP
tel (0870) 1919980 *fax* (0870) 6077720
email enquiries@redhouse.co.uk
website www.redhouse.co.uk

The children's arm of the UK's largest supplier of cut-price books, The Book People. Red House specialises in providing a huge selection of books to children at competitive prices through a catalogue and their website. It is not a book club as there is no commitment to buy every month. Sponsors of the Red House Children's Book Award.

Red House International Schools Book Club (ISBC)

Scholastic Ltd, Villiers House, Clarendon Avenue, Leamington Spa, Warks. CV32 5PR
tel (01993) 893474 *fax* (01993) 708159
email intschool@scholastic.co.uk

International book club and book fair service for schools worldwide.

Scholastic Book Clubs

Scholastic Ltd, Villiers House, Clarendon Avenue, Leamington Spa, Warks. CV32 5PR
tel (0845) 6039091
email scbenquiries@scholastic.co.uk
website www.scholastic.co.uk

Schools-based clubs offering children a wide range of books specially selected for their age group from most major publishers. There are 5 Children's Book Clubs: Seesaw for 3–5 year-olds, Firefly for 5–7 year-olds, Lucky for 7–9 year-olds, Arrow for 9–11 year-olds and Cover2Cover for 11–14 year-olds. Mail order leaflets are sent direct to schools 2–3 times a term.

Scholastic Book Fairs

website www.scholastic.co.uk/bookfairs

Pre-selected choice of books delivered to schools for children/parents/teachers to purchase.

Travelling Book Company

(also known as Troubadour)
Express House, Crow Arch Lane, Ringwood, Hants. BH24 1PD
tel (0800) 7315758
email customer.services@travellingbooks.co.uk
website www.travellingbooks.co.uk

Book fair operation selling books to children in schools in the UK (Celtic Travelling Book Company in Ireland) through easy-to-manage, well-stocked bookcases containing a wide range of books for all age groups. An editorial team works closely with teachers and parents to ensure a balanced collection and is headed up by Fiona Walker, the well-known writer, reviewer, publisher and bookseller.

Children's bookshops

The bookshops in the first part of this list specialise in selling new children's books and are good places for writers and illustrators to check out the marketplace. Most of them are members of the Booksellers Association and are well known to publishers. A list of secondhand and antiquarian children's bookshops follows.

Arcade Bookshop

3–4 The Arcade, Eltham High Street, London SE9 1BE
tel 020-8850 7803 *fax* 020-8850 4950

A specialist children's bookseller providing services to schools in the area.

Askews

218–222 North Road, Preston, Lancs. PRI 1SV
tel (01772) 254860 *fax* (01772) 254860
website www.askews.co.uk

Libraries and schools supplier with particular emphasis on children's books. Sponsors of the Askews Torchlight Award.

Bags of Books

1 South Street, Lewes, East Sussex BN7 2BT
tel (01273) 479320 *fax* (01273) 478404
website www.bags-of-books.co.uk
Contact Paul Waller

Specialist children's bookshop including a mail-order service for audio tapes. Also distributes big books and some hard-to-get US children's books.

Balloons Children's Boookshop

41A Killigrew Street, Falmouth, Cornwall TR11 3PW
tel/fax (01326) 211505
Contact John Williams

School bookshop and book fair service. Also accommodates class visits and caters for special needs. Stocks dual language and storytapes.

Barnsley Bookworm

2–4 The Arcade, Barnsley, South Yorkshire S70 2QN
tel (01226) 215263 *fax* (01226) 215265
Contact Mr D. I. Smith

The Big Friendly Bookshop

8 Camden Road, Tunbridge Wells, Kent TN1 2PT
tel (01892) 528795
website www.bigfriend@aol.co.uk

Newly established independent children's bookshop.

Blackwells Too

8 Broad Street, Oxford OX1 3BQ
tel (01865) 792792 *fax* (01865) 794143

Children's branch of this well-known Oxford bookshop.

Blast-Off Books

103 High Street, Linlithgow, Scotland EH49 7EQ
tel (01506) 844645 *fax* (01506) 844346
email blastoff.books@virgin.net
website www.blastoffbooks.co.uk

A dedicated children's bookshop for babies through to young adults, also stocking support materials for the Standard Grades and Highers. An important aspect of the shop is the range of materials for parents of, and teachers working with, children with specific learning needs such as dyslexia, autism, ADHD and Down's Syndrome.

The Book House

93 High Street, Thame, Oxon 0X9 3HJ
tel (01844) 213032 *fax* (01844) 213311
Manager Brian Pattinson

Books for Children

97 Wandsworth Bridge Road, London SW6 2TD
tel 020-7384 1821 *fax* 020-7736 0915

Bookspread Ltd

Trident Centre, Bickersteth Road, London SW17 9SH
tel 020-8767 6377 *fax* 020-8767 7628
website www.bookspread.co.uk
Contact Judy Hall

A bookshop run by ex-teachers who offer advice and consultation as well as a mobile book service for schools. Also organises workshops and author visits to schools. Works in conjunction with the educational charity, the Children's Discovery Centre.

BfS (Books for Students)

Bird Road, Heathcote, Warwick CV34 6TB
tel (01926) 436436 *fax* (01926) 436437
website www.bfs.co.uk

Supplies children's books, support materials and author profiles to schools and colleges, and operates an approval service for public libraries. Offers advice on setting up and running school bookshops.

Bookworm

1177 Finchley Road, London NW11 0AA
tel 020-8201 9811 *fax* 020-8201 9311
Contact Ruth Swindon

Brook Green Bookshop
72 Blythe Road, Brook Green, London W14 0HB
tel 020-7603 5999

Children's bookshop started by former Macmillan sales director Michael Halden and his wife Loma Slater in spring 2003, situated in West London.

Charlotte's Web
59 Newton Road, Mumbles, Swansea SA3 4BL
tel (01792) 366654

Children's Book Centre
237 Kensington High Street, London W8 6SA
tel 020-7937 7497 *fax* 020-7938 4968
website www.childrensbookcentre.co.uk

Children's books, videos, tapes, audiobooks, toys and multimedia products.

The Children's Book Company
11 The Green, High Street, London W5 5DA
tel 020-8567 4324

The Children's Bookshop
1 Red Lion Parade, Bridge Street, Pinner, Middlesex HA5 3JD
tel 020-8866 9116 *fax* 020-8866 9116
Proprietor Judy Lever-Chain

Children's Bookshop (Huddersfield)
37–39 Lidget Street, Lindley, Huddersfield, West Yorkshire HD3 3JF
tel (01484) 658013 *fax* (01484) 460020
Contact Sonia Benster

Children's Bookshop (Muswell Hill)
29 Fortis Green Road, London N10 3HP
tel 020-8444 5500 *fax* 020-8883 8632
Contact Lesley Agnew

Daisy & Tom Ltd
181 Kings Road, London SW3 5EB
tel 020-7349 5814 *fax* 020-7349 5818
Contact Sally-Ann Campbell

Daisy & Tom Ltd
118 Deansgate, Manchester M3 2QR
tel 0161-835 5000 *fax* 0161-834 6608
Contact Janet Rawnsley

Enchanted Wood
3–5 Kings Road, Shalford, Guildford, Surrey GU4 8JU
tel (01483) 570088 *fax* (0870) 7052342
Contact Ann Ferguson and Jane Colman

The Golden Treasury (Fulham)
95–97 Wandsworth Bridge Road, London SW6 2TD
tel 020-7384 1821 *fax* 020-7736 0916
Contact Susan Foster

Golden Treasury (Southfields)
27 Replingham Road, London SW18 5LT
tel 020-8333 0167
Contact Pippa Gray

Harrods Children's Books
4th Floor, Harrods, Knightsbridge, London SW1X 7XL
tel 020-7225 5721 *fax* 020-7225 5611
Contact Jane Robertson

Jubilee Books
Eltham Green School Complex, Middle Park Avenue, London SE9 5EQ
tel 020-8850 7676 *fax* 020-8294 0345
email enquiries@jubileebooks.co.uk
website www.jubileebooks.co.uk
Contact Edward Burnett

Offers a wide range of books and resources to schools. Organises book-related events including visits by the bookbus, author/illustrator sessions and creative workshops for schools, LEAs and other education organisations. Established 1996.

Kendrake Children's Bookshop
Shop Unit 2, 16 St Nicholas Way, Sutton, Surrey SM1 1AX
tel 020-8255 7744 *fax* 020-8255 7744
website www.kendrakebooks.co.uk
Owners Anna Parsley and Roy Flowers, *Manager* Ruth Boxhall

Independent children's bookshop selling books for all ages, including wide range of preschool books and teachers' resources. Allows customers access to search their database for titles.

Madeleine Lindley Ltd,
Broadgate, Broadway Business Park, Chadderton, Oldham OL9 9XA
tel 0161-683 4400 *fax* 0161-682 6801
website www.madeleinelindley.com
Contact Mike Lindley
Supplies children's books to schools, provides information services and runs open days for teachers. Hosts author/publisher events for teachers and children.

The Lion and Unicorn Bookshop
19 King Street, Richmond, Surrey TW9 1ND
tel 020-8940 0483 *fax* 020-8332 6133
email enquiries@lionunicornbooks.co.uk
website www.lionunicornbooks.co.uk
Owner Jenny Morris, *Manager* Tony West

Holds author/illustrator events for parents, children and teachers to promote books and reading.

Publishers of *The Roar*, a termly newsletter for customers and local schools, featuring author interviews and reviews of children's books. Founded in 1977 and voted Independent Bookseller of the Year in 2000 – the first time the award had been offered to a children's bookshop.

Norfolk Children's Book Centre

Alby, Norwich NR11 7HB
tel (01263) 761402 *fax* (01263) 768167
website www.ncbc.co.uk
Contact Marilyn Brocklehurst
Specialist children's bookshop for readers of all ages. Offers services to schools in East Anglia including storytelling, talks to children and parents, approval services and INSET for teachers.

Oundle School Bookshop

13 Market Place, Oundle, Peterborough PE8 4BA
tel (01832) 273523 *fax* (01832) 274611
Contact Alice Pooley

Peters Bookselling Services

120 Bromsgrove Steet, Birmingham B5 6RL
tel 0121-666 6646 *fax* 0121-666 7033
Libraries and schools supplier which provides book-related promotional material for schools such as posters, information booklets and magazines, including *Author Zone* and *tBkmag*.

Rhyme & Reason

681 Ecclesall Road, Sheffield S11 8TG
tel 0114-266 1950 *fax* 0114-266 1950
email richard@rhyme-reason.co.uk
website www.rhyme-reason.co.uk
New books for children of all ages.

River Books Children's Bookshop

25 High Street, Dunblane, Scotland FK15 0EE
tel (01786) 826917 *fax* (01786) 823695
Contact Anna Fenge

Roving Bookshop

3 Kirkby Road, Desford LE9 9GL
tel (01455) 822 192 *fax* (01455) 822 192
website www.rovingbooks.com
Contact Mr J. D. Wright
Schools and libraries supplier. Runs book fairs, the Jolly Roger Book Club and promotional events.

Toys and Tales

37 Church Street, Enfield, Middlesex EN2 6AJ
tel 020-8363 9319 *fax* 020-8363 5053
Contact Joy Sykes

Willesden Bookshop

Willesden Green Library Centre, 95 High Road, London NW10 4QU
tel 020-8451 7000 *fax* 020-8830 1233
email books@willesdenbookshop.co.uk
website www.willesdenbookshop.co.uk
Specialist supplier of multicultural children's books (including many unusual and imported titles) to schools, nurseries, libraries and professional development agencies.

Young Browsers Bookshop

33 The Thoroughfare, Woodbridge, Suffolk IP12 1AH
tel (01394) 382832
Contact Simon Robertson-Young

Children's booksellers for collectors

Ampersand Books

Ludford Mill, Ludlow, Shrops. SY8 1PP
tel (01584) 877813 *fax* (01584) 877519
email ampersand.books@mcmail.com
website www.ampersand.books.mcmail.com
Contact Michael Dawson
The only dealer in Britain specialising exclusively in three-dimensional and interactive books, with a permanent stock of about 1000 pop-ups, movables, panoramas, carousels, peepshows, split-page and flick books – in fact, all types of paper-engineering, whether antiquarian, secondhand, remaindered or new. Ampersand Books also repair, research and write about books of this sort. Private premises: open at any time but strictly by prior appointment. Established 1982.

Blackwell's Rare Books

48–51 Broad Street, Oxford OX1 3BQ
tel (01865) 333555 *fax* (01865) 794143
email rarebooks@blackwellsbookshops.co.uk
website www.rarebooks.blackwell.co.uk
The Rare Books Department within Blackwell's deals in early and modern first editions of children's books, among other subjects. Catalogues are issued periodically, which include modern and antiquarian children's books.

Bookmark Children's Books

Firtnight, Wick Down Broad, Hinton, Swindon, Wilts. SN4 9NR
tel (01793) 731693 *fax* (01793) 731782
email leonora.excell@btinternet.com
Contact Leonora and Anne Excell
A mail-order bookseller, specialising in books for collectors, ranging from antiquarian to modern. A wide range of first editions, novelty and picture books, chap-books, ABCs, annuals, etc. Also a selection of nursery china, dolls, toys and games. Catalogues of children's books and related juvenilia will be issued. Book search service available within

this specialist area. Member of PBFA, exhibiting at PBFA book fairs in London, Oxford and Bath. Established 1973.

Mary Butts Books

219 Church Road, Earley, Reading, Berks. RG6 1HW
tel 0118-926 1793
email mary@mbutts.fsnet.co.uk

Secondhand bookseller specialising in 19th- and 20th-century children's books for readers and students rather than collectors. Mainly postal business, but bookroom available on request. Free book search.

Paul Embleton

12 Greenfields, Stansted, Essex CM24 8AH
tel (01279) 812627
email paulembleton@btconnect.com

Sells by post via the internet (some stock is on ABE) and sends subject lists to regular customers. Receives visitors by appointment. Specialises in books and ephemera for the picture postcard collector and maintains a good stock of children's books and ephemera, mostly Victorian and Edwardian chromolithographic by such publishers as Nister and Raphael Tuck, and items of any age by collectable illustrators.

Ian Hodgkins & Co Ltd

Upper Vatch Mill, The Vatch, Slad, Stroud, Glos. GL6 7JY
tel (01453) 764270 *fax* (01453) 755233
email i.hodgkins@dial.pipex.com
Contact Simon Weager

Dealer in rare and out-of-print books and related material. Specialist in Beatrix Potter and fairy tales and 19th-century British art and literature. Free catalogues in all specialist areas published regularly.

Robert J. Kirkpatrick

6 Osterley Park View Road, London W7 2HH
tel 020-8567 4521

Secondhand bookseller specialising in stories about boys' schools from 1800 to the present day. Also public school studies, histories, etc.

Marchpane Children's Books

16 Cecil Court, Charing Cross Road, London WC2N 4HE
tel 020-7836 8661 *fax* 020-7497 0567

Specialises in illustrated children's books. Open Mon–Sat 10.30am–6.30pm.

Plurabelle Books

77 Garden Walk, Cambridge CB4 3EW
tel (01223) 366680 *fax* (01223) 571105
email books@plurabelle.co.uk
website www.plurabelle.co.uk
Contact Michael Cahn

Secondhand bookseller (private premises) specialising in academic books on literature, reading, history of education and children's literature. Free book search for out-of-print books. Catalogue published three times a year.

Jo Ann Reisler Ltd

360 Glyndon St, NE Vienna, VA22180, USA
tel 703-938-2967 *fax* 703-938-9057
email reisler@clark.net
website www.clark.ne/pub/reisler
Contact Don Reisler

Specialist in fine and collectible children's books, illustrated books, paper dolls, manuscript materials and original illustrations from the late 1700s to the present. Items available in English, French, German, Russian, Swedish, Norwegian, Japanese, etc. Primarily focused on materials that are characterised by their physical beauty and collectible nature. The business is conducted via mail or telephone order, by appointment only. Full-colour illustrated catalogues issued several times a year. Children's books and fine original art purchased, either individual items or entire collections. Member of ABAA, ILAB. Located in suburb of Washington, DC. Established 1970.

M & D Reeve Children's Books

PO Box 16, Wheatley, Oxford OX33 1RD
tel (01865) 874383 *fax* (01865) 872442
email MDReeve@btinternet.com
website www.reevebooks.com
Contact Dr M.K. Reeve

Mail-order business specialising in the sale of antiquarian and out-of-print children's books from pre-Victorian times to the present. Four catalogues per annum sent free worldwide, each listing in detail over 700 children's books plus related ephemera, china and games. Brief Wants Lists welcomed. Children's books purchased anywhere in the UK. Member of the Antiquarian Booksellers Association and the Provincial Booksellers Fairs Association. Established 1981.

Ripping Yarns Bookshop

355 Archway Road, London N6 4EJ
tel 020-8341 6111 *fax* 020-7482 5056
email yarns@rippingyarns.co.uk
website www.rippingyarns.co.uk

Bookshop specialising in children's books – particularly in 19th and 20th century children's fiction – annuals, Puffins and picture books.

Rose's Books

14 Broad Street, Hay-on-Wye, Herefordshire HR3 5DB
tel (01497) 820013 *fax* (01497) 820031

email enquiries@rosesbooks.com
website www.rosesbooks.com
Contact Maria Goddard

Bookshop specialising solely in rare out-of-print children's books and located in the international book town of Hay-on-Wye. Stock available via website. Catalogues and specialist lists issued on a regular basis. Open daily 9.30am–5.00pm. Free book search service. Children's books purchased – single items or collections. Established 1986.

Henry Sotheran Limited

2–5 Sackville Street, Piccadilly, London W1X 2DP
tel 020-7439 6151 *fax* 020-7434 2019
Contact Rosie Hodge

A large showroom with hundreds of important children's books spanning two centuries, specialising in first editions and attractive illustrated works by pivotal artists. Issues two specialist children's book catalogues free, on request.

Talatin Books

21 Parkstone Avenue, Emerson Park, Hornschurch, Essex RM11 3LX
tel (01708) 447561 *fax* (01708) 442238
email talatin-books@talk21.com
Contact Maggie Stevenson

Dealer in antiquarian and modern children's books. A wide range available, including reference books. Visitors are welcome by appointment (private premises, parking at door). Catalogues sent worldwide. Exhibits at the occasional book fair. Member of PBFA.

Unicorn Books

56 Rowlands Avenue, Hatch End, Pinner, Middlesex HA5 4BP
tel 020-8420 1091 *fax* 020-8428 0125
email sheila@unicornbooks.co.uk
website www.unicornbooks.co.uk

Specialises in illustrated and children's books. Private premises – appointment necessary. Books available through catalogue and internet.

John Williams

93 Goddard Avenue, Swindon, Wilts. SN1 4HT
tel (01793) 533313 *fax* (01793) 533313
email john.william24@virgin.net
website www.jwbooks.com
Contact John Williams

A dealer in secondhand and antiquarian children's and illustrated books and a specialist in 20th-century children's authors and illustrators. Free mailing list for catalogues (3 p.a.). Collections/individual items purchased. Private premises: visitors welcome by prior appointment. For full details see website.

A word from J.K. Rowling

J.K. Rowling shares her first experience of becoming a writing success.

I can remember writing *Harry Potter and the Philosopher's Stone* in a café in Oporto. I was employed as a teacher at the language institute three doors along the road at the time, and this café was a kind of unofficial staffroom. My friend and colleague joined me at my table. When I realised I was no longer alone I hastily shuffled worksheets over my notebook, but not before Paul had seen exactly what I was doing. 'Writing a novel, eh?' he asked wearily, as though he had seen this sort of behaviour in foolish young teachers only too often before. '*Writers' & Artists' Yearbook*, that's what you need,' he said. 'Lists all the publishers and… stuff' he advised before ordering a lager and starting to talk about the previous night's episode of *The Simpsons*.

I had almost no knowledge of the practical aspects of getting published; I knew nobody in the publishing world, I didn't even know anybody who knew anybody. It had never occurred to me that assistance might be available in book form.

Nearly three years later and a long way from Oporto, I had almost finished *Harry Potter and the Philosopher's Stone*. I felt oddly as though I was setting out on a blind date as I took a copy of the *Writers' & Artists' Yearbook* from the shelf in Edinburgh's Central Library. Paul had been right and the *Yearbook* answered my every question, and after I had read and re-read the invaluable advice on preparing a manuscript, and noted the time-lapse between sending said manuscript and trying to get information back from the publisher, I made two lists: one of publishers, the other of agents.

The first agent on my list sent my sample three chapters and synopsis back by return of post. The first two publishers took slightly longer to return them, but the 'no' was just as firm. Oddly, these rejections didn't upset me much. I was braced to be turned down by the entire list, and in any case, these were real rejection letters – even real writers had got them. And then the second agent, who was high on the list purely because I like his name, wrote back with the most magical words I have ever read: 'We would be pleased to read the balance of your manuscript on an exclusive basis…'

See also...

- *Spotting talent*, page 68
- *How it all began*, page 102
- *Out of the slush pile*, page 72
- *The amazing picture book story*, page 145
- *Fiction for 6–9 year-olds*, page 79
- *Teenage fiction*, page 85
- *Getting started*, page 1

Spotting talent

Publishers and literary agents are not looking for what *they* like but for what children will like. Barry Cunningham famously accepted the manuscript of the first Harry Potter book which – as everyone knows – turned out to be the first of an international bestselling series. He explains here what he is looking for when he reads a new manuscript.

I'm a fan: I love reading and I love great stories. My background is in sales and marketing, and for many years I travelled with Penguin the length and breadth of the country – on tours with authors like Roald Dahl, to schools with the Puffin Book Club or to lonely writers' festivals.

It was during that time that I learnt the most important part of my trade – how children react to the books they love, the authors that they adore, and how they put up with the material that they are coerced into reading. Reluctant readers indeed!

So what I'm looking for is what *they* want, not what I like or what you think is good. More of this later.

First steps

All publishers get streams of brown envelopes – especially, like divorces, after Christmas or the summer holidays – when writers finally feel something must be done with that story they've been working on.

We read some part of everything we get. But, be warned, not every publisher does. So, ring up and find out what the publisher wants: sample, complete manuscript, or perhaps they won't accept it at all!

For most editors, first on the reading list are the submissions from agents, manuscripts recommended by other authors or by someone whose judgement they trust. So, if you know someone who knows someone – use the contact.

Next, know a little about the list you are submitting to: look at their catalogue or read some of their books. Let publishers know how much you like their publications (we all like those sorts of comments!) and how you think your novel might sit with the rest of their titles.

Then, write a short snappy synopsis – a page will do (I've had some that are as long as half the novel itself!). It should tell the publisher what the book is about, its characters and why they should read it.

Also include a little bit about you, the author. Don't forget that. It can be almost as important as anything else in these days of marketing and personality promotion (no, you don't *have* to be a vicar or an ex-glamour model, but it does give an impetus to read on…).

I worked with a very famous editor in my first job who was talking one day about her regular advice to first-time writers. Her advice began with a simple question – 'Have you thought of starting at Chapter 2?'

Strangely, I find myself repeating this regularly. Often I find the first chapter is tortured and difficult, before the writer relaxes into the flow of the story in Chapter 2. And often things improve if we start straight into the action, and come back and explain later. But more importantly, first novels often fail because the editor doesn't get past a poor opening section. Beginnings are crucial, because I know children won't persevere if the story has a poor start, either.

So what am I looking for?

Back to the heart of things...

There are writers who know a lot about children – they might be teachers or parents – so does this mean they can write more relevantly for young people? There are authors who know nothing about modern children, don't even really like children – does this mean they will never understand what a child wants? There are 'crossover' books that don't appear to be for real children at all. There are books with children in them that aren't children's books. Confused?

To me it's simple. Books that really work for children are written from a child's perspective through an age-appropriate memory of how the author felt and dreamed and wondered. The best children's writers carry that childhood wonder, its worry and concern, or even its fear and disappointment, around with them. They have kept the child within alive – so writing is not a professional task of storytelling for tiny tots but a simple glorious act of recreating the excitement of childhood.

That's part one of what you need. Part two, in my view, is a concentration on your audience. I've worked with adult writers too and there is a difference here. Children's authors are creating for a distinctly different readership – they need to think in a more *humble* way than if their work was for their contemporaries. What I mean is that they have to be mindful of how their work will impact on children. Characters must have convincing voices, descriptions must be good enough for children to visualise, and authors must be aware of things like children's attention span when it comes to detailed explanations.

But perhaps even more important is an awareness of the emotional effect of a story on a child. We must always remember their hunger for hope and a bright tomorrow, the closeness and importance of relationships – how easily a world can be upset by parents, or loss of an animal or a friend – and the way in which action really does speak to children, for fantasy and adventure is part of the process of literally growing an imagination.

(If all this means nothing to you, and writing for children is just another category, then I don't think you should bother. That's not to say all this should operate consciously in the mind of the new writer – but that's what a publisher seeks, and that's what I'm looking for.)

Categories and concepts

Everyone has read about the older children's market, and its lucrative crossover into the kind of children's book that adults buy for themselves. I think this will continue to be a growing phenomenon – but the best books in the field will still be clear in their intent: not looking 'over their shoulder' at adults, but true to themselves and their subjects.

I'm sure fantasy will continue to hold a firm following – but with the best books based around character and not simply wild lands and strange people.

And historical fiction is poised for a come back for older children – showing the rich material and heritage we have in our shared everyday culture, as well as the 'big battles' of yore!

At last all kinds of young adult fiction has found a firm market and any number of clear voices: hard edged, romantic, comic, or a wild mixture of all three! Both here and in the United States the 13–17 age group has really started buying for themselves, and this is sure to demand more than just conventional 'problem issues' fare.

But my favourite category is the most neglected – real stories and novels for the 7–9 year-olds. This really was once the classic area of children's books, with the biggest names and the greatest longevity of appeal. Sadly, it has become the haunt of derivative series and boring chapter books. I predict a considerable revival, and it will be a great area for new talent.

Picture books seem to have had a much quieter time lately and are, perhaps, awaiting a revival with some newer attitudes. The success of cartoon novels and graphic story treatments for older readers must also hint at a new market here.

Language and setting

It's often said that, like exams, children's books are getting easier, that the language is getting 'younger' while the plots are getting more sophisticated. I don't think this is true. Certainly, for all markets, dialogue is more important than ever – and less time is taken in description.

Children are used to characters who say what they mean, and whose motivations and subtleties emerge in speech. But largely I think this makes for more interpretation and imagination. Descriptions now concentrate on setting and atmosphere, rather than telling us authoritatively what the hero or heroine feels. All to the good in my view, and something new writers for children should absorb.

Also welcome in contemporary children's books is the freeing up of the adult! These characters are no longer confined to small walk-on parts and 'parental' or 'villainous' roles. Nowadays, adults in children's novels are as well drawn as the children, sometimes as touchingly vulnerable people themselves. But as in life, the most potent and frightening image in any children's book remains the bad or exploitative parent.

International scope

Children's literature is truly one of our most glorious 'hidden exports'. British writers continue to be very successful around the world, particularly in the USA and Europe. It is worth remembering this – while setting is not so important as inspiration, obviously UK-centred plots, regional dialogue and purely domestic issues, if not absolutely necessary, are best avoided. But there is no need either – like a creaky old British film – to introduce 'an American boy' or mid-Atlantic slang to your work to appeal to another audience. This seldom works and is often excruciating!

The marketplace

The market still remains delightfully unpredictable. It is hopeless to look at last year's trends and try to speculate. The sound and timelessly good advice is to find your own voice and, above all, to write from the heart. If you can touch what moved you as a child or still moves the child within you, then there's your 'market appeal'. Whether it's aboard the frigate of your imagination or in the quieter, but equally dangerous seas of the lonely soul, skill and inspiration will win you your readership.

Oh, and finally, don't give up. As I once said to a certain young woman about a boy called Harry…

Barry Cunningham was the editor who originally signed J.K. Rowling to Bloomsbury Children's Books. He now runs his own company, The Chicken House, specialising in introducing new children's writers to the UK and USA. Notable recent successes include Cornelia Funke and Kevin Brooks.

See also...

- *A word from J.K. Rowling*, page 67
- *Getting started*, page 1
- *Out of the slush pile*, page 72
- *Fiction for 6–9 year-olds*, page 79
- *What does an editor do?* page 88
- *How it all began*, page 102
- *The amazing picture book story*, page 145

Out of the slush pile

Victoria Lloyd recounts how her book came to be published.

With a title like 'Out of the slush pile', I feel under a certain amount of pressure to hand down wise words of advice. And what qualifies me to offer them? Well, to be perfectly honest, not a lot. My first book, 'a chapter book for confident young readers' called *Pants on Fire* is, as I write this, coming out in about six weeks' time. It was plucked from the HarperCollins Children's Books' slush pile about a year and a half before by an editorial assistant, and taken up by their Roaring Good Reads imprint.

It's not the best basis for offering advice. But getting to that point was an interesting, exhilarating and at times frustrating process.

How did it happen?

I had a bit of a head start, I think, because a year before I had briefly worked for another publishing company. I'd absorbed all sorts of useless information about submitting manuscripts which, though it may not actually make a difference to the 'yes' or 'no' at the end, did make me feel a lot more confident in sending my own manuscripts off.

So armed with my manuscript formatting skills, a real love of children's books, and an idea that I thought was very funny, I sat and wrote over several weekends until I had something that I was pleased with.

I also read as much as I could about getting published. I scoured the web and found an extremely useful (and of course American!) website run by an author who struggled her way out of the slush pile. If you haven't found it already do look it up because it's invaluable in terms of motivation and plain common sense – www.verlakay.com.

I didn't hear back about the story I'd sent to the publisher for at least a couple of months. Then I had an email from an editor who'd read my manuscript. She liked my piece and wanted to take it to an acquisitions meeting. At this meeting a committee made up of editors, marketing and sales representatives and usually someone from the rights department all look at the projects that are currently being considered for publication, and make a judgement based not just on whether they like your work, but whether they think they can sell it.

I got very excited. We exchanged a flurry of emails. Could I make changes? I made changes. Could I make some more?

The story went off to the meeting, and I sat at work and kept my fingers firmly crossed. Then I received a less exciting email: the people at the acquisitions meeting liked it, but not enough to publish it.

So I tried again...

I wrote something else, set it out nicely, and sent it off. This was *Pants on Fire*, a cautionary tale about a boy who discovers a pair of magical underpants which enable him to hypnotise adults into believing any lies that come into his head.

And an editorial assistant at HarperCollins Children's Books picked it up, and liked it enough to take it to an editor, who liked it enough to take it to the acquisitions committee, who this time liked it enough to agree to publish it as a highly illustrated chapter book for children just starting to read on their own.

A contract

From there I got (in this order) a publication date – February 2004 – which at the time felt like a lifetime away. An offer of an advance against royalties (gratefully accepted). A contract (signed before they could change their minds). And then nothing for about six months while the book took its place in the queue for publication.

The publication process

Time passed. So much so, that my parents actually started to doubt whether the book was really going to be published. 'Never mind', my dad said, 'they've paid you for it already.' He's a practical man.

But, to my dad's relief, and I suspect surprise, about eight months before the publication date that had been set way back when the book had first been accepted, the cogs turned and suddenly *Pants on Fire* was due to go into production, and the publication process proper began. Suddenly it actually felt like my story was going to be made into a book.

Being edited

The editing process itself was a bit surreal. There was a lot of discussion about wording. 'There are too many "lies"', the editor said, which seemed a bit unfair for a book called *Pants on Fire*. But I bowed to her superior judgement, and some of the 'lies' became 'fibs'. I found myself trying to decide whether 'knitted' or 'made' makes more sense, and found out that the system of numbering primary school classes has changed since my own school days. The 8–9 year-old target audience wouldn't want to read about class three babies, and so Class 3M became Class 5M. Little bits of the text disappeared. Some bits that I thought were quite good. Some bits I didn't even notice going.

Design and illustrations

The next step was for the text to be typeset so that it would fit the 64-page layout and for an illustrator to provide the illustrations.

The designer went through and chose the bits of the story she thought would make good, interesting, relevant places for illustrations. Then the text was shaped around where the illustrations would go.

I got sent a version to look at, and it looked pretty strange – lots of white holes with directions for the illustrator, including the memorable instruction 'nothing too top shelf' when the main character has to hide his modesty while wearing only a t-shirt. It was hard to imagine what the final pages would look like.

In the meantime, the illustrator, Scott Walker, had started working on the cover. I was sent a rough mock-up – which showed the cover layout perfectly, but gave the main character the bulbous red nose of a 60 year-old man with a heavy sherry addiction. Then a few weeks later came the cover proof, which was unutterably gorgeous – and it had my name on it! And not a red nose in sight.

Getting proofs

Shortly after that, I was sent another set of page proofs, this time with pictures where the blank spaces had been before. The illustrations looked great, but they also added a lot to the text. It was amazing to see my characters come to life in someone else's imagination.

A published author at last!

So by the time I received the first copy of the actual book, I had seen it in all of its stages from my monitor screen, to the typeset page proofs. It was still quite a mental jump to see it finally finished. Bound. Covered. And most importantly available for sale in all good bookshops!

Victoria Lloyd is a Broadcast Assistant for BBC Radio 4 working on comedy programmes such as *The Museum of Everything* and *Absolute Power*. Her first children's book, *Pants on Fire*, was published by HarperCollins Children's Books in 2004.

See also...

- *A word from J.K. Rowling*, page 67
- *Spotting talent*, page 68
- *Fiction for 6–9 year-olds*, page 79
- *Writing humour for young children*, page 82
- *Teenage fiction*, page 85
- *What does an editor do?* page 88
- *The amazing picture book story*, page 145

Books for babies

Books for babies can be wonderfully enjoyable for both infant and reader, and can give the child a head start in learning to learn. Wendy Cooling looks at what makes a successful book for a baby.

Over the last few years reading has become big news with the phenomenal success of the *Harry Potter* series, *His Dark Materials*, *Lord of the Rings* and such memorable events as the National Year of Reading, World Book Day and the Big Read. Children's books are now being read by adults and people outside the book business have stopped asking in sympathetic voices: 'Do you ever do anything with adult books?'. Within this context the baby book market has been an area of real growth.

For babies

Publishers are not the kinds of people who miss opportunities and they have responded with great creativity to this growing market. For five years the Sainsbury's Baby Book Award (now the Booktrust Early Years Awards – see page 279) has celebrated the rich achievements of this publishing and looked at what it is that makes a good book for a baby. The first winner was Helen Oxenbury's *Tickle, Tickle* (Walker Books); it has been hugely successful and demonstrates many of the ingredients that add up to a really good book for a baby. The text is a joy to read aloud – very necessary as anyone with children will know that favourite books must be read again, and again, and again. Children don't understand all the words but they respond to the sound of the voice of someone who loves them and to the sound of the words. 'Splish, splash' and 'Tickle, tickle' resonate in the head because they sound good, they're great words to say and help the very youngest children to develop an ear for language that will later take them into reading. The invitation to adult and child to join in with the 'Tickle, tickle' is a winner too as the shared reading experience is always better if there's an element of fun and interaction. The illustrations are a delight as babies rule in this book; they fill every page as they squelch in the mud, splash in the bath and take readers through the pages to bedtime. Helen Oxenbury draws wonderful babies, both black and white, yet children just starting to talk will point to every one of them saying, 'Me, me, me, me.' So this is a book, a tough board book, for a baby to listen to, look at, play with and enjoy in the first two years of life. And, for those parents who worry excessively about learning, children who've enjoyed this book will find that they understand such things as alliteration and onomatopoeia when they come to them at school!

Even before *Tickle, Tickle* babies needed books made from cloth, books for the bath and books with no words at all. Helen Oxenbury's wordless books, first published in 1981, are still the best as her pictures are perfectly observed yet deceivingly simple. *Dressing* (Walker Books) is a good example as it really encourages the adult to talk as each page reveals a clear picture of a toddler progressing with the very complicated business of getting dressed. Many others have tried the wordless book but to do it well is no easy task. My favourite bath book is a small duck-shaped book *My First Duck* (published long ago by Blackie and now sadly out of print). It fits into a baby's hand and feels squidgy and wonderful when wet; it's a great first book as it tells a simple story in clear words and pictures. With a book like this babies learn to love books before they have any real idea about what books and stories – and ducks – are. They just know that the experience is fun and the voice of mum or dad is lovely and they want more of it!

Cloth books too are quite a creative challenge. A good one is *Farm* (Baby Campbell), a stuffed cloth book that crackles and crinkles as it's touched and uses black and white alongside just a little red – colours good for the very young child to pick out.

For innovation it's hard to beat another Baby Book Award winner, *Baby Faces* (Baby Campbell). This is a small board book with round pages joined by a string on which there is also a rattle. You can't move this book, or even turn a page without it making a noise – great, for shared reading with tiny children is often not quiet time! The title of this book describes it accurately as each round page reveals a baby's face and a minimal text as babies say 'hello', demonstrate moods and say 'goodbye'. This time the illustrations are black and white photographs, by Sandra Lousada, and they really do appeal to babies. The publisher has put lots of thought into this, picked up on the research that tells us that babies can focus on black and white long before they can pick out colours, and produced a superb first book for any baby. Baby Campbell also gave us another winning innovation – the buggy buddies – a series of tiny board books that can be attached to a buggy, cot or high chair and so always be accessible to the baby. These books look good and are very close to being toys but with them babies and toddlers learn how books work, learn to turn the pages and to look at the pictures even when no one has time to read to them.

Nursery rhymes

Nursery rhymes, traditional songs and action rhymes are great for all preschool children but there are never enough good, small collections for the very young. Some rhymes are quite violent but many are ideal to start with – hopefully they remind adults of the rhymes they listened to when they were young, because of course talking and singing to children is just as good as reading to them. Too often, nursery rhyme books are packed so full of words and pictures that they're too much for the early years, although children will of course love all the detail on the page as they get older. *Head, Shoulders, Knees and Toes*, illustrated by Annie Kubler (Child's Play), another prize-winner, is a good example for the youngest of children. It is quite a large board book and Annie Kubler's babies fill every page as they touch their head, shoulders, and laugh and giggle as they do it! This is a book that absolutely demands participation and is totally focused on the baby and on fun!

For a more sophisticated edition of a well-known rhyme there's *Twinkle, Twinkle!* (Templar). 'Twinkle, twinkle little star' is told on uncluttered backgrounds with star-shaped cut-outs that are perfect for little fingers to feel and explore. This is a tough and stylish board book that invites talk about shapes as it introduces a traditional poem – it's part of the excellent amazing baby series.

For a big nursery rhyme book it's hard to beat Sam Childs' *The Rainbow Book of Nursery Rhymes* (Hutchinson), for its generous page design, clear and warm pictures and wide range of rhymes – this is a book to last, a book for the bookshelf so it can be dipped into again and again well up to starting school. There is, however, no doubt that babies under one year old prefer the small book that they can hold themselves and keep in the toy box.

For toddlers

As babies grow into toddlers and develop better coordination there's nothing they like more than the lift-the-flap book – unless it's the touch-and-feel book! A newish one for really young children is Debi Gliori's *Where, oh where, is Baby Bear?* (Orchard Books), offering a good introduction to her positive dad character, Mr Bear. Mr Bear is searching for Baby Bear and there's a flap to be lifted on every page until Baby Bear is discovered on the last page – and in the most obvious place. This is great for under one year-olds, with its delicious pictures and good rhyming text that children will try and gurgle along with before they start to talk. There are several bigger board books featuring Mr Bear for babies to move on to.

It's probably not necessary to mention two long-time winning lift-the-flap titles but I must. Eric Hill's *Where's Spot?* (Puffin) shows exactly what it takes to make a lasting baby book and so does *Dear Zoo* by Rod Campbell (Macmillan and Puffin) These books are worth examining by all would-be authors and illustrators of books for babies. What is it that makes children want to look and listen again and again once they know exactly where Spot is, and what will make the perfect pet?

Young children love to find characters they can read more and more about. As well as Spot and Mr Bear, current stars are Lucy Cousins' Maisy (Walker), Mick Inkpen's Kipper (Hodder), David McKee's Elmer (Andersen) and Tony Ross' Little Princess (Andersen). These characters all appear in board books as well as picture books and will still be enjoyed as children start school. *Weather*, a Little Princess board book, is one of the most delightful non-fiction books ever produced for babies; children who know her will happily learn with her many of the important things of life. All the characters mentioned are drawn with charm and love; all are very original and have the capacity to become friends. Many characters lack these qualities and never get beyond the third book. An interesting new one to look out for is Ted Dewan's *Bing*, a slightly anarchic character with great appeal to one and two year-olds – watch out for him!

What makes a classic picture book?

Babies who experience these exciting early books – and there are many more I could have mentioned – will soon be taking off into wonderful classic picture books such as *Each Peach Pear Plum* by Janet and Allan Ahlberg, *Where the Wild Things Are* by Maurice Sendak, *We're Going on a Bear Hunt* by Michael Rosen and Helen Oxenbury, and Eric Carle's *The Very Hungry Caterpillar*. If you're contemplating a career as an author and/or illustrator of picture books, look at these and at other great picture books carefully for there's a lot to learn – not least that every single word counts in a book for the very young.

What doesn't make a good picture book? The perfect picture book that has been reduced to board book format (why do publishers do it?) simply doesn't work – picture books are more sophisticated than that. Texts that lack rhythm and so really can't be read aloud should not be used. Crowded pages packed with the sort of detail that will intrigue a six year-old are obviously inappropriate for babies. Illustration that lacks quality and offers no interest to the child – and certainly none to the adult – should be abandoned.

So what *does* make a good picture book? Let's have great language packed with fine-sounding words that children will enjoy listening to. Let's have rhythm and rhyme that makes the reader want to turn the page and look/read on. Let's remember that the books are for the babies – it helps if adults enjoy them too but the baby must be at the heart of it. Let's value books for babies and celebrate them – they take children into a love of books and the start of a life as readers, and what could be more important? The right books can be nothing but good for babies, parents, carers, authors, illustrators and publishers – they make commercial and social sense.

About Bookstart

We've always known that an enormous amount of learning takes place in the preschool years and that reading books to babies can do nothing but good. Yet it took the Bookstart research to really prove to us all that sharing books with children from a very early age can give them a positive advantage when they start school and can change family attitudes to books and book-buying. Bookstart was piloted by Booktrust in Birmingham in 1992 and aimed simply to give books to families when they attended the 7–9 month health check at their Health Centre, and to invite them to join the local public library.

Professor Barrie Wade and Doctor Maggie Moore of Birmingham University evaluated the project and continue to follow the progress of the first babies involved with Bookstart. When they started school this group of children were way ahead of the control group in all literacy-based tests and, rather unexpectedly, in all the numeracy tests. The children who had been read to at home were really ready for school and were able to start with confidence. They knew about stories, about rhyme and rhythm, and about shapes and numbers and most importantly, they knew that books could give great pleasure and that sharing could be fun – their learning from this early book experience was accidental, but very important learning.

Bookstart became established and grew into a nationwide project as the Government was extending nursery education and starting the Surestart scheme – a brilliant initiative working with disadvantaged families. Not all those Bookstart parents have enrolled their babies at the library but many more than ever before have, and many are buying books whether it be in bookshops, by mail order or at car boot sales, which has to be good for books and for babies.

Wendy Cooling is a highly respected children's book consultant and reviewer. She taught English in Inner London comprehensives for many years before becoming head of the Children's Book Foundation (now Booktrust) where she initiated the Bookstart project. She is a regular guest on book-related radio and television programmes, and is the compiler of several children's fiction and poetry anthologies.

Fiction for 6–9 year-olds

Alison Stanley is an experienced commissioning editor of young fiction. She gives here what she regards as essential components of a good fiction book for younger readers.

When teaching six year-olds in the mid-1970s, 'reading' was something that involved a queue of children at my desk, waiting to be heard struggling through their less than stimulating reading-scheme books. There had to be a better way of developing reading skills, especially as the delight of sharing real books with the children during 'storytime' at the end of the day, was such a marked contrast. I had no idea in those days about the business of publishing, and I certainly never imagined that many years later I would be commissioning books for that very same age group to read and enjoy. But without that classroom experience, I doubt that I would have begun to appreciate the needs of the young beginner reader. Nor would I have experienced that magical moment when a child just breaks through the reading skills barrier and begins to read unaided for the very first time. The anticipation in excitedly turning over the page to find out what happens next; the thrill of a guessed word being right; and the beginning of reading for pleasure are all magical moments to witness.

Beginner readers

What makes a good book for children just beginning to read on their own – one that will stimulate and motivate them, and let them know that reading is an enjoyable and rewarding activity?

Firstly and simply – beginner readers need good stories. Strong plots that are easy to follow, so that when faced with an unrecognisable word, the child can predict what is going to happen and be able to have a go at reading that 'difficult' word. Lively and appealing characters are essential too, especially if featured in more than one book.

Beginner readers like stories that reflect their experiences of the world but also ones that will stretch their imaginations. Stories with a fantasy element rooted in the real world where something ordinary becomes extraordinary in a familiar world, are always popular. The language of the stories should be rhythmic with plenty of repetition and alliteration. Sentences need to be short enough so they don't get split by a page turn, but long enough so that the story doesn't read in a stilted fashion.

Books for beginner readers require a generous typeface and good clear layout with plenty of illustrations giving clues to the text. This will help make the transition from shared picture books to reading alone a smooth one.

Last, but definitely not least, there is one vital thing to remember when writing stories for the beginner reader… beginner readers read *slowly*. Wacky, fast-paced humour within the text does not work when read word for word, very slowly. Humour in the text needs to be obvious, relate to the child's world and work when read at a snail's pace (see *Writing humour for young children* on page 82 for inspirational advice on writing funny fiction).

Top 10 questions

To summarise, the 10 questions I ask when assessing manuscripts for younger readers are:

Plot
- Is it a good story?
- Will it make sense when read slowly?
- Will it keep the reader wanting to turn over the pages?
- Is the story strong enough to stand up to the competition?

Setting
- Is the story set in a world that children will be familiar with?
- Are there events in the story that children will relate to?

Characters
- Are the characters appealing and original?
- Are the characters rounded enough for the beginner reader to want further books about them?

Language
- Is the vocabulary suitable for the young beginner reader?
- Is there plenty of repetition, alliteration and rhythmic writing?

I would also want to know about the author. I'd want to know if the manuscript was written by a published author, and if so, do his or her books sell? (Never forget that publishing is a commercial venture!) If it is a new author, I'd like to know if he or she is seen to be a major new talent who will progress to write further books.

The editorial process can help with many of these points, but the originality and uniqueness of a story belong to the author. Because there are so many books written for this age group, it takes a special author to create something new and appealing, something that will stand the test of time.

Books for younger readers

Here are some of my favourite books for younger readers that have stood the test of time. Read them and you'll know what I mean!

Happy Families series by Janet and Allan Ahlberg (Puffin)

Horrid Henry by Francesca Simon (Orion)

The Littlest Dragon by Margaret Ryan (Collins)

Mr Majeika by Humphrey Carpenter (Puffin)

The Worst Witch by Jill Murphy (Puffin)

Spider McDrew by Alan Durant (Collins)

The Black Queen by Michael Morpurgo (Random House)

Morris the Mouse Hunter by Vivian French (Collins)

Clarice Bean by Lauren Child (Orchard Books)

Lizzie Zipmouth by Jacqueline Wilson (Random House)

There's a Viking in My Bed by Jeremy Strong (Puffin)

Confident readers

Once children become fluent readers, there's usually no stopping them in their quest to read more, and soon move on to longer novels. It's at this stage that they are exploring the different genres – humour, horror, adventure, or themes such as school stories, animal stories and football stories, amongst others. They're also finding out which authors they like to read and will be actively seeking out new books by that author. Confident readers come in all shapes, sizes, ages and with different backgrounds and personalities and it is essential that this is reflected in a broad range of reading matter.

Alison Stanley was a commissioning editor at Puffin Books and at HarperCollins Children's Books, where she was responsible for developing the younger end of the fiction list.

See also...

- *Writing humour for young children*, page 82
- *Getting started*, page 1

Writing humour for young children

Like most adults, children love humour. But in both cases the joke will fall flat unless it is aimed at the right audience. Jeremy Strong has 10 rules for writing humour for young children.

The snappy bit: some simple rules

1. Never allow your bum to become gratuitous.
2. Write wrong.
3. Self mutilation is highly recommended.
4. Words are essential.
5. Pulchritude? No way.
6. Inside every 20-plus there's an eight year-old trying to get out.
7. You calling me a wozzer? Mankynora!
8. Just who do you think you're talking to?
9. Surprise!
10. Ha! I laugh at death.

The expansive bit. We begin at the beginning, with ***Rule Nine. Surprise!*** Ha ha! That's pretty much self explanatory.

Rule Six: Inside every 20-plus there's an eight year-old trying to get out.

Years ago, when I first began writing for children, I was often asked (by adults) why it was that the stories I wrote seemed to appeal to children. You have to imagine an adult asking this question, in a tone of voice that mixes one part admiration to 10 parts complete bewilderment. I used to answer, fairly truthfully, that only my exterior had aged along with my chronological age, and that I was still aged about eight inside. The adult would usually laugh and would go away as bewildered as they were before they'd asked the question. The point here is, I think, that it isn't possible to really understand except from a child's viewpoint. If you have forgotten what it was like to be a child then you're unlikely to understand.

Rule One: Never allow your bum to become gratuitous.

To make matters worse, adults often think the things that make children laugh are puerile. To some extent this is true and it is easy to make a child laugh by playing 'lowest common denominator' jokes – jokes that refer to farts, snot, bums, knickers, etc. But whilst employing these guaranteed tickle-sticks it is easy to forget that children also like quite sophisticated jokes.

As for the bums and farts, it's okay to pop them in here and there but, for the sake of at least some self respect, keep them to a minimum. Never let your bum be gratuitous.

Rule Four: Words are essential.

Children love word play, and they love 'knowing' jokes – for example, jokes that are aware of how bad they are, or referential jokes that make use of things familiar to them, the things that mark out their lives, such as school, parents, family.

Then there is the matter of what children can read and understand. Obviously, this is going to vary not only with age but with ability. Anyone who has taught junior age children knows that there are children of six who can read like 11 year-olds, and vice versa, with all shades in between and quite frequently further beyond. Nevertheless, as a writer, you need to aim towards the centre. In this article I am going to concentrate on 6–11 year-olds because those are the ages I taught for 17 years.

Let's look at language. Things need to be fairly simple. Shorter, rather than longer sentences work best. But like all rules this one can be deliberately misused. For example, at some appropriate point in a story you might wish to hurl yourself into some ever-increasing sentence that just seems to plunge on and on at a relentless pace and with reckless abandon like a runaway car because that happens to be one of the best ways your writing can capture the manic activity that is going on in your story at that particular point. Maybe it is a description of a runaway car. You get the point. Children respond to this positively because, anchored as it is in a normally short and simple style of writing, the over-long sentence becomes not only a writing device, but also a source of humour.

Rule 10: Ha! I laugh at death.

As with comedy for other age groups, nothing is held sacred. You will, however, have to obey the obvious rules that generally apply to writing for children, and also steer clear of the PC police. You can be smutty, but not dirty. You can be unkind to animals, but they mustn't be in a circus, unless you're a signed up freedom fighter for 'Say no! to performing dumb creatures'.

You can laugh about death. (It's an emotional release. Honest.) You can even have stereotypes and clichés – but in this instance don't expect to get published.

Rule Two: Write wrong.

Children love to recognise things that are wrong, and this is where word play often has great effect. Characters that get their words or spellings wrong are a good source of humour, not only because it is funny in its own right, but because children love the empowerment of recognising what's wrong. (You will, incidentally, lose brownie points for using words like 'empowerment'.)

Rule Seven: You calling me a wozzer? Mankynora!

Invented words can also be a terrific source of enjoyment for both writer and reader, especially when they are used as expletives – sort of coded (and therefore safe) swear words. Mankynora! Wozzer yourself! Let's also take a look at sophistication. You have to ask yourself, am I writing a joke for an adult or a child? I know for a fact that I am guilty of putting jokes for adults in some stories – jokes I know only an adult will understand. (Or sometimes a joke that a child will get on one level, but where the adult will see a second 'hidden' joke or implication.) The reason I do this is because (a) I can't resist the temptation if it's a good one, (b) I like to remember that many of my books are read to children by adults, and so I am putting in something to make it more enjoyable for them, and (c) I don't do it often and I make sure that the vast majority of the humour is firmly in the child's grasp.

Rule Five: Pulchritude? No way.

Whilst on the subject of sophistication it is worth thinking about the words you use. With each word you need to ask yourself: can a child of 'x' years read and understand this word? Apply a bit of common sense. There are some words a child might not understand but it might be worthwhile introducing it to them, allowing the context to help reveal its meaning.

The word sophistication itself is a reasonable example. Many junior children would not understand it but, although it's long, it's not too difficult to work out what it says and you could argue that it's a good word for a child to know. On the other hand, the word 'pulchritudinous' is not only very hard for a child to work out but it is extremely unlikely you would need to use such a word when writing for junior children and if you do then you seriously need to reconsider what you are doing.

Rule Three: Self mutilation is highly recommended.

You have to be rigorously self disciplined about this. No matter how good a joke is you have to cut it out if it's not actually funny to your audience. The humour also needs to arrive and leave quickly. Anything that takes pages to set up is not worth it and the longer it takes the more likely it is that your writing will become increasingly false and unnatural as you struggle with all the scaffolding you require to hold up the joke.

Rule Eight: Just who do you think you're talking to?

It is a mistake to think that the things adults laugh at in children make good material for children's books. They don't, for the simple reason that it's funny to the adult watching the child, and not the other way round. All of this points to one of the cardinal rules for writing anything: be aware of your audience. Keep that firmly in mind and you can't go far wrong. I was going to finish by writing: May the fart be with you. Then I realised that it would be out of place and one fart too many. See what I mean?

Jeremy Strong's humorous fiction is hugely popular with 8–11 year-olds. His books include *The Karate Princess* titles, and three Viking stories which were made into a popular television series. Jeremy won the Federation of Children's Book Groups Children's Book Award for *The Hundred-Mile-an-Hour Dog*. Recent books include *Pirate School – The Birthday Bash* and *Let's Do The Pharoah*, all published by Puffin.

See also...

- *Writing comedy for children's television*, page 217
- *Fiction for 6–9 year-olds*, page 79

Teenage fiction

Gillie Russell writes about teenage fiction from a publisher's pespective.

People often ask what the difference is between writing for teenagers and writing for adults. For me, the one significant difference is that teenagers come to books without a life experience. They are on the brink of self discovery, never having been plunged into the everyday grind of earning a living. They are open, honest and questioning as an audience and this, I believe, is why so many terrific writers want to write for this age group. Teenagers are challenging to write for and satisfyingly able to digest complex ideas. This often means that there are far too many 'issue'-based books on the market – not that these are badly written, often completely the reverse. But every major book fair will offer teenage books on incest, bullying, sibling rivalry, parental separation and drugs. Of course these kinds of books are important, but teenagers, like adults, need a varied diet. Teenagers like well-crafted stories in many genres – they love humour and history and fantasy, just as much as they like books which reflect their own worlds. They like inspirational and aspirational books where they can identify with the protagonists in a real way.

Getting teenagers to read

To lump teenage readers into one, all-encompassing bracket is not only dangerous but will ultimately reduce the choice of books available to them. We all know that teenagers who read don't necessarily want to continue reading 'children's books', that some seem to move seamlessly on to authors as varied as Agatha Christie and Isobel Allende, Ian Rankin and Margaret Atwood. This is partly because, though there are many wonderful writers for teenagers, no self-respecting young adult wants to venture into the 'children's' section of a bookshop – they would much rather hang out in Body Shop or HMV, or find books in the adult book displays or, sadly, stop reading books, entirely.

To attract teenagers to read at all is difficult; they don't like to feel manipulated, and life in secondary school nowadays makes it difficult to find time to read anything other than the books they are studying, The lead-up to major exams and the required reading tends to dominate their lives. This is why it is so important for children to develop the reading habit and reading stamina earlier in their lives – something which, hopefully, will never leave them, and the desire to lose themselves in a book.

As teenagers move away from the influence of their parents, it is important that, as well as having teachers to motivate and inspire them to read, there are bookshops which do the same. In the USA, for example, there are large areas devoted to 'young adult' books, sections of the bookshops which feel right for them, and are 'cool' places to be. Here in the UK it is sadly not the case. In most of the high street chains the children's areas are dominated by books for the much younger child. Hidden in amongst the books for the 8–12 year-olds there may be a few 'teenage' gems – but few teenagers venture into these areas and discover them. How about bookshops ranging teenage books like CDs, for example – in a rack, facing outwards – and organised by theme, with some short reviews?

Variety is the key

It is true that when we talk about books for teenagers, we tend to think automatically of gritty, contemporary fiction – rather like Melvyn Burgess's *Junk*, for example. But there are lots of books that young people like that are not specially written for teenagers. We need to remember that books for teenagers are any books, any genres, for the 12-plus age group. This band of children – from 12 up to young adult – can have any variety of tastes; they may like historical fiction, such as Celia Rees's *Witch Child*, humour, like Louise Rennison's *Angus, Thongs and Full Frontal Snogging* (to name just one of her deliciously funny and timeless teenage books), Philip Pullman's *His Dark Materials*, and David Almond's *Skellig*. A variety of genres, easy visibility in bookshops, the right covers and 'packaging' – all these things are hugely important to attract teenage readers. They are an intelligent and discerning audience, and when they discover an author they like, extremely loyal. Surely this is reason enough to make retailers think about being more imaginative in attracting teenage buyers?

The 'crossover' book

We talk a great deal these days of the 'crossover' book where an adult market has been identified for a children's book, a phenomenon which started with Harry Potter. Perhaps this is because publishers are desperately trying to attract a bigger section of the market for their authors, to make a double killing with one book. How true this *actually* is, I'm not sure, though occasionally a book which is stunningly original and exceptional, like *The Curious Incident of the Dog in the Night-Time*, can appeal to both markets, and even be successful in two editions. Another example of a 'crossover' book is *Across the Nightingale Floor* by Lian Hearn, which to some may feel more 'adult' than 'child', but which is hugely appealing to teenagers and doesn't feel at all patronisingly like a 'children's' book marketed at teens. How we market, package and position these 'crossover' books, such as Isobel Allende's *City of Beasts*, for example, occupies publishers constantly. Should they do one edition, sold into both adult and children's sections, or should there be two separate editions, one following the other? Or will teenagers who read discover Isobel Allende anyway, and thus make the publishing of a 'children's' edition completely redundant? Publishers certainly don't want to cannibalise their own book sales.

Is reading cool?

What we can say, post Harry Potter, is that reading is still 'cool' – that it is OK to be seen with a book on a bus or train. This can only be a good thing. It can only be fantastically exciting that there are queues outside bookshops for authors like Jacqueline Wilson, Philip Pullman, Darren Shan and, of course, J.K. Rowling.

Where do we go from here?

So where does this leave teenage fiction? How do we enable wonderful writers to reach their target audience? We try to keep publishing the talented authors who are offered to us, people like Mark Haddon who make a difference, who may write about 'issues' but don't set out to do so, but simply set out to write an engaging and compelling book. We keep trying to persuade retailers to recognise the importance of good teenage books – and I sincerely believe this is ultimately empowering, liberating and vital to their adult lives – and we have to be as innovative and imaginative as possible in the ways we think about presenting these books to our readers. Fewer books, better publishing, strong authors writing in different genres – this can be the only way forward. We have to keep on trying to publish the culturally important with the commercially successful in order to be able to produce books for our teenagers. We need to remember that, even in this relatively small area of our market, children need variety, complexity and vitality; they need adventure and fantasy and history and thrillers, humour and grit – everything, of course, that adult readers need, too.

We are privileged in our country to have truly wonderful authors writing for the teenage market – Michael Morpurgo's *Private Peaceful*, for example, which shows how world events impact on ordinary lives; Adele Geras, whose novel *Troy* is better than any history lesson; Peter Dickinson, Anthony Horovitz, Sherry Ashworth, Melvyn Burgess, Kevin Brooks, Nicky Singer… one can go on and on. There is new talent emerging all the time. Children's authors are now dominating the market in a way that was unheard of a few years ago, and this can only be a thrilling time for teenage fiction.

Gillie Russell is Fiction Publishing Director at HarperCollins Children's Books.

See also...

- *Getting started*, page 1
- *A word from J.K. Rowling*, page 67
- *How it all began*, page 102
- *What does an editor do?* page 88

What does an editor do?

Yvonne Hooker describes the varied and exciting aspects to an editor's job.

What does an editor do? Good question. Answers have ranged from reading all day to drawing the illustrations. However, baldly put, an editor's job is to acquire new titles and to oversee a book's progress from acquisition to publication, bringing the book in on time and on budget. Where the book goes, the editor follows – from finance and contracts, through design and production, to sales and publicity – making sure that their book, their baby, is getting the best possible treatment and the maximum attention. An editor is the book's champion throughout its life.

Acquiring

The demise of the publisher's slush pile in recent years means that most new books now come via agents. No editor wants to miss out on seeing the latest find from an agent. It's always possible that she will turn down a manuscript that will later become a runaway bestseller – publishing remains a gambling business – but the worst scenario of all is just not to have been offered the book in the first place. So, it is absolutely vital for the editor to be on close terms with all the relevant agents. She must make sure that the agent knows her tastes and is generally confident of her editorial skills and judgements, so that when a real plum of a book arrives, the agent will immediately think, 'Ah, *x* is just the editor for this,' and send it off.

No one can be an editor and not thrill to the sight of a new manuscript, so finding something you want to publish is a pulse-racing moment. What the editor has to do immediately is to get everyone else's pulse racing as well. She has to start the internal buzz. No book is going to succeed unless all the publishing departments are firmly behind it and it is the editor's job to get the enthusiasm going by talking the book up to key figures, and by presenting the book at the publisher's acquisitions meetings.

The editor will probably have to prepare some kind of financial spreadsheet showing that the book can be expected to make a profit. Figures are needed from sales, marketing, rights and so on and, in order to get the best possible forecasts, the editor has to convince all these other departments that here is a terrific new book which is an absolute must for the list.

In the meantime, the editor will have rung the agent to express her enthusiasm. Usually agents will say whether they are sending books to other publishers as well, but it's always prudent to check and to find out if interest has been expressed from any other quarter. If it has, and an auction situation is developing, then the editor has to make sure that everyone is aware of this, and that the offer is going to be ready on time. In these circumstances, the editor may prepare a particular pitch for the book: a presentation which will convince the author that this is the true home for the book with people who really understand it.

Although many other departments will be involved in the mechanics of the offer, it is the editor who will present it to the agent and who will negotiate all the terms of advance, royalties and rights. It would be rare for an offer for a book by a new author to be accepted as it stands. A certain amount of haggling will be expected and this is one instance where a cool head will serve an editor rather better than unbridled enthusiasm.

Sometimes, before the deal is concluded, the agent will want to have a beauty parade and take the author round to meet competing publishers. This is the editor's chance to woo the author face-to-face and, very often, though not always, the choice of editor will be the deciding factor. The author should be well aware that this is the person with whom he or she will be working most closely and that this will be a vital and all-important relationship. It is, of course, a professional one, and it is perfectly possible for author and editor to work together harmoniously even if they would never choose each other's company outside of publishing, but it does help to have a sense of rapport. No one else has as much contact with the author, and no one else fights as fiercely for the author's voice to be heard. Once the book is hers, the editor will be the author's champion. But she also has to remember that the book is required to make money for the publisher as well as the author.

Editing

The first stage the manuscript of the book goes through is editing: the process to arrive at a final text which is agreed upon by both the editor and the author. This is, rightly, a stage largely hidden from the rest of the world though, for both author and editor, it is the most rewarding part of the whole process. The editor is the first professional reader of the manuscript and her aim is to make the book the best it can possibly be. She will read it with a fine critical eye, checking for problems and seeing what can be done to put them right. These can range from the simple glitch (a week that lasts 10 days or a dog that changes breed in the course of the story), to the emotional core (does a relationship have enough depth, would this character actually do or say this, is the emotional focus clear enough?) and the overall narrative structure (is the beginning punchy enough, does it take too long to get going, does it feel rushed at the end?).

This is the stage which cements the relationship between editor and author. It is a curiously intimate process, relying as it does on a basis of trust and a sharing of the creative process. There has to be absolute trust between author and editor. The author has to feel that he or she can rely upon the editor's critical skill and judgement; the editor has to feel that the author will receive editorial suggestions with serenity. It is taken for granted that editors will not make changes for the sake of it. Nor will they try to rewrite the book as they would have written it. It is, and will remain, the author's book. The whole process should be one of discussion and cooperation, with author and editor working together to make the book the very best it can be.

Every author has a different way of working with his or her editor. Some like to submit a finished manuscript, while others like to send in first ideas and chapters for editorial input as they go along. Any way the author wants to play it is fine with the editor. Sometimes, even the most experienced authors get stuck for some reason – finding the right voice, for instance – and it helps to meet with and talk to the editor. This is a vital and important part of the editorial role as writing is an incredibly lonely occupation and to be able to talk problems through with an interested and experienced reader can be a lifeline. The author–editor relationship can develop to the point where the editor will be one of the first people to be told about quite personal things – impending marriages and babies – and her advice can be sought about things which have nothing to do with work: the best way to cook roast potatoes, for instance (this has actually happened!). Editorial trust can extend beyond the book!

Copy-editing and proofing

When a final manuscript has been agreed between the author and editor, the text is ready to be copy-edited. Not many editors do this themselves nowadays, though most will have copy-editorial experience. This is not just because they do not have the time but it's good to have a fresh eye on the manuscript at this stage. The copy-editor marks up the manuscript for the typesetter, checks the grammar and spelling and acts as a safety net for any glitches which may have slipped through. Any word changes are checked with the author and, in any case, most authors are given the opportunity of seeing the copy-edited manuscript. This is the last opportunity to get everything right before the manuscript is typeset (and changes start costing money) so it is vitally important that everyone should be happy with it at this stage.

The copy-edited manuscript will then go off to be typeset. The editor, with the designer or text designer, will have chosen an appropriate text setting and any flourishes to chapter heads. If the book is to be illustrated, the editor will have marked appropriate places in the text for the illustrations. Both editor and author will be involved in choosing an illustrator, but this aspect is the responsibility of the design department.

When the proofs arrive from the typesetter a set will be sent to the author and another set will be proofread by a professional proofreader. The editor will see the proofs but will very rarely proofread the text, though every editor has the skill. This is a last opportunity for another fresh eye on the text to check for any errors.

While all this is going on, the editor will be busy with other aspects of the book. Having a final manuscript or bound proofs, if there are any, is an opportunity to remind everyone how good the book is, making sure it's not forgotten as other, newer titles are coming through. The editor may send the book out to well-known people in the hope of getting a useful quote for publicity purposes.

The cover

Getting the right cover for a book is of paramount importance. Although this is the design department's province, the editor has a vital role to play. She will need to discuss the book with the designer, and with the sales and marketing teams. Together they will decide on the approach to take, though the choice of artist will generally be in the hands of the designer. The editor may also have to write the cover copy if the publishing house does not have a separate blurb-writing department.

Because getting the right cover is so important, other departments such as sales and marketing will be involved and will have to approve. Of course, publishers want authors to be happy with the covers but authors very rarely have final approval of covers; it is generally accepted that this is an area where the publisher's judgement is final. It is the editor's job to send roughs and visuals of the cover to the author and, in rare cases of disagreement, to persuade them that the cover is absolutely the right one, or to suggest acceptable compromises.

Proof covers have to be ready at least six months before publication to allow for sell-in time. If that date slips, then the publication date has to move, so getting the cover through on time is a major editorial preoccupation.

Publication

Once the cover is done and the final text is going through, the editor's major work on the book is done. But she must keep it in the forefront of everyone's minds and keep the internal buzz growing. She will present the book at internal launch meetings and possibly also at sales conferences and presentations of lead and highlight titles. She will also be liaising with publicity and marketing on their plans to launch the book and will make sure that the author knows the publisher's publicity contact.

About a month before publication, early finished copies of the book will arrive on the editor's desk, hopefully looking wonderful. The editor will check through to make sure that everything is all right, and send an early copy to the author.

All the editor has to do then is to send the author a card on publication day, raise a glass at the launch party if there is one, read the reviews circulated by the publicity department, and make sure that the book is entered for every relevant prize going.

An editor has to have sound judgement, a fine critical eye and enormous funds of patience and sensitivity. It also helps to be a fast reader! Above all, she must be a consummate juggler, handling books at all their different stages – yet be able to drop everything in a crisis to concentrate on the one thing that matters: getting an author's book absolutely right, the book that he or she always hoped it would be.

Yvonne Hooker is Senior Editor at Puffin Books.

See also...

- *Getting started*, page 1
- *A word from J.K. Rowling*, page 67
- *How it all began*, page 102
- *Marketing, publicising and selling children's books*, page 92

Marketing, publicising and selling children's books

The way in which books for children are marketed and publicised is different to the way the adult market is targeted. Rosamund de la Hey identifies the target audience for children's books and explains the various ways in which publishers can reach that audience.

What is marketing?

Marketing can be seen as an umbrella term that includes all the work a publisher does to promote or sell a book. Many people are not clear about the difference between marketing and publicity. Traditionally, marketing is categorised as anything paid for (posters, advertising, catalogues, etc) and publicity (such as review coverage and radio interviews) is free. There is a useful saying that every book must be sold three times – by the editor to the rest of the company, by the sales/marketing/publicity departments to the bookseller, and by the bookseller to the consumer.

How can authors help?

There are many ways authors can help to market their books from the start. Most publishers will send out an author questionnaire soon after acquiring the book. This will generally ask for information ranging from the name of his or her local bookshop, to background details which may offer a marketing or publicity hook. It can help to think of a biography as a series of tabloid headlines – for instance, a children's novelist whose previous career was that of a fighter pilot would be very interesting to teenage magazine editors with a young male readership. On the other hand, if there are areas an author would rather the press did not know about, he or she should tell the publicist, as otherwise innocent, but upsetting, mistakes may happen. Sometimes a mock interview with the publisher's publicist may help the author.

If a book covers a specialist area or issue – for example, Benjamin Zephaniah's *Face* deals with severe facial scarring – it's likely that the author will be able to give the publisher information about relevant organisations which would be interested in hearing about the book, and whose members may indeed buy it.

Events can form a crucial part of promoting a children's book. However, it's worth remembering that not all authors are comfortable in front of a room full of six year-olds.

Marketing children's books

One of the differences between marketing children's books and marketing adults' books is the timescale. Adult book launches are all tied round a very specific window of publication, whereas a children's publication, even if there is a splashy launch, tends to work more like a slow-burn candle.

Children's advertising is also dictated by both the target market – children and their parents – and by more limited budgets. While adult campaigns can assume that adults read a newspaper, take public transport and go shopping, children's sphere of influence tends to be more limited – school, the local sports centre, the library, the internet or television. Publishers must also decide whether they are targeting the child or the parent in advertising.

Publicity

In publicity terms, children's review space is more limited than for adult books, so the coverage happens when the space allows. Additionally, many of the important reviews for children's books happen in specialist magazines such as *Books for Keeps* and *Carousel* which are published only bimonthly or quarterly.

Libraries

Libraries often receive the books some time after publication as each book needs to be adapted for library use. In school libraries, budgets can also be very tight so it may be months or years after publication that a school can afford to stock new titles.

Events

Unlike adult authors who will normally only do a book tour around publication, many children's authors and illustrators spend a great deal of their time doing events and workshops in schools and bookshops, and at the numerous literary festivals around the country throughout the year (see *Children's literature festivals and trade fairs* on page 285). For those who do get involved, the word-of-mouth benefits are well worth the effort. One of the best examples of this is Jacqueline Wilson, who was visiting schools up to three times a week long before her books became bestsellers. She still visits schools regularly year round, as well as touring bookshops and festivals with her new publications.

Direct marketing to schools

The children's market lends itself to direct marketing more than many other areas of trade publishing. This is largely because there is a captive market sitting in school for much of the year. However, marketing directly to schools does have its drawbacks. Teachers are very busy people who have to wade through enough paperwork without being sent endless publishers' catalogues. So, it is important for publishers to be clear and realistic about why they are sending material to schools. A children's educational publisher which also publishes a trade fiction list, may be more likely to be picked up by the Head of English because he or she is expecting to order course books from that catalogue.

Mailing a full trade publisher catalogue to every primary school headteacher in the country is also a very expensive exercise, for potentially little return. Some publishers do have a schools sales force who sell their list directly into schools; others use freelance reps to sell a limited selection from their list into schools. The appropriateness of either of these approaches will depend entirely on the type of list a publisher has.

World Book Day, however, provides many trade publishers with a positive platform to market to schools. For the past few years, a schools' pack has been sent out giving information to teachers and their pupils about World Book Day. Publishers that support World Book Day have the opportunity to insert marketing material (flyers, posters, etc) into the schools pack and know that the investment is more likely to pay dividends because it's more targeted.

Advertising in schools

Media agencies now sell poster sites within schools themselves. Books are arguably the perfect 'product' to advertise in this way – the teachers are keen to encourage reading and hopefully the advertisement will spark the interest of the children. This is an example of where jacket design is crucial. If the jacket is not sufficiently strong, it's unlikely to make an eye-catching design that will stand up to the advertising-savvy children.

This type of advertising is not cheap and so is likely to be used rarely and be carefully timed. *Holes* by Louis Sachar, although winner of the prestigious Newbury Medal in the USA, was unknown in the UK until 1999. Bloomsbury marketed the hardback with a successful publicity-led campaign and when the paperback was published nine months later it targeted schools and ran a poster campaign within secondary schools. It is always hard to gauge the exact response to advertising of this type without commissioning expensive research (which is often more expensive than the original advertising costs). However, *Holes* has now sold half a million copies, helped in no small way by being extensively read for course work in schools.

Playground marketing

The phrase 'playground marketing' was widely used after the publication of *Harry Potter and the Philosopher's Stone* in 1997 and partly as a result of the book winning the Gold Smarties Book Prize that year. It is very hard to pin down exactly how playground marketing works except to say that it is a combination of many factors: school events, word of mouth, in-school advertising and the prizes network all play their part. The latter is especially important when the children themselves are involved in selecting the winner of a book prize. This now happens for many prizes, from the big national ones such as the Smarties and the Children's Book Award, to strongly championed local prizes such as the Angus Book Award (see *Children's book and illustration prizes and awards* on page 278).

Playground marketing only works in tandem with mainstream publicity and child-focused campaigns. For example, when *Harry Potter and the Prisoner of Azkaban* was released in 1999, it was timed for 3.45pm, just after school finished for the day. This caused massive publicity as children streamed out of school and into bookshop queues to buy the book, giving the television cameras a visual hook.

Internet marketing

Many children's publishers are putting more emphasis on internet marketing. The reasons for this are fairly straightforward. In general, children are far more internet-aware than their parents, and tend to spend a lot more time on their computers than reading a book.

Most publishers have their own website and it's worth having a look at some examples to get an idea about what's out there. Some lead titles will be marketed on a specially created independent site as a key part of the overall marketing plan. For example, fantasy fiction often inspires addictive online games and quizzes, such as www.faeriewars.co.uk and www.artemisfowl.co.uk. However, these are expensive to set up and a great deal can be done to promote a book on the existing publisher website. Many publishers also use their sites to run readers' clubs and offer information to teachers.

Design

One of the key marketing tools for any book is the jacket image. If the book is fantastic but has a dull, or inappropriate jacket, not only will the bookseller be unwilling to stock it, but the reader will not be attracted to it, nor understand what kind of a reading experience it's 'selling'.

A good example of where a jacket can help to raise an already successful writer to the next level, is *Witch Child* by Celia Rees. Staring out of the jacket is the beautiful face of a young girl who commands the passer-by's attention with her piercing stare. The book jacket was cited by many booksellers as one of the key reasons why customers picked it up and it was subsequently shortlisted for the British Book Awards in their Book Cover image of the year.

Book jacket design is not only important in bookshops, it is also crucial in advertising. This is true for all advertising from standing out in a small trade advert in *The Bookseller* or *The School Librarian*, to staring down from the side of a London bus.

Trade sales and marketing

Sales and marketing have become more and more closely allied since the demise of the Net Book Agreement (NBA). This was abolished in 1995 and has meant the inexorable rise of the big discount as a way for booksellers to market to the consumer. The knock-on effect of this in the high street has been for publishers to compete with one another for their books to claim valued places in bookshop promotions, be they '3 for 2' offers or '£2 off' schemes. Although these do almost always generate higher sales for a title, they come at a price, and more and more publishers' marketing budgets are being devoted to funding bookshops to run these promotions.

As a result, the trend is for big books to get bigger and small titles to get lost and often disappear without trace. This in turn is polarising publishers' lists and making it a much harder business to break into.

Non-traditional book markets

Another knock-on effect of the NBA's demise is the rise of the supermarket as bookseller. Big supermarket chains such as Asda, Tesco and Sainsbury's are getting more and more involved in selling books, and it is now almost impossible to get onto the general bestseller lists without a supermarket presence for your title. They usually stock a very narrow range of titles but some, such as Asda, will occasionally try less well-known authors who publishers are pushing strongly. Bearing in mind that the likes of Tesco have in the region of 800 stores, this can transform the sales of a title on the basis of one retailer.

Book clubs/direct marketing sales

Book clubs have always marketed themselves using price and heavy advertising in the national press. Usually they offer deals whereby if you join you get several books very cheaply and you are then tied into a minimum level of book buying through the club for a specific period. Direct marketing companies such as The Book People have been incredibly successful in selling to customers in their workplace and through catalogues.

In the children's world, book clubs are especially important as there are more clubs devoted to children and their parents than there are for adults (see *Children's book clubs* on page 60). The children's market also has schools as a captive audience. Several clubs, including Scholastic and Troubadour, are set up to run 'book fairs' in schools in tandem with their mail order operations. They offer a hand-picked selection of what the club deems to be the most commercial and appropriate selection of titles. It is therefore crucial that any children's publisher has a very strong relationship with the clubs. They may stock a more narrow range than the high street, but they order in bulk and in many cases that one order can radically improve the viability of a book's print run.

The changing face of the children's marketplace

The past five or six years has seen a huge change in attitudes to children's publishing. One of the effects of this has been to generate far more high-profile – and expensive – marketing campaigns to launch new writers such as Eoin Colfer and Lemony Snicket. In the past, these authors might have expected a publicity campaign and perhaps a poster for bookshops and libraries. However, for a small number of lead titles, now you will see major 'outdoor' advertising and read about them as front page news. Children's books are now winning the big prizes and taking up the kind of column inches that used to be reserved for the Salman Rushdies of this world.

However, this can distort the market and it should be emphasised that, generally speaking, children's books attract smaller marketing budgets than adults' books. This is down to simple economics: in general, children's books cost less than their adult equivalent. On the positive side, all this publicity has meant that the public awareness of good children's writing has been massively raised by the success of authors such as Rowling, Pullman and Wilson.

The 'crossover' book

The rise of the children's book prompted adults to find out what all the fuss is about and as a result the 'crossover' book was born. When Bloomsbury first published the Harry Potter books for the adult market with a specially designed discreet black and white jacket in 1998, it was for several reasons. Firstly, anecdotal evidence suggested that adults were reading the books already but that some felt embarrassed to be seen in public with a children's book. Secondly, even when *Harry Potter and the Chamber of Secrets* reached number one in the overall bestseller charts, booksellers refused to stock the books at the front of store. And finally, as a marketing concept, for fun, to see if it worked.

The results speak for themselves with the advent of adult editions of the

Philip Pullman trilogy *His Dark Materials*, *Holes* by Louis Sachar and *Face* by Benjamin Zephaniah, the 'crossover' book has become a recognised marketing strategy that works when used for the right book.

This theory has been taken a step further by the simultaneous publication of Mark Haddon's *The Curious Incident of the Dog in the Night-Time* in 2003 when Jonathan Cape and David Fickling Books brought out editions for both markets. This has proved a huge critical and commercial success.

Champion the book

One thing that will never change in marketing children's books is the very first sale that is made – by the editor to the publishing company. He or she must be able to inspire people to read and love the book they champion. In children's books, as with adult books, a very great deal comes down to the individual championing of one book above all others. This passion can make all the difference in marketing and selling, and it costs nothing.

Rosamund de la Hey was formerly Children's Marketing Director of Bloomsbury Publishing plc and has been responsible for marketing J.K. Rowling's *Harry Potter* books, as well as other notable successes such as *Holes* by Louis Sachar and *Witch Child* by Celia Rees. She now manages the children's trade sales at Bloomsbury.

See also...

- *Getting started*, page 1
- *What does an editor do?* page 88
- *Children's books and the US market*, page 98
- *Magazines about children's literature and education*, page 212

Children's books and the US market

Richard Scrivener outlines the possibilities for breaking into the US children's book market.

As L.P. Hartley once said of the past, America is a foreign country, they do things differently there. It is the biggest territory in the world for books, with immense opportunities, but with just as many pitfalls. Of course, the Brits have those US senators to thank, who some 200 years ago decided to make English the national language of their young nation. This does give British writers an edge over their Italian and French counterparts, although the competition for places is intense. So this article will briefly consider and note the general state of the US market, and then offer some general thoughts on what awaits a British writer who finds themselves about to be published in the United States of America.

Getting through the door

It's an old joke: the British and the Americans find their respective sandwiches very amusing. We think theirs are ridiculously big, they think ours are ridiculously small. The good news for authors is the 'big sandwich culture' has an enormous sales potential. The even better news is that, unlike their rock and pop counterparts, British authors have a brilliant track record in doing very well 'over there'. From A.A. Milne to J.K. Rowling, from Beatrix Potter to Philip Pullman, time and again the US market has shown itself more than receptive to the stories written on these wet islands. The knack is how to get in through the door.

I wouldn't recommend that a writer research the American market, then write a novel with that specifically in mind. One would most likely end up with a series of novels featuring a Christian wizard who loved *Star Trek* and looked after horses. No. As a writer, you simply have to write what you think is right. Practicalities say that you should begin with a UK publisher and editor in mind. However, you may choose to avoid subjects that might alienate the American market, though it's probably true to say the same issues apply in the UK.

The US market

Here are some basic facts and figures. (With apologies if this is a little like an economics lesson.) The US market is six times bigger than the UK's. The US publish just about the same number of titles as in the UK – somewhere a little north of 110,000, of which around a quarter are children's books in various formats. The independent bookshop is still viable in the US, and that's despite the massive growth of online sales via Amazon and the growing importance of retail chains such as Barnes and Noble and Borders. The library and institutional market whilst having suffered severe funding issues of late, still plays a stronger role in US publishing than its much ravaged British counterpart. The area of the greatest volume at retail, the mass market, is dominated by a couple of key players, with Walmart by far the largest company. The Asda-owning supermarket behemoth has a turnover larger than most countries. When it takes a book it will sell in great quantities.

Immediately one can see parallels with the UK, yet there is one noticeable difference and it's a crucial one for authors. In the delightful vicious pond that is the UK publishing market, publishers and retailers agree different discounts depending on the size of the account. In the US you can't do that. It's basically the same discount if you're Mr Barnes Books of Biloxi or if you're Mr Barnes and Noble, though of course there are various legitimate ways around this. Nonetheless it sets the tone for the business.

As in the UK, the US is dominated by the big 'conglomerate' publishers: Random House, Penguin, HarperCollins and Scholastic. They all carry large lists, publishing sometimes as many as 800 books a year. Hardback publication is still the much preferred initial route for most novels and picture books with a paperback following sometime later. Review coverage in the US for children's books is noticeably better than in the UK. *Publishers Weekly* (the US equivalent of *The Bookseller*; see *Magazines about children's literature and education* on page 212) always carries a children's section and features many thoughtful – and detailed – reviews. It would certainly be worth getting hold of a few copies of this excellent magazine to get a sense of the US market.

Alongside the usual names are other publishers which are less well known in the UK, but highly respected in the US: Harcourt Brace, Farrar Straus-Giroux, Houghton Mifflin and Little, Brown. Some of these publishers have affiliates in the UK, others are part of major media companies. They have considerable clout in the marketplace and can certainly make things happen. For example: Farrar Strauss-Giroux is the US publisher of Louis Sachar's *Holes* and sold it to Bloomsbury in the UK which then published it to great acclaim. And then there was the film…

There are also a host of small hardback houses, independent general publishers who have children's lists, as well as mass market publishers who service the supermarkets. There is plethora of choice, each company with its own dynamic and ethos.

So how do I make it over there?

The principal question of interest to any author is how do I get published in the US? As Bill Clinton used to say: that depends. If your book has been sold in the UK and the publisher has world rights and if that publisher has a US affiliate then most likely the affiliate will be the first port of call. This has the advantage of them knowing who to send it to and the fact that it's being published in the UK by the sister company will help. There should be a financial benefit to the author too – in that the royalty is paid 'straight through'. From a marketing perspective it could also mean that the publisher feels a global ownership of the author, and that would certainly help justify the necessary marketing investment.

But publishing isn't always that simple. The US affiliate may not like your book but this needn't be an issue *per se*. Nor indeed should it be a problem if the UK publisher doesn't have a US office because a good rights department will look to sell the title elsewhere. The cost of doing this for the publisher and the author is reflected in the cut of the deal retained by publisher.

If you have an agent, he or she may suggest selling US rights separately, in which case your manuscript or book will be submitted direct to US publishers.

If you're really lucky, the agent may even be able to conduct an auction, but you have to be confident the book concerned will generate sufficient interest. There's nothing more embarrassing than a one-publisher auction.

In the case of picture books – there is no question of the publisher *not* getting world rights. Co-editions will need to be set up, so as broad a territory as possible is required to offset the high origination costs of publishing in full colour.

Changes, changes

Once your book has been sold, be prepared for further editorial comments! American editors nearly always make changes to the text to Americanise it. For example, rubbish becomes garbage, nappy becomes diaper and sausage becomes hot dog. And it's not unusual for a US editor to give more line by line comments and even request a different ending. Take these in your stride, sometimes it will help sell the book. On other occasions you may think it's a bridge too far. You'll have to take each battle as it comes.

Covers, too, require a sharp intake of breath. Invariably the US cover will be different. For reasons no one can understand, British and American cover sensibilities vary considerably. It's best really to let them get on with it. You have to trust that the publisher will know what sells in Des Moines. It may not look pretty to you, but if it sells, does it matter?

As in the UK, marketing is a critical factor in determining a book's success. Dumpbins, publicity, review coverage all add to the mix. The key thing is to have an editor who's supportive and a publishing organisation which supports the editor. The best marketing plans in the world can fall flat, whilst the unexpected bestseller can come from nowhere.

Being published in the US means you'll get US fanmail! And, unless you happen to live there, you won't have that 'I'll just the check the stock in my local bookshop' opportunity, that is unless you have American friends prepared to do it for you. (Though if you ring your US publisher to tell them about this, expect the same frosty response as you'd get from your UK publisher.)

Schools

Another point of difference with the US is the schools market. And at this point I should declare I work for the company I'm about to refer to. School book clubs and book fairs are enormously important sales channels in the US. A typical order quantity would be 75,000 units. Through club mailings and touring fairs, the principal player in this market is Scholastic, reaching virtually every American child at some stage or other. These titles are often discounted and acquired under licence from US publishers who grant schools rights. Royalties are generated via the net receipts from the sale of those rights and the ongoing sale of the book. And of course there is a promotional benefit in having your book displayed in schools.

How did they do it?

It all sounds very exciting doesn't it? So how do I get invited to the party? Luck as much as anything plays an important part. Certainly you can't sit down and think I'm going to write a children's bestseller. Did J.K. Rowling ever think: 'I bet kids in Montana are going to love a story about an orphan trainee wizard attending a summer public school?' Who would have thought that Philip Pullman's version of *Paradise Lost* in which religion is castigated and God dies, would have been so popular in a country with such a wide Bible Belt?

So write what you want to write. Certainly it might be an idea to have more than one book in mind. America is after all the ultimate consumer country, if they like one, they'll want another – quickly. Though not what it once was, series publishing is still popular in the US. *Goosebumps* holds the record for the largest number of books sold, at its peak subscribing over a million copies on publication. Lemony Snicket is currently king of this castle, but there's always something else around the corner. And most likely a popular series will be made into a television show or even film – and then there's merchandising. But that's a whole other story.

Genres

As anywhere in the publishing world, genres come and go out of fashion. Fiction has been a hot category for some time now, with a particular emphasis on fantasy. It may well be this bubble will burst as publishers' lists fill with titles featuring weird creatures in various forms. Picture books have had a tough few years, but that said there are writers and artists who continue to sell very well in the US. Again it will depend on the strength of the book – it will have to be outstanding. Probably the most difficult area is publishing for the 5–8 year-olds. These books tend to feature school scenarios or make assumptions about reading levels. It is very difficult to sell these books in the US, so I wouldn't have high hopes if that's your milieu. That's not saying, like a local wine, that there's anything wrong with it – it just doesn't travel long distances.

Teenage books have actually found a much greater audience in recent years. That's as much a British thing as an American factor. Though I personally would avoid writing what I call 'My Dad killed my Step Mum' fiction, there are plenty of American writers doing that. Non-fiction certainly can travel extremely well – although for some reason, humorous non-fiction is less successful.

In short, there are many reasons to be interested in the American market. And the obvious point is the sales potential. Imagine if all of Europe spoke English – okay they do, but at least no American cities have been trashed by English football fans. The infrastructure of US publishing is immensely impressive, it's full of talented and dedicated people who, like their British counterparts, love books. Find a home. Find an editor. Find a publisher. If you get all three in the US, you'd be lucky, you may earn a few pennies. But whatever, if you're successful you'll have the satisfaction of knowing you're better than Oasis and Robbie Williams. *You* made it in America.

Richard Scrivener is Publisher of Scholastic Children's Books UK.

How it all began

Eoin Colfer shares his first experience of becoming a writing success.

I have in my time purchased several copies of the *Writers' & Artists' Yearbook*, yet there is only one copy on my bookshelf. This, I suspect, is a condition common to most authors. When other writers visit my bat-cave – sorry, office – they don't bother asking for a signed first edition of my book, instead they make off with my *Yearbook* secreted up their jumpers. This inevitably happens shortly after I have completed the laborious task of attaching colour-coded paperclips to pages of interest. I know what you're thinking. Colour-coded paperclips. That explains a lot.

My obsession with the *Yearbook* began in the dark era of glitter eye shadow and ozone-puncturing hairdos known as the Eighties. I had recently finished college, and like all males in their twenties, knew all there was to know about the world. The population in general, I decided with humble altruism, deserved the benefit of my wisdom. And the best way to reach my prospective public was through literature.

So I wrote a book. Not content with that, I designed the cover. Multi-tasking even before the phrase was coined. This book qualified as a book because it had many words and quite a few pages. Secure in my sublime self delusion, I got hold of an industrial stapler, bound the whole lot together and crammed a copy into the nearest postbox. One copy would be sufficient, to the country's foremost publishers. I settled back on the family chaise longue and waited for the publisher's helicopter to land in the garden.

Seasons passed and the helicopter never materialised. Not so much as a postcard from the honoured house. Sighing mightily I widened my net, sending copies of my book to several other publishers. I got some replies this time. Would that I had not. Most were civil enough. We regret to inform you, etc … the opening phrase that haunts every writer's dreams. Still, at least they were polite. But a few less generic replies dropped onto my doormat. There was one note in which the handwriting deteriorated in spots, as the editor suffered from sporadic fits of laughter. A pattern was beginning to emerge. Could it be possible that my manuscript was flawed? Was there a chance that my presentation was not all that it could be? Did genius have to be packaged?

Help arrived in the form of an editor's response. "We regret to inform you …" it began. Nothing new there. I was becoming inured. But there was an addendum pencilled below the type. Get the *Writers' & Artists' Yearbook*. It's worth the investment.

Reluctant as any Irish man in his twenties is to take advice from anyone besides his mother, I decided to act on this particular recommendation. The *Yearbook* paid for itself almost immediately. The mere act of purchasing the fat volume made me feel like a legitimate writer. I left the shop, making certain that my grip did not obscure the book title.

At home, I was amazed to discover that the *Yearbook* was not just a list of publishers. Every possible scrap of information needed by the upcoming or established writer was included (for more details buy the book. And if there are paperclips on this book, it is mine: please return it!) but what I needed to know was detailed under the heading 'Submitting material'. Next time, I vowed. Next time.

Next time turned out to be nearly a decade later. My self esteem had recovered sufficiently to brave the sae trail once more. So I wrote an introductory letter and an interesting summary of the book, and included the first 50 pages – double-spaced.

It worked. Two weeks later I had a publisher. Now I can't put the entire thing down to the *Yearbook*, but it certainly played its part. In public of course, I take all the credit myself. I am a writer after all. But packaging and presentation in my opinion made the difference between desktop and trash, to use a computer analogy.

A few years later my brothers advised me that I needed an agent, as they were running short on beer money. Once again the *Yearbook* was consulted. Not only were the agents listed but they were categorised. These *Yearbook* people were cut from the same cloth as myself. I could almost imagine their desks stacked with coloured paperclips.

My research paid off, and within weeks I was sitting in a top-class hotel treating my new agent to a flute of champagne. Although she insists it was a glass of Guinness in a Dublin pub and she paid.

Since then, I haven't looked back. Things are going well enough for me to be invited to write this Foreword. If you are published and reading this book, hide it away and beware those with baggy jumpers. If you are as yet unpublished, then keep the faith and make sure that all around you can see the title.

Eoin Colfer has written several bestselling children's novels, including the *Artemis Fowl* series. The books have been translated into 38 languages and have won awards including British Children's Book of the Year, WHSmith Children's Book of the Year, Bisto Merit Awards and the South African Book Club Book of the Year. The first *Artemis Fowl* film is currently in production.

See also...

- *Spotting talent*, page 68
- *How it all began*, page 102
- *Out of the slush pile*, page 72
- *The amazing picture book story*, page 145
- *Fiction for 6–9 year-olds*, page 79
- *Teenage fiction*, page 85
- *Getting started*, page 1

Children's evergreens and bestsellers

Alex Hamilton presents his view on children's bestsellers and children's books that have enduring appeal. His charts on pages 106–109 enable easy comparison.

In 2003 Nestlé bought 4.5 million Puffin paperbacks to give away in *Cheerio* cereal packets. Presumably the children, spotting them through the cute window in the packet, read rather than ate them, and found them tasty. Mothers were delighted to find, instead of a tawdry plastic item, something that would, in Dr Johnson's phrase, stretch and stimulate their little minds. That Potterish total, divided evenly among six titles such as *Ten in a Bed* and *Attack of the Tentacled Terror*, would place them high on any chart. But I've ruled out promos – despite the power of cereals.

Book charts are never flexible enough to give everything a fair shake. Publishers may use these as sales tools, as with all bestseller lists, but they're not meant to be competitive. The chart on pages 106–107 lists home sales for 2003, with all formats, ages and original dates welcomed; the big numbers of the other (pages 108–109) include a sampling of evergreens for 'lifetime' sales, though some had previous lives with different publishers, or their figures are lost in antique archives. Computers, alas, have no folk memory. Furthermore, one title in different guises may collect many ISBNs. These charts, showing publishers' figures, are not about Stage 3, SATS or study aids, nor encyclopedias (Usborne have seven information and puzzle works each selling more than a million since 1991), nor bibles (Parragon have sold 831,500 of *My First Bible*), nor babies' prayer books. They're general books, mostly fiction, sold in schools and to libraries and through book clubs, and possibly a hundred independent children's bookshops, along with supermarkets and the trade in the high street. (Nearly half this maze of distribution is not covered by the Nielsen Bookscan system that posts its bestseller lists in magazines and newspapers.)

In a chart, defining children's books by age group is more important than the adult classification by genre. It begins in the pram with *Buggie Buddies* and *Fairy Phones*, novelties with widgety bits of the kind produced by Campbell Books, through board books, flats and pop-ups for school, short stories that ease into 'chapter books', and longer novels for pre-teen, before flowing into the estuary of 12 and up, teenage and 'crossover' books. Altogether these cover 10,000 titles (a rise last year of 2000) out of a total of 125,000 books published each year in the UK.

Nevertheless there are genres. They come, they go. Series that sold in millions, like *Fighting Fantasy* and *Dungeons and Dragons*, were inspired by electronic games and were eventually overwhelmed by them. Among the most popular books there's always a seesaw between reality partnered by humour, and fantasy partnered by horror. Just now fantasy is riding high. Witchcraft has cast a glamour on the scene. Children's publishers, whom Peter de Vries once described in a novel as 'the furry people', are brisk and bushy-tailed. Tolkien is virtually a posthumous business on his own. J.K. Rowling is a billionaire (albeit a lowly one) with a turnover like a small nation (albeit Third World). You can buy broomsticks in the Rowling district of Hamley's toyshop. Philip Pullman goes tête-à-tête with the Archbishop of Canterbury. HarperCollins' reissue of the Chrestomanci series by Diana Wynne Jones, the influence most often cited by young witchcraft writers, has sold 742,000 copies.

The force behind children's books

What drives children's book sales? In a literary agency, it's finding they're not all low-income; in a publishing house, the editor feeling she's not alone, that her colleagues are on board. At the London and Bologna Book Fairs it's the illustrations. Children's books over a century have saved the art of literary illustration. For a colossal bestseller, the perfect marriage between author and illustrator is made in the art director's office.

In a school, it's the authors, especially Stakhanovites such as Jacqueline Wilson, and swarms who in return for a coffee doggedly build up their fan-base school by school (there are 25,000 junior schools in the UK). The writers were always poorly paid, and the majority still are. In addition to bookselling services and specialist school suppliers, Scholastic, originally a US schools bookselling operation, provides 'book fair' weeks in schools, where children buy at a discount, with teachers collecting and despatching the money. School book clubs are likewise cost effective, with publishers filling a hundred orders in one box. Every publisher dreams of selling direct in schools, but trying to administer 25,000 small accounts would be a nightmare. Send in debt collectors to defaulters? Unthinkable.

Directors of children's publishing – such as Philippa Dickinson of Random House, Sally Gritten of HarperCollins, Kate Wilson of Macmillan and Elaine McQuade of Puffin – believe that many teachers also need introducing to children's books, and with the Arts Council on side, they lobby the Min of Ed for teacher training to add a course on children's literature to the existing one on literacy. Given that children's publishing embraces, in Dickinson's words, 'the best writers in the universe', that shouldn't be a hardship.

David Fickling, with his own imprint under the Random House umbrella, rather blames the education system: 'the increased speed, the level of activity needed to report back about, which takes away from the teaching… and the quite terrible loop between educational publishers, government and teachers, making a huge mound of books that are a great enemy to anybody liking a book at all.'

In the high street, promotional support comes with the retailer feeling he's ahead of the game and backed by publishing money. A common publishing view of the chains is that they are doing better but still have a long way to go, as they try to fit the selling of children's books into the adult model. They do the usual promotional things – 3-for-2, book-of-the-month, etc – to get children's books up front, all effective techniques for people who go into bookshops. Unfortunately most people don't go into bookshops. It's still a very fragmented market. Success of many wonderful books results primarily from librarians and grass roots movements.

For a headline launch, invent a stunt creating maximum hysteria among

No	Title	Author	Imprint	Age group
1	Harry Potter & Order of Phoenix	J.K. Rowling	Bloomsbury	9+
2	Northern Lights	Philip Pullman	Scholastic	12+
3	The Lion King	Disney	Disney	5–7
4	The Subtle Knife	Philip Pullman	Scholastic	12+
5	The Amber Spyglass	Philip Pullman	Scholastic	12+
6	Finding Nemo: Book of the Film	Disney	Disney	5–7
7	So You Think You Know H. Potter	Clive Gifford	Hodder	8+
8	Jungle Book 2: Book of the Film	Audrey Daly	Disney	5–7
9	The Shadowmancer	G.P. Taylor	Faber	11+
10	Secrets	Jacqueline Wilson	Corgi	9–11
11	Midnight	Jacqueline Wilson	Doubleday	9–11
12	Mr Christmas	Roger Hargreaves	Egmont	3+
13	Eagle Strike (Alex Rider 4)	Anthony Horowitz	Walker	8+
14	Maisy's Colours	Lucy Cousins	Walker	2–5
15	An Eye for an Eye	Malorie Blackman	Corgi	12+
16	The Twits	Roald Dahl	Puffin	7+
17	Duck's Day Out	Jez Alborough	HarperCollins	0–7
18	The Worry Website	Jacqueline Wilson	Corgi	9–11
19	Charlie & the Chocolate Factory	Roald Dahl	Puffin	8+
20	The Wee Free Men	Terry Pratchett	Doubleday	12+
21	Gruffalo	Donaldson/Scheffler	Macmillan	3–5
22	Artemis Fowl: Eternity Code	Eoin Colfer	Puffin	10+
23	Barbie Annual 2004	Mattel	Egmont	3+
24	George's Marvellous Medicine	Roald Dahl	Puffin	7+
25	Rent-A-Genius	Gillian Cross	Puffin	7+
26	The Carnivorous Carnival	Lemony Snicket	Egmont	8+
27	The English Roses	Madonna	Puffin	6+
28	Lyra's Oxford	Philip Pullman	David Fickling	12+
29	The Hostile Hospital	Lemony Snicket	Egmont	8+
30	Artemis Fowl: Arctic Incident	Eoin Colfer	Puffin	10+
31	The Last Polar Bears	Harry Horse	Puffin	9+
32	Three Little Pigs	Traditional	Ladybird	3–7
33	Goldilocks and the Three Bears	Traditional	Ladybird	3–7
34	The Bad Beginning	Lemony Snicket	Egmont	8+
35	The Elves & the Shoemaker	Brothers Grimm	Ladybird	3–7
36	First Readers: Lost and Found	Disney	Disney	3+
37	The Very Hungry Caterpillar	Eric Carle	Puffin	5+
38	The Tale of Peter Rabbit	Beatrix Potter	Warne	3–7
39	Invitation to the Ballet	Holabird/Craig	Puffin	4–7
40	Artemis Fowl	Eoin Colfer	Puffin	10+
41	Princess Diaries: Give Me Five	Meg Cabot	Macmillan	12+
42	Princess Diaries	Meg Cabot	Macmillan	12+
43	Princess Doll Dressing Up Book	Disney	Disney	3–5
44	Horrid Henry's Underpants	Francesca Simon	Dolphin	7+
45	Princess Diaries: Take Two	Meg Cabot	Macmillan	12+
46	The Smartest Giant in Town	Donaldson/Scheffler	Macmillan	3–5
47	Molly Moon's Incredible Hypnotism	Georgia Byng	Macmillan	8–12
48	Mr Peabody's Apples	Madonna	Puffin	6+
49	Nicola and the Viscount	Meg Cabot	Macmillan	12+
50	Stormbreaker (Alex Rider 2)	Anthony Horowitz	Walker	8+

Format	Date	UK sale	Notes: Children's bestsellers 2003
Hb	June 2003	2,987,194	Harry Potter I–IV total in 2003: 1,424,506
Pb	Oct 1994	343,002	*The Guardian* Award
Mini Hb	May 2003	291,267	
Pb	Oct 1998	279,607	
Pb	Sept 2001	270,963	Whitbread prize
Mini Hb	Sept 2003	265,986	Plus 479,023 in 7 other *Nemo* titles in 2003
Pb	June 2002	258,769	Quiz book – WHSmith special
Mini Hb	Apr 2003	254,287	
Pb	June 2003	239,501	Lunatic evil cleric plots to rule the world
Pb	Mar 2003	209,735	Top 10 *Wilson* titles total in 2003: 1.205,604
Hb	Oct 2003	197,555	
Pb	Aug 2003	192,835	Top 10 *Mr Men* total in 2003: 544,673
Pb	Apr 2003	186,260	Latest in light Bond-for-kids type series
Pb	Aug 1999	185,005	
Pb	Feb 2003	184,001	Written for World Book Day 2003
Pb	Apr 2001	178,018	Reissue
Pb	Mar 2003	170,954	World Book Day
Pb	June 2003	170,787	
Pb	Apr 2001	169,767	His second book, 1964, and bestseller
Hb	May 2003	167,958	
Pb/Hb	1999/2002	167,858	Originally World Book Day paperback
Hb	May 2003	167,102	
Hb	July 2003	163,439	Mattel: world's largest maker of women's gear
Pb	Apr 2001	161,210	Top 10 Dahl titles in 2003: 1,485,561
Pb	June 2003	156,000	
Hb	Oct 2003	150,774	9 *Unfortunate Events* total in 2003: 819,571
Pb	Sept 2003	148,720	
Hb	Nov 2003	140,023	Lyra is the protagonist of *His Dark Materials*
Hb	May 2003	137,373	*Unfortunate Events* title
Pb	Mar 2003	136,845	
Pb	Feb 2003	127,189	World Book Day
Mini Hb	Mar 1999	123,605	One of dozens of Ladybird traditional tales...
Mini Hb	Mar 1999	118,599	...many selling in 6 figures
Hb	June 2001	118,259	*Unfortunate Events* title
Mini Hb	Mar 1999	118,127	First appeared in Britain c. 1823
Mini Hb	Apr 2001	117,067	
Pb	Sept 1994	115,885	First published 1970
Hb	reissue 02	114,683	40 Beatrix Potter titles total in 2003: 385,250
Pic/Hb	Oct 2003	113,672	
Pb	Mar 2002	109,164	
Tpb	Oct 2003	107,091	
Pb	June 2001	104,746	
Pb	Feb 2003	91,098	
Pb	Aug 2003	87,171	
Pb	Sept 2001	85,462	Top 5 *Princess* titles total in 2003: 456,120
Pb	Sept 2003	85,347	
Pb	May 2003	84,365	
Pic/Hb	Nov 2003	81,061	
Pb	Jan 2003	79,679	
Pb	Oct 2000	78,237	

Children's books: evergreen sampler

Author	Title	1st Date	Imprint today
Richard Adams	Watership Down	1972	Puffin
Enid Blyton	21 Famous Five titles	1942	Hodder
Raymond Briggs	The Snowman	1975	Puffin
Eric Carle	The Very Hungry Caterpillar	1970	Puffin
Lucy Cousins	Maisy: 40 titles	1991	Walker
Lucy Daniels	Animal Ark: c. 60 titles	1994	Hodder
Roald Dahl	29 titles	1964	Puffin
Terry Deary	22 Horrible Histories titles	1993	Scholastic
Anne Frank	Diary of a Young Girl	1950	Puffin
Jostein Gaarder	Sophie's World	1995	Phoenix
Martin Handford	5 Where's Wally? titles	1989	Walker
Roger Hargreaves (and son)	43 Mr Men titles	1971	Egmont
Anthony Horowitz	4 Alex Rider titles	2000	Walker
Ted Hughes	The Iron Man	1968	Faber
Clive King	Stig of the Dump	1963	Puffin
C.S. Lewis	The Lion, the Witch and...	1950	HarperCollins
Sam McBratney	Guess How Much I Love You	1996	Walker
Michelle Magorian	Goodnight Mr Tom	1981	Puffin
A.A. Milne	Winnie the Pooh	1926	Egmont
Jill Murphy	The Worst Witch	1974	Puffin
Jan Ormerod	Peekaboo!	1997	Bodley Head
Parragon	13 My Dolly Dressing titles	2001	Parragon
Parragon	17 I Can Draw titles	2000	Parragon
Terry Pratchett	9 children's titles	1988	Corgi
Philip Pullman	Northern Lights	1995	Scholastic
Philip Pullman	The Subtle Knife	1997	Scholastic
Philip Pullman	The Amber Spyglass	2000	Scholastic
Arthur Ransome	Swallows and Amazons	1930	Random House
Rosen/Oxenbury	We're Going on a Bear Hunt	1991	Walker
J.K. Rowling	Harry Potter I–V	1997	Bloomsbury
Francesca Simon	Horrid Henry series	1995	Dolphin
Lemony Snicket	10 Unfortunate Events titles	1999	Egmont
R.L. Stine	100 plus Goosebumps titles	1992	Scholastic
J.R.R. Tolkien	The Hobbit	1937	HarperCollins
Jacqueline Wilson	All titles	1993	Corgi

children and inconvenience for parents, deadline it nationwide for midnight. Be ready, like Jacqueline Wilson in Bournemouth, to sign 3000 copies in an eight-hour day. (Really? Six a minute? Practise!) A loaded title helps: Walker's *Guess How Much I Love You* is boosted by Valentine's Day, while Puffin's *The Snowman* sells like warm underwear every winter.

For the media, big awards are sexy, such as the overall Whitbread, or news of a large advance. (£150,000 is high, but occasionally there's more for a three-book contract – hence, perhaps, the spate of trilogies and chronicles doing well: Lemony Snicket's *Unfortunate Events*, Eoin Colfer's *Artemis Fowl*, Pullman's *His Dark Materials*, Crossley-Holland's *Arthur*, and diTerlizzi's *Spiderwick*.) Then there's the good 'back story', such as the precocity and looks of home-educated

Sales	Comment
3,982,194	Carnegie Medal, *The Guardian* Award 1973
5,072,608	Last 10 years. Led by *Fire on a Treasure Island*, 405,544
2,396,617	Excluding many spin-offs. Annual Christmas bestseller
2,964,895	'The perfect stand-alone book', a hardy perennial
19,266,253	Including export: 16,053,791
7,380,534	Led by *Kitten in the Kitchen*, 234,883. Lucy Daniels is a team
c. 40,000,000	Allen & Unwin was Dahl's first publisher, also Tolkien's
6,351,513	Led by *The Terrible Tudors*, 559,493
797,858	Since 1997. First published posthumously, by Macmillan
c. 1,500,000	Very crossover
42,223,312	Including export: 37,653,326
c. 70,000,000	At £1.99 bought like peanuts in supermarkets
1,112,634	Including export: 166,999
1,260,000	Late Poet Laureate's 'Story in five nights' read to his children
1,426,816	Next book *22 Letters*, 'written specially for Puffin'
3,613,002	First of the *Narnia* series of 7 books
15,927,380	Including export: 14,011,960
1,110,000	*The Guardian* Award 1982
c. 50,000,000	And a Poohsticks bridge is a tourist destination
3,216,914	Pre-Rowling witches' boarding school
459,975	Classic baby lift-the-flap
1,717,040	World sale. Name 'Parragon' based on founder Guy Parr
1,522,092	World sale. Parragon books are created in-house
3,400,000	Led by *Truckers*, 446,604. Adult books 20,500,000
1,303,341	*The Guardian* Award 1996
1,050,603	Second in *His Dark Materials* trilogy
916,976	Trilogy concluded, but it's not over yet. Whitbread Award
644,000	Sales from 1993. Ransome left *The Guardian* staff to write this
2,861,724	Including export: 1,911,470
18,775,427	...and counting. Scholastic US in print: 97,000,000
c. 1,600,000	Beastly child, bit like William. 620,000 sold in 2003
c. 2,000,000	Prolific young American author of bouncing comedies
c. 260,000,000	Worldwide. Source: *Guinness Book of Records*
844,433	Sales in the last 10 years
c. 15,000,000	Led by *Double Act*, 620,088

American Christopher Paolini, who began at 15, and at 19 has a trilogy fantasy contract and a million US sale of his boy-and-dragon fantasy, *Eragon*. Young genius stories don't always work: when French publishers extolled eight year-old poet Minou Drouet as a 'child of genius' Jean Cocteau retorted, 'All children have genius, except Minou Drouet.'

Does all this – five children's authors in the top 10 library borrowings, Big Read hype, enviable prizes – owe everything to the awareness created by the Potter craze? Some feel it has lifted fiction, if nothing else. Others have reservations as to whether individual success does translate to other people. Book Marketing's figures suggest that if you strip the Potter figures out, you're not actually looking at something different.

Richard Scrivener of Scholastic, publisher of a wildly diverse range across the *Goosebumps* and *Horrible Histories* series, and Philip Pullman, says, 'It's children's books becoming more like adult books. Publishers are being sent a synopsis and told "We need your offer by six o'clock. We're looking for a six-figure advance, and we're offering rights in Essex and Suffolk." People worry whether this is the next Big Hit, can they afford to let it go? But I think it'll blow itself out.' Philippa Dickinson, overseeing eight separate children's imprints, used to sweat over £50,000, but these days stays calm facing six figures. 'In the last 10 years children's publishing has grown up at last, and we know what we're doing. All the big publishers do, with older books – question is, how do we do it with younger fiction?'

Scrivener says that while children have a great relish for comic grotesque, 'like when in *The Terrible Tudors* your guts explode if you had the plague, or whatever,' and that at his peak R.L. Stine's horror stories were a unique publishing tidal wave (a million units a month in the USA), 'reading about sex would make them feel pretty uncomfortable. They think, "I don't want to deal with this."' What they are interested in, he believes, apart from horror and the grotesque, and the anarchy in a book that's not their real-life experience, is the illusion of power that allows them to assert themselves over adults. Dickinson, who first worked with Kaye Webb at Puffin in the 1970s, recalls publishing inhibition in those days. 'But now, so many read explicit magazines and watch explicit TV – boys are perhaps more often embarrassed than girls, who tend to mature earlier.'

Children's publishing is a world without celebrities, unless Madonna or McCartney drop by. Only Dahl has thought his life would interest children enough to write a whole book about it (he guessed right, *Going Solo* sold another 115,982 in 2003). It's a feel-good society, providing an amusing or exciting base for a future reader's private culture. It's a mixture of skills, compared with the adult publisher's search for 'the next great paper-burger'. Plus Bologna Book Fair is so much more pleasant than Frankfurt – and in Bologna, books for nodding off to are a commercial asset.

Alex Hamilton is a journalist and award-winning travel writer, and the author of several novels and volumes of short stories. Each year Alex writes about the top one hundred paperback fastsellers of the previous year and, together with his compiled Top 100 chart, is included in the *Writers' & Artists' Yearbook*.

Poetry

Riding on the poetry roundabout

Poet and anthologist John Foster writes about the difficulties involved in getting children's poetry published and offers some practical advice.

Today's children's poetry roundabout started spinning in the 1960s, when it was given a push-start by Spike Milligan, gathered momentum in the 1970s and 1980s with helping hands from the likes of Roger McGough, Allan Ahlberg and Michael Rosen, and has been gathering speed ever since. You would think, therefore, that it might be easier for a newcomer to break in and to get their poems published these days than it was when I started anthologising and writing poetry some 25 years ago. Yet, in spite of the upsurge in children's poetry publishing in recent decades, for the aspiring children's poet it can seem as hard as ever to get your poems published.

One reason, of course, is that there are now many more people specialising in writing children's poetry than there used to be and the competition is more fierce. Another is that there's an increasing number of established children's poets and that those people inevitably stand much more chance of getting a collection of their poems into print than someone who is unknown.

That said, anthologists like myself are always on the lookout for new voices, and if a good poem is submitted for an anthology, it doesn't matter who has written it – it will go in. When you're starting out, you have far more chance of getting one or two of your poems into some of the anthologies that are published annually than you have of getting a complete collection of your poems published. So if you are keen to find a ride on the poetry roundabout, it is better to discover what anthologies are in the pipeline and what specific poems are required than to try to place a single author collection. I had been anthologising and contributing poems to other anthologies for over 10 years before my first book of original poems, *Four O'Clock Friday*, was accepted. And there are some very good children's poets – Julie Holder and John Kitching, for example – who have contributed to anthologies for many years, yet have never had collections of their own published.

Ask a publisher why there are many more anthologies than single poet collections and they will give you a simple answer: anthologies sell more copies. It is much easier to sell an anthology of school poems, such as 'Why do we have to go to school today?' than it is to sell 'The Very Best of A.N.Other Children's Poet'.

Get inspired by children

If you are undaunted by what I have said so far and still determined that you are going to write children's poetry and get it published, what tips can I offer?

Starting with the most obvious, get to know children's language. If you are writing poems about children's experiences from a child's point of view you must get the language right. It is, perhaps, not surprising that many of the most successful children's poets are from a teaching background – for example, Tony Mitton, Wes Magee, Judith Nicholls, Paul Cookson and Brian Moses. Teachers not only know what children's interests are, but they also know how children think and how they express themselves. So steep yourself in children's language, not just the language of your children or the children of friends, but of children from all sorts of backgrounds and cultures.

Try to arrange to visit schools in different areas. But always go through the correct channels with a letter to the literacy coordinator, copied to the head teacher, explaining the reasons you would like to visit. Schools these days are, quite rightly, very security-conscious. Visiting schools will give you the opportunity not only to talk with children, but to try out your poems too. There's nothing like a deafening wall of silence greeting that punchline you thought they would find so amusing to let you know that, in fact, the poem doesn't work!

Schools are also a good source of ideas. Many a poem comes from a child's tale or a teacher's comment. In one school I met a teacher called Mr Little, who was six foot six inches tall. He told me a story about a girl who had asked him: Were you big when you were little? This led to my poem 'Size-Wise' (below).

Our teacher Mr Little's really tall.
He's twice the size of our helper Mrs Small.
'Were you big when you were little?'
Sandra asked him.
'I was Little when I was little,
but I've always been big!'
he said with a grin.
'Have you always been small?'
Sandra asked Mrs Small.
'No,' said Mrs Small.
'I was Short before I got married,
then I became Small.
But,' she added, 'I've always been little.'
'That's the long and the short of it,'
said Mr Little.
'I've always been big and Little,
but she used to be little and Short,
and now she's little and Small.'

Visiting schools is worthwhile, too, because you can bring yourself up to date with how poetry is being used in the classroom. The National Literacy Strategy requires that children be introduced in the primary years to a wide range of poetic forms. There is an educational as well as a trade market for children's poems and it is worth knowing what the educational publishers might be looking out for.

Anthologies

Successful children's poets will tell you that many of their poems have been triggered by an anthologist's request for a poem on a particular theme. What then is the secret of getting a poem into an anthology?

It may seem to be stating the obvious but the first thing to do is to read the submissions letter closely. My filing cabinets are full of poems that have been given only a cursory glance, because it has become apparent from the first line that they are neither relevant to the theme of the anthology in question nor appropriate for the age group at which the anthology is aimed.

Having read the letter, one's first impulse is to consider whether any of the poems you have already written are suitable. There may well be one or two, particularly among those that are already published, but simply trawling through your file of unpublished poems to see if some of them can be made to fit in with the anthologist's demands is less likely to be successful than actually writing something new.

The key very often is to come up with something slightly different. Let's say you have been asked to contribute to a book of poems about pirates. You probably stand more chance of getting your poem selected if you write a poem about pirates who have become film stars, specialising in gangster parts, than if you write a poem about traditional pirates burying their treasure or making a captive walk the plank. Similarly, if you are writing about dragons, you are more likely to succeed in placing a poem about young dragons having a flying lesson (as I have done myself), or about a young dragon doing his party trick of lighting the candles on his birthday cake (as Ian McMillan has done) than a poem about a dragon fighting a knight. The wackier and more bizarre your idea is, the more chance you will have of your poem being chosen.

Another way of making your poem stand out from the crowd is to write it in a more unusual form. For example, instead of writing your poem about St George and the dragon in couplets, you could write it in the form of an encyclopedia entry, as a series of extracts from St George's diary or even as a text message. The more contemporary the form, the more likely it is to appeal, both to the anthologist and the reader.

Getting the idea is, of course, the hardest part. If you are stuck for a humorous idea, one way of trying to find one is to look in a book of jokes. I was racking my brains to come up with a new poem for a book of magic poems, when I came across this joke: Why are the ghosts of magicians no good at conjuring? Because you can see right through their tricks! This led to:

The ghost of the magician said:
'I'm really in a fix.
The trouble is the audience
Sees right through all my tricks!'

A word of caution: whereas it can pay to be risqué, both in terms of getting your poem selected and entertaining your readers, don't be rude just for the sake of it and, especially, don't be crude. Besides, you could easily get yourself labelled! During a performance in Glasgow, I included one or two poems which made references to 'bottoms' and 'knickers', getting the usual delighted response from the audience. However, I was taken aback when I asked them to suggest why the publishers won't allow me to illustrate my poetry books. Instead of giving me the expected – and correct – answer that my drawings are no good, the first boy I asked said: 'Because your poems are dirty!'

Before sending off your poems, make sure your name and contact details are given clearly beneath every poem. It is usually better, too, to put each poem on a separate page. Check with the anthologist before you submit your poems by email. Many anthologists prefer to receive hard copies, since they assemble the anthology by hand, rather than on the computer, and it saves them the chore of having to print out the poems themselves.

Also, don't send too many poems. As a rule of thumb it's usually best to send about five, and not more than 10. Of course, you will include what you think is your best and most suitable poem. But don't be surprised if it's not chosen and another one is. I'm constantly being asked why that happens. Usually it's because someone else has written a poem that's similar in content or form to your best one and it would not be appropriate to include two such similar poems. Whereas, with regard to your other poem, it either looks at the topic from a different angle or fills a gap that needs to be filled.

You won't make a fortune from getting your poem into an anthology, but once it is in print there's also the chance that it will be picked up and used by another anthologist. So my advice is: be prepared to accept any minor changes that the editor proposes, even if you prefer your original version of the poem. My own experience is that nine times out of 10 any changes that have been suggested to my poems have actually improved them. One established poet actually calls me 'the poetry surgeon' because on several occasions I have suggested cutting whole verses from some of his poems. Professional that he is, he has agreed to accept the cuts, even if privately he knows, and I know, that he does not totally agree with them. And, of course, he has pocketed the fee!

Finally, the big question: how do you get yourself onto the anthologists' mailing lists? A simple request to have your name added won't necessarily do the trick. The anthologist needs to know that it is worth taking the time to send you a letter. So it's worth sending a sample of your poems (about five is enough) with a covering letter. But don't expect to be flooded with requests. There are only a limited number of anthologies published annually. However, if the anthologist thinks your poems have potential, your name will be added to the list – the first step towards getting a ride on the children's poetry roundabout.

John Foster's latest collection of his own poems, *Our Teacher's Gone Bananas*, is published by Oxford University Press. 'Size-Wise' is from *Making Waves* (Oxford University Press) ©John Foster; 'The Ghost of the Magician' ©John Foster.

Poetry organisations

Poetry is one of the easiest writing art forms to begin with, though the hardest to excel at or earn any money from. Many organisations offer advice, information and resources to writers and readers at all levels, and as many as possible are included here. Jules Mann, Director of the Poetry Society, lists below the organisations which can help poets take their poetry further.

Where to get involved

The Poetry Society

22 Betterton Street, London WC2H 9BX
tel 020-7420 9880 *fax* 020-7240 4818
email info@poetrysociety.org.uk
website www.poetrysociety.org.uk

The Poetry Society was set up to help poetry and poets thrive in Britain and is a registered charity funded by the Arts Council England. The Society offers advice and information to all, with a more comprehensive level of information available to members. Membership is open to anyone interested in poetry and includes 4 issues each of the magazine *Poetry Review* and the newsletter *Poetry News*. The Society's website offers an excellent interactive regional guide to poetry organisations, venues, publishers and bookshops around the UK through its Poetry Landmarks of Britain section.

The Society also publishes education resources (see later); promotes National Poetry Day; runs a critical service called Poetry Prescription (£50 for 100 lines – 20% discount to members); provides an education advisory and training service, school membership, youth membership and a thriving website. A range of events and readings take place at the Poetry Café and the Poetry Studio at the Society's headquarters in Covent Garden.

Competitions run by the Society include the National Poetry Competition, the largest open poetry competition in Britain each year with a first prize of £5000, the biannual Corneliu M. Popescu Prize for European Poetry Translation and the Foyle Young Poets of the Year Award. Membership: £35 full, £25 concessions. Founded 1909.

Poetry Ireland

120 St Stephen's Green, Dublin 2,
Republic of Ireland
tel (01) 478 9974 *fax* (0) 478 0205
email poetry@iol.ie
website www.poetryireland.ie

Poetry Ireland is the national organisation dedicated to developing, supporting and promoting poetry throughout Ireland. It is a resource and information point for any member of the public with an interest in poetry and works towards creating opportunities for poets working or living in Ireland. It is grant-aided by both the Northern and Southern Arts Councils of Ireland and is a resource centre with the Austin Clarke Library of over 10,000 titles. It publishes the quarterly magazine *Poetry Ireland Review* and the bi-monthly newsletter *Poetry Ireland News*. Poetry Ireland organises readings in Dublin and nationally, and runs a Writers-in-Schools Scheme.

The Poetry Book Society

Book House, 45 East Hill,
London SW18 2QZ
tel 020-8870 8403 *fax* 020-8870 0865
email info@poetrybooks.co.uk
website www.poetrybooks.co.uk
Chair Daisy Goodwin, *Director* Chris Holifield

This unique book club for readers of poetry was founded in 1953 by T.S. Eliot, and is funded by the Arts Council England. Every quarter, selectors choose one outstanding publication (the PBS Choice), and recommend 4 other titles. Members can receive some or all of these books free and are also offered substantial discounts on other poetry books. The Poetry Book Society also administers the T.S. Eliot Prize, produces the quarterly membership magazine, the *Bulletin*, and has an education service providing teaching materials for primary and secondary schools. Write for details.

The British Haiku Society

Lenacre Ford, Woolhope, Hereford HR1 4RF
Secretary David Walker
tel (01432) 860328
email davidawalker@btinternet.com
website www.britishhaikusociety.org

The Society runs the prestigious annual James W. Hackett International Haiku Award, the Nobuyuki Yuasa Annual International Award for Haibun and the bienniel Sasakawa Prize worth £2500 for original contributions in the field of haikai. It is active in promoting the teaching of haiku in schools and colleges, and is able to provide readers, course/workshop leaders and speakers for poetry groups, etc. It has created a haiku teaching/learning kit for schools. Write for membership details. Founded 1990.

Survivors Poetry

Diorama Arts Centre, 34 Osnaburgh Street,
London NW1 3ND
tel 020-7916 5317 *fax* 020-7916 0830
email survivor@survivorspoetry.org.uk

Survivors Poetry provides poetry workshops, performances, readings, publishing, networking and training for survivors of mental distress in London and the UK. Survivors Poetry is funded by the Arts Council England and was founded in 1991 by 4 poets who have had first-hand experience of the mental health system. It works in partnership with local and national arts, mental health, community, statutory and disability organisations. Its outreach project has established a network of 30 writers' groups in the UK.

Where to get information

Your local library should have information about the local poetry scene. Many libraries are actively involved in promoting poetry as well as having modern poetry available for loan. Local librarians promote writing activities with, for example, projects like Poetry on Loan and Poetry Places information points in West Midlands Libraries.

The Poetry Library

Level 5, Royal Festival Hall, London SE1 8XX
tel 020-7921 0943/0664 *fax* 020-7921 0939
email poetrylibrary@rfh.org.uk
website www.poetrylibrary.org.uk

The principal roles of the Poetry Library are to collect and preserve all poetry published in the UK since about 1912 and to act as a public lending library. The Library also keeps a wide range of international poetry. It has 2 copies of each title available and a collection of about 40,000 titles in English and English translation. The Library also provides an education service (see page 118).

Founded in 1953 by the Arts Council, the Library runs an active information service, which includes a unique noticeboard for lost quotations, and tracing authors and publishers from extracts of poems. Current awareness lists are available for magazines, publishers, competitions, bookshops, groups and workshops, evening classes and festivals on receipt of a large sae. The Library also stocks a full range of British poetry magazines as well as a selection from abroad. When visiting the Library, look out for the Voice Box, a performance space for literature; a programme is available from 020-7921 0906. Open 11am–8pm Tuesday to Sunday. Membership: free with proof of identity and current address.

The Northern Poetry Library

County Library, The Willows, Morpeth,
Northumberland NE61 1TA
tel (01670) 534514 (poetry enquiries)
tel (01670) 534524 (poetry dept)

The Northern Poetry Library has over 14,000 titles and magazines covering poetry published since 1945. For information about epic through to classic poetry, a full text database is available of all poetry from 600–1900. A postal lending service is available to members, who pay for return postage. Membership is free to anyone living in the areas of Tyne and Wear, Durham, Northumberland, Cumbria and Cleveland. Founded 1968.

The Scottish Poetry Library

5 Crichton's Close, Canongate,
Edinburgh EH8 8DT
tel 0131-557 2876 *fax* 0131-557 8393
email inquiries@spl.org.uk
website www.spl.org.uk

The Scottish Poetry Library is run along similar lines to the Poetry Library in London. It specialises in 20th century poetry written in Scotland, in Scots, Gaelic and English. It also collects some pre-20th-century poetry and contemporary poetry from all over the world. Information and advice is given, and visits by individuals, groups and schools are welcome. Borrowing is free of charge and there is a membership scheme (£20 p.a.), which includes use of the members' reading room and a regular newsletter. It has branches in libraries and arts centres throughout Scotland and also runs a library touring service. Readings and exhibitions are regularly organised, particularly during the Edinburgh Festival. Founded 1984.

Arts Council England

website www.artscouncil.org.uk

Arts Council England has 9 regional offices and local literature officers can provide information on local poetry groups, workshops and societies (see page 262). Some give grant aid to local publishers and magazines and help fund festivals, literature projects and readings, and some run critical services.

The internet

You can get many links with good internet poetry magazines through the following:

The Poetry Kit

website www.poetrykit.org

The Poetry Society of America

website www.poetrysociety.org

Where to get poetry books

See the Poetry Book Society on page 115. The Poetry Library provides a list of bookshops which stock poetry. For second-hand mail order poetry books try:

The Poetry Bookshop

The Ice House, Brook Street,
Hay-on-Wye HR3 5BQ
tel (01497) 821812

Peter Riley

27 Sturton Street, Cambridge CB1 2QG
tel (01223) 576422
email priley@dircon.co.uk

Where to celebrate poetry

Festival information should be available from Arts Council England offices (see page 262). See also *Children's literature festivals and trade fairs* on page 285.

The British Council

Information Officer, Literature Dept,
The British Council, 11 Portland Place,
London W1N 4EJ
tel 020-7930 8466 *fax* 020-7389 3199
website www.britishcouncil.org/arts/literature

Send a large sae or visit the website for a list of forthcoming festivals.

Where to perform

In London, Express Excess and Vice Verso are 2 of the liveliest venues and they regularly feature the best performers, while Poetry Unplugged at the Poetry Café is famous for its weekly open mike nights (Tuesdays 7.30pm). Other performance venues listed below have readings. For up-to-date information, read *Time Out* and *What's On in London*).

For venues outside London, check local listings, ask at libraries and Arts Council England offices, and visit the Landmarks of Britain section of the Poetry Society's website (www.poetrysociety.org.uk).

Apples and Snakes Performance Poetry

Battersea Arts Centre, Lavender Hill,
London SW11
tel 020-7223 2223

Coffee House Poetry

Troubadour Coffee House, 265 Old Brompton Road,
London SW5
tel 020-7370 1434

Express Excess

The Enterprise, 2 Haverstock Hill, London NW3
tel 020-7485 2659

Poetry Café

22 Betterton Street, London WC2
tel 020-7420 9888

Vice Verso

Bread and Roses, 68 Clapham Manor Street,
London SW4
tel 020-8341 6085

Voice Box

Level 5, Royal Festival Hall, London SE1
tel 020-7960 4242

Competitions

There are now hundreds of competitions to enter and as the prizes increase, the highest being £5000 (first prize in the National Poetry Competition and the Arvon Foundation International Poetry Competition), so does the prestige associated with winning such competitions.

To decide which competitions are worth entering, make sure you know who the judges are and think twice before paying large sums for an anthology of 'winning' poems which will only be read by entrants wanting to see their own work in print. The Poetry Library publishes a list of competitions each month (available free on receipt of a large sae).

Literary prizes are given annually to published poets and as such are non-competitive. An A–Z guide to literary prizes can be found on the Booktrust website (www.booktrust.org.uk).

Where to write poetry

The Arvon Foundation

Lumb Bank – The Ted Hughes Arvon Centre
Hebden Bridge, West Yorkshire HX7 6DF
tel (01422) 843714 *fax* (01422) 843714
website www.arvonfoundation.org
The Arvon Foundation at Totleigh Barton
Sheepwash, Beaworthy, Devon EX21 5NS
tel (01409) 231338 fax (01409) 231144
The Arvon Foundation at Moniack Mhor
Teavarren, Kiltarlity, Beauly,
Inverness-shire IV4 7HT
tel (01463) 741675 *fax* (01463) 741733
The Hurst – The John Osborne Arvon Centre
Clunton, Craven Arms, Shrops. SY7 0JA
tel (01588) 640658 *fax* (01588) 640509
email hurst@arvonfoundation.org

The Arvon Foundation's 4 centres run 5-day residential courses throughout the year to anyone over the age of 16, providing the opportunity to live and work with professional writers. Writing genres explored include poetry, narrative, drama, writing for children, song writing and the performing arts. Bursaries are available to those receiving benefits. Founded in 1968.

The Poetry School

1a Jewel Road, London E17 4QU
tel/fax 020-8223 0401 *tel* 020-8985 0090
email thepoetryschool@phonecoop.coop
website www.poetryschool.com

Using London venues, the Poetry School offers a core programme of tuition in reading and writing poetry. It provides a forum to share experience, develop skills and extend appreciation of both traditional and innovative aspects of poetry.

The Poet's House/Teach na hÉigse

Clonbarra, Falcarragh, County Donegal, Republic of Ireland
tel (074) 65470 *fax* (074) 65471
email phouse@iol.ie

Runs 3 10-day poetry courses in July and August. An MA degree in creative writing is validated by Lancaster University, and the Irish Language Faculty includes Cathal O'Searcaigh. The faculty comprises 30 writers, including Paul Durcan and John Montagu.

Ty Newydd

Taliesin Trust, Ty Newydd, Llanystumdwy, Criccieth, Gwynedd LL52 0LW
tel (01766) 522811 *fax* (01766) 523095
email post@tynewydd.org
website www.tynewydd.org

Ty Newydd runs week-long writing courses encompassing a wide variety of genres, including poetry, and caters for all levels, from beginners to published poets. All the courses are tutored by published writers. Writing retreats are also available.

Groups on the internet

It is worth searching for discussion groups and chat rooms on the internet. There are plenty of them; John Kinsella's is highly recommended, which is junk mail-resistant and highly informative:

John Kinsella's

email poetryetc@jiscmail.ac.uk

The Poetry Kit

website www.poetrykit.org/wkshops2.htm

Local groups

Local groups vary enormously so it is worth shopping around to find one that suits your poetry. Up-to-date information can be obtained from Art Council England regional offfices (see page 262).

The Poetry Library publishes a list of groups for the Greater London area which will be sent out on receipt of a large sae.

Help for young poets and teachers

National Association of Writers in Education (NAWE)

PO Box 1, Sheriff Hutton, York YO60 7YU
tel/fax (01653) 618429
email paul@nawe.co.uk
website www.nawe.co.uk

NAWE is a national organisation, which aims to widen the scope of writing in education, and coordinate activities between writers, teachers and funding bodies. It publishes the magazine *Writing in Education* and is author of a writers' database which can identify writers who fit the given criteria (e.g. speaks several languages, works well with special needs, etc) for schools, colleges and the community. Publishes *Reading the Applause: Reflections on Performance Poetry by Various Artists*. Write for membership details.

The Poetry Library

Children's Section, Royal Festival Hall, London SE1 8XX
tel 020-7921 0664
website www.poetrylibrary.org.uk

For young poets, the Poetry Library has about 4000 books incorporating the SIGNAL Collection of Children's Poetry. It also has a multimedia children's section, from which cassettes and videos are available to engage children's interest in poetry.

The Poetry Library has an education service for teachers and writing groups. Its information file covers all aspects of poetry in education. There is a separate collection of books and materials for teachers and poets who work with children in schools, and teachers may join a special membership scheme to borrow books for the classroom.

Poetry Society Education

The Poetry Society, 22 Betterton Street, London WC2H 9BX
tel 020-7420 9894 *fax* 020-7240 4818
email education@poetrysociety.org.uk
website www.poetrysociety.org.uk

For over 30 years the Poetry Society has been introducing poets into classrooms, providing teachers' resources and producing colourful, accessible publications for pupils. A publication celebrating National Poetry Day is sent free to schools, giving an insight into the best of contemporary poetry.

Schools membership (£50 secondary, £30 primary) offers publications, training opportunities for teachers and poets, a free subscription to *Poems on the Underground* and a consultancy service giving advice on working with poets in the classroom. *Poetryclass*, an INSET training project funded by the DfES, employs poets to train teachers at primary and secondary level. People aged 11–18 can join the Society and receive poetry books and posters, quarterly copies of *Poetry News*, and a Young Writer's Pack giving advice on developing writing skills.

Poetry Society publications for schools include *The Poetry Book for Primary Schools* and *Jumpstart Poetry in the Secondary School*, a young poets pack and posters for school Key Stage 1 to GCSE requirements. A full catalogue of poetry resources, details of youth membership, the Foyle Young Poets of the Year Award, school membership and education residencies are available from the Education Department.

Young poetry competitions

Children's competitions are included in the competition list provided by the Poetry Library (free on receipt of a large sae).

Foyle Young Poets of the Year Award

The Poetry Society, 22 Betterton Street, London WC2H 9BX
tel 020-7420 9894 *fax* 020-7240 4818
email education@poetrysociety.org.uk
website www.poetrysociety.org.uk

Free entry for 11–18 year-olds with unique prizes.

Christopher Tower Poetry Prize

Tower Poetry, Christ Church, Oxford OX1 1DP
tel/fax (01865) 286591
email info@towerpoetry.org.uk
website www.towerpoetry.org.uk/prize/index.html

An annual poetry competition from Christ Church, Oxford, open to 16–18 year-olds in UK schools and colleges. The poems should be no longer than 48 lines, on a different chosen theme each year. Prizes: £1500 (1st), prize £750 (2nd), £500 (3rd). Every winner also receives a prize for their school. Highly commended entries each receive £200.

Further reading

Baldwin, Michael, *The Way to Write Poetry*, Hamish Hamilton, 1982, o.p.
Chisholm, Alison, *The Craft of Writing Poetry*, Allison & Busby, 1997, repr. 2001
Chisholm, Alison, *A Practical Poetry Course*, Allison & Busby, 1997
Corti, Doris, *Writing Poetry*, Writers News Library of Writing/Thomas & Lochar, 1994
Fairfax, John, and John Moat, *Creative Writing: The Way to Write*, Elm Tree Books, 2nd edn revised, 1998
Finch, Peter, *How to Publish Your Poetry*, Allison & Busby, 2nd edn, 1998
Forbes, Peter, *Scanning the Century*, Penguin Books, 2000
Hamilton, Ian, *The Oxford Companion to Twentieth Century Poetry in English*, OUP, 1996
Hyland, Paul, *Getting into Poetry*, Bloodaxe, 2nd edn, 1997
Livingstone, Dinah, *Poetry Handbook for Readers and Writers*, Macmillan, 1992
O'Brien, Sean, *The Firebox*, Picador, 1998
Reading the Applause: Reflections on Performance Poetry by Various Artists, NAWE, 1999
Riggs, Thomas (ed.), *Contemporary Poets*, St James Press, 7th edn, 2000
Roberts, Philip Davies, *How Poetry Works*, Penguin Books, 2nd edn, 2000
Sansom, Peter, *Writing Poems*, Bloodaxe, 1994, reprinted 1997
Sweeney Matthew, and John Williams, *Teach Yourself Writing Poetry*, Hodder and Stoughton, 2003
Whitworth, John, *Writing Poetry*, A & C Black, 2001

USA

Breen, Nancy, *Poet's Market*, Writer's Digest Books, USA, 2004 (due Aug 2003)
Fulton, Len, *Directory of Poetry Publishers*, Dustbooks, USA, 19th edn, 2003–4
Fulton, Len, *The International Directory of Little Magazines and Small Presses*, Dustbooks, USA, 39th edn, 2003–4
Preminger, Alex, *New Princeton Encyclopedia of Poetry and Poetics*, Princeton University Press, 3rd edn, 1993

Literary agents

How to get an agent

Because children's publishing is highly competitive and the market is crowded, in this article Philippa Milnes-Smith explains that finding an agent isn't child's play.

If you are currently just experiencing a vague interest in being a writer or illustrator, stop now. You are unlikely to survive the rigorous commercial assessment to which your work will be subjected. If you are a children's writer or illustrator, do not think that the process of getting published will be any easier than for the adult market. It's just as tough, if not tougher, partly because a lot of writers and would-be writers see writing for children as an easy option. It can't be that difficult to write a kid's book, can it? After all, it is just for kids…

Nowadays, too, there is extra competition in the children's field: the high profile of successes such as J.K. Rowling's *Harry Potter* series and Philip Pullman's *His Dark Materials* have drawn the attention of many professional writers who have previously only written for the adult market and who see it as a new and lucrative area for their talents. So, before embarking on a children's book/script/proposal for an exciting new children's character, remember that it is a highly competitive and crowded market you are entering.

So, what is a literary agent and why would I want one?

You will probably already have noticed that contacts for many publishers are provided in the *Children's Writers' & Artists' Yearbook*. This means that there is nothing to prevent you from pursuing publishers directly yourself. Indeed, if you can answer a confident 'yes' to all the questions below, and have the time and resources to devote to this objective, you probably don't need an agent.

- Do you have a thorough understanding of the publishing market and its dynamics?
- Do you know who are the best publishers for your book and why? Can you evaluate the pros and cons of each?
- Are you financially numerate and confident of being able to negotiate the best commercial deal available in current market conditions?
- Are you confident of being able to understand fully and negotiate a publishing or other media contract?
- Do you enjoy the process of selling yourself and your work?
- Do you want to spend your creative time on these activities?

An agent's job is to deal with all of the above on your behalf. A good agent will do all of these well.

Is that all an agent does?

Agents aren't all the same. Some will provide more editorial and creative support; some will help on longer-term career planning; some will be subject specialists; some will involve themselves more on marketing and promotion. Such extras may well be taken into consideration in the commission rates charged.

If I am writing and/or illustrating for children's books, do I need a specialist children's agent?

Most specialist children's agents would probably say you definitely need a specialist; many general agents will say you don't really need a specialist. In the end you will have to make up your own mind about whether an individual agent is right for your work and right for you as an individual. Knowledge, experience and excellent industry contacts (in the right companies and the right categories) are essential qualities in an agent who is going to represent you. If you are writing younger fiction, an agent whose expertise is in adult books with a few forays into young adult fiction probably won't have a full grasp of its potential. If your project is really something specifically for the schools and educational market it may well require different representation than a project for the consumer market: the audience (children) may be the same but projects for educational publishers tend to have to be tailored to the educational syllabus in a very particular way. You will need an agent who understands this (and there are very few).

If you are only interested in illustrating work by other people rather than developing your own projects and would like to try illustration work across a broad range of genres and formats, you may be best served by an artists' agent rather than a literary agent (see *Illustrators' agents* on page 154).

I am writing a text for an illustrated book – do I need to send illustrations with it for an agent to consider it?

No, not unless you are an accomplished illustrator or intend to do the illustrations yourself. The wrong illustrations will put off an agent as they will a publisher. A good text should be able to speak for itself. And never, in any case, send in original artwork, only send copies.

What if I have a brilliant novelty proposal, like a pop-up book? Do I need to show how it is going to look it its finished state?

If you can do it competently and it helps demonstrate how different and exciting your project is, you can certainly do this. But be prepared for the fact that you may need to make more than one, as the original runs the risk of getting damaged through handling or, when the worst comes to the worst, getting lost.

I have decided I definitely do want an agent. Where do I begin?

When I left publishing and talked generally to the authors and illustrators I knew, a number of them said it was now more difficult to find an agent than a publisher. Why is this? The answer is a commercial one. Running an agency is a costly thing and an agent will only take someone on if they can see how and why they are going to make money for the client and themselves (and, of course, a client who is making no money tends quickly to become an unhappy client). To survive just the basic costs, an agent needs to make commission and if an agent needs to fund sales trips on clients' behalf, often internationally, they need more commission. An agent also knows that if he or she cannot and does not sell a client's work, the relationship isn't going to last long.

So the agent just thinks about money?

Well, some agents may just think about money. And it is certainly what some authors and artists think about a lot. *But* good agents do also care about the quality of work and the clients they take on. They are professional people who commit themselves to doing the best job they can. They also know that good personal relationships count – and that they help everyone enjoy business more. This means that, if and when you get as far as talking to a prospective agent, you should ask yourself the questions: 'Do I have a good rapport with this person? Do I think we will get along? Do I understand and trust what they are saying?' Follow your instinct – more often than not it will be right.

So how do I convince them that I'm worth taking on?

Start with the basics. Make your approach professional. Make sure you only approach an appropriate agent who deals with the category of book you are writing/illustrating. Phone to check to whom you should send your work and whether there are any particular ways your submission should be made (if it's not clear from the listings in this *Yearbook* – see page 129). Only submit neat typed work on single-sided A4 paper. Send a short covering letter with your manuscript explaining what it is, why you wrote it, what the intended audience is and providing any other *relevant* context. Always say if and why you are uniquely placed and qualified to write a particular book. Also, provide a CV (again, neat, typed, relevant). Think of the whole thing in the same way as you would a job application, for which you would expect to prepare thoroughly in advance. You might only get one go at making your big sales pitch to an agent. Don't mess it up by being anything less than thorough.

And if I get to meet them?

Treat it like a job interview (although hopefully it will be more relaxed than this). Be prepared to talk about your work and yourself. An agent knows that a prepossessing personality in an author is a great asset for a publisher in terms of publicity and marketing – they will be looking to see how good your interpersonal skills are. Do also take the chance to find out, if you are discussing children's projects in particular, how and where they submit their clients' work and how well they understand the children's market themselves. Also check that they have good relationships with the sort of publishers/media companies with whom you think your work belongs. Don't be afraid to question them on their credentials and track record. And if you have personal recommendations and referrals from other writers, publishers and other industry contacts, do follow these up. Ask, too, about representation overseas and at the key trade children's book fair(s) such as the one held annually in Bologna. If appropriate, ask about representation in other media. Is this agent going to get their clients' work noticed by the right people in the right places and sold for the best market rates?

Will they expect me to be an expert on children and the children's market?

Not as such, but they might reasonably expect you to have an interest in what children like and enjoy and show an understanding of a child's eye view of the world. Basically, an agent will be looking for a writer/illustrator who is in sympathy with the target audience. It also won't do any harm if you spend time at your local bookshop and/or library and befriend your local librarian or specialist children's bookseller to find out what books and authors are working well and if anyone is doing exactly what you plan to do. It's good, basic market research, as is browsing what else is available through internet retailers. For example, if you are planning a series of picture books about a ballet-dancing mouse you need to be aware that *Angelina Ballerina* is already out there.

And if they turn my work down? Should I ask them to look again? People say you should not accept rejection.

No means no. Don't pester. It won't make an agent change his or her mind. Instead, move on to the next agency who might feel more positive towards your work. The agents who reject you may be wrong. But the loss is theirs.

Even if they turn my work down, isn't it worth asking for help with my creative direction?

No. Agents will often provide editorial advice for clients but won't do so for non-clients. Submissions are usually sorted into two piles of 'yes, worth seeing more' and 'rejections'. There is not another pile of 'promising writer but requires further tutoring'. To get teaching and advice, creative writing courses (see page 248) and writers' and artists' groups are better options to pursue. It is, however, important to practise and develop your creative skills. You wouldn't expect to be able to play football without working at your ball skills or practise as a lawyer without studying to acquire the relevant knowledge. If you are looking to get your work published, you are going to have to compete with professional writers and artists – and those who have spent years working at their craft.

There are particular considerations that need to be given in the craft of writing children's books. In a picture book, the text needs to work specifically with the illustrations: the fewer words there are, the more they matter. In writing fiction for a young age group, where language and sentence construction have to be simple enough for a seven year-old child, the writer often has to work much harder to generate emotion and excitement and give the story personality. When illustrating children's poetry, the artist has to be able to develop and enhance the meaning of the words to just the right level. Children's books are a demanding business.

Good luck!

Philippa Milnes-Smith is a literary agent and children's specialist at the agency LAW (Lucas Alexander Whitley). She was previously Managing Director of Puffin Books.

Do you *have* to have an agent to succeed?

Bestselling children's author Philip Ardagh has over 60 titles to his credit but chooses not have a literary agent to represent him. In this article he tells us why.

There are a lot of people out there who think that they're children's writers ('I was a child myself once, you know') and who send unsolicited manuscripts directly to publishers in their hundreds – possibly thousands – every year. These manuscripts usually end up on what is called the 'slush pile'. Some publishers won't even read them. Some do but, usually, only after a very long time. Many manuscripts are very badly written or very badly presented. Some are perfectly good but a little too much like something already out there in the bookshops, or they lack that indefinable something that makes them stand out from the crowd. Others are perfectly good but are sent to completely the wrong publisher. The best children's fantasy novel ever isn't going to appeal to a publisher specialising in adult DIY manuals, is it? Getting an agent cuts through this process.

Having an agent

Firstly, if an agent submits a manuscript it's going to be to the publisher they think that it's best suited to, and probably to the most suitable editor within that company – more often than not someone they know or have had dealings with in the past. So your manuscript is being seen by the right people at the right place. It's also neatly bypassed the slush pile. It will actually get read. Hurrah! The agent has acted as a filter. The publisher knows that, if you've been taken on by a reputable agent, your words are probably *worth* reading. You're ahead of the game.

And if a publisher wants to publish your work, an agent knows the ins and outs of advances, royalties, escalators, foreign rights, and a million and one other things that makes the humble writer's head spin. Agents know the 'going rates' and will get you the very best deal they can. And, should there be problems further down the line, your agent can play the bad guy on your behalf – renegotiating contracts and doing the number crunching – whilst you only deal with the nice fluffy creative side with your editor.

That's the theory, of course, and much of it is true. They take their 10%–15% but they're not a charity and, if they're on a percentage of your earnings, it's generally in their interest to make you as much money as possible, isn't it?

The question is: is it possible to be a successful children's author without an agent? Of course it is. Anything's possible. I'm an agentless author and I'm doing okay, but not without help, advice, common sense, good luck and, as time has passed, experience.

So what are the disadvantages of having an agent? If you've got the right agent, the answer is probably very few, if any. Sure, you're not earning the full advance or royalty because you're giving them a percentage but your manuscript may never have become a book (or the advance and royalty may have been much lower) if they didn't represent you in the first place. If you don't have an agent you don't get directly involved in every aspect of negotiation and discussion with your publisher because you've handed that role over. And if you like the on-hands approach (for that read 'are a control freak'), you may miss out on that but, over all, the pros seem to outweigh the cons.

If you're *not* happy with your agent, though, it can be a very different story. You're not your agent's only client and you may feel – rightly or wrongly – that they're not giving you enough attention. Many is the writer and illustrator I know who has said, 'I find more work for myself than my agent does', or who isn't happy with the advance they've received and said, 'I'm not sure why my agent was so keen for me to agree to this deal.' Another familiar lament is, 'She seemed so enthusiastic when I first signed up, but now she's gone really quiet.' Your filter has become a barrier.

There may also be jobs which your agent is reluctant for you to take. In children's non-fiction, many authors are still paid flat fees, and small ones at that. Many agents will tell you not to touch them with a barge pole but – if you are at the beginning of your career – who knows what that little job might lead to? I once wrote the text to a book that owed its subsequent international success not to the beauty of my prose but to the illustrations and brilliant paper engineering. My fee was peanuts and, in immediate financial terms, it made no difference if the book sold three copies or 300,000. But it did my writing career the power of good. My name was associated with a successful title, I got known by various people within that particular publishing house, I went on to write many more books for them *with* royalties, and added to my reputation, generating interest from other publishers.

Going it alone

I enjoy that getting-to-know aspect of developing a relationship with publishers and, when it comes to contracts, I have a very useful not-so-secret secret weapon. I may not have an agent but I can call on the contracts experts at the Society of Authors (see page 255). As a member of the Society, they'll go through a contract line by line for me, free and for nothing, offering comments, suggestions and advice. They also publish excellent easy-to-understand pamphlets on various aspects of publishing. If you're not already a member, rush out and join immediately! If you don't understand something, don't be afraid to ask.

Remember, whatever impression a publisher might give, there is very rarely such thing as a standard contract, written in stone, that can't be altered; sometimes significantly. Be prepared to concede some minor points, maybe, in return for sticking to your guns over a point which may really matter to you. (Different things matter to different writers.)

My big break came by luck, but luck borne out of developing contacts and making real friendships in the course of my agentless foray into the children's publishing world. The bulk of my 60-or-more titles are non-fiction, but the bulk of my income and 95% of my recognition comes from my fiction, but one grew from the other. Because I was involved and enthusiastic, I was invited to promote one of my non-fiction titles at a sales conference. As a result of how I ad libbed at the conference, following a mighty cock-up, I was asked if I wrote fiction. *Awful End* (my first Eddie Dickens book) was pulled out of the drawer and a deal was done. One thing had, indeed, led to another. Eddie's adventures are now in 25 languages and read around the world, picking up a few literary awards along the way. An option for a series of Eddie Dickens films has been signed with Warner Bros.

Your rights

Publishers love to have world rights to your books. Agents love to sell the rights separately. You can see why. An agent will argue that they can get more for you (and therefore more for them) by selling foreign rights separately to foreign publishers – perhaps creating a US auction for your fabulous book, for example – rather than your signing everything over to your UK publisher in one fell swoop. If, however, you sell the world rights to your publisher, and you have a good relationship with them, they're in effect acting as your agent on foreign deals and can still negotiate some excellent ones *in consultation with you*. And, having your world rights, they can share in your international success when it comes, so may be more keen to nurture you (and your money-generating, recognition-building world rights) in the future than, possibly, another writer whom they only publish in the UK.

And remember, an advance is an advance of royalties. If the advance is small and the book is a success, it simply means that the advance is earned out sooner and the cheques start rolling in. My advance for *Awful End* was just a four figure sum, but the money I've earned from additional royalties have been very-nice-thank-you-very-much. And my advance for the latest Eddie Dickens books are significantly larger.

Making the right decision

I know from friends and colleagues that, when you're starting out, you can find it as hard to get an agent as a publisher, which is why some people choose to go straight for the publishing houses. My advice – and this may surprise some of you – is to stick at trying to get an agent. If I was starting out now, I'd do that. Having an agent from the beginning makes sense.

If you're dead against the idea, feeling convinced that you can do a great job (see Philippa Milnes-Smith's check list on page 121) or are exhausted trying, there are a few obvious things you can do. Even now, I sometimes ask myself 'Am I getting the very best deal?' and 'Could an agent do better for me?' Financially, the answers to these are probably 'Maybe not' and 'Yes', but are these the right questions? Surely what I need to ask is: 'Am I happy with this deal?' 'Is it a reasonable sum reflecting what I think I'm worth and showing the commitment and understanding of the publisher?' And the answer to that is, more often than not, 'yes'. And remember, money ain't the be all and end all. A good working relationship with an editor and publisher who understand you, consult with you, nurture you and your writing, promote and market you in a way you're happy with is beyond price!

Approaching a publisher

But let's not get ahead of ourselves. One of the most important, important *important* – it's important, get it? – things you need to be sure of before sending a manuscript to an agent *or* a publisher is that it's ready to be seen. Some unpublished writers are so keen to show their work to others in the hope of getting it published as soon as possible that it's still in a very raw state. They're not doing themselves any favours. In fact, they could be ruining their chances. Sure, there is such a thing as overworking a piece, but you really need to be confident that it's about as good as it's going to get, especially if you're bypassing the agent route and going direct to the publisher. With no agent 'filter', you've got to be sure that you're representing yourself, through your work, in the very best possible light.

Look in bookshops to find out who publishes what. Once you've chosen a publisher, look them up in this *Yearbook*, find out their submissions procedure and ring them up. Ask the receptionist the name of the person you should send your manuscript or sample chapters to. This way you can address and write a letter to a particular person, rather than taking the 'Dear Sir/Madam' approach.

The covering letter you should write to the publisher is almost identical to the one Philippa Milnes-Smith outlines for writing to a prospective agent on page 123 except, of course, that you should also include the reason why you think they'd be right people to publish your work.

Finally, do treat the business side of selling yourself as a business. It's not simply that 'the writing's the important bit' and that it'll 'sell itself'. Network, send in invoices on time, get in touch when you say you'll get in touch and be contactable (there's no excuse for dropping off the radar in this age of emails and mobile phones). If you're shy or don't like parties, still go to the ones you're invited to by your publisher. You never know what that chance meeting with that rather scruffy bloke by the chilli dips might lead to. He could end up turning your book into a 24-part television series.

Oh, and one last thing: never admit that, secretly, you enjoy writing so much that you'd happily be published for nothing. Ooops. Me and my big mouth!

Agented or agentless, good luck.

Philip Ardagh has been a full-time writer for over 12 years. His non-fiction includes *The Truth About Christmas*; whilst his novels comprise the very silly *Eddie Dickens* adventures, now in 25 different languages and being developed by Warner Bros. for a proposed series of films. *The Fall of Fergal*, the first of his *Unlikely Exploits*, has been serialised on Radio 4. He is currently collaborating with Sir Paul McCartney and Geoff Dunbar on the children's book *High in the Clouds*.

See also...

- *How to get an agent*, page 121
- *Out of the slush pile*, page 72
- *The amazing picture book story*, page 145

Children's literary agents UK and Ireland

*Full member of the Association of Authors' Agents

The Agency (London) Ltd*

24 Pottery Lane, London W11 4LZ
tel 020-7727 1346 *fax* 020-7727 9037
email info@theagency.co.uk
Executives Stephen Durbridge, Leah Schmidt, Sebastian Born, Julia Kreitman, Bethan Evans, Hilary Delamere (children's books), Katie Haines, Ligeia Marsh, Faye Webber, Nick Quinn

Novelty books, picture books, fiction for 5–8 and 9–12 year-olds, teenage fiction and series fiction (home 10%). All adult writers for theatre, film, TV and radio. No unsolicited MSS. No reading fee. Will suggest revision. Works in conjunction with agents in USA and overseas.

Children's authors include Neil Arksey, Steve Barlow and Steve Skidmore, Elisabeth Beresford, Malorie Blackman, Michael Bond, Tony Bradman, Janet Burchett and Sara Vogler, Simon Cheshire, Terrance Dicks, Fiona Dunbar, Joyce Dunbar, Alan Durant, Heather Dyer, Jim Eldridge, Paeony Lewis, Karen McCombie, Beverley Naidoo, Andrew Norriss, Amanda Swift, Bob Wilson, David Henry, Wilson, Estate of Mabel Lucie Attwell and Estate of Barbara Sleigh.

Children's author/illustrators include Ian Beck, Richard Brassey, Raymond Briggs, Martin Chatterton, Helen Cooper, Ted Dewan, Deborah Fajerman, Caroline Glicksman, Mini Grey, Penny Ives, Lara Jones, Moira Kemp, Lydia Monks, Hilda Offen, Ant Parker, Guy Parker-Rees, Graham Rawle, Lucy Su and Steve Webb. *Paper engineers* include Nick Denchfield and Maggie Bateson. Founded 1995.

Gillon Aitken Associates Ltd*

18-21 Cavaye Place, London SW10 9PT
tel 020-7373 8672 *fax* 020-7373 6002
email reception@gillonaitken.co.uk
Director Clare Alexander, *Agent* Kate Shaw

Children's fiction (home 10–15%, overseas 20%). Handles fiction for 5–8 and 9–12 year-olds and teenage fiction. Also handles adult fiction and non-fiction; 15% of list is for the children's market. Send preliminary letter with a short synopsis and 3–5 sample chapters with a sae. No reading fee. Will suggest revision.

Children's authors include Helen Fox, Manjula Padma and Louise Rennison. Founded 1977.

Darley Anderson Literary, TV and Film Agency*

Estelle House, 11 Eustace Road, London SW6 1JB
tel 020-7385 6652 *fax* 020-7386 5571
email enquiries@darleyanderson.com
website www.darleyanderson.com
Contacts Darley Anderson, Lucie Whitehouse (foreign rights), Elizabeth Wright (women's fiction, thrillers and crime), Julia Churchill (non-fiction and children's books), Rosi Bridge (finance)

Commercial fiction and non-fiction; children's fiction; selected scripts for film and TV (home 15%, USA/translation 20%, film/TV/radio 20%). No poetry or academic books.

Send preliminary letter, synopsis and first 3 chapters. Return postage/sae essential for reply. Disk and emailed submissions cannot be considered. Overseas associates: APA Talent & Literary Agency (LA/Hollywood), Liza Dawson Literary Agency (New York) and 21 leading foreign agents worldwide.

Author Literary Agents

53 Talbot Road, London N6 4QX
tel 020-8341 0442 *mobile* (07989) 318245
email agile@authors.co.uk
Contact John Havergal

Send half–one-page outline, plus first chapter/scene/section only for initial appraisal (home 15%, overseas/ translations 25%). Sae essential for reply. No reading fee. Also thought-through game, toy, animation, picture, graphics and children's concepts, for book and screen (25% + VAT). Founded 1997.

Felicity Bryan*

2A North Parade, Banbury Road, Oxford OX2 6LX
tel (01865) 513816 *fax* (01865) 310055

Fiction for children aged 8–14, and adult fiction and general non-fiction (home 10%, overseas 20%). Translation rights handled by Andrew Nurnberg Associates; works in conjunction with US agents. No unsolicited submissions.

Children's authors include Julie Hearne, Liz Kessler, Katherine Langrish, Meg Rosoff.

Celia Catchpole

56 Gilpin Avenue, London SW14 8QY
tel 020-8255 7200 *fax* 020-8288 0653
website www.celiacatchpole.co.uk

Specialises exclusively as agent for children's writers and illustrators (home 10%, overseas 20%). Handles picture books and fiction to age 12. No reading fee. Will suggest revision. Founded 1996.

Conville & Walsh Ltd*

118–120 Wardour Street, London W1V 3LA
tel 020-7287 3030 *fax* 020-7287 4545

email firstname@convilleandwalsh.com
Directors Clare Conville, Patrick Walsh, Peter Tallack

Picture books, fiction for 5–8 and 9–12 year-olds, teenage fiction, series fiction and film/TV tie-ins (home 10–15%, overseas 20%). Also handles adult literary and commercial fiction and non-fiction. No reading fee.

Children's authors include John Burningham, Kate Cann, P.J. Lynch, Jacqui Murhall, Nicky Singer. Founded 2000.

Curtis Brown Group Ltd*

Haymarket House, 28–29 Haymarket, London SW1Y 4SP
tel 020-7396 6600 *fax* 020-7396 0110
email cb@curtisbrown.co.uk
Chairman Paul Scherer, *Group Managing Director* Jonathan Lloyd, *Financial Director* Mark Collingbourne, *Australia: Managing Director* Fiona Inglis, *Books London* Jonathan Lloyd, Anna Davis, Jonny Geller, Hannah Griffiths, Ali Gunn, Camilla Hornby, Anthea Morton-Saner, Peter Robinson, Vivienne Schuster, Janice Swanson (children's), John Saddler

Agents for the negotiation in all markets of novels, general non-fiction, children's books (home 10%, overseas 20%) and associated rights (including multimedia), as well as film, theatre, TV and radio scripts. Outline for non-fiction and short synopsis for fiction with 2–3 sample chapters and autobiographical note. No reading fee. Return postage essential. Also represents directors, designers and presenters. Return postage essential. Founded 1899.

Eddison Pearson Ltd

10 Corinne Road, London N19 5EY
tel 020-7700 7763 *fax* 020-7700 7866
email info@eddisonpearson.com
Contact Clare Pearson

Children's books and scripts, literary fiction and non-fiction, poetry (home 10%, overseas 15%). No unsolicited MSS. Enquire by letter enclosing brief writing sample and sae. Email enquiries welcome but no email submissions please. No reading fee. May suggest revision where appropriate.

Authors include Valerie Bloom, Sue Heap, Sally Lloyd-Jones, Robert Muchamore, Mary Murphy, Ruth Symes.

Fraser Ross Associates

6 Wellington Place, Edinburgh EH6 7EQ
tel/fax 0131-553 2759, 0131-657 4412
email lindsey.fraser@tiscali.co.uk, kjross@tiscali.co.uk
Partners Lindsey Fraser, Kathryn Ross

Writing and illustration for children's books, but not exclusively (home 10%). No reading fee. Will suggest revision, depending on individual submission. Founded 2002.

Futerman, Rose & Associates*

Heston Court Business Park, 19 Camp Road, London SW19 4UW
tel 020-8947 0188 *fax* 020-8605 2162
email guy@futermanrose.co.uk
website www.futermanrose.co.uk
Contact Guy Rose

Children's books and animation. Also scripts for film and TV; commercial fiction and non-fiction with film potential, biography, show business (15–20%). No unsolicited MSS, science fiction or fantasy. Send preliminary letter with a brief résumé, detailed synopsis and sae. Overseas associates.

Children's clients include Terry Candy, Michael Walker, Ian Osbourne, Toyah Wilcox. Founded 1984.

Annette Green Authors' Agency*

1 East Cliff Road, Tunbridge Wells, Kent TN4 9AD
tel (01892) 514275 *fax* (01892) 518124
email annettekgreen@aol.com
website www.annettegreenagency.co.uk
Partners Annette Green, David Smith

Full-length MSS (home 15%, overseas 20%). Literary and general fiction and non-fiction, popular culture, history, science, teenage fiction. No dramatic scripts, poetry, science fiction or fantasy. No reading fee. Preliminary letter, synopsis, sample chapter and sae essential.

Children's authors include Julia Bell, Meg Cabot, Mary Hogan. Founded 1998.

Greene & Heaton Ltd*

37 Goldhawk Road, London W12 8QQ
tel 020-8749 0315 *fax* 020-8749 0318
website www.greeneheaton.co.uk
Contacts Carol Heaton, Judith Murray, Antony Topping, Linda Davis (children's)

Children's fiction and non-fiction (home/overseas 10–15%). Handles picture books, fiction for 5–8 and 9–12 year-olds, teenage fiction, series fiction, poetry and non-fiction. Also handles adult fiction and non-fiction. Send a covering letter, synopsis and the first 50pp (or less) with an sae and return postage. Email enquiries will be answered but submission attached to emails will not be considered.

Children's authors include Helen Craig. Founded 1963.

Marianne Gunn O'Connor Literary Agency

Morrison Chambers, Suite 17, 32 Nassau Street, Dublin 2, Republic of Ireland
email mariannegunn@eircom.net
Contact Marianne Gunn

Non-commercial and literary fiction, non-fiction – biography, Mind, Body & Spirit, health, children's fiction (UK 15%, overseas 20%, film/TV 20%). No reading fee.

Antony Harwood Ltd

103 Walton Street, Oxford OX2 6EB
tel (01865) 559615 *fax* (01865) 310660
email mail@antonyharwood.com
Contacts Antony Harwood, James Macdonald Lockhart

General and genre fiction; general non-fiction (home 15%, overseas 20%). Will suggest revision. No reading fee.

Children's authors include Garth Nix. Founded 2000.

A.M. Heath & Co. Ltd*

79 St Martin's Lane, London WC2N 4RE
tel 020-7836 4271 *fax* 020-7497 2561
website www.amheath.com
Directors William Hamilton (managing), Sara Fisher, Sarah Molloy, Victoria Hobbs

Fiction and non-fiction from age 5 to young adult (home 10–15%, USA 20%, translation 20%). Handles picture books, fiction for 5–8 and 9–12 year-olds, teenage fiction, series fiction, film/TV tie-ins and non-fiction. Also handles adult literary and commercial fiction and non-fiction; 20% of list is for the children's market. Submit synopsis and sample chapters. No reading fee. Will suggest revision. Overseas associates in USA, Europe, South America, Japan and the Far East.

Children's authors include Joan Aiken, Nicholas Allan, Helen Cresswell, Nick Gifford, Joanna Nadin, Susan Price, Maggie Prince, John Singleton, Rose Wilking, Leslie Wilson, Estate of Noel Streatfeild. Founded 1919.

David Higham Associates Ltd*

5–8 Lower John Street, Golden Square, London W1F 9HA
tel 020-7434 5900 *fax* 020-7437 1072
email dha@davidhigham.co.uk
website www.davidhigham.co.uk
Managing Director Anthony Goff, *Books* Veronique Baxter, Anthony Goff, Bruce Hunter, Jacqueline Korn, Lizzy Kremer, Caroline Walsh, *Foreign Rights* Ania Corless, *Film/TV/Theatre* Gemma Hirst, Nicky Lund, Georgina Ruffhead

Children's fiction, picture books and non-fiction (home 15%, USA/translation 20%). Handles novelty books, picture books, fiction for 5–8 and 9–12 year-olds, teenage fiction, series fiction, poetry, plays, film/TV tie-ins, non-fiction, audio and CD-Roms. Also handles adult fiction, general non-fiction, plays, film and TV scripts; 35% of list is for the children's market. Submit synopsis and 2–3 sample chapters with a covering letter. For picture books, send complete MS, CV and sae. Address all children's submissions to Lucy Firth. No reading fee. Represented in all foreign markets.

Also represents 21 illustrators for children's book publishing (home 15%). Submit colour copies of artwork by post or via email. Include samples that show children 'in action' and animals.

Clients (children's market) include Jenny Alexander, Caroline Anstey, Elizabeth Arnold, Antonia Barber, Julie Bertagna, Tim Bowler, Henrietta Branford, Charles Causely, Kathryn Cave, Catherine Charley, Lauren Child, David Clement-Davies, Peter Collington, W.J. Corbett, Anne Cottringer, Cressida Cowell, Berlie Doherty, Ruth Dowley, Jonathan Emmett, Jan Fearley, Anne Fine, Susan Gates, Jamila Gavin, Hannah Giffard, Kes Gray, Ann Halam, Carol Hedges, Peter Hepplewhite, Meredith, Hooper, Julia Jarman, Brenda Jobling, Richard Kidd, Clive King, Bert Kitchen, Rebecca Lisle, Geraldine McCaughrean, Richard MacSween, Jan Mark, Simon Mason, James Mayhew, William Mayne, Pratima Mitchell, Tony Mitton, Nicola Moon, Bel Mooney, Michael Morpurgo, Jan Needle, Jenny Nimmo, Martine Oborne, June Oldham, David Pelham, Liz Pichon, Tamora Pierce, Gina Pollinger, Chris Powling, Gwyneth Rees, Adrian Reynolds, Georgie Ripper, Catherine Robinson, Jenny Samuels, Carolyn Sloan, Emily Smith, Jane Stemp, Jeremy Strong, Alan Temperley, Frances Thomas, Theresa Tomlinson, Neil Tonge, Caroline Uff, Martin Waddell, Nick Warburton, Gina Wilson, Jacqueline Wilson, David Wojtowycz and Philip Wooderson. Founded 1935.

The Inspira Group

5 Bradley Road, London EN3 6ES
tel 020-8292 5163 *fax* (0870) 139 3057
email darin@theinspiragroup.com
website www.theinspiragroup.com
Managing Director Darin Jewell

Humour, lifestyle, fiction and children's (home 15%, overseas 15%). No reading fee. Will suggest revision. Founded 2001.

Johnson & Alcock*

Clerkenwell House, 45–47 Clerkenwell Green, London EC1R 0HT
tel 020-7251 0125 *fax* 020-7251 2172
email info@johnsonandalcock.co.uk
Contacts Michael Alcock, Andrew Hewson, Anna Power, Merel Reinink

Full-length MSS (home 15%, US and translation 20%). Literary and commercial fiction, children's fiction; general non-fiction including current affairs, biography and memoirs, history, lifestyle, health and personal development. No poetry, screenplays, science fiction, technical or academic material. No unsolicited MSS; approach by letter in the first instance giving details of writing and other media experience, plus synopsis. For fiction send one-page synopsis and first 3 chapters. Sae esssential for response. No reading fee. Founded 1956.

Juvenilia

Avington, Winchester, Hants SO21 1DB
tel (01962) 779656 *fax* (01962) 779656
email juvenilia@clara.co.uk
Contact Rosemary Bromley

Full-length MSS for the children's market, fiction and non-fiction (home 10%, overseas from 15%), illustration (10%), performance rights (10%). Short stories only if specifically for picture books, radio or TV. No unsolicited MSS; preliminary letter with sae and full details essential. Postage for acknowledgement and return of material imperative. No fax, telephone or email enquiries. Founded 1973.

LAW Ltd*

14 Vernon Street,
London W14 0RJ
tel 020-7471 7900 *fax* 020-7471 7910
email firstname@lawagency.co.uk
Contacts Mark Lucas (adult), Julian Alexander (adult), Araminta Whitley (adult), Philippa Milnes-Smith (children's)

Children's books (home 15%, overseas 20%). Handles novelty books, picture books, fiction for 5–8 and 9–12 year-olds, teenage fiction, series fiction, film/TV tie-ins, poetry, non-fiction, reference and audio. Also handles adult commercial and literary fiction and non-fiction; 20–25% of list is for the children's market. Send brief covering letter, short synopsis and 2–3 sample chapters. For picture books, send complete text and/or copies of sample artwork. Do *not* send original artwork. Sae essential. No email submissions. Overseas associates worldwide. Founded 1996.

The Christopher Little Literary Agency*

10 Eel Brook Studios, 125 Moore Park Road,
London SW6 4PS
tel 020-7736 4455 *fax* 020-7736 4490
email info@christopherlittle.net
website www.christopherlittle.net
Contact Christopher Little

Fiction for 9–12 year-olds and teenage fiction (home 15%, overseas 20%); no illustrated children's or short stories. Also handles adult fiction and non-fiction. Send synopsis and first 3 chapters with an sae. No reading fee.

Children's authors include J.K. Rowling and Darren Shan. Founded 1979.

London Independent Books

26 Chalcot Crescent, London NW1 8YD
tel 020-7706 0486 *fax* 020-7724 3122
Proprietor Carolyn Whitaker

Specialises in teenage fiction (home 10–15%, overseas 20%). Handles fiction for 9–12 year-olds, teenage fiction and non-fiction. Also handles adult fiction, show business and travel; approx. one-third of list is for the children's market. Submit 2 chapters and a synopsis with return postage. No reading fee. Will suggest revision of promising MSS.

Authors include Simon Chapman, Chris Wooding. Founded 1971.

Jennifer Luithlen Agency

88 Holmfield Road, Leicester LE2 1SB
tel 0116-273 8863 *fax* 0116-273 5697
Agents Jennifer Luithlen, Penny Luithlen

Not looking for new clients. Children's books; adult fiction: crime, historical, saga (home 10%, overseas 20%), performance rights (15%). Founded 1986.

Frances McKay Illustration – see Illustrators' agents

Eunice McMullen Children's Literary Agent Ltd

Low Ibbotsholme Cottage, Off Bridge Lane,
Troutbeck Bridge, Windermere,
Cumbria LA23 1HU
tel (01539) 448551 *fax* (01539) 442289
email eunicemcmullen@totalise.co.uk
Director Eunice McMullen

Specialises exclusively in children's books, especially picture books (home 10%, overseas 15%). Handles novelty books, picture books, fiction for 5–8 and 9–12 year-olds, teenage fiction, series fiction and audio. No unsolicited scripts. Telephone enquiries only. No reading fee.

Authors include Wayne Anderson, Sam Childs, Caroline Jane Church, Jason Cockcroft, Ross Collins, Charles Fuge, Maggie Kneen, David Melling, Angela McAllister, Angie Sage and Susan Winter. Founded 1992.

Andrew Mann Ltd*

1 Old Compton Street, London W1D 5JA
tel 020-7734 4751 *fax* 020-7287 9264
email manuscript@onetel.net.uk
Contacts Anne Dewe, Tina Betts, Sacha Elliot

Children's fiction and non-fiction (home 15%, overseas 20%). Handles picture books, fiction for 5–8 and 9–12 year-olds, teenage fiction, series fiction, film/TV tie-ins and non-fiction. Also handles adult scripts for TV, cinema, radio and theatre; 20% of list is for the children's market. Submit synopsis and first 20pp plus a sae. No email submissions. No reading fee. Will suggest revision. Founded 1968.

Children's authors include Gina Douthwaite, Joe Hackett, Judith Heneghan, Shirley Isherwood, Kate Lennard and Jude Wisdom.

Sarah Manson Literary Agent

6 Totnes Walk, London N2 0AD
tel 020-8442 0396
email submissions@smliteraryagent.com
Proprietor Sarah Manson

Specialises exclusively in fiction for children and young adults (home 10%, overseas 20%). Send letter, brief author biography, one-page synopsis, first 3 chapters with sae. Or send brief email enquiry with no attachment. Founded 2002.

Marjacq Scripts

34 Devonshire Place, London W1G 6JW
tel 020-7935 9499 *fax* 020-7935 9115
email enquiries@marjacq.com
website www.marjacq.com
Contact Philip Patterson (books), Luke Speed (film/TV)

All full-length MSS (home 10%, overseas 20%), including commercial and literary fiction and non-fiction, crime, thrillers, commercial, women's fiction, children's, science fiction, history, biography, sport, travel, health. No poetry. Send first 3 chapters with synopsis. May suggest revision. Film and TV rights, screenplays, radio plays, documentaries, screenplays/radio plays: send full script with 1–2 page short synopsis/outline. Strong interest in writer/directors: send show reel with script. Also looking for documentary concepts and will accept propoals from writer/directors. Sae essential for return of submissions. Founded 1974.

Martinez Literary Agency

60 Oakwood Avenue, London N14 6QL
tel 020-8886 5829
Contacts Françoise Budd, Mary Martinez

Fiction, children's books, arts and crafts, interior design, autobiographies, popular music, sport and memorabilia (home 15%; USA, overseas and translation 20%; performance rights 20%). Not accepting any new writers. Founded 1988.

William Morris Agency (UK) Ltd*

52–53 Poland Street, London W1F 7LX
tel 020-7534 6800 *fax* 020-7534 6900
website www.wma.com
Managing Director Stephanie Cabot

Worldwide theatrical and literary agency with offices in New York, Beverly Hills, Nashville and Miami. Handles film and TV scripts, TV formats; fiction and general non-fiction (film/TV 10%, UK books 15%, USA books and translation 20%). No unsolicited material; MSS only when preceded by letter. No reading fee. London office founded 1965.

Maggie Noach Literary Agency*

22 Dorville Crescent, London W6 0HJ
tel 020-8748 2926 *fax* 020-8748 8057
email m-noach@dircon.co.uk

Fiction for 9–12 year-olds and teenage fiction (home 15%, USA 20%). Also handles adult fiction; approx. one-third of list is for the children's market. Send letter plus synopsis and 3 chapters. Will not accept submissions by email or fax but initial enquiry may be made by email.

Children's authors include David Almond, Anthony Horowitz, Graham Marks, Linda Newbery, Katherine Roberts, Jean Ure. Founded 1992.

PFD*

Drury House, 34–43 Russell Street, London WC2B 5HA
tel 020-7344 1000 *fax* 020-7836 9539
email postmaster@pfd.co.uk
website www.pfd.co.uk
Joint Chairmen Anthony Jones and Tim Corrie, *Managing Director* Anthony Baring, *Books* Caroline Dawnay, Michael Sissons, Pat Kavanagh, Charles Walker, Rosemary Canter (children's), Rosemary Scoular, Robert Kirby, Simon Trewin, James Gill, *Serial* Pat Kavanagh, Carol Macarthur, *Film/TV* Tim Corrie, Anthony Jones, Norman North, Charles Walker, St John Donald, Natasha Galloway, Louisa Thompson, Jago Irwin, Lynda Mamy, *Actors* Maureen Vincent, Dallas Smith, Lindy King, Ruth Cooper, Ruth Young, Lucy Brazier, Kathryn Fleming, Duncan Hayes, *Theatre* Kenneth Ewing, St John Donald, Nicki Stoddart, Rosie Cobbe, *Children's* Rosemary Canter, *New Media* Rosemary Scoular, *Translation Rights* Intercontinental Literary Agency, *US Illustrators' Representation* Harriet Kasak, *PFD New York* Zoë Pagnamenta, Mark Reiter

Handles the full range of books including fiction, children's and non-fiction as well as scripts for film, theatre, radio and TV, actors and multimedia projects (home 10%; USA and translation 20%). Has 75 years of international experience in all media. Send a full outline for non-fiction and short synopsis for fiction with 2–3 sample chapters and autobiographical note. Screenplays/TV scripts should be addressed to the 'Film & Script Dept'. The Children's Dept accepts unsolicited written material in the form of a covering letter, brief plot summary and 3 chapters of text; submissions from illustrators are also welcome. Material submitted on an exclusive basis preferred; in any event it should be disclosed if material is being submitted to other agencies or publishers. Return postage essential. No reading fee. No guaranteed response to submissions by email. See website for detailed submissions guidelines.

Pollinger Ltd*

9 Staple Inn, Holborn, London WC1V 7QH
tel 020-7404 0342 *fax* 020-7242 5737
email info@pollingerltd.com
website www.pollingerltd.com
Chairman Paul Woolf, *Managing Director* Lesley Pollinger, *Rights Manager* Katy Loffman, *Consultants* Gerald Leigh Pollinger, Joan Deitch

All types of general trade adult and children's fiction and non-fiction books; intellectual property developments, illustrators/photographers (home 15%, translation 20%). Overseas, media and theatrical associates. No unsolicted material.

Children's clients include Bridget Crowley, Catherine Fisher, Phillip Gross, Frances Hendry, Catherine Johnson, Kelly McKain, Sue Mongredien. Founded 2002.

The Lisa Richards Agency

46 Upper Baggot Street, Dublin 4, Republic of Ireland
tel (01) 660 3534 *fax* (01) 660 3545
email fogrady@eircom.net
Contact Faith O'Grady

Fiction and general non-fiction (home 10%, UK 15%, US and translation 20%, Film and TV 15%). Approach with proposal and sample chapter for non-fiction, and 3–4 sample chapters and synopsis for fiction (sae essential). Translation rights handled by the Marsh Agency Ltd. No reading fee. Founded 1998.

Rogers, Coleridge & White Ltd*

20 Powis Mews, London W11 1JN
tel 020-7221 3717 *fax* 020-7229 9084
Directors Deborah Rogers, Gill Coleridge, Patricia White (USA, children's), David Miller, Laurence Laluyaux, *Consultant* Ann Warnford-Davis

Children's fiction and non-fiction (home 10%, USA 15–20%). Handles novelty books, picture books, fiction for 5–8 and 9–12 year-olds, teenage fiction, series fiction, non-fiction and reference. Also handles adult MSS. No unsolicited MSS. No submissions by fax or email. No reading fee. Will suggest revision.

Children's authors include Mary Hoffman, Valerie Mendes, Karen Wallace. Founded 1967.

Elizabeth Roy Literary Agency

White Cottage, Greatford, Nr Stamford, Lincs. PE9 4PR
tel (01778) 560672 *fax* (01778) 560672

Children's fiction and non-fiction – writers and illustrators (home 10–15%, overseas 20%). Send preliminary letter, synopsis and sample chapters with names of publishers and agents previously contacted. Return postage essential. No reading fee. Founded 1990.

Uli Rushby-Smith Literary Agency

72 Plimsoll Road, London N4 2EE
tel 020-7354 2718 *fax* 020-7354 2718
Director Uli Rushby-Smith

Fiction and non-fiction, literary and commercial (home 15%, USA/foreign 20%). No poetry, plays or film scripts. Send outline, sample chapters (no disks) and return postage. No reading fee. UK representatives of Curtis Brown Ltd, New York (children's books) and Penguin Canada, Penguin South Africa, Columbia University Press (USA), Alice Toledo Agency (Netherlands). Founded 1993.

Rosemary Sandberg Ltd

6 Bayley Street, London WC1B 3HB
tel 020-7304 4110 *fax* 020-7304 4109
Directors Rosemary Sandberg, Ed Victor

Children's writers and illustrators, general fiction and non-fiction. Absolutely no unsolicited MSS: client list is full. Founded 1991.

Caroline Sheldon Literary Agency*

London office 71 Hillgate Place, London W8 7SS
tel 020-7727 9102
mailing address for MSS Thorley Manor Farm, Thorley, Yarmouth, Isle of Wight PO41 0SJ
tel (01983) 760205
Proprietor Caroline Sheldon

Specialises in full-length children's novels, picture books and authors and artists with a substantial body of work (home 10%, overseas 20%). Handles novelty books, picture books, fiction for 5–8 and 9–12 year-olds, teenage fiction and series fiction. Also handles adult general and women's fiction; 50% of list is for the children's market. Submit first 3 chapters of a novel with a synopsis or photocopies of illustration work. Always enclose with material an intelligent letter of introduction and an sae. No reading fee. Will suggest revision. Founded 1985.

Dorie Simmonds Agency

67 Upper Berkley Street, London W1H 7QZ
tel 020-7486 9228 *fax* 020-7486 8228
email dhsimmonds@aol.com
Contact Dorie Simmonds

Children's books, general non-fiction – particularly historical biographies – commercial fiction and associated rights (UK and USA 15%; translation 20%). No reading fee but sae required. For non-fiction send an outline; for fiction send a short synopsis, 2–3 sample chapters and a CV.

Abner Stein*

10 Roland Gardens, London SW7 3PH
tel 020-7373 0456 *fax* 020-7370 6316
Contacts Abner Stein, Arabella Stein

Full-length and short MSS (home 10%, overseas 20%). No reading fee, but no unsolicited MSS; preliminary letter and return postage required.

United Authors Ltd

11–15 Betterton Street, London WC2H 9BP
tel 020-7470 8886 *fax* 020-7470 8887
email editorial@unitedauthors.co.uk

Fiction, non-fiction, children's, biography, travel. Full-length MSS (home 12%, overseas 15%), short MSS (12%/20%), film and radio (15%/20%), TV (15%/15%). Will suggest revision.

Ed Victor Ltd*

6 Bayley Street, Bedford Square,
London WC1B 3HE
tel 020-7304 4100 *fax* 020-7304 4111
email sophie@edvictor.com
Executive Chairman Ed Victor, *Joint Managing Directors* Sophie Hicks, Margaret Phillips, *Directors* Carol Ryan, Graham C. Greene CBE, Leon Morgan, Hitesh Shah, *Editorial Director* Philippa Harrison

Children's picture books, fiction for 5–8 and 9–12 year-olds, teenage fiction, series fiction, film/TV tie-ins, non-fiction and audio (home 10%, overseas 20%). No short stories or poetry. Also handles adult fiction and non-fiction. Submit sample chapters with a covering letter. No reading fee.

Children's authors include Mary Arrigan, Herbie Brennan, Eoin Colfer, David Lee Stone and Kate Thompson. Founded 1976.

Watson, Little Ltd*

Capo Di Monte, Windmill Hill, London NW3 6RJ
tel 020-7431 0770 *fax* 020-7431 7225
email enquiries@watsonlittle.com
Directors Sheila Watson (children's), Amanda Little, Sugra Zaman

Adult and children's fiction and non-fiction (home 15%, translation 19%, film/video/TV 10%). Fiction: commercial women's, crime and literary. Non-fiction special interests: history, science, popular psychology, self-help, business and general leisure books. No short stories, TV/play/film scripts or poetry. Not interested in exclusively academic writers. Send informative preliminary letter and synopsis with return postage. No unsolicited MSS. No reading fee. Works in conjunction with worldwide agents. Film and TV associates: the Sharland Organisation Ltd and Hurley Lowe Management.

Children's authors include Stephen Biesty, Margaret Mahy and Lynne Reid Banks.

A.P. Watt Ltd*

20 John Street, London WC1N 2DR
tel 020-7405 6774 *fax* 020-7831 2154 (books), 020-7430 1952 (drama)
email apw@apwatt.co.uk
website www.apwatt.co.uk
Directors Caradoc King, Linda Shaughnessy, Derek Johns, Georgia Garrett, Nick Harris, Natasha Fairweather, Shelia Crowley

Adults' and children's full-length MSS; dramatic works for all media (home 10%, USA and foreign 20% including commission to foreign agent). No poetry. No reading fee. No unsolicited MSS.

Authors include Zizou Corder, Grace Dent, Helen Dunmore, Sarah Harrison, Philip Kerr, Dick King-Smith, Jill Murphy, Philip Pullman, Philip Ridley. Founded 1875.

Eve White

Irish Hill House, Hamstead Marshall,
Newbury RG20 0JB
tel (01488) 657656
email evewhite@btinternet.com
Contact Eve White

Children's fiction and picture books (home 15%, overseas 20%). Handles picture books, fiction for 5–8 and 9–12 year-olds, teenage fiction and film/TV tie-ins. Also handles adult commercial and literary fiction and non-fiction; 70% of list is for the children's market. Send synopsis and sample page with a covering letter and biography. Include email address. No submissions by email. No reading fee. Will suggest revision where appropriate.

Children's authors include Deanne Ashman, Peter J. Murray and Diana Raffle. Founded 2003.

Children's literary agents overseas

Before submitting material, writers are advised to send a preliminary letter with an sase or IRC (International Reply Coupon) and to ascertain terms.

*Member of the Association of Authors' Representatives

USA

Maria Carvainis Agency Inc.*

1350 Avenue of the Americas, Suite 2905, New York, NY 10019
tel 212-245-6365 *fax* 212-245-7196
President Maria Carvainis, *Executive Vice President* Frances Kuffel

Adult fiction and non-fiction (home 15%, overseas 20%). Fiction: all categories except science fiction and fantasy, especially literary and mainstream; mystery, thrillers and suspense; historical, Regency, contemporary women's, young adult. Non-fiction: politics and film history, biography and memoir, medicine and women's issues; business, finance, psychology, popular science. Works in conjunction with foreign, TV and movie agents. No reading fee. Query first; no unsolicited MSS. No queries by fax or email.

Curtis Brown Ltd*

10 Astor Place, New York, NY 10003
tel 212-473-5400
Branch office 1750 Montgomery Street, San Francisco, CA 94111
tel 415-954-8566
President Peter Ginsberg, *Ceo* Timothy Knowlton
Contact Query Department

Fiction and non-fiction, juvenile, film and TV rights. No unsolicited MSS; query first with sase. No reading fee; no handling fees.

Dunham Literary, Inc.*

156 Fifth Avenue, Suite 625, New York, NY 10010-7002
website www.dunhamlit.com
Contact Jennie Dunham

Children's books (home 15%, overseas 20%). Handles picture books, fiction for 5–8 and 9–12 year-olds and teenage fiction. Also handles adult literary fiction and non-fiction; 50% of list is for the children's market. Send query letter in first instance by post, not by fax or email. Do not send full MS. No reading fee. Will suggest revision. Founded 2000.

Dystel & Goderich Literary Management*

One Union Square West, New York, NY 10003
tel 212-627-9100 *fax* 212-627-9313
website www.dystel.com
Contacts Jane D. Dystel, Miriam Goderich, Stacey Glick, Michael Bourret, Jim McCarthy, Jessica Papin

Children's fiction and non-fiction (home 15%, overseas 19%). Handles picture books, fiction for 5–8 and 9–12 year-olds, teenage fiction, series fiction and non-fiction. Looking for quality young adult fiction. Also handles adult fiction and non-fiction. Send a query letter with a synopsis and up to 50pp of sample MS. No reading fee. Will suggest revision.

Children's authors include Deb Levine, Kelly McWilliams, Soyung Pak, Anne Rockwell, Bernadette Rossetti. Founded 1994.

Peter Elek Associates/The Content Company, Inc.

5111 JFK Boulevard East, West New York, NJ 07093
tel 201-558-0323 *fax* 201-558-0307
email info@theliteraryagency.com
website www.theliteraryagency.com
Directors Peter Elek, Helene W. Elek *Submissions* Lauren Mactas

Full-length fiction/non-fiction. Illustrated adult non-fiction: style, culture, popular history, popular science, current affairs; juvenile picture books (home 15%, overseas 20%), performance rights (20%); will sometimes suggest revision. Works with overseas agents. No reading fee. Experienced in licensing for multimedia, online and off-line. Founded 1979.

Barry Goldblatt Literary Agency

320 Seventh Avenue, Apt. 266, Brooklyn, New York, NY 11215
tel 718-832-8787 *fax* 718-832-5558
email bgliterary@earthlink.net
Contact Barry Goldblatt

Specialises in young adult and middle grade fiction, but also handles picture book writers and illustrators. No non-fiction. Has a preference for quirky, offbeat work. Unsolicited MSS must be accompanied by a sase.

Ashley Grayson Literary Agency

1342 18th Street, San Pedro, CA 90732
tel 310-548-4672 *fax* 310-514-1148
email carolynadg@mac.com
Contact Ashley Grayson, Carolyn Grayson

Commercial fiction and literary fiction for adults and children. Handles foreign rights. No unsolicited MSS. Submit query letter and first 3 pages of MSS. No calls or queries. No reading fee.

Clients include Bruce Coville, J.B. Cheany, David Lubar, Christopher Pike. Established 1976.

John Hawkins & Associates Inc.*

71 West 23rd Street, Suite 1600, New York, NY 10010
tel 212-807-7040 *fax* 212-807-9555
website www.jhaliterary.com
President John Hawkins, *Vice-President* William Reiss, *Foreign Rights* Moses Cardona, *Other Agents* Warren Frazier, Anne Hawkins

Fiction, non-fiction, juvenile. No reading fee. Founded 1893.

Barbara S. Kouts, Literary Agent*

PO Box 560, Bellport, NY 11713
tel 631-286-1278 *fax* 631-286-1538

Full-length MSS. Fiction and non-fiction, children's and adult (home 15%, overseas 20%); will suggest revision. Works with overseas agents. No reading fee. Send query letter first. Founded 1980.

McIntosh & Otis Inc.*

353 Lexington Avenue, New York, NY 10016
tel 212-687-7400 *fax* 212-687-6894
Head of Children's Dept Tracey Adams

Children's fiction and non-fiction (home 15%, overseas 20%). Handles picture books, fiction for 5–8 and 9–12 year-olds, teenage fiction, series fiction, poetry and non-fiction. Also handles adult fiction and non-fiction. No unsolicited MSS for novels; query first with outline, sample chapters and sase. For picture books, send with sase. No submissions by email. No reading fee. Will suggest revision. Founded 1928.

William Morris Agency Inc.*

1325 Avenue of the Americas, New York, NY 10019
tel 212-586-5100
Executive VP Owen Laster, *Senior VPs* Jennifer Rudolph Walsh, Suzanne Gluck, Virginia Barber, Joni Evans, Mel Berger, *Agents* Manie Barron, Jay Mandel, Tracy Fisher, *Foreign Rights Director* Tracy Fisher, *Foreign Rights Coordinator* Shana Kelly, *First Serial and Audio Manager* Karen Gerwin

General fiction and non-fiction (home 15%, overseas 20%, performance rights 15%). Will suggest revision. No reading fee.

The Norma-Lewis Agency

311 West 43rd Street, Suite 602, New York, NY 10036
tel 212-664-0807
Contact Norma Liebert

Fiction for young adults. No unsolicited MSS. Query first with sase. No reading fee. No phone calls: contact by mail only. Founded 1980.

Susan Schulman Literary & Dramatic Agents Inc.*

454 West 44th Street, New York, NY 10036
tel 212-713-1633 *fax* 212-581-8830
email schulman@aol.com
2 Bryan Plaza, Washington Depot, CT 06794

Agents for negotiation in all markets (with co-agents) of fiction, general non-fiction, children's books, academic and professional works, and associated subsidiary rights including plays and film (home 15%, UK 7.5%, overseas 20%). No reading fee. Return postage required.

Wecksler-Incomco

170 West End Avenue, New York, NY 10023
tel 212-787-2239 *fax* 212-496-7035
email jacinny@aol.com
President Sally Wecksler, *Associate* Joann Amparan-Close

Children's books (home 15%, overseas 20%). Handles picture books, fiction for 5–8 and 9–12 year-olds, teenage fiction, series fiction, non-fiction and reference. Also handles adult non-fiction and some literary fiction; 40% of list is for the children's market. No reading fee. No submissions by fax or email: only hard copy will be read.

Children's authors include Diane Allison, Ellen Leroe, Marie Snyder, Richard Stein, Candace Whitman. Founded 1971.

Writers House LLC*

21 West 26th Street, New York, NY 10010
tel 212-685-2400 *fax* 212-685-1781
President Albert Zuckerman, *Executive Vice-President* Amy Berkower

Fiction and non-fiction, including all rights; film and TV rights. No screenplays or software. Send a one-page letter in the first instance, saying what's wonderful about your book, what it is about and why you are the best person to write it. No reading fee. Founded 1974.

AUSTRALIA

Altair-Australia Literary Agency

PO Box 475, Blackwood SA 5051
tel (8) 8278 8995 *fax* (8) 8278 5585
email altair-australia@altair-australia.com
Agent Robert N. Stephenson

Specialises in science fiction and fantasy; also children's literature, mainstream literature, crime and mystery and action/adventure fiction (15%–20%). Non-fiction material may be considered if queried first.

Submission details Submit the first 3 chapters (up to 15,000 words) and a 2-page synopsis for fiction/novel. Send whole MS plus reference details for non-fiction (do not include original graphics, films or photographs). Allow at least 12 weeks before querying. Founded 1997.

Australian Literary Management

2A Booth Street, Balmain, New South Wales 2041
tel (9) 818 8557 *fax* (9) 818 8569
email alpha@austlit.com
website www.austlit.com

Fiction, non-fiction, fantasy, young readers and cartoons (home 15%). Telephone first, then submit a short synopsis and 2 chapters. No reading fee. Do not email. Does not suggest revision.

Children's authors include Pamela Freeman, Chrsitine Harris, Glyn Parry-Ranulfo, Laurie Stiller. Established 1980.

Bryson Agency Australia Pty Ltd

PO Box 226, Finders Lane PO, Melbourne 8009
tel (613) 9620 9100 *fax* (613) 9621 2788
email agency@bryson.com.au
website www.bryson.com.au
Contact Fran Bryson

Represents writers operating in all media: print, film, TV, radio, the stage and electronic derivatives; specialises in representation of book writers. Unsolicited MSS must include sample first chapters (5000 words max.), a synopsis, CV and return postage. Query first before sending.

Jenny Darling & Associates

Suite 1, Level 1, 464 Toorak Road, Toorak, Victoria 3142
postal address PO Box 413, Toorak, Victoria 3142
tel (03) 9827 3883 *fax* (03) 9827 1270
email mail@jd-associates.com.au
Contact Jenny Darling, Jacinta Di Mase

Represents only a few children's authors. Open to all genres and ages. For picture books and up to end primary school, send the complete MS. For young adult, send the first 3 chapters or 50pp in the first instance. Submit material by post, including return postage.

Golvan Arts Management

PO Box 766, Kew, Australia 3101
tel (03) 9853 5341 *fax* (03) 9853 8555
website www.golvanarts.com.au
Manager & Director Debbie Golvan, *Director* Colin Golvan

Children's fiction and non-fiction (10%+GST). Handles picture books, fiction for 5–8 and 9–12 year-olds, teenage fiction, series fiction, film/TV tie-ins, non-fiction and plays; educational – primary, secondary and tertiary. Also handles adult fiction and non-fiction, plays, feature film and TV scripts, visual artists and composers; 60% of list is for the children's market. Read 'general information' section on website before sending a brief letter. No reading fee. Will suggest revision. Works with Chinese and Korean agents.

Children's authors include Bronwyn Bancroft, Vicki Bennett, Nan Bodsworth, Kim Caraher, Terry Denton, Janine Fraser, Helen Lunn, Gilly McInnes, Paty Marshall-Stace, David Miller, Sally Morgan, Kevin Nemeth, Wendy Orr, Greg Pyers, Ben Redlich, Mark Svendsen. Founded 1989.

CANADA

Melanie Colbert

17 West Street, Holland Landing, Ontario L9N 1L4
tel 905-853-2435
Contact Melanie Colbert

Children's authors and illustrators. Please send initial query; no unsolicited MSS. Established 1985.

Pamela Paul Agency

12 Westrose Avenue, Toronto, Ontario M6P 2S5
tel 416-410-4395
email ppainc@interlog.com
Contact Pamela Paul

Children's fiction only. Please send query. No unsolicited MSS. Established 1989.

Carolyn Swayze Literary Agency

WRPO Box 39588, White Rock, British Columbia V4B 5L6
tel 604-538-3478
email cswaze@direct.ca
website www.swayzeagency.com
Proprietor Carolyn Swayze

Literary and commercial fiction, some juvenile and teen books. No romance, science fiction, poetry, screenplays, or picture books. Eager to discover lively, thought-provoking narrative non-fiction, especially in the fields of science, history, travel, politics, and memoir.

Submission details No telephone calls: make contact either by post or send short queries by email, providing a brief resumé which describes who you are. Include publication credits, writing awards, education and experience relevant to your book project. Include a one-page synopsis of the book and – if querying via post – include sase for the return of your materials. Do not include original photographs or artwork. Include sase if acknowledgement of receipt of materials is required. Will not open unsolicited attachments. Allow 6 weeks or longer for a reply. Founded 1994.

Transatlantic Literary Agency

77 Glengowan Road, Toronto, Ontario MGN 1G4
tel 416-488-9214 *fax* 416-488-4531
email tla@netcom.ca
Contact David and Lynn Bennet

Specialises exclusively in children's and young adult books: fiction, non-fiction, illustrated books and picture books. No unsolicited MSS. Founded 1993.

NEW ZEALAND

Glenys Bean Writer's Agent

PO Box 60509, Titirangi, Auckland
tel (09) 812 8486 *fax* (09) 812 8188
email g.bean@clear.net.nz

Adult and children's fiction, educational, non-fiction, film, TV, radio (10–20%). Send preliminary letter, synopsis and sae. No reading fee. Represented by Sanford Greenburger Associates Ltd (USA). Translation/foreign rights: the Marsh Agency Ltd. Founded 1989.

Michael Gifkins & Associates

PO Box 6496, Wellesley Street PO, Auckland 1000
tel (09) 523-5032 *fax* (09) 5235033
email michale.gifkins@xtra.co.nz
Director Michael Gifkins

Literary and popular fiction, fine arts, children's and young adult fiction, substantial non-fiction (non-academic) co-publications (home 15%, overseas 20%). No reading fee. Will suggest revision. Founded 1985.

Richards Literary Agency

11 Channel View Road, Campbells Bay, Auckland 11
postal address PO Box 31-240, Milford, Auckland 9
tel (09) 479-5681 *fax* (09) 479-5681
email rla.richards@clear.net.nz
Partners Ray Richards, Nicki Richards Wallace

Children's fiction and non-fiction (home/overseas 15%). Handles picture books, fiction for 5–8 and 9–12 year-olds, teenage fiction, series fiction, film/TV tie-ins, non-fiction and reference; educational (primary). Also handles adult fiction and non-fiction, and film, TV and radio; approx. 50% of list is for the children's market. Concentrates on New Zealand authors. Send book proposal with an outline and biography. No reading fee.

Children's authors include Joy Cowley and Maurice Gee – the agency has approx. 50 on books. Founded 1977.

TFS Literary Agency

PO Box 29-023, Ngaio, Wellington
tel (04) 479-6746
email tfs@elsewhere.co.nz

Children's books, general fiction and non-fiction. No poetry or short stories. No reading fee. Member of the New Zealnd Association of Literary Agents (NZALA). Make initial enquiry first. No unsolicited MSS.

SOUTH AFRICA

Cherokee Literary Agency

3 Blythwood Road, Rondebosch, Cape 7700
tel (021) 671 4508
email dklee@mweb.co.za
Director D.K. Lee

Children's picture books in translation (home 10%). Founded 1988.

Illustrating for children

Eight great tips to get your picture book published

Tony Ross gives some sound advice for illustrators and writers of children's picture books.

I have always had the uncomfortable feeling that if I can get published, anyone can. A belief that being published is something that only happens to other people, holds some very good writers and illustrators back.

Assuming you have drawings – or a story – to offer, there are several ways to go about it. Probably the best way is to have a publishing house in the family! Failing that, all is not lost.

Work can be sent directly to a publisher's office. Most editors receive a good amount of unsolicited work, so be patient with them for a reply. A stamped addressed envelope for its return is always appreciated, bearing in mind that the majority of work submitted is refused. At the beginning of a career, refusal is quite normal and a great deal about yourself and your talent can be gleaned from this experience. Sometimes, advice gained at this stage can change your future.

Starting on a drawing career is an exciting time and I think it's a good idea to get yourself in perspective. Visit the library and some bookshops to look at all the styles that are around. Get a sense for what's out there: you don't want to regurgitate it, but to get a feel for the parameters. You can learn a lot, maybe more than you learned at art school, from looking at great artists such as Edward Ardizzone, E.H. Shepherd, Maurice Sendak and Chris Van Allsberg.

Great Tip No 1: Use black and white

There is great appeal in working in full colour but it's good to remember black and white. Sometimes a publisher may have a black and white project waiting for an illustrator, while all of the big interest is going into the coloured picture book list. Some of the greatest children's books are illustrated in black and white – A.A. Milne and E.H. Shepherd made one of the greatest partnerships with those tiny black ink drawings contributing so much to a great classic. Not a bad place to start, eh?

Ink drawing is simple, in the hands of a master, but not easy. That unforgiving fluid! Wonder at the uncomplicated, straightforwardness of the Pooh drawings. Consider Toad in *The Wind in the Willows*. When he applied to do the illustrations, Kenneth Graham said to Shepherd: 'I have seen many artists who can draw better than you, but you make the animals live.' Can you learn anything from that? Look at Ardizzone's ability to draw mood. He can show a summer afternoon, or a cold November morning, both using black ink. There is so much to look at, so much to learn from.

Try to include black and white work in your folder. Also include a series of perhaps 30 drawings, such as a fully illustrated story, where you show your ability to be consistent with the characters and the style, without repetition or irrelevance (like the radio programme *Just a Minute*!).

It is a duty of an illustrator to be able to read – that is to try and understand the writer's aims – and to help them rather than to inflict a totally different angle onto the book (think of the Milne and Shepherd partnership). Much of this comes down to being sensitive enough to recognise the tone of the writing, and skilful enough to draw in the same tone. So the importance of really taking an interest in the story cannot be overstressed. In the text, there will be either clues, or blatant instructions to help the drawings gel. Be very aware.

Great Tip No 2: Experiment

I have known illustrators who convinced themselves that they couldn't use black ink. Mostly this was because they were using the wrong ink, the wrong pen, and/or the wrong paper. Types of black ink vary: waterproof behaves differently from water soluble. Fine nibs and broad nibs each give a totally different result, as does an old fountain pen or a sharpened stick. Try 10 different inks, 50 different nibs, odd sticks and all the papers you can find: tracing, layout, calendered, five different cartridges, smooth and rough watercolour, handmade, wrapping paper, anything at all. It's a case of finding the combination that suits your hand and your intention. Your own genius, unrecognised at art school, could surprise you.

Many of the points I've made about black and white work also apply to colour. The marriage of image to text will be in your hands, but it must work.

Great Tip No 3: Choose the right words

I am hesitant to give advice to writers. After all, there are few rules, and the next J.K. Rowling may read this. My own view is really quite simple, and rather obvious. I write mainly for under eight year-olds, so my stories are as short as I can make them. I feel that it is good to have a magnetic first sentence, and an ending that EXPLODES WITH SURPRISE. I think that the ending is the most important part of the story. The bit in the middle should waft the reader along, remembering that the *sound* of words and sentences can be a useful tool.

I like stories to be either funny or scary. *Very* funny, or *very* scary. To be dull is the worst thing in the world! That sounds so obvious, but it gets overlooked. If you are not excited with your work, maybe nobody else will be either.

A picture book has about 23 pages of text (but this can be flexible). I think those pages should have fewer than 2000 words; 1000–1500 is good. One word per page would be great, if the one word was brilliant. As brilliant as the story. Don't be frightened of editing out surplus words. One brilliant one will work better than a dozen mundane ones.

Don't fall into the mindset that writing for children is easy. It has all the disciplines of writing for adults, with the added problem of understanding a child's mind and world. The great writers have a passport to a child's world – think of Roald Dahl. I have seen many brilliant ideas, with less than brilliant pictures, make wonderful books. I have seen a bad idea saved by wonderful illustrations. So, writing style apart, be your own concept's greatest critic. It is quite natural to be protective of your baby, of your story. But try to remember that there are a lot of good editors out there and it will be in your own interest to consider their advice. So don't be a young fogey: be flexible, listen, understand experienced points of view. This can be a good time to change for the better, and to start a relationship with one publishing house that may serve you for a lifetime.

Great Tip No 4: Choose what you draw

Don't plan huge drawing problems into your submitted roughs. They may be accepted, and the editor will expect the final art to be better than the roughs.

I illustrate my own writing. This appeals to me for all sorts of reasons, few of them noble. Firstly, I get all of the available fee or/and royalty. I don't have to let half or more go to a writer. Secondly, if there is something I don't like to draw, I don't write about it! For instance, most of my stories take place in the summer, because I prefer to handle trees with their leaves on.

Illustrations being worked on to be published is not the place to practise your drawing. *Practise, change, experiment* all the time, but not in a publishing project. Your finished illustrations must be as good as you can make them. I know an illustrator who won't draw feet, always hiding the ends of legs in grass, water, behind rocks, etc. This is okay if the text will allow; a well-drawn puddle is better than a badly drawn foot any day. It is better to think around a drawing problem, than just to go along with it.

Great Tip No 5: Experiment with your main character

Before you start, try drawing your main character (the most important visual element of the story) in all sorts of ways. A day spent doing this can be so valuable. Getting the main character right can indicate ways to proceed with the whole book.

Great Tip No 6: Think global

Remember that editors react well to stories with wide appeal, rather than minority groups. Foreign sales are in everyone's interest, so try to allow your work to travel. Rhyme is sometimes difficult to translate, as are unusual plays on words.

Great Tip No 7: Plan the whole book

Do little mock-up books for yourself to plan what text goes on which page. This helps to get the story right throughout the book. A 32-page children's book (the most common extent for a picture book) includes covers, end papers, title and half-title pages. This leaves you 23–25 pages to play with. These little mock-ups are for your own use, not to be presented as roughs, so they can be quite work-a-day.

By working out what text goes on which page you will get some sort of an idea of which illustrations go where. Just as the drawings are creative, so is their use on the page. If you use a full double-page spread, another can be expected on the next page. But imagine the effect if the next page explodes with huge typography, and tiny pictures? I am not suggesting you do this, only reminding you that pages of a book are there to be turned, and the turning can be unpredictable and adventurous. Book design is important, along with everything else.

Great Tip No 8: Persevere

So much to do, so much to remember. The main thing is, every children's illustrator and writer I know who has kept trying has got there in the end and been published. But I've also seen great talents give up far too early. Remember that rejection is normal: it's only someone's point of view. Some great books have had long hunts for a publisher. Be open to change and always bear in mind that editors have the experience that you may lack and an editor's advice is meant to help you, not choke you off. However, not all of their advice may apply in your case, so try to recognise what applies to you. When I worked in advertising, I had an art director who said: 'Half of what I say is rubbish. Trouble is, I don't know which half.'

And a reminder

Don't waste time by sending work to publishers who don't publish material like yours. Libraries and bookshops are worth exploring to familiarise yourself with which publishing houses favour what types of work. Research of this kind is time well spent.

Try to show your work in person so that you get a chance to talk, and learn. Do not, however, just drop in. Make an appointment first and hope that these busy people have some time available.

There are also agents prepared to represent new talent (see *Illustrators' agents* on page 154). Of course, an agent will charge a percentage of work sold, but my dad used to say, 'Seventy-five per cent of something is better than 100% of nothing.'

I am troubled by giving advice. I can't help thinking of the young composer who approached the slightly older Mozart and asked, 'Maestro, how should I compose a concerto?' to which Mozart replied 'You are very young, perhaps you should start with a simple tune'. The young composer frowned, and argued. 'But, Maestro, *you* composed a concerto when you were still a child!' 'Ah yes,' said Mozart, 'but I didn't have to ask how?'

Tony Ross is a renowned illustrator of international repute and the creator of such classics as *The Little Princess* and *I Want My Potty*. His first book was published in 1976 and since then he has illustrated more than 700 books including the *Dr Xargle* series, created with the author Jeanne Willis and the *Horrid Henry* series written by Francesca Simon.

See also...

- *Cartoons and deadlines*, page 199
- *The amazing picture book story*, page 145
- *Illustrating for children's books*, page 150

The amazing picture book story

Oliver Jeffers tells the story of how his first picture book came to be published.

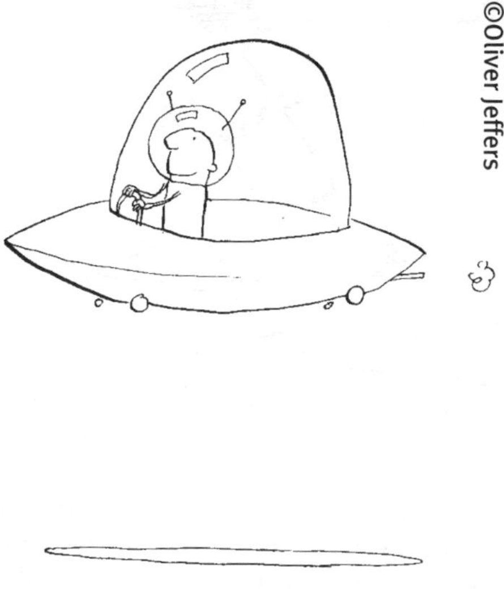
©Oliver Jeffers

In this, the 21st century, anything is possible. We drive flying cars, live in bubbles, go to the moon for our summer holidays and we can freeze and heat things instantly. People can do whatever they want, and in some cases get paid for it, even writing and illustrating children's books. And in this age of possibility, they can even be picked from the slush pile. That's what happened to me. Although I still believe I'm one of the luckiest people alive, and this article isn't much beyond bragging, hindsight and other people would suggest there is more to it than that. One thing that hasn't changed with all our technological advancements is the fundamental need for children's picture books on a number of levels. From educating enquiring young minds, and entertaining both children and adults alike at bedtime (and not just adults who have children, and not just at bedtime) to pushing the boundaries of style and content within the broader worlds of both art and literature. Children's books are art, and all true artists do what they love first and hope to make a living second. Creating a piece of work to the absolute best of an ability is an artist's priority. Getting paid is a bonus. The same goes for those who create children's books. (I bet if you were to ask someone like Tony Ross, if he wasn't getting paid to make children's books, would he do it anyway and just be poor? He'd probably say 'yes' but also have a second job working at the moon resort.)

Anyway, so back to me bragging about how I'm one of the luckiest people in the world and get to do what I love for a living. Actually, I'm going to retract that, as my first book is only just out and I have no idea whether I'm going to make any money, but I do have a contract saying that a publisher is going to publish my picture book and I'm going to tell you how that happened. The story itself is actually quite business-like and boring so I'll throw in a few creative exaggerations for effect.

The story begins

It all started when I had just defeated the Admiral of the Swiss Navy in a sword fight, and sat at the edge of the pier at the Sydney fish market for a think. I had known all along that I liked to draw pictures and I liked to write, and I had been putting the two together for a while in my paintings. I even bought and collected

©Oliver Jeffers

children's picture books both for my own enjoyment and as research for my paintings. But it wasn't until my good friend Ben suggested I attempt a children's book of my own that I seriously considered it as a direction to take my life. So, as I sat there dangling my legs off the pier, I had my first idea for a children's book, about a boy who tries to catch the reflection of a star in the water, much like the Brer Rabbit story of the *Moon and the Mill Pond*.

After a year out, I carried the idea into my final year studying Visual Communication (specialising in illustration) at the University of Ulster in Belfast in 2000, having to hold down a second job as a racecar driver to pay for my tuition. I developed self-portrait doodles to narrate my thesis that year, which eventually developed into the character used in the book. In the second half of my final year I used my picture book concept as a piece of coursework, deciding to see how far I could take it to a finished product. This involved getting the words right, and the pictures right, and more importantly, the balance between the two right.

Looking, thinking children's books

To get the words right, I read my manuscript to as many six year-olds as I could find (you'd be amazed how many there are: I reckon if they were all to jump at once something big would break, like London Bridge or at least a phone box or two), slowly tweaking the story based on the feedback I was getting. To get the pictures right I used the unending help of my older brother Rory who basically has a lot more sense than I do. And to get the balance right we both looked at hundreds of other picture books to see what everyone else had done. That was when the earthquake happened and Rory had to balance 58 books on his head to save them from falling down a crack to the molten core of the earth.

In the process of getting the balance right, I noticed a few things about how good picture books seem to work. The one that sticks out most is about how they seem to appeal across all ages without being forced. They aren't condescending, but at the same time they aren't inaccessible. There just seems to be a natural universal appeal to both children and adults – and let's face it, they need to appeal to adults, as however well a six year-old is doing, they're unlikely to stick their hand in their pocket and pull out a tenner in a bookshop!

OK, so in the second half of 2001, after I had finished developing my idea and finished my degree, and after the initial euphoria of never having to write another thesis in my life wore off, and during that slightly intimidating, 'I actually have to do something with my life now!' phase, I decided I would get my book published. I looked at what was around in the bookshops and thought that what I had created was as good as, if not better, than anything else that was out there, and confidence and self belief are important tools when you need to be self motivated. My first step was to buy the *Writers' & Artists' Yearbook* (and it's great to see this *Children's Writers' & Artists' Yearbook* out now) and I then began to look at which publisher would be lucky enough to receive my manuscript. Alright, I wasn't that confident, in fact, having worked in Waterstones for a few years and armed with a very minimal knowledge of the publishing world, I knew I was in for a long and trying road of numerous attempts contacting publishers, repeatedly saying 'have you read it yet?'

Apart from using the *Yearbook* to research which publishers I should send my idea to, I also referred to my own collection of children's picture books, the collection that would make any six year-old jealous. I looked to see who had published what, paying particular attention to my favourites, and which publishers popped up more often.

My next step was to figure out what exactly to send them. There are hundreds and thousands of unsolicited ideas that reach publishers every year and my objective was to stand out among those. To be noticed. By asking, I found that what publishers like to see in a proposal for a new book was the manuscript and a few samples of the illustrations to give a broad idea of the feel for the book. I invested a bit of money into producing 100 copies of a small spiral bound 'sample', with the manuscript at the start and 10 full-colour illustrations after, which I put into an envelope with a letter outlining who I was and what I was

©Oliver Jeffers

trying to do, and a self-addressed envelope for them to contact me. I also included a small portfolio (and I mean small, eight prints that were 14cm square each) of other examples of my paintings and illustrations in the hope that if a particular publisher didn't pick up on my book idea, at least I might be able to get a few commissions while I was waiting.

A few phone calls later and I had found out who looked after the children's division in each appropriate publishing house, and addressed my envelope to them. The point being that it would arrive at a real person's desk instead of an anonymous room that was only used for hostage situations or when they ran out of chairs. I spent a while drawing up a big chart showing which publishers I had sent an envelope to, their contact name and number, date last contacted, and room for comments. I sent an envelope to the 10 biggest publishers in the UK, and the 10 biggest in USA, figuring I'd start at the top and work my way down.

The envelopes were opened

Expecting a healthy dose of being ignored and avoided, you can perhaps imagine my surprise when, the next afternoon, as I was entertaining the Sultan of Brunei and his wonderful wife Delilah, I received a phone call from a publisher in London during the course of which they expressed their desire to publish my book. It had arrived on the desk of a young editorial assistant: she had opened it, liked what she saw, and had immediately decided to do something about it. That offer was followed a week later by one from a US publisher in New York City, where something similar happened. I forgave the US publisher for their delay, as they are geographically further away.

And it was as simple as that. I met with both publishers, and between the three of us we were able to devise a cunning plan that would enable both of them to publish the book.

Told you I was lucky, I may as well have won the lottery. But as someone wiser than me once said, 'It's all about healthy measures of luck and hard work!' or was that 'work and hard luck?' I can't remember, but the point is that I set myself an objective and was quite methodical and logical in my efforts to get there. Like most businesses, I had an idea, I developed it, then invested time, thought, and money in selling it. But if I hadn't already sold it, I'd still be trying to, and I'd still be having the same ideas for my next books, only wearing cheaper shoes, eating Weetabix for dinner, and maybe sending off an application to the moon resort too.

The end. Or rather, the beginning...

Oliver Jeffers graduated from the University of Ulster in 2001 with a First Class Honours degree in Visual Communication. He has exhibited paintings around the globe and worked as a freelance illustrator in both New York City and Sydney, Australia. His first children's picture book *How to Catch a Star* is published by HarperCollins Children's Books in the UK and by Philomel (Penguin Group) in the USA.

See also...

- *Getting started*, page 1
- *Out of the slush pile*, page 72

Illustrating for children's books

The world of children's publishing is big business. The huge range of books published each year all carry artwork. Maggie Mundy offers guidance for people who are at the start of their career in illustrating for children's books.

The portfolio

Your portfolio should reflect the best of you and your work, and should speak for itself. Keep its content simple – if too many styles are included, for instance, your work will not leave a lasting impression.

Include some artwork other than those carried out for college projects, e.g. an illustration from a timeless classic to show your abilities, and something modern which reflects your own taste and the area in which you wish to work.

If your strength is for black and white illustration, include pieces with and without tone and with or without a wash. Some publishers want line and tone and some want only line. As cross hatching and stippling can add a lot of extra time to an illustration deadline, it might be advisable to leave out these samples. If you can, include a selection of humour as it can be used effectively in educational books and elsewhere. It is best not to sign and date your work: some artworks can stand the test of time and still look good after a year or two, but if it looks dated … so is the illustrator!

An A3 portfolio is probably the ideal size. Place your best piece of artwork on the opening page and your next best piece on the last page.

Looking at the market

Start by looking thoroughly at what is being published today for children. Take your studies to branches of big retail chains, some independent bookshops, as well as your local library (a helpful librarian should be able to tell you which are the most borrowed books). Absorb the picture books, explore the novelty books, look at the variety of colour covers, and note the range of black line illustrations inside books for children and teenagers. Make a list of the publishers you think may be able to use your particular style.

By making these investigations you will gain an insight into not only the current trends and styles but also the much favoured, oft-published classic children's literature. Most importantly, it will help you identify your market.

In books for a young age range every picture must tell the story – some books have no text and the illustrations say it all. Artwork should be uncluttered, shapes clear, and colour bright. If this does not appeal to you, go up a year or two and note the extra details that are added to the artwork (which still tells the story). Children now need to see more than just clear shapes: they need extra details added to the scene – e.g. a quirky spider hanging around, or a mouse under the bed.

Children are your most critical audience: never think that you can get away with 'any old thing'. Indeed, at the Bologna Book Fair it is a panel of children which judges what they consider to be the best picture book.

Current trends

Innovative publishers are always on the lookout for something new in illustration styles: something completely different from the tried and tested. More and more they are turning to European and overseas illustrators, often sourced from the Bologna Book Fair exhibitions and illustrators catalogue.

Always strive to improve on your work. Don't be afraid to try out something different and to work it up into acceptable examples. Above all, don't get left behind.

Making approaches for work

With your portfolio arranged and your target audience in mind, compile a list of publishing houses, packagers and magazines which you think may be suitable for your work.

An agent should know exactly where to place your work, and this may be the easier option (see below). However, you may wish to market yourself by making and going to appointments until you crack your first job.

Alternatively, you could make up a simple broadsheet comprising a black and white and two or three colour illustrations, together with your contact details, and have it colour photocopied or printed. Another inexpensive option is to have your own CDs made up and to send them instead. Send a copy to either the Art Director, the Creative Director or the Senior Commissioning Editor (for picture books) of each potential client on your list. Try to find out the name of the person you would like to see your work. Wait at least a week and then follow up your mailing with a phone call to ask if someone would like to see your portfolio.

Also consider investing in your own website which you can easily update yourself.

Know your capabilities

Know your strengths, but be even more aware of your weaknesses. You will gain far more respect if you admit to not being able to draw something particularly well than by going ahead and producing an embarrassing piece of artwork and having it rejected. You will be remembered for your professional honesty and that client may well try to give you a job where you can use your expertise.

Publishers need to know that you can turn out imaginative, creative artwork while closely following a text or brief, and be able to meet their deadline. It may take an illustrator three weeks to prepare roughs for 32 pages, three weeks to finish the artwork, plus a week to make any corrections. In addition, time has to be allowed for the roughs to be returned. On this basis, how many books can an illustrator realistically take on? Scheduling is of paramount importance (see below).

You will need to become familiar with 'publishing speak' – terms such as gutters, full bleed, holding line, overlays, vignettes, tps, etc. If you don't know the meaning of a term, ask – after all, if you have only recently left college you will not be expected to know all the jargon.

In the course of your work you will have to deal with such issues as contracts, copyright, royalties, public lending rights, rejection fees, etc. The Association of Illustrators, which exists to give help to illustrators in all areas, is well worth joining.

Organising your workload

When you have reached the stage when you have jobs coming through on a fairly regular basis, organise a comprehensive schedule for yourself so you do not overburden yourself with work. Include on it when roughs have to be submitted, how much work you can fit in while waiting for their approval, the deadline for the artwork, and so on. A wall chart can be helpful for this but another system may work better for you. It is totally unacceptable to deliver artwork late. If you think that you might run over time with your work, let your client know in advance as it may be possible to reach a new agreement for delivery.

Payment

There are two ways in which an illustrator may be paid for a commission for a book: a flat fee on receipt and acceptance of the artwork, or by an advance against a royalty of future sales. The advance offered could be less than a flat fee but it may result in higher earnings overall. If the book sells well, the illustrator will receive royalty payments twice a year for as long the book is in print.

You need to know from the outset how you are going to be paid. If it is by a flat fee, you may be given an artwork order with a number to be quoted when you invoice. Always read through orders to make sure you understand the terms and conditions. If you haven't been paid within 30 days, send a statement to remind the client, or make a quick phone call to ask when you can expect to receive payment.

With a royalty offer, a contract will be drawn up and this must be checked carefully. One of the clauses will state the breakdown of how and when you will be paid.

Once you have illustrated your first book you should register with the Public Lending Right Office (see page 176) so that you can receive a yearly payment on all UK library borrowings. You will need to cooperate with the author regarding percentages before submitting your own form. The PLR office will give you a reference number, and you then submit details to them of each book you illustrate. It mounts up and is a nice little earner!

Agents

The role of the agent is to represent the illustrator to the best of their ability and to the illustrator's best advantage. A good agent knows the marketplace and will promote illustrators' work where it will count. An agent may ask you to do one or two sample pieces to strengthen your portfolio, giving them a better chance of securing work for you.

Generally speaking, agents will look after you, your work schedules, payments, contracts, royalties, copyright issues, and try to ensure you have a regular flow of work which you not only enjoy but will stretch your talents to taking on bigger and better jobs. Without exposing your weaknesses, check that you have adequate time in which to do a job and that you are paid a fair rate for the work.

Some illustrators manage well without an agent, and having one is not necessarily a pathway to fame and fortune. Choose carefully: you need to both like and trust the agent and vice versa.

Agents' charges range from 25% to 30%. Find out from the outset how much a prospective agent will charge.

Finally

Do not be downhearted if progress is at first slow. Everyone starts by serving an apprenticeship, and it is a great opportunity to learn, absorb and soak up as much of the business as possible. Ask questions, get all the advice you can, and use what you learn to improve your craft and thereby your chances of landing a job. Publishers are always on the lookout for fresh talent and new ideas, and one day your talent will be the one they want.

Maggie Mundy has been representing illustrators for children's books since 1983. Her agency represents 25 European and British illustrators for children's books.

See also...

- *Children's book publishers UK and Ireland,* page 5
- *Children's book packagers,* page 54
- *Children's literary agents UK and Ireland,* page 129
- *Illustrators' agents,* page 154

Illustrators' agents

Before submitting work, artists are advised to make preliminary enquiries and to ascertain terms of work. Commission varies but averages 25–30%. The Association of Illustrators (see page 263) provides a valuable service for illustrators, agents and clients.

*Member of the Society of Artists Agents
†Member of the Association of Illustrators

Advocate†

Advocate Gallery, 372 Old York Road,
London SW18 1SP
tel (07000) 238622 *fax* 020-8874 7661
email mail@advocate-art.com
website www.advocate-art.com
Director Edward Burns

Represents 110 artists with 6 agents. Recently launched *Devil's Advocate*, representing alternative illustrators. Supplies work to book publishers, design and advertising agencies, greeting card and fine art publishers, ceramic manufacturers and potteries, and supplies editorial illustrations. Also has an original art gallery, a stock library and licensing agency for its art character 'Newton's Law'. Founded as a co-operative in 1996.

Allied Artists

The Gallery at Richmond,
63 Sheen Road,
Richmond upon Thames TW9 1YJ
tel 020-8334 1010 *fax* 020-8334 9900
email info@alliedartists.uninev.co.uk,
mary@umbrellapublishing.ca
websites www.alliedartists.uninev.co.uk,
www.umbrellapublishing.ca
Contacts Gary Mills, Mary Burtenshaw

Represents over 40 artists, all of whom produce children's material. Produces material for all markets. Specialisms include highly finished realistic figure illustrations and stylised juvenile illustrations for children's books. Extensive library of stock illustrations. Commission: 33%. Founded 1998.

Arena*†

Quantum Artists Ltd, 108 Leonard Street,
London EC2A 4RH
tel 020-7613 4040 *fax* 020-7613 1441
email info@arenaworks.com
website www.arenaworks.com
Contact Tamlyn Francis

Represents 35 artists, half of whom produce children's material. Produces illustrations for picture books and children's fiction for all ages; also for book covers and design groups. Average commission 20%. Founded 1970.

The Artworks*†

70 Rosaline Road, London SW6 7QT
tel 020-7610 1801 *fax* 020-7610 1811
email info@theartworksinc.com
website www.theartworksinc.com
Director Lucy Scherer
Consultant Allan Manham

Represents 30 artists. Undertakes artwork for illustrated gift books and children's books. Commission: 20%. Founded 1982.

Associated Freelance Artists Ltd

124 Elm Park Mansions, Park Walk,
London SW10 0AR
tel 020-7352 6890 *fax* 020-7352 8125
email pekes.afa@virgin.net
Directors Eva Morris, Doug FitzMaurice

Freelance illustrators mainly in children's educational fields, and some greeting cards.

Beehive Illustration†

42A Cricklade Street, Cirencester, Glos. GL7 1JH
tel (01285) 885149 *fax* (01285) 641291
email info@beehiveillustration.co.uk
website www.beehiveillustration.co.uk
Contact Paul Beebee

Represents 60 artists specialising in education and general children's publishing illustration. Commission: 25%. Founded 1989.

Celia Catchpole Ltd

56 Gilpin Avenue, London SW14 8QY
tel 020-8255 7200 *fax* 020-8288 0653
Proprietor Celia Catchpole

Represents 9 artists specialising in artwork for picture books for ages 0–12. Submit samples as A4 photocopies. Commission: 15%. Founded 1996. See also entry in *Children's literary agents UK and Ireland*.

The Copyrights Group Ltd

23 West Bar, Banbury, Oxon OX16 9SA
tel (01295) 672050 *fax* (01295) 672060
email enquiries@copyrights.co.uk
website www.copyrights.co.uk
Kanalstr. 38-22085 Hamburg, Germany
tel (40) 2271160 *fax* (40) 22711640

email enquiries@copyrightseur.de
website www.copyrightseur.de
Chairman & Ceo Nicholas Durbridge, *Licensing Manager* Ulla Lane-Rowley, *Managing Director, Europe* Andre Martin, *Managing Director, UK* Peter Woodhead

Leading independent licensing organisation with an international team of staff working together to represent writers, artists and the owners of quality characters, fine art and brand names for licensing to manufacturers of consumer products and for consumer promotions. Properties include *Benjamin the Elephant, Dr Seuss, Flower Fairies, The Herbs, Ivory Cats, Maisy, Paddington Bear, Peter Rabbit, Spot, The Snowman* and *The Wombles*.

Graham-Cameron Illustration†

The Studio, 23 Holt Road, Sheringham, Norfolk NR26 8NB
tel (01263) 821333 *fax* (01263) 821334
and Duncan Graham-Cameron, Graham-Cameron Illustration, 59 Redvers Road, Brighton BN2 4BF
tel (01273) 385890
email duncan@graham-cameron-illustration.com
website www.graham-cameron-illustration.com
Partners Mike Graham-Cameron, Helen Graham-Cameron, Duncan Graham-Cameron

Represents 37 artists. Undertakes all forms of illustration for publishing and communications. Specialises in educational, information and children's books. Send A4 copies of sample illustrations with sae. No MSS. Founded 1985.

David Higham Associates Ltd – see Children's literary agents UK and Ireland

John Hodgson Agency

38 Westminster Palace Gardens, Artillery Row, London SW1P 1RR
tel 020-7580 3773 *fax* 020-7222 4468

Represents 6 artists producing children's material. Specialises in children's picture books for 0–8 year-olds. Phone before sending samples. Enclose an sae with samples. Commission: 25%. Founded 1965.

The Illustration Cupboard

401 Langham House, 302 Regent Street, London W1B 3HH
tel/fax 020-7610 5481
email illustrationcupboard@yahoo.com
website www.illustrationcupboard.com
Chief Executive John Huddy

Represents over 50 artists, most of whom produce children's material for ages 12–16. Specialises in the exhibition and sale of original contemporary book illustration from around the world. Exhibitions are arranged throughout the year in the UK and abroad, and are also featured on the website. Founded 1996.

The Inkshed*†

98 Columbia Road, London E2 7QB
tel 020-7613 2323 *fax* 020-7613 2726
email makecontact@inkshed.co.uk
website www.inkshed.co.uk
Partners Tim Woolgar, Jacqueline Hollister, *Contact* Melanie Grimshaw, Abby Glassfield (agents)

Represents 31 artists who work across the board – advertising, design, publishing, editorial. Commission: 25%. Founded 1985.

Kathy Jakeman Illustration†

Richmond Business Centre, 23–24 George Street, Richmond, Surrey TW9 1HY
tel 020-8973 2000 *fax* (07071) 225 115
email kathy@kji.co.uk
website www.kji.co.uk

Represents 15 artists producing illustrations for children's publishing. Send samples by post only, *not* by email. Commission: 25%. Founded 1990.

Juvenilia

Avington, Winchester, Hants SO21 1DB
tel (01962) 779656 *fax* (01962) 779656
email juvenilia@clara.co.uk
Contact Rosemary Bromley, Colin Bromley

Represents 11 artists producing children's material for all areas of children's publishing. Send letter, CV and samples of illustrations. Commission: 10%. Founded 1973.

LAW Ltd (Lucas Alexander Whitley)

14 Vernon Street, London W14 0RJ
tel 020-7471 7900 *fax* 020-7471 7910
email firstname@lawagency.co.uk
Contacts Philippa Milnes-Smith (children's), Mark Lucas (adult), Julian Alexander (adult), Araminta Whitley (adult)

Illustrations for children's publishing for ages 0–16. Submit copies of samples (not originals) together with an sae for their return plus a covering letter and CV. Commission: 15% (20% overseas). Founded 1996.

David Lewis Illustration Agency

Worlds End Studios, 134 Lots Road, London SW10 0RJ
tel 020-7435 7762, *mobile* (07931) 824674
fax 020-7435 1945
email davidlewis34@hotmail.com
website www.davidlewisillustration.com
Director David Lewis, *Associate Director* Robin Broadway

All kinds of material for all areas of children's publishing, including educational, merchandising and toys. Represents approx. 25 artists, half of whom produce children's material. Send A4 colour or b&w copies of samples with return postage. Do not send CDs or emails. Commission: 30%. Founded 1974.

Frances McKay Illustration

14A Ravensdon Street, London SE11 4AR
tel 020-7582 2327 *mobile* 07703 344334
fax 020-7735 3303
email frances@francesmckay.com
website www.francesmckay.com
Proprietor Frances McKay

Represents 16 artists producing children's material, largely for book publishers and packagers. Also considers MSS for young children. Submit illustrations for age 7 with an original slant, either as Jpeg files on CD, as low-res scans by email or send copies by post with sae. Commission: 25%. Founded 1999.

John Martin & Artists†

12 Haven Court, Hatfield Peverel, Chelmsford, Essex CM3 2SD
tel (01245) 380337 *fax* (01245) 382055
email bernardjma@aol.com
website www.jm-a.co.uk
Contact Bernard Bowen-Davies

Represents 25 illustrators, mainly producing artwork for children's fiction/non-fiction and educational books. Include return postage with submissions. Founded 1956.

Maggie Mundy Illustrators' Agency

14 Ravenscourt Park Mansions, Dalling Road, London W6 0HG
tel 020-8748-2391
email maggiemundy@compuserve.com

Represents 20 artists in varying styles of illustration for children's books. The Agency's books are closed.

NB Illustration†

40 Bowling Green Lane, London EC1R 0NE
tel 020-7278 9131 *fax* 020-7278 9121
email info@nbillustration.co.uk
website www.nbillustration.co.uk
Directors Joe Najman, Charlotte Berens, Paul Najman

Represents 35 artists, of whom 10% produce children's material for picture books and educational publishing. Submit samples either as 72 dpi Jpegs by email or by post with an sae. Commission: 30%. Founded 2000.

The Organisation*†

The Basement, 69 Caledonian Road, London N1 9BT
tel 020-7833 8268 *fax* 020-7833 8269
email lorraine@organisart.co.uk
website www.organisart.co.uk
Contact Lorraine Owen

Represents 60 artists, 75% of whom produce children's material for all age ranges. Both traditional and digital illustration can be supplied to cover all markets, including the children's and educational book markets. Also produces illustrations for other print markets, advertising, packaging and editorial. Before submitting samples research the website. New artists must not have a similar style to one already represented. Send samples either by email or on a CD by post, or send printed images with sae. Average commission: 30%. Founded 1987.

Oxford Designers & Illustrators Ltd

Aristotle House, Aristotle Lane, Oxford OX2 6TR
tel (01865) 512331 *fax* (01865) 512408
email richardcorfield@odi-illustration.co.uk
website www.o-d-i.com
Directors Peter Lawrence (managing), Richard Corfield, Andrew King

Studio of 20 artists, three-quarters of whom produce preschool to A level educational book illustration. Also produces work for other publishers, business and industry. Submit samples by email. Not an agency. Commission: 20%. Founded 1968.

PFD – see Children's literary agents UK and Ireland

Sylvie Poggio Artists' Agency†

36 Haslemere Road, London N8 9RB
tel 020-8341 2722 020-8374 1725
website www.sylviepoggio.com

Represents a wide spectrum of professional artists who work in the fields of contemporary, conceptual, cartoony, realistic and digital illustrations.

Linda Rogers Associates†

PO Box 330, 163 Half Moon Lane, London SE24 9WB
tel 020-7501 9106 *fax* 020-7501 9175
email lr@lindarogers.net
website www.lindarogers.net
Partners Linda Rogers, Peter Sims, Jess Sims

Represents approx. 75 illustrators producing children's material. Specialises in books and magazines, all types, all ages. Looking for contemporary, multi-racial, figurative work. Submit artwork samples by post with sae for their return, *not* by email. Will not view artists' websites. Commission: 25%. Founded 1973.

Elizabeth Roy Literary Agency

White Cottage, Greatford, Nr Stamford, Lincs. PE9 4PR
tel/fax (01778) 560672

Handles illustrations for children's books. Only interested in exceptional material. Illustrators should research the children's book market before sending samples, which must include figure work. Send by post with return postage; no CD, disk or email submissions. Founded 1990. See also entry in *Children's literary agents UK and Ireland.*

SGA Illustration Agency†

18 High Street, Hadleigh, Suffolk IP7 5AP
tel (01473) 824083 *fax* (01473) 827846
email info@sgadesignart.com
website www.sgadesignart.com

Represents over 50 illustrators, all of whom produce children's material. They work mainly within publishing: early learning board books through all ages to teenage, picture books, and educational and trade material. Also manages projects from conception to final film. Especially interested in figurative artists. Submit samples as Jpegs or printed copies by post with an sae. Commission: 30%. Founded 1985.

Specs Art†

93 London Road, Cheltenham, Glos. GL52 6HL
tel (01242) 515951
email roland@specsart.com
website www.specsart.com
Partners Roland Berry, Stephanie Prosser

Represents 30 artists, all of whom produce children's material for all ages. High-quality illustration and animation work for advertisers, publishers and all other forms of visual communication. Specialises in licensed character illustration. Submit about 6 Jpegs by email. Commission: 25%. Founded 1982.

Temple Rogers Artists' Agency

120 Crofton Road, Orpington, Kent BR6 8HZ
tel (01689) 826249 *fax* (01689) 896312
Contact Patrick Kelleher

Illustrations for children's educational books and magazine illustrations. Commission: by arrangement.

Vicki Thomas Associates

195 Tollgate Road, London E6 5JY
tel 020-7511 5767 *fax* 020-7473 5177
email vickithomasassociates@yahoo.co.uk
website www.vickithomasassociates.com
Consultant Vicki Thomas

Represents approx. 50 artists, three-quarters of whom produce children's material for all ages. Specialises in designing gift products and considers images for publishing, toys, stationery, clothing decorative accessories, etc. Submit samples as photocopies with a covering letter. Commission: 25–30%. Founded 1985.

Wildlife Art Ltd†

The Lodge, Cargate Lane, Saxlingham Thorpe, Norwich NR15 1TU
tel (01508) 471500 *fax* (01508) 470391
website www.wildlife-art.co.uk

Represents 35 artists, of whom 60% produce material for children of all ages. Illustrations produced are only of all things natural, including wildlife, natural history, gardening and food. Markets include children's picture books, children's stories, packaging, adult reference books and magazine series. Clients range from children's/adults' books to design and advertising agencies. Sae must be included with work submitted for consideration. Phone before emailing portfolios. Commission: 30%. Founded 1992.

Winning the greeting card game

The UK population spends £1.2 billion a year on greeting cards yet finding a route into this fiercely competitive industry is not always easy. Jacqueline Brown steers artists through the greeting card maze. fee and how to negotiate one to your best advantage.

The UK greeting card industry leads the world on two counts – design and innovation and per capita send. On average people in the UK send 50 cards a year, 85% of which are bought by women.

But just how do you, as an artist, go about satisfying this voracious appetite of the card-sending public? There are two main options: either to become a greeting card publisher yourself or to supply existing greeting card publishers with your artwork and be paid a fee for doing so.

The idea of setting up your own greeting card publishing company may sound exciting, but this decision should not be taken lightly. Going down this route will involve taking on all the set up and running costs of a publishing company as well as the production, selling and administrative responsibilities. This often leaves little time for you to do what you do best – creating the artwork.

There are estimated to be around 800 greeting card publishers in the UK, ranging in size from one-person operations to multinational corporations, roughly 200 of which are regarded as 'serious' publishers (see page 162). Not all of them accept freelance artwork, but a great many do. Remember, whatever the size of the company, all publishers rely on good designs.

Finding the right publishers

While some publishers concentrate on producing a certain type of greeting card (e.g. humorous, fine art or juvenile), the majority publish a variety of greeting card ranges. Unfortunately, this makes it more difficult for you as an artist to target the most appropriate potential publishers for your work. There are various ways in which you can research the market, quickly improve your publisher knowledge and, therefore, reduce the amount of wasted correspondence:

• **Go shopping.** Browse the displays in card shops, newsagents and other high street shops, department stores and gift shops. This will not only give you an insight into what is already available but also which publishers

Some greeting card language

Own brand/bespoke publishers. These design specific to a retailer's needs.

Spring Seasons. The industry term to describe greeting cards for Valentine's Day, Mother's Day, Easter and Father's Day. Publishers generally launch these ranges all together in June/July.

Greeting card types. Traditional; cute or whimsical; contemporary/quirky art; juvenile; handmade or hand-finished; fine art; photographic, humorous.

Finishes and treatments. Artists will not be expected to know the production techniques and finishes, but a working knowledge is often an advantage. Some of the most commonly used finishes and treatments include: embossing (raised portion of a design), die-cutting (where the card is cut into a shape or includes an aperture), foiling (metallic film) and flitter (a glitter-like substance).

may be interested in your work. Most publishers include their contact details on the backs of the cards.

- **Trade fairs.** There are a number of trade exhibitions held during the year at which publishers exhibit their greeting card ranges to retailers and overseas distributors. By visiting these exhibitions, you will gain a broad overview of the design trends in the industry, as well as the current ranges of individual publishers. Some publishers are willing to meet artists and look through their portfolios on the stand but others are not. If you believe your work could be relevant for them, ask for a contact name and follow it up afterwards. Have a supply of business cards handy, perhaps illustrated with some of your work, to leave with publishers.

Types of publishers

There are two broad categories of publisher – wholesale and direct-to-retail – each employing a different method of distribution to reach the retailer.

Wholesale publishers distribute their products to the retailer via greeting card wholesalers or cash-and-carry outlets. They work on volume sales and have a rapid turnover of designs, many being used with a variety of different captions. For example, the same floral design may be used for cards for mothers, grandmothers, aunts and sisters. It is therefore usual for the artist to leave a blank space on the design to accommodate the caption. Until recently, wholesale publishers were generally only interested in traditional, cute and juvenile designs, but they now publish across the board, including contemporary and humorous ranges.

Direct-to-retail (DTR) publishers supply retailers via sales agents or reps. Most greeting cards sold through specialist card shops and gift shops are supplied by DTR publishers, which range from multi-national corporations down to small, trendy niche publishing companies. These publishers market series of ranges based on distinctive design themes or characters. Categories of DTR cards include contemporary art/fun, fine art, humour, children's, photographic, traditional and handmade.

Approaching a publisher

Unfortunately, there is no standard way of approaching and submitting work to a card publisher. The first step is to establish that the publisher you wish to approach accepts work from freelance artists; then find out their requirements for submission and to whom it should be addressed.

It is always better to send several examples of your work to show the breadth of your artistic skills. Some publishers prefer to see finished designs while others are happy with well-presented sketches. Never send originals: instead send photocopies, laser copies or photographs, and include at least one design in colour. Never be tempted to sell similar designs to two publishers – a bad reputation will follow you around.

Some publishers will be looking to purchase individual designs for specific sending occasions while others will be more intent on looking for designs which could be developed to make up a range. Bear in mind that publishers work a long way in advance, e.g. Christmas ranges are launched to the retailers in January.

Further information

The Greeting Card Association

United House, North Road, London N7 9DP
tel 020-7619 0396
email gca@max-publishing.co.uk
website www.greetingcardassociation.org.uk

The UK trade association for greeting card publishers. Its website contains leaflets on freelance designing and writing for greeting cards complete with lists of publishers which accept freelance work.

Trade fairs

Spring & Autumn Fairs Birmingham, NEC

Contact TPS *tel* 020-8277 5830
Takes place 5–8 Sept 2004, 6–10 Feb 2005, 4–7 Sept 2005

Top Drawer, Earls Court

Contact Clarion Events *tel* 020-7370 8374
Takes place 12–14 Sept 2004, 16–18 Jan, 22–25 May 2005

Home and Gift, Harrogate

Contact Clarion Events *tel* 020-7370 8374
Takes place 17–20 July 2005

Trade magazines

Greetings Today

(formerly Greetings Magazine)
Lema Publishing, Unit No. 1, Queen Mary's Avenue, Watford, Herts. WD18 7JR
tel (01923) 250909 *fax* (01923) 250995
Publisher-in-Chief Malcolm Naish, *Editor* Vicky Denton
Monthly £45 p.a. (other rates on application)

Articles, features and news related to the greetings card industry. Includes Artists Directory for aspiring artists wishing to attract the eye of publishers. Runs seminars for small publishers and artists.

Progressive Greetings Worldwide

Max Publishing, United House, North Road, London N7 9DP
tel 020-7700 6740 *fax* 020-7607 6411
12 p.a. (£40 p.a.)

The official magazine of the Greeting Card Association. Provides an insight to the industry, including an up-to-date list of publishers, a new product section and a free showcase for artists and illustrators. Special supplements include *Focus on Art Cards, Focus on Humorous Cards, Focus on Words & Sentiments, Focus on Kids* and *Focus on Giftwrap*.

Hosts The Henries, the greeting card industry awards. The September edition includes details of the finalists in the different categories and the November issue features the winners.

Development of a range may take up to six months prior to launching.

Also remember that cards in retail outlets are rarely displayed in their entirety. Therefore, when designing a card make sure that some of the 'action' appears in the top half.

When interest is shown

Some publishers respond to submissions from artists immediately while others prefer to deal with them on a monthly basis. A publisher's response may be in the form of a request for more submissions of a specific design style or of a specific character. This speculative development work is usually carried out free of charge. Always meet your deadline (news travels fast in the industry).

A publisher interested in buying your artwork will probably then issue you with a contract. This may cover aspects such as the terms of payment; rights of usage of the design (e.g. is it just for greeting cards or will it include giftwrap and/or stationery?); territory of usage (most publishers want worldwide rights); and ownership of copyright or license period.

There is no set industry standard rate of pay for greeting card artists. Publishers pay artists either on a per design or per range basis in one of the following ways:

- **Flat fee.** A one-off payment is made to the artist for ownership of a design for an unlimited period. The industry standard is around £200–£250 for a single design, and payment on a sliding scale for more than one design.
- **Licensing fee.** The publisher is granted the right to use a piece of artwork for a specified number of

years, after which the full rights revert to the artist. Payment to the artist is approximately £150 upwards per design.

- **Licensing fee** plus royalty. As above plus a royalty payment on each card sold. Artists would generally receive a minimum of £100 for the licensing fee plus 3% of the trade price of each card sold.
- **Advance royalty deal.** A goodwill advance on royalties is paid to the artist. In the case of a range, the artist would receive a goodwill advance of say £500–£1000 plus 5% additional royalty payment once the threshold is reached.
- **Royalty only.** The artist receives regular royalty payments, generally paid quarterly, based on the number of cards sold. Artists should expect a sales report and royalty statement.

The fees stated above should only be regarded as a rough guideline. Fees and advances are generally paid on completion of artwork. Publishers which have worldwide rights pay royalties for sales overseas to artists, although these will be on a pro rata basis to the export trade price.

Jacqueline Brown is editor of *Progressive Greetings Worldwide* and general secretary of the Greeting Card Association.

Card and stationery publishers

Before submitting work, artists are advised to write giving details of the work they have to offer, and asking for requirements.

*Member of the Greeting Card Association

Card Connection Ltd*

Park House, South Street, Farnham, Surrey GU9 7QQ
tel (01252) 892300 *fax* (01252) 892363
email ho@card-connection.co.uk
website www.card-connection.co.uk
Managing Director Simon Hulme, *Senior Product Manager* Alison Mahoney

Everyday and seasonal designs. Styles include cute, fun, traditional, floral, contemporary, graphic, art, photography. Submit colour copies. Humour designs and jokes. Sentiment verse. Founded 1992.

Carlton Cards Ltd*

Mill Street East, Dewsbury,
West Yorkshire WF12 9AW
tel (01924) 465200
website www.carltoncards.co.uk
Marketing Director Keith Auty, *Creative Director* Linda Marshall

All types of artwork, any size; submit as colour roughs, colour copies or transparencies. Especially interested in humorous artwork and ideas.

Carte Blanche Greetings Ltd

Unit 3, Chichester Business Park, Tangmere, Chichester, West Sussex PO20 2FT
website www.metoyou.co.uk
Contact Stephen Haines

Greetings cards, gifts and stationery in the *Me to You* brand, featuring the toy bear with the blue nose. Founded 1987.

Caspari Ltd*

9 Shire Hill, Saffron Walden, Essex CB11 3AP
tel (01799) 513010 *fax* (01799) 513101
Managing Director Keith Entwisle

Traditional fine art/classic images; 5 x 4in transparencies. No verses. Founded 1990.

Charity Christmas Card Council*

221 St John Street, London EC1V 4LY
tel 020-7702 5090 *fax* 020-7702 5092
email karnthorsson@charitycards.org
website www.charitycards.org

Traditional and contemporary Christmas cards for the corporate market. Submit artwork on CD-Rom or 5 x 4in transparencies. No verses. Charitable not-for-profit organisation. Founded 1966.

Simon Elvin Ltd

Wooburn Industrial Park, Wooburn Green, Bucks HP10 0PE
tel (01628) 526711 *fax* (01628) 53148
website www.simonelvin.com
Senior Design Managers Isabel Scott Evans, Roger Kingshott

Female/male cute wedding/anniversary, birth congratulations (boy/girl), humour, good luck/ congratulations, fine art, exam pass, Christmas photographic, florals/domestic animals, Easter gift wrap designs, Valentine's Day, Father's Day, Mother's Day, traditional female sympathy, traditional male get well, juvenile boy/girl new home.

In general terms, the company is looking for submissions that have flair and imagination. Artists should first familiarise themselves with the range, style and content and make sure their designs broadly complement them. Send a small collection of good quality colour copies or prints (no original artwork) and include an sae for return of work.

Gallery Five Ltd*

Regent House, 24 Nutford Place, London W1H 5YN
tel 020-8741 3891 *fax* 020-8741 4444

Send samples of work FAO 'Gallery Five Art Studio'. Colour photocopies, Mac-formatted zip/CD acceptable, plus sae. Founded 1961.

Gemma International Ltd*

Linmar House, 6 East Portway, Andover, Hants. SP10 3LU
tel (01264) 388400 *fax* (01264) 366243
website www.gemma-international.co.uk
Directors L. Rudd-Clarke, M. Rudd-Clarke, A. Parkin, T. Rudd-Clarke, W. O'Loughlin, R. Howard, K. Bishop

Cute, contemporary, leading-edge designs for children, teens and young adults, and mainstream adult humour. Considers humorous verses. Founded 1984.

Gibson Greetings International Ltd

Gibson House, Hortonwood 30, Telford, Shrops. TF1 7YF
tel (01952) 608333 *fax* (01952) 605259
email jan_taylor@gibson-greetings.co.uk
Product Director Jan Taylor

All everyday and seasonal illustrations: cute, humorous, juvenile, traditional and contemporary designs, as well as surface pattern. Greeting card traditional and humorous verse. Founded 1991.

Hallmark Cards Plc*

Hallmark House, Bingley Road,
West Yorkshire BD9 8SD
email 1willi2@hallmark-uk.com
website www.hallmark.com
Submissions Katy Jones

Illustrations: all subjects considered. Submit colour copies and/or transparencies but not original artwork. Ensure that all work is named and includes an sae. Words: humour only will be considered.

Hanson White – UKG Speciality Products

9th Floor, Wettern House, 56 Dingwall Road,
Croydon, Surrey CR0 0XH
tel 020-8260 1200 *fax* 020-8260 1213
email hannah.turpin@ukgsp.co.uk,
sally.hipkins@ukgsp.co.uk
Submissions Editors Hannah Turpin, Sally Hipkins

Humorous artwork and cartoons for greeting cards, including Christmas, Valentine's Day, Mother's Day and Father's Day. Humorous copy lines, punchline jokes, poems and rhymes; guidelines available. Founded 1958.

Jarrold Publishing

incorporating Pitkin and Unichrome brands
Whitefriars, Norwich NR3 1JR
tel (01603) 763300 *fax* (01603) 662748
email publishing@jarrold.co.uk
website www.jarrold-publishing.co.uk
Directors Margot Russell-King (managing), David Lombe (finance), Steve Plackett (supply chain gift and stationery)

UK tourism and heritage guidebooks and souvenirs, calendars, diaries and gift stationery. Unsolicited MSS, synopses and ideas welcome but approach in writing before submitting to Marketing Department. Founded 1770.

The Monster Factory*

Unit 207, Welsbach House, 3–9 Broomhill Road,
London SW18 4JQ
tel 020-8875 9988 *fax* 020-8870 4488
email info@themonsterfactory.com
website www.themonsterfactory.com
Directors Martin Grix, Kate Eagar

Publishers of innovative stationery with a funky, design-led feel. Specialises in handmade ranges, unusual printing techniques and quirky illustration. Will consider original new concepts and fresh artwork styles with bags of character and humour. Do not send original artwork. No verses. Founded 2000.

The Paper House Group plc*

Waterwells Drive, Gloucester, Glos. GL2 2PH
tel (01452) 888999 *fax* (01452) 888912
email dewi.morris@paperhouse.co.uk
website www.paperhouse.co.uk
Product Director Chris Wilcox

Publishers of greeting cards specialising in cartoon humour illustration, contemporary art styles and traditional verse design in special occasions and family birthday.

Paperlink Ltd*

356 Kennington Road, London SE11 4LD
tel 020-7582 8244 *fax* 020-7587 5212
email info@paperlinkcards.com
website www.paperlinkcards.com
Directors Louise Tighe, Jo Townsend, Tim Porte, Tim Purcell

Publishers of ranges of humorous and contemporary art greetings cards. Produce products under licence for charities. Founded 1986.

Paper Rose Ltd

18 Queens Bridge Road, Nottingham NG2 1WS
Submissions Artists Submissions, Mabel Street, Nottingham NG2 3ED
tel 0115-986 0115 *fax* 0115-986 0116
email philipburley@paperrose.co.uk,
newartists@paperrose.co.uk (submissions)
website www.paperrose.co.uk
Marketing Director Alan Hankes

Innovative contemporary greetings cards. Portfolio includes a broad mix of contemporary art and fine art styles (no photography). Always looking for children's artists for various card ranges (ages 0–8). Popular designs include male/female characters, cats, flowers, presents, birthday cakes, balloons, birds, hearts, fish. Send colour photocopies of a representative selection of artwork addressed to 'Artists Submissions'. Alternatively send via email but size must not exceed 5MB. Founded 1982.

Pepperpot

Royston Road, Duxford, Cambridge CB2 4QY
tel (01223) 836825 *fax* (01223) 833321
Publishing Controller Linda Worsfold

Gift stationery, photo albums, gift cards. Colour illustrations; cute/traditional/floral. Division of Copywrite Designs Ltd.

Pineapple Park*

58 Wilbury Way, Hitchin, Herts. SG4 0TP
tel (01462) 442021 *fax* (01462) 440418
email info@pineapplepark.co.uk
website www.pineapplepark.co.uk
Directors Peter M. Cockerline, Sarah M. Parker

Illustrations and photographs for publication as greetings cards. Contemporary, cute, humour:

submit artwork or laser copies with sae. Photographic florals always needed. Humour copy/jokes accepted without artwork. Also concepts for ranges. Founded 1993.

Nigel Quiney Publications Ltd*

Cloudesley House, Shire Hill, Saffron Walden, Essex CB11 3FB
tel (01799) 520200 *fax* (01799) 520100
website www.nigelquiney.com
Contact Ms J. Arkinstall, Product & Marketing Director

Everyday and seasonal greetings cards and giftwrap including fine art, photographic, humour, fun art, contemporary and cute. Submit colour copies, photographs or transparencies: no original artwork.

Rainbow Cards Ltd*

Kingswood Business Park, Holyhead Road, Albrighton, Wolverhampton, West Midlands WV7 3AU
tel (01902) 376000 *fax* (01902) 376001
email sales@rainbowcards.co.uk
website www.rainbowcards.co.uk

Artwork for humorous and traditional greetings cards. Founded 1976.

Really Good*

The Old Mast House, The Square, Abingdon, Oxon OX14 5AR
tel (01235) 537888 *fax* (01235) 537779
website www.reallygood.uk.com
Director David Hicks

Always looking for fun and funny artwork in a quirky or modern way to publish on cards, stationery or gifts. Send samples on paper rather than on disk, etc. Allow plenty of time for review. Founded 1987.

Santoro Graphics Ltd

Rotunda Point, 11 Hartfield Crescent, London SW19 3RL
tel 020-8781 1100 *fax* 020-8781 1101
email enquiries@santorographics.com
website www.santorographics.com
Directors Lucio Santoro, Meera Santoro (art)

Publishers of innovative and award-winning designs for greetings cards, giftwrap and gift stationery. Bold contemporary images with an international appeal. Subjects covered: quirky and humorous, whimsical, Fifties, Seventies, futuristic! Styles include traditional to stylised. Submit samples as colour photocopies, transparencies or on CD, or via email as Jpegs or PDF files. Founded 1985.

Wishing Well Studios Ltd*

Kellet Close, Martland Park, Wigan, Lancs. WN5 0LP
tel (01942) 218888 *fax* (01942) 218899
email studio@wishingwell2.demon.co.uk
website www.wishingwell.co.uk
Directors David Evans, Brian Phillips, *Contact* Susie Riley

Rhyming and prose verse 4–24 lines long; also jokes. All artwork styles considered but do not send originals.

Publishing practice

Publishing agreements

Before signing a publisher's agreement, it should be thoroughly checked. Caroline Walsh introduces the key points of this very important contract.

So, you've done the difficult bit and persuaded a publisher to make an offer to publish your book. But how do you know if you're getting a fair deal? And what should you be looking out for on the contract? I would always advise an author or illustrator to engage an agent. An agent will ensure that the contract gives you the best possible chance of maximising your income from a book. Alternatively, the Society of Authors (see page 255) and the Writers' Guild of Great Britain (see page 277) will both check publishing agreements for their members. In addition, there are lawyers who specialise in publishing contracts and for those who prefer to go it alone, there are some useful books on the subject listed at the end of this article.

What follows is a whistle-stop tour around the key points of a publishing contract, especially for those writing for children. To begin, the offer from the publisher should come in writing clearly setting out exactly what rights the publisher wants to license and what they are willing to pay for those rights. A contract is a business agreement for the supply of goods or performance of work at a specified price. Normally, that payment comes as an advance against royalties. Occasionally, a flat fee payment is appropriate, but a royalty allows the author to share in the income from a book throughout its life and is therefore generally preferable. Perhaps the most important point of all is that you make sure you fully understand which rights are being licensed under the contract and aren't seduced merely into worrying about the advance and royalty (tempting though they may be!)

Publishers' agreements often have useful headings for each clause and I've used some of those headings here for ease of reference.

Licence

The very first thing to be clear about is what is being licensed to the publisher. For a new book one expects to grant to the publisher, for the legal term of copyright, the exclusive right to publish and sell the work in certain forms. The standard grant is of 'volume form', which means all book forms (hardback, paperback, other formats). However, the offer or contract may also state other forms, for example serial (newspaper and magazine rights) or audio rights. Some publishers' contracts include all-encompassing wording such as 'all media forms currently in existence and hereinafter invented'. This in effect hands control to the publisher of a wide range of rights, including electronic, dramatic (film, television, radio), merchandising and so on. In such a case, it's likely that the author's share of income from such rights will be less than it would be were the author to reserve those rights and have them handled separately.

Territory

Territory states *where* the publisher has the right to sell or sub-license the book. For picture books of all kinds, fiction and non-fiction, UK publishers generally require world rights as the UK market alone is not large enough to sustain the costs of four-colour printing. US publishers are lucky enough to have a sufficiently large home market to mean they are not reliant on foreign sales and therefore will not always require world rights.

For fiction (i.e. novels) a judgement needs to be made about which territories should be granted to the publisher. English language rights are made up of two large mutually exclusive territories: the UK and Traditional British Commonwealth (including or excluding Canada) on the one hand and the USA, its dependencies and the Philippines on the other. The rest of the world is considered an open market. One could grant Traditional British Commonwealth rights in the English Language to a publisher, thereby reserving American and translation rights to be sold separately. Or one could grant World English Language rights, so the publisher can sell on US rights while translation rights are held in reserve to be sold separately. Or again, one could grant world rights to the originating publisher.

When thinking of granting a wide range of territories to a publisher, it is worth checking out how proactive and successful their foreign rights department is. It may be possible to speak to the foreign rights manager and find out for yourself if they have a good track record. An agent will have an informed view on a publisher's expertise in this area and furthermore, they will probably either be experienced themselves in selling foreign and US rights, or will work with associate agencies in all the different language territories. Publishers will take 15%–30% share on US and foreign sales and, if you have an agent too, their commission will also be deducted before you receive your percentage. Agents will generally charge 15%–20% on US and foreign sales.

Advances

We've all read the newspaper headlines about huge advances, but the fact is most children's book advances currently fall within the range of £1000–£25,000. For books that will be published in the trade (i.e. by a mainstream publishing house and where the book will appear in bookshops) most offers are framed as an advance against royalties. Advances may be paid in one go, on signature, but don't be surprised if the publisher proposes paying half on signature and half on publication, or in thirds (signature, delivery and publication), or even in quarters (signature, delivery, hardback publication, paperback publication), though the latter is more common when the advance offered is substantial.

Royalties

As a very basic rule of thumb, hardbacks attract a 10% base royalty and paperbacks 7.5%. Bear in mind that on picture books these figures will be shared between author and illustrator. Sometimes, children's black and white illustrated fiction titles also bear a small royalty for the illustrator, which will come out of the total royalty. Most novelty books, including board books, work on a smaller royalty, for example 5% or even less because of the high production costs and relatively low retail price.

Ideally, the royalty will escalate to a higher level when a certain number of sales have been achieved and this can prove to be very important if a book becomes a long-running success.

For a trade book the royalties should ideally be based on the recommended retail price for home sales. Export sales and sales to book clubs or book fairs are usually calculated on the publisher's price received (or net receipts). The contract should set out each type of sale and list the appropriate royalty rate. Nowadays particular attention needs to be paid to 'high discount' clauses in contracts. However good the main home sales royalty is, a disadvantageous high discount clause can mean that disappointingly few of the sales attract the full royalty and consequently revenues will be much reduced. This is especially important now because retailers are pushing publishers hard on discounts. An agent will be used to negotiating carefully on precisely this kind of area to secure the best possible terms.

Co-edition royalties

As previously mentioned, picture books in the UK are very dependent upon publishers selling American and foreign language co-editions. Therefore, it is important to note on the contract what the author's share of any such co-edition deals will be. These generally fall under two categories in the contract:

- If the UK publisher prints for the foreign publisher, the books are usually sold for a fixed price per copy as 'royalty inclusive' and the author's and artist's share will be expressed as a percentage of the publisher's price received. These deals help to get the book published by bringing the unit cost down and they begin the process of earning out the advance.
- US and foreign language sales also fall under the heading of subsidiary rights. In this case, the UK publisher may or may not print the books, but the US or foreign publisher will have agreed to pay an advance and royalty for the right to sell the book in their territory (a 'royalty exclusive' deal). The author's and artist's share in this instance shouldn't be less than 50% and it could be much more. If a book is particularly sought after by foreign or US publishers, such a royalty exclusive deal could mean that the original UK advance is earned out immediately.

Subsidiary rights

Other subsidiary rights include reprint rights (large print, book club, paperback reprint, etc), serial rights (the right to publish in newspapers and magazines), anthology and quotation rights, educational rights, audio rights and so on. There will usually be a percentage listed against each right and that is the author's share of any deal. Generally the author receives at least 50% on these deals and more in the case of serial, US and translation rights. The rights listed in the sub-rights clause should be checked against the opening grant of rights clause to see that they conform.

Delivery and publication

There should be clauses in the contract that state the agreed delivery date of the book and give some indication of what is expected, for example 'a work for children to be written and illustrated by the said author to a length of not more than 25,000 words plus approximately 50 black and white line illustrations'. There should also be an undertaking by the publisher to publish the work within a stated time period, for example 'within 12 months from delivery of the complete typescript and artwork'. There might also be an indication of what the published price will be.

Copyright and moral rights

As you are licensing your work, you should retain copyright and there should be a clause that obliges the publisher to include a copyright line in every edition of the work published or sub-licensed by them. The author's moral rights are also often asserted within the contract.

Production

Though the publishers will generally insist on having the final decision regarding details of production, publication and advertising, they should agree to consult meaningfully with the author over the blurb, catalogue copy, jacket and cover design. There should also be an undertaking to supply the author with proofs for checking and enough time for the author to check those proofs.

Accounts

Publishers usually account to authors twice a year for royalties earned. Even if the advance has not earned out, the publishers should still send a royalty statement. Royalty statements are notoriously enigmatic and vary from publisher to publisher. Mistakes on royalty statements are more common than one might like to think and an agent will be used to checking royalty statements carefully and taking up any anomalies with the publisher.

In addition to the twice-yearly accounting, once the initial advance has been earned out, an agent will be able to ensure that any substantial income from sub-rights deals (e.g. in excess of £100) will be paid immediately.

Electronic rights

The electronic book market is in its infancy and norms have not yet been established. If a publisher insists on including these rights in the contract, one should aim to negotiate a royalty of 50% of the publisher's price received or, at the very least, leave the royalty rate to be mutually agreed at a later date.

Reversion

It's important to ensure that the author can get back the rights to their book if the publisher either fails to stick to the terms of the contract or lets the book go out of print and leaves it out of print for six to nine months after receiving a written request to reprint it. It is well worth reclaiming rights to out of print books as it may be possible to re-license them later on.

Assignment

A small but important clause that may need to be added states that the publishers shall not assign the rights granted to them without the author's express written consent. This gives the author at least a degree of control over the book's destiny if the publishing company runs into trouble or is sold.

Educational publishers' contracts

Many children's authors begin as writers for educational publishers and quite a number continue to work in this field alongside producing books for the trade market. Educational publishers usually commission tightly briefed work. Advances are generally modest and the royalties are based on the publishers' price received. However, substantial sums can eventually be earned. Educational publishers usually expect to be granted a very wide range of rights and while it makes sense to grant audio or electronic rights where the publisher has the capacity to produce or license such formats for their market, it may be possible and desirable to reserve, for example, dramatic and merchandising rights. However, discretion is needed here. If, for example, the publisher is commissioning writers to create stories about a given set of characters created by the publisher, then the publisher will rightly expect to control such rights.

That really is a scratching of the surface of publishing agreements. Do take advice if you don't feel confident that the contract presented to you is fair. It seems a very obvious thing to say but always read a publishing agreement carefully before signing it and if anything in it isn't clear, ask for an explanation. Remember, too, that it's a negotiation and that despite publishers' talk of 'standard terms' and 'standard agreements', it is always possible to make amendments to contracts.

Caroline Walsh is a literary agent and a director of David Higham Associates Ltd (www.davidhigham.co.uk). She specialises in the children's book market.

Useful reading

The following books provide useful advice on publishing agreements – but don't forget to engage that agent!

Clark, Charles (ed.), *Publishing Agreements: A Book of Precedents*, Tolley, 6th edn, 2002

Flint, Michael F., *A User's Guide to Copyright, Butterworths*, 5th edn, 2000

Legat, Michael, *An Author's Guide to Publishing, Robert Hale*, 3rd edn revised, 1998

Legat, Michael, *Understanding Publishers' Contracts*, Robert Hale, 2nd edn revised, 2002

FAQs about ISBNs

The Standard Book Numbering Agency receives a large number of enquiries about the ISBN system. The most frequently asked questions are answered here.

What is an ISBN?

An ISBN (International Standard Book Number) is a 10-digit product number used by publishers, booksellers and libraries for ordering, listing and stock control purposes. It enables them to identify a specific edition of a specific title in a specific format from a particular publisher. The 10 digits are always divided into four parts, separated by spaces or hyphens. The four parts can be of varying length and are as follows:

- Group Identifier – Identifies a national, geographic or language grouping of publishers. It tells you which of these groupings the publisher belongs to (not the language of the book).
- Publisher Prefix – Identifies a specific publisher or imprint.
- Title Number – Identifies a specific edition of a specific title in a specific format.
- Check Digit – This is always and only the final digit which mathematically validates the rest of the number. It is calculated using a Modulus 11 system with weights 10–2.

Do all books need to have an ISBN?

There is no legal requirement for an ISBN and it conveys no form of legal or copyright protection. It is a product number.

What can be gained from using an ISBN?

If you wish to sell your publication through major bookselling chains, or internet booksellers, they will require you to have an ISBN to assist their internal processing and ordering systems. The ISBN also provides access to Bibliographic Databases such as Whitaker BookBank, which are organised using ISBNs as references. These databases are used by the book trade and libraries to provide information for customers. The ISBN therefore provides access to additional marketing tools which could help sales of your product.

Where can we get an ISBN?

ISBN prefixes are assigned to publishers in the country in which the publisher is based by the national agency for that country. In the UK and Republic of Ireland this agency is the Standard Book Numbering Agency Ltd. The Agency introduces new publishers to the system, assigns prefixes to new and existing publishers and deals with any queries or problems in using the system. The Standard Book Numbering Agency Ltd was the first ISBN Agency in the world. Publishers based elsewhere will not be able to get numbers from the UK Agency but should contact them for details of the relevant Agency.

Who is eligible for ISBNs?

Any publisher which is publishing a qualifying product for general sale or distribution to the market is eligible (see 'Which products do not qualify for ISBNs?').

What is a publisher?

It is sometimes difficult to decide who the publisher is and who their agent may be, but the publisher is generally the person or body which takes the financial risk in making a product available. For example, if a product went on sale and sold no copies at all, the publisher is usually the person or body which loses money. If you get paid anyway, you are likely to be a designer, printer, author or consultant of some kind.

How long does it take to get an ISBN?

In the UK the Standard service time is 10 working days. There is also a Fast Track service, which is a three-working day processing period.

How much does it cost to get an ISBN?

In the UK there is a registration fee which is payable by all new publishers. The fees are £60 plus VAT for the Standard service and £96 plus VAT for the Fast Track service. A publisher prefix unique to you will be provided and allows for 10 ISBNs. Larger allocations are available where appropriate.

ISBNs are only available in blocks. The smallest block is 10 numbers. It is not possible to obtain a single ISBN.

Which products do not qualify for ISBNs?

Calendars; diaries; greetings cards, videos for entertainment; documentaries on video/CD-Rom; computer games; computer application programs; items which are available to a restricted group of people, e.g. a history of a golf club which is only for sale to members, or an educational course book only available to those registered as students on the course.

Can I turn my ISBN into a barcode?

Where a product carries a barcode and an ISBN, the barcode is derived from the ISBN and includes the Bookland Prefix (978). The barcode also contains a check digit which is derived by a different calculation method from that used for ISBNs. Further information about barcoding for books is available on the Book Industry Communication website (www.bic.org.uk).

Contact details

ISBN Agency
3rd Floor, Midas House, 62 Goldsworth Road, Woking GU21 6LQ
tel (0870) 777 8712 *fax* (0870) 777 8714
email isbn@nielsenbookdata.co.uk
website www.whitaker.co.uk/isbn.htm

What is an ISSN?

An International Standard Serial Number is the numbering system for journals, magazines, periodicals, newspapers and newsletters. It is administered by the British Library (*tel* (01937) 546959).

Public Lending Right

Under the PLR system, payment is made from public funds to authors (writers, translators, illustrators and some editors/compilers) whose books are lent out from public libraries. Payment is made once a year, and the amount authors receive is proportionate to the number of times (established from a sample) that their books were borrowed during the previous year (July to June).

The legislation

PLR was created, and its principles established, by the Public Lending Right Act 1979 (HMSO, 30p). The Act required the rules for the administration of PLR to be laid down by a scheme. That was done in the Public Lending Right Scheme 1982 (HMSO, £2.95), which includes details of transfer (assignment), transmission after death, renunciation, trusteeship, bankruptcy, etc. Amending orders made in 1983, 1984, 1988, 1989 and 1990 were consolidated in December 1990 (SI 2360, £3.90). Some further amendments affecting author eligibility came into effect in December 1991 (SI 2618, £1), July 1997 (SI 1576, £1.10), December 1999 (SI 420, £1) and July 2000 (SI 933, £1.50).

How the system works

From the applications he receives, the Registrar of PLR compiles a register of authors and books which is held on computer. A representative sample of book issues is recorded, consisting of all loans from selected public libraries. This is then multiplied in proportion to total library lending to produce, for each book, an estimate of its total annual loans throughout the country. Each year the computer compares the register with the estimated loans to discover how many loans are credited to each registered book for the calculation of PLR payments. The computer does this using code numbers – in most cases the ISBN printed in the book.

Parliament allocates a sum each year (£7,200,000 for 2003–4) for PLR. This Fund pays the administrative costs of PLR and reimburses local authorities for recording loans in the sample libraries. The remaining money is then divided by the total registered loan figure in order to work out how much can be paid for each estimated loan of a registered book.

Limits on payments

Bottom limit. If all the registered interests in an author's books score so few loans that they would earn less than £5 in a year, no payment is due.
Top limit. If the books of one registered author score so high that the author's PLR earnings for the year would exceed £6000, then only £6000 is paid. No author can earn more than £6000 in PLR in any one year.

Money that is not paid out because of these limits belongs to the Fund and increases the amounts paid that year to other authors.

The sample

The basic sample represents only public libraries (no academic, school, private or commercial libraries are included) and only loans made over the counter (not

Summary of the 21st year's results

Registration: authors. When registration closed for the 21st year (30 June 2003) the number of shares in books registered was 366,565 for 36,362 authors and assignees.

Eligible loans. Of the 377 million estimated loans from UK libraries, 169 million belong to books on the PLR register. The loans credited to registered books – 45% of all library borrowings – qualify for payment. The remaining 55% of loans relate to books that are ineligible for various reasons, to books written by dead or foreign authors, and to books that have simply not been applied for.

Money and payments. PLR's administrative costs are deducted from the fund allocated to the Registrar annually by Parliament. Operating the Scheme this year cost £812,000, representing some 11.3% of the PLR fund. The Rate per Loan for 2003–4 increased to 4.85 pence and was calculated to distribute all the £6,400,000 available. The total of PLR distribution and costs is therefore the full £7.2 million which the Government provided in 2003–4.

The numbers of authors in various payment categories are as follows:

*354	payments at	£5000–6000
350	payments between	£2500–4999.99
767	payments between	£1000–2499.99
910	payments between	£500–999.99
3,875	payments between	£100–499.99
12,507	payments between	£5–99.99
18,763	TOTAL	

* includes 280 authors where the maximum threshold applied.

consultations of books on library premises). It follows that only those books which are loaned from public libraries can earn PLR and make an application worthwhile.

The sample consists of the entire loans records for a year from libraries in more than 30 public library authorities spread through England, Scotland, Wales and Northern Ireland. Sample loans represent around 20% of the national total. Several computerised sampling points in an authority contribute loans data ('multi-site' sampling). This change has been introduced gradually, and began in July 1991. The aim has been to increase the sample without any significant increase in costs. In order to counteract sampling error, libraries in the sample change every two to three years. Loans are totalled every 12 months for the period 1 July to 30 June.

An author's entitlement to PLR depends, under the 1979 Act, on the loans accrued by his or her books in the sample. This figure is averaged up to produce first regional and then finally national estimated loans.

ISBNs

PLR depends on the use of code numbers to identify books lent and to correlate loans with entries on the register so that payment can be made. The system uses the International Standard Book Number (ISBN), which is required for all new registrations. Different editions (e.g. 1st, 2nd, hardcover, paperback, large print) of the same book have different ISBNs.

Authorship

In the PLR system the author of a book is the writer, illustrator, translator, compiler, editor or reviser. Authors must be named on the book's title page, or be able to prove authorship by some other means (e.g. receipt of royalties). The ownership of copyright has no bearing on PLR eligibility.

Co-authorship/illustrators. In the PLR system the authors of a book are those writers, translators, editors, compilers and illustrators as defined above. Authors must apply for registration before their books can earn PLR. This can now be done online through the PLR website. There is no restriction on the number of authors who can register shares in any one book as long as they satisfy the eligibility criteria.

Writers and/or illustrators. At least one must be eligible and they must jointly agree what share of PLR each will take. This agreement is necessary even if one or two are ineligible or do not wish to register for PLR. Share sizes should be based on contribution. The eligible authors will receive the share(s) specified in the application. PLR can be any whole percentage. Detailed advice is available from the PLR office.

Translators. Translators may apply, without reference to other authors, for a 30% fixed share (to be divided equally between joint translators).

Editors and compilers. An editor or compiler may apply, either with others or without reference to them, to register a 20% share. Unless in receipt of royalties an editor must have written at least 10% of the book's content or more than 10 pages of text in addition to normal editorial work. The share of joint editors/compilers is 20% in total to be divided equally. An application from an editor or compiler to register a greater percentage share must be accompanied by supporting documentary evidence of actual contribution.

Dead or missing co-authors. Where it is impossible to agree shares with a co-author because that person is dead or untraceable, then the surviving co-author or co-authors may submit an application without the dead or missing co-author but must name the co-author and provide supporting evidence as to why that co-author has not agreed shares. The living co-author(s) will then be able to register a share in the book which will be 20% for the illustrator (or illustrators)

Most borrowed children's authors

1. Jacqueline Wilson
2. Mick Inkpen
3. R.L. Stine
4. Janet & Allan Ahlberg
5. Lucy Daniels
6. Roald Dahl
7. Enid Blyton
8. Nick Butterworth
9. Eric Hill
10. Dick King-Smith
11. Terry Deary
12. Martin Waddell
13. J.K. Rowling
14. Lucy Cousins
15. Shirley Hughes
16. Sally Grindley
17. David McKee
18. Debi Gliori
19. Jenny Dale
20. Colin McNaughton

These two lists are of the most borrowed authors in UK public libraries. They are based on PLR sample loans in the period July 2002–June 2003. They include all writers, both registered and unregistered, but not illustrators where the book has a separate writer. Writing names are used; pseudonyms have not been combined.

Most borrowed authors (adult fiction)

1. Danielle Steel
2. Josephine Cox
3. Catherine Cookson
4. Agatha Christie
5. Audrey Howard
6. Jack Higgins
7. James Patterson
8. John Grisham
9. Dick Francis
10. Ian Rankin
11. Ruth Rendell
12. Lynda M. Andrews
13. Emma Blair
14. Mary Higgins Clark
15. Joan Jonker
16. Bernard Cornwell
17. Patricia Cornwell
18. Maeve Binchy
19. Anne Perry
20. Barbara Taylor Bradford

and the residual percentage for the writer (or writers). If this percentage is to be divided between more than one writer or illustrator, then this will be in equal shares unless some other apportionment is requested and agreed by the Registrar.

The PLR Office keeps a file of missing authors (mostly illustrators) to help locate co-authors. Help is also available from publishers, the writers' organisations, and the Association of Illustrators.

Life and death. Authors can only be registered for PLR during their lifetime. However, for authors so registered, books can later be registered if first published within one year before their death or 10 years afterwards. New versions of titles registered by the author can be registered posthumously.

Residential qualifications. With effect from 1 July 2000, PLR is open to authors living in the European Economic Area (i.e. EU member states plus Norway, Liechtenstein and Iceland). A resident in these countries (for PLR purposes) has his or her only or principal home there. The United Kingdom does not include the Channel Islands or the Isle of Man.

Eligible books

In the PLR system each separate edition of a book is registered and treated as a separate book. A book is eligible for PLR registration provided that:

- it has an eligible author (or co-author);
- it is printed and bound (paperbacks counting as bound);
- copies of it have been put on sale (i.e. it is not a free handout and it has already been published);
- it is not a newspaper, magazine, journal or periodical;
- the authorship is personal (i.e. not a company or association) and the book is not crown copyright;
- it is not wholly or mainly a musical score;
- it has an ISBN.

Notification and payment

Every registered author receives from the Registrar an annual statement of estimated loans for each book and the PLR due.

Sampling arrangements

To help minimise the unfairnesses that arise inevitably from a sampling system, the Scheme specifies the eight regions within which authorities and sampling points have to be designated and includes libraries of varying size. Part of the sample drops out by rotation each year to allow fresh libraries to be included. The following library authorities have been designated for the year beginning 1 July 2004 (all are multi-site authorities):

- London – Harrow, Kingston upon Thames, Bexley, Brent;
- Metropolitan Boroughs – Bolton, North Tyneside, Coventry, The Wirral, Leeds;
- Counties: Northern – Nottinghamshire/Nottingham, Derbyshire/Derby, Lancashire, Northumberland;
- Counties: South West – Hampshire, Worcestershire, Devon, Stoke on Trent;
- Counties: South East – Bedfordshire/Luton, Kent, Milton Keynes/Bucks, West Sussex, Windsor and Maidenhead;
- Scotland – Orkney, Dundee, South Lanarkshire, Fife;
- Northern Ireland – all five Education and Library Boards;
- Wales – Carmarthenshire, Pembrokeshire, Conwy.

Participating local authorities are reimbursed on an actual cost basis for additional expenditure incurred in providing loans data to the PLR Office. The extra PLR work mostly consists of modifications to computer programs to accumulate loans data in the local authority computer and to transmit the data to the PLR Office at Stockton-on-Tees.

Reciprocal arrangements

Reciprocal PLR arrangements now exist with the German and Dutch PLR schemes. Authors can apply for German and Dutch PLR through the Authors' Licensing and Collecting Society. (Further information on PLR schemes internationally and recent developments within the EC towards wider recognition of PLR is available from the PLR Office or on the international PLR website.)

Further information

Public Lending Right

PLR Office, Richard House, Sorbonne Close, Stockton-on-Tees TS17 6DA
tel (01642) 604699 *fax* (01642) 615641
websites www.plr.uk.com, www.plrinternational.com
Contact The Registrar

Application forms, information, publications and a copy of its *Annual Report* are all obtainable from the PLR Office. See website for further information on eligibility for PLR, loans statistics and forthcoming developments.

PLR Advisory Committee

Advises the Secretary of State for Culture, Media and Sport and the Registrar on the operation of the PLR scheme.

Copyright

Copyright questions

Copyright is a vital part of any writer's assets, and should never be assigned or sold without due consideration and the advice of a competent authority, such as the Society of Authors, the Writers' Guild of Great Britain, or the National Union of Journalists. Michael Legat answers some of the most commonly asked questions about copyright.

Is there a period of time after which the copyright expires?

Copyright in the European Union lasts for the lifetime of the author and for a further 70 years from the end of the year of death, or, if the work is first published posthumously, for 70 years from the end of the year of publication. In most other countries of the world copyright exists similarly for the lifetime and for either 50 years or 70 years after death or posthumous publication.

If I want to include an extract from a book, poem or article, do I have to seek copyright? How much may be used without permission? What happens if I apply for copyright permission but do not get a reply?

It is essential to seek permission to quote from another author's work, unless that author has been dead for 70 years or more, or 70 years or more has passed from the date of publication of a work published posthumously. Only if you are quoting for purposes of criticism or review are you allowed to do so without obtaining permission, and even then the Copyright, Designs and Patents Act of 1988 restricts you to 400 words of prose in a single extract from a copyright work, or a series of extracts of up to 300 words each, totalling no more than 800 words, or up to 40 lines of poetry, which must not be more than 25% of the poem. However, a quotation of no more than, say, half a dozen words may usually be used without permission since it will probably not extend beyond a brief and familiar reference, as, for example, Rider Haggard's well-known phrase, 'she who must be obeyed'. If in doubt, always check. If you do not get a reply when you ask for permission to quote, insert a notice in your work saying that you have tried without success to contact the copyright owner, and would be pleased to hear from him or her so that the matter could be cleared up – and keep a copy of all the relevant correspondence, in order to back up your claim of having tried to get in touch.

If a newspaper pays for an article and I then want to sell the story to a magazine, am I free under the copyright law to do so?

Yes, provided that you have not granted copyright or exclusive use to the newspaper. When selling your work to newspapers or magazines make it clear, in writing, that you are selling only First or Second Serial Rights, not your copyright.

If I agree to have an article published for no payment do I retain any rights over how it appears?

Whether or not you are paid for the work has no bearing on the legal situation. However, the Moral Rights which apply to books, plays, television and radio scripts, do not cover you against a failure to acknowledge you as the author of an article, nor against the mutilation of your text, when it is published in a newspaper or magazine.

I want to publish a photograph that was taken in 1950. I am not sure how to contact the photographer or even if he is still alive. Am I allowed to go ahead and publish it?

The Copyright, Designs and Patents Act of 1988 works retrospectively, so a photograph taken in 1950 is bound to be in copyright until at least 2020, and the copyright will be owned by the photographer, even though, when it was taken, the copyright would have belonged to the person who commissioned it, according to the laws then in place. You should therefore make every effort to contact the photographer, keeping copies of any relevant correspondence, and in case of failure take the same course of action as described above in relation to a textual extract the copyright owner of which you have been unable to trace.

I recently read an article on the same subject as one I have written. It contained many identical facts. Did this writer breach my copyright? What if I send ideas for an article to a magazine editor and those ideas are used despite the fact that I was not commissioned? May I sue the magazine?

Facts are normally in the public domain and may be used by anyone. However, if your article contains a fact which you have discovered and no one else has published, there could be an infringement of copyright if the author who uses it fails to attribute it to you. There is no copyright in ideas, so you cannot sue a writer or a journal for using ideas that you have put forward; in any case you would find it very difficult to prove that the idea belonged to you and to no one else. There is also no copyright in titles.

Does being paid a kill fee affect my copyright in a given piece?

No, provided that you have not sold the magazine or newspaper your copyright.

Do I need to copyright a piece of writing physically – whether an essay or a novel – or is it copyrighted automatically? Does it have to carry the © symbol?

Anything that you write is your copyright, assuming that it is not copied from the work of someone else, as soon as you have written it on paper or recorded it on the disk of a computer or on tape, or broadcast it. It is not essential for the work to carry the © symbol, although its inclusion may act as a warning and help to stop another writer from plagiarising it.

Am I legally required to inform an interviewee that our conversation is being recorded?

The interviewee owns the copyright of any words that he or she speaks as soon as they are recorded on your tape. Unless you have received permission to use those words in direct quotation, you could be liable to an action for infringement of copyright. You should therefore certainly inform the interviewee that the conversation is being recorded and seek permission to quote what is said directly.

More and more newspapers and magazines have versions both in print and on the internet. How can I ensure that my work is not published on the internet without my permission?

Make sure that any clause granting electronic rights to anyone in any agreement that you sign in respect of your work specifies not only the proportion of any fees received which you will get, but that your agreement must be sought before the rights are sold. Copyright extends to electronic rights, and therefore to publication on the internet, in just the same way as to other uses of the material.

I commissioned a designer to design a business card for me, and I paid her well. Does the design belong to me or to her?

Copyright would belong to the designer, and not to the person who commissioned it (as is also true in the case of a photograph, copyright in which belongs to the photographer). However, copyright in the business card might be transferred to you if a court considered you to have gained beneficially from the card.

Michael Legat became a full-time writer after a long and successful publishing career. He is the author of a number of highly regarded books on publishing and writing.

See also...

- *UK copyright law*, page 180
- *Authors' Licensing and Collecting Society*, page 194
- *Design and Artists Copyright Society*, page 197
- *The Copyright Licensing Agency Ltd*, page 192

UK copyright law

Amanda Michaels describes the main types of work which may qualify for copyright protection, or related protection as a design, together with some of the main problems which may be faced by readers of this Yearbook in terms of protecting their own works or avoiding infringement of existing works in the UK. This is a technical area of the law, and one which is constantly developing; in an article of this length, it is not possible to deal fully with all the complexities of the law. It must also be emphasised that copyright is national in scope, and whilst works of UK authors will be protected in many other countries of the world, and works of foreign authors will generally be protected in the UK, foreign laws may deal differently with questions of subsistence, ownership and infringement.

Copyright is a creation of statute, now shaped and influenced significantly by EU harmonisation measures. On 1 August 1989, the Copyright, Designs & Patents Act 1988 ('the Act') replaced the Copyright Act 1956, which in turn replaced the Copyright Act 1911. All three Acts are still relevant to copyright today. Whilst the Act to a large degree restated the existing law, it was also innovative, in particular in the creation of a new 'design right' offering protection (generally speaking in lieu of copyright) for many industrial or commercial designs, and in the wider protection of moral rights.

The law has changed further since 1989, largely as a result of EU directives. An important change occurred on 1 January 1996, when the duration of copyright protection in respect of most works (see below) was extended from 'life of the author' plus 50 years to life plus 70 years. Further changes came into force on 1 January 1998, when a new 'database right' was created. New Community design rights were brought into effect in 2003 and numerous other amendments were made, in particular to the rules on fair dealing with copyright works, by the Copyright and Related Rights Regulations 2003 (see below).

Continuing relevance of old law

In this article, I discuss the law as it currently stands, but where a work was created prior to 1 August 1989 it will always be necessary to consider the law in force at the time of creation (or possibly first publication) in order to assess the existence or scope of any rights. Particular difficulties may arise with foreign works, which may qualify for protection in the UK as a matter of international obligation. Each Act has contained transitional provisions and these, as well as the substantive provisions of any relevant earlier Act, will need to be considered where, for instance, you wish to use an earlier work and it is necessary to decide whether permission is needed and if so, who may grant it. Publishing or licence agreements designed for use under older Acts and prior to the development of modern technologies may be unsuitable for current use.

Copyright protection of works

Copyright protects the particular form in which an author's idea has been expressed, not the idea itself. Generally speaking, plots or artistic ideas are not protected by copyright, but what is protected is the particular manner in which the idea is presented. See *Designers Guild Limited* v. *Russell Williams (Textiles) Limited* [2001] FSR 113 in which a fairly simple fabric design was found to be original and to have been copied. Of course, if someone has written an outline, script or screenplay for a television show, film, etc and that idea is confidential, then dual protection may arise in the confidential idea embodied in the documents and in the literary (and sometimes artistic) works in which the idea has taken material form. If the idea is used, but not the form, this might give rise to an action for breach of confidence, but not for infringement of copyright. Copyright prevents the copying of the *material form* in which the idea has been presented, or of a substantial part of it, measured in terms of quality, not quantity.

Section 1 of the Act sets out a number of different categories of works which can be the subject of copyright protection. These are:

- original literary, dramatic, musical or artistic works,
- sound recordings, films, broadcasts or cable programmes, and
- typographical arrangements of published editions.

These works are further defined in ss.3–8 (see box for examples).

However, no work of any description enjoys copyright protection until it has been reduced into or recorded in a tangible form, as s.3(2) provides that no copyright shall subsist in a literary, musical or artistic work until it has been recorded in writing or otherwise.

On the other hand, all that is required to achieve copyright protection is to record the original work in an appropriate medium. Once that has been done, copyright will subsist in the work (assuming that the qualifying features set out below are present) without any formality of registration or otherwise. There is, for instance, no need to publish a work to protect it. Please note, however, that the law of the United States does differ on this.

Nonetheless, there can be a real benefit in keeping a proper record of the creation of a work. Drafts or preliminary sketches should be kept and dated, so as to be able to show the development of a work. It may also be beneficial (especially where works are to be submitted to potential publishers or purchasers) to take a complete copy of the documents and send them to oneself or lodge them with a responsible third party, sealed and dated, so as to be able to provide cogent evidence of the form or content of the work at that date. Such evidence may help prove one's independent title either as claimant or defendant in a copyright infringement (or indeed breach of confidence) action.

Originality

In order to gain copyright protection, literary, dramatic, artistic and musical works must be original. Sound recordings or films which are copies of pre-existing sound recordings or films, broadcasts which infringe rights in another broadcast or cable programmes which consist of immediate retransmissions of broadcasts are not protected by copyright.

Just as the law protects the form, rather than the idea, originality relates to the 'expression of the thought', rather than to the thought itself. A work need not be original in the sense of showing innovative artistic, literary or cultural merit, but must have been the product of skill and labour on the part of the author. This can be seen for instance in the definition of certain artistic works, and in the fact that copyright protects works such as compilations (like football pools coupons or directories) and tables (including mathematical tables).

There may be considerable difficulty, at times, in deciding whether a work is of sufficient originality, or has original features, where there is a series of similar designs or amendments of existing works. See *L.A. Gear Inc.* [1992] FSR 121 and *Biotrading* [1998] FSR 109. A new edition or an adaptation of an existing work may obtain a new copyright depending upon the scope of the changes to the work; this will not affect the earlier copyright protection. See *Cala Homes* [1995] FSR 818. What is clear, though, is that merely making a 'slavish copy' of a work will not create an original work: see *Interlego AG* [1989] AC 217. On the other hand, if the work gives particular expression to a commonplace idea or an old tale, copyright may subsist in it (e.g. *Christoffer* v. *Poseidon Film Distributors Limited* (6/10/99) in which it was held that a script for an animated film of a story from Homer's *Odyssey* was an original literary work). Copyright protection will be limited to the original features of the work, or those features created or chosen by the author's input of skill and labour.

'Works' such as the titles of books or periodicals, or advertising slogans, which may have required a good deal of original thought, generally are not accorded copyright protection, because they are too short to be deemed literary works.

Definitions under the Act

Literary work is defined as: 'any work, other than a dramatic or musical work, which is written, spoken or sung, and accordingly includes: (a) a table or compilation other than a database, (b) a computer program, (c) preparatory design material for a computer program and (d) a database.'

A musical work means: 'a work consisting of music, exclusive of any words or action intended to be sung, spoken or performed with the music.'

An artistic work means: '(a) a graphic work, photograph, sculpture or collage, irrespective of artistic quality, (b) a work of architecture being a building or model for a building, or (c) a work of artistic craftsmanship.'

These categories of work are not mutually exclusive, e.g. a film may be protected both as a film and as a dramatic work. See *Norowzian* v. *Arks* [2000] FSR 363.

Qualification

The Act is limited in its effects to the UK (and to colonies to which it may be extended by Order). It is aimed primarily at protecting the works of British citizens, or works which were first published here. However, in line with the requirements of various international conventions, copyright protection in the UK is also accorded to the works of nationals of many foreign states, as well as to works first published in those states, on a reciprocal basis.

As for works of nationals of other member states of the European Union, there is a principle of equal treatment, so that protection must be offered to such works here: see *Phil Collins* [1993] 3 CMLR 773.

The importance of these rules mainly arises when one is trying to find out whether a foreign work is protected by copyright here, for instance, if one wishes to make a film based upon a foreign novel.

Ownership

The general rule is that the copyright in a work will first be owned by its author, the author being the creator of the work. In most cases this is self-explanatory, but the definition of 'author' in relation to films and sound recordings has changed over the years; currently, the author of a sound recording is its producer, and the authors of a film are the producer and principal director.

One important exception to the general rule is that the copyright in a work made by an employee in the course of his or her employment will belong to their employer, subject to any agreement to the contrary. However, this rule does not apply to freelance designers, journalists, etc, and not even to nominally self-employed company directors. This obviously may lead to problems if the question of copyright ownership is not dealt with when an agreement is made to create, purchase or use a work (see box, page 185).

Where a work is produced by several people who collaborate in such a way that each one's contribution is not distinct from that of the other(s), then they will be joint authors of the work. Where two people collaborate to write a song, one producing the lyrics and the other the music, there will be two separate copyright works, the copyright of which will be owned by each of the authors separately. But where two people write a play, each rewriting what the other produces, there will be a joint work.

The importance of knowing whether the work is joint or not arises:

- in working out the duration of the copyright, and
- from the fact that joint works can only be exploited with the agreement of all the joint authors, so that all of them have to join in any licence, although each of them can sue for infringement without joining the other(s) as a claimant in the proceedings.

Duration of copyright

As a result of amendments brought into effect on 1 January 1996, copyright in literary, dramatic, musical or artistic works expires at the end of the period of 70 years from the end of the calendar year in which the author dies (s.12(1)). Where there are joint authors, then the 70 years runs from the death of the last of them to die. If the author is unknown, there will be 70 years protection from the date the work was first made or (where applicable) first made available to the public. Previously, the protection was for 'life plus 50'.

The extended 70-year term also applies to films, and runs from the end of the calendar year in which the death occurs of the last to die of the principal director, the author of the screenplay or the dialogue, or the composer of any music created for the film (s.13B). This obviously may be a nightmare to establish, and there are certain presumptions in s.66A which may help someone wishing to use material from an old film.

However, sound recordings are still protected by copyright only for 50 years from the year of making or release (s.13A); similarly, broadcasts, cable programmes and computer-generated works still get only 50 years protection.

The new longer term applies without difficulty to works created after 1 January 1996 and to works in copyright on 31 December 1995. The owner of that extended copyright will be the person who owned it on 31 December 1995, unless that person had only a limited term of ownership, in which case the extra 20 years will be added on to the reversionary term.

Where copyright had expired here, but the author died between 50 and 70 years ago, the position is more complicated. EC Directive 93/98 provided that if a work was protected by copyright anywhere in the European Union on 1 July 1995, copyright would revive for it in any other state until the end of the same 70-year period. This may make it necessary to look at the position in the states offering a longer term of protection, namely Germany, France and Spain.

Licensing

A licence is granted to another to exploit the right whilst the licensor retains overall ownership.

Licences do not need to take any form in particular, and may indeed be granted orally. However, an exclusive licence (i.e. one which excludes even the copyright owner himself from exploiting the work) must be in writing, if the licensee is to enjoy rights in respect of infringements concurrent with those of the copyright owner.

Ownership of the revived term of copyright will belong to the person who was the owner of the copyright when the initial term expired, save that if that person died (or a company, etc, ceased to exist) before 1 January 1996, then the revived term will vest in the author's personal representatives, and in the case of a film, in the principal director's personal representatives.

Any licence affecting a copyright work which subsisted on 31 December 1995 and was then for the full term of the copyright continues to have effect during any extended term of copyright, subject to any agreement to the contrary (paragraph 21 of the Regulations).

The increased term offered to works of other EU nationals as a result of the Term Directive is not offered automatically to the nationals of other states, but will only apply where an equally long term is offered in their state of origin.

Where acts are carried out in relation to such revived copyright works, pursuant to things done whilst they were in the public domain, protection from infringement is available. A licence as of right may also be available, on giving notice to the copyright owner and paying a royalty.

Dealing with copyright works

Ownership of the copyright in a work confers upon the owner the exclusive right to deal with the work in a number of ways, and essentially stops all unauthorised exploitation of the work. Ownership of the copyright is capable of being separated from ownership of the material form in which the work is embodied, depending upon the terms of any agreement or the circumstances. Even buying an original piece of artwork will not in general carry with it the legal title to the copyright, as an effective assignment must be in writing signed by the assignor (although beneficial ownership might pass: see page 185).

Assignments

In an assignment, rights in the work are sold, with the owner retaining no interest in it (except, possibly, for payment by way of royalties).

An assignment must be in writing, signed by or on behalf of the assignor, but no other formality is required. One can make an assignment of future copyright (under s.91). Where the author of a projected work agrees in writing that he will assign the rights in a future work to another, the copyright vests in the assignee immediately upon the creation of the work, without further formalities.

These rules do not affect the common law as to beneficial interests in copyright. One possibility may be that a court will, in the right circumstances, find or infer an agreement to assign the copyright in a work, e.g. where a sole trader who had title to the copyright used in his business later incorporated the business and allowed the company to exploit the software as if it were its own, an agreement to assign was inferred (see *Lakeview Computers plc* 26/11/99). Alternatively, if the court finds that a work was commissioned to be made, and that there was a common intention that the purchaser should own the copyright, the court may order the author to assign the copyright to him. 'Commission' in this context means only to order a particular piece of work to be done: see *Apple Corps Ltd* v. *Cooper* [1993] FSR 286 (a 1956 Act case).

Copyright works can be exploited by their owners in two ways:

- Assignment: rights in a work may be sold, with the owner retaining no interest in it (except, possibly, for payment by way of royalties or some reversionary rights in certain agreed circumstances) – see box; or
- Licensing: the owner may grant a licence to another to exploit the right, whilst retaining overall ownership (see box).

Agreements dealing with copyright should make it clear whether an assignment or a licence is being granted. There may be significant advantages for the author in granting a licence rather than an assignment, for where the assignee's rights pass to a third party, for instance on his insolvency, the author cannot normally enforce the original agreement to pay royalties, etc against the purchaser (*Barker* v. *Stickney* [1919] 1 KB 121). If the agreement is unclear, the Court is likely to find that the grantee took the minimum rights necessary for his intended use of the work, very probably an exclusive licence rather than an assignment (*Ray* v. *Classic FM plc* [1998] FSR 622). The question of moral rights (see below) will also have to be considered by the parties.

Assignments and licences often split up the various rights contained within the copyright. So, for instance, a licence might be granted to one person to publish a novel in book form, another person might be granted the film, television and video rights, and yet another the right to translate the novel into other languages.

Assignments and licences may also confer rights according to territory, dividing the USA from the EU or different EU countries one from the other. Any such agreement should take into account divergences between different national copyright laws. Furthermore, when seeking to divide rights between different territories of the EU there is a danger of infringing the competition rules of the EU. Professional advice should be taken, as breach of these rules may attract a fine and can render the agreement void in whole or in part.

Licences can, of course, be of varying lengths. There is no need for a licence to be granted for the whole term of copyright. Well-drafted licences will provide for termination on breach, including the failure of the licensee to exploit the work, and on the insolvency of the licensee and will specify whether the rights may be assigned or sub-licensed.

Copyright may be assigned by will. A bequest of an original document, etc embodying an unpublished copyright work will carry the copyright.

Infringement

The main type of infringement is what is commonly thought of as plagiarism, that is, copying the work. In fact, copyright confers on the owner the exclusive right to do a number of specified acts, so that anyone doing those acts without his permission will infringe. It is important to note that it is not necessary to copy a work exactly or use all of it; it is sufficient if a substantial part is used. That question is to be judged on a qualitative not a quantitative basis, bearing in mind that it is the skill and labour of the author which is to be protected (see *Ravenscroft* v. *Herbert* [1980] RPC 193 and *Designers Guild*). It is important to note that primary infringement, such as copying, can be done innocently of any intention to infringe.

The form of infringement common to all forms of copyright works is that of copying. This means reproducing the work in any material form. Infringement may occur where an existing work provides the inspiration for a later one, if copying results, for example by including edited extracts from a history book in a novel (*Ravenscroft*), using a photograph as the inspiration for a painting (*Baumann* v. *Fussell* [1978] RPC 485), or words from a verse of one song in another (*Ludlow Music* v. *Williams* [2001] FSR 271). Infringement will not necessarily be prevented merely by the application of significant new skill and labour by the infringer, nor by a change of medium.

In the case of a two-dimensional artistic work, reproduction can mean making a copy in three dimensions, and vice versa. However, s.51 of the Act provides that in the case of a 'design document or model' (for definition, see page 189) for something which is not *itself* an artistic work, it is no infringement to make an article to that design. This means that whilst it would be an infringement of copyright to make an article from a design drawing for, say, a sculpture, it will not be an infringement of copyright to make a handbag from a copy of the design drawing for it, or from a handbag which one has purchased. Instead, such designs are generally protected by design right or as registered designs (for both see below).

Copying a film, broadcast or cable programme can include making a copy of the whole or a substantial part of any image from it (see s.17(4)). This means that copying one frame of the film will be an infringement. It is not an infringement of copyright in a film to reshoot the film (*Norowzian*) (though there would doubtless be an infringement of the copyright in underlying works such as the literary copyright in the screenplay).

Copying is generally proved by showing substantial similarities between the original and the alleged copy, plus an opportunity to copy. Surprisingly often, minor errors in the original are reproduced by an infringer.

'Secondary' infringements

Secondary infringements consist not of making infringing copies, but of dealing with existing infringing copies in some way. It is an infringement to import an infringing copy into the UK, and to possess in the course of business, or to sell, hire, offer for sale or hire, or distribute in the course of trade an infringing copy. However, none of these acts will be an infringement unless the alleged infringer knew or had reason to believe that the articles were infringing copies. What is sufficient knowledge will depend upon the facts of each case (see *LA Gear Inc.* [1992] FSR 121, *ZYX Records* v. *King* [1997] 2 All ER 132 and *Pensher Security* [2000] RPC 249). Merely putting someone on notice of a dispute as to ownership of copyright may not suffice to give him or her reason to believe in infringement for this purpose: *Hutchison* [1995] FSR 365.

Other secondary infringements consist of permitting a place to be used for a public performance in which copyright is infringed and supplying apparatus to be used for infringing public performance, again, in each case, with safeguards for innocent acts.

Copying need not be direct, so that, for instance, where the copyright is in a fabric design, copying the material without ever having seen the original drawing will still be an infringement, as will 'reverse engineering' of industrial designs, for example to make unlicensed spare parts (*British Leyland* [1986] AC 577; *Mars* v. *Teknowledge* [2000] FSR 138).

Issuing copies of a work to the public when they have not previously been put into circulation in the UK is also an infringement of all types of work.

Other acts which may amount to an infringement depend upon the nature of the work. It will be an infringement of the copyright in a literary, dramatic or musical work to perform it in public, whether by live performance or by playing recordings. Similarly, it is an infringement of the copyright in a sound recording, film, broadcast or cable programme to play or show it in public. Many copyright works will also be infringed by the rental or lending of copies of the work.

One rather different form of infringement is to make an adaptation of a literary, dramatic or musical work. An adaptation includes, in the case of a literary work, a translation, in the case of a non-dramatic work, making a dramatic work of it, and vice versa. A transcription or arrangement of a musical work is an adaptation of it.

There are also a number of 'secondary' infringements – see box.

Exceptions to infringement

The Act provides a large number of exceptions to the rules on infringement which were extended and amended with effect from 31 October 2003 by the Copyright and Related Rights Regulations 2003. They are far too numerous to be dealt with here in full, but they include:

- fair dealing with literary, dramatic, musical or artistic works for the purpose of non-commercial research or private study (s.29);
- fair dealing for the purpose of criticism or review or reporting current events, as to which see e.g. *Pro Sieben Media* [1999] FSR 610; *Hyde Park* v. *Yelland* [2001] Ch. 143; *NLA* v. *Marks & Spencer Plc* [2002] RPC 4) (s.30);
- incidental inclusion of a work in an artistic work, sound recording, film, broadcast or cable programme (s.31);

- educational exceptions (ss.32–36A);
- exceptions for libraries (ss.37–44A) and public administration (ss.45–50);
- making transient copies as part of a technological process (s.28A) and backing-up, or converting a computer program or accessing a licensed database (s.50A–D);
- dealing with a work where the author cannot be identified and the work seems likely to be out of copyright (s.57);
- public recitation, if accompanied by a sufficient acknowledgement (s.59).

The effect of the Human Rights Act on copyright in relation to the right to free speech seems likely to be limited, as sufficient protection is to be found in the fair dealing provisions: *Ashdown* v. *Telegraph Group Limited* [2002] Ch. 149.

There is no defence of parody.

Remedies for infringements

The copyright owner will usually want to prevent the repetition or continuation of the infringement and he will want compensation.

In almost all cases an injunction will be sought to stop the infringement. The Courts have useful powers to grant an injunction at an early stage, indeed even before any infringement takes place, if a real threat of damage can be shown. Such an interim injunction can be applied for on three days' notice (or without notice in appropriate cases), but will not be granted unless the claimant has a reasonably good case and can show that he would suffer 'unquantifiable' damage if the defendant's activities continued pending trial. Delay in bringing an interim application may be fatal to its success. An injunction may not be granted where the claimant clearly only wants financial compensation (*Ludlow Music*).

Financial compensation may be sought in one of two forms. Firstly, damages. These will usually be calculated upon evidence of the loss caused to the claimant, sometimes based upon loss of business, at others upon the basis of what would have been a proper licence fee for the defendant's acts. Additional damages may be awarded in rare cases for flagrant infringements. See for example *Notts. Healthcare* v. *News Group Newspapers* [2002] RPC 49.

Damages will not be awarded for infringement where the infringer did not know, and had no reason to believe, that copyright subsisted in the work. This exception is of limited use to a defendant, though, in the usual situation where the work was of such a nature that he should have known that copyright would subsist in it.

The alternative to damages is an account of profits, that is, the net profits made by the infringer by virtue of his illicit exploitation of the copyright. Where an account of profits is sought, no award of flagrant damages can be made. See *Redrow Homes Limited* [1999] 1 AC 197.

A copyright owner may also apply for delivery up of infringing copies.

Finally, there are various criminal offences relating to the making, importation, possession, sale, hire, distribution, etc of infringing copies.

Design right

Many industrial designs are excluded from copyright protection by s.51. Alternatively, the term of copyright protection is limited to 25 years from first industrial exploitation, by s.52. However, they may instead be protected by the 'design right' created by ss.213–64. Like copyright, design right does not depend upon registration, but upon the creation of a suitable design by a "qualifying person".

Design right is granted to original designs consisting of the shape or configuration (internal or external) of the whole or part of an article, not being merely 'surface decoration'. A design is not original if it was commonplace in the design field in question at the time of its creation. In *Farmers Build* [1999] RPC 461, 'commonplace' was defined as meaning a design of a type which would excite no 'peculiar attention' amongst those in the trade, or one which amounts to a run-of-the-mill combination of well-known features. Designs are not protected if they consist of a method or principle of construction, or are dictated by the shape, etc of an article to which the new article is to be connected or of which it is to form part, the so-called 'must-fit' and 'must-match' exclusions. In *Ocular Sciences* [1997] RPC 289, these exclusions had a devastating effect upon numerous design rights claimed for contact lens designs.

Design right subsists in designs made by or for qualifying persons (see, broadly, 'Qualification' on page 182) or first marketed in the UK or EU or any other country to which the provision may be extended by Order.

Design right lasts only 15 years from the end of the year in which it was first recorded or an article made to the design, or (if shorter) 10 years from the end of the year in which articles made according to the design were first sold or hired out. During the last five years of the term of protection, a licence to use the design can be obtained 'as of right' but against payment of a proper licence fee. Hence, design right may give only five years 'absolute' protection, as opposed to the 'life plus 70' of copyright.

The designer will be the owner of the right, unless it was commissioned, in which case the commissioner will be the first owner. An employee's designs made in the course of employment will belong to the employer.

The right given to the owner of a design right is the exclusive right to reproduce the design for commercial purposes. The rules as to assignments, licensing and infringement, both primary and secondary, are substantially similar to those described above in relation to copyright, as are the remedies available.

There have recently been significant changes to the law on registered designs, which coexist with the right given by the unregistered design right discussed above. The Registered Design Act 1949 has been amended (and expanded) in line with EU legislation, and now permits the registration of designs consisting of the appearance of the whole or any part of a product resulting from features of the product itself, such as shape, materials, etc or from the ornamentation of the product. It covers industrial or handicraft items, their packaging or get-up, etc. Designs must be novel and not solely dictated by function. The range of designs which may be registered is wider than under the old law, and designs need not necessarily have 'eye appeal'. Such designs provide a monopoly right renewable for up to 25 years. For further explanation see the useful guidance on the Patent Office website.

EU Regulation 6/2002 has created two new Community design regimes, one for registered and one for unregistered designs. It is not possible in the space available here to describe these new regimes in detail but the Regulation is available online at www.europa.ue.int/eur-lex. In brief, such designs (which are *very* broadly defined in Article 3) must be 'new' and have 'individual character'. The registered right, available from April 2003, may be enjoyed for up to 25 years in five-year tranches, but an unregistered Community design right lasts only three years. The unregistered right protects the design from copying, but the registered right gives 'absolute' exclusivity, in that it may be infringed without copying.

Moral rights

The Act also provides for the protection of certain 'moral rights'.

The right of 'paternity' is for the author of a copyright literary, dramatic, musical or artistic work, or the director of a copyright film, to be identified as the author/ director, largely whenever the work is commercially exploited (s.77).

However, the right does not arise unless it has been 'asserted' by appropriate words in writing, or in the case of an artistic work by ensuring that the artist's name appears on the frame, etc (see end). There are exceptions to the right, in particular where first ownership of the copyright vested in the author's or director's employer.

The right of 'integrity' protects work from 'derogatory treatment', meaning an addition to, deletion from, alteration or adaptation of a work which amounts to distortion or mutilation of the work or is otherwise prejudicial to the honour or reputation of the author/director.

Again, infringement of the right takes place when the maltreated work is published commercially or performed or exhibited in public. There are various exceptions set out in s.81 of the Act, in particular where the publication is in a newspaper, etc, and the work was made for inclusion in it or made available with the author's consent.

Where the copyright in the work vested first in the author's or director's employer, he or she has no right to 'integrity' unless identified at the time of the relevant act or on published copies of the work.

These rights subsist for as long as the copyright in the work subsists.

A third moral right conferred by the Act is not to have a literary, dramatic, musical or artistic work falsely attributed to one as author, or to have a film falsely attributed to one as director, again where the work in question is published, etc. This right subsists until 20 years after a person's death.

None of these rights can be assigned during the person's lifetime, but all of them either pass on the person's death as directed by his or her will or fall into his residuary estate.

A fourth but rather different moral right is conferred by s.85. It gives a person who has commissioned the taking of photographs for private purposes a right to prevent copies of the work being issued to the public, etc.

The remedies for breach of these moral rights again include damages and an injunction, although s.103(2) specifically foresees the granting of an injunction qualified by a right to the defendant to do the acts complained of, if subject to a suitable disclaimer.

Moral rights are exercisable in relation to works in which the copyright has revived subject to any waiver or assertion of the right made before 1 January 1996 (see details as to who may exercise rights in paragraph 22 of the Regulations).

Useful websites

www.patent.gov.uk/index.htm
Website of the Patent Office.

www.intellectual-property.gov.uk

www.wipo.int
Website of the World Intellectual Property Organisation.

www.baillii.org
A website containing judgements from UK courts and with links to equivalent foreign websites. Legislation on the site may be in an unamended form.

NOTICE
AMANDA LOUISE MICHAELS hereby asserts and gives notice of her right under s.77 of the Copyright, Designs & Patents Act 1988 to be identified as the author of the foregoing article.

AMANDA MICHAELS

Amanda L. Michaels is a barrister in private practice in London, and specialises in copyright, designs, trade marks, and similar intellectual property and 'media' work. She is author of *A Practical Guide to Trade Mark Law* (Sweet & Maxwell, 3rd edn 2002).

Further reading

Garnett, Rayner James and Davies, *Copinger and Skone James on Copyright*, Sweet & Maxwell, 14th edn, 1999 and Supplement 2002
Laddie, Prescott and Vitoria, *The Modern Law of Copyright*, Butterworths, 3rd edn, 2000
Flint, *A User's Guide to Copyright*, Butterworths, 5th edn, 2000
Bainbridge, David, *Intellectual Property*, Pearson Education, 5th edn, 2002

Copyright Acts

Copyright, Designs and Patents Act 1998 (but it is vital to use an up-to-date amended version)
The Duration of Copyright and Rights in Performances Regulations 1995 (SI 1995 No 3297)
The Copyright and Related Rights Regulations 2003 (SI 2003 No 2498)
see also Numerous Orders in Council

The Copyright Licensing Agency Ltd

The Copyright Licensing Agency (CLA) collects and distributes money on behalf of artists, writers and publishers for the copying, scanning and emailing of their work. CLA operates on a non-profit basis, and issues licences to schools, further and higher education, business and government bodies so that such organisations can access the copyright material in books, journals, law reports, magazines and periodicals.

Why was CLA established?

CLA was established in 1982 by its members, the Authors' Licensing and Collecting Society (ALCS) and the Publishers Licensing Society (PLS) to promote and enforce the intellectual property rights of British rightsholders both at home and abroad. CLA also has an agency agreement with the Design and Artists Copyright Society (DACS), which represents artists and illustrators.

ALCS has two corporate members – the Society of Authors and the Writers' Guild of Great Britain. It also has a large number of individual authors as members and affiliations with the National Union of Journalists and the Chartered Institute of Journalists. PLS members are the Publishers Association, the Periodical Publishers Association and the Association of Learned and Professional Society Publishers.

How CLA helps artists and writers

CLA allows licensed users access to over 16 million titles worldwide. In return CLA ensures artists and writers, along with publishers, are fairly recompensed by the licence fees, which CLA collects and forwards to its members for onward distribution to artists, writers and publishers.

The collective management of licensing schemes means that CLA can provide users with the simplest and most cost-effective means of obtaining authorisation for photocopying, while copy limits ensure fair recompense is maintained for rightsholders.

CLA is has developed licences which enable digitisation of existing print material. The licence enables users to scan and electronically send extracts from copyright works. Scanning and email distribution is only available for UK works at present.

Licence to copy

CLA's licensees fall into three main categories:

- education (schools, further and higher education);
- government (central, local, public bodies); and
- business (business, industry, professionals).

CLA develops licences to meet the specific needs of each sector and groupings within each sector. Depending on the requirement, there are both blanket and transactional licences available. Every licence allows the photocopying of most books, journals, magazines and periodicals published in the UK.

An international dimension

Many countries have established equivalents to CLA and the number of such agencies is set to grow. Nearly all these agencies, including CLA, are members of the International Federation of Reproduction Rights Organisations (IFRRO).

Through reciprocal arrangements with these organisations, any CLA licence also allows copying from an expanding list of publications in other countries. Currently these countries are: Australia, Canada (including Quebec), Denmark, Finland, France, Germany, Greece, Iceland, Ireland, The Netherlands, New Zealand, Norway, South Africa, Spain, Sweden, Switzerland and the USA.

CLA receives monies from these organisations for the copying of UK material abroad and forwards it to rightsholders.

Further information

The Copyright Licensing Agency Ltd
90 Tottenham Court Road, London W1T 4LP
tel 020-7631 5555 *fax* 020-7631 5500
email cla@cla.co.uk
website www.cla.co.uk
CBC House, 24 Canning Street, Edinburgh EH3 8E9
tel 0131-272 2711 *fax* 0131-272 2811
email clascotland@cla.co.uk

Distribution

The fees collected from licensees are forwarded to artists, authors and publishers via ALCS, DACS and PLS respectively, and are based on statistical surveys and records of copying activity. For the year ending 31 March 2003 in excess of £36 million was returned to rightsholders.

Respecting copyright

CLA also believes it is important to raise awareness of the copyright in published material and the need to protect the creativity of artists, authors and publishers. To this end, CLA organises a range of activities such as copyright workshops in schools, seminars for businesses and institutions and an extensive exhibition programme. A comprehensive website is regularly updated and a bi-annual newsletter, *Clarion*, is posted to all licensees and to those individuals and groups concerned with copyright.

Protecting creativity

CLA believes in working together with all sectors to take into account their differing needs, meaning legal action is rare. However, organisations – especially in the business sector – need to be made aware that copyright is a legally enforceable right enshrined in statute law, not a voluntary option. CLA's recently restructured compliance division aims to continue the education programme. However, as a last resort it has the power to take legal proceedings on behalf of rightsholders.

Authors' Licensing and Collecting Society

The Authors' Licensing and Collecting Society (ALCS) is the rights management society for all UK writers.

The Authors' Licensing and Collecting Society (ALCS) is the UK collective rights management society for writers. Established in 1977, the Society represents the interests of all UK writers and aims to ensure that they are fairly compensated for any works that are copied, broadcast or recorded.

A non-profit company, ALCS was set up in the wake of the campaign to establish a Public Lending Right to help writers protect and exploit their collective rights. Today, it is the largest writers' organisation in the UK with a membership of over 44,000 and an annual distribution of over £12 million in royalties to writers.

The Society is committed to ensuring that the rights of writers, both intellectual property and moral, are fully respected and fairly rewarded. It represents all types of writers and includes educational, research and academic authors drawn from the professions; scriptwriters, adaptors, playwrights, poets, editors and freelance journalists, across the print and broadcast media.

Internationally recognised as a leading authority on copyright matters and authors' interests, ALCS is committed to fostering an awareness of intellectual property issues among the writing community. It maintains a close watching brief on all matters affecting copyright both in the UK and internationally and makes regular representations to the UK government and the European Union.

ALCS works closely with the Writers' Guild of Great Britain (see page 277), the Society of Authors (see page 252) and by reciprocal agreement with over 50 collecting societies overseas. Owned and controlled by writers, it is governed by a non-executive board of 12 directors, all of whom are working writers. Four of these directors are nominated by the Writers' Guild of Great Britain and four by the Society of Authors. The other four independent members are elected directly by ALCS Ordinary Members.

The Society collects fees that are difficult, time-consuming or legally impossible for writers and their representatives to claim on an individual basis, money that is nonetheless due to them. To date, it has distributed over £80 million in secondary royalties to writers.

Over the years, ALCS has developed highly specialised knowledge and sophisticated systems that can track writers and their works against any secondary use for which they are due payment. A network of international contacts and reciprocal agreements with foreign collecting societies also ensures that British writers are compensated for any similar use overseas.

The primary sources of fees due to writers are secondary royalties from the following:

Photocopying

The single largest source of income, this is administered by the Copyright Licensing Agency (CLA – see page 192). Created in 1982 by ALCS and the Publishers Licensing Society (PLS), the CLA grants licences to users for the copying of books, periodicals and journals. This includes schools, colleges, universities, central and local government departments as well as the British Library, businesses and other institutions. Licence fees are based on the number of people who benefit and the number of copies made. The revenue from this is then split between the rightsholders: authors, publishers and artists. Money due to authors is transferred to ALCS for distribution. ALCS also receives photocopying payments from foreign sources.

Digitisation

In 1999, the CLA launched its licensing scheme for the digitisation of printed texts. It offers licences to organisations for storing and using digital versions of authors' printed works, which have been scanned into a computer. Again, the fees are split between authors and publishers.

Foreign Public Lending Right

The Public Lending Right (PLR) system pays authors whose books are borrowed from public libraries. Through reciprocal agreements with VG Wort (the German collecting society) and Stichting Leenrecht (the Dutch collecting Society), ALCS members receive payment whenever their books are borrowed from German and Dutch libraries. (Please note that ALCS does not administer the UK Public Lending Right, this is managed directly by the UK PLR Office; see page 176.)

ALCS also receives other payments from Germany. These cover the loan of academic, scientific and technical titles from academic libraries; extracts of authors' works in textbooks and the press, together with other one-off fees.

Simultaneous cable retransmission

This involves the simultaneous showing of one country's television signals in another country, via a cable network. Cable companies pay a central collecting organisation a percentage of their subscription fees, which must be collectively administered. This sum is then divided by the rightsholders. ALCS receives the writers' share for British programmes containing literary and dramatic material and distributes this to them.

The BBC

ALCS licenses BBC Worldwide Ltd for the inclusion of material within the ALCS repertoire. The licence covers the direct reception and cable retransmission of BBC Prime, a satellite entertainment channel, in Europe and Africa and other countries.

Educational recording

ALCS, together with the main broadcasters and rightsholders, set up the Educational Recording Agency (ERA) in 1989 to offer licences to educational establishments. ERA collects fees from the licensees and pays ALCS the amount due to writers for their literary works.

Other sources of income include a blank tape levy and small, miscellaneous literary rights.

Tracing authors

ALCS is dedicated to protecting and promoting authors' rights and enabling writers to maximise their income. It is committed to ensuring that royalties due to writers are efficiently collected and speedily distributed to them. One of its greatest challenges is finding some of the writers for whom it holds funds and ensuring that they claim their money.

Any published author or broadcast writer could have some funds held by ALCS for them. It may be a nominal sum or it could run in to several thousand pounds. Either call or visit the ALCS website – see box for further details.

Membership

Authors' Licensing and Collecting Society Ltd

14-18 Holborn, London EC1N 2LE
tel 020-7395 0600 *fax* 020-7395 0660
email alcs@alcs.co.uk
website www.alcs.co.uk
Chief Executive Jane Carr

ALCS membership is open to all writers and successors to their estates at a current annual subscription fee of £10 for Ordinary members. Members of the Society of Authors and the Writers' Guild of Great Britain have free Ordinary membership of ALCS. In addition, members of the National Union of Journalists, Chartered Institute of Journalists, British Association of Journalists and the British Comedy Writers' Association have free Associate membership of ALCS. You may also register direct with ALCS for free Associate membership.

ALCS operations are primarily funded through a commission levied on distributions and membership fees. The commission on funds generated for Ordinary members is currently 11%. Writers do not have to become Ordinary members of ALCS to receive funds due to them for the reproduction of their works; however, for Associate members such funds are subject to a levy of 14%. Most writers will find that this, together with a number of other membership benefits, provides excellent value to membership.

Design and Artists Copyright Society

The Design and Artists Copyright Society (DACS) is a not-for-profit membership organisation which exists to protect and promote the copyright of visual creators in the UK and worldwide.

About DACS

DACS was established in 1984 and is the UK's copyright licensing and collecting society for visual creators. It acts as an agent for its members, offering a Primary Licensing service for copyright consumers wishing to license artistic works. It negotiates a share of revenue from Collective Licensing schemes on behalf of all visual creators and distributes this through the its Payback scheme.

DACS membership represents over 36,000 international fine artists as well as 16,000 commercial visual creators for collective licensing only. It is a not-for-profit organisation and retains only 25% of licensing revenue to cover costs, so 75% goes to visual creators.

DACS Licensing Services

Copyright in artistic works is governed in the UK by the Copyright, Designs & Patents Act 1988 (as amended).

What is Primary Licensing?

A primary licence is a one-off use, for example when a publisher wants to reproduce an artistic work in a book. DACS offers licences for many uses and charges fees according to the type, purpose and extent of the reproduction. Its fees are set on a rate card, or by negotiation for merchandising or advertising uses.

What is collective licensing of secondary uses?

Secondary uses of artistic works are often collectively administered under blanket licences, for example when a business needs to photocopy pages of books or magazines. Primary licences may not be practical so DACS offers collective licences, either directly or through appointed agents. It negotiates a share of the revenue from these schemes on behalf of visual creators and pays it out via Payback.

Membership

Membership of DACS is open to all visual creators, their heirs and beneficiaries working in any medium. It manages their copyright by negotiating terms and collecting fees on their behalf. Its experienced licensing staff work closely with both artists and consumers to ensure the best balance of interests is achieved when licensing works. DACS provides licences for a wide range of primary uses, both commercial and non-commercial, in academic and business environments.

Other benefits

DACS belongs to an international network of collecting societies in 27 countries. Visual creators' rights are administered on the same basis in all these countries and they will receive royalties when their work has been reproduced overseas.

DACS is committed to protecting copyright. In some circumstances, it may be able to investigate infringement of an artist's copyright.

Because DACS is an authoritative voice for visual creators' rights in the UK, new members who join will be strengthening the presence of visual creators and their rights in the copyright community as a whole. DACS also gives its members access to a range of services.

Contact details

Design and Artists Copyright Society (DACS)
Parchment House, 13 Northburgh Street, London EC1V 0JP
tel 020-7336 8811 *fax* 020-7336 8822
email info@dacs.org.uk
website www.dacs.org.uk

Copyright

- Copyright is a right granted to creators under law.
- Copyright in all artistic works is established from the moment of creation – the only qualification is that the work must be original.
- There is no registration system in the UK; copyright comes into operation automatically and lasts the lifetime of the visual creator plus a period of 70 years after their death.
- After death, copyright is usually transferred to the visual creator's heirs or beneficiaries. When the 70-year period has expired, the work then enters the public domain and no longer benefits from copyright protection.
- The copyright owner has the exclusive right to authorise the reproduction (or copy) of a work in any medium by any other party.
- Any reproduction can only take place with the copyright owner's consent. Permission is usually granted in return for a fee, which enables the visual creator to derive some income from other people using his or her work.
- If a visual creator is commissioned to produce a work, he or she will usually retain the copyright unless an agreement is signed which specifically assigns the copyright. When visual creators are employees and create work during the course of their employment, the employer retains the copyright in those works.

See also...

- *Copyright questions*, page 177
- *UK copyright law*, page 180

Magazines and newspapers

Cartoons and deadlines

A good cartoon needs only a glance to take in its message. But what makes a good cartoonist? Ros Asquith introduces the world of drawing cartoons for a living.

If anyone had told me, when I was 10 years old, that I'd earn a living by drawing pictures, I'd have thought they were mad. I'd also have believed that I'd never be good enough. After spending nearly 20 years as a cartoonist and illustrator I still worry that both those things might be true – and I live in fear of being found out. I once worked for a newspaper editor who received a letter that said 'My four year-old can draw better than Ros Asquith'. He replied, paraphrasing Groucho Marx: 'Astonishing – send me your four year-old's work post haste.' I was lucky to have such an editor. I could just as easily have been sacked.

I've been both dismissed and defended countless times and if you really want to be a cartoonist you need to learn to take criticism as gracefully as praise. A cartoon is an immediate statement. It must make itself understood in one glance and is therefore more vulnerable to criticism than any article. The phrase 'saw your cartoon' has a very different meaning from 'saw your article'. It means the reader has seen, understood, liked or disliked, all at once. And there will always be readers who dislike or are offended by your work – and a great many of them who think they could do it better.

Not surprising then, that a distinguished colleague once gave the following pearls of wisdom to an eager young woman hoping to get started in the business, 'I always have just two words of advice for young cartoonists: take poison.' And who can blame him? We cartoonists are paid to play and we have to make it look difficult just in case other people get the idea they might be able to do it too.

How do you get started?

First, you must love to draw. Secondly, you must be brimming with ideas. Thirdly, a sense of humour is an asset. But love of drawing, the sheer sensual joy of holding a pencil and the pleasure of guiding it across the page, the endless magic of creating something out of nothing, is the major qualification. Perhaps it's not surprising that I've ended up doing what I do, since my earliest memories are linked to the pictures I drew as a child. I illustrated my own life from an early age, whether the adventures I drew were real or imaginary.

You may say that love of drawing is not enough, surely you must also be *good* at drawing? That's debatable. Almost all small children love to draw but sadly the way we teach art in primary schools soon weeds out those who 'can draw' from those who 'can't'. This is a nail in the coffin of talent for everyone who can't make things look realistic at an early age. If they were encouraged, by peers as well as teachers, to pursue expressiveness and ideas rather than striving for realism, perhaps children would not abandon drawing by the age of 11. We lose a vast amount of creative talent in this way, but it usually means that anyone considering cartooning or illustration as a career is already settled into the little box labelled 'can draw.' You need more than this. If you are someone who can't imagine a day without drawing, then go for it.

There are as many routes to cartooning as there are cartoonists. One thing we have in common, though, is heads full of heroes. I grew up devouring cartoons in every form: Leo Baxendale's fantastic Bash Street Kids in the *Beano*, Ronald Searle's ferocious St Trinian's schoolgirls, Thelwell's recalcitrant ponies, all the *New Yorker* cartoonists but especially James Thurber, Charles Addams (whose fiendish gallows humour inspired the long-running *Addams Family* series on television), and the endlessly inventive, wordlessly eloquent Saul Steinberg. I revelled in the artistry of *Batman* comics and could have probably won *Mastermind* with Superman as my subject when I was about 12. I was a huge fan of Reg Smythe's Andy Capp and my favourite cartoonist ever was the gentle giant of *The Express*, Giles, who could not only draw better than anyone on the planet, but whose drawings also conveyed a huge affection for humanity in all its whimsical and tremulous attempts to make sense of itself. These heroic figures captured for me the essence of the human condition, the little person against the tyrant, whether the tyranny be that of a dictatorship, a cruel boss, or merely a wilful domestic appliance.

Now I'm lucky enough to draw in the same paper as my later heroes: Steve Bell, Posy Simmonds, David Austin, Nicola Jennings and Andrjez Krause.

How on earth did that happen?

Despite drawing all the time, I'd hoped to become a graphic designer. Cartooning was not a career that occurred to me and it still surprises me how few women do it. (In fact I have several letters to 'Rob' or 'Rod' Asquith, which proves that even when you sign your name to a cartoon, people think you're a bloke.) My first cartoons came about by mistake, when I was working for Inter-Action Trust. The director, Ed Berman, wanted some jokes to replace the advertisements on the upper deck of the Fun Art Bus, a magnificent old Route master that had a cinema downstairs, a theatre upstairs, a driver who played keyboard on the bonnet and tickets that were poems. The bus ran a normal route and you could ride it for free. This was art in the community. I did some jokes about dogs. They were pasted up inside the bus and to my amazement the passengers laughed.

I made the drawings into a book (photocopied and spiral bound at Instant Print) and sold some at a dog show(!) and some through *The Times'* late great cartoonist Mel Calman, who was very encouraging when I nervously approached him. He agreed to sell some in his Bloomsbury shop.

But still it never occurred to me to take my drawings further into the marketplace – I spent the next few years as a mural painter, photographer and theatre critic and only started drawing again in desperation. I was asked to write an article for *Time Out* magazine about why there were no West End plays written by women, but I couldn't think of anything to write that I hadn't written already, so I drew a full-page feminist cartoon instead, which had a much greater impact than anything I'd ever written.

This led to my drawing for a number of publications alongside reviewing theatre. But it was having babies that finally made me turn back to drawing – after all, I didn't want to go out reviewing theatre every night any more. My children made me laugh so much I couldn't resist drawing jokes about them. Optima published these drawings in a collection originally titled *BABY! (the highs, the lows, the runny nose)* and Alan Rusbridger, (now *The Guardian's* editor, but then launching the *Weekend* magazine) liked them and asked me to do a strip.

My favourite creation, Doris, was born. Doris was a cleaner who never spoke but gently satirised the chattering classes (or *Guardian* readership) for whom she worked. I have since been told that cartoons should be recognisable in silhouette (think of Mickey Mouse or Bart Simpson) and, unconsciously, that was true of Doris, whose spotted headscarf and simple profile – I always drew her facing sideways – appeared weekly in *The Guardian* for 10 years. No doubt the readership was divided over Doris – she wasn't perhaps at the cutting edge of political satire and I expect some people found her bland, but I still get a lot of people asking after her – and that is a wonderful reason for becoming a cartoonist. Like an author, you can create a character people feel they know. Myself, I find it difficult not to believe the Simpsons live in a parallel universe and that I might bump into them some day. I've continued to enjoy drawing for sections of *The Guardian* regularly ever since.

My drawings for children's books (usually ones I've written myself) have, like Doris, instantly recognisable trademarks: Trixie Tempest's bunches, or the Teenage Worrier Letty Chubb's hair and nose, or Rover the Cat's pointy ears and whiskers.

Practical tips

If you are doing a strip, it's useful to have something that you'll be able to draw easily time and again, with clothes or hair that readers instantly latch onto: Andy Capp's cap, Claire in the Community's pony tail, Wendy Weber's huge round glasses, Bristow's bowler hat, Tin Tin's quiff. Draw something you will find easy to reproduce again and again. There's no sense giving yourself a hard time.

Your own route to success will be unique but initially you must have lots of ideas about absolutely everything. You need a sense of humour and a love of the absurd, obviously, but who knows if your gags are funny? Humour is as diverse as humanity – as everyone who's argued over a sitcom knows – and since no one can please everyone, you must have the courage to pursue your own vision, however eccentric, and hope there'll be enough takers for it in the real world. Try to find your own style, which should become as instantly recognisable as your signature.

Practise with different styles and ideas. Experiment with all kinds of pencils and pens and all kinds of colours and textures and papers. Doodle on the computer, but don't expect miracles. Be playful. See what suits you. Then, be serious and pursue it!

Most cartoonists draw in pencil and then ink over it – it must be the simplest profession in terms of tools. But still, when cartoonists gather, they will talk of nibs and inks, in search of the elusive pen, the freer flowing, quicker drying inks. (When you're drawing to deadlines, you need a hair dryer handy.)

Research the market to see what's out there in terms of newspapers and magazines. What do you want to draw? What do you find funny? What do you know a lot about? Are you political? Domestic? Wry? Romantic? Surreal? Can you encompass an idea without any words? Or do you need punchlines? Do you want to do strips? Or single gags?

I'd like a hot meal for everyone who's asked me if I write the words to my cartoons – of course I do. But if you feel you can draw but can't write, then there are a number of successful partnerships who work that way.

Presenting your portfolio

Take a subject. It could be gardening, DIY, giving birth, cats, Shakespeare. Preferably all of these. Then discipline yourself to come up with at least six gags on each subject as this is what you'll have to do if you work on a newspaper. Then you'll give your rough ideas to the editor who will either sneer and send you off to do some more roughs (or possibly another job entirely, like floor sweeping) or will smile enigmatically and choose one. If your editor actually laughs, you will feel foolishly happy – and that is about as near as you are likely to get to your audience. If you want to hear an audience laughing, you would be better off becoming a stand-up comedian.

Once you've created your portfolio of roughs and finished sketches, take it to newspapers and magazines which you think might be interested in your work. Set up appointments in advance as newspapers and magazines are extremely busy places. I think it's better to meet people face to face than to fax or email them, as you can then gauge what they really think of your work and might even pick up some helpful tips.

On the left are examples of roughs I did recently for the letters page in the *Saturday Review* section of *The Guardian*. And above is the final artwork of the one they chose. See? Couldn't be simpler.

Listen to what editors say. They will not always be right about your work, because illustration and cartooning are matters of taste, but they are much more often right than not – and they certainly know more about their particular readership than you do, so don't try to tell them how to do their jobs. Good art editors will certainly give helpful advice about presentation and ideas, but what they are looking for is professionalism, vision, and originality.

Don't be put off by rejection. (Everyone knows that Harry Potter was rejected by several editors – you will be too!) Keep trying. Keep improving. Aim your work at suitable places. There are racks and racks of magazines to choose from. Remember that a picture is worth a thousand words and editors like a laugh as much as you do.

A final word of advice: if the names Gary Larsen, Posy Simmonds, Jules Feiffer, James Thurber, Steve Bell and Matt Groening, mean nothing to you, you may be barking up the wrong tree.

Or you may be that genius I've yet to meet who needs no outside inspiration.

Ros Asquith is a cartoonist and an author. Her cartoons appear regularly in *The Guardian* where her comic strip Doris featured for many years. She wrote and illustrated the bestselling *Teenage Worrier* series (Corgi), which has been translated into 12 languages. Her most recent children's books are about the Trixie Tempest, Tweenage Tearaway character (HarperCollins) and her teenage novel, *Love, Fifteen*, is to be published by Corgi in February 2005.

Magazines and newspapers for children

Listings of magazines about children's literature and education start on page 212.

Absolutely Boys

RNIB, PO Box 173, Peterborough PE2 6W7
tel (01733) 375336 *fax* (01733) 375001
email editorial@rnib.org.uk
website www.rnib.org.uk
Fortnightly

Braille magazine for blind and partially sighted men aged 16–19. Also available in disk and email formats. Includes features on the music scene, sport, interviews with personalities and a problem page. Will consider unsolicited material but most material has previously appeared in mainstream print magazines.

Absolutely Girls

RNIB, PO Box 173, Peterborough PE2 6WS
tel (01733) 375336 *fax* (01733) 375001
email editorial@rnib.org.uk
website www.rnib.org.uk
Editor Chris James
Fortnightly

Braille magazine for blind and partially sighted girls aged 16–19. Also available in disk and email formats. Includes real life stories, celebrity interviews and beauty features. Will consider unsolicited material but most material has previously appeared in mainstream print magazines.

Action Hero

BBC Worldwide Ltd, BBC Woodlands, 80 Wood Lane, London W12 0TT
tel 020-8433 2000 *fax* 020-8749 0538
website www.bbcworldwide.com
Every 4 weeks £1.50

Magazine for boys aged 4–7 featuring popular TV characters and toys joining forces to fight evil. Content includes stories, makes, games, posters, news and reviews of the best toys available and a competition.

Adventure Box

Bayard, 1st Floor, 2 King Street, Peterborough PE1 1LT
tel (01733) 565 858 *fax* (01733) 427 500
email contact@bayard-magazines.co.uk
website www.bayard-magazines.co.uk
Editor-in-chief Simona Sideri, *Art Director* Pat Carter
10 p.a. £37.50 p.a.

Aimed at 7–9 year-old children starting to read on their own. Each issue contains an illustrated chapter story plus games, an animal feature, nature activity and a cartoon. Length: 2500–3000 words (stories). Specially commissions most material. Founded 1996.

After Hours

RNIB, PO Box 173, Peterborough PE2 6WS
tel (01733) 375000 *fax* (01733) 375001
email editorial@rnib.org.uk
website www.rnib.org.uk
Editor Racheal Jarvis
Every 2 months 65p discounted/£1.86 full

Braille magazine for blind and partially sighted children aged 11–14. Short stories (fiction).

Animals and You

D.C. Thomson & Co Ltd, Albert Square, Dundee DD1 9QJ
tel (01382) 223131 *fax* (01382) 225511
185 Fleet Street, London EC4A 2HS
tel 020-7400 1030 *fax* 020-7400 1089
Monthly (Fri) £1.75

Features, stories and pin-ups for girls who love animals. Founded 1998.

Aquila

New Leaf Publishing Ltd, PO Box 2518, Eastbourne, East Sussex BN21 2BB
tel (01323) 431313 *fax* (01323) 731136
email info@aquila.co.uk
website www.aquila.co.uk
Editor Jackie Berry
Monthly £35 p.a. (£25 6 months)

Dedicated to encouraging children aged 8–13 to reason and create, and to develop a caring nature. Short stories and serials of up to 4 parts. Occasional features commissioned from writers with specialist knowledge. Approach in writing with ideas and sample of writing style, with sae. Length: 700–800 words (features), 1000–1100 words (stories or per episode of a serial). Illustrations: colour and b&w, cartoons. Payment: £75 (features); £90 (stories), £80 (per episode). Founded 1993.

Art Crazy!

De Agostini UK Ltd, Griffin House, 161 Hammersmith Road, London W6 8SD
tel 020-8600 2015, (08707) 299 399 (customer services) *fax* 020-8741 8927
email enquiries@deagostini.co.uk
website www.deagostini.co.uk
Weekly £2.50

Magazine series containing cool crafts to make, drawing and painting projects, information on how to create art with a computer and how to be a cartoonist.

BBC Learning is Fun!

BBC Worldwide Ltd, BBC Woodlands,
80 Wood Lane, London W12 0TT
tel 020-8433 2000 *fax* 020-8749 0538
website www.bbcworldwide.com
Editor Anna Bassi
Every 4 weeks £1.99

An award-winning magazine which aims to support children as they progress through Key Stage 1 of the National Curriculum, Literacy and Numeracy strategies. Each school subject is depicted in an exciting, fun and stimulating way with colourful illustrations, photographs of children and stunning pictures. It includes a pull-out guide for parents/carers which highlights the key educational points covered in the issue and suggests extension activities. In addition, there is a regular feature, written by the Education Editor, which tackles parent/school/child issues.

BBC The Magic Key

BBC Worldwide Ltd, BBC Woodlands,
80 Wood Lane, London W12 0TT
tel 020-8433 2000 *fax* 020-8749 0538
website www.bbcworldwide.com
Every 4 weeks £180

Devised specifically to help develop the literacy skills of young readers, its pages are packed with stories and activities designed to support the reading and writing skills of 5–7 year-olds, encouraging children to develop an interest in words, an understanding of language and a love of reading. Both the National Curriculum and Literacy Strategy at Key Stage 1 have been used as a guide to the educational content with the notes on each page enabling parents to support and extend their child's learning. Features the popular children's characters from the Oxford Reading Scheme.

BBC Toybox Teach Me

BBC Worldwide Ltd, BBC Woodlands,
80 Wood Lane, London W12 0TT
tel 020-8433 2000 *fax* 020-8749 0538
website www.bbcworldwide.com
Every 4 weeks £150

Magazine formulated to help 3–5 year-olds progress through the Early Learning Goals for Reading, Writing and Numbers in preparation for Key Stage 1 of the National Curriculum. Content includes popular BBC characters such as *Bob the Builder*, *Tweenies* and *Postman Pat* featuring in simple, educational puzzles and activities all aimed at making learning fun.

The Beano

D.C. Thomson & Co. Ltd, Albert Square,
Dundee DD1 9QJ
tel (01382) 223131 *fax* (01382) 322214
185 Fleet Street, London EC4A 2HS
tel 020-7400 1030 *fax* 020-7400 1089
Editor Euan Kerr
Weekly 65p

Comic strips for children aged 6–12. Series, 11–22 pictures. Payment: on acceptance.

Fun Size Beano

2 p.m. 90p

Founded 1997.

Blast Off!

RNIB, PO Box 173, Peterborough PE2 6WS
tel (01733) 375000 *fax* (01733) 375001
email editorial@rnib.org.uk
website www.rnib.org.uk
Editor Racheal Jarvis
Monthly 20p subsidised/82p full

Braille general interest magazine for blind and partially sighted children aged 7–11. Also available on disk.

Bliss

EMAP Media, Endeavour House,
189 Shaftesbury Avenue, London WC2H 8JG
tel 020-7437 9011 *fax* 020-7208 3591
website www.blissmag.co.uk
Editor Charlotte Crisp
Monthly £1.90

Glamorous young women's glossy magazine. Bright intimate American-style format, with real life stories and reports, beauty, fashion, talent, advice, quizzes. Payment: by arrangement. Founded 1995.

Bob the Builder

BBC Worldwide Ltd, BBC Woodlands,
80 Wood Lane, London W12 0TT
tel 020-8433 2000 *fax* 020-8749 0538
website www.bbcworldwide.com
Editor Andrea Wickstead
Monthly £1.50

Stories, puzzles, competitions and activities built around Bob and his team for children aged 4–6 and their parents.

Braille at Bedtime

RNIB, PO Box 173, Peterborough PE2 6WS
tel (01733) 375000 *fax* (01733) 375001
email editorial@rnib.org.uk
website www.rnib.org.uk
Editor Racheal Jarvis
Every 2 months 65p discounted/£1.86 full

Braille short fiction magazine for blind and partially sighted children aged 7–11.

Brownie

Warners Group Publications plc, Manor Lane,
Bourne, Lincs. PE10 9PH
tel (01778) 391124

website www.girlguiding.org.uk
Editor Marion Thompson
Monthly £1.40

Official Magazine of The Guide Association. Short articles for Brownies (7–10 year-old girls); fiction with Brownie background (700–800 words); puzzles; 'things to make', etc. Illustrations: colour. Payment: £50 per 1000 words; varies for illustrations.

Children's Express UK

Exmouth House, 3–11 Pine Street,
London EC1R 0JH
tel 020-7833 2577 *fax* 020-7278 7722
email enquiries@childrensexpress.btinternet.com
website www.childrens-express.org
Chief Executive Christopher Wyld, *Chairman* Stephanie Williams, *Editor* Fiona Wyton

An award-winning charity that offers young people aged 8–18 the opportunity to write on issues of importance to them, for newspapers, radio and TV. It operates after school and at weekends. Founded 1995.

Commando

D.C. Thomson & Co. Ltd, Albert Square,
Dundee DD1 9QJ
tel (01382) 223131 *fax* (01382) 322214
8 p.m. £1

Fictional war stories told in pictures. Scripts: about 135 pictures. Synopsis required as an opener. New writers encouraged; send for details. Payment: on acceptance.

Cosmogirl

National Magazine House, 72 Broadwick Street,
London W1F 9EP
tel 020-7439 5081 *fax* 020-7439 5400
email cosmogirl.mail@natmags.co.uk
website www.cosmogirl.co.uk
Editor Celia Duncan, *Send material to* Miranda Eason
Monthly £2

Little sister to *Cosmopolitan*. Features 'to inspire teenage girls to be the best they can be'. Specially commissions most material. Welcomes ideas for articles and features. Length: 600 words. All illustrations commissioned. Founded 2001.

Cricket Magazine

Carus Publishing Company, Cricket Magazine Group, P0 Box 300, Peru, IL 61354, USA
tel 815-224-5830 *fax* 815-224-6615
email mmiklavcic@caruspub.com
website www.cricketmag.com
Editor Marianne Carus, *Art Director* Ron McCutchan
12 p.a. $35.97

USA award-winning fun magazine for 9–14 year-olds with literary content including original stories, poems and articles by the world's best authors for children (*not* about cricket the sport!). Also includes puzzles, games, activities, plays, music and art. Welcomes ideas for articles and features. Founded 1973.

Submission details Do not query first. Send sase or IRCs with submissions. Allow 12 weeks for a reply. Length: 200–2000 words (stories), 200–1500 words (articles); poems up to 50 lines. Payment: up to 25 cents per word (stories and articles), up to $3 per line (poems). Illustrations: welcomes b&w and colour artwork but do not send originals. Payment by arrangement.

The Dandy

D.C. Thomson & Co. Ltd, Albert Square,
Dundee DD1 9QJ
tel (01382) 223131 *fax* (01382) 322214
185 Fleet Street, London EC4A 2HS
tel 020-7400 1030 *fax* 020-7400 1089
Weekly 65p

Comic strips for children. 10–12 pictures per single page story, 18–20 pictures per 2-page story. Promising artists are encouraged. Payment: on acceptance.

Funsize Dandy

2 p.m. 90p
Founded 1997.

Dare

BBC Worldwide Ltd, BBC Woodlands,
80 Wood Lane, London W12 0TT
tel 020-8433 2000 *fax* 020-8749 0538
website www.bbcworldwide.com
Fortnightly £1.60

Feisty, flirty magazine for girls aged 10–14. Content ranges from gritty investigative features to the hottest celebrities, relationship worries and up-to-the-minute fashions.

Discovery Box

The Children's Magazine Company Ltd,
Tower House, Soverign Park, Lathkill Street,
Market Harborough, Leics. LE94 7ZT
tel (01858) 435319 *fax* (01858) 434958
email childrens.magazines@bayard-presse.com
website www.bayard-magazines.co.uk
Editor Sophie Delbert
10 p.a. £34.75

Photographs and short texts to introduce children aged 8–12 to animals and their habitats. Includes historical events retold as picture stories and a range of topics and experiments to develop children's scientific knowledge; also photographs showing the variety of lifestyles around the world. Plus games, fun facts, short story, recipe, quizz, cartoon. Specially commissions most material. Founded 1996.

Disney Girl
BBC Worldwide, Woodlands, Wood Lane, London W12 0TT
tel 020-8433 1845 *fax* 020-8433 2941
website www.bbcworldwide.com
Editor Samantha McEvoy, *Art Director* Carol Gook, *Send material to* Bea Appleby
Monthly £1.50

Magazine of Walt Disney cartoons and characters for girls 5–8 year-old girls. Contains short stories, dressing up, fashion, craft activities, competitions, readers' letters, puzzles. Length: 500 words (fiction). Payment: £75. All material is specially commissioned. Founded 2002.

Disney Princess
De Agostini UK Ltd, Griffin House, 161 Hammersmith Road, London W6 8SD
tel 020-8600 2015, (08707) 299 399 (customer services) *fax* 020-8741 8927
email enquiries@deagostini.co.uk
www.deagostini.co.ukFornightly £5.99

Classic fairytales that bring Disney Princesses and enchanted worlds to life. Includes activities and quizzes.

Elle Girl
Hachette Filipacchi UK Ltd, 64 North Row, London W1K 7LL
tel 020-7150 7000 *fax* 020-7150 7670
Editor Claire Irwin
Monthly £2.20

Little sister to *Elle*. Glossy fashion and beauty magazine for teenage girls aiming to be sweet, stylish and spirited. Aimed at 12–17 year-old girls but has a core audience aged 14–16. Founded 2001.

Fimbles
BBC Worldwide Ltd, BBC Woodlands, 80 Wood Lane, London W12 0TT
tel 020-8433 2000 *fax* 020-8749 0538
website www.bbcworldwide.com
Monthly £1.45

Magazine aimed at 2–4 year-olds. The *Fimbles* are always trying to find out new things and the magic of discovery accompanies everything they do.

The Funday Times
1 Pennington Street, London E98 1ST
tel 020-7782 7415 *fax* 020-7782 7416
email funday.news@sunday-times.co.uk
Editor Dave Coombs, *Art Director* Ed White
Free with *The Sunday Times* (£1.40)

Supplement for 8–12 year-old boys and girls. Content is a lively mix of news, features, sport, music and readers' views plus cartoons, puzzles and quizzes. Specially commissions most material but considers unsolicited material and welcomes ideas for articles and features. Length: 300 words (articles), 600 words (features), 100 words (news). Payment: 40p per word. Illustrations: colour transparencies, prints, artwork, cartoons. Founded 1989.

Funsize Dandy
2 p.m. 90p

Founded 1997.

Girl Talk
BBC Worldwide, Woodlands, Wood Lane, London W12 0TT
tel 020-8433 1845 *fax* 020-8433 2941
email girltalk.magazine@bbc.co.uk
website www.bbcworldwide.com
Editor Samantha McEvoy, *Art Director* Carol Gook, *Send material to* Bea Appleby
Fortnightly £1.20

Magazine for children aged 7–12 years old. Contains pop, TV and film celebrity features, personality features, quizzes, fashion, competitions, stories. Length: 500 words (fiction). Payment: £75. All material is specially commissioned. Founded 1997.

Go Girl Magazine
Egmont Magazines, 184 Drummond Street, London NW1 3HP
tel 020-7380 6430
website www.egmontmagazines.co.uk
Editor Sarah Delmege
13 p.a. £1.60

Magazine for 7–11 year-old girls including fashion, beauty, celebrity news and gossip. Payment: by arrangement. Founded 2003.

Guiding Magazine
17–19 Buckingham Palace Road, London SW1W 0PT
tel 020-7834 6242 *fax* 020-7828 5791
website www.girlguiding.org.uk
Editor Wendy Kewley
Monthly £21.60

Official magazine of Girlguiding UK. Articles of interest to women of all ages, with special emphasis on youth work and the Guide Movement. Articles on simple crafts, games and the outdoors especially welcome. Length: up to 600 words. Illustrations: line, half-tone, colour. Payment: £70 per 1000 words.

It's HOT!
BBC Worldwide Ltd, BBC Woodlands, 80 Wood Lane, London W12 0TT
tel 020-8433 2000 *fax* 020-8749 0538
website www.bbcworldwide.com
Editor Peter Hart
Monthly £1.95

Entertainment magazine for 9–13 year-old girls covering TV, pop, films and gossip. Includes 3 comic strips (*EastEnders*, *S Club 7* and the *Top Of The Pops Star Bar*) and a day-by-day diary of cool stuff to do. Founded 2002.

Kids Alive! (The Young Soldier)

The Salvation Army,
101 Newington Causeway,
London SE1 6BN
tel 020-7367 4910 *fax* 020-7367 4710
email kidsalive@salvationarmy.org.uk
Editor Ken Nesbitt
Weekly 50p (£25 p.a. including free membership of the Kids Alive! Club)

Children's magazine: stories, pictures, cartoon strips, puzzles, etc; Christian-based with emphasis on education regarding addictive substances. Payment: by arrangement. Illustrations: half-tone, line and 4-colour line, cartoons. Founded 1881.

Learning Land

De Agostini UK Ltd,
Griffin House, 161 Hammersmith Road,
London W6 8SD
tel 020-8600 2015, (08707) 299 399 (customer services) *fax* 020-8741 8927
email enquiries@deagostini.co.uk
website www.deagostini.co.uk

Interactive CD-Rom and magazine series for children at preschool and Key Stage 1 to discover and play on a PC. Includes games to learn numbers, letters and about nature.

Mizz

IPC Magazines Ltd, King's Reach Tower,
Stamford Street, London SE1 9LS
tel 020-7261 6319 *fax* 020-7261 6032
email mizz@ipcmedia.com
website www.ipcmedia.com
Editor Sharon Christal
Fortnightly £1.50

Articles on any subject of interest to girls aged 10–14. Approach in writing. Payment: by arrangement. Illustrated. Founded 1985.

myBOOKSmag

guise, 15 Scots Drive, Wokingham,
Berks. RG41 3XF
tel 0118-962 9528
email guy@newbooksmag.com
website www.newbooksmag.com
Editor Helen Davies *Send material to* Guy Pringle, Publisher
Quarterly £1

Activities and extracts from the best new books for 5–7 year-olds. Specially commissions all material. Founded 2001.

my first magazine

BBC Worldwide Ltd, BBC Woodlands,
80 Wood Lane, London W12 0TT
tel 020-8433 2000 *fax* 020-8749 0538
website www.bbcworldwide.com
Monthly £1.50

Magazine for preschool childen encouraging them to play, discover and learn

The Newspaper

Young Media Ltd, PO Box 121, Tonbridge,
Kent TN12 5ZR
tel (01622) 871297 *fax* (01622) 871927
email editor@thenewspaper.org.uk
website www.thenewspaper.org.uk
Editor Jenny MacDonald
6 p.a. Free

Newspaper aimed at 8–14 year-old schoolchildren for use as part of the National Curriculum. Contains similar columns as in any national daily newspaper. Length: 800–1000 words for features and short stories (non-fiction). Payment: £250 per item. Illustrations: colour. Founded 1999.

Noddy

BBC Worldwide Ltd, BBC Woodlands,
80 Wood Lane, London W12 0TT
tel 020-8433 2000 *fax* 020-8749 0538
website www.bbcworldwide.com
Managing Editor Helen Mitchell
13 p.a. £1.75

Activities, stories, puzzles and games built around the *Noddy* character. Founded 1992.

Pony Magazine

Headley House, Headley Road, Grayshott,
Surrey, Surrey GU26 6TU
tel (01428) 601020 *fax* (01428) 601030
Editor Janet Rising
Monthly £2.10

Lively articles and short stories with a horsy theme aimed at readers aged 8–16 . Technical accuracy and young, fresh writing essential. Length: up to 800 words. Payment: by arrangement. Illustrations: drawings (commissioned), photos, cartoons. Founded 1949.

Pop Girl

BBC Worldwide, Woodlands, Wood Lane,
London W12 0TT
tel 020-8433 1845 *fax* 020-8433 2941
email girltalk.magazine@bbc.co.uk
website www.bbcworldwide.com
Editor Samantha McEvoy, *Art Director* Carol Gook, *Send material to* Bea Appleby
Monthly £1.50

Magazine for girls aged 7–12 years old. Contains pop, TV and film celebrity interviews, pop star style, fan fiction, puzzles, competitions, readers' letters. Length: 500 words (fiction). Payment: £75. All material is specially commissioned. Founded 2003.

Scooby-Doo World of Mystery!

De Agostini UK Ltd, Griffin House,
161 Hammersmith Road, London W6 8SD
tel 020-8600 2015, (08707) 299 399 (customer services) *fax* 020-8741 8927
email enquiries@deagostini.co.uk
website www.deagostini.co.uk
Weekly £1.99

Scooby and the gang go on spooky adventures around the world, every week in a different country. Includes country facts, comics, mysterious site information, scrapbooks and puzzles and games.

Scouting Magazine

Gilwell House, Gilwell Park, London E4 7QW
tel 020-8433 7100 *fax* 020-8433 7103
Editor Anna Sorensen
Monthly £2.15

Magazine of the Scout Association. Ideas, news, views, features and programme resources for Leaders and Supporters. Training material, accounts of Scouting events and articles of general interest with Scouting connections. Illustrations: photos – action shots preferred rather than static posed shots for use with articles or as fillers or cover potential, cartoons. Payment: on publication by arrangement.

Shoot Monthly

IPC Magazines Ltd, King's Reach Tower,
Stamford Street, London SE1 9LS
tel 020-7261 6287 *fax* 020-7261 6019
Editor Colin Mitchell
Monthly £2.95

Football magazine for fans of all ages. Features, profiles of big names in football. Length: 500–2000 words (features). Illustrations: colour transparencies. Payment: negotiable. Founded 1969.

Shout

D.C. Thomson & Co. Ltd, Albert Square,
Dundee DD1 9QJ
tel (01382) 223131 *fax* (01382) 200880
email shout@dcthomson.co.uk
185 Fleet Street, London EC4A 2HS
tel 020-7400 1030 *fax* 020-7400 1089
Editor-in-Chief Jackie Brown
Fortnightly £1.80

Colour gravure magazine for 11–14 year-old girls. Pop, film and 'soap' features and pin-ups; general features of teen interest; emotional features, fashion and beauty advice. Illustrations: colour transparencies. Payment: on acceptance. Founded 1993.

Slugs and Snails

RNIB, PO Box 173, Peterborough PE2 6WS
tel (01733) 375000 *fax* (01733) 375001
email editorial@rnib.org.uk
website www.rnib.org.uk
Editor Racheal Jarvis
Monthly 38p discount/£1.49 full

Braille general interest magazine for blind and partially sighted boys aged 12–15. Also available on disk.

Smash Hits

EMAP Performance, Mappin House,
4 Winsley Street, London W1W 8HF
tel 020-7312 8718 *fax* 020-7636 5792
email letters@smashhits.net
Editor Lisa Smosarski
Fortnightly £1.90

News, interviews and posters of pop, TV and film stars. Illustrations: colour photos. Payment: varies.

Storybox

The Children's Magazine Company Ltd,
Tower House, Soverign Park, Lathkill Street,
Market Harborough, Leics. LE94 7ZT
tel (01858) 435319 *fax* (01858) 434958
email childrens.magazines@bayard-presse.com
website www.bayard-magazines.co.uk
Editor-in-chief Simona Sideri
10 p.a. £34.75 p.a.

Aimed at 3–6 year-old children. A range of stories with rhyme and evocative pictures to stimulate children's imagination and introduce them to the delights of reading. Each issue presents a new, full-colour, 24-page story created by teams of internationally acclaimed writers and illustrators for laptime reading. A non-fiction section linked to a theme in the story follows, together with pages of games and craft ideas. Includes games, an animal feature, science and a cartoon. Founded 1996.

Submission details Length: 500–1000 words (stories). Requirements: rhyme, repetition, interesting language. Specially commissions most material. Payment: by arrangement.

Sugar

Hachette Filipacchi, 64 North Row,
London W1K 7LL
tel 020-7150 7000 *fax* 020-7150 7001
Acting Editor Nick Chalmers
Monthly £2.20

Magazine for young women aged 12–17. Fashion, beauty, entertainment, features. Send synopsis first. Will consider unsolicited material. Interested in real-life stories (1200 words), quizzes. Payment: negotiable. Founded 1994.

Sugar and Spice

RNIB, PO Box 173, Peterborough PE2 6WS
tel (01733) 375000 *fax* (01733) 375001
email editorial@rnib.org.uk
website www.rnib.org.uk
Editor Racheal Jarvis
Monthly 38p discount/£1.86 full

Braille general interest magazine for blind and partially sighted girls aged 12–15. Also available on disk.

tBkmag

guise, 15 Scots Drive, Wokingham, Berks. RG41 3XF
tel 0118-962 9528
email guy@newbooksmag.com
website www.newbooksmag.com
Editor Helen Davies *Send material to* Guy Pringle, Publisher
Quarterly £1

Extracts and activities from the best new books for 8–12 year-olds. Specially commissions all material. Founded 2001.

Teletubbies

BBC Worldwide Ltd, BBC Woodlands, 80 Wood Lane, London W12 0TT
tel 020-8433 2000 *fax* 020-8749 0538
website www.bbc.co.uk/teletubbies
Editor Helen Mitchell
13 p.a. £1.99

Magazine for very young children (18 months+) who love the *Teletubbies*. The activities included are designed to build children's confidence, creativity and imagination and are clear, colourful and entertaining. Founded 1997.

Thomas & Friends

De Agostini UK Ltd, Griffin House, 161 Hammersmith Road, London W6 8SD
tel 020-8600 2015 *fax* 020-8741 8927
website www.deagostini.co.uk
Fortnightly £4.99

Magazine series to encourage the imagination and creativity. Includes stories, puzzles and games, stickers. A new engine or accessory comes with each issue.

Top of the Pops

BBC Worldwide Ltd, BBC Woodlands, 80 Wood Lane, London W12 0TT
tel 020-8433 2000 *fax* 020-8749 0538
website www.bbcworldwide.com
Editor Corinna Scaffer
Monthly £1.95

The pop music bible for teenagers. Primarily aimed at teenage girls (ages 11–19), the magazine strives to provide all the pop knowledge growing teenagers could want. It aims to make the reader feel part of an exclusive club, to transport them behind the scenes so they get a real sense of what really goes on in the world of music. Founded 1995.

Toxic Magazine

Egmont Magazines, 184 Drummond Street, London NW1 3HP
tel 020-7380 6430
website www.egmontmagazines.co.uk
Editor Matthew Yeo
3-weekly £1.75

Topical monthly lifestyle magazine for 7–12 year-old boys. Includes competitions, pull-out posters, reviews and jokes. Covers boys' entertainments, sports, video games, films, TV, music, fashion and toys. Slapstick humour. Showcases latest products, events and trends. Payment: by arrangement. Founded 2002.

Toybox

BBC Worldwide Ltd, BBC Woodlands, 80 Wood Lane, London W12 0TT
tel 020-8433 2000 *fax* 020-8749 0538
website www.bbcworldwide.com
Preschool Publisher Wendy Bryan, *Managing Editor* Helen Mitchell
Monthly 99p

Fun and interactive magazine for 3–5 year-olds with stories, activities, games and colouring-in. Features a variety of star characters from the BBC.

Tweenies

BBC Worldwide Ltd, BBC Woodlands, 80 Wood Lane, London W12 0TT
tel 020-8433 2000 *fax* 020-8749 0538
website www.bbcworldwide.com
13 p.a. £1.50

Magazine based around the *Tweenies* for children aged 18 months–3 years, with stories and activities including songs to sing, things to make and colouring-in.

Young Writer

Glebe House, Weobley, Herefordshire HR4 8SD
tel (01544) 318901 *fax* (01544) 318901
email editor@youngwriter.org
website www.youngwriter.org
Editor Kate Jones
3 p.a. £3.50 (£10 for 3 issues)

Specialist magazine for young writers under 18 years old: ideas for them and writing by them. Includes interviews by children with famous writers, fiction and non-fiction pieces, poetry; also explores words and grammar, issues related to writing (e.g. dyslexia), plus competitions with prizes. Length: 750 or 1500 words (features), up to 400 words (news), 750 words (short stories – unless specified otherwise in a competition), poetry of any length. Illustrations: colour – drawings by children, snapshots to accompany features. Payment: most children's material is published without payment; £25–£100 (features); £15 (cover cartoon). Free inspection copy. Founded 1995.

Your Cat Magazine

BPG (Stamford) Ltd, Roebuck House,
33 Broad Street, Stamford, Lincs. PE9 1RB
tel (01780) 766199 *fax* (01780) 766416
email s.parslow@bournepublishinggroup.co.uk
Editor Sue Parslow
Monthly £2.75

Practical advice on the care of cats and kittens, general interest items and news on cats, and true life tales and fiction. Length: 800–1500 words (articles), 200–300 (news), up to 1000 (short stories). Illustrations: colour transparencies and prints. Payment: £80 per 1000 words. Founded 1994.

Your Dog Magazine

BPG (Stamford) Ltd, Roebuck House,
33 Broad Street, Stamford, Lincs. PE9 1RB
tel (01780) 766199 *fax* (01780) 766416
email swright@bourneppublishinggroup.co.uk
Editor Sarah Wright
Monthly £2.95

Articles and information of interest to dog lovers; features on all aspects of pet dogs. Length: approx. 1500 words. Illustrations: colour transparencies, prints and line drawings. Payment: £80 per 1000 words. Founded 1994.

Your Horse

Emap Active, Bretton Court, Bretton,
Peterborough PE3 8DZ
tel (01733) 264666 *fax* (01733) 465100
email amanda.stevenson@emap.com
Editor Natasha Simmonds
Every 4 weeks £2.75

Practical horse care and riding advice for the leisure rider and horse owner. Send feature ideas with examples of previous published writing. Specially commissions most material. Welcomes ideas for articles and features. Length: 1500 words. Payment: £120 per 1000 words. Founded 1983.

Magazines about children's literature and education

Listings of magazines and newspapers for children start on page 204.

Armadillo

Greystones, 37 Lawton Avenue, Carterton, Oxon OX18 3JY
tel (01993) 841219 *fax* (01993) 845116
email armadillo@worldash.demon.co.uk
website www.armadillomagazine.com
Editor Mary Hoffman
4 p.a.

Magazine about children's books, including reviews, interviews, features and profiles. After 5 years of publication as a paper magazine posted to subscribers, *Armadillo* is now available only online. New issues will be posted at the end of March, June, September and December. Some material will be accessible as a free sample but full access to the magazine is by subscription (see website for rates). New reviewers and writers are always welcome but the magazine does not pay a fee; reviewers keep the books. Publishers please note: books are *not* to be sent to the editor; she instructs reviewers to obtain specific titles direct from publishers. Founded 1999.

AuthorZone

Peter's Bookselling Services, 120 Bromsgrove Street, Birmingham B5 6RL
Editor Peter Sheldon, *Art Directors* Roger Berry, Peter Sheldon
tel 0121-666 6646 *fax* 0121-666 7033
email psheldon@peters-books.co.uk
website www.peters-books.co.uk
Occasional £6.95

Magazine about children's authors and illustrators designed for children aged 9+, parents, teachers, librarians and anyone interested in children's books. Approx. 50 authors are featured in each issue with pictures, biographies, Q&As and articles. Welcomes ideas for articles.

The Bookseller

VNU Entertainment Media Ltd, 5th Floor, Endeavour House, 189 Shaftesbury Avenue, London WC2H 8TJ
tel 020-7420 6006 *fax* 020-7420 6103
email letters.to.editor@bookseller.co.uk
website www.thebookseller.com
Editor Nicholas Clee
Weekly £175 p.a.

Journal of the UK publishing and bookselling trades. The *Children's Bookseller* supplement is published regularly and there is news on the children's book business in the main magazine. Produces the *Children's Buyer's Guide*, which previews children's books to be published in the following 6 months. The website holds news on children's books, comment on the children's sector, author interviews and children's bestseller charts. Founded 1858.

Books for Keeps

6 Brightfield Road, London SE12 8QF
tel 020-8852 4953 *fax* 020-8318 7580
email booksforkeeps@btinternet.com
website www.booksforkeeps.co.uk
Editor Rosemary Stones, *Send material to* Richard Hill
Bi-monthly £21.75

Features, reviews and news on children's books. Readership is both professionals and parents. Founded 1980.

Booktrusted News

Booktrust, Book House, 45 East Hill, London SE18 2SQ
tel 020-8516 2977 *fax* 020-8916 2978
email publications@booktrust.org.uk
website www.booktrusted.com
Editor Sarah Harrington, *Send material to* Edeardo Zaehini
Quarterly £20 (on subscription)

Features, news and views on various aspects of the children's book world. Each issue concentrates on a particular theme and contains a related book list. Also included are author and illustrator profiles, information about book prizes, reviews of new titles and a variety of articles about children's books and reading. Specially commissions most material but welcomes ideas for articles and features. Length: 4000 words (articles and features). Founded 2002.

Carousel – The Guide to Children's Books

The Saturn Centre, 54–76 Bissell Street, Birmingham B5 7HX
tel 0121-622 7458 *fax* 0121-666 7526
email carousel.guide@virgin.net
website www.carousel.guide.co.uk
Editor Jenny Blanch
3 p.a. £10.50 p.a. (£15 p.a. Europe; £18 p.a. rest of world)

Reviews of fiction, non-fiction and poetry books for children, plus in-depth articles; profiles of authors and illustrators. Length: 1200 words (articles); 150 words (reviews). Illustrations: colour and b&w. Payment: by arrangement. Founded 1995.

Child Education

Scholastic Ltd, Villiers House, Clarendon Avenue, Leamington Spa, Warks. CV32 5PR
tel (01926) 887799 *fax* (01926) 883331
website www.scholastic.co.uk
Acting Editor Michael Ward
Monthly £3.75

For teachers concerned with the education of children aged 4–7. Articles by specialists on practical teaching ideas and methods. Length: 600–1200 words. Payment: by arrangement. Profusely illustrated with photos and artwork; also A1 full colour picture poster. Founded 1924.

Cricket Magazine – see page 206

Early Childhood Today

Scholastic Canada Ltd, 175 Hillmount Road, Markham, Ontario L6C 1Z7
website www.scholastic.com
Addresses and anticipates the needs of early childhood educators (pre-K–K). Each thematic issue focuses on a specific aspect of early childhood development, such as literacy or creativity, and provides a 'mini-workshop' on that topic: updates on current research, interviews with leading experts, and easy-to-implement activities broken down by age group.

Early Years Activity Bank

Scholastic Ltd, Villiers House, Clarendon Avenue, Leamington Spa, Warks. CV32 5PR
tel (01926) 887799 *fax* (01926) 883331
email earlyyears@scholastic.co.uk
website www.scholastic.co.uk
Editor Sarah Sodhi
6 p.a. £75 p.a.

Support material for early years professionals. A bank of play-based activities and resources including term-by-term activities with seasonal links, practical ideas covering the Stepping Stones and Early Learning Goals, colour posters and gameboards. Illustrations: transparencies and colour artwork. Length: 500 words (articles). Founded 2000.

Mary Glasgow Magazines

Mary Glasgow Magazines/Scholastic ELT, Commonwealth House, 1–19 New Oxford Street, London WC1A 1NU
020-7421 9050 020-7421 9051
email @maryglasgowmags.co.uk

Publisher of 17 magazines for learners of English, French, German, and Spanish. Also publishes a series of resource books for teachers of English as a foreign language. Wholly-owned subsidiary of Scholastic Inc.

Infant Projects

Scholastic Ltd, Villiers House, Clarendon Avenue, Leamington Spa, Warks. CV32 5PR
tel (01926) 887799 *fax* (01926) 337322
Editor Michael Ward
Bi-monthly £3.75

Practical articles suggesting project activities for teachers of children aged 4–7; material mostly commissioned. Length: 500–1000 words. Illustrations: colour photos and line illustrations, colour posters. Payment: by arrangement. Founded 1978.

Inis – The Children's Books Ireland Magazine

Children's Books Ireland, 17 Lower Camden Street, Dublin 2, Replublic of Ireland
tel/fax 8725854
email inis@childrensbooksireland.com
website www.childrensbooksireland.com
Editors Siobhan Parkinson, Valerie Coghlan
Quarterly €4

Reviews and articles on Irish and international children's books. Readership of teachers, librarians and children's books specialists. Founded 1989.

Instructor

Scholastic Canada Ltd, 175 Hillmount Road, Markham, Ontario L6C 1Z7
website www.scholastic.com
Professional magazine for elementary (Grades 1–8) classroom teachers that keeps educators abreast of the latest and best ideas about how children learn, and translates that thinking into effective classroom practice. Includes tips, activities, and strategies to better meet the needs of teachers.

Junior Education

Scholastic Ltd, Villiers House, Clarendon Avenue, Leamington Spa, Warks. CV32 5PR
tel (01926) 887799 *fax* (01926) 883331
email juniored@scholastic.co.uk
Editor Tracy Kewley
Monthly £3.75

For teachers of 7–11 year-olds. Articles by specialists on practical teaching ideas, coverage of primary education news; posters; photocopiable material for the classroom. Length: 800–1000 words. Payment: by arrangement. Illustrated with photos and drawings; includes colour poster. Founded 1977.

Junior Focus

Scholastic Ltd, Villiers House, Clarendon Avenue, Leamington Spa, Warks. CV32 5PR
tel (01926) 887799 *fax* (01926) 883331
email jfocus@scholastic.co.uk
Editor Tracy Kewley
Monthly £3.75

Aimed at teachers of 7–11 year-olds, each issue is based on a theme, closely linked to the National Curriculum. Includes A1 and A3 full-colour posters, 12 pages of photocopiable material and 16 pages of articles. All material commissioned. Length: 800 words. Illustrations: photos and drawings. Payment: £100 per double-page spread; varies for illustrations. Founded 1982.

Junior Magazine

Beach Magazines & Publishing Ltd, 4 Cromwell Place, London SW7 2JE
tel 020-7761 8900 *fax* 020-7761 8901
email editorial@juniormagazine.co.uk
website www.juniormagazine.co.uk
Editor Catherine O'Dolan
Monthly £2.90

Glossy up-market parenting magazine aimed at mothers of children aged 0–8 and reflects the shift in today's society towards older mothers and fathers who have established their careers and homes. Intelligent and insightful features and the best in fashion. Specially commissions most material. Welcomes ideas for articles and features. Payment: £150 per 1000 words (articles/features/short fiction), £300 per feature (colour and b&w photos/artwork). Founded 1998.

Literacy

UK Literary Association, Unit 6, 1st Floor, The Maltings, Green Drift, Royston, Herts. SG8 5AY
tel (01763) 241188 *fax* (01763) 243785
email admin@ukla.org
websites www.ukla.org, www.blackwellpublishing.com
Editor Henrietta Dombey, School of Education, University of Brighton, Falmer, Brighton BN1 9PH
email h.dombey@brighton.ac.uk
3 p.a. (subscription only)

The official journal of the United Kingdom Literacy Association (see page 275) and is for those interested in the study and development of literacy. Readership comprises practitioners, teachers, educators, researchers, undergraduate and graduate students. It offers educators a forum for debate through scrutinising research evidence, reflecting on analysed accounts of innovative practice and examining recent policy developments. Length: 2000–6000 words (articles). Illustrations: b&w prints and artwork. Formerly known as *Reading – Literacy and Language*. Published by Blackwell Publishing. Founded 1966.

Literacy Time

Scholastic Ltd, Villiers House, Clarendon Avenue, Leamington Spa, Warks. CV32 5PR
tel (01926) 887799 *fax* (01926) 883331
website www.scholastic.co.uk

A selection of posters for class and group work and multiple children's leaflets, created to meet specific teachers' objectives for the Literacy Hour, term by term. There are 3 levels: *Literacy Times Years 1/2*, *Literacy Times Years 3/4* and *Literacy Times Years 5/6*.

NATE News (National Association for the Teaching of English)

NATE, 50 Broadfield Road, Sheffield S8 OXJ
tel 0114-255 5419 *fax* 0114-255 5296
email info@nate.org.uk
website www.nate.org.uk
Editor Julie Sellwood
5 p.a.

The official newsletter of the National Association for the Teaching of English (NATE), available as part of its membership. The newsletter is a topical mix of news, views and reviews on all aspects of English at all phases. NATE researches the teaching of English and is involved in curriculum development initiatives with the Arts Council and the National Council for Educational Technology (see page 270).

Nursery Education

Scholastic Ltd, Villiers House, Clarendon Avenue, Leamington Spa, Warks. CV32 5PR
tel (01926) 887799 *fax* (01926) 883331
email earlyyears@scholastic.co.uk
website www.scholastic.co.uk
Editor Susan Sodhi
Monthly £3.75

Practical theme-based activities for educators working with 3–5 year-olds. All ideas based on the Early Learning Goals. Material mostly commissioned. Length: 500–1000 words. Illustrations: colour and b&w; colour posters. Payment: by arrangement. Founded 1997.

Nursery World

Admiral House, 66–68 East Smithfield, London E1W 1BX
tel 020-7782 3120
Editor Liz Roberts
Weekly £1.30

For all grades of primary school, nursery and child care staff, nannies, foster parents and all concerned with the care of expectant mothers, babies and young children. Authoritative and informative articles, 800 or 1300 words, and photos, on all aspects of child welfare and early education, from 0–8 years, in the UK. Practical ideas, policy news and career advice. No short stories. Payment: by arrangement. Illustrations: line, half-tone, colour.

Parent & Child

Scholastic Canada Ltd, 175 Hillmount Road, Markham, Ontario L6C 1Z7
website www.scholastic.com

Covers the essential topics that parents need to know about their child's growth and development (pre-K–K), with expert advice on everything from school transitions to understanding children's feelings to promoting learning at home. Features include Ask the Doctor, Weekend Activities, and a Sibling Sharing Page.

Publishers Weekly

Publishers Weekly, 360 Park Avenue South, New York, NY 10010
tel 646-746-6758 *fax* 646-746-6631
website www.PublishersWeekly.com
Editor-in-chief Nora Rawlinson, *Editorial Director* John F. Baker
Contact Isabell Taylor for general editorial enquiries *tel* 646-746-6758, *email* i.taylor@reedbusiness.com
Children's Books Department: Senior Editor Diane Roback *tel* 646-746-6768 *fax* 646-746-6738

The international news magazine of the $23 billion book industry. Covers all segments involved in the creation, production, marketing and sale of the written word in book, audio, video and electronic formats. In addition to reaching publishers worldwide, it influences all media dealing with the acquisition, sale, distribution and rights of intellectual and cultural properties.

Children's Books Books for review, from preschool to young adult, should be sent to Diane Roback, Children's Books Editor – all reviews are prepublication. Also send her story suggestions on children's publishing, new trends, author or illustrator interviews, etc for the weekly *Children's Books*. Diane also edits the listings for new children's books twice a year for the Spring and Fall Children's Announcements issues. Please fax (do not email) any story pitches or queries concerning review submissions of children's books, review enquiries and editorial guidelines for submission of children's books for review. Founded 1873.

Right Start

McMillan-Scott plc, 10 Savoy Street, London WC2E 7HR
tel 020-7878 2338 *fax* 020-7379 6261
Editor Lynette Lowthian
Bi-monthly £2.10

Features on all aspects of preschool and infant education, child health and behaviour. No unsolicited MSS. Length: 800–1500 words. Illustrations: colour photos, line. Payment: varies. Founded 1989.

Scholastic Canada Ltd

Scholastic Canada Ltd, 175 Hillmount Road, Markham, Ontario L6C 1Z7
website www.scholastic.com

Classroom magazines to provide curriculum support. They include current events and engaging stories through to hands-on maths and science investigations.

PreK-K/Primary: *Let's Find Out*, *Clifford*. Elementary/Junior: *DynaMath* (Grade 3–6), *SuperScience* (Grade 3–6), *Storyworks* (Grade 3–6). Intermediate/Secondary: *Scholastic Math* (Grade 7–9), *Science World* (Grade 7–10), *New York Times Upfront* (Grade 7–12), *Scope* (Grade 7–9). Struggling Reader: *Action* (Grade 7–12), *Literary Cavalcade* (Grade 9–12), *Choices* (Grade 7–12), *Scholastic Art* (Grade 7–12).

The School Librarian

The School Library Association, Unit 2, Lotmead Business Village, Lotmead Farm, Wanborough, Swindon SN4 0UY
tel (01793) 791787 *fax* (01793) 791786
email info@sla.org.uk
website www.sla.org.uk
Editor Ray Lonsdale, DILS, University of Wales, Aberystwyth, Ceredigion SY23 3AS
Quarterly Free to members (£55 p.a.)

Official journal of the School Library Association. Articles on school library management, use and skills, and on authors and illustrators, literacy, publishing. Reviews of books, CD-Roms, websites and other library resources from preschool to adult. Length: 1800–3000 words (articles). Payment: by arrangement. See also page 273. Founded 1937.

TES Cymru

Sophia House, 28 Cathedral Road, Cardiff CF11 9LJ
tel 029-206 60201 *fax* 029-206 60207
website www.tes.co.uk
Editor Karen Thornton
Weekly £1.20

Education newspaper. Articles on education, about special knowledge or teaching experience and short news items about Welsh educational affairs. Length: up to 800 words (articles). Illustrations: line, half-tone. Payment: by arrangement. Founded May 2004.

The Times Educational Supplement

Admiral House, 66–68 East Smithfield, London E1W 1BX
tel 020-7782 3000 *fax* 020-7782 3202 (news),

020-7782 3199(features)
email friday@tes.co.uk (feature outlines), teacher@tes.co.uk (curriculum-related outlines)
website www.tes.co.uk
Editor Bob Doe
Weekly £1.20

Education newspaper. Articles on education written with special knowledge or experience; news items; books, arts and equipment reviews. Check with the news or picture editor before submitting material. Outlines of feature ideas should be faxed or emailed. Illustrations: suitable photos and drawings of educational interest, cartoons. Payment: standard rates, or by arrangement.

TES Teacher
Weekly Free with *TES*

Practical ideas and resources for teachers to inspire more successful lessons.

Times Educational Supplement Scotland

Scott House, 10 South St Andrew Street, Edinburgh EH2 2AZ
tel 0131-557 1133 *fax* 0131-558 1155
Editor Neil Munro
Weekly £1.20

Education newspaper. Articles on education, preferably 800–1000 words, written with special knowledge or experience. News items about Scottish educational affairs. Illustrations: line, half-tone. Payment: by arrangement. Founded 1965.

Young People Now

Haymarket Publishing Ltd, 174 Hammersmith Road, London W6 7JP
tel 020-8267 4707 *fax* 0116-285 3775
email ypn.editorial@haynet.com
website www.ypnmagazine.com
Editor Steve Barrett
Weekly £1.75

Informative articles, highlighting issues of concern to all those who work with young people, including youth workers, probation and social services, Connexions Service, teachers and volunteers. Guidelines for contributors available on request. Founded 1989.

Young Writer – see page 210

Television, film and radio

Writing comedy for children's television

Adam Bromley looks at types of comedy, the parameters of writing comedy for children's television and describes the commissioning process.

Writing comedy for children's television presents numerous challenges: it is both liberating and restrictive. Today, this target audience is more discerning than ever and they have a wide choice of television channels and entertainment options. If a comedy show doesn't deliver in a few minutes viewers will look elsewhere and perhaps channel surf or switch on a games console. Budgets for making programmes are ratcheted downwards than upwards. Also, editorial restrictions for children's television are extensive and need to be considered at every stage in the writing process.

But don't be disheartened by these challenges because children are more imaginative than adults and as an audience they will bc more receptive to more outlandish ideas than conservative adult audiences.

The first question

Before you start on the time-consuming, frustrating and drawn-out process of 'making it' as a comedy writer, there's one question you should ask yourself: 'Can I write funny material?' It's surprising how many aspiring comedy writers never take a moment to be objective about their own work. You have to be tough on yourself because the chances of getting a show commissioned are low. The majority of scripts never get past the initial filtering process by producers and script readers. At every stage the numbers are whittled down. So the odds of any given script actually becoming a television programme are stacked against a writer from day one. Hard work and dedication will take you a long way, but if you can't deliver the comedy then think again. Try out what you've written on children and observe their reaction. You can rely on children to display their honest opinions. Don't rely on adults to give you mere confidence-boosting words of encouragement about your work. You don't need to wow your audience with the first thing you write. But you do need to raise a laugh somewhere along the way. If, after looking at yourself objectively, you do reckon that you may have that potential, the next step is to find out more about your chosen medium.

Budgets and briefs

Children's television has two special features that a writer should be aware of at every stage of writing: low budgets and a restrictive editorial brief. Budgets for programmes are around a fifth of comparable adult television shows so it's worth considering programme budgets when devising an idea. Commissioners are more likely to be attracted to proposals that can be realised on these lower sums than shows with a cast of hundreds and requiring numerous special effects.

But don't make the mistake of thinking that a lower budget means lower quality. For example, Monty Python's *Life of Brian* was shot on a very low budget. The use of coconuts clapped together in place of horses for the knights was an ingenious way of overcoming the lack of funds for the horses. Whilst it's not a writer's job to get mired in the detail of how a scene could be shot, you should try to get a sense of what to avoid. Complex ideas which require large casts, major set builds and extensive use of special effects or large amounts of expensive post production are the obvious pitfalls.

The other unique aspect to children's television is its editorial concerns, which are wide ranging and can be tricky to master. In terms of content, swearing, sexual references, blasphemy or realistic violence are absolutely taboo. Your point of reference should be the content of a U or PG-rated film at the cinema. Watch a good variety of children's television and films to get an innate sense of what the boundaries are. As with the budgets, it's more productive to see these editorial rules as something that will force you to be a better writer than just a burden. Often new comedy writers rely on dark, violent scenarios because mastering a scene that relies on word play and a clever premise is beyond them. This tighter control of content means that the writer cannot fall back on shock tactics or explicit language to achieve a reaction which is, in the long run, a better way to progress.

There is an additional concern known as 'imitative behaviour'. Children are more suggestible and have a lower sense of risk and personal safety. In anything you write avoid any action that, if copied by children, might harm them, for example swallowing lots of tablets, forcing things into their mouths, throwing household objects at people. This may pose problems if you've got slapstick gags, which are a reliable mainstay of children's comedy. Be wary of any highly realistic scenarios as opposed to cartoonish ones. If the above sounds limiting, the flipside is that children will readily make greater leaps of imagination than adults. Don't forget that you're writing for an audience that remains fresh and open-minded in a way few adults are. Working within these ground rules is a small price to pay for an appreciative audience.

Comedy writing itself naturally divides into three main areas: sketches, scripted comedy and gag writing.

Scripted comedy

Scripted comedy covers a number of forms, including comedy narrative that has an unfolding story which links week by week and sitcom in which each episode is largely self contained. The three keys to writing good scripted comedy are number one: character; number two: character; and number three: character.

Everything starts and ends with your principal characters. Witty one-liners and elaborate plot structures are worthless unless they flow from strong central characters. For creating comedy characters, it's useful to think of them as embodying certain key personality traits and to make that inform everything they do. As we're dealing with comedy, don't make your characters too pleasant. There's nothing very amusing, for example, about a family sitcom where everyone gets on wonderfully well, is understanding, supportive and helpful. That may be a good environment to raise children, but it makes for tedious television. Characters don't work in isolation so put together a mix of characters that will spark against one another. Comedy, like drama, needs tension. So if you have a dysfunctional family that lives in a house so huge they never need to interact with one another, there's no friction for comedy to happen. But if you put them in a pokey flat where they're always getting in one another's way, then you've got fertile comic territory.

If you want to devise characters that will appeal to a children's audience, a mix of adults and children will be the most likely to work, preferably of different generations. Children won't be interested in mid-life crises, office politics or single women in their twenties looking for love. Generational conflict with families is an ideal starting point. But as with everything, there are no rules.

So long as your audience can find some point of connection, there's no reason why your lead couldn't be an alien or from another century. It all depends on how that character is presented so consider how your characters will connect with the wider audience. A child's frame of reference is different to that of an adult and children want comedy that reflects that. Remembering that you're writing not just for yourself but for hundreds of thousands of strangers will help guide you towards broader, more accessible characters. Make sure that the comedy flows from the characters themselves and doesn't just happen around them. Your comic leads need to initiate much of the action. In comedy things should go wrong most of the time so the leads should be the authors of their own misfortunes rather than having random events simply happen.

Sketch writing

Sketch writing presents other challenges, not least that many ideas have been done before. Common mistakes new writers make with a sketch is to start with a confused or muddled premise. Alternatively, they have a good premise and do nothing with it. The premise of a sketch is the one-line summary of a funny idea. If you can't summarise the sketch into one line and if that summary doesn't make you laugh, then there's probably something at fault with the original idea. Once you've got a promising sketch idea, it should develop as the piece unfolds. Even though the sketch may be only two minutes of airtime, you'll have to give some kind of twist or progression to sustain the audience's interest over that period. Even 10 seconds of dead air in a television programme can feel like an eternity. Write your sketches longer and then trim them back. Another good rule is to not let a sketch run for longer than two minutes.

Gag writing

Gag writing is a discipline all of its own. When writing standalone jokes, practise does make perfect and it's critical that you test your material on audiences. It can be intimidating but there's no better way to find out if what you've written makes audiences laugh. Your main avenue for gag writing is the scripted links in entertainment shows.

The commissioning process

Once you have material ready to submit, understanding the commissioning process can save a lot of wasted effort. The first hurdle for a writer is to get anyone, whether it's a producer or an agent, to take an interest in their work. Getting a programme commissioned is a long, frustrating process and it's integral to that process to have someone promoting your cause – typically a producer.

From a new writer's perspective, agents can help from an the early stage to get your script past the initial filtering stage. Producers and development executives are generally more receptive to scripts sent to them by agents, as they act as a form of quality control. Don't despair, if you send an unsolicited script or proposal to a producer or editor, it will be read… eventually.

One mistake writers often make is to send out copies of their script to every producer working in children's television with a general covering letter. This is never a good idea. It sends out a signal that the writer in question couldn't be bothered to do some research on who might be interested in their script. Finding out who makes which shows is relatively easy as all the major channels have information lines if you miss the end credits of shows. A bit of research goes a long way. You should follow up that script with a phone call or email. Although your script may represent months of hard toil to you, remember that producers work on other shows and that reading scripts is a low priority for them.

If you are able to get a producer to take an interest in your work, often the next natural step is not to immediately pitch your own programme ideas but to work on existing shows, perhaps writing episodes of a long-running sitcom, devising sketch ideas or writing additional material for entertainment shows. This is a good bridging stage as you'll get a better feel of the production and commissioning process. It's also a great opportunity to improve your writing craft without the exposure of a solo project. Nearly all comedy writers started out writing on other people's shows. The longer you spend writing in a professional environment, the better you'll get. Meeting deadlines and turning work around in a short time frame are not disciplines new writers acquire by writing on their own but they are an important part of being a successful television writer. Being funny on demand is a tough task and it's part of the craft.

In the long run most writers are more interested in getting their own solo ideas commissioned. Be prepared for a lot of frustration and disappointment if you follow this route. There are relatively few programme slots available in any given year. Commissioners tend to favour tried and tested writers over new names. There's no conspiracy to exclude new talent, however. When money is in short supply, opting for a safe pair of hands is a form of insurance policy. All of which means that, as a new writer, you'll have to be that much more impressive than an established one to get noticed. In spite of all this, if you deliver funny, original and accessible scripts, sooner or later you'll be noticed and they will make it on screen.

Adam Bromley is a producer for BBC Entertainment. Recent credits include *The Now Show, The Problem with Adam Bloom* and *Think the Unthinkable* for BBC Radio 4 and *Tiny and Mr Duk's Huge Show*. He is currently producing a 10-part sketch show for *CBBC Stupid* which is due to air in November 2004.

Children's literature on radio and audio

The spoken word and the written word in literature require different handling. Neville Teller looks at the radio and audiobook media and explores what a writer for the microphone needs to know and how to break into this market.

'Read me a story' – one of childhood's perennial calls. Parents found little relief from this cry (palming it off on grandma or auntie was perhaps the best bet) until radio appeared on the scene. But from its very beginning radio included in its schedules stories read aloud for children, and the loudspeaker, for part of the time at least, was able to provide a fair substitute for mummy or daddy by presenting professional actors reading literature specially prepared for performance at the microphone.

Very early on, actors learned that performing at the microphone was a new skill that had to be acquired – the techniques were quite different from those required on the stage. Writers, too, had to acquire a whole range of new skills in preparing material for radio. Two things quickly became apparent. First, literature simply read aloud from the printed page often failed to 'come across' to a listening audience, because material produced to be scanned by the eye is often basically unsuited to the requirements of the microphone. Secondly, the time taken to read a complete book on the air would be far too long to be acceptable, and in consequence most books would need to be abridged.

Today there are two main outlets in this country for aspiring radio/audio writers for children: BBC radio and audiobook publishers.

How has this market reached its present position?

Radio

Children's radio in the UK has certainly had its ups and downs. It came into existence in December 1922, just a few weeks after the BBC itself was born, and for some 40 years the daily Children's Hour became an established and much-cherished feature of life in this country. It is no exaggeration to say that during its heyday its presenters, and those who made its programmes, created an indelible impression on the childhood of millions of people.

However, in the 1960s the imminent death of radio was a generally accepted prognostication. So, starting in 1961, children's radio was slowly but surely strangled on the dubious, if not specious, grounds that children no longer had the time or inclination to listen to radio. Television, it was argued, was their medium of choice. So first the much-loved title 'Children's Hour' was dropped, then the time allotted to programmes 'For the Young' (as it was then called) was cut back. Finally, in March 1964, the programme was put out of its agony.

The demise of children's radio naturally evoked a massive groundswell of protest. In response – although the BBC of the day had clearly lost faith in it – they did grant some sort of reprieve. Stories had always featured strongly in its schedules, and *Story Time* – a programme of abridged radio readings – started life in the old Children's Hour slot with a strong bias towards children's literature. After a few years, however, its character changed. More general literature began to be selected, and then the programme was moved to earlier in the afternoon. That decision, despite a brief experiment with a programme called *Fourth Dimension* and the continued existence of *Listen with Mother* till 1982, effectively left the Radio 4 schedules for nearly 20 years bereft of any specifically children's programmes.

The comeback started slowly, and then suddenly gathered momentum. Early in the new millennium the BBC – moved, doubtless, by mounting evidence of the undiminished popularity of radio – decided to reintroduce a regular programme for children. All they could offer at the time was a 30-minute programme each Sunday evening on Radio 4 called *Go4It*, a magazine-type show that would include a 10-minute reading. Children's literature had – to mix metaphors and create a glorious vision – re-established a toehold on the airwaves and abridgements of books ranging from *The Lion, the Witch and the Wardrobe* by C.S. Lewis to *The Fall of Fergal* by Philip Ardagh were aired.

Much more was to follow, for in the autumn of 2002 the BBC launched its new digital radio channel, BBC7, which included in its schedules, as a basic ingredient, daily programmes for children using live performers and incorporating readings from children's literature, both current and classic. These abridgements are specially prepared and read for the two daily shows: *The Big Toe Radio Show* for older children and – it goes without saying – *The Little Toe Radio Show* for the youngsters. I was delighted to have prepared, amongst others, *Artemis Fowl* by Eoin Colfer, *Stormbreaker* by Anthony Horowitz and *The Prince and the Pauper* by Mark Twain.

Audiobooks

Audiobooks are literary works of all types, some abridged, some unabridged, read by actors and made available in audiocassette or CD form. They are a rapidly growing market: from what was virtually a standing start in the late 1980s, annual sales are now around £70 million. No less than five million audiobooks were purchased in the UK last year and children's literature forms a significant proportion of that total.

Over the past decade and a half an enormous backlist of children's literature has been built up in audiobook format. Nowadays, moreover, it is common for major publishers to launch a fair number of their new books in printed and audiobook form simultaneously. Children's publishers are also increasingly developing the 'twin pack' concept – packaging book and audiobook together – so that children can read and listen at the same time. This development is bound to mushroom, because Customs and Excise decided in 2003 that such products could be zero-rated for VAT.

It was in May 2000 that a consortium thought of putting one modern development (audiobooks) together with another (digital radio), and came up with a revolutionary new radio concept. Oneword is a digital radio channel concerned above all with literature. The core of its programming is the transmission of audiobook readings, both abridged and unabridged, streamed into various segments throughout the day. Its schedules (which, like BBC7's, are regularly included in *Radio Times* as well as in several newspapers) include classical and new books for children.

Writing for the microphone

Putting unabridged audiobook readings to one side, what does the aspiring radio/audio children's writer need to know, and how can he or she break into the rather specialised world of abridging children's literature for the microphone?

As in all professional fields, the tyro is faced with the classic Catch-22 situation: radio producers and audio publishers are reluctant to offer commissions to people without a track record, while it is of course impossible to gain a track record without having won a commission or two. The only advice is to keep plugging away, hoping for that elusive lucky break – and the only consolation on offer is that even the most experienced of today's professionals was once a complete novice.

But what of the techniques that need to be applied in converting material produced for the printed page into a series of scripts that can be performed by an actor with ease at the microphone, and bring real listening pleasure to the child at the other end?

Getting to grips with abridging books for the microphone requires, in the first instance, the application of some simple arithmetic. Take a book of around 70,000 words. Children's radio these days usually devotes about 10 minutes' airtime to its reading slot, and producers allow up to 14 episodes for each book. In 10 minutes, an actor can read about 1450 words. It is clear, therefore, that normally the abridger will be required to reduce the wordage from 70,000 to no more than 20,300 words. In other words, one can be required to remove up to 70% of the original.

The audio field has different requirements. Most books abridged for audio are still published in the form of two double-sided cassettes, though the changeover to CDs is well under way. Each of the four cassette sides runs for about 45 minutes and uses 7000 words. Thus the normal audiobook contains some 28,000 words. CDs can accommodate well over 60 minutes of airtime, so the 180-minute abridgement is often also presented in the form of three CDs.

An abridgement – is that the same as a précis? I think not. A précis writer's objective is to reproduce the sense of an original in fewer words. The skill of the abridger lies in doing that while, in addition and quite as important, retaining the character of the original writing. That demands the capacity to respond sympathetically to the feel of an author's style and to be able to preserve it, even when large chunks of the original are being cut away. Abridging for radio goes beyond even this, for the writer must fulfil his or her commission through the medium of that highly technical artefact, the radio script.

Some abridgements intended for the printed page are able to boast 'only the words of the original are used'. Radio or audio abridgements that followed that principle could be disastrous. The requirements of eye and of ear do not always coincide; a message easily absorbed from the printed page can become surprisingly garbled if transmitted unamended at the microphone.

In crafting a radio/audio script the needs of the listener must be a prime consideration. The needs of the actor who will read it at the microphone are another. The writer must keep in the forefront of the mind the fact that the script has to be performed. The words must 'flow trippingly on the tongue'.

With audio the listener is in control, and can switch on or off whenever convenient. However, a radio script needs shape. On the air, 10 minutes on an emotional plateau can be pretty boring. *Crescendi* and *diminuendi* are called for. A good plan is to provide a modest peak of interest about halfway through the script, and work up to a climax at the end, leaving the listener anxious for more of the story.

Principles, principles – what about practice? A modest illustration.

'How are you going?' Harriet said, stifling a yawn.

'The Oxford bus,' returned Pam.

Nothing wrong with that – on the printed page. If faced with it, though, the experienced radio or audio writer would feel it necessary to present it somewhat along the following lines:

Harriet stifled a yawn.

'How are you going?'

'The Oxford bus,' said Pam

Why? Let's take the points in order.

Harriet said.

If the speaker's name instantly follows a piece of reported speech, and especially a question, a moment of confusion can arise in the listener's mind. In this instance, it could be unclear for a second whether 'Harriet' is included in, or excluded from, the question. It might be: *'How are you going, Harriet... ?'*

The meaning is soon resolved, of course, but impediments to understanding are best eliminated.

'Stifling a yawn' is an indication of the way in which the words were said. If the actor is to provide that indication, he or she needs to know ahead of the speech how it is to be delivered. Moreover, taking the original version, if the actor stifles a yawn while saying Harriet's speech, and then reads 'said Harriet, stifling a yawn,' the passage becomes tautologous.

For this reason it is best to cut back to a bare minimum all indications in the text of how speeches are delivered. It is better to leave it to the actor and the producer to interpret most of them.

There are no apostrophes on the air. By and large, 'said' is the best radio indicator of speech. An alternative is to precede speech by some description of the speaker, and to insert the words spoken with no further indication of who is speaking. Thus:

Harriet stifled a yawn.

'How are you going?'

It is clearly Harriet speaking.

'The Oxford bus,' returned Pamela.

Two points here. Almost all the literary variants of 'said' ring false through the loudspeaker or headphones – cried, riposted, remarked, answered, etc. For reading purposes, most are best replaced with 'said' (or better, wherever possible, omitted altogether) and the speech in question left to the actor to interpret. In this instance, '*returned*' is particularly difficult for the listener – again, for no more than a moment – but is 'returned' part of the speech? '*The Oxford bus returned... ?*' It is surely best to eliminate obstacles to understanding.

This peek into the radio/audio abridger's toolbox might leave one thinking that the business is all gimmick and no heart – noses pressed up so hard against tree trunks that there is no time for the wood. It is certainly necessary that in this field, as in any other, basic techniques have to be acquired and then absorbed to the point where they become second nature. Only then can they be applied to ensure that the radio and audio media are used to interpret a writer's intentions as fully and as honestly as possible.

It is, though, equally essential that the abridger of children's books reproduces, as far as possible, the plot, atmosphere and character of the original. The aim must be to leave the listener with as complete a feeling of the original book as possible, given the technical limitations of time and wordage. It is, in short, an essential aspect of the radio/audio writer's craft to keep faith with the author.

Neville Teller has been contributing to BBC radio for over 40 years. He has well over 250 abridgements for radio readings to his credit, some 50 radio dramatisations and over 150 audiobook abridgements. His most recent children's adaptations include *Artemis Fowl* by Eoin Colfer, *Stig of the Dump* by Clive King, *The BFG* by Roald Dahl, *The Wolves of Willoughy Chase* by Joan Aiken and *Stormbreaker* by Anthony Horovitz. Neville Teller is Chairman of the Society of Authors' Broadcasting Committee. He is also on the Committee of the Spoken Word Publishing Association and chairs the SWPA's Contributors' Committee. He is Guest Playwright for Shoestring Radio Theatre, San Francisco.

See also...

- *Children's audio publishers*, page 51
- *Writing to a brief*, page 226

Writing to a brief

Writing to a brief is an exacting process in which the writer has to produce work to satisfy others as opposed to exploring their own project ideas. The writer may work with others as part of a team when script writing or collaborate with an artistic director when adapting a play. Diane Redmond looks at three aspects of writing to a brief for children.

Writing to a brief is enormous fun! I never know what's going to land on my desk – it could be anything: a children's animation series, a set of books, a live action drama script or a stage play. For this kind of writing you must have the ability to absorb a lot of material quickly and you also have to be capable of putting your own ideas on the back burner. You can't twist the brief in order to accommodate what you want to write as opposed to what the commissioner is *paying* you to write.

Animation

Script writing for animation is energising writing – it makes you think in pictures and images which you have to transcribe into words. An animation series is usually commissioned in blocks of 26 or 52 10-minute episodes. Once you've been invited to work on the series, background material is usually sent to you by the commissioning body. This outlining material is often referred to as the 'bible' and it contains everything the writer needs to know in order to write the manuscript: the number of characters, locations, props, sets and costumes. The 'bible' might contain a fully executed script, which is really useful as you can read for yourself a script that's been approved by the commissioner and thereafter use it as a guideline.

The writing team

The writing team meet with the commissioner (the person or company funding the show) to go through the 'bible' in some detail. The commissioner will be looking for scripts that contain humour, warmth, clarity and a real understanding of the age group the writers are pitching at. As a writer, you should never allow yourself to lose track of the main character and the central theme: if it's about garden gnomes then keep it in the garden; if it's about a builder then the building job will be essential to *every* story; if it's about a postman then he has to do his post round. I know it's obvious but you'd be astonished how often writers stray from the central plot in their obsession to create their *own* story! Most scripts, even if they're only 10 minutes long, have a main plot and a sub-plot which have to reconciled. Make sure your sub-plot doesn't swamp your main plot and make doubly sure your main plot echoes the criteria of the series.

Storylines

Sometimes a few storylines are developed when the writing team is together – just enough to get the team kick-started. The writers may be invited to choose a storyline that excites them and develop it into a three- or four-page treatment, i.e. a scene-by-scene breakdown of the 10-minute episode. Alternatively, writers may be asked to think up and develop more storylines at home. When writing like this on a commission your contract should ensure that you're paid for each stage of the writing process.

The very first outline is often the hardest one of all. The writer may have seen the artwork, may even have seen a pilot script and heard a snatch of the opening music but she's coming to the first story *cold*. The characters aren't alive yet – it's the writer at this vital initial stage who breathes life into them. After a couple of scripts, and certainly after a series of 13 episodes, the characters will be alive and kicking! They will have taken up a space in your imagination and will inspire you with ideas for 10 more series! You know what makes them tick because you've created them in the very act of writing. You'll find that within the writing team writers will favour particular characters and bring out the best in that character. It's a heart-lifting experience to work with a team of writers who are open and generous and willing to share their thoughts. By pooling your joint strengths and resources you generate ideas so don't hold back at the writers' meeting. If you've come up with one good idea, think of it as a springboard because you'll need at least another dozen hot on the heels of the first!

The script editor

The script editor is *vital*. He or she coordinates the scripts and makes sure the series has one voice. Four writers will have different styles, which is exactly why they've been chosen to do the job. However, the series itself has the voice – be it that of a ballerina, a robot, or a kind-hearted mule. The script editor has an overall view of the show and will make small changes to scripts so that idiosyncrasies are ironed out. She also has the sensitive task of liaising with the commissioner and the producer on the writers' behalf. Sometimes you *don't* want to see the notes the producer has made: they may be too abrupt or confusing. The script editor will expand and clarify these notes then pass them on to the writers who can then make the necessary alterations to their scripts based on the producer's wishes. The script editor should be valued because she does *a lot* for the writers in the team.

Stages of writing

After the initial idea, followed by a detailed outline (I usually précis mine scene by scene) you may be asked to reconstruct your outline based on changes the animators or the producer have requested. For instance, if you have written an elephant into your script and if that frame (containing your elephant puppet) will cost £8000 you can guarantee someone will want it to go! It's best to sort out all practical problems at this stage and a good producer will go through a script outline with a fine comb, looking for potential problem areas. The animators will tell you what they, in practical terms, can and cannot do so be prepared for notes from them and remember they're the ones who will be shooting the episode when you've been paid off. I usually find animators incredibly helpful, sometimes inspirational as they'll push their puppeteering to the limit and give me brilliant ideas in the process.

Writers expect to get detailed notes on their first draft scripts and shorter notes on their second draft scripts but if problems have been sorted out at the outline stage it's usually a wrap after two drafts. When you get the go-ahead to write the script the real *fun* begins! I have sat at my desk and laughed till I cried at some of the characters I've written for. Behind the lively dialogue there are other things happening simultaneously: movement within the set, expressions, little mutters and mumbles and music too. Sometimes your instructions to camera can be three times as long as a simple piece of dialogue like, 'Oh, all right then.' Occasionally you may wonder, 'How am I going to get all of that information to camera in such a small space?' It's an exacting rigour, which ultimately strengthens your overall writing skills. When your script is approved you get such a sweet feeling of relief. But then you'll start to miss your characters and so begin work on another script idea – and the business starts all over again.

Stage plays

As well as writing my own stage plays I've also adapted stage plays from the classics such as *Hard Times* by Charles Dickens and Homer's *Odyssey*. The Dickens play was commissioned by the Cambridge Youth Theatre for the Edinburgh Festival with a cast of 30, and *The Odyssey* was staged in 1990 and 1994 at the Polka Theatre for Children in London with a cast of six!

When briefed by an artistic director writers should listen hard to his or her requirements and it is imperative that they take on board the limitations of the budget. Theatres usually have to work on a shoestring budget. If too much is spent on props and costumes it may be at the cost of the funding for an actor, so be prepared to adapt and compromise.

Adapting from the classics

Adapting from a text such as a classic is an exacting exercise. The two books I adapted couldn't have been more different but the process was exactly the same. I read both books until I knew them backwards: with that knowledge under my belt I felt at liberty to explore the plotlines within the stories and look for modern day angles on how to dramatise them.

The brief for *The Odyssey* was to write a 90-minute play with a 10-minute interval for children aged between eight and 12 years old. There's a lot of sex in *The Odyssey*. For instance, Odysseus loiters too long with Circes and nearly dies in his desire to reach the Sirens! In order not to shock my young audience I found a way around this sensitive area by bringing in the crew who made humorous references to Odysseus' behaviour. In one of my scenes Eurylochus says, 'It's time we set sail.' Castor nods towards Odysseus locked in the arms of Circes the Witch and says, 'I don't think the captain's ready for that yet, mate!' The language of Homer is hauntingly beautiful but certainly not pitched at children. The hardest part of writing the play was adapting the language and the plot so that the audience could understand what was going on without destroying the nobility of the original piece. Working closely with the artistic director, it took three drafts to get the tone of the play right but by that time I was so familiar with the gods and heroes of Ancient Greece that they felt like my extended family! It's a knowledge I've never lost and have since written three books based on classical Greek heroes. That's another great thing about writing: you can transpose a story from one art form to another!

Book series

A book series may be commissioned as a result of a writer pitching an idea to a publisher, or a publisher may have spotted a gap in the market which a writer has been invited to fill. The books vary in length depending on the age range – they could be anything from 2000 words to 40,000 words.

I've written three series of books based on football which I knew nothing about but finished up the world's expert on the offside trap! I went on to write several more series based on show jumping, a stage school, a veterinary practice, a drama queen, and an eight-book series based on bridesmaids! A lot of research goes into my books. With my show-jumping series I virtually lived at the livery yard, trailing the head groom and asking questions like, 'Where do show jumpers go when they're not show jumping? How do you treat a lame horse? What's the best fitness diet? Do show jumpers need special shoes and saddles?' I've always been very lucky in finding professionals who allowed me into their lives and let me watch them at work, though I have had a few nasty shocks in the process. Once I found myself masked and gloved in a vast operating theatre at a vet's surgery watching a Newmarket racehorse under the scalpel; but I fled the premises (and my note taking) when a couple brought in a large snake that needed treatment! You *really* do have to know your subject when you're writing this kind of specialist book. The readers certainly know their stuff and are very critical of any inaccuracies. I know this first hand because of all the letters I get from children who've read my series and appreciated the accuracy of them.

Diane Redmond has written numerous scripts including *Bob the Builder*, *Angelina Ballerina*, *Magic Key*, *Tweenies* and *The Hoobs*. She has also written for radio, the stage and live action television dramas. She has published over a hundred books and is presently completing a children's thriller based on murder and counter espionage in the court of Elizabeth I.

See also...

- *Children's literature on radio and audio*, page 221
- *What does an editor do?* page 88

BBC children's television

During the day, BBC1 runs two children's channels – Cbeebies for a preschool audience and CBBC for older children. Both have designated early morning and afternoon time slots but programmes run continuously on individual channels on digital, cable and satellite networks. These channels have a combined budget of £20 million. To find out about the commissioning process visit www.bbc.co.uk/commissioning

BBC Learning and Education

BBC White City, 201 Wood Lane,
London W12 7TS
tel 020-8752 5252
websites www.bbc.co.uk/schools,
www.bbc.co.uk/learning

The BBC runs a wide range of programmes and websites for schools to encourage children to learn (it also has a separate service for adults.) The programmes aim to inspire learning more broadly and informally on topics such science, history and children's entertainment. The BBC uses interactive TV and internet for these learning services. This department commissions and produces a broad range of online and interactive factual output and is actively looking for new writers.

Controller Liz Cleaver
Creative Director, Learning Nick Ware
Controller, Children's Education Frank Flynn

CBBC

Television Centre, Wood Lane, London W12 7RJ
tel 020-8743 8000
email cbbconline@bbc.co.uk
Submissions CBBC Treatments & Scripts, Development Executive, CBBC Creates, Room E1200, East Tower, BBC Television Centre, Wood Lane, London W12 7RJ
email amanda.gabbitas@bbc.co.uk
website www.bbc.co.uk/cbbc

Digital channel aimed at 6–12 year-olds (it does not cater for teenagers). Produced by the BBC under the CBBC brand. Broadcasts 7am–7pm on BBC1, BBC2 (known as CBBC1 and CBBC2) and cable/satellite channels. Offers a complete TV and online experience by offering a broad range of content made specifically for the 6–12 age group which is relevant to their daily lives and helps them make sense of the world.

There are opportunities for new writers in this highly competitive area. Unsolicited programme proposals from individual writers and independent production companies are passed to the relevant genre head. The CBBC department is searching for new writing and screen presenting talent, across the CBBC output. CBBC prefer treatments of programme ideas to be sent via email. Presenter enquiries need to send a showreel of approximately 3 minutes on VHS.

Controller, CBBC Dorothy Prior
Head of Entertainment Anne Gilchrist
Head of Drama Elaine Sperber
Head of On-Air Paul Smith
Head of Education Sue Nott
Head of CBBC News & Factual Programmes Roy Milani
Head of Preschool Clare Elstow
Head of Acquisitions Michael Carrington
Development Executive Amanda Gabbitas

Cbeebies is CBBC's sister channel for younger viewers. Launched 2002.

Cbeebies

Television Centre, Wood Lane, London W12 7RJ
tel 020-8743 8000
email cbeebiesonline@bbc.co.uk
website www.bbc.co.uk/cbeebies

Channel produced by the BBC and aimed at children under 6 years old. A range of preschool learning programmes designed to encourage learning through play. Programmes include *The Tweenies* and *Teletubbies*. It transmits on BBC1, BBC2 and the Cbeebies cable/satellite channel, 6am–7pm and features a Cbeebies Bedtime Hour between 6pm and 7pm. The approach is to entertain and engage children so they learn through play, and to stimulate and encourage participation. CBBC is its sister channel for older viewers. Launched 2002.

Independent children's television

A broad range of independently commissioned and scheduled programmes is available on terrestrial and digital, cable and satellite television networks. ITV, Channel 4 and Channel 5, have allocated children's morning, afternoon and weekend time slots, whereas the digital channels run back-to-back programmes between 12 and 24 hours a day. For channel information, contact Ofcom (www.ofcom.org.uk).

Boomerang

Turner House, 16 Great Marlborough Street, London W1F 7HS
tel 020-7693 1000
email toon.pressoffice@turner.com
website www.cartoonnetwork.com/boomerang

Shows classic animated cartoons mainly from Warner Brothers, Hanna-Barbera and MGM archives; also shows *Thunderbirds*. Owned by The Cartoon Network.

Channel 5 Broadcasting Ltd

22 Long Acre, London WC2E 9LY
tel 020-7550 5555, (08457) 050505 (comments)
fax 020-7550 5554
email leatherp@five.tv.co.uk (press office)
websites www.five.tv.co.uk, www.five.tv/programmes/milkshake, www.five.tv/programmes/shake
Director of Programmes Kevin Lygo

The fifth and last national 'free-to-air' terrestrial 24-hour TV channel. Commissions a wide range of programmes to suit all tastes.

Milkshake! is Channel 5's weekday children's programme slot, 6.30–9.25am. Programmes include *Noddy, Hi-5, Funky Valley* and *Peppa Pig*. Established 1997.

Channel 4 Television Corporation

124 Horseferry Road, London SW1P 2TX
tel 020-7396 4444, 020-7306 8333 (viewer enquiries), 020-7396 4444 (E4 and FilmFour information)
fax 020-7306 8347
website www.channel4.com/entertainment/t4
Director of Programmes Kevin Lygo

Commissions and purchases programmes for broadcast during the whole week throughout the UK (except Wales). Also broadcasts subscription film channel FilmFour and digital entertainment channel E4.

Children's early morning viewing is approx. 6–7am and *The Hoobs* and *Spider-man* are programmes shown regularly. Programmes catering for the teenagers, such as *Friends, Hollyoaks, The O.C.* and *Big Brother*, are shown during weekday early evenings and on the weekend show *T4*.

CiTV

200 Gray's Inn Road, London WC1X 8HF
tel 020-7843 8000 *fax* 020-7843 8158
website www.citv.co.uk

ITV1 devotes 3.15–5pm and Saturday and Sunday mornings to children's programmes. It offers a broad mix of programmes over a range of genres including drama, factual, entertainments, preschool (Little CiTV) and animation.

Discovery Kids

Discovery Networks Europe, 160 Great Portland Street, London W1W 5QA
tel 020-7462 3600
email mail_us@discovery-europe.com
website www.kids.discovery.co.uk
Contact Valerie Taylor

Satellite and cable network showing mainly science, documentary and nature programmes, such as *Mystery Hunters, History Busters* and *Sci-Busters*. Part of the Discovery Channel and owned by Discovery Communications.

Disney Channel UK

Beaumont House, Avonmore Road, London W14 8ST
tel 020-7605 2401
email tdc_talk@studio.disney.com
websites www.disney.co.uk/disneychannel, www.disney.co.uk/DisneyChannel/toondisney, www.disney.co.uk/DisneyChannel/playhouse

A cable and satellite network run by the Walt Disney Company. Disney Channel comprises 4 channels: Disney Channel, Disney Channel+1, Toon Disney and Playhouse Disney. Features family-orientated programmes aimed at pre-teens and younger adolescents. Surprisingly, it does not feature many classic Disney cartoons but newer programmes such as *Lizzie McGuire, Boy Meets World* and the *Proud Family*. Established 1973; UK version launched 1990s.

Fox Kids Europe

338 Euston Road, London NW1 3AZ
tel 020-7554 9000 *fax* 020-7554 9005
email info@foxkidseurope.com
website www.foxkids.co.uk

Broadcasts programmes for children aged 2–14 in 57 countries in Europe and the Middle East. Programmes are specifically aimed at the needs of different markets, viewing habits, parental sensitivities and cultural trends. Also offers localised websites. Launched 1996.

GMTV

London Television Centre, Upper Ground, London SE1 9TT
tel 020-7827 7000 *fax* 020-7827 7001
email talk2us@gmtv.co.uk
website www.gmtv.co.uk
Director of Programmes Peter McHugh

GMTV1 is ITV's national breakfast TV service, 6.00–9.25am, 7 days a week. GMTV2 is GMTV's digital, satellite and cable channel shown on ITV2 daily 6.00–9.25am. GMTV's preschool children's slot is on Saturday (6–7am), and the slot for older children is *Diggin' It* and runs on Saturdays (7.00–9.25am) and Sundays (7.45–8.25am). On weekdays children's programmes are shown on GMTV2.

ITV Network Ltd/ITV Association

200 Gray's Inn Road, London WC1X 8HF
tel 020-7843 8000 *fax* 020-7843 8158
email info@itv.com
website www.itv.co.uk
Managing Director (Granada) Mick Desmond, *Managing Director (Carlton)* Clive Jones, *Director of Programmes* Nigel Pickard

Comprises 16 independent regional TV licensees, broadcasting across 15 regions of the UK. Commissions and schedules its own programmes and from independent production companies, shown across the ITV network. The ITV terrestrial channel is ITV1. See also CiTV (listed) and the following websites:

Anglia
website www.angliatv.co.uk

Border
website www.border-tv.co.uk

Carlton London, Central and West Country
website www.carlton.com

Channel Television
website www.channeltv.co.uk

Grampian
website www.grampiantv.co.uk

Granada
website www.granadatv.co.uk

HTV Wales
website www.htvwales.co.uk

HTV West
website www.htvwest.co.uk

London Weekend
website www.lwt.co.uk

Meridian
website www.meridian.co.uk

Scottish
website www.scottishtv.co.uk

Tyne Tees
website www.tyneteestv.co.uk

Ulster
website www.u.tv

Yorkshire
website www.yorkshire-television.co.uk

MTV Network Europe

United Kingdom House, 180 Oxford Street, London W1D 1DS
tel 020-7284 7777
email pressinfo@mtvne.com
website www.mtv.co.uk

Europe's largest 24-hour music TV network. It has 5 cable/satellite/digital channels in the UK: MTV Dance, Base, Hits, MTV2, VH1 Classic which show popular rock and music videos. All channels except VH1 Classic are aimed at adolescents and young adults. The company also produces other shows, including animated cartoons such as *Beavis and Butthead* and *Daria*, as well as reality shows and sitcoms such as *The Osbournes*. Owned by Viacom.

Nick Jr.

Nickelodeon House, 15–18 Rathbone Place, London W1
tel 020-7462 1000
email letterbox@NickJr.co.uk
website www.nickjr.co.uk

Programmes for preschool children to promote social and thinking skills through playful entertainment. Nick Jr. policy is 'play to learn'. Programmes include *Maisy, Kipper, Maggie and the Ferocious Beast* and *Angelina Ballerina*.

Nickelodeon UK

Nickelodeon House, 15–18 Rathbone Place, London W1H 1HU
tel 020-7462 1000
website www.nick.co.uk

American cable/satellite network known for its innovative children's programming. There are 4 channels in the UK: Nickelodeon, Nicktoons TV, Nick Jr and Nick Replay. Programmes include *Sabrina the Teenage Witch* and *My life as a Teenage Robot*. Established in the US in 1979; launched in UK 1993. Owned by Viacom.

Nicktoons TV

Nickelodeon House, 15–18 Rathbone Place, London W1
tel 020-7462 1000
website www.nick.co.uk/toons

Channel solely devoted to Nick's own produced children's cartoons (e.g. *Rugrats*).

S4C

Parc Ty Glas, Llanishen, Cardiff CF14 5DU
tel 029-20747444 *fax* 029-20754444
email s4c@s4c.co.uk
website www.s4c.co.uk
Chief Executive Huw Jones, *Director of Programmes* Iona Jones

The Welsh Fourth Channel. S4C's analogue service broadcasts 32 hours per week in Welsh: 22 hours are commissioned from independent producers and 10 hours are produced by the BBC. Most of Channel 4's output is rescheduled to complete this service. S4C's digital service broadcasts 12 hours per day in Welsh.

It runs the same children's programmes as Channel 4 but includes Welsh language programmes for both older and younger viewers such as *Bardd Plant Cymru, Mas Draw* and *Triong!*.

Smash Hits Channel

Mappin House, 4 Winsley Street, London W1W 8HF
tel 020-7436 1515
website www.smashhits.net

24-hour, non-stop music channel for children and teenagers where the viewer decides what is played. All songs can be viewed online.

The Cartoon Network (TCN)

Turner Entertainments Network Ltd, 16 Great Marlborough Street, London W1F 7HS
tel 020-7693 1000
email toon.pressoffice@turner.com
website www.cartoonnetwork.co.uk

Channel dedicated to showing cartoons by Warner Bros, Hanna-Barbera and MGM cartoons, e.g. *Dexter's Laboratory* and *The Powderpuff Girls*. Created by Turner Broadcasting and bought by Time Warner in 1996; now owned by Time Warner. Established 1992.

Trouble

Flextech Television, 160 Great Portland Street, London W1W 5QA
tel (0870) 043 4027
email enquiries@trouble.co.uk
website www.trouble.co.uk

Channel for teenagers. Shows US programmes such as *2 Guys & a Girl* and UK programmes such as *Date my Mate* and *Playing Tricks*. Also has interactive programmes such as *Talk to the Hand*. The website claims to have some of the busiest teen chatrooms. Owned by Flextech Television, the content division of Telewest Braodband.

Children's television and film producers

The recommended approach for submitting material is through a literary agency. However, if you choose to submit material direct, first check with the company that they may be interested in your work and whether they would like to receive it.

Aardman Animations

Gas Ferry Road, Bristol BS1 6UN
tel 0117-984 8485 *fax* 0117-984 8486
email mail@aardman.com
website www.aardman.com
Head of Script Development Mike Cooper, *Development Executive (Shorts & Series)* Helen Brunsdon

Produces animated TV series, TV specials, short films, feature films, interstitials and commercials. Half of its programmes/films are aimed at children (40% family, 10% adult). Specialists in model animation. Considers screenplays for cinema and TV. No unsolicited submissions. Only considers proposals via an agent. Founded 1972.

ACP Television

Crosshands, Coreley, Ludlow, Shrops. SY8 3AR
tel (01584) 890893 *fax* (01584) 890810
email mair@acptv.com
website www.acptv.com
Contact Sandra Keating

Documentaries for children aged 12–16. Founded 1993.

Carlton Television Productions

35–38 Portman Square, London W1H 0NU
tel 020-7486 6688 *fax* 020-7486 1132
Director of Programmes Steve Hewlett

Comprises Carlton Television Productions, Planet 24 and Action Time and makes programmes for all UK major broadcasters (ITV, BBC, Channel 4, Channel 5 and Sky) and regional programmes for Carlton Central, Carlton London and Carlton Westcountry. Carlton Television Productions' Drama department encourages the submission of scripts and outlines from professional writers through an agent.

Children's Film and Television Foundation Ltd

Elstree Film and Television Studios, Borehamwood, Herts. WD6 1JG
tel 020-8953 0844 *fax* 020-8207 0860
email annahome@cftf.onyxnet.co.uk
Chief Executive Anna Home

Involved in the development and co-production of films for children and the family, both for the theatric market and for TV. Will consider screenplays for cinema. Founded 1951.

Collingwood O'Hare Entertainment

10–14 Crown Street, London W3 8SB
tel 020-8993 3666 *fax* 020-8993 9595
email info@crownstreet.co.uk
Contact Helen Stroud, Head of Development

Children's animation series for TV for ages 0–8, e.g. *Yoko! Jakamoko! Toto!*. Will only consider material submitted via an agent. Founded 1988.

The Comedy Unit

Glasgow TV & Film Studios, The Media Park, Craigmont Street, Glasgow G20 9BT
tel 0141-305 666 *fax* 0141-305 6600
email general@comedyunit.co.uk
Contact Niall Clark, Script Editor

Comedy and entertainment programmes for radio, TV and film. Approx. 20% of output is aimed at children aged 5–12. Will consider scripts for plays, comedy drama scripts for TV or film, and treatments for live-action and animation. Aims to significantly develop children's output. Submit material by post or email. Allow approx. one month for response. Founded 1996.

Contender TV

The Contender Entertainment Group, 48 Margaret Street, London W1W 8SE
tel 020-7907 3773 *fax* 020-7907 3777
website www.contendergroup.com

A new division of the Contender Entertainment Group, its first animated series for children, *Tractor Tom*, has been broadcast.

Cosgrove Hall Films Ltd

8 Albany Road, Chorlton-Cum-Hardy, Manchester M21 0AW
tel 0161-882 2500 *fax* 0161-882 2555
email animation@chf.co.uk
Contact Nicola Davies, Assistant Script Editor

Screenplays for cinema and TV for animation (drawn, model or CGI) or a 'live action'/animation mix. Series material especially welcome, preschool to adult. Founded 1976.

The Walt Disney Company Ltd

3 Queen Caroline Street, London W6 9PE
tel 020-8222 1000 *fax* 020-8222 2795

Screenplays not accepted by London office. Must be submitted by an agent to The Walt Disney Studios in Burbank, California.

Diverse Productions

Gorleston Street, London W14 8AX
tel 020-7603 4567 *fax* 020-7603 2148
website www.diverse.co.uk

Documentaries, science, business history, travel, the arts, music, entertainment, children's.

Endemol

Shepherd's Building Central, Charechrost Way, London W14 0EE
tel (0870) 333 1700 *fax* (0870) 333 1800

Entertainment, documentary, drama, children's arts, news, current affairs, religion.

Fairwater Films Ltd

68 Vista Rise, Llandaff, Cardiff CF5 2SD
tel 029-2057 8488 *fax* 029-2057 8488
email tbarnes@netcomuk.co.uk
Managing Director Tony Barnes

Animation for cinema and TV; live action entertainment. All material should be submitted through an agent. Founded 1982.

The Jim Henson Company

30 Oval Road, London NW1 7DE
tel 020-7428 4000 *fax* 020-7428 4001
website www.henson.com
President, Jim Henson Television Europe Angus Fletcher, *Director of Development, Jim Henson Television* Sophie Finston, *International Development Co-ordinator* Clare Lewis

Screenplays for cinema and TV; fantasy, family and children's programmes – usually involving puppetry or animatronics. All material should be submitted through an agent. Founded 1979.

HIT Entertainment plc

5th Floor, Maple House, 149 Tottenham Court Road, London W1T 7NF
tel 020-7554 2500 *fax* 020-7388 9321
website www.hitentertainment.com

One of the world's leading children's entertainment companies. Its activities span TV and video production (with studios in the US and the UK), publishing, consumer products, licensing (properties include *Bob the Builder*, *Thomas the Tank Engine*, *Barney*, *Angelina Ballerina*, *Pingu* and *Guinness World Records*) and live events. Founded 1989.

Lion Television

191 Askew Road, London W12 9AX
tel 020-8735 4000

Light entertainment, documentaries, drama, children's, the arts, news/current affairs, religion.

Loonland UK Ltd

72–74 Dean Street, London W1V 6AE
tel 020-7434 1478 *fax* 020-7434 1578
email info@loonland.com
website www.loonland.com

See also Telemagination.

Lupus Films Ltd

Studio 107, Blackbull Yard, 24–28 Hatton Wall, London EC1N 8JH
tel 020-7419 0997 *fax* 020-7404 9474
email info@lupusfilms.net
website www.lupusfilms.net
Head of Development Ruth Fielding

High-quality children's programming across a variety of genre, from preschool animation to live-action family drama for up to 12 year-olds. Produces 1–2 programmes/films a year. Will consider screenplays for cinema and TV and for other TV programmes submitted *only* from reputable agents or publishers. 'Strong and original ideas will always push through. Watch children's TV and be aware of different channels' preferences and scheduling trends.' The company was set up by Camilla Deakin and Ruth Fielding, formerly the commissioning team for Arts and Animation at Channel 4 Television. Lupus prides itself on being the 'head not the hands' of the animation production process, acting not as a studio but as a production company, seeking out the best ideas and putting together talented teams by accessing their many useful contacts in the industry. Founded 2002.

Millimages

6 Broadstone Place, London W1U 7EN
tel 020-7486 9555 *fax* 020-7486 9666
email info@millimages-uk.com
website www.millimages.com
Managing Director John Reynolds

One of the main children's animation production companies in Europe.

Pearson

1 Stephen Street, London W1F 1PJ
tel 020-7691 6000 *fax* 020-7691 6100

Light entertainment, drama and children's TV programmes.

Penguin Television

80 Strand, London WC2R 0RL
tel 020-7010 3000 *fax* 020-7010 6643
email info@penguintv.com
website www.penguintv.com
Marketing Executive Laura Jones

Children's, documentaries/factual, lifestyle and educational programmes. Produces approx. 3 programmes a year (about half the total output) for children aged 0–12. Will consider screenplays for TV and other TV programmes and non-broadcast TV scripts. Send material to Production Dept. Founded 2000.

Planet 24 Productions Ltd

35–38 Portman Square, London W1H 0NU
tel 020-7486 6268 *fax* 020-7612 0679
website www.planet24.com
Managing Director Ed Forsdick

Light entertainment, factual entertainment, music, features and computer animation. Wholly owned subsidiary of Carlton Communications Plc.

Ragdoll Productions

Timothy's Bridge Road,
Statford-upon-Avon CV37 9NQ
tel (01753) 631800
email pinewood@ragdoll.co.uk
website www.ragdoll.co.uk

Company set up by Anne Wood and best-known for *Teletubbies, Rosie and Jim, Badjelly the Witch, Boohbah, Brum* and *Pob*. Initiated Open Door, a unique international exchange of 5-minute films without words that focus on the perceptions and needs of young children worldwide.

Screentiger Ltd

First Floor, 53 Greek Street, London W1D 3DR
tel 020-7434 2487 *fax* 020-7287 7204
email claudine.massin@virgin.net

Animation for TV.

Telemagination

Royalty House, 3rd Floor, 72–74 Dean Street, London W1V 6AE
tel 020-7434 1551 *fax* 020-7434 3344
email mail@tmation.co.uk
websites www.telemagination.co.uk, www.loonland.com
Head of Production Beth Parker, *Director of Animation* Alan Simpson

Producer of animated TV series for children such as *The Telebugs* and *The Animals of Farthing Wood*. One of the UK's leading full-service animation studios, the company has particular experience in large-scale international co-productions. Owned by TV-Loonland, a leading international producer and distributor of TV series and animation in the programming market for children, youth and families. Established 1984; bought by Loonland in 2000.

Twofour Productions Ltd

Quay West Studios, Old Newnham,
Plymouth PL7 5BH
tel (01752) 333900 *fax* (01752) 344224
email enq@twofour.co.uk
website www.twofour.co.uk
Contact Melanie Leach, Development Dept

Factual, factual entertainment, leisure and lifestyle, and children's TV programmes. Founded 1987.

WarkClements Children's and Youth

45–49 Mortimer Street, London W1W 8HX
tel 020-7470 1335 *fax* 020-7636 1955
email info@warkclements.co.uk
website www.warkclements.com/childrens
Head of Children's & Youth Richard Langridge

Award-winning children's division of WarkClements. Programmes include *Captain Abercromby* and *Jepordy*, both commissioned by the BBC. Currently planning further ventures in children's programming in all areas, including comedy, factual and drama and family films. Founded 2001.

Children's radio

The BBC is the main outlet for radio writers with its strong relationship with children's literature. In addition to storytelling, the BBC commissions and produces dramatisations of children's classics and historically based fiction, as well as a wide range of significant works by contemporary children's authors.

BBC radio

BBC Schools Radio

Room 340, Henry Wood House,
3 & 6 Langham Place, London W1 1AA
tel (0870) 830 8000 *fax* (0870) 830 8002
email bbc@twoten.press.net
website www.bbc.co.uk/schools/guide/radio_schedule.sht

Audio resources to support teaching across a wide range of primary curriculum areas. The programmes offer a varied and flexible, convenient resource with learning outcomes which carefully target curriculum objectives. Programmes are available in 3 ways: as prerecorded cassettes and CDs (due to rights restrictions these are only available to schools in the UK); as 'audio on demand' using the internet site; and transmission. It is intended that programmes are prerecorded for use in the classroom.

CBBC Radio

BBC7, Room 1003, BBC Broadcasting House,
London W1 1AA
tel (08700) 100700 *textphone* (07958) 100700
email bigtoe@bbc.co.uk
website www.bbc.co.uk/music/childrens

Programmes available on the children's radio player include: *Big Toe* – features, music, interviews, Top 40; *Little Toe* (*Big Toe's* little brother or sister) – stories. *Go4It* – Radio 4's weekly show hosted by Barney Harwood, with stories competitions and special features; *Making Tracks* – music show presented by CBBC's Angellica Bell and Adrian Dickson; and *Smile* – pop and urban sounds from the show.

Independent radio producers

The Comedy Unit

Glasgow TV & Film Studios, The Media Park,
Craigmont Street, Glasgow G20 9BT
tel 0141-305 666 *fax* 0141-305 6600
email general@comedyunit.co.uk
Contact April Chamberlain, Joint Managing Director

Comedy and entertainment programmes for radio, TV and film. Approx. 20% of output is aimed at children aged 5–12. Submit material by post or email. Allow approx. one month for response. Founded 1996.

Crosshands Ltd/ACP Television

Crosshands, Coreley, Ludlow, Shrops. SY8 3AR
tel (01584) 890893 *fax* (01584) 890893
email mail@acptv.com
Contact Richard Uridge

Radio and TV documentaries.

CSA Word

6A Archway Mews, London SW15 2PE
tel 020-8871 0220 *fax* 020-8877 0712
email info@csaword.co.uk
website www.csaword.co.uk
Audio Manager Victoria Williams

Produces readings, plays and features/documentaries. Allowapprox. 2 months for response to submissions. Founded 1992.

Loftus Productions Ltd

2A Aldine Street, London W12 8AN
tel 020-8740 4666
email ask@loftusproductions.co.uk
website www.loftusproductions.co.uk
Contact Nigel Acheson

Produces features, documentaries and readings (no drama) for BBC Radio. Programmes are mostly for adults with approx. 5% of output for children aged 5–12, usually documentaries. Also produces audio guides for museums and galleries, some specifically for children. Founded 1996.

Pennine Productions LLP

2 Grimeford Lane, Anderton, Chorley, Lancs. PR6 9HL
tel (01257) 482559
email mike@pennine.biz
website www.pennine.biz
Contact Mike Hally

Wide range of features for BBC Radio. Book readings for Radio 4 from Autumn 2004. No unsolicited material – phone/email/write first. Founded 2000.

Lou Stein

14A Tavistock Place, London WC1H 9RD
email loustein@yahoo.com
Contact Lou Stein

Plays for BBC Radio. Founded 2000.

Theatre

Theatre for children

London and provincial theatres are listed below; listings of touring companies start on page 241.

London

Polka Theatre for Children

240 The Broadway, London SW19 1SB
tel 020-8545 8320 *fax* 020-8545 8365
email info@polkatheatre.com
website www.polkatheatre.com
Artistic Director Annie Wood, *Contact* Richard Shannon, Director of New Writing

Exclusively for children between 18 months and 16 years of age, the Main Theatre seats 300 and the Adventure Theatre seats 80. It is programmed for 18 months to 2 years in advance. Theatre of new writing, with targeted commissions. Founded 1967.

Soho Theatre and Writers' Centre

21 Dean Street, London W1D 3NE
tel 020-7287 5060 *fax* 020-7287 5061
email writers@sohotheatre.com
website www.sohotheatre.com
Artistic Director Abigail Morris

Produces or co-produces 6–7 new plays each year but none are for children. For children, STWC hosts one visiting production company a year, e.g. *Something Else* by Tall Stories Touring Company, adapted from the book by Kathryn Cave and Chris Riddell. Welcomes unsolicited scripts of new plays but not for children.

Unicorn Theatre for Children

Admin offices St Mark's Studios, Chillingworth Road, London N7 8QJ
tel 020-7700 0702 *fax* 020-7700 3870
email admin@unicorntheatre.com
website www.unicorntheatre.com
Administrative Director Christopher Moxon, *Artistic Director* Tony Graham, *Associate Director* Rebecca Gatward, *Literary Manager* Carl Miller, *Associate Artist (Literary)* Charles Way

At the end of 2005 Unicorn will move into its new London home near Tower Bridge, where it will produce a year-round programme of theatre for children aged 4–12, their families and schools. Eight in-house productions of full-length plays with professional casts and production teams will be staged across 2 auditoriums alongside visiting companies and education work.

Unicorn rarely commissions plays from writers who are new to it. However, it is keen to hear from writers who are interested to work with Unicorn in the future. Its aim is for its work to be artistically led, truthful, and insistent on the primacy of imagination. It asks: does the play matter to children; does it have a sense of poetry; does it contain a child's perspective; is it drama; can it transcend and transform?

Do not send unsolicited MSS as Unicorn does not have the resources to read and respond to them in appropriate detail. Send a short statement describing why you would like to write for Unicorn and a CV or a summary of your relevant experience.

Young Vic Theatre Company

Chester House, Kennington Park, Brinnen Estate, 1–3 Brixton, London SW9
tel 020-7922 8400 *fax* 020-7922 8401
email info@youngvic.org
website www.youngvic.org
General Manager Mark Feakins

Metropolitan producing theatre producing classic plays. Founded 1969.

Provincial

The Byre Theatre of St Andrews

Abbey Street, St Andrews KY16 9LA
tel (01334) 476288 *fax* (01334) 475370
email enquiries@byretheatre.com
website www.byretheatre.com
Artistic Director Stephen Wrentmore

Offers an exciting year-round programme of contemporary and classic drama, dance, concerts, comedy and innovative education and community events. Operates a blend of in-house and touring productions. Maintains a policy of producing new and established work. Education programme caters for all ages with Youth workshops and Haydays (for 50+). Offers support for new writing through the Byre Writers, a well-established and successful playwrights group.

Chichester Festival Theatre Ltd

Chichester Festival Theatre, Oaklands Park, Chichester, West Sussex PO19 4AP

tel (01243) 784437 *fax* (01243) 787288
email admin@cft.org.uk
website www.cft.org.uk
Artistic Directors Martin Duncan, Ruth Mackenzie, Steven Pimlott

Festival Season April–Oct in Festival and Minerva Theatres together with a year-round education programme.

Contact Theatre Company

Oxford Road,
Manchester M15 6JA
tel 0161-274 3434 *fax* 0161-274 0640
email info@contact-theatre.org.uk
Artistic Director John E. McGrath

Interested in working with and for young people aged 13–30. Send sae for writers' guidelines.

Everyman Theatre

Regent Street, Cheltenham,
Glos. GL50 1HQ
tel (01242) 512515 *fax* (01242) 224305
email admin@everymantheatre.org.uk
website www.everymantheatre.org.uk
Chief Executive Philip Bernays, *Artistic Director* Sue Colverd

Regional presenting and producing theatre promoting a wide range of plays. Small-scale experimental, youth and educational work encouraged in The Other Space studio theatre. Contact the Artistic Director before submitting material.

Haymarket Theatre Company

The Haymarket Theatre,
Wote Street, Basingstoke,
Hants RG21 7NW
tel (01256) 323073 *fax* (01256) 357130
email info@haymarket.org.uk
website www.haymarket.org.uk

Produces up to 8 main house shows a year plus a full and integrated education programme. Interested in co-producing and up to 4 visiting shows. Introduced a 3-year ensemble acting company-in-residence from August 2003. New writing needs to fit the season. Contact the theatre before sending a synopsis.

The Haymarket Youth Theatre is a vibrant group of young performers aged 12–18. It is led by a professional director and meets weekly on Thursday evenings, 6.00–8.30pm during term time. As well as rehearsing for productions, students are trained in drama skills and theatre practice, involving workshops, visiting specialist tutors and residential courses. Entry is by audition only which is in workshop style (no solo performances required!) and lasts about 2 hours. For further information contact Barbara Lilley on (01256) 323073 or barbara@haymarket.org.uk

Leeds Children's Theatre

c/o Leeds Civic Theatre, Cookridge Street,
Leeds LS2 8BH
tel 0113-214 5338 *fax* 0113-214 5347
email info@leeds-childrens-theatre.co.uk
website www.leeds-childrens-theatre.co.uk
Secretary T. Hutchinson

One of the many amateur dramatic societies based at the Leeds Civic Theatre. A member of the Leeds Civic Arts Guild, Leeds Children's Theatre stages 2 shows at the Leeds Civic Theatre each year. It is dedicated to the principle of quality, affordable children's entertainment in order to encourage the introduction of the theatrical experience to young children. It covers most aspects of theatrical production. Membership is open to all young people. Saturday morning drama workshops offer an excellent introduction but there is currently a waiting list for places. Adult membership is also available. Founded 1935.

Leighton Buzzard Children's Theatre

12 Linslade Road, Heath and Reach,
Leighton Buzzard, Beds. LU7 0AU
tel (01525) 237469
email sally@lbct.freeserve.co.uk
website www.lbct.org

A community-based group which exists to introduce young people to the joy of theatre, to develop theatre craft and to enhance enjoyment of performance through community involvement. It offers a unique opportunity to young people aged 5–18 to act, sing, dance, improvise, communicate, have fun and learn.

Library Theatre Company

St Peter's Square, Manchester M2 5PD
tel 0161-234 1913 *fax* 0161-228 6481
email ltc@libraries.manchester.gov.uk
website www.librarytheatre.com
Contact Artistic Director

Produces mostly contemporary drama with a major play for children and families at Christmas. A recent children's production was *The Ghosts of Scrooge* by Charles Way with a cast of 8. Aims to produce drama which illuminates the contemporary world. Will consider scripts from new writers. Allow 4 months for response. Founded 1952.

Queen's Theatre, Hornchurch

Billet Lane, Hornchurch, Essex RM11 1QT
tel (01708) 462362 *fax* (01708) 462363
email info@queens-theatre.co.uk
website www.queens-theatre.co.uk
Artistic Director Bob Carlton

500-seat producing theatre serving outer East London with permanent company of actors/musicians presenting 8 mainhouse and 3 TIE productions each year. Treatments welcome; unsolicited scripts may be returned unread. Queen's Theatre Writer's Group showcases new work Sept–March; contact Education & Outreach Manager for details.

The Queen's Youth Theatre Programme provides the opportunity for young people aged 7–18 to become involved in drama. There is no selection process on the basis of experience or ability.

The Sherman Theatre

Senghennydd Road, Cardiff CF24 4YE
tel 029-2064 6901 *fax* 029-2064 6902
email admin@shermantheatre.demon.co.uk
website www.shermantheatre.co.uk
General Manager Margaret Jones
Contact Programme Coordinator

Regional repertory theatre producing a third of its plays for children. Produces work for the very young (under 5s) and Christmas productions for 6–12 year-olds and teenagers. Also participatory work with youth theatres for 15–25 age range. Recent children's productions include *The Borrowers* by Charles Way with a cast of 6, and *Pinocchio*, adapted by Mike Kenny with a cast of 3. No unsolicited submissions. Founded 1987.

Touring companies

Actors Touring Company

Alford House, Aveline Street, London SE11 5DQ
tel 020-7735 8311 *fax* 020-7735 1031
email atc@atc-online.com
website www.atc-online.com
Executive Producer Emma Dunton

Small to medium-scale company producing innovative contemporary work for young audiences.

The Hiss & Boo Company Ltd

1 Nyes Hill, Wineham Lane, Bolney, West Sussex RH17 5SD
tel (01444) 881707 *fax* (01444) 882057
email ian@hissboo.co.uk

Not much scope for new plays, but will consider comedy thrillers/chillers and plays/musicals for children. No unsolicited scripts – telephone first. Plays/synopses will be returned only if accompanied by an sae.

Imaginate

45A George Street, Edinburgh EH2 2HT
tel 0131-225 8050 *fax* 0131-225 6440
email info@imaginate.org.uk
Director Tony Reekie, *General Manager* Tessa Rennie

Imaginate is an arts agency committed to promoting and developing performing arts for children in Scotland. See page 268 for further information.

The Little Angel Theatre

14 Dagmar Passage, London N1 2DN
tel 020-7226 1787 *fax* 020-7359 7565
email info@littleangeltheatre.com
website wwwlittleangeltheatre.com
Artistic Director Steve Tiplady

The theatre is committed to working with children and families, both through schools and the local community. It is developing innovative projects to improve access to their work, offer opportunities for participation, and stimulate learning and creativity for all using puppetry. Every term it runs activities for children, families and schools, including the Saturday Morning Puppet Club, family workshops and schools projects such as the highly successful Pupper Power.

The Little Angel shows last about an hour and they tour many of their shows to schools, theatres, arts centres and festivals. Its Education Programme works with schools, youth groups and Education Authorities; it is a strategic plank in the theatre's ongoing work with children and young people. In 2003 the Little Angel gave 579 performances to a total audience of over 63,000 children and adults.

M6 Theatre Company (Studio Theatre)

Hamer C.P. School, Albert Royds Street, Rochdale, Lancs. OL16 2SU
tel (01706) 355898 *fax* (01706) 711700
email info@m6theatre.co.uk
Contact Jane Milne

Theatre-in-education company providing high-quality theatre for children, young people and community audiences.

Oily Cart

Smallwood School Annexe, Smallwood Road, London SW17 OTW
tel 020-8672 6329 *fax* 020-8672 0792
email oilies@oilycart.org.uk
website www.oilycart.org.uk
Artistic Director Tim Webb

Touring company staging 2 children's productions a year. Multi-sensory, highly interactive work is produced, often in specially constructed installations for 2 specific audiences: children from 6 months to 6 years and young people with profound and multiple learning disabilities. Considers scripts from new writers but at present all work is generated from within the company. Founded 1981.

Proteus Theatre Company

Queen Mary's College, Cliddesden Road, Basingstoke, Hants RG21 3HF
tel (01256) 354541 *fax* (01256) 356186
email info@proteustheatre.com
website www.proteustheatre.com

Artistic Director Mark Helyar, *Associate Director* Deborah Wilding, *General Manager* Julie Bladon

Small-scale touring company particularly committed to new writing and new work, education and community collaborations. Produces 3 touring shows per year plus several community projects. Founded 1979.

Quicksilver National Touring Theatre

4 Enfield Road, London N1 5AZ
tel 020-7241 2942 *fax* 020-7254 3119
email talktous@quicksilvertheatre.org
website www.quicksilvertheatre.org
Joint Artistic Director/Ceo Guy Holland, *Joint Artistic Director* Carey English

A professional touring theatre company which brings live theatre to theatres and schools all over the country. Delivers good stories, original music, kaleidoscopic design and poignant, often humorous, new writing to entertain and make children and adults think. Two to three new plays a year for 3–5 year-olds, 7–11 year-olds and 6+ years and families. Founded 1977.

Red Ladder Theatre Company

3 St Peters Buildings, York Street, Leeds LS9 8AU
tel 0113-245 5311 *fax* 0113-245 5351
email wendy@redladder.co.uk
website www.redladder.co.uk
Artistic Director Wendy Harris

Theatre performances for young people (14–25) in youth clubs and small-scale theatre venues. Commissions at least 2 new plays each year. Runs the Asian Theatre School, an annual theatre training programme for young Asians in Yorkshire.

Snap People's Theatre Trust

29 Raynham Road, Bishop's Stortford, Herts. CM23 5PE
tel (01279) 461607 *fax* (01279) 506694
email info@snaptheatre.co.uk
Contact Gill Bloomfield

Produces 2 new plays for children and young adults each year. Recent children's productions include *Stepping on the Cracks* by Mike Kenny with a cast of 2, and *Starlight – The Dreamcatchers* by Diane Hancock with a cast of 3. Welcomes scripts from new writers. Allow a few months for response. Founded 1978.

Theatre Centre

Units 7 & 8, Toynbee Workshops, 3 Gunthorpe Street, London E1 7RQ
tel 020-7377 0379 *fax* 020-7377 1376
email admin@theatre-centre.co.uk
website www.theatre-centre.co.uk
Director Rosamunde Hutt

New writing company producing 3 plays a year and touring nationally and internationally. All productions are for children and/or young people, staged in schools, arts centres and other venues. Recently produced *A Spell of Cold Weather* by Charles Way with a cast of 4. Keen to hear from writers from ethnic minority groups. Response time to submissions can be lengthy. Founded 1953.

Theatre Workshop

34 Hamilton Place, Edinburgh EH3 5AX
tel 0131-225 7942 *fax* 0131-220 0112
Contact Robert Rae

Cutting edge, professional, inclusive theatre company. Plays include new writing/community/children's/disabled. Scripts from new writers considered.

Tiebreak Theatre Company

Heartsease High School, Marryat Road, Norwich NR7 9DF
tel (01603) 435 209 *fax* (01603) 435 184
email info@tiebreak-theatre.com
website www.tiebreak-theatre.com
Contact Kaja Holloway

Independent theare producer and touring company. Presents 2–3 productions per year of new work and/or adaptations, usually with music, for children up to age 8. Recently staged the *Nightingale* by David Farmer, adapted from the story by Hans Christian Andersen, with a cast of 2. Founded 1982.

Resources for children's writers

Learning to write for children

Many people have what they consider to be brilliant ideas for children's books but have no experience of writing. But lack of experience need not get in the way of bringing an idea to fruition as there is guidance available in the form of courses. Alison Sage demystifies what happens on a writing course for children and outlines the benefits to be gained.

Can you teach people to write for children?

There are quite a few who think you can't. There is an implicit idea that writing is a talent you are born with and that one day, sitting at the word processor in your kitchen (why is it always the kitchen?) your innate ability will suddenly surface like a lottery ticket, and you will write a bestseller that will pay your mortgage and take you on exotic holidays for life.

After many years working in publishing and talking to would-be writers, I have come to the conclusion that this is only a tiny fraction of the truth. Writing is like any other talent and it improves with being used. Dancers dance, musicians play and writers have to write and write and write to get better.

There is no doubt that some people have more aptitude for writing than others. But besides natural talent, a writer must have something to say.

Next, a writer needs to have the persistence and self belief to continue to write through all kinds of distractions and discouragement. And finally, if a writer wants to be published successfully, he or she needs a certain amount of luck.

The role of writing classes

First and most importantly, writing classes can give the writer a chance to explore different kinds of writing in a non-judgemental atmosphere. It is the job of the teacher to help students to experiment until they find what suits them.

Students can also meet other people in the same situation. Writing can be a very lonely pursuit. A writer's friends are usually embarrassed to give their honest opinion about a story because it is a recipe for falling out. Every writer knows the despair of writing something which at first sounds wonderful and then on re-reading sounds rubbish. Where can writers find an independent judgement? Whoever they ask must be someone they can trust to be impartial, someone who can suggest where their good ideas become woolly and perhaps even how they might go about improving things. However, these must always be *suggestions*. It is the writer who must decide how, where, and in what way to alter the manuscript.

In an ideal world, the publisher's editor would help new writers endlessly until they achieved a bestselling novel. The reality is that publishers' editors are too busy to nurture every single would-be talent. Therefore, it is up to the writer either to go it alone – which many do – or to find someone else to act as a sounding board. This is where writing classes can help.

Who benefits most from writing classes?

It is impossible to guess at the beginning of a course how far students will develop their talent or even who will actually get published. Obviously, different teachers suit different people, but I have found an astonishing range amongst my students. That is what makes it so exciting and rewarding – and so unpredictable. The only student who is unlikely to be happy is the one who says: 'Teach me to write a bestseller.' This is frankly impossible and anyone who believes that writing is an exact science is bound to be disappointed.

Interestingly enough, the one thing that can indicate how far a student will get – apart from their persistence, of course – is how flexible they are. Often, people who are highly educated are actually at a disadvantage. They believe they have been taught how to write correctly – and that there is a 'right' and a 'wrong' way to do it. Nothing could be further from the truth, particularly when writing for children. Therefore, I have seen an Oxford graduate watch enviously as another student, still at school, sends the whole class into fits of laughter with a perfect story. I have had students who were models, refugees, counsellors, puppeteers, housewives, diplomats, postmen, soldiers, office managers, nurses, with children, without children or simply out of work. One of my best students left school aged 15. He is now editing a magazine and I still wonder if he will ever write his children's novel… Another is now a published author/illustrator, through his own talent and a great deal of effort. Yet another is looking after her children – and one day perhaps the quiet brilliance of her writing will find a publisher.

A typical course outline

Every course is different because every student is asked what they hope to achieve and this obviously affects what we do. However, certain things are always included in some form.

It may sound self evident, but central to a writing course is getting students to write. Students develop through putting new ideas into practice. Therefore, every class includes about 15 minutes' writing time and students read out and talk about what they have written. Most students are nervous at first, because they feel they are unprepared. But this rarely lasts because writing on the spot seems to bring the group closer together. It also relaxes everyone, as no one can be expected to write a bestseller in 15 minutes and at this point, students invariably have brilliant ideas and express them unbelievably well. If anyone gets stuck, they simply explain that the topic hasn't worked for them. Different students shine at different topics and this helps to steer them towards what they ultimately want to write.

Finding a story

The first place to look for a story is in your own experience. All students are asked to write something about their first memories of their baby brothers or sisters because when students genuinely remember their own childhood, their language becomes simpler, their writing more powerful and direct. They write in a way they never would if they were consciously trying to 'write for children'. This is a very important step in trying to discover what is your own voice. Writers need to know not only what they want to say, but also how they are going to put it over.

The class then usually discusses what kinds of story are appropriate for different ages. Perhaps one of the most common mistakes made by new children's writers is that they write about very young topics in a very sophisticated fashion. If you are aiming to write a picture book for a three year-old, you need to understand a little of what a three year-old can cope with. It is no use writing a story that is 10,000 words long.

However, a nine year-old is not going to be interested in stories designed for a three year-old – even if technically they are suitable. In fact, a good rule of thumb is that children are interested in most of the things that adults are – except they are not used to dealing with concepts. A child may love a book about a character who is alone, or brave, or funny. They will not be so interested in loneliness, heroism or humour in the *abstract*. Children are also not very comfortable with irony until they are about nine or 10 years old, tending to take the printed word at its face value. However, when they *do* discover it, they love it.

The beginning

The next thing to stress is the importance of the beginning. Many students think that page one is where a writer finds his feet and that the story proper starts about page six. This is not true. The first paragraph of a book is crucial. Children invest a lot of energy in reading a book and they want to be convinced pretty quickly that this effort is going to be worthwhile. A dull first page means that the book will be put down, never to be opened again. Even more to the point, perhaps, a busy editor reading an unsolicited manuscript will also lose interest if the beginning of the story is dull or confusing and they will make this the excuse they need to return it immediately. The beginning must draw the reader in. If a story is the solving of a problem, then the beginning must make that problem sound exciting and tantalising.

At this point, it is usually a good idea for the class to discuss strategies for keeping going with a story. Finishing a story gives a student a great boost and in itself, is a huge learning curve. Different strategies are helpful for different people. Some students need a writing routine – a special chair or table or cup of coffee. For others this is either no use or impossible to maintain. Some find writing notes at the end of each writing session is helpful, so that they can more easily get into the flow of ideas where they broke off. And most people find a notebook helpful, where they can record interesting ideas and experiences to be used as the raw material for future stories. If you are able to go into a school and help with reading, this can be a great eye opener as you will see first hand which stories children struggle over and which really work.

A vital ingredient

Another vital topic usually covered at this stage of the course is tension. Tension is what makes you want to continue reading and without tension, a story is as dull as a meal without salt. Just as a joke falls flat if the timing is wrong, so a fascinating story can become boringly muddled if the author does not build to a climax. It is about choosing selective details and using the reader's own imagination to create suspense. A description of the monster's claw grasping from behind the door is far more terrifying than a complete run-down of the whole creature.

If you think of your own favourite childhood story, it is often not the end that sticks in your mind. It is the bit just before the climax. That is when the tension and suspense should be strongest. At the end of the story, you can ask a question or add a twist, to give the impression that your characters will continue even after the book has been shut.

Talk about getting published

Finally, most students are interested in the mechanics of getting published, and this is a minefield for would-be authors. It is difficult to get your work singled out from a pile of unsolicited manuscripts and while (eventually) good writers are usually discovered, it can be a long and tortuous process.

There are things you can do to improve your chances and while they are mostly common sense, this is probably an area where a good writing class can help. Look in your local bookshop for the publishers which produce the kind of books you admire. There is an outside chance that if you like them, they might like you. Far too many good manuscripts are sent to the wrong places and if a publisher produces medical books, he or she is not likely to be interested in a children's manuscript, even if it is *Harry Potter*.

Sharing an interest

Perhaps the most important thing is to enjoy writing and to meet other people who are also interested. That way, students can keep each other going through the rejections and at the very least, improve at something they want to do. There are a great many courses which cater for all different kinds of interests, attitudes and expectations. The best place to look is probably at the local adult education institute. If there is no course specifically listed for writing for children, it is worth ringing up and asking if they would like to start one. You could also put up a notice in your local library for anyone else who might be interested and as soon as you are a group, the authority will take notice of you. You could even start your own independent writing group!

There are also several residential courses (such as the Arvon Foundation courses), and they are a very enjoyable and relaxing way to take your ambitions further. Look on the internet, as these courses constantly change and new ones are added every year. Several universities and colleges also run long and short courses in children's writing and you can achieve a diploma in Writing for Children, although this would take you at least a year.

So can writing be taught?

The debate will certainly continue, as people point out that teachers on courses rarely become as famous as some of their students. However, there *are* things which are helpful to discover when you are starting out as a children's writer. And perhaps the encouragement of the group will make sure that you continue writing until instead of your returned manuscript, it is the publisher's contract that drops through your letterbox!

Alison Sage is an experienced commissioning editor of children's books and has worked for a variety of publishers including Oxford University Press, HarperCollins and Random House. Alison is also a writer and anthologist and her *Treasury of Children's Literature* won the NIBBY – the Children's Book of the Year Award in 1995. She has run many courses on creative writing for children for Kensington & Chelsea and Hammersmith adult education institutes.

See also...

- *Children's writing courses and conferences*, page 248
- *Online resources about children's books*, page 250

Children's writing courses and conferences

Anyone wishing to participate in a writing course should first satisfy themselves as to its content and quality. For day and evening courses consult your local Adult Education Centre.

Annual Writers' Conference

Chinook, Southdown Road, Shawford, Winchester, Hants SO21 2BY
tel (01962) 712307
email Writerconf@aol.com
website www.gmp.co.uk/writers/conference
Conference Director Barbara Large MBS, FRSA
Takes place King Alfred's College, Winchester, 24–26 June 2005

Mini courses and workshops, lectures, seminars, one-to-one appointments with agents and commissioning editors, bookfair, 15 writing competitions; followed by one-week workshops June–4 July. Pitstop Refuelling Writers' Weekend Workshops planned for 18–20 March 2005 and 21–23 October 2005, and How to Self Publish Your Book day courses in May and October 2005.

The Arvon Foundation

Lumb Bank, Heptonstall, Hebden Bridge, West Yorkshire HX7 6DF
tel (01422) 843714 *fax* (01422) 843714
email l-bank@arvonfoundation.org
website www.arvonfoundation.org
Contact Ann Anderton
Moniack Mhor, Teavarran, Kiltarlity, Beauly, Inverness-shire IV4 7HT
tel (01463) 741675 *fax* (01463) 741733
email m-mhor@arvonfoundation.org
Contact Chris Aldridge
The Arvon Foundation, Totleigh Barton, Sheepwash, Beaworthy, Devon EX21 5NS
tel (01409) 231338 *fax* (01409) 231144
email t-barton@arvonfoundation.org
Contact Julia Wheadon
The Hurst – The John Osborne Arvon Centre Clunton, Craven Arms, Shropshire SY7 0JA
tel (01588) 640658 *fax* (01588) 640509
email hurst@arvonfoundation.org

Children's Literature International Summer School

University of Surrey Roehampton, Digby Stuart College, London SW15 5PH
tel 020-8392 3008 *fax* 020-8392 3819
email ncrcl@roehampton.ac.uk
website www.ncrcl.ac.uk/cliss
Takes place July

Leading academics and authors from the world of children's literature gather for this biennial 5-day event organised by the National Centre for Research in Children's Literature (NCRCL). The purpose of the summer school is to provide a forum in which participants and researchers in the field can exchange ideas and broaden their knowledge of the subject. There is also an optional Creative Writing module. There are places for 100 participants and en-suite accommodation is available on campus.

Essex Literature Development

Cultural Services, Essex County Council, PO Box 47, Chelmsford CM2 6WN
tel (01245) 436156 *fax* (01245) 436841
email kaveri.woodward@essexcc.gov.uk
website www.essexlivelit.org.uk
Contact Kaveri Woodward

One-day seminars covering fiction genres, writing for children, biography, non-fiction, poetry, scriptwriting and editing. Writers will include Michael Holroyd, Martina Cole, Peter Forbes, Brian Keaney and Julia Bell.

The Federation of Children's Book Groups Conference

Details Pat Tate, 51 Highwood Avenue, Solihull, West Midlands B92 8QY
email p.tate@virgin.net
website www.fcbg.org.uk
Takes place 3 days in April

Held annually, guest speakers include well-known children's authors as well as experts and publishers in the field of children's books. Publishers also exhibit their newest books and resources.

IBBY Congress

Nonnenweg 12, Postfach, CH-4003-Basel, Switzerland
tel (4161) 272 2917 *fax* (+4161) 272 2757
email ibby@eye.ch
website www.ibby.org
British Section c/o National Centre for Research in Children's Literature
tel 020-8392 3008
email ibby@roehampton.ac.uk
A biennial international congress for IBBY (International Board on Books for Young People)

members and other people involved in children's books and reading development. Every other year a different National Section of IBBY hosts the congress and several hundred people from all over the world attend the professional programme.

Forthcoming congresses: 5–9 September 2004 (29th Congress) to be held in Cape Town, South Africa, on the theme of Books for Africa; 20–24 September 2006 (30th Congress) to be held in Beijing, China, on the theme of Children's Literature and its Development. See also page 269.

NCLL Annual Conference

University of Reading, Bulmershe Court,
Reading RG6 1HY
tel 0118-931 8820
email ncll@reading.ac.uk
website www.ncll.org.uk
Takes place October

Annual one-day conference held at the National Centre for Language and Literacy, Bulmershe Court, Reading. Includes guest speakers, lectures and workshops; also courses on writing fiction and non-fiction, and dramatising stories for young children.

NCRCL British IBBY Conference

University of Surrey Roehampton,
Digby Stuart College, London SW15 5PH
tel 020-8392 3008 *fax* 020-8392 3819
email ncrcl@roehampton.ac.uk
website www.ncrcl.ac.uk

Conference held annually in November on a specific theme.

Oxford University Day and Weekend Schools

Department for Continuing Education,
Oxford University, Rewley House,
1 Wellington Square, Oxford OX1 2JA
tel (01865) 270368
email ppdayweek@conted.ox.ac.uk
Contact Administrative Assistant

Effective Writing: a series of one-day accredited courses for biography and travel.

Ty Newydd

Ty Newydd, National Creative Writing Centre of Wales, Llanystumdwy, Cricieth, Gwynedd LL52 0LW
tel (01766) 522811 *fax* (01766) 523095
email post@tynewydd.org
website www.tynewydd.org

YLG Conference

Bedington Central Library, Civic Way, Bebington,
Wirral CH63 7PN
tel 0151-643 7232 *fax* 0151-643 7231
email bebington.childrens@merseymail.com
website www.cilip.org.uk/groups/ylg
Secretary Sue Roe
Takes place September

This annual conference run by the Youth Libraries Group (YLG) of CILIP is a forum for discussion and debate on current issues for everyone working with and for children in libraries. It also provides an opportunity for experts, authors, illustrators, publishers and all those involved in the children's book trade to meet informally.

Postgraduate course

King Alfred's College

School of Cultural Studies, King Alfred's College,
Winchester SO22 4NR
tel (01962) 827235 *fax* (01962) 827406
website www.kingalfreds.ac.uk
Contact The Admissions Office

MA in English: Writing for Children.

Online resources about children's books

This is a representation of some of the many websites relating to children's books and reading. Individual author websites can be accessed via the ACHUKA or Booktrusted websites.

About Children's Books

www.childrensbooks.about.com

Part of About.com, this site holds international information on children's books plus a newsletter.

ACHUKA Children's Books UK

www.achuka.co.uk

The most up-to-date and comprehensive online guide to children's books and what's new in children's publishing. With author interviews, children's book news across the globe plus links to many other sites.

Armadillo

email armadillo@siliconhenge.com
website www.armadillomagazine.com
Editor Mary Hoffman, *Website Editor* Rhiannon Lassiter
£5 for 4 issues

Magazine about children's books, including reviews, interviews, features and profiles. After 5 years of publication as a paper magazine posted to subscribers, *Armadillo* is now available only online. New issues will be posted at the end of March, June, September and December. Some material will be accessible as a free sample but full access to the magazine is by subscription. New reviewers and writers are always welcome but the magazine does not pay a fee; reviewers keep the books. Publishers please note: books are *not* to be sent to the editor; she instructs reviewers to obtain specific titles direct from publishers. Founded in 1999 by author Mary Hoffman as a review publication for children's books.

Amazon

www.amazon.co.uk, www.amazon.com

UK and US online bookstore with more than 3 million books available on their websites at discounted prices, plus a personal notification service of new releases, reader reviews, bestsellers and book information.

BBC Education

www.bbc.co.uk/schools

Information about UK schools' curriculum. Essential for those wishing to write for educational publishers but also for keeping abreast of curricular topics.

BBC Teens

www.bbc.co.uk/teens

The Best Kids Book Site

www.thebestkidsbooksite.com

US site 'where children's books, crafts and collectibles intersect with your interests.' Useful links to Children's Book Awards, children's series fiction and author websites. Also gives access to the Book Wizard, an information tool to help track down children's books.

Quentin Blake

www.quentinblake.com

The official Quentin Blake website. Find out about the illustrator who brought many favourite children's characters to life, from Mister Magnolia and Mrs Armitage to the BFG and Matilda. There's also news and information on new books and exhibitions, downloads for children and suggestions for teachers on using books in the classroom. A great site for children, parents, teachers and aspiring children's books' illustrators.

Book Reviews by Kids

www.bookreviewsbykids.com

Website dedicated to children's book reviews written only by children. A great website for children to get their say on the books that they read.

Booktrusted

www.booktrusted.co.uk

Dedicated children's division of Booktrust and an essential site for professionals working with young readers. Information on events, prizes, books, authors, etc.

Bookheads

www.bookheads.org.uk

The website of the Booktrust Teenage Prize aims to encourage teenagers to express their views on their favourite books. It features celebrity interviews and details of past, present and future Booktrust Teenage Prize shortlists and winners. A good way of finding out what teenagers really like to read!

Books4Publishing

www.books4publishing.co.uk

Shropshire-based e-agent which showcases authors' synopsis and first chapter and then auto-targets publishers and agents for a £49.95 fee.

Canadian Children's Book Centre

www.bookcentre.ca

The site of the Canadian Children's Book Centre includes profiles of authors, illustrators, information on recent books, a calendar of upcoming Canadian events, information on publications and tips from Canadian children's authors.

Children's BBC

www.bbc.co.uk/cbbc

'Kid culture' website. Has a section on books, including a behind-the-scenes visit to, and information on, the Blue Peter Book Awards.

The Children's Book Council

www.cbcbooks.org

The Children's Book Council in the USA is an organisation dedicated to encouraging literacy and the enjoyment of children's books. The website includes reviews of children's books published in the USA, forthcoming publications, author profiles and features 'sneek peeks at publishers' newest and hottest titles.' A good site for checking out the US marketplace.

Children's Literature

www.childrenslit.com

The aim of this US site is to help teachers, librarians, childcare providers and parents make appropriate literary choices for children. Each month there are featured interviews with children's authors and illustrators and several sets of themed reviews. (These are licensed to Barnes & Noble and Borders for use on their websites.)

Contemporary Writers

www.contemporarywriters.com

Searchable database containing up-to-date profiles of some of the UK and Commonwealth's most important living writers – biographies, bibliographies, critical reviews, prizes and photographs.

Cool Reads

www.cool-reads.co.uk

Find out what children think are cool reads! A website set up by teenagers with reviews, genres, ideas and much more.

Roald Dahl Club

www.roalddahlclub.com

Everything you ever wanted to know about Dahl's books with a section for teachers, children's activities plus the online Roald Dahl Club magazine *The Gobblefunk Gazette.*

enCompass

www.enCompassCulture.com

The British Council's online worldwide reading group is divided into 3 sections: books for children (ages 3–12), books for ages 12–18 and books for adults. It aims to provide up-to-date information about the contemporary UK and Commonwealth literature that is being talked about. There is the opportunity to read or write book reviews, follow related web links, read about books and to chat with the online reader-in-residence. Books can be selected from the best of contemporary UK and Commonwealth literature.

The Guardian

www.educationguardian.co.uk

The Guardian's education pages online.

Kids' Bookline

www.cllc.org.uk/PAL2002/Kids_Bookline/HTML_ENG/FramesKB.html

Part of the Welsh Books Council's Children's Books Department. Activities for children, in both Welsh and English.

Kids' Open Book

www.kidsopenbook.co.uk

Independent site of online reviews of children's books and multimedia, set up by an experienced UK bookseller. Selective titles and personal choices.

Kids' Reads and Teen reads

www.kidsreads.com, www.teenreads.com

Two excellent US websites with information, reviews, author links and features on children's and teenage books. Part of The Book Report Network.

Mrs Mad's Book-a-Rama

www.mrsmad.com

Children's book reviews from an independent reviewer – great fun and informative.

Graham Marks

www.marksworks.co.uk

Children's feature writer for *Publishing News* now has his own website with author features and general children's books trade news.

National Curriculum Online

www.nc.uk.net

This site links every National Curriculum programme of study requirement to resources on the Curriculum Online.

National Grid for Learning

www.ngfl.gov.uk

The government's gateway to educational resources on the internet. Provides a network of selected links to websites that offer high-quality content and information.

National Grid for Learning: Scotland

www.ngflscotland.gov.uk

National Literacy Trust

www.literacytrust.org.uk

Details of all the NLT's initiatives plus lots of news and information about children's books.

National Reading Campaign

www.readon.org.uk

Information and networking for reading practitioners about promoting reading for all ages and abilities throughout the community. Government funded and part of the National Literacy Trust.

Reading is Fundamental, UK

www.rif.org.uk

An initiative of the National Literacy Trust that helps children and young people (aged 0–19) to realise their potential by motivating them to read.

School Zone

www.schoolzone.co.uk

Well-used education website, receiving up to a million hits each month. According to *The Times* it is 'an excellent and professional website offering educational and emotional support to teachers, parents, pupils and schools'.

Scottish Writers Website

www.slainte.org.uk

Linked to the Scottish Writers project that provides a forum for young readers and Scottish professionals to exchange literary ideas. Includes online writers-in-residence.

Stories from the Web

www.storiesfromtheweb.org

A development between Leeds, Bristol and Birmingham Library Services and the UK office for Library and Information Networking to provide information on library clubs, stories, and a chance to e-mail authors.

Storybook Web

www.itsscotland.org.uk/storybook

Access to Scottish Children's authors and book-related activities for children.

Storyzone

www.storyzone.uk

An e-publishing site that makes contemporary children's stories available to the internet generation. Brand new stories as well as old favourites from well-known authors are available. Useful for those nowhere near a bookshop or library. It costs £5 to download up to 5 stories; £10 for 12; £20 for 25 stories and £40 for 50.

UK Children's Books

www.ukchildrensbooks.co.uk

Directory of authors, illustrators and publishers involved in children's books and reading promotion.

The Word Pool

www.wordpool.co.uk

Independent website which profiles authors of children's books and gives information and advice for aspiring writers. Access to the free monthly newsletter.

Young Writer Magazine

www.mystworld.com/youngwriter

Online version of this magazine subtitled 'The Magazine for Children with Something to Say'. Presents young people's writing and their favourite authors.

YouthBOOX

www.boox.org.uk

A joint venture between The Reading Agency and National Youth Agency to promote reading for pleasure for teenagers through building on their own interests.

Write4Kids

www.Write4Kids.com

US site with articles and information about the art of writing children's books. Also *Children's Book Insider* newsletter.

Books about children's books

There are many books written about children's books. Some offer practical advice on selecting books. Others provide invaluable research material for those pursuing degrees and diplomas in children's literature. Here is a small selection.

Best Book Guide For Children and Young Adults

Published by Booktrust
Paperback pub. annually

Booktrust's independent annual 'pick of the best' in children's paperback fiction published in the previous calendar year. It is designed to help parents, teachers, librarians, booksellers and anyone interested in children's reading to select books for children, from babies to teenagers. Printed in full colour, each book featured has a short review, colour coding to indicate reading age and interest level, and bibliographic information.

The Book about Books

by Chris Powling
Published by A & C Black Publishers Ltd
ISBN 0 7136 5479 1
Paperback 2001

Using interviews with authors and illustrators, this book asks: what makes a classic? How do you get a book published? How do writers come up with their ideas? A light-hearted and informative book for children, perfect as a resource for Children's Book Week.

The Cambridge Guide to Children's Books in English

Edited by Victor Watson
Published by Cambridge University Press
ISBN 0 5215 5064 5
Hardback 2001

Reference work providing a critical and appreciative overview of children's books written in English across the world. It includes the history of children's books from pre-Norman times to the present, taking on board current developments in publishing practices and in children's own reading. Entries on TV, comics, annuals and the growing range of media texts are included.

The Oxford Companion to Children's Literature

Edited by Humphrey Carpenter and Mari Prichard
Published by Oxford University Press
ISBN 0 1986 0228 6
Paperback 1999

An indispensable reference book for anyone interested in children's books. Over 900 biographical entries deal with authors, illustrators, printers, publishers, educationalists and others who have influenced the development of children's literature. Genres covered include myths and legends, fairy tales, adventure stories, school stories, fantasy, science fiction, crime and romance. This book is of particular interest to librarians, teachers, students, parents and collectors.

The Reading Bug – and how you can help your child to catch it

by Paul Jennings
Published by Penguin Books
ISBN 0 14 131840 6
Paperback 2004

Paul Jennings is a well-known children's author. This book explains, in his unique humorous style, how readers can open up the world through a love of books. He cuts through the jargon and the controversies to reveal the simple truths, which should enable adults to infect children with the reading bug.

The Rough Guide to Books for Teenagers

Edited by Nicholas Tucker and Julia Eccleshare
Published by Rough Guides
ISBN 1 84353 138 0
Paperback 2003

A resource for teenagers who love reading, this *Guide* is also ideal for adults looking to recommend and buy books for teenagers. More than 200 books are reviewed – mainly fiction – ranging from classics such as *Wuthering Heights* to more controversial and bestselling titles such as Melvin Burgess's *Junk* and Judy Blume's *Forever*. Graphic novels and some narrative non-fiction are also included.

The Rough Guide to Children's Books 0–5

Edited by Nicholas Tucker
Published by Rough Guides
ISBN 1 85828 787 1
Paperback 2002

Comprises reviews of books for this youngest of age groups, including picture books for babies through alphabets and nursery rhymes to classic stories. Each book has a brief synopsis and an evaluation of its special qualities and educational advantages.

The Rough Guide to Children's Books 5–11

Edited by Nicholas Tucker
Published by Rough Guides
ISBN 1 85828 788 X
Paperback 2002

With over 200 entries, this book contains reviews of recommended titles from poetry, non-fiction and classic tales, to fiction dealing with contemporary issues. Each book is roughly subdivided by the different ages within each age band, and by subject matter and genre.

Sticks and Stones: The Troublesome Success of Children's Literature from Slovenly Peter to Harry Potter

by Jack Zipes
Published by Routledge
ISBN 0415938805
Paperback 2002

Jack Zipes – translator of the Grimm tales, teacher, storyteller, and scholar – questions whether children ever really had a literature of their own. He sees children's literature in many ways as being the 'grown-ups' version' – a story about childhood that adults tell kids. He discusses children's literature from the 19th century moralism of Slovenly Peter (whose fingers get cut off) to the wildly successful *Harry Potter* books. Children's literature is a booming market but its success, this author says, is disguising its limitations. *Sticks and Stones* is a forthright and engaging book by someone who clearly cares deeply about what and how children read.

The Ultimate Book Guide

by Anne Fine
Edited by Daniel Hahn
Published by A & C Black Publishers Ltd
ISBN 0 7136 6718 4
Paperback 2004

Over 600 entries covering the best books for children aged 8–12, from classics to contemporary titles published up to the end of 2003. Funny, friendly and frank recommendations written for children by their favourite and best-known authors including Anthony Horowitz, Jacqueline Wilson, Celia Rees, Darren Shan, David Almond and Dick King-Smith. Plus features on the most all the popular genres.

Societies, prizes and festivals

The Society of Authors

The Society of Authors is an independent trade union, representing writers' interests in all aspects of the writing profession, particularly publishing, but also broadcasting, television and films, theatre and translation.

Founded over 100 years ago, the Society now has more than 7500 members. It has a professional staff, responsible to a Management Committee of 12 authors, and a Council (an advisory body meeting twice a year) consisting of 60 eminent writers.

Specialist groups

There are specialist groups within the Society to serve particular needs: the Academic Writers Group, the Broadcasting Group, the Children's Writers and Illustrators Group (see below), the Educational Writers Group, the Medical Writers Group and the Translators Association. There are also groups representing Scotland and the North of England.

The Children's Writers and Illustrators Group

The Children's Writers and Illustrators Group (CWIG) was formed in 1963. Besides furthering the interests of writer and artist and defending them whenever they are threatened, the Group seeks to bring members together professionally and socially, and in general to raise the status of children's books.

The Group has its own Executive Committee with representation on the Management Committee of the Society of Authors. Meetings and socials are held on a regular basis. Speakers have so far included publishers, librarians, booksellers and reviewers, and many distinguished writers and illustrators for children.

The annual subscription to the Society of Authors includes membership of all its groups. Membership of the CWIG is open to writers and illustrators who have had at least one book published by a reputable British publisher, five short stories or more than 20 minutes of material broadcast on national radio or television. Election is at the discretion of the Committee. For further details contact the Secretary, Jo Hodder at jhodder@societyofauthors.org

What the Society does for members

Through its permanent staff (including a solicitor), the Society is able to give its members a comprehensive personal and professional service covering the business aspects of authorship, including:

- providing information about agents, publishers, and others concerned with the book trade, journalism, broadcasting and the performing arts;
- advising on negotiations, including the individual vetting of contracts, clause by clause, and assessing their terms both financial and otherwise;

- helping with members' queries, major or minor, over any aspect of the business of writing;
- taking up complaints on behalf of members on any issue concerned with the business of authorship;
- pursuing legal actions for breach of contract, copyright infringement, and the non-payment of royalties and fees, when the risk and cost preclude individual action by a member and issues of general concern to the profession are at stake;
- holding conferences, seminars, meetings and social occasions;
- producing a comprehensive range of publications, free of charge to members, including the Society's quarterly journal, *The Author*. *Quick Guides* cover many aspects of the profession such as: copyright, publishing contracts, libel, income tax, VAT, authors' agents, permissions, indexing, and the protection of titles. The Society also publishes occasional papers on subjects such as film agreements, packaged books, revised editions, multimedia, and vanity publishing.

Further membership benefits

Members have access to:

- the Retirement Benefit Scheme;
- a group Medical Insurance Scheme with BUPA;
- the Pension Fund (which offers discretionary pensions to a number of members);
- the Contingency Fund (which provides financial relief for authors or their dependents in sudden financial difficulties);
- free membership of the Authors' Licensing and Collecting Society (ALCS);
- books and other products at special rates;
- membership of the Royal Over-Seas League at a discount.

The Society frequently secures improved conditions and better returns for members. It is common for members to report that, through the help and facilities offered, they have saved more, and sometimes substantially more, than their annual subscriptions (which are an allowable expense against income tax).

What the Society does for authors

The Society lobbies Members of Parliament, Ministers and Government Departments on all issues of concern to writers. Recent issues have included the operation and funding of Public Lending Right, the threat of VAT on books, copyright legislation and European Union initiatives. Concessions have also been obtained under various Finance Acts.

The Society litigates in matters of importance to authors. For example, the Society backed Andrew Boyle when he won his appeal against the Inland Revenue's attempt to tax the Whitbread Award.

The Society campaigns for better terms for writers. With the Writers' Guild, it has negotiated 'minimum terms agreements' with many leading publishers. The translators' section of the Society has also drawn up a minimum terms agreement for translators which has been adopted by Faber & Faber, and has been used on an individual basis by a number of other publishers.

The Society is recognised by the BBC for the purpose of negotiating rates for writers' contributions to radio drama, as well as for the broadcasting of published material. It was instrumental in setting up the ALCS (see page 194), which collects and distributes fees from reprography and other methods whereby copyright material is exploited without direct payment to the originators.

The Society keeps in close touch with the Arts Councils, the Association of Authors' Agents, the British Council, the Institute of Translation and Interpreting, the Department for Culture, Media and Sport, the National Union of Journalists, the Publishers Association and the Writers' Guild of Great Britain.

The Society is a member of the European Writers Congress, the British Copyright Council and the National Book Committee.

Membership

The Society of Authors

84 Drayton Gardens, London SW10 9SB
tel 020-7373 6642
email info@societyofauthors.org
website www.societyofauthors.org
General Secretary Mark Le Fanu

Membership is open to authors who have had a full-length work published, broadcast or performed commercially in the UK and to those who have had a full-length work accepted for publication, but not yet published; and those who have had occasional items broadcast or performed, or translations, articles, illustrations or short stories published. The owner or administrator of a deceased author's copyrights can become a member on behalf of the author's estate. Writers who have been offered a contract seeking a contribution towards publication costs may apply for one year's associate membership and have the contract vetted.

The annual subscription (which is tax deductible) is £80 (£75 by direct debit after the first year). There is a special rate for partners living at the same address. Authors under 35 not yet earning a significant income from writing, may pay a lower subscription of £56. Authors over 65 may pay at the reduced rate after their first year of membership.

Contact the Society for a membership booklet and copy of *The Author*.

Awards

The Society of Authors administers:

- Travelling Scholarships which give honorary awards;
- four prizes for novels: the Betty Trask Awards, the Encore Award, the McKitterick Prize and the Sagittarius Prize;
- two prizes for a full-length published work: the Somerset Maugham Awards and *The Sunday Times* Young Writer of the Year Award;
- two poetry awards: the Eric Gregory Awards and the Cholmondeley Awards;
- the Tom-Gallon and Olive Cook Awards for short story writers;
- the Authors' Foundation and Kathleen Blundell Trust, which give grants to published authors working on their next book;
- the Richard Imison Award for a writer new to radio drama;
- awards for translations from French, German, Italian, Dutch, Portuguese, Spanish and Swedish into English;
- the Francis Head Bequest for assisting authors who, through physical mishap, are temporarily unable to maintain themselves or their families;
- medical book awards.

Booktrust

Booktrust is the largest literature organisation in the United Kingdom. It is supported by Arts Council England and has a broad range of activities aimed at promoting books and reading.

Booktrust is an independent charity bringing books and people together. It exists to open up the world of books and reading to people of all ages and cultures. Its services and activities include the Book Information Service, a unique specialist information service for all queries on books and reading (business callers are charged at £1.50 per minute on 0906-516 1193, weekdays 10am–1pm). Booktrust administers a number of literary prizes, including the Orange and Commonwealth prizes for adults and the Booktrust Teenage and Nestlé Smarties prizes for children (see *Children's book and illustration prizes and awards*, page 278), as well as promoting books for all ages through numerous campaigns such as Get London Reading.

Further information

Contact Booktrust, Book House, 45 East Hill, London SW18 2QZ
tel 020-8516 2977 *fax* 020-8516 2978
email childrens@booktrust.org.uk
websites www.booktrusted.com, www.booktrust.org.uk, www.bookheads.org.uk

Contact Booktrust for subscription details.

Booktrust and children

The Children's Literature Team at Booktrust offers advice and information on all aspects of children's reading and books.

- The 'booktrusted' website gives invaluable information on children's books and resources, including annotated booklists; information about organisations concerned with children's books; publishers; children's book news; and events listings for readings, festivals and other children's book events throughout the UK.
- Booktrust also coordinates the national Bookstart (books-for-babies) programme which gives free advice and books to parents/carers attending their baby's health checks (see *Books for babies*, page 75).
- Booktrust produces *Booktrusted News*, a quarterly magazine featuring news and views on various aspects of the children's book world. Each issue concentrates on a particular theme and contains a related pull-out booklist. Also included are author and illustrator profiles, information about book prizes, reviews of new titles from baby books to teenage reads, and a variety of articles about children's books and reading.
- Booktrust publishes the annual *Best Book Guide for Children and Young Adults*, which details the best in children's paperback fiction published in the previous calendar year.
- Booktrust now runs the Booktrust Early Years Awards (formerly the Sainsbury's Baby Book Award) which aims to celebrate, publicise and reward the exciting range of books being published today for babies, toddlers and preschool children. With Bookstart, Booktrust hopes to promote and make these books accessible to as wide an audience as possible.

The Children's Book Circle

Rachel Wade and Miranda Baker of the Children's Book Circle introduce the organisation.

Are you passionate about children's books? The Children's Book Circle (CBC) provides an exciting forum in which you can develop your interest, build your contacts and enrich your engagement with the children's book world. The CBC's membership consists of publishers, librarians, authors, illustrators, agents, teachers, booksellers and anyone with an active interest in the field.

Further information

Contact Nicola Wilkinson, Children's Book Circle, Egmont Books Ltd, 239 Kensington High Street, London W8 6SA
tel 020-7761 3699
email nicola.wilkinson@euk.egmont.com

Membership of the Children's Book Circle costs £15 per year for those within the M25 and £12 for those outside the M25. If you would like to join, or require additional information, then please contact Nicola Wilkinson.

If you're an aspiring author or illustrator, you'll already know how important it is to become as knowledgeable as possible about the current marketplace for children's books. The CBC is the ideal place to broaden your knowledge. It's not the place to try for a publishing contract, but it will give you the opportunity to take part in discussions with people from the industry in an informal and enjoyable context.

The CBC meets regularly at a variety of venues in London. At our speaker meetings, invited guest speakers debate key issues relating to children's books. The wide membership base ensures that these meetings are exciting occasions. Recent events have included a discussion between the bestselling author Paul Stewart and illustrator Chris Riddell about their working relationship and a debate about the relevance of fairy tales, with contributions from Viv French, Elizabeth Laird and Nicholas Tucker.

Members also have the opportunity to attend the annual Eleanor Farjeon Award reception and the Patrick Hardy Lecture. The Eleanor Farjeon Award is awarded for an outstanding contribution to the world of children's books, either by an individual or an organisation. Recent winners include Philip Pullman and editor Miriam Hodgson. The Patrick Hardy Lecture is delivered each year by a distinguished speaker on a relevant topic of their choice. Past speakers have included Anne Fine, David Almond and Jacqueline Wilson.

Other highlights of the CBC calendar include a summer and Christmas party. The summer party offers members a chance to show off their children's book knowledge in a challenging quiz. The Christmas party is a chance for members to get together for an end-of-year celebration based upon a theme – last year's party was a celebration of children's illustration.

The Children's Book Circle is a non-profit making organisation and is run entirely by volunteers.

Federation of Children's Book Groups

The aim of the Federation of Children's Book Groups is to bring children and books together and have fun. David Blanch introduces the organisation.

The Federation of Children's Book Groups (now a registered charity) was formed in 1968 by Anne Wood to coordinate the work of the many different children's book groups that were coming together across the country. Over the next eight years the organisation expanded and a system of regionalisation was introduced to link groups together in each part of the country.

In 1976 National Tell-A-Story-Week was introduced and became an immediate success. This has now grown into National Share-A-Story-Month and takes place in May. It enables groups to focus on the power of story and to hold events which celebrate this. Each year the National Launch is held in a different part of the country. In 2004 Leeds Armories hosted the event, organised by the Airedale Group.

The following year, 1977, saw the publication of the first Federation anthology and since then there have been six more titles. The next will be launched at the Federation's Annual Conference in St Albans in 2005.

In 1981 the Federation inaugurated one of its most successful ventures, the Children's Book Award. It is a prize given for the best book of the year, judged entirely by children. The first winner was *Mr Magnolia* by Quentin Blake and the 2004 winner is Michael Morpurgo for *Private Peaceful*. The award is presented at an annual gala lunch in London in June. Children from all over the country come together to celebrate all that is best in children's books. For the past three years the award has been supported by Red House Children's Books. Their financial commitment has enabled the award to go from strength to strength, providing opportunities for children all over the country, who are not members of the Federation, to become involved in the final round of judging.

Each year the Federation invites one of its affiliated groups to organise the annual conference. This ensures that the conference moves around the country year by year and that its organisation involves many different members. Venues have included Edinburgh, Bradford, Plymouth, Stratford-upon-Avon, Brighton and Cirencester. The 2004 conference was held in Birmingham and was organised by five of the region's groups working together. Over 300 delegates attended during the weekend and listened to speakers as diverse as Brian Wildsmith, Niki Daly, Eoin Colfer and the Children's Laureate, Michael Morpurgo. The 2005 conference will take place in Hertfordshire.

A new venture in 2004 is to sponsor a day at the *The Guardian* Hay Literary Festival (see page 286), where once again the Federation's aim – to bring children and books together and have fun – will be at the forefront of the day's activities.

The Children's Book Groups

So where are the groups and who are its members? Federation Groups exist in many parts of England, Scotland and Wales; from Plymouth to Dundee; from Grantham to St David's and from York to Lewes. Membership of a group is made up of parents, carers, teachers, librarians and, in some cases, children's authors and illustrators. The passion of Federation members for bringing books and children together is the reason that the organisation has continued and developed over the past 36 years.

Each of the member groups is self supporting in terms of money and organisation, but has the advantage of a parent body to support and encourage its activities. These are as varied and diverse as the groups themselves, serving their own community's needs. They might include author visits, children's events and celebrations. But above all the Federation is an organisation that is passionate about children's books, bringing together ordinary book-loving families, empowering parents, grandparents, carers and their children to become enthusiastic and excited about all kinds of good books. Local groups encourage everyone to talk about books and reading, and thus enthusiasm for good children's literature is passed on at all levels.

Further information

Federation of Children's Book Groups
2 Bridge Wood View, Horsforth, Leeds LS18 5PE
tel 0113-2588910 *fax* 0113-2588920
email info@fcbg.org.uk
website www.fcbg.org.uk
Registered Charity No 268289

David Blanch joined the Federation in 1969 and helped set up the Birmingham Children's Book Group. He is a committee member of that group and has also been Chair of the National Executive. He is currently Publicity Officer for the Federation.

Societies, associations and organisations

The societies and associations listed here include appreciation societies devoted to specific authors (see also online resources on page 250), professional bodies and national institutions. Some also offer prizes and awards (see page 278).

Academi (Welsh Academy)

Main Office 3rd Floor, Mount Stuart House, Mount Stuart Square, Cardiff CF10 5FQ
tel 029-2047 2266 *fax* 029-2049 2930
email post@academi.org
website www.academi.org
North West Wales Office Ty Newydd, Llanystumdwy, Cricieth, Gwynedd LL52 0LW
tel (01766) 522817 *fax* (01766) 523095
email academi.gog@dial.pipex.com
South West Wales Office Dylan Thomas Centre, Somerset Place, Swansea SA1 1RR
tel (01792) 463980 *fax* (01792) 463993
Chief Executive Peter Finch
Membership Associate: £15 p.a. (waged), £7.50 (unwaged)

Academi is the trading name of Yr Academi Gymreig, the Welsh National Literature Promotion Agency and Society of Writers. With funds mostly provided from public sources, it has been constitutionally independent since 1978. It runs courses, competitions (including the Cardiff International Poetry and Book of the Year Competition), conferences, tours by authors, festivals and represents the interests of Welsh writers and Welsh writing both inside Wales and beyond. Its publications include *Taliesin* (3 p.a.), a literary journal in the Welsh language; *A470* (bi-monthly), a literature information magazine; *The Oxford Companion to the Literature of Wales*, *The Welsh Academy English–Welsh Dictionary*, and a variety of translated works.

Academi administers a range of schemes including Writers on Tar, Writers Residencies and Writing Squads for young people. Academi also runs services for writers in Wales such as bursaries, critical advice and mentoring. Founded 1959.

AccessArt

38 Mill Lane, Impington, Cambridge CB4 9XN
tel (01223) 520213
email info@accessart.org.uk
website www.accessart.org.uk

A fun, creative and dynamic learning tool for pupils across all the key stages, and for home-users of all ages. AccessArt gives users access to arts educational activities that would otherwise reach only a small audience.

Arts Council England

14 Great Peter Street, London SW1P 3NQ
tel (0845) 300 6200 *textphone* 020-7973 6564
fax 020-7973 6590
email enquiries@artscouncil.org.uk
website www.artscouncil.org.uk
Chief Executive Peter Hewitt, *Chair* Prof Christopher Frayling

The national development agency for the arts in England, distributing public money from the National Lottery and Government. Its main funding programme is Grants for the Arts, which is open to individuals, arts organisations, national touring companies and other people who use the arts in their work. The Council has one national and 9 regional offices with a single contact telephone and email address for general enquiries (see above).

East

Eden House, 48–49 Bateman Street, Cambridge CB2 1LR
textphone (01223) 306893 *fax* (0870) 242 1271

East Midlands

St Nicholas Court, 25–27 Castle Gate, Nottingham NG1 7AR *fax* 0115-950 2467

London

2 Pear Tree Court, London EC1R 0DS
textphone 020-7608 4101 *fax* 020-7608 4100

North East

Central Square, Forth Street, Newcastle upon Tyne NE1 3PJ
textphone 0191-255 8500 *fax* 0191-230 1020

North West

Manchester House, 22 Bridge Street, Manchester M3 3AB
textphone 0161-834 9131 *fax* 0161-834 6969

South East

Sovereign House, Church Street, Brighton BN1 1RA
textphone (01273) 710659 *fax* (0870) 2421257

South West

Bradninch Place, Gandy Street, Exeter EX4 3LS
textphone (01392) 433503 *fax* (01392) 229229

West Midlands

82 Granville Street, Birmingham B1 2LH
textphone 0121-643 2815 *fax* 0121-643 7239

Yorkshire

21 Bond Street, Dewsbury, West Yorkshire WF13 1AX
textphone (01924) 438585 *fax* (01924) 466522

The Arts Council/An Chomhairle Ealaíon

Literature Officer, 70 Merrion Square, Dublin 2, Republic of Ireland
tel (01) 6180200 *fax* (01) 6761302
website www.artscouncil.ie
Literature Officer Sinéad MacAodha, *Visual Arts Officer* Oliver Dowling

The national development agency for the arts in Ireland. Founded 1951.

Arts Council of Northern Ireland

MacNeice House, 77 Malone Road, Belfast BT9 5JW
tel 028-9038 5200 *fax* 028-90661715
website www.artscouncil-ni.org
Chief Executive Roisín McDonough, *Literature Officer* Robbie Meredith, *Visual Arts Officer* Iain Davidson

Promotes and encourages the arts throughout Northern Ireland. Artists in drama, dance, music and jazz, literature, the visual arts, traditional arts and community arts, can apply for support for specific schemes and projects.

The Arts Council of Wales

9 Museum Place, Cardiff CF10 3NX
tel 029-2037 6500 *minicom* 029-2039 0027
fax 029-2022 1447
email info@artswales.org.uk
website www.artswales.org.uk
Chairman Geraint Talfan Davies, *Chief Executive* Peter Tyndall

National organisation with specific responsibility for the funding and development of the arts in Wales. ACW receives funding from the National Assembly for Wales and also distributes the National Lottery funds in Wales to the arts. It undertakes this work in both the English and Welsh languages.

North Wales Regional Office

36 Princes Drive, Colwyn Bay LL29 8LA
tel (01492) 533440 *minicom* (01492) 532288
fax (01492) 533677

Mid and West Wales Regional Office

6 Gardd Llydaw, Jackson Lane, Carmarthen SA31 1QD
tel (01267) 234248 *minicom* (01267) 223469
fax (01267) 233084

South Wales Office

9 Museum Place, Cardiff CF10 3NX
tel 029-2037 6525 *minicom* 029-2039 0027
fax 029-2022 1447

Association for Scottish Literary Studies

c/o Dept of Scottish History, 9 University Gardens, University of Glasgow G12 8QH
tel 0141-330 5309
email office@asls.org.uk
website www.asls.org.uk
Hon. President Alan MacGillivray, *Hon. Secretary* Bill Aitken, *Publishing Manager* Duncan Jones
Membership £38 p.a. individulas, £10 UK students, £67 corporate

Promotes the study, teaching and writing of Scottish literature and furthers the study of the languages of Scotland. Publishes annually an edited text of Scottish literature, an anthology of new Scottish writing, a series of academic journals and a Newsletter (2 p.a.). Also publishes *Scotnotes* (comprehensive study guides to major Scottish writers), literary texts and commentary cassettes designed to assist the classroom teacher, and a series of occasional papers. Organises 3 conferences a year.

Association of American Publishers Inc.

71 Fifth Avenue, New York, NY 10003, USA
tel 212-255-0200 *fax* 212-255-7007
website www.publishers.org
President and Ceo Patricia S. Schroeder

The Association of Authors' Agents

20 John Street, London WC1N 2DR
tel 020-7405 6774 *fax* 020-7831 2154
email aaa@lutyensrubinstein.co.uk
website www.agentsassoc.co.uk
President Derek Johns, *Vice President* Sara Fisher, *Treasurer* Paul Marsh, *Secretary* Simon Trewin

Maintains a code of professional practice to which all members commit themselves. Founded 1974.

Association of Authors' Representatives Inc.

PO Box 237201, Ansonia Station, New York, NY 10023, USA
tel 212-252-3695
website www.aar-online.org

Association of Canadian Publishers

161 Eglinton Avenue East, Suite 702, Toronto, Ontario M4P 1J5, Canada
tel 416-487-6116 *fax* 416-487-8815
email info@canbook.org
website www.publishers.ca
Executive Director John P. Pelletier

The Association of Illustrators

81 Leonard Street, London EC2A 4QS
tel 020-7613 4328 *fax* 020-7613 4417
website www.theaoi.com
Contact Membership Secretary

Exists to support illustrators, promote illustration and encourage professional standards in the industry. Publishes bi-monthly magazine; presents an annual programme of events; annual competition, exhibition and tour of Images – the Best of British Illustration (call for entries: late spring). Founded 1973.

Australia Council

PO Box 788, Strawberry Hills, NSW 2012, Australia
located at 372 Elizabeth Street, Surry Hills, NSW 2010, Australia
tel (02) 9215 9000 *fax* (02) 9215 9111
email mail@ozco.gov.au
website www.ozco.gov.au
Chairperson David Gonski

Provides a broad range of support for the arts in Australia, embracing music, theatre, literature, visual arts, crafts, Aboriginal arts, community and new media arts. It has 8 major Boards: Literature, Visual Arts/Craft, Music, Theatre, Dance, New Media, Community Cultural Development, Major Performing Arts, as well as the Aboriginal and Torres Strait Islander Arts Board.

The Literature Board's chief objective is to support the writing of all forms of creative literature – novels, short stories, poetry, plays and literary non-fiction. It also assists with the publication of literary magazines, has a book publishing subsidies programme, and initiates and supports projects of many kinds designed to promote Australian literature both within Australia and abroad.

Australian Copyright Council

PO Box 1986, Strawberry Hills, NSW 2012, Australia
tel (02) 9318 1788 *fax* (02) 9698 3536
email info@copyright.org.au
website www.copyright.org.au

An independent non-profit organisation which aims to assist creators and other copyright owners to exercise their rights effectively. The Council comprises 23 organisations or associations of owners and creators of copyright material, including the Australian Society of Authors, the Australian Writers Guild and the Australian Book Publishers Association. Founded 1968.

Australian Publishers Association (APA)

60–89 Jones Street, Ultimo, NSW 2007, Australia
tel (02) 9281 9788 *fax* (02) 9281 1073
email apa@publishers.asn.au
website www.publishers.asn.au
Chief Executive Susan Bridge

Australian Writers' Guild (AWG)

8/50 Reservoir Street, Surry Hills, NSW 2010
tel (02) 9281 1554 *fax* (02) 9281 4321
email admin@awg.com.au
website www.awg.com.au

The professional association for all performance writers, i.e. writers for film, TV, radio, theatre, video and new media. The AWG is recognised throughout the industry in Australia as being the voice of performance writers. Established 1962.

Authors' Licensing and Collecting Society Ltd – see page 194

Bethnal Green Museum of Childhood

Cambridge Heath Road, London E2 9PA
tel 020-8980 2415 (24-hour Information Line)
fax 020-8983 5225
website www.museumofchildhood.org.uk

Holds one of the largest and oldest collections of toys and childhood artefacts in the world. As well as its permanent displays, the museum has temporary exhibitions, and every weekend, has art activities for children aged 5+ and soft play for under 5 year-olds, with additional activities during school holidays.

Enid Blyton Society

93 Milford Hill, Salisbury, Wilts. SP1 2QL
tel (01722) 331937
email info@enidblytonsociety.co.uk
website www.enidblytonsociety.co.uk
Contact Anita Bensoussane

To provide a focal point for collectors and enthusiasts of Enid Blyton through its magazine *The Enid Blyton Society Journal* (3 p.a.) and the annual Society Day which attracts in excess of a hundred members each year. Founded 1995.

Book Publishers Association of New Zealand Inc.

PO Box 36477, Northcote, Auckland 1309, New Zealand
tel (09) 480-2711 *fax* (09) 480-1130
email bpanz@copyright.co.nz
website www.bpanz.org.nz
President Elizabeth Caffin

The Booksellers Association of the United Kingdom & Ireland Ltd

272 Vauxhall Bridge Road, London SW1V 1BA
tel 020-7802 0802 *fax* 020-7802 0803
email mail@booksellers.org.uk
Chief Executive T.E. Godfray

Founded 1895.

Booktrust – see page 258

The British Council

10 Spring Gardens, London SW1A 2BN
tel 020-7930 8466 *fax* 020-7839 6347
website www.britishcouncil.org
Chair Baroness Helena Kennedy QC, *Director-General* David Green, *Director Literature* Margaret Meyer, *Director Arts* Sue Harrison

The British Council connects people worldwide with learning opportunities and creative ideas from the UK, and builds lasting relationships between the UK and other countries. It works in 109 countries, where it has over 180 libraries and information centres, each catering to the needs of the local community with print and electronic resources. British Council libraries not only provide information and materials to users, but also promote the latest UK publications.

Working in close collaboration with book trade associations, British Council offices organise book and electronic publishing exhibitions ranging from small, specialist displays to participation in major international book fairs. Other projects include Global Publishing Information, a collection of online publishing market reports on international markets compiled in collaboration with the Publishers Association.

Details of the British Council's many publications are available online (www.britishcouncil.org/publications/index.htm). The British Council is the agent for the Department for International Development (DFID) for book aid projects in developing countries, and is an authority on teaching English as a second or foreign language. It also gives advice and information on curriculum, methodology, materials and testing.

The British Council promotes British literature overseas through writers' tours, academic visits, seminars and exhibitions. It publishes *New Writing*, an annual anthology of unpublished short stories, poems, extracts from works in progress and essays; and a series of literary bibliographies. The British Council's Literature Dept provides an overview of UK literature and a range of online resources (www.britishcouncil.org/arts/ literature). This includes a literary portal (www.literature.britishcouncil.org), directories of courses in literature and creative writing, a directory of literary conferences and information about UK and Commonwealth authors (www.contemporarywriters.com, www.literarytranslation.com). There is a worldwide online book club and reading group for adults, teenagers and children (www.encompassculture.com) and a website for young European translators (www.youngtranslators.com).

The Visual Arts Department, part of the British Council's Arts Group, develops and enlarges overseas knowledge and appreciation of British achievement in the fields of painting, sculpture, printmaking, design, photography, the crafts and architecture, working closely with the British Council's overseas offices and with professional colleagues in the UK and abroad.

British Museum

Great Russell Street, London WC1B 3DG
tel 020-7323 8000
email information@thebritishmuseum.ac.uk
website www.thebritishmuseum.ac.uk

Children's Compass

website www.thebritishmuseum.ac.uk/compass

Children's Compass enables children to explore the British Museum's collections online. It incorporates a special children's search, activities and quizzes for use in the classroom, noticeboards for children's work, 'Ask the Expert' and articles written specially for 7–11 year-olds. Compass is also available on terminals in the Reading Room in the Museum's Great Court. Access to Compass is free. Alongside these terminals are quiz sheets for children and family groups. Children are encouraged to find objects on Compass and then go and look at them in the galleries in order to complete the quiz. . Launched in February 2002.

Canadian Authors Association

PO Box 419, Campbellford, Ontario K0L 1L0, Canada
tel 705-653-0323, 866-216-6222 (toll free)
fax 705-653-0593
email canauth@redden.on.ca
website www.CanAuthors.org/national.html
President Ishbel Moore, *Administrator* Alec McEachern

Canadian Magazine Publishers Association

425 Adelaide Street West, Suite 700, Toronto, Ontario M5V 3C1, Canada
tel 416-504-0274 *fax* 416-504-0437
email cmpainfo@cmpa.ca
website www.cmpa.ca www.magomania.com
President Mark Jamison

Canadian Publishers' Council

250 Merton Street, Suite 203, Toronto, Ontario M4S 1B1, Canada
tel 416-322-7011 *fax* 416-322-6999
email pubadmin@pubcouncil.ca
website www.pubcouncil.ca
Executive Director Jacqueline Hushion

CANSCAIP (Canadian Society of Children's Authors, Illustrators & Performers)

40 Orchard View Boulevard, Suite 101, Toronto, ON M4R 1B9, Canada
tel 416-515-1559
email office@canscaip.org
website www.cansaip.org
Office Manager Lena Coakley
Membership $75 p.a. Full member (published authors and illustrators), $45 Insitutional Friend, $35 Friend

A non-profit support network for children's artists. Promotes children's literature and performances in Canada and internationally. Founded 1977.

Careers Writers' Association

Membership Secretary Anne Goodman, 16 Caewal Road, Llandaff, Cardiff CF5 2BT
tel 029-2056 3444 *fax* 029-2065 8190
email anne.goodman5@ntlworld.com
website www.careerswriters.co.uk
Membership £20 p.a.

Society for established writers on the inter-related topics of education, training and careers. Holds occasional meetings on subjects of interest to members, and circulates details of members to information providers. Founded 1979.

The Lewis Carroll Society

Secretary Alan White, 69 Cromwell Road, Hertford, Herts. SG13 7DP
email alanwhite@tesco.net
website www.lewiscarrollsociety.org.uk
Membership £13 p.a. UK, £15 Europe, £17 elsewhere; special rates for institutions

Aims to promote interest in the life and works of Lewis Carroll (Revd Charles Lutwidge Dodgson) and to encourage research. Activities include regular meetings, exhibitions, and a publishing programme that includes the first annotated, unexpurgated edition of his diaries in 9 volumes, the Society's journal *The Carrollian* (2 p.a.), a newsletter, *Bandersnatch* (quarterly) and the *Lewis Carroll Review* (occasional). Founded 1969.

Lewis Carroll Society (Daresbury)

Secretary Kenn Oultram, Clatterwick House, Little Leigh, Northwich, Cheshire CW8 4RJ
tel (01606) 891303 (office), 781731 (evening)
Membership £5 p.a.

Aims to encourage an interest in the life and works of Lewis Carroll, author of *Alice's Adventures*. Meetings take place at Carroll's birth village (Daresbury, Cheshire). Elects an annual 'Alice', who is available for public engagements. Founded 1970.

Centre for Literacy in Primary Education (CLPE)

Webber Street, London SE1 8QW
tel 020-7401 3382/3 *fax* 020-7928 4624
email info@clpe.co.uk
website www.clpe.co.uk

A centre for children's language, literacy, literature and educational assessment which provides in-service training for teachers and contains a library of children's books plus teachers' resources. CLPE also publishes teaching resources relating to literacy in the primary classroom and the journal *Language Matters*.

Centre for the Children's Book

18 Quay Level, St Peter's Marina, Newscastle upon Tyne NE6 1TZ
email info@centreforthechildrensbook.org.uk
website www.centreforthechildrensbook.org.uk

In 2005 the first British centre to celebrate children's books is due to open in a converted Victorian mill in the Ouseburn Valley. It will house an interactive gallery, a library, an exhibitions and seminar space and a coffee shop.

Plans range from unconventional exhibitions to entertaining and challenging events and activities, some inspired by the Centre's growing collection of original manuscripts and artwork which celebrates the creative process and others introducing works from abroad.

The Children's Book Circle

c/o Rachel Wade, Hodder Children's Books, 338 Euston Road, London NW1 3BH
tel 020-7873 6000 *fax* 020-7873 6477
email rachel.wade@hodder.co.uk
Membership Secretary Nicola Wilkinson, Egmont Children's Books, 239 Kensington High Street, London W8 6SA
tel 020-7761 3500 *fax* 020-7761 3510
email nicola.wilkinson@ukegmont.com
Membership £15 p.a. if working inside M25; £12 outside

Provides a discussion forum for anybody involved with children's books. Meetings are addressed by a panel of invited speakers and topics focus on current and controversial issues. Holds the annual Patrick Hardy lecture and administers the Eleanor Farjeon Award. See also page 259. Founded 1962.

Children's Books History Society

Secretary Ms Sarah Mahurter, 66 Idmiston Square, Worcester Park, Surrey KT4 7SY
tel 020-8830-6084 *fax* 020-8830-6084
email sjamahuter@hotmail.com
Membership £10 p.a.; apply for overseas rates

Aims 'to promote an appreciation of children's books, and to study their history, bibliography and literary content'. Holds approx. 6 meetings and produces 3 substantial *Newsletters* and an occasional paper per year. The Harvey Darton Award is given biennially for a book that extends knowledge of British children's literature of the past. Founded 1969.

Children's Books Ireland

17 Lower Camden Street, Dublin 2, Republic of Ireland
tel/fax (01) 8725854
email info@childrensbooksireland.com
website www.childrensbooksireland.com
Administrative Officer Liz Marshall
Membership €25/£18 p.a. individual, €35/£26 p.a. institution, €45/£40 p.a. overseas, €15/£11 p.a. student

Committed to raising awareness of the value and importance of children's books and to playing a central role in promoting, celebrating and supporting all aspects of children's books. Formed in 1996.

Children's Writers and Illustrators Group – see The Society of Authors, page 255

CLÉ: The Irish Book Publishers' Association

19 Parnell Square, Dublin 1, Republic of Ireland
tel (056) 7756 333 *fax* (056) 7756 333
email info@publishingireland.com
website www.publishingireland.com
President Fergal Tobin, *Adminstrator* Jolly Ronan

Comhairle nan Leabhraichean/The Gaelic Books Council

22 Mansfield Street, Glasgow G11 5QP
tel 0141-337 6211 *fax* 0141-353 0515
email fios@gaelicbooks.net
website www.gaelicbooks.net
Chair Prof Donald E. Meek

Stimulates Scottish Gaelic publishing by awarding publication grants for new books, commissioning authors and providing editorial services and general assistance to writers and readers. Has its own bookshop of all Gaelic and Gaelic-related books in print and runs a book club; catalogue available. Founded 1968.

Curiosity & Imagination 4 Children

Bellerive House, 3 Muirfield Crescent, London E14 9SZ
tel 020-7522 6919 *fax* 020-7512 2010
email info@curiosityandimagination.org.uk
website www.curiosityandimagination.org.uk
Manager Alison Coles, *Communications Officer* Nick Austin

Promotes an approach to children's learning which:
• harnesses the power of playful, hands-on experience as a tool for learning;
• empowers parents and carers to support their children's learning;
• encourages community ownership of the provision, giving children a central role in decision-making;
• draws in expertise from local partners across a range of sectors.

This approach fosters children's natural curiosity, stimulating them to discover more about themselves, other people and the world around them. It also inspires children's imaginations, helping them to see what is possible in the future. See website for further information.

Cyngor Llyfrau Cymru – see Welsh Books Council/Cyngor Llyfrau Cymru

Roald Dahl Foundation

92 High Street, Great Missenden, Bucks. HP16 OAN
tel (01494) 890465
websites www.roalddahl.com, www.roalddahlclub.com

A UK-based registered charity offering a programme of grant-giving to charities, hospitals and individuals in the UK. It supports many varied projects, in the same way Roald Dahl did when he was alive, offering practical assistance to children and families in 3 areas: neurology, haematology and literacy.

The Foundation's websites are illustrated with the artworks of Quentin Blake, Roald Dahl's principal illustrator and include full information about the author, his life and his works. The Foundation also operates a website club for children and the online magazine *The Gobblefunk Gazette*.

Roald Dahl's Children's Gallery

tel (01296) 331441
website www.buckscc.gov.uk/museum/dahl/index.stm
An exciting hands-on gallery for children. A visit is a step into the magical world of Roald Dahl. Booking is advised to avoid disappointment.

Discover

1 Bridge Terrace, London E15 4BG
tel 020-8536 5555
email team@discover.org.uk
website www.discover.org.uk

Discover is designed for children aged 0–8 years and their families, carers and teachers. Discover is about story-building – making stories together. Story-building helps children to use their imaginations and express themselves, both to each other and to grown-ups, through play. Speaking, listening, writing and acting become easy activities. Story-building is fun and breaks down barriers.

Discover has been running its outreach programmes to schools, libraries and community centres since 2000. The Story Garden opened in 2002 and the Story Trail opened in June 2003 in a renovated Edwardian building in the centre of Stratford. Story Trail is full of unique hands-on exhibits. Children's input at every stage of Discover's work is fundamental.

Educational Publishers Council

The Publishers' Association, 29B Montague Street, London WC1B 5BH
tel 020-7691 9191 *fax* 020-7691 9199
email mail@publishers.org.uk

Represents publishers of school and textbooks. It works closely with the DfES on the provision of text books in schools, school libraries and colleges of further education, the school curriculum, the National Grid for Learning and IT in schools. It represents members' interests in copyright licensing negotiations covering photocopying and electronic copying in schools and colleges.

Educational Writers Group – see The Society of Authors, page 255

Department for Education and Skills

Sanctuary Buildings, Great Smith Street, London SW1P 3BT
tel (0870) 000 2288 *minicom* (01928) 794274
fax (01928) 794248
email info@dfes.gsi.gov.uk
website www.dfes.gov.uk

Aims to help build a competitive economy and inclusive society by creating opportunities for everyone to develop their learning potential and achieve excellence in standards of education and levels of skills. The department's main objectives are to give children an excellent start in education and enable young people and adults to develop and equip themselves with the skills, knowledge and personal qualities needed for life and work.

The Department also sponsors 11 non-departmental public bodies across a variety of professional disciplines and educational services.

English Association

University of Leicester, University Road, Leicester LE1 7RH
tel 0116-252 3982 *fax* 0116-252 2301
email engassoc@le.ac.uk
website www.le.ac.uk/engassoc/
Chair Elaine Treharne, *Chief Executive* Helen Lucas

Aims to further knowledge, understanding and enjoyment of English literature and the English language, by working towards a fuller recognition of English as an essential element in education and in the community at large; by encouraging the study of English literature and language by means of conferences, lectures and publications; and by fostering the discussion of methods of teaching English of all kinds.

Federation of Children's Book Groups – see page 260

The Gaelic Books Council – see Comhairle nan Leabhraichean/The Gaelic Books Council

The Greeting Card Association

United House, North Road, London N7 9DP
tel 020-7619 0396
website www.greetingcardassociation.org.uk
Administrator Sharon Little

See website for information on freelance designing and writing for greeting cards. Official magazine: *Progressive Greetings Worldwide* (see page 160).

Hayward Gallery

Belvedere Road, London SE1 8XZ
tel 020-7960 5226 *fax* 020-7401 2664
website www.hayward.org.uk

The Hilliard Society of Miniaturists

The Executive Officer Pauline Warner, Priory Lodge, 7 Priory Road, Wells, Somerset BA5 1SR
tel (01749) 674472 *fax* (01749) 674472
website www.art-in-miniature.org
President Heather O. Catchpole RMS, PHSF, MASSA, MASF
Membership From £25 p.a.

Founded to increase knowledge and promote the art of miniature painting. Annual Exhibition held in June at Wells; seminars; Young People's Awards (11–19 years); Newsletter. Member of the World Federation of Miniaturists. Founded 1982.

Imaginate

45A George Street, Edinburgh EH2 2HT
tel 0131-225 8050 *fax* 0131-225 6440
email info@imaginate.org.uk
Director Tony Reekie, *General Manager* Tessa Rennie

Imaginate is an arts agency committed to promoting and developing performing arts for children in Scotland. Its vision is that all children, by the age of 12, will have had a positive experience of performing arts. Its mission is to act as an advocate for the provision of high-quality performing arts for children across Scotland. Imaginate produces an annual programme of events and initiatives.

Imaginate creates and produces the Bank of Scotland International Children's Festival for children and young people (see page 285). This annual event attracts an audience of children, their teachers, parents, carers and friends from across Scotland. An outreach programme takes live theatre into schools and communities in Edinburgh and the Lothians during the Festival. It also takes international theatre invited by Imaginate to perform at the Festival to venues across Scotland reaching children in communities from Shetland to Dumfriesshire to the Borders.

Imaginate produces WYSIWYG – What You See Is What You Get, Scotland's annual showcase of children's theatre for funders, artists, producers, programmers, arts and education workers.

In addition, Imaginate brings together practitioners from home and abroad to collaborate, develop skills and share experiences for the future benefit of young audiences. It identifies and develops opportunities and activities to support the growth and development of the performing arts sector for children and young people in Scotland. It has a range of resources accessible to the children's theatre sector.

Imperial War Museum

Lambeth Road, London SW7 5BD
tel 020-7942 500
website www.iwm.org.uk

International Board on Books for Young People (IBBY)

Nonnenweg 12, Postfach, CH-4003-Basel, Switzerland
tel (4161) 272 2917 *fax* (+4161) 272 2757
email ibby@eye.ch
website www.ibby.org
British Section c/o National Centre for Research in Children's Literature
tel 020-8392 3008
email ibby@roehampton.ac.uk

IBBY is a non-profit organisation which represents an international network of people from all over the world who are committed to bringing books and children together. Its aims are:

- to promote international understanding through children's books;
- to give children everywhere the opportunity to have access to books with high literary and artistic standards;
- to encourage the publication and distribution of quality children's books, especially in developing countries;
- to provide support and training for those involved with children and children's literature;
- to stimulate research and scholarly works in the field of children's literature.

IBBY is composed of more than 68 National Sections all over the world and represents countries with well-developed book publishing and literacy programmes, and other countries with only a few dedicated professionals who are doing pioneer work in children's book publishing and promotion. Founded in Zurich, Switzerland in 1953.

The Irish Book Publishers' Association

– see CLÉ: The Irish Book Publishers' Association

The Kipling Society

Hon. Secretary Jane Keskar, 6 Clifton Road, London W9 1SS
email jane@keskar.fsworld.co.uk
website www.kipling.org.uk

For everyone interested in the prose and verse, and life and times, of Rudyard Kipling (1865–1936). Expert knowledge is not needed: most members simply share an enthusiasm for Kipling's writings and an interest in the times through which he lived. This is one of the most active and enduring literary societies in Britain and, as the only one which focuses on Kipling and his place in English literature, attracts a worldwide membership. The Society is a Registered Charity and a voluntary, non-profit-making organisation. Founded in 1927.

C.S. Lewis Society (Oxford)

Pusey House, St Giles, Oxford OX1 3LZ
email cslewis@sable.ox.ac.uk

Meets 8.15pm, Tuesday term-time at Pusey House, to promote knowledge of C.S. Lewis and the writers who influenced him, including J.R.R. Tolkein, Charles Williams, Dorothy L. Sayers, G.K. Chesterton and George MacDonald. Open to non-University members.

The C.S. Lewis Society (New York)

Secretary Clare Sarrocco, 84–23 77th Avenue, Glendle, NY 11385-7706, USA
email subscribe@nycslsociety.com
website www.nycslsociety.com

The oldest society for the appreciation and discussion of C.S. Lewis. Founded 1969.

Little Theatre Guild of Great Britain

Public Relations Officer Michael Shipley, 121 Darwen Road, Bromley Cross, Bolton BL7 9BG
tel (01204) 304103

Aims to promote closer cooperation amongst the little theatres constituting its membership; to act as coordinating and representative body on behalf of the little theatres; to maintain and advance the highest standards in the art of theatre; and to assist in encouraging the establishment of other little theatres. Its yearbook is available to non-members for £5.

The Livesey Museum for Children

682 Old Kent Road, London SE15 1JF
tel 020-7639 5604 *fax* 020-7277 5384
email info@liveseymuseum.org.uk
website www.liveseymuseum.org.uk

An all-new interactive exhibition is shown every year for children under 12 years old, their families, carers and teachers. Children can learn things by experimenting and investigating, by using their imaginations – and by having fun! Exhibitions are designed to support the National Curriculum at Foundation Stage, Key Stage 1 and Key Stage 2.

Museum of London

London Wall, London EC2Y 5HN
tel 020-7600 3699 *fax* 020-7600 1058
email info@museumoflondon.org.uk
website www.museumoflondon.org.uk

National Art Library

Victoria and Albert Museum, South Kensington, London SW7 2RL
website www.nal.vam.ac.uk

A major reference library and the Victoria and Albert Museum's curatorial department for the art, craft and design of the book.

National Association for the Teaching of English (NATE)

50 Broadfield Road, Sheffield S8 0XJ
tel 0114-255 5419 *fax* 0114-255 5296
email info@nate.org.uk
website www.nate.org.uk

Supports subject teachers of English at all phases of education in the UK. NATE provides information about current developments, publications and resource materials. It also funds research, in-service training and holds an annual and regional conferences. Annual membership gives members 5 copies of NATE's journal, newsletter and pupil age-related magazines and well as discounts on publications, courses and conferences.

National Association of Writers' Groups

Headquarters The Arts Centre, Biddick Lane, Washington, Tyne and Wear NE38 2AB
Secretary Diane Wilson, 40 Burstall Hill, Bridlington, East Yorkshire YO16 7GA
tel (01262) 609228 *fax* (01262) 609228
email nawg@tesco.net
website www.nawg.co.uk
Membership £25 p.a. plus £5 registration per group; £10 Associate individuals

Aims 'to advance the education of the general public throughout the UK, including the Channel Islands, by promoting the study and art of writing in all its aspects.' Publishes *Link* bi-monthly magazine. Annual Festival of Writing held in Durham 3–5 Sept 2005. Annual Creative Writing Competition. Founded 1995.

National Association of Writers in Education (NAWE)

PO Box 1, Sheffield Hutton, York YO6 7YU
website www.nawe.co.uk

Represents and supports writers, teachers and all those involved in the development of creative writing in education. Useful resource of writers who work in schools and communities is held on the website.

National Centre for Language and Literacy (NCLL)

University of Reading, Bulmershe Court, Reading RG6 1HY
tel 0118-931 8820
email ncll@reading.ac.uk
website www.ncll.org.uk

An independent organisation concerned with all aspects of language and literacy learning. The Centre supports teachers, parents and governors through its unique collection of resources, its publications, an extensive programme of courses and conferences, ongoing research and a membership scheme designed to meet the needs of individual schools.

National Centre for Research in Children's Literature (NCRCL)

University of Surrey Roehampton, Digby Stuart College, London SW15 5PH
tel 020-8392 3008 *fax* 020-8392 3819
email ncrcl@roehampton.ac.uk
website www.ncrcl.ac.uk

Facilitates and supports research exchange in the field of children's literature, and is the headquarters of the UK branch of the International Board on Books for Young People. The NCRCL is based in the University of Surrey Roehampton, which houses several collections held in the Children's Literature Centre and in the Froebel Archive for Childhood Studies. The website provides information on resources, activities and children's literature-related individuals and links to websites.

National Galleries of Scotland

National Gallery of Scotland, The Mound, Edinburgh EH2 2EL
Scottish National Portrait Gallery, 1 Queen Street, Edinburgh EH2 1JD
Scottish National Gallery of Modern Art, Belford Road, Edinburgh EH4 3DR
The Dean Gallery, Belford Road, Edinburgh EH4 3DS
tel 0131-624 6200, 0131-624 6332 (press office)
fax 0131-343 3250 (press office)
email pressinfo@nationalgalleries.org
website www.nationalgalleries.org

National Gallery

Trafalgar Square, London WC2N 5DN
tel 020-7747 2885 *fax* 020-7747 2423
email information@ng-london.org.uk
website www.nationalgallery.org.uk

National Library for the Blind (NLB)

Far Cromwell Road, Bredbury, Stockport SK6 2SG
tel 0161-355 2000 *minicom* 0161-355 2043
fax 0161-355 2098
email enquiries@nlbuk.org
website www.nlb-online.org

A registered charity giving visually impaired adults and children access to books and information. The NLB houses Europe's largest collection of Braille and Moon books. It also publishes magazines for children and teenagers (see *Magazines and newspapers for children*) and spearheads the Right to Read campaign.

National Literacy Association

Office No 1, The Magistrates Court, Bargates, Christchurch, Dorset BH23 1PY
tel (01202) 484079/89 *fax* (01202) 484079
email nla@argonet.co.uk
websites www.nla.org.uk, www.literacyguide.org

Campaigns to raise awareness of the needs of underachievers and aims to ensure that 99% of school leavers will have adequate literacy for their needs in daily life. Produces publications and other resources including *The Guide to Literacy Resources*, which is distributed free to schools, parent groups, libraries and others.

National Literacy Trust

Swire House, 59 Buckingham Gate,
London SW1E 6AJ
tel 020-7828 2435 *fax* 020-7931 9986
email contact@literacytrust.org.uk
websites www.literacytrust.org.uk, www.rif.org.uk, www.readon.org.uk
Director Neil McClelland, *PA* Jacky Taylor

Independent registered charity dedicated to building a literate nation in which everyone enjoys the skills, self-esteem and pleasures that literacy can bring. The only organisation concerned with raising literacy standards for all age groups throughout the UK. Maintains an extensive website with literacy news, summaries of key issues, research and examples of practice nationwide; organises an annual conference, courses and training events; publishes a quarterly magazine, *Literacy Today*, and runs a range of initiatives to turn promising ideas into effective action. Initiatives include the National Reading Campaign, funded by the government; Reading is Fundamental, UK, which provides free books to children; Reading The Game, involving the professional football community; the Talk To Your Baby campaign; and the Literacy and Social Inclusion Project, a partnership with the Basic Skills Agency. Founded 1993.

National Museums and Galleries of Wales/Amgueddfeydd Ac Orielau Cenedlaethol Cymru

Cathays Park, Cardiff CF10 3NP
tel 029-2039 7951 *fax* 029-2037 3219
website www.nmgw.ac.uk

National Museums Liverpool

PO Box 33, 127 Dale Street,
Liverpool L69 3LA
tel 0151-207 0001 *fax* 0151-478 4790

National Museums of Scotland

Chambers Street,
Edinburgh EH1 1JF
tel 0131-225 7534 *fax* 0131-220 4819
website www.nms.ac.uk

National Portrait Gallery

St Martin's Place, London WC2H 0HE
tel 020-7306 0055 *fax* 020-7306 0056
website www.npg.org.uk

National Society for Education in Art and Design

The Gatehouse, Corsham Court, Corsham,
Wilts. SN13 0BZ
tel (01249) 714825 *fax* (01249) 716138
website www.nsead.org
General Secretary Dr John Steers NDD, ATC, AE, PhD

The leading national authority concerned with art, craft and design across all phases of education in the UK. Offers the benefits of membership of a professional association, a learned society and a trade union. Has representatives on National and Regional Committees concerned with Art and Design Education. Publishes *Journal of Art and Design Education* (3 p.a.; Blackwells) and *Start* magazine for primary schools. Founded 1888.

The Natural History Museum

Cromwell Road, London SW7 5BD
tel 020-7942 5000
website www.nhm.ac.uk

The Edith Nesbit Society

21 Churchfields, West Malling, Kent ME19 6RJ
email mmccarthy30@hotmail.com
website www.therailway-children.co.uk
Membership £6 p.a.; £12 organisations/overseas

Aims to promote an interest in the life and works of Edith Nesbit (1858–1924) by means of talks, a regular newsletter and and other publications, and visits to relevant places. Founded 1996.

New Writing North

2 School Lane, Whickham,
Newcastle upon Tyne NE16 4SL
tel 0191-488 8580 *fax* 0191-488 8576
email mail@newwritingnorth.com
website www.newwritingnorth.com
Director Claire Malcolm, *Administrator* Silvana Michelini, *Education Director* Anna Summerford

The literature development agency for the North East. Offers advice and support to writers of poetry, prose and plays. See website. Founded 1996.

Office for Standards in Education (OFSTED)

Alexandra House, 33 Kingsway,
London WC2B 6SE
tel 020-7421 6800 *fax* 020-7421 6707

A non-ministerial Government department established under the Education (Schools Act) 1992. Since April 2001 OFSTED has been responsible for inspecting all educational provision for 16–19 year-olds to establish and monitor an independent inspection system for maintained schools in England. Its inspection role also includes the inspection of local educational authorities, teacher training institutions and youth work. In September 2001, OFSTED took over the regulation of childcare providers, from 150 local authorities.

The Poetry Book Society

Book House, 45 East Hill, London SW18 2QZ
tel 020-8870 8403 *fax* 020-8870 0865
email info@poetrybooks.co.uk
website www.poetrybooks.co.uk
Chair Daisy Goodwin, *Director* Chris Holifield

Foremost in getting books of new poetry to readers through quarterly selections, special offers, and 300-strong backlist which it sells at favourable rates to members. Website features over 1000 post-1950s poetry books for sale. Publishes *Bulletin* (quarterly) and runs the annual T.S. Eliot Prize for the best collection of new poetry. Operates as a charitable Book Club with annual membership (£10, £32, £125) open to all. Education resources for secondary schools and Children's Poetry Bookshelf for primary schools and libraries. Also plays role in promoting and stimulating sales of poetry books.

The Poetry Library – see page 116

The Poetry Society

22 Betterton Street, London WC2H 9BX
tel 020-7420 9880 *fax* 020-7240 4818
email info@poetrysociety.org.uk
website www.poetrysociety.org.uk
Subscriptions Subscriptions and Membership Dept, Freepost 5410, London WC2H 9BR
tel 020-7420 9881 *fax* 020-7240 4818
Chair Richard Price, *Director* Jules Mann
Membership Open to all; national membership

Aims to help poets and poetry thrive in Britain today. Publishes *Poetry Review* (quarterly) and *Poetry News* (quarterly), has an information and imagination service, runs promotions and educational projects, helps to coordinate National Poetry Day and the annual National Poetry Competition. Provides a unique critical service, Poetry Prescription, where poetry of up to 100 lines is appraised by a chosen poet. Runs the Poetry Café at its premises in Covent Garden, which is also a venue for regular and one-off events, and is also available for hire for small readings and seminars (contact Jess York, *tel* 020-7420 9887). Founded 1909.

Poetry Society Education – see page 118

The Beatrix Potter Society

Secretary Sidney Blackmore, 9 Broadfields, Harpenden, Herts. AL5 2HJ
tel (01582) 769755
email beatrixpottersociety@tiscali.co.uk
website www.beatrixpottersociety.org.uk
Membership £15 p.a. UK, £20 overseas

Promotes the study and appreciation of the life and works of Beatrix Potter as author, artist, diarist, farmer and conservationist. Founded 1980.

The Publishers Association

29B Montague Street, London WC1B 5BW
tel 020-7691 9191 *fax* 020-7691 9199
email mail@publishers.org.uk
website www.publishers.org.uk
Chief Executive Ronnie Williams OBE, *Director of International and Trade Divisions (BDCI)* Ian Taylor, *Director of Educational, Academic and Professional Publishing* Graham Taylor

Founded 1896.

Qualifications and Curriculum Authority (QCA)

83 Piccadilly, London W1J 8QA
tel 020-7509 5555 *fax* 020-7509 6666
email info@qca.org.uk
website www.qca.org.uk
Chairman Sir Anthony Greener, *Chief Executive* Dr Ken Boston

An independent government agency funded by the DfES. It is responsible for ensuring that the curriculum and qualifications available to young people and adults are of a high quality and are coherent and flexible. Its remit ranges from the under-fives to higher level vocational qualifications.

The Arthur Ransome Society Ltd (TARS)

Abbott Hall Museum, Kendal, Cumbria LA9 5AL
tel (01539) 722464
email tarsinfo@authur-ransome.org
website www.authur-ransome.org
President Norman Willis

Formed for people of all ages who have enjoyed the *Swallows and Amazons* books. Until her death, the Society's President was Brigit Sanders, who was the youngest member of the family to whom Arthur Ransome dedicated *Swallows and Amazons* because they were the inspiration for the crew of the *Swallow*. Founded 1990.

REACH: National Advice Centre for Children with Reading Difficulties

California Country Park, Nine Mile Ride, Finchampstead, Berks. RG40
tel (0845) 604 0414 (Helpline) *fax* 0118-973 7575

Offers advice and assistance on children's reading disability and a comprehensive resource collection of books and materials in a user-friendly environment for both children and adults. Phone first for an appointment during opening hours (Mon–Fri 10am–5pm).

Readathon

Hele Mill, Marham Church, Bude, Devon EX23 OJA
tel (0870) 240 1124
website www.readathon.org

Readathon was set up to encourage children to read more books. Children undertake to read books, or do other literacy-based activities, in return for pledges of money, for charity, from family and friends. Thousands of schools have contributed to this success, and have made the Readathon campaign Britain's largest sponsored literary event. On joining, a free starter pack containing everything needed to run a successful Readathon is supplied.

Since it began, Readathon has raised well over £10 million, which has been shared equally between two charities, the Roald Dahl Foundation and Sargent Cancer Care for Children. Fundraising costs are kept to a minimum because Readathon receives support from booksellers, children's publishers, and many organisations concerned with books and reading. And because Readathon is primarily a literacy initiative, it also receives funding from the Arts Councils of England, Scotland and Northern Ireland. Founded 1984.

Reading is Fundamental, UK

National Literacy Trust, Swire House, 59 Buckingham Gate, London SW1E 6AJ
tel 020-7828 2435 *fax* 020-7931 9986
email rif@literacytrust.org.uk
website www.rif.org.uk

An initiative of the National Literacy Trust that helps children and young people (aged 0–19) to realise their potential by motivating them to read. Working with volunteers, it delivers targeted literacy projects that promote: the fun of reading; the importance of book choice; and the benefits to families of sharing books at home. Children in each project choose up to 3 free books a year to keep at special events involving families and local volunteers; receive a book bag, bookmark, bookplates and stickers; and enjoy fun activities that highlight the pleasures of reading and often involve authors, poets, storytellers and illustrators.

Established in 1996 following the success of RIF Inc. (the largest children's and family literacy programme in the USA), RIF, UK has distributed 510,000 books to over 170,000 children and young people, and currently supports around 300 projects reaching 20,000 children. RIF, UK projects are set up in schools, libraries, football clubs, early years centres, bookshops, after-school and study support centres, women's refuges, prisons and parents' groups.

Scattered Authors Society

Secretary Anne Cassidy, 150 Wanstead Lane, Ilford, Essex IG1 3SG
email anne.cassidy4@btopenworld.com

Aims to provide a forum for informal discussion, contact and support for professional writers in children's fiction. Founded 1998.

School Library Association

Unit 2, Lotmead Business Village, Lotmead Farm, Wanborough, Swindon SN4 OUY
tel (01793) 791787 *fax* (01793) 791786

Promotes the development of school libraries as being central to the curriculum. It publishes guidelines for library and resource centres, a quarterly journal and provides training and an information service.

Science Museum

Exhibition Road, London SW7 2DD
tel (0870) 870 4868
email sciencemuseum@nmsi.ac.uk
website www.sciencemuseum.org.uk

Scottish Arts Council

12 Manor Place, Edinburgh EH3 7DD
tel 0131-226 6051
email help.desk@scottisharts.org.uk
website www.scottisharts.org.uk
Chairman James Boyle, *Director* Graham Berry, *Head of Literature* Gavin Wallace, *Head of Visual Arts* Amanda Catto

Principal channel for government funding of the arts in Scotland, the Scottish Arts Council is funded by the Scottish Executive. It aims to develop and improve the knowledge, understanding and practice of the arts, and to increase their accessibility throughout Scotland. It offers about 1300 grants a year to artists and arts organisations concerned with the visual arts, drama, dance and mime, literature, music, festivals, and traditional, ethnic and community arts. It is also the distributor of National Lottery funds to the arts in Scotland.

Scottish Book Trust (SBT)

Sandeman House, 55 High Street, Edinburgh EH1 1SR
tel 0131-524 0160 *fax* 0131-524 0161
email info@scottishbooktrust.com
website www.scottishbooktrust.com

With a particular responsibility towards Scottish writing, SBT exists to promote literature and reading, and aims to reach (and create) a wider reading public than has existed before. It also organises exhibitions, readings and storytellings, administers the Live Literature Scotland Scheme, operates an extensive children's reference library available to everyone and provides a book information service. SBT has a range of publications and advises other relevant art organisations. Founded 1960.

Scottish Publishers Association

Scottish Book Centre, 137 Dundee Street,
Edinburgh EH11 1BG
tel 0131-228 6866 *fax* 0131-228 3220
email enquiries@scottishbooks.org
website www.scottishbooks.org
Director Lorraine Fannin, *Administrator* Carol Lothian, *Member Services Manager* Liz Small, *Information and Development Administrator* Katherine A. Naish

Founded 1973.

Screenwriters' Workshop

Suffolk House, 1–8 Whitfield Place,
London W1T 5JU
tel 020-7387 5511
email screenoffice@tisali.co.uk
website www.lsw.org.uk
Contact Administrator
Membership £40 p.a.

Forum for contact, information and tuition, the SW helps new and established writers work successfully in the film and TV industry, and organises a continuous programme of activities, events, courses and seminars, all of which are reduced to members and open to non-members at reasonable rates. The SW is the largest screenwriting group in Europe and supports Euroscript, a Media II-funded organisation developing scripts for film and TV throughout the EU. Founded 1983.

Society for Editors and Proofreaders (SfEP)

Office Riverbank House, 1 Putney Bridge Approach, London SW6 3JD
tel 020-7736 3278
email admin@sfep.org.uk
website www.sfep.org.uk

Works to promote high editorial standards and achieve recognition of its members' professional status, through local and national meetings, an annual conference, an email discussion group, a regular newsletter and a programme of reasonably priced workshops/training sessions. These sessions help newcomers to acquire basic skills, enable experienced editors to update their skills or broaden their competence, and also cover aspects of professional practice or business for the self-employed. An annual Directory of members' services is available. The Society supports moves towards recognised standards of training and accreditation for editors and proofreaders and has developed its own Accreditation in Proofreading qualification. It has close links with the Publishing Training Centre and the Society of Indexers, is represented on the BSI Technical Committee dealing with copy preparation and proof correction (BS 5261), and works to foster good relations with all relevant bodies and organisations in the UK and worldwide. Founded 1988.

Society for Storytelling (SfS)

PO Box 2344, Reading, Berks. RG6 7FG
tel 0118-935 1381
email sfs@fairbruk.demon.co.uk
website www.sfs.org.uk

For anyone with an interest in oral storytelling, whether teller, listener, beginner or professional. The SfS aims to provide information on oral storytelling and organises festivals and conferences and a National Storytelling Week each year in February. It is a network for everyone interested in storytelling and to increase public awareness of the art. The SfS produces a members' magazine, *Storylines* (quarterly), a catalogue of storytelling tapes and a *Directory of Storytellers*. Founded 1993.

Society of Artists Agents

21c Montpellier Row, London SE3 0RL
tel (07870) 628 709
email jennieward@btopenworld.com
website www.thesaa.com
Contact Jennifer Ward

Formed to promote professionalism in the illustration industry and to forge closer links between clients and artists through an agreed set of guidelines. The Society believes in an ethical approach through proper terms and conditions, thereby protecting the interests of the artists and clients. Founded 1992.

The Society of Authors – see page 255

Society of Children's Book Writers and Illustrators (SCBWI)

Flat 3, 124 Norwood Road, London SE24 9AY
tel 020-8671 7539
email scbwi_bi@hotmail.com
website www.wordpool.co.uk/scbwi
Regional Adviser Natascha Biebow
Membership £44 p.a. plus a one-off fee of £7

An international network for the exchange of knowledge between professional writers, illustrators, editors, publishers, agents, librarians, educators, booksellers and others involved with literature for young people. Sponsors 2 annual conferences on writing and illustrating books and multimedia – in New York (February) and Los Angeles (summer) – as well as dozens of regional conferences and events throughout the world. Publishes a bi-monthly newsletter, *The Bulletin*, and information publications, and awards grants for works in progress. The SCBWI also presents the annual Golden Kite Award for the best fiction and non-fiction books, which is open both to published and unpublished writers and illustrators.

The SCBWI British Isles region meets quarterly for a speaker or workshop event. Also sponsors local critique groups and publishes *Words and Pictures* quarterly newsletter, which includes up-to-date events and marketing information and articles on the craft of children's writing and illustrating in the British Isles. The yearly Writer's Day and Illustrator's Day includes workshops and the opportunity to meet publishing professionals. Founded 1971.

Society of Editors

Director Bob Satchwell, University Centre, Granta Place, Mill Lane, Cambridge CB2 1RU
tel (01223) 304080 *fax* (01223) 304090
email info@societyofeditors.org
website www.societyofeditors.org
Membership £230 p.a.

Formed from the merger of the Guild of Editors and the Association of British Editors, the Society has more than 450 members in national, regional and local newspapers, magazines, broadcasting, new media, journalism education and media law, campaigning for media freedom. Publishes *Briefing* (monthly). Founded 1999.

Society of Indexers

Blades Enterprise Centre, John Street, Sheffield S2 4SU
tel 0114-292 2350 *fax* 0114-292 2351
email admin@indexers.org.uk
website www.indexers.org.uk
Administrator Wendy Burrow
Registrar Elizabeth Wallis *tel* 020-8940 4771
Membership £60 p.a. UK/Europe, £75 overseas; £120 corporate

An *Occasional paper* on indexing children's books is available. Visit the website or contact the Administrator for further information. Publishers and authors seeking to commission an indexer should consult *Indexers Available* on the website or contact the Registrar.

Society of Young Publishers

Contact The Secretary, c/o The Bookseller, Endeavour House, 189 Shaftesbury Avenue, London WC2H 8TJ
email thesyp@thesyp.org.uk
website www.thesyp.org.uk
Membership Open to anyone employed in publishing or hoping to be soon; Associate membership available to those over the age of 35

Organises monthly speaker meetings at which senior figures talk on topics of key importance to the industry today, and social and other events. Runs a job database which matches candidates with potential employers. Meetings are held in Central London, usually on the last Wednesday of the month at 6.30pm. Also a branch in Oxford. Founded 1949.

Southwest Scriptwriters

Secretary John Colborn
tel 0117-909 5522
email southwest_scriptwriters@hotmail.com
website www.southwest-scriptwriters.co.uk
Membership £5 p.a.

Workshops members' drama scripts for stage, screen, radio and TV with the aim of improving their chances of professional production, meeting at the Bristol Old Vic. Also hosts regular talks by professional dramatists. Presents short annual seasons of script-in-hand performances of members' work at a major Bristol venue. Bi-monthly newsletter. Founded 1994.

Speaking of Books

9 Guildford Grove, London SE10 8VJ
tel 020-8692 4704

Arranges school visits by writers, illustrators and storytellers and book-related in-service training activities and bookstalls.

Tate

Tate Britain, Millbank, London SW1P 4RG
tel 020-7887 8008, 020-7887 8000 (admin)
email information@tate.org.uk
website www.tate.org.uk
Tate Modern, Bankside, London SE1 9TG
tel 020-7887 8008
Tate Liverpool, Albert Dock, Liverpool L3 4BB
tel 0151-702 7400
Tate St Ives, Porthmeor Beach, St Ives, Cornwall TR26 1TG
tel (01736) 796226

Theatre Museum

National Museum of the Performing Arts, 1E Tavistock Street, London WC2E 7PR
tel 020-7943 4700 *fax* 020-7943 4777
website www.theatremuseum.org

In addition to extensive public displays on live entertainment and education programme, the Museum has an unrivalled collection of programmes, playbills, prints, photos, videos, texts and press cuttings relating to performers and productions from the 17th century onwards. Available by appointment (book 3 weeks in advance), free of charge through the Study Room. Open Wed–Fri 10.30am–4.30pm. Reprographic services available.

The Tolkien Society

Secretary Sally Kennett, 210 Prestbury Road, Cheltenham, Glos. GL52 3ER
website www.tolkiensociety.org
Membership Secretary Trevor Reynolds, 65 Wentworth Crescent, Ash Vale, Surrey GU12 5LF
email trevor@caerlas.demon.co.uk

United Kingdom Literacy Association (UKLA)

Unit 6, 1st Floor, The Maltings, Green Drift, Royston, Herts. SG8 5DB
tel (01763) 241188 *fax* (01763) 243785
email admin@ukla.org
website www.ukla.org

UKLA is a registered charity, which has as its sole object the advancement of education in literacy. It is committed to promoting good practice nationally and internationally in literacy and language teaching and research. Its activities include:
• a conference programme of international, national and local conferences reflecting language and literacy interests.
• an active publications committee. Members are kept up to date via UKLA journals and website. Members receive a copy of both the newsletter, *UKLA News* (3 p.a.), and the recently renamed journal *Literacy* (see *Magazines about children's literature and education*, page 212). For an additional subscription, members can receive the *Journal of Research in Reading.* Both of the UKLA journals are refereed and include research reports, both qualitative and quantitative research, and critiques of current policy and practice as well as discussions and debates about current issues. UKLA also produces a range of books, written mainly with teachers and students in mind.
• regular responses to national consultations, including those organised through the DfES or QCA. Consequently, the UKLA often seeks information and responses from its members, as well as establishing a UKLA response to particular issues.
• promoting and disseminating research: provides support and small grants for literacy research.
• networking – UKLA helps its members to network both in the UK and through its worldwide contacts. UKLA's affiliation to the International Reading Association enables it to keep members in touch with events and ideas in other parts of the world. UKLA is also involved in specific international projects such as Project Connect, for which it provides some support for literacy education in Uganda.

Founded in 1963 as the United Kingdom Reading Association; renamed the United Kingdom Literacy Association in 2003.

Victoria and Albert Museum

South Kensington, London SW7 2RL
tel 020-7942 2000
email www.vanda@vam.ac.uk
website www.vam.ac.uk

Welsh Books Council/Cyngor Llyfrau Cymru

Castell Brychan, Aberystwyth, Ceredigion SY23 2JB
tel (01970) 624151 *fax* (01970) 625385
email castellbrychan@cllc.org.uk
website www.cllc.org.uk, www.gwales.com
Director Gwerfyl Pierce Jones

A national body funded directly by the Welsh Asssembly Government which provides a focus for the publishing industry in Wales. Awards grants for publishing in Welsh and English. Provides services to the trade in the fields of editing, design, marketing and distribution. The Council is a key enabling institution in the world of books and provides services and information in this field to all who are associated with it. Founded 1961.

Working Group Against Racism in Children's Resources

460 Wandsworth Road, London SW8 3LX
tel/fax 020-7627 4594

A registered charity dedicated to training anyone working with children in the identification and elimination of racist images, language and sterotypes in children's books, resources and play materials.

Writernet

Cabin V, Clarendon Buildings, 25 Horsell Road, London N5 1XL
tel 020-7609 7474 *fax* 020-7609 7557
email writernet@btinternet.com
website www.writernet.org.uk
Executive Director Jonathan Meth
Membership Rates on application

Works with all new writing in all performance contexts. Provides writers for all forms of live and recorded performance – working at any stage of their career – with a range of services which enable them to pursue their careers better. Aims to network writers into and through the industry, principally by providing information, advice, guidance and career development training to meet the requirements of writers and producers alike. Also provides a wide range of producers who employ writers with the opportunity to make more informed choices to meet their needs. Writernet is an innovative interface between the writer and producer. Founded 1985.

The Writers Advice Centre for Children's Books

The Courtyard Studio, 43A Lesbourne Road, Reigate, Surrey RH2 7JS
tel (01737) 242999
email WritersAdvice@aol.com
Director Cherith Baldry

Editorial and marketing advice to children's writers. Founded 1994.

Writers' Circles Handbook

Contact Jill Dick, Oldacre, Horderns Park Road, Chapel-en-le-Frith, High Peak SK23 9SY
tel (01298) 812305

email oldacre@bt.internet.com
website www.btinternet.com/~oldacre

Handbook for writers' circles with information, articles, and a comprehensive list of all known circles and groups meeting in the UK. Some overseas entries too. Regular free updates available after initial purchase. Cost: £5 post free.

The Writers' Guild of Great Britain

15 Britannia Street, London WC1X 9JN
020-7833 0777 *fax* 020-7833 4777
email admin@writersguild.org.uk
website www.writersguild.org.uk
General Secretary Bernie Corbett
Membership Open to all persons entitled to claim a single piece of written work of any length for which payment has been received under written contract in terms not less favourable than those existing in current minimum terms agreements negotiated by the Guild. Candidate membership (£75) is open to all those who are taking their first steps into writing but who have not yet received a contract. The minimum subscription is currently £150, or 1% of an author's income earned from professional writing sources in the previous calendar year, with a cap of £1500. All Full members are automatically members of the Authors Licensing and Collecting Society (ALCS). The Guild is a corporate member of the ALCS and maintains its links through representation on its board.

A trade union for all professional writers working in TV, radio, film, theatre, books and multimedia. It is affiliated to the Trades Union Congress (TUC) and has over 2000 members. The Guild represents writers over matters such as terms of pay and credits for their work. The Minimum Terms Agreements and advice services aim to safeguard writers against exploitation. Also offered are professional, cultural and social activities to help provide writers with a sense of community, making writing a less isolated occupation.

Members receive the *Writers' Bulletin*, which carries articles, letters and reports written by members, plus an email newsletter every Friday. Other benefits include free entry to the British Library reading rooms, and reduced entry to the National Film Theatre and regional film theatres. Founded in 1958.

Youth Libraries Group (YLG)

Bedington Central Library, Civic Way, Bebington, Wirral CH63 7PN
tel 0151-643 7232 *fax* 0151-643 7231
email bebington.childrens@merseymail.com
Secretary Sue Roe

The YLG is open to all members of the Chartered Institute for Library and Information Professionals (CILIP) who are interested in children's work. At a national level, its aims are:

- to influence the provision of library services for children and the provision of quality literature;
- to inspire and support all librarians working with children and young people; and
- to liaise with other national professional. organisations in pursuit of such aims.

At a local level, the YLG organises regular training courses, supports professional development and provides opportunities to meet colleagues. It holds an annual conference and judges the CILIP Carnegie and Kate Greenaway Awards. It also produces the journal *Youth Library Review* (2 p.a.) and produces various publications and posters.

Children's book and illustration prizes and awards

This list provides details of prizes, competitions and awards for children's writers and artists.

The Hans Christian Andersen Awards

Details International Board on Books for Young People, Nonnenweg 12, Postfach, CH-4003 Basel, Switzerland
tel (61) 272 29 17 *fax* (61) 272 27 57
email ibby@ibby.org
website www.ibby.org

The Medals are awarded every 2 years to a living author and an illustrator who by the outstanding value of their work are judged to have made a lasting contribution to literature for children and young people. 2004 award winners: Martin Waddell (author) and Max Velthuijs (illustrator).

Angus Book Award

Details Moyra Hood, Educational Resources Librarian, Educational Resources Service, Angus Council, Leisure Services, Bruce House, Wellgate, Arbroath DD11 3TL
tel (01241) 435008
email hood@angus.gov.uk
website www.angus.gov.uk/bookaward

An annual award originally set up as an Angus Council initiative to encourage pupils to read and enjoy quality teenage fiction. It is based on pupils not only voting for the winner but actively participating in all aspects of the award from selection of the shortlist to the award ceremony. The award involves 3rd-year pupils from all 8 secondary schools in Angus in reading 5 shortlisted titles. The shortlist is selected by teachers, librarians and pupils from books appropriate for the 14–15 year-old age group, written by authors living in the UK and published in paperback between July and June of the preceding year. Titles are chosen that reflect the range of themes which interest teenagers whilst challenging and interesting both committed and less enthusiastic readers. As part of the shortlisting process authors agree to visit schools and attend the Award ceremony, which takes place in May. The winner receives a miniature replica of the Aberlemno Serpent stone and £250. 2004 winner: *The Edge* by Alan Gibbons (Orion). Launched 1996.

Arts Council England Writers' Awards

The Literature Dept, Arts Council England, 14 Great Peter Street, London SW1P 3NQ
tel 020-7973 6442
email info.literature@artscouncil.org.uk
website www.artscouncil.org.uk

Arts Council England offers 15 awards annually of £7000 each for writers who need finance for a period of concentrated work on their next book. These Awards are open to writers who have been previously published in book form. Poetry, fiction, autobiography, biography, drama intended for publication, literature for young people, and other creative works are eligible. At least one award will be reserved specifically for a writer of Literature for Young People and the Clarissa Luard Award will be made to a fiction writer under 35 years of age. The Award winners will be determined by a panel of 3 judges, who are themselves writers.

Askews Torchlight Children's Book Award

Details Rob Sanderson, Askews Children's Book Awards, 218–222 North Road, Preston, Lancs. PR1 1SY
tel (01772) 555947
email roberts@askews.co.uk
website www.askews.co.uk

To highlight quality fiction for 9–12 year-olds, written by authors who have not already been shortlisted for major awards. 2004 winner: *How to Train your Dragon* by Cressida Cowell (Hodder Children's Books).

The Aventis Prizes for Science Books

Details The Royal Society, 6–9 Carlton House Terrace, London SW1Y 5AG
tel 020-7451 2513 *fax* 020-7451 2693
email scott.keir@royalsoc.ac.uk
website www.aventissciencebookprizes.com

These annual prizes reward books that make science more accessible to readers of all ages and backgrounds. Prizes of up to a total of £30,000 are awarded in 2 categories: General (£10,000) for a book with a general readership; and Junior (£10,000) for a book written for people aged under 14. Up to 5 shortlisted authors in each category receive £1000.

Eligible books should be written in English and their first publication in the UK must have been between 1 January and 31 December 2004. Seven copies of each entry should be supplied with a fully completed entry form. Publishers may submit any number of books for each prize. Entries may cover any aspect of science and technology but educational textbooks published for professional or specialist audiences are not eligible. 2004 prize-winners: Junior – *Really Rotten Experiments* by Nick Arnold and illustrated by Tony de Saulles (Scholastic); General – *The Short History of Nearly Everything* by Bill Bryson (Doubleday/Transworld). The Prizes are managed by the Royal Society in cooperation with the sponsor, Aventis. Founded 1988.

The Bisto Book of the Year Awards

Details The Administrator, Children's Books Ireland, 17 Lower Camden Street, Dublin 2, Republic of Ireland
tel (01) 872 5854 *fax* (01) 872 5854
email info@childrensbooksireland.com, bistoawards@childrensbooksireland.com

Annual awards open to authors and/or illustrators who were born in Ireland, or who were living in Ireland at the time of a book's publication.

The Bisto Book of the Year Award

An award of €3000 is presented to the overall winner (text and/or illustration). 2004 award winner: *Wings Over Delft* by Aubrey Flegg (O'Brien Press).

Bisto Merit Awards

A prize fund of €2400 is divided between 3 authors and/or illustrators. 2004 award winners: Anita Jeram for her illustrations on *You Can Do It, Sam* (Walker), Kate Thompson for *Origins* (Bodley Head) and Niamh Sharkey for *Ravenous Beast* (Walker).

Bisto Eilís Dillon Award

An award of €1000 is presented to an author for a first children's book. 2004 award winner: Alan Titley for *Amach* (An Gum).

Closing date: 15 January 2005 for work published between 1 January and 31 December 2004. Founded 1990.

Blue Peter Children's Book Awards

Details Fraser Ross Associates, 6 Wellington Avenue, Edinburgh EH6 7EQ
tel 0131-524 0160 *fax* 0131-524 0161
website www.scottishbooktrust.com, www.bbc.co.uk/bluepeter

Awarded annually and judged by a panel of celebrities and children. There are 3 categories: the Best Book to Keep Forever, the Book I Couldn't Put Down and the Best Book to Read Aloud. The Best Book of the Year is chosen from the winners of the 3 categories. Books must be published between 1 May and 31 April the preceding year. Winners are announced in December on a Blue Peter special broadcast by CBBC. Best Book of the Year 2003: *Mortal Engines* by Philip Reeve (Scholastic).

BolognaRagazzi Award

Piazza Costituzione 6, 40128 Bologna, Italy
tel (051) 282242/282361 *fax* (051) 6374011
email bookfair@bolognafiere.it
website www.bookfair.bolognafiere.it
Takes place April

Winners of the BolognaRagazzi Award are displayed at the Bologna Children's Book Fair. Prizes are given to encourage excellence in children's publishing in the categories of fiction, non-fiction and 'new horizons' (books from emerging countries). The books are judged on the basis of their creativity, educational value and artistic design.

Booktrust Early Years Awards

Details Booktrust, Book House, 45 East Hill, London SW18 2QZ
tel 020-8516 2973 *fax* 020-8516 2978
email kate@booktrust.org.uk, tarryn@booktrust.org.uk
Contact Kate Mervyn Jones, Tarryn McKay

The winners of each of 2 categories, Best Picture Book for Pre-School Children and the Best New Illustrator Award, will each receive a cheque for £2000. Closing date: June 2005. Winner 2003 (formerly called Sainsbury's Baby Book Award): *Happy Dog, Sad Dog* by Sam Lloyd (Little Tiger Press).

The Booktrust Teenage Prize

Details Booktrust, Book House, 45 East Hill, London SW18 2QZ
tel 020-8516 2986 *fax* 020-8516 2978
email hannah@booktrust.org.uk
Contact Hannah Rutland

The first annual national book prize to recognise and celebrate the best in young adult fiction. The author of the best book for teenagers receives £1500 and is chosen from a shortlist of 6. Eligible books must be fiction, aimed at teenagers between the ages of 13 and 16 and written in English by a citizen of the UK, or an author resident in the UK. The work must be published between 1 July and 30 June.

2003 winner: *The Curious Incident of the Dog in the Night-Time* by Mark Haddon (David Fickling Books). 2004 shortlist: *The Dark Beneath* by Alan Gibbons, *Looking for JJ* by Anne Cassidy, *Deep Secret* by Berlie Doherty, *Rani and Sukh* by Bali Rai, *Boy Kills Man* by Matt Whyman, *Fat Boy Swim* by Catherine Forde, *The Opposite of Chocolate* by Julie Bertagna, *Unique* by Alison Allen-Gray. Established 2003.

The Branford Boase Award

Details The Administrator, 8 Bolderwood Close, Bishopstoke, Eastleigh SO50 5PG
tel (01962) 826658 *fax* (01962) 856615
email anne@marleyhcl.freeserve.co.uk

An annual award is made to a first-time writer of a

full-length children's novel (age 7+) published in the preceding year; the editor is also recognised. Its aim is to encourage new writers for children and to recognise the role of perceptive editors in developing new talent. The Award was set up in memory of the outstanding children's writer Henrietta Branford and the gifted editor and publisher Wendy Boase who both died in 1999. Closing date for nominations: end of March of each year. 2004 winner: Mal Peet for *Keeper*, edited by Paul Harrison (Walker Books). Founded 2000.

British Book Awards

Details Merric Davidson, PO Box 60, Cranbrook, Kent TN17 2ZR
tel (01580) 212041 *fax* (01580) 212041
email nibbies@mdla.co.uk
website www.britishbookawards.com

Presented annually, major categories include: Author of the Year, Publisher of the Year, Bookseller of the Year, Children's Book of the Year (2004 winner: *The Curious Incident of the Dog in the Night-Time* by Mark Haddon, David Fickling Books). Founded 1989.

Carnegie Medal – see The CILIP Carnegie and Kate Greenaway Awards

The Children's Award

Details Charles Hart, Literature Dept, Arts Council England, 14 Great Peter Street, London SW1P 3NQ
tel 020-7973 6431
email charles.hart@artscouncil.org.uk
website www.artscouncil.org.uk

This award of £6000 is for playwrights who write plays of at least 45 minutes long for children up to the age of 12. Plays must have been professionally produced between 1 July 2004 and 30 June 2005. 2004 award winner: Charles Way for *Red Red Shoes* (Unicorn Theatre/The Place).

Children's Writers' & Artists' Yearbook 2005 Children's Story Competition – see page viii

The CILIP Carnegie and Kate Greenaway Awards

email marketing@cilip.org.uk
website www.ckg.org.uk

Recommendations for the following 2 awards are invited from members of CILIP (the Chartered Institute of Library and Information Professionals), who are asked to submit a preliminary list of not more than 2 titles for each award, accompanied by a 50-word appraisal justifying the recommendation of each book. The awards are selected by the Youth Libraries Group of CILIP.

Carnegie Medal

Awarded annually for an outstanding book for children (fiction or non-fiction) written in English and first published in the UK during the preceding year or co-published elsewhere within a 3-month time lapse. 2003 winner: *Ruby Holler* by Sharon Creech. 2004 shortlist: *The Fire Eaters* by David Almond (Hodder), *A Gathering Light* by Jennifer Donnelly (Bloomsbury), *The Curious Incident of the Dog in the Night-Time* by Mark Haddon (David Fickling), *The Garbage King* by Elizabeth Laird (Macmillan), *Private Peaceful* by Michael Morpurgo (HarperCollins) and *Sisterland* by Linda Newbery (David Fickling).

Kate Greenaway Medal

Awarded annually for an outstanding illustrated book for children first published in the UK during the preceding year or co-published elsewhere within a 3-month time lapse. Books intended for older as well as younger children are included, and reproduction will be taken into account. The Colin Mears Award (£5000) is awarded annually to the winner of the Kate Greenaway Medal. 2003 Medal winner: *Jethro Byrde, Fairy Child* by Bob Graham. 2004 shortlist: *The Shape Game* by Anthony Browne (Doubleday), *Beegu* by Alexis Deacon (Hutchinson), *Always and Forever* by Debi Gliori (written by Alan Durant) (Doubleday), *The Pea and the Princess* by Mini Grey (Red Fox), *Ella's Big Chance* by Shirley Hughes (Bodley Head), *Two Frogs* by Chris Wormell (Red Fox), *Bob Robber and Dancing Jane* by Bee Willey (written by Andrew Matthews) (Jonathan Cape) and *The Wolves in the Wall* by David McKean (written by Neil Gaiman) (Bloomsbury).

The CLPE Poetry Award

Details CLPE, Webber Street, London SE1 8QW
tel 020-7401 3382/3 *fax* 020-7928 4624
website www.clpe.co.uk/poetry

A new award that aims to honour excellence in children's poetry. Organised by the Centre for Literacy in Primary Education, it is to be presented annually in May/June for a book of poetry published in the preceding year. The book can be a single-poet collection, an anthology, an important critical work about children's poetry or the body of work of one contemporary poet writing for children. 2004 winner: *All the Best: Selected Poems* by Roger McGough (Puffin). Submissions deadline: end of February.

The Eleanor Farjeon Award

An annual prize of (minimum) £750 may be given to a librarian, teacher, author, artist, publisher, reviewer, TV producer or any other person working with or for children through books. Instituted in 1965 by the Children's Book Circle for distinguished services to children's books and named after the much-loved children's writer. 2003 award winner: Miriam Hodgson.

Foyle Young Poets of the Year Award – see page 119

Kate Greenaway Medal – see The CILIP Carnegie and Kate Greenaway Awards

The Guardian Children's Fiction Prize

tel 020-7239 9694
email books@guardian.co.uk

The Guardian's annual prize of £1500 is for a work of children's fiction (for children over 8; no picture books) published by a British or Commonwealth writer. The winning book is chosen by the Children's Book Editor together with a team of 3–4 other authors of children's books. 2003 winner: *The Curious Incident of the Dog in the Night-Time* by Mark Haddon (David Fickling Books).

Killie Writing Competition

Details Killie Writing Competition, Kilmarnock College KA3 7AT
tel (01355) 302160
email editor@killie.co.uk
website www.killie.co.uk

Annual competition usually with 4 categories: 5–7 year-olds, 8–11 year-olds, 12–16 year-olds, adults. Free expessive writing (poetry or fiction) with no limit on subject, word count, style or format. See website for guidelines. Work submitted must have been previously unpublished. Various prizes with the overall best entry receiving £1000 and a trophy. Closing date: April. Founded 2000.

Lancashire County Library Children's Book of the Year Award

Details Lancashire Country Library Headquarters, PO Box 61, County Hall, Preston PR1 8RJ
tel (01772) 264040 *fax* (01772) 264043
email library@lcl.lancscc.gov.uk

A prize of £500 and an engraved decanter is awarded to the best work of fiction for 12–14 year-olds, written by a UK author and first published between 1 September and 31 August of the previous year. The winner is announced in June. 2004 winner: *Poison* by Chris Wooding (Scholastic).

Literary Review Grand Poetry Prize

44 Lexington Street, London W1F 0LW
tel 020-7437 9392 *fax* 020-7734 1844
email litrev@dircon.co.uk

Literary Review runs a competition each month for poems on a given subject which are no more than 24 lines, rhyme, scan and make sense. The Grand Prize of £5000 is awarded to the best of these each year. Closing date: September. Founded 1990.

London Writers Competition

Details Arts Office, Room 224A, Wandsworth Town Hall, High Street, London SW18 2PU
tel 020-8871 8711
email arts@wandsworth.gov.uk
website www.wandsworth.gov.uk

Open to writers who live, work or study in the Greater London Area. Awards are made annually in 4 classes (Poetry, Short Story, Fiction for Children and Play) and prizes total £1000 in each class. Entries must be previously unpublished work. Judging is under the chairmanship of Francine Stock.

The Macmillan Prize for Children's Picture Book Illustration

Applications Imogen Blundell, Macmillan Children's Books, 20 New Wharf Road, London N1 9RR
tel 020-7014 6124
email i.blundell@macmillan.co.uk

Three prizes are awarded annually for unpublished children's book illustrations by art students in higher education establishments in the UK. Prizes: £1000 (1st), £500 (2nd) and £250 (3rd). 2004 winners: 1st – Emily Gravett (Brighton University) for *Wolves*; 2nd – Katherine Leake (NEWI School of Art and Design) for *The Best Chip*; 3rd – Daniel Taylor (UCE Birmingham) for *Mike and the Moon Kangaroo*.

Marsh Award for Children's Literature in Translation

Administered by National Centre for Research in Children's Literature, Digby Stuart College, University of Surrey Roehampton, Roehampton Lane, London SW15 5PU
tel 020-8392 3008
Contact Dr Gillian Lathey

This biennial award of £1000 is given to the translator of a book for children (aged 4–16) from a foreign language into English and published in the UK by a British publisher. Electronic books, and encyclopedias and other reference books, are not eligible. Next award: January 2005. 2003 award winner: Anthea Bell for *Where were you Robert?* (*Wa warst du, Robert?* by Jans Magnus Enzensberger). Founded 1996.

NASEN & TES Special Educational Needs Book Awards

Details Kerry Paige, NASEN/TES Book Awards, Admiral House, 66–68 East Smithfield, London E1W 1BX
email 020-7782 3403
email kerry.paige@newsint.co.uk
website www.specialneedsexhibition.co.uk

The Awards have been created to recognise the authors and publishers of high-quality books that inspire both children with special educational needs and their teachers. The awards will be presented in 3 categories: the Special Educational Needs Children's Book Award; the Special Educational Needs Academic Book Award; and the Books for Teaching and Learning Award. A prize of £500 will be awarded to the winning author of each category and to the publisher a quarter-page advertisement in the *TES* worth £1200 at a ceremony to be held at the NASEN & TES Special Needs Exhibition.

All books submitted for entry in any category must have been published in the UK between 21 July 2003 and 20 July 2004. A maximum of 3 books can be submitted per publisher. Closing date: July. 2003 award winner: *Freaks, Geeks & Asperger's Syndrome* by Luke Jackson (Jessica Kingsley).

The Nestlé Smarties Book Prize

Details Booktrust, Book House, 45 East Hill, London SW18 2QZ
tel 020-8516 2973/2972 *fax* 020-8516 2978
email kate@booktrust.org.uk, tarryn@booktrust.org.uk
Contact Kate Mervyn-Jones, Tarryn McKay

Three prizes (Gold, Silver and Bronze) are awarded to the 3 shortlisted books in each category (5 and under, 6–8 and 9–11 years). The Gold Award winners each receive £2500, the Silver Award winners receive £1500, and the Bronze Award winners receive £500. Eligible books must be published in the UK in the 12 months ending 30 September of the year of presentation and be a work of fiction or poetry for children written in English by a citizen or resident of the UK. Closing date for entries: contact Administrator. Sponsored by Nestlé Smarties. 2003 winners: 5 and under: *The Witch's Children and the Queen* by Ursula Jones and Russell Ayto (Orchard); 6–8 years: *Varjak Paw* by S.F. Said (David Fickling); 9–11 years: *The Fire Eaters* by David Almond (Hodder). Established in 1985.

New Zealand Post Book Awards for Children and Young Adults

Details c/o Booksellers New Zealand, PO Box 13248, Johnsonville, Wellington, New Zealand
tel (04) 478-5577 *fax* (04) 478-5519
email jayne.wasmuth@booksellers.conz
website www.booksellers.co.nz

Annual awards to celebrate excellence in, and provide recognition for, the best books for children and young adults published annually in New Zealand. Awards are presented in 4 categories: non-fiction, picture book, junior fiction and young adult fiction. The winner of each category wins $5000. One category winner is chosen as the *New Zealand Post* Book of the Year and receives an additional $5000. Eligible authors' and illustrators' books must have been published in New Zealand in the calendar year preceding the awards year. Closing date: December. Founded 1990.

North East Book Award

Details Eileen Armstrong, Cramlington High School, Cramlington, Northumberland NE23 6BN
tel (01670) 712311 *fax* (01670) 730598
website www.nebaonline.co.uk

Awarded to a book first published in paperback between April and the end of March the following year. The shortlist is selected by librarians and teachers and final winner by Year 10 students. Winner announced in January. 2004 award winner: *Blue* by Sue Mayfield (Hodder).

Nottingham Children's Book Awards

Nottingham City Libraries and Information Services, Leisure and Community Services, Isabella Street, Nottingham NG1 6AT
tel 0115-915 8727
website www.nottinghamchildrensbookaward.co.uk
Contact Elaine Dykes, Deborah Sheppard

Children's librarians in Nottingham form a long list of new fiction, divided into age categories: Foundation Stage, 5–7 year-olds, 8–9 year-olds and 10–11 year-olds. They then work with a panel of children to create the shortlist and children vote for their favourite book at their local library or in school. Winners are announced March. Organised by Nottingham City Libraries in partnership with Experian. 2004 winners – 3–4 year-olds: *Smile, Crocodile, Smile* by An Vrombout (OUP); 5–7 year-olds: *Dirty Birtie* by David Roberts (Little Tiger Press); 8–9 year-olds: *The Great Brain Robbery* by Alan Macdonald and Lizzie Finlay (Scholastic); 10–11 year-olds: *Molly Moon's Incredible Book of Hypnotism* by Georgia Byng (Macmillan). Launched 1999.

Peterloo Poets Open Poetry Competition

Details Peterloo Poets, The Old Chapel, Sand Lane, Calstock, Cornwall PL18 9QX

This annual competition offers a first prize of £2000 and 14 other prizes totalling £2100. There is also a 15–19 age group section with 5 prizes each of £100. Closing date: 1 March 2005. Founded 1986.

The Red House Children's Book Award

Details Marianne Adey, The Old Malt House, Aldbourne, Marlborough, Wilts. SN8 2DW
tel (01672) 540629 *fax* (01672) 541280
email marianneadey@aol.com

This award is given annually to authors of works of fiction for children published in the UK. Children participate in the judging of the award. 'Pick of the Year' booklist is published in conjunction with the award. 2004 winners: overall winner and winner older readers – *Private Peaceful* by Michael Morpurgo; category winner younger children – *Billy's Bucket* by Kes Gray and Gary Parsons (Red Fox); category winner younger readers – *The Mum Hunt* by Gwyneth Rees (Macmillan). Founded in 1980 by the Federation of Children's Book Groups.

RSPCA Young Photographer Awards

Details Publications Department, RSPCA, Wilberforce Way, Southwater, Horsham, West Sussex RH13 9RS
tel (0870) 7540455 *fax* (0870) 7530455
email publications@rspca.org.uk
website www.rspca.org.uk

Annual awards are made for animal photographs taken by young people in 2 age categories: under 12 and 12–18 year-olds. Prizes: overall winner (£250 cash, digital camera), age group winners (£100 cash, camera). Four runners-up in each age group receive a camera and £50 cash. Closing date for entries: 17 September 2004. Sponsored by Olympus and Truprint. 2003 award winner: Gareth Newton for his photograph of a hippopotamus under water. Founded 1990.

Sainsbury's Baby Book Award – see Booktrust Early Years Awards

Scottish Arts Council

Contact Gavin Wallace, Head of Literature, Scottish Arts Council, 12 Manor Place, Edinburgh EH3 7DD
tel 0131-226 6051
email gavin.wallace@scottisharts.org.uk

A limited number of writers' bursaries – up to £15,000 each – are offered to enable professional writers based in Scotland, including writers for children, to devote more time to writing. Priority is given to writers of fiction and verse and playwrights, but writers of literary non-fiction are also considered. Applications may be discussed with Gavin Wallace.

Scottish Book Awards

Up to 7 awards ranging from £2000 to £10,000 are made in the spring to new and established authors of published books in recognition of high standards of writing, for both adults and children. Preference is given to literary fiction and poetry, but literary non-fiction is also considered. Authors should be Scottish, resident in Scotland or have published books of Scottish interest. Entries from publishers only. Guidelines available on request.

Sheffield Children's Book Award

Details Book Award Co-ordinator, Schools Library Service, Sheffield
tel 0114-250 6843
email bookaward@dial.pipex.com
website www.sheffieldchildrensbookaward.org.uk

Presented annually in November to the book chosen as the most enjoyable by the children of Sheffield. Three category winners and one overall winner. 2003 award winner: *Molly Moon's Incredible Book of Hypnotism* by Georgia Byng (Macmillan).

WHSmith 'People's Choice' Awards

Details WHSmith PLC, Nations House, 103 Wigmore Street, London W1U 1WH
tel 020-7514 9623 *fax* 020-7514 9635
email elizabeth.walker@WHsmith.co.uk
website www.WHSmithbookawards.co.uk
Contact Elizabeth Walker, Group Events Marketing Manager

Now in their fourth year, WHSmith were the first UK book awards to have the winners voted for entirely by the public. Teams of celebrity and public judges choose the shortlists but any book published during the calendar year can be voted for. There are 9 Award categories in total, and 8 are voted for by the public: Fiction; Debut Novel; Lifestyle; Autobiography/Biography, Travel Writing; Business; Factual and Teen Choice. The public can vote in WHSmith stores, in libraries, by text, by Freepost or via the website. Voting starts in January and lasts 6 weeks, and the winners are announced in March.

The 9th category is the long-standing WHSmith Literary Award, the prize for good writing. This is not put out to public vote but is decided by a panel led by the Professor of English Literature at Merton College, Oxford and Chief Book Reviewer for *The Sunday Times*, John Carey. Three members of the public join at the shortlist stage to help decide the winner. Each winning author receives a trophy and £5000. 2004 Fiction winner: *Harry Potter and the Order of the Phoenix* by J.K. Rowling (Bloomsbury); 2004 Teen Choice winner: *The Wee Free Men* by Terry Pratchett (Corgi).

South Lanarkshire Book Award

Details Literacy Development Co-ordinator, Libraries and Community Learning
tel (01355) 248581 *fax* (01355) 229365
email margaret.cowan@southlanarkshire.gov.uk
website www.slc-learningcentres.org.uk

Awarded to the best teenage book. The initial selection is by librarians and the final winner is chosen by a panel of school students. The shortlist is announced in December and the winner announced in March the following year. 2004 award winner: *Malarkey* by Keith Gray (Red Fox).

The Spoken Word Awards

Contact The Spoken Word Publishing Association, c/o Zoe Howes, Macmillan Publishers Ltd, 20 New Wharf Road, London N1 9RR
tel 020-7014 6041 *fax* 020-7014 6141
email z.howes@macmillan.co.uk
website www.swpa.co.uk

Annual awards are made for excellence in the spoken word industry. There are over 40 judges from all areas of the industry including audiobook reviewers, radio broadcasters, producers, abridgers, etc. Closing date: April. Award winners: 6 and under category: *Horrid Henry's Stinkbomb* by Francesca Simon, narrated by Miranda Richardson (Orion); Over 6: *The Curious Incident of the Dog in the Night-Time* by Mark Haddon, narrated by Ben Tibber (Random); Classic fiction: *Chitty Chitty Bang Bang* by Ian Fleming, narrated by Andrew Sachs (Puffin).

Tir Na N-og Awards

Details Welsh Books Council, Castell Brychan, Aberystwyth, Ceredigion SY23 2JB
tel (01970) 624151 *fax* (01970) 625385
email menna.lloydwilliams@cllc.org.uk
website www.cllc.org.uk

There are 3 annual awards to children's authors and illustrators: best original Welsh-language fiction, including short stories and picture books – 2004 winner: *Iawn Boi?);-* by Caryl Lewis (Y Lolfa); best original Welsh-language non-fiction book of the year – 2004 winner: *Stori Dafydd ap Gwilym* by Gwyn Thomas and Margaret Jones (Y Lolfa); best English book with an authentic Welsh background – 2004 winner: *The Battle of Mametz Wood, 1916*, Robert Phillips (CAA). Total prize value is £3000. Founded 1976.

Christopher Tower Poetry Prize – see page 119

UKLA Children's Book Awards

Details Debbie Wright
tel (01491) 836631
email debbie.wright@oxfordshire.gov.uk
website www.ukla.org
Submissions Administrative Secretary, United Kingdom Literacy Association, Upton House, Baldock Street, Royston, Herts. SG8 5AY

Biennial awards are presented for excellence in the field of literacy. 'Literacy is interpreted here as being about the expression of meaning and ideas through challenging use of language, imaginative expression, illustration and other graphics.' Three copies of each book should be submitted. The awards are presented at the United Kingdom Literacy Association International Conference in July.

The V&A Illustration Awards

Enquiries The Word & Image Department, Victoria and Albert Museum, London SW7 2RL
tel 020-7942 2414
website www.nal.vam.ac.uk
Contact Annemarie Riding *tel/fax* 020-7942 2381
email a.riding@vam.ac.uk

These annual awards are given to practising book and magazine illustrators, for work first published in Great Britain in the 12 months preceding the judging of the awards. There are 6 awards, including for the first time in 2004, a new prize for book covers. A first and second prize winner will be chosen from the 3 following award categories: book illustration, book cover and jacket illustration, and editorial illustration. Of the 3 category winners, one will be selected to receive the Premier Award of £2500 as the best overall illustration. The other 2 winners will each receive £1000; while the 3 second prize winners will each be awarded £500. Closing date for submissions: mid July. 2003 award winner: Nick Maland for *You've Got Dragons* by Kathryn Cave (Hodder).

Whitbread Book Awards

Details Anna O'Kane, The Booksellers Association, Minster House, 272 Vauxhall Bridge Road, London SW1V 1BA
tel 020-7802 0802 *fax* 020-7802 0803
email anna.okane@booksellers.co.uk
website www.whitbreadbookawards.co.uk

The awards celebrate and promote the most enjoyable contemporary British writing. Judged in 2 stages and offering a total of £50,000 prize money, the awards are open to 5 categories: Novel, First Novel, Biography, Poetry and Children's. They are judged by a panel of 3 judges and the winner in each category receives an award of £5000. Nine final judges then choose the Whitbread Book of the Year from the winners of all categories. The winner receives a cheque for £25,000. Writers must have lived in Great Britain or Ireland for 3 or more years. Submissions must be received from publishers. Closing date: early July.

2004 Children's Award winner: *The Fire Eaters* by David Almond (Hodder); Whitbread Book of the Year: *The Curious Incident of the Dog in the Night-Time* by Mark Haddon (Jonathan Cape).

Write A Story for Children Competition

Entry forms The Academy of Children's Writers, PO Box 95, Huntingdon, Cambs. PE28 5RL
tel (01487) 832752
email per_ardua@lycos.co.uk

Three prizes (1st £1000, 2nd £200, 3rd £100) are awarded annually for a short story for children, maximum 1000 words, by an unpublished writer of children's fiction. Send sae for details. Founded 1984.

Young Writers' Programme

Details Young Writers' Programme, Royal Court Young Writers' Programme, Sloane Square, London SW1W 8AS
tel 020-7565 5034 *fax* 020-7565 5001

Anyone aged 13–25 can submit a play on any subject. A selection of plays are professionally presented by the Royal Court Theatre with the writers fully involved in rehearsal and production. Pre-Festival Development Workshops are run by professional theatre practitioners and designed to help everyone attending to write a play. Playwriting projects run all year round.

Children's literature festivals and trade fairs

We give here a selection of literature festivals and general arts festivals which include literature events for children.

Bank of Scotland Children's International Theatre Festival

45A George Street, Edinburgh EH2 2HT
tel 0131-225 8050 *fax* 0131-225 6440
email info@imaginate.org.uk
Director Tony Reekie, *General Manager* Tessa Rennie
Takes place Last week of May and first week of June

This annual event attracts an audience of children, teachers, parents, carers and friends from across Scotland. If offers the more international theatre for children and young people than any other event in the UK. An outreach programme takes live theatre into schools and communities in Edinburgh and the Lothians during the Festival. It also takes international theatre from the Festival to perform at venues across Scotland reaching children in communities from Shetland to Dumfriesshire to the Borders. See also Imaginate on page 268. Founded 1990.

Bath Literature Festival

Bath Festivals Trust, 5 Broad Street, Bath BA1 5LJ
tel (01225) 462231, (01225) 463362 (box office)
fax (01225) 445551
email info@bathfestivals.org.uk
website www.bathlitfest.org.uk
Director Sarah LeFanu
Takes place 26 Feb–6 March 2005

An annual festival with leading guest writers. Includes readings, debates, discussions and workshops, and events for children and young people. Programme available from box office in December.

Bologna Children's Book Fair

Piazza Costituzione 6, 40128 Bologna, Italy
tel (051) 282242/282361 *fax* (051) 6374011
email bookfair@bolognafiere.it
website www.bookfair.bolognafiere.it
Takes place April

Held annually, the Bologna Children's Book Fair is the leading children's publishing event. Publishers, authors and illustrators, literary agents, TV and film producers and many other members of the children's publishing community meet in Bologna to buy and sell copyrights, establish new contacts and strengthen their professional relationships, discover new illustrators, develop new business opportunities, learn about the latest trends and developments and explore children's educational materials, including new media products.

Approximately 4000 professionals active in children's publishing attend from 70 countries. For most of the week, entry is restricted to those in the publishing trade, but there is one open day for the public to attend.

Selected by a jury, the Bologna Illustrators Exhibition showcases fiction and non-fiction children's book illustrators, both new and established, from all over the world. Many illustrators also visit the Fair to show their latest portfolios to publishers.

Winners of the BolognaRagazzi Award are displayed. Prizes are given to encourage excellence in children's publishing in the categories of fiction, non-fiction and 'new horizons' (books from emerging countries), and books are judged on the basis of their creativity, educational value and artistic design. The Hans Christian Andersen Award is announced at the Fair.

The Bologna Children's Book Fair, working with The Association of Educational Publishers (US), has created the Global Learning Initiative (GLA), an international business-to-business event created by and for educational publishers serving the K–12 market. The GLA provides a rights and commercial centre specifically for the growing international community of supplemental educational publishers.

Book Now!

Education, Arts & Leisure Department, Orleans House Gallery, Riverside, Twickenham TW1 3DJ
tel 020-8831 6000 *fax* 020-8744 0507
website www.richmond.gov.uk
Takes place Throughout Nov

An annual literature festival covering a broad range of subjects. Leading British and overseas guest writers and poets hold discussions, talks, debates and workshops and give readings. There are also exhibitions, storytelling sessions and a schools programme.

Cheltenham Festival of Literature

Town Hall, Imperial Square, Cheltenham, Glos. GL50 1QA
tel (01242) 227979 (box office), 237377 (brochure), 263494 (festival office) *fax* (01242) 256457
email adam.pushkin@cheltenham.gov.uk
website www.cheltenhamfestivals.co.uk
Artistic Director Christopher Cook
Takes place October and April each year

This annual festival is the largest of its kind in Europe. Events include talks and lectures, poetry readings, novelists in conversation, exhibitions, discussions, workshops and a large bookshop. *Book It!* is a festival for children within the main festival with an extensive programme of events and a multimedia room. Brochures are available in August.

Chester Festivals – Literature

8 Abbey Square, Chester CH1 2HU
tel (01244) 319985 *fax* (01244) 341200
email freda@chesterfestivals.co.uk
Festival Administrator Freda Hadwen
Takes place 2–29 2004, 8–29 Oct 2005

An annual festival commencing the first weekend in October. Events featuring international, national and local writers and poets are part of the programme, as well as a literary lunch and festival dinner. There is a poetry competition for school children, events for children and workshops for adults. A Cheshire Prize for Literature is awarded each year; only residents in Cheshire are eligible.

Children's Book Festival

Festival Office, Children's Books Ireland, 17 Lower Camden Street, Dublin 2, Republic of Ireland
website www.childrensbooksireland.com
Contact Emma Walsh, Festival Co-ordinator
Takes place 14–31 October 2004

Annual nationwide celebration of reading and books in Ireland with the emphasis being on fun!

Children's Book Week

Book House, 45 East Hill, London SW18 2QZ
tel 020-8516 2977 *fax* 020-8516 2998
email info@booktrust.org.uk
websites www.booktrust.org.uk, www.booktrusted.com
Takes place First full week of October

The annual National Children's Book Week celebrates the wonderful world of children's books. It is an annual focus on the enjoyment of reading, with the aim of encouraging as many children as possible to get into books. The Week is based on the belief that designating a special day or week at school, in libraries and at home, for fun book activities can help children to see reading as a source of pleasure – as well as trying to encourage them to write themselves, to discuss and share books and to explore libraries and bookshops. All over the UK, schools, libraries and bookshops hold events and activities.

Edinburgh International Book Festival

Scottish Book Centre, 137 Dundee Street, Fountainbridge, Edinburgh EH11 1BG
tel 0131-228 5444 *fax* 0131-228 4333
email admin@edbookfest.co.uk
website www.edbookfest.co.uk
Director Catherine Lockerbie
Takes place 13–29 Aug 2005

Now established as Europe's largest book event for the public. In addition to a unique independent bookselling operation, over 600 writers contribute to the programme of events. Programme details available in June.

Global Learning Initiative – see Bologna Children's Book Fair

The Guardian Hay Festival

Festival Office, The Drill Hall, 25 Lion Street, Hay-on-Wye HR3 5AD
tel (01497) 821217, (01497) 821299 (box office)
fax (01497) 821066
email admin@hayfestival.co.uk
website www.hayfestival.com
Takes place May/June

This annual festival aims to celebrate the best in writing and performance from around the world, to commission new work, and to promote and encourage young writers of excellence and potential. Over 200 events in 10 days with leading guest writers. Programme published April.

Guildford Book Festival

c/o Tourist Information Office, 14 Tunsgate, Guildford GU1 3QT
tel (01483) 225388
email book-festival-director@surrey.ac.uk
website www.guildford.org.uk, www.guildfordbookfestival.co.uk
Festival Director Glenis Pycraft
Takes place 17–31 Oct 2004

An annual festival with a varied programme of over 60 events held at different venues in Guildford, including readings, discussions, literary lunches and teas, performance poetry, workshops, competitions. High-profile authors and many children's events. Its aim is to involve, instruct and entertain all who care about literature and to encourage in children a love of reading. Founded 1990.

Hay Festival – see The Guardian Hay Festival

Lowdham Book Festival

4th Floor, Arts, County Hall, West Bridgford, Nottingham NG2 7QP
tel 0115-977 4435
email ross.bradshaw@nottscc.gov.uk
website www.lowdhambookfestival.co.uk
Contact Ross Bradshaw, Literature Officer
Takes place June

An annual 10-day festival of literature events for adults and children with a daily programme of high-profile national writers. There is a writer-in-residence and a book fair on the last Saturday.

Northern Children's Book Festival

22 Highbury, Jesmond, Newcastle Upon Tyne NE2 3DY
tel 0191-2813289
email annkey@waitrose.com
website www.ncbf.org.uk
Chairperson Ann Key
Takes place 10–22 Nov 2004

An annual festival to bring authors, illustrators, poets and performers to children in schools, libraries and community centres across the North East of England. About 36 authors visit the North East over the 2-week period for 2–8 days, organised by the 12 local authorities. The climax of the festival is a huge public event in a different part of the North East each year when over 4000 children and their families visit to take part in author seminars, drama workshops, and to enjoy a variety of book-related activities. The Gala Day will be on 20 November 2004.

Off the Shelf Literature Festival

Central Library, Surrey Street, Sheffield S201 1XZ
tel 0114-273 4716 *fax* 0114-273 5009
email offtheshelf@sheffield.gov.uk
website www.offtheshelf.org.uk
Contacts Maria de Souza, Su Walker
Takes place 16–30 Oct 2004

The festival comprises a wide range of events for adults and children, including author visits, writing workshops, storytelling, competitions, theatre performances and exhibitions. Programme available in September.

Oxford Literary Festival – see The Sunday Times Oxford Literary Festival

Poetry International

Literature Section, Royal Festival Hall, South Bank Centre, London SE1 8XX
tel 020-7921 0906 *fax* 020-7928 2049
email awhitehead@rfh.org.uk
website www.rfh.org.uk
Contact Angela Whitehead
Takes place Oct 2004, 2006 (biennial)

The biggest poetry festival in the British Isles, bringing together a wide range of poets from around the world. It includes readings, workshops, discussions and events for children. The Literature Section also runs a year-round programme of readings, talks and debates.

Readathon

Hele Mill, Marham Church, Bude, Devon EX23 OJA
tel (0870) 240 1124
website www.readathon.org

Often run in schools and libraries during Children's Book Week, children undertake to read books, or do other literacy-based activities, in return for pledges of money for charity. See page 273.

Royal Court Young Writers' Festival

The Royal Court Young Writers' Programme, Sloane Square, London SW1W 8AS
tel 020-7565 5050
Contact The Administrator
Takes place Biennially

A national festival which anyone aged 13–25 can enter. Promising plays which arise from the workshops are then developed and performed at the Royal Court's Theatre Upstairs (see page 285).

The Sunday Times Oxford Literary Festival

301 Woodstock Road, Oxford OX2 7NY
tel (01865) 514149 *fax* (01865) 514804
email oxford.literary.festival@ntlworld.com
website www.sundaytimes-oxfordliteraryfestival.co.uk
Festival Directors Angela Prysor-Jones, Sally Dunsmore
Takes place 2 weeks prior to Easter

An annual 6-day festival for both adults and children. Presents topical debates, fiction and non-fiction discussion panels, and adult and children's authors who have recently published books. Topics range from contemporary fiction to discussions on politics, history, science, gardening, food, poetry, philosophy, art and crime fiction.

Tales & Trails

Mythstories Museum, The Morgan Library, Aston Street, Wem, Shrops. SY4 5AU
tel (01939) 235500
email tandt@mythstories.com
website www.mythstories.com
Contact Del Quarréll, Curator/Storyteller
Takes place Three times a year: March, May, Sept

A strolling festival of storytelling with morning storywalks and evening story concerts featuring Britain's top storytellers and the cream of Border storytellers.

World Book Day

World Book Day, 66 Burlington Lane, London W4 2RR
tel 020-7631 2666 *fax* 020-7631 2699
email pr@colmangettypr.co.uk
website www.worldbookday.com
Contact Cathy Schofield
Takes place Early March

An annual celebration of books and reading aimed at promoting their value and creating the readers of the future. Every schoolchild in full-time education receives a £1 book token. Events take place all over the UK in schools, bookshops, libraries and arts centres.

World Book Day was designated by UNESCO as a worldwide celebration of books and reading, and is marked in over 30 countries. It is a partnership of publishers, booksellers and interested parties who work together to promote books and reading for the personal enrichment and enjoyment of all.

A main aim of World Book Day is to encourage children to explore the pleasures of books and reading by providing them with the opportunity to have a book of their own. To support this aim, a Schools' Pack full of ideas and activities, display material and information about how to get involved in World Book Day is mailed to schools from mid-January. There are a range of activities and events organised by thousands of people around the country.

Thanks to the generosity of National Book Tokens Ltd and numerous participating booksellers, schoolchildren are entitled to receive a World Book Day £1 Book Token (or equivalent Euro Book Token in Ireland). The Book Token can be exchanged for one of the 6 specially published World Book Day £1 Books (while stocks last), or is redeemable against any one of the Recommended Reads, or a book or audiobook of their choice at a participating bookshop or book club. Details of the £1 Books and Recommended Reads can be found in the Resources section of the website. See also World Book Day Online Festival and Readathon entries.

World Book Day Online Festival

website www.worldbookdayfestival.com
Takes place March

Readers of every age across the world have the opportunity to chat online with famous children's authors (see website for details), watch specially commissioned films, and join in online chats and discussion forums. Transcripts of the web chats are archived at the website so they can be revisited. The Festival site attracts three-quarters of a million hits from over 60 countries on World Book Day; and readers in 100 countries continue to use the site via the Festival archive.

The Festival is funded by Arts Council England and is a partnership of publishers, booksellers and interested parties who work together to promote books and reading for the personal enrichment and enjoyment of all.

Young Readers Birmingham

Children's Office, Central Library, Chamberlain Square, Birmingham B3 3HQ
tel 0121-303 3368 *fax* 0121-464 1004
email patsy.heap@birmingham.gov.uk
website www.birmingham.gov.uk/youngreaders
Contact Patsy Heap
Takes place 21 May–4 June 2005

An annual festival targeted at young people aged 0–19 and adults who care for or work with them. It aims to motivate them to enjoy reading and through this to encourage literacy; to provide imaginative access to books, writers and storytellers; to encourage families to share reading for pleasure; to provide a national focus for the celebration of books and reading for children and young people and help raise the media profile of children's books and writing. Approximately 150 events take place.

Finance for writers and artists

FAQs for writers

Peter Vaines, a chartered accountant and barrister, addresses some questions frequently asked by writers.

What can a working writer claim against tax?

A working writer is carrying on a business and can therefore claim all the expenses which are incurred wholly and exclusively for the purposes of that business. A list showing most of the usual expenses is contained on page 295 of this *Yearbook* but there will be other expenses which can be allowed in special circumstances.

Strictly, only expenses which are incurred for the sole purpose of the business can be claimed; there must be no 'duality of purpose' so an item of expenditure cannot be divided into private and business parts. However, the Inland Revenue is usually quite flexible and is prepared to allow all reasonable expenses (including apportioned sums) where the amounts can be commercially justified.

Allowances can also be claimed for the cost of business assets such as a motor car, personal computers, fax, copying machines and all other equipment (including books) which may be used by the writer. An allowance of 25% of the cost can be claimed on the reducing balance each year and for most assets (except cars) an allowance of 40% can be claimed in the first year of purchase. This is increased to 50% for the year ending 5 April 2005. Some expenditure on information technology now benefits from a special 100% allowance. See page 297 for further details of the deductions available in respect of capital expenditure.

Can I request interest on fees owed to me beyond 30 days of my invoice?

Yes. A writer is like any other person carrying on a business and is entitled to charge interest at a rate of 8% over bank base rate on any debt outstanding for more than 30 days – although the period of credit can be varied by agreement between the parties. It is not compulsory to claim the interest; it is up to you to decide whether to enforce the right.

What can I do about bad debts?

A writer is in exactly the same position as anybody else carrying on a business over the payment of his or her invoices. It is generally not commercially sensible to insist on payment in advance but where the work involved is substantial (which will normally be the case with a book), it is usual to receive one third of the fee on signature, one third of the fee on delivery of the manuscript and the remaining one third on publication. On other assignments, perhaps not as substantial as a book, it could be worthwhile seeking 50% of the fee on signature and the other 50% on delivery. This would provide a degree of protection in case of cancellation of the assignment because of changes of policy or personnel at the publisher.

What financial disputes can I take to the Small Claims Court?

If somebody owes you money you can take them to the Small Claims Section of your local County Court, which deals with financial disputes up to £5000. The procedure is much less formal than normal court proceedings and involves little expense. It is not necessary to have a solicitor. You fill in a number of forms, turn up on the day and explain the background to why you are owed the money. Full details of the procedure can be found on: www.courtservice.gov.uk

If I receive an advance, can I divide it between two tax years?

Yes. There used to be a system known as 'spreading' but in 2001 a new system called 'averaging' was introduced. This enables writers (and others engaged in the creation of literary, dramatic works or designs) to average the profits of two or more consecutive years if the profits for one year are less than 75% of the profits for the highest year. This relief can apply even if the work takes less than 12 months to create. Both the spreading relief and the averaging relief allow the writer to avoid the higher rates of tax which might arise if the income in respect of a number of years' work were all to be concentrated in a single year.

How do I make sure I am taxed as a self-employed person so that tax and National Insurance Contributions are not deducted at source?

To be taxed as a self-employed person under Schedule D you have to make sure that the contract for the writing cannot be regarded as a contract of employment. This is unlikely to be the case with a professional author. The subject is highly complex but one of the most important features is that the publisher must not be in a position to direct or control the author's work. Where any doubt exists, the author might find the publisher deducting tax and National Insurance Contributions as a precaution and that would clearly be highly disadvantageous. The author would be well advised to discuss the position with the publisher before the contract is signed to agree that he or she should be treated as self employed and that no tax or National Insurance Contributions will be deducted from any payments. If such agreement cannot be reached, professional advice should immediately be sought so that the detailed technical position can be explained to the publisher.

Is it a good idea to operate through a limited company?

It can be a good idea for a self-employed writer to operate through a company but generally only where the income is quite large. The costs of operating a company can outweigh any benefit if the writer is paying tax only at the basic rate. Where the writer is paying tax at the higher rate of 40%, being able to retain some of the income in a company at a tax rate of only 19% is obviously attractive. However, this will be entirely ineffective if the writer's contract with the publisher would otherwise be an employment. The whole subject of operating through a company is complex and professional advice is essential.

When does it become necessary to register for VAT?

Where the writer's self-employed income (from all sources, not only writing) exceeds £58,000 in the previous 12 months or is expected to do so in the next 30 days, he or she must register for VAT and add VAT to all his/her fees. The publisher will pay the VAT to the writer, who must pay the VAT over to the Customs and Excise each quarter. Any VAT the writer has paid on business expenses and on the purchase of business assets can be deducted. It will be possible for some authors to take advantage of the simplified system for VAT payments which applies to small businesses. This involves a flat rate payment of VAT without any need to keep records of VAT on expenses.

If I make a loss from my writing can I get any tax back?

Where a writer makes a loss, the Inland Revenue may suggest that the writing is only a hobby and not a professional activity thereby denying any relief or tax deduction for the loss. However, providing the writing is carried out on a sensible commercial basis with an expectation of profits, any resulting loss can be offset against any other income the writer may have for the same or the previous year.

Income tax

Despite attempts by successive Governments to simplify our taxation system, the subject has become increasingly complicated. Peter Vaines, a chartered accountant and barrister, gives a broad outline of taxation from the point of view of writers and other creative professionals. The proposals in the April 2004 Budget are broadly reflected in this article.

How income is taxed

Generally

Authors are usually treated for tax purposes as carrying on a profession and are taxed in a similar fashion to other professionals, i.e. as self-employed persons taxed under Schedule D. This article is directed to self-employed persons only, because if a writer is employed he or she will be subject to the much less advantageous rules which apply to employment income.

Attempts are often made by employed persons to shake off the status of 'employee' and to attain 'freelance' status so as to qualify for the advantages of Schedule D, such attempts meeting with varying degrees of success. The problems involved in making this transition are considerable and space does not permit a detailed explanation to be made here – individual advice is necessary if difficulties are to be avoided.

Particular attention has been paid by the Inland Revenue to journalists and to those engaged in the entertainment industry with a view to reclassifying them as employees so that PAYE is deducted from their earnings. This blanket treatment has been extended to other areas and, although it is obviously open to challenge by individual taxpayers, it is always difficult to persuade the Inland Revenue to change its views.

There is no reason why employed people cannot carry on a freelance business in their spare time. Indeed, aspiring authors, painters, musicians, etc, often derive so little income from their craft that the financial security of an employment, perhaps in a different sphere of activity, is necessary. The existence of the employment is irrelevant to the taxation of the freelance earnings although it is most important not to confuse the income or expenditure of the employment with the income or expenditure of the self-employed activity. The Inland Revenue is aware of the advantages which can be derived by an individual having 'freelance' income from an organisation

Arts Council category A awards

- Direct or indirect musical, design or choreographic commissions and direct or indirect commission of sculpture and paintings for public sites.
- The Royalty Supplement Guarantee Scheme.
- The contract writers' scheme.
- Jazz bursaries.
- Translators' grants.
- Photographic awards and bursaries.
- Film and video awards and bursaries.
- Performance Art Awards.
- Art Publishing Grants.
- Grants to assist with a specific project or projects (such as the writing of a book) or to meet specific professional expenses such as a contribution towards copying expenses made to a composer or to an artist's studio expenses.

of which he or she is also an employee, and where such circumstances are contrived, it can be extremely difficult to convince an Inspector of Taxes that a genuine freelance activity is being carried on. Where the individual operates through a company or partnership providing services personally to a particular client, and would be regarded as an employee if the services were supplied directly by the individual, additional problems arise from the notorious IR35 legislation and professional advice is essential.

For those starting in business or commencing work on a freelance basis the Inland Revenue produces a very useful booklet, *Starting in Business (IR28)*, which is available from any tax office.

Income

For income to be taxable it need not be substantial, nor even the author's only source of income; earnings from casual writing are also taxable but this can be an advantage, because occasional writers do not often make a profit from their writing. The expenses incurred in connection with writing may well exceed any income receivable and the resultant loss may then be used to reclaim tax paid on other income. There may be deducted from the income certain allowable expenses and capital allowances which are set out in more detail below. The possibility of a loss being used as a basis for a tax repayment is fully appreciated by the Inland Revenue, which sometimes attempts to treat casual writing as a hobby so that any losses incurred cannot be used to reclaim tax; of course by the same token any income receivable would not be chargeable to tax. This treatment may sound attractive but it should be resisted vigorously because the Inland Revenue does not hesitate to change its mind when profits begin to arise. In the case of exceptional or non-recurring writing, such as the autobiography of a sports personality or the memoirs of a politician, it could be better to be treated as pursuing a hobby and not as a professional author. Sales of copyright cannot be charged to income tax unless the recipient is a professional author. However, the proceeds of sale of copyright may be charged to capital gains tax, even by an individual who is not a professional author.

Arts Council category B awards

- Bursaries to trainee directors.
- Bursaries for associate directors.
- Bursaries to people attending full-time courses in arts administration (the practical training course).
- In-service bursaries to theatre designers and bursaries to trainees on the theatre designers' scheme.
- In-service bursaries for administrators.
- Bursaries for actors and actresses.
- Bursaries for technicians and stage managers.
- Bursaries made to students attending the City University Arts Administration courses.
- Awards, known as the Buying Time Awards, made not to assist with a specific project or professional expenses but to maintain the recipient to enable him or her to take time off to develop his personal talents. These at present include the awards and bursaries known as the Theatre Writing Bursaries, awards and bursaries to composers, awards and bursaries to painters, sculptures and print makers, literature awards and bursaries.

Royalties

Where the recipient is a professional author, a series of cases has laid down a clear principle that sales of copyright are taxable as income and not as capital receipts. Similarly, lump sums on account of, or in advance of royalties are also taxable as income in the year of receipt, subject to a claim for averaging relief (see below).

Copyright royalties are generally paid without deduction of income tax. However, if royalties are paid to a person who normally lives abroad, tax must be deducted by the payer or his agent at the time the payment is made unless arrangements are made with the Inland Revenue for payments to be made gross under the terms of a Double Taxation Agreement with the other country.

Arts Council grants

Persons in receipt of grants from the Arts Council or similar bodies will be concerned whether or not such grants are liable to income tax. The Inland Revenue has issued a Statement of Practice after detailed discussions with the Arts Council regarding the tax treatment of the awards. Grants and other receipts of a similar nature have now been divided into two categories (see boxes) – those which are to be treated by the Inland Revenue as chargeable to tax and those which are not. Category A awards are considered to be taxable; awards made under category B are not chargeable to tax.

This Statement of Practice has no legal force and is used merely to ease the administration of the tax system. It is open to anyone in receipt of a grant or award to disregard the agreed statement and challenge the Inland Revenue view on the merits of their particular case. However, it must be recognised that the Inland Revenue does not issue such statements lightly and any challenge to their view would almost certainly involve a lengthy and expensive action through the Courts.

The tax position of persons in receipt of literary prizes will generally follow a decision by the Special Commissioners in connection with the Whitbread Literary Award. In that case it was decided that the prize was not part of the author's professional income and accordingly not chargeable to tax. The precise details are not available because decisions of the Special Commissioners were not, at that time, reported unless an appeal was made to the High Court; the Inland Revenue chose not to appeal against this decision. Details of the many literary awards which are given each year start on page 278, and this decision is of considerable significance to the winners of each of these prizes. It would be unwise to assume that all such awards will be free of tax as the precise facts which were present in the case of the Whitbread award may not be repeated in another case; however it is clear that an author winning a prize has some very powerful arguments in his or her favour, should the Inland Revenue seek to charge tax on the award.

Allowable expenses

To qualify as an allowable business expense, expenditure has to be laid out wholly and exclusively for business purposes. Strictly there must be no 'duality of purpose', which means that expenditure cannot be apportioned to reflect the private and business usage, e.g. food, clothing, telephone, travelling expenses, etc. However, the Inland Revenue does not usually interpret this principle strictly and is prepared to allow all reasonable expenses (including apportioned sums) where the amounts can be commercially justified.

It should be noted carefully that the expenditure does not have to be 'necessary', it merely has to be incurred 'wholly and exclusively' for business purposes. Naturally, however, expenditure of an outrageous and wholly unnecessary character might well give rise to a presumption that it was not really for business purposes. As with all things, some expenses are unquestionably allowable and some expenses are equally unquestionably not allowable – it is the grey area in between which gives rise to all the difficulties and the outcome invariably depends on negotiation with the Inland Revenue.

Great care should be taken when claiming a deduction for items where there may be a 'duality of purpose' and negotiations should be conducted with more than usual care and courtesy – if provoked the Inspector of Taxes may well choose to allow nothing. An appeal is always possible although unlikely to succeed as a string of cases in the Courts has clearly demonstrated. An example is the case of *Caillebotte* v. *Quinn* where the taxpayer (who normally had lunch at home) sought to claim the excess cost of meals incurred because he was working a long way from his home. The taxpayer's arguments failed because he did not eat only in order to work, one of the reasons for his eating was in order to sustain his life; a duality of purpose therefore existed and no tax relief was due.

Other cases have shown that expenditure on clothing can also be disallowed if it is the kind of clothing which is in everyday use, because clothing is worn not only to assist the pursuit of one's profession but also to accord with public decency. This duality of purpose may be sufficient to deny relief – even where the particular type of clothing is of a kind not otherwise worn by the taxpayer. In the case of *Mallalieu* v. *Drummond* a barrister failed to obtain a tax deduction for items of sombre clothing that she purchased specifically for wearing in Court. The House of Lords decided that a duality of purpose existed because clothing represented part of her needs as a human being.

Allowances

Despite the above, Inspectors of Taxes are not usually inflexible and the following list of expenses are among those generally allowed.

(a) Cost of all materials used up in the course of preparation of the work.

(b) Cost of typewriting and secretarial assistance, etc; if this or other help is obtained from one's spouse then it is entirely proper for a deduction to be claimed for the amounts paid for the work. The amounts claimed must actually be paid to the spouse and should be at the market rate although some uplift can be made for unsocial hours, etc. Payments to a wife (or husband) are of course taxable in her (or his) hands and should therefore be most carefully considered. The wife's earnings may also be liable for National Insurance contributions and it is important to take care because otherwise you may find that these contributions may outweigh the tax savings. The impact of the National Minimum Wage should also be considered.

(c) All expenditure on normal business items such as postage, stationery, telephone, email, fax and answering machines, agent's fees, accountancy charges, photography, subscriptions, periodicals, magazines, etc, may be claimed. The cost of daily papers should not be overlooked if these form part of research material. Visits to theatres, cinemas, etc, for research purposes may also be permissible (but not the cost relating to guests). Unfortunately, expenditure on all types of business entertaining is specifically denied tax relief.

(d) If work is conducted at home, a deduction for 'use of home' is usually allowed providing the amount claimed is reasonable. If the claim is based on an appropriate proportion of the total costs of rent, light and heat, cleaning and maintenance, insurance, etc (but not the Council Tax), care should be taken to ensure that no single room is used 'exclusively' for business purposes, because this may result in the Capital Gains Tax exemption on the house as the only or main residence being partially forfeited. However, it would be a strange household where one room was in fact used exclusively for business purposes and for no other purpose whatsoever (e.g. storing personal bank statements and other private papers); the usual formula is to claim a deduction on the basis that most or all of the rooms in the house are used at one time or another for business purposes, thereby avoiding any suggestion that any part was used exclusively for business purposes.

(e) The appropriate business proportion of motor running expenses may also be claimed although what is the appropriate proportion will naturally depend on the particular circumstances of each case; it should be appreciated that the well-known scale benefits, whereby one is taxed according to the size and cost of the car, do not apply to self-employed persons.

(f) It has been long established that the cost of travelling from home to work (whether employed or self-employed) is not an allowable expense. However, if home is one's place of work then no expenditure under this heading is likely to be incurred and difficulties are unlikely to arise.

(g) Travelling and hotel expenses incurred for business purposes will normally be allowed but if any part could be construed as disguised holiday or pleasure expenditure, considerable thought would need to be given to the commercial reasons for the journey in order to justify the claim. The principle of 'duality of purpose' will always be a difficult hurdle in this connection – although not insurmountable.

(h) If a separate business bank account is maintained, any overdraft interest thereon will be an allowable expense. This is the only circumstance in which overdraft interest is allowed for tax purposes and care should be taken to avoid overdrafts in all other circumstances.

(i) Where capital allowances (see below) are claimed for a personal computer, fax, modem, television, video, CD or tape player, etc, used for business purposes the costs of maintenance and repair of the equipment may also be claimed.

Clearly many other allowable items may be claimed in addition to those listed. Wherever there is any reasonable business motive for some expenditure it should be claimed as a deduction although it is necessary to preserve all records relating to the expense. It is sensible to avoid an excess of imagination as this would naturally cause the Inspector of Taxes to doubt the genuineness of other expenses claimed.

The question is often raised whether the whole amount of an expense may be deducted or whether the VAT content must be excluded. Where VAT is reclaimed from the Customs and Excise by someone who is registered for VAT, the VAT element of the expense cannot be treated as an allowable deduction. Where the VAT is not reclaimed, the whole expense (inclusive of VAT) is allowable for income tax purposes.

Capital allowances

Allowances

Where expenditure of a capital nature is incurred, it cannot be deducted from income as an expense – a separate and sometimes more valuable capital allowance being available instead. Capital allowances are given for many different types of expenditure, but authors and similar professional people are likely to claim only for 'plant and machinery'; this is a very wide expression which may include motor cars, personal computers, fax and photocopying machines, modems, televisions, CD, video and cassette players used for business purposes. Plant and machinery generally qualify for a 40% allowance in the year of purchase (which has been increased to 50% for the year 2004/05) and 25% of the reducing balance in subsequent years. Expenditure on information technology for the purposes of the business now benefits from a special 100% allowance in the year of purchase. Where the useful life of an asset is expected to be short, it is possible to claim special treatment as a 'short life asset' enabling the allowances to be accelerated.

The reason these allowances can be more valuable than allowable expenses is that they may be wholly or partly disclaimed in any year that full benefit cannot be obtained – ordinary business expenses cannot be similarly disclaimed. Where, for example, the income of an author does not exceed his personal allowances, he would not be liable to tax and a claim for capital allowances would be wasted. If the capital allowances were to be disclaimed their benefit would be carried forward for use in subsequent years. Careful planning with claims for capital allowances is therefore essential if maximum benefit is to be obtained.

As an alternative to capital allowances, claims can be made on the 'renewals' basis whereby all renewals are treated as allowable deductions in the year; no allowance is obtained for the initial purchase, but the cost of replacement (excluding any improvement element) is allowed in full. This basis is no longer widely used, as it is considerably less advantageous than claiming capital allowances as described above.

Leasing is a popular method of acquiring fixed assets, and where cash is not available to enable an outright purchase to be made, assets may be leased over a period of time. Whilst leasing may have financial benefits in certain circumstances, in normal cases there is likely to be no tax advantage in leasing an asset where the alternative of outright purchase is available. Indeed, leasing can be a positive disadvantage in the case of motor cars with a new retail price of more than £12,000. If such a car is leased, only a proportion of the leasing charges will be tax deductible.

Books

The question of whether the cost of books is eligible for tax relief has long been a source of difficulty. The annual cost of replacing books used for the purposes of one's professional activities (e.g. the cost of a new *Children's Writers' & Artists' Yearbook* each year) has always been an allowable expense; the difficulty arose because the initial cost of reference books, etc (e.g. when commencing one's profession) was treated as capital expenditure but no allowances were due as the books were not considered to be 'plant'. However, the matter was clarified by the case of *Munby* v. *Furlong* in which the Court of Appeal decided that the initial cost of law books purchased by a barrister was expenditure on 'plant' and eligible for capital allowances. This is clearly a most important decision, particularly relevant to any person who uses expensive books in the course of exercising his or her profession.

Pension contributions

Personal pensions

Where a self-employed person pays annual premiums under an approved personal pension policy, tax relief may now be obtained each year for the following amounts:

Age at 6/4/2003	Maximum %
35 and under	17.5% (max) £17,850
36 – 45	20% (max) £20,400
46 – 50	25% (max) £25,500
51 – 55	30% (max) £30,600
56 – 60	35% (max) £35,700
61 – 74	40% (max) £40,800

These figures do not apply to existing retirement annuity policies; these remain subject to the old limits which are unchanged.

These arrangements can be extremely advantageous in providing for a pension as premiums are usually paid when the income is high (and the tax relief is also high) and the pension (taxed as earned income when received) usually arises when the income is low and little tax is payable. There is also the opportunity to take part of the pension entitlement as a tax-free lump sum. It is necessary to take into account the possibility that the tax advantages could go into reverse. When the pension is paid it could, if rates rise again, be taxed at a higher rate than the rate of tax relief at the moment. One would be deferring income in order to pay more tax on it later. However, this involves a large element of guesswork, and many people will be content simply with the long-term pension benefits.

Since April 2001 it has been possible for up to £3600 to be paid into a Stakeholder pension without the need for any earnings.

Class 4 National Insurance contributions

Allied to pensions is the payment of Class 4 National Insurance contributions, although no pension or other benefit is obtained by the contributions; the Class 4 contributions are designed solely to extract additional amounts from self-employed persons and are payable in addition to the normal Class 2 (self-employed) contributions. The rates are changed each year and for 2004/05 self-employed persons will be obliged to contribute 8% of their profits between the range £4745–£31,720 per annum. This amount is collected in conjunction with the Schedule D income tax liability.

From 6 April 2003 there is a further 1% charge on earnings above £31,720 limit to correspond with the increase in employees' contributions.

Averaging relief

Relief for copyright payments

For many years special provisions enabled authors and similar persons engaged on a literary, dramatic, musical or artistic work for a period of more than 12 months, to spread certain amounts received over two or three years depending on the time spent in preparing the work.

On 6 April 2001 a simpler system of averaging was introduced. Under these rules, professional authors and artists engaged in the creation of literary, dramatic works or designs may claim to average the profits of two or more consecutive years if the profits for one year are less than 75% of the profits for the highest year. This new relief can apply even if the work took less than 12 months to create and is available to people who create works in partnership with others.

The purpose of the relief is to enable the creative artist to utilise his allowances fully and to avoid the higher rates of tax which might apply if all the income were to arise in a single year.

Collection of tax

Self-assessment

In 1997, the system of sending in a tax return showing all your income and the Inland Revenue raising an assessment to collect the tax was abolished. So was the idea that you pay tax on your profits for the preceding year. Now, when you send in your tax return you have to work out your own tax liability and send a cheque; this is called 'self-assessment'. If you get it wrong, or if you are late with your tax return or the payment of tax, interest and penalties will be charged.

Under this system, the Inland Revenue rarely issue assessments; they are no longer necessary because the idea is that you assess yourself. A colour-coded tax return was created, designed to help individuals meet their tax obligations. This is a daunting task but the term 'self-assessment' is not intended to imply that individuals have to do it themselves; they can (and often will) engage professional help. The term is only intended to convey that it is the taxpayer, and not the Inland Revenue, who is responsible for getting the tax liability right and for it to be paid on time.

The deadline for sending in the tax return is 31 January following the end of the tax year; so for the tax year 2004/05, the tax return has to be submitted to the Inland Revenue by 31 January 2006. If for some reason you are unwilling or unable to calculate the tax payable, you can ask the Inland Revenue to do it for you, in which case it is necessary to send in your tax return by 30 September 2005.

Income tax on self-employed earnings remains payable in two instalments on 31 January and 31 July each year. Because the accurate figures may not necessarily be known, these payments in January and July will therefore be only payments on account based on the previous year's liability. The final balancing figure will be paid the following 31 January together with the first instalment of the liability for the following year.

When the Inland Revenue receives the self-assessment tax return, it is checked to see if there is anything obviously wrong; if there is, a letter will be sent to you immediately. Otherwise, the Inland Revenue has 12 months from the filing date of 31 January in which to make further enquiries; if it doesn't, it will have no further opportunity to do so and your tax liabilities are final – unless there is something seriously wrong such as the omission of income or capital gains. In that event, the Inland Revenue will raise an assessment later to collect any extra tax together with appropriate penalties. It is essential for the operation of the new system that all records relevant to your tax returns are retained for at least 12 months in case they are needed by the Inland Revenue. For the self-employed, the record-keeping requirement is much more onerous because the records need to be kept for nearly six years. One important change in the rules is that if you claim a tax deduction for an expense, it will be necessary to have a receipt or other document proving that the expenditure has been made. Because the existence of the underlying records is so important to the operation of self-assessment, the Inland Revenue treats them very seriously and there is a penalty of £3000 for any failure to keep adequate records.

Interest

Interest is chargeable on overdue tax at a variable rate, which at the time of writing is 6.5% per annum. It does not rank for any tax relief, which can make the Inland Revenue an expensive source of credit.

However, the Inland Revenue can also be obliged to pay interest (known as repayment supplement) tax-free where repayments are delayed. The rules relating to repayment supplement are less beneficial and even more complicated than the rules for interest payable but they do exist and can be very welcome if a large repayment has been delayed for a long time. Unfortunately, the rate of repayment supplement is only 2.5%, much lower than the rate of interest on unpaid tax.

Value added tax

The activities of writers, painters, composers, etc are all 'taxable supplies' within the scope of VAT and chargeable at the standard rate. (Zero rating which applies to publishers, booksellers, etc on the supply of books does not extend to the work performed by writers.) Accordingly, authors are obliged to register for VAT if their income for the past 12 months exceeds £58,000 or if their income for the coming month will exceed that figure.

Delay in registering can be a most serious matter because if registration is not effected at the proper time, the Customs and Excise can (and invariably do) claim VAT from all the income received since the date on which registration should have been made. As no VAT would have been included in the amounts received during this period the amount claimed by thc Customs and Excise must inevitably come straight from the pocket of the author.

The author may be entitled to seek reimbursement of the VAT from those whom he or she ought to have charged VAT but this is obviously a matter of some difficulty and may indeed damage his commercial relationships. Apart from these disadvantages there is also a penalty for late registration. The rules are extremely harsh and are imposed automatically even in cases of innocent error. It is therefore extremely important to monitor the income very carefully because if in any period of 12 months the income exceeds the £58,000 limit, the Customs and Excise must be notified within 30 days of the end of the period. Failure to do so will give rise to an automatic penalty. It should be emphasised that this is a penalty for failing to submit a form and has nothing to do with any real or potential loss of tax. Furthermore, whether the failure was innocent or deliberate will not matter. Only the existence of a 'reasonable excuse' will be a defence to the penalty. However, a reasonable excuse does not include ignorance, error, a lack of funds or reliance on any third party.

However, it is possible to regard VAT registration as a privilege and not a penalty, because only VAT registered persons can reclaim VAT paid on their expenses such as stationery, telephone, professional fees, etc, and even typewriters and other plant and machinery (excluding cars). However, many find that the administrative inconvenience – the cost of maintaining the necessary records and completing the necessary forms – more than outweighs the benefits to be gained from registration and prefer to stay outside the scope of VAT for as long as possible.

Overseas matters

The general observation may be made that self-employed persons resident and domiciled in the United Kingdom are not well treated with regard to their overseas work, being taxable on their worldwide income. It is important to emphasise that if fees are earned abroad, no tax saving can be achieved merely by keeping the money outside the country. Although exchange control regulations no longer exist to require repatriation of foreign earnings, such income remains taxable in the UK and must be disclosed to the Inland Revenue; the same applies to interest or other income arising on any investment of these earnings overseas. Accordingly, whenever foreign earnings are likely to become substantial, prompt and effective action is required to limit the impact of UK and foreign taxation. In the case of non-resident authors it is important that arrangements concerning writing for publication in the UK, e.g. in newspapers, are undertaken with great care. A case concerning the wife of one of the great train robbers who provided detailed information for a series of articles in a Sunday newspaper is most instructive. Although she was acknowledged to be resident in Canada for all the relevant years, the income from the articles was treated as arising in this country and fully chargeable to UK tax.

The United Kingdom has double taxation agreements with many other countries and these agreements are designed to ensure that income arising in a foreign country is taxed either in that country or in the UK. Where a withholding tax is deducted from payments received from another country (or where tax is paid in full in the absence of a double taxation agreement), the amount of foreign tax paid can usually be set off against the related UK tax liability. Many successful authors can be found living in Eire because of the complete exemption from tax which attaches to works of cultural or artistic merit by persons who are resident there. However, such a step should only be contemplated having careful regard to all the other domestic and commercial considerations and specialist advice is essential if the exemption is to be obtained and kept; a careless breach of the conditions could cause the exemption to be withdrawn with catastrophic consequences.

Further information concerning the precise conditions to be satisfied for exemption for tax in Eire can be obtained from the Revenue Commissioners, Blocks 3–10, Dublin Castle, Dublin 2, or from their website (www.revenue.ie).

Companies

When an author becomes successful the prospect of paying tax at the higher rate may drive him or her to take hasty action such as the formation of companies, etc, which may not always be to his advantage. Indeed some authors seeing the exodus into tax exile of their more successful colleagues even form companies in low tax areas in the naive expectation of saving large amounts of tax. The Inland Revenue is fully aware of the opportunities and have extensive powers to charge tax and combat avoidance. Accordingly, such action is just as likely to increase tax liabilities and generate other costs and should never be contemplated without expert advice; some very expensive mistakes are often made in this area which are not always able to be remedied.

To conduct one's business through the medium of a company can be a most effective method of mitigating tax liabilities, and providing it is done at the right time and under the right circumstances very substantial advantages can be derived. However, if done without due care and attention the intended advantages will simply evaporate. At the very least it is essential to ensure that the company's business is genuine and conducted properly with regard to the realities of the situation. If the author continues his or her activities unchanged, simply paying all the receipts from his work into a company's bank account, he cannot expect to persuade the Inland Revenue that it is the company and not himself who is entitled to, and should be assessed to tax on, that income.

It must be strongly emphasised that many pitfalls exist which can easily eliminate all the tax benefits expected to arise by the formation of the company. For example, company directors are employees of the company and will be liable to pay much higher National Insurance contributions; the company must also pay the employer's proportion of the contribution and a total liability of over 23% of gross salary may arise. This compares most unfavourably with the position of a self-employed person. Moreover, on the commencement of the company's business the individual's profession will cease and the possibility of revisions being made by the Inland Revenue to earlier tax liabilities means that the timing of a change has to be considered very carefully.

The tax return

No mention has been made above of personal reliefs and allowances; this is because these allowances and the rates of tax are subject to constant change and are always set out in detail in the explanatory notes which accompany the Tax Return. The annual Tax Return is an important document and should be completed promptly with extreme care, particularly since the introduction of self-assessment. If filling in the Return is a source of difficulty or anxiety, comfort may be found in the Consumer Association's publication *Money Which? – Tax Saving Guide*; this is published in March of each year and includes much which is likely to be of interest and assistance.

Peter Vaines FCA, ATII, barrister, is a partner in the international law firm of Haarmann Hemmelrath and writes and speaks widely on tax matters. He is Managing Editor of *Personal Tax Planning Review*, on the Editorial Board of *Taxation*, and tax columnist of the *New Law Journal* and author of a number of books on taxation.

Social security contributions

In general, every individual who works in Great Britain either as an employee or as a self-employed person is liable to pay social security contributions. The law governing this subject is complicated and Peter Arrowsmith FCA gives here a summary of the position. This article should be regarded as a general guide only.

All contributions are payable in respect of years ending on 5 April. See box (below) for the classes of contributions.

Employed or self-employed?

The question as to whether a person is employed under a contract *of* service and is thereby an employee liable to Class 1 contributions, or performs services (either solely or in partnership) under a contract for service and is thereby self-employed liable to Class 2 and Class 4 contributions, often has to be decided in practice. One of the best guides can be found in the case of *Market Investigations Ltd* v. *Minister of Social Security* (1969 2 WLR 1) when Cooke J. remarked:

'... the fundamental test to be applied is this: "Is the person who has engaged himself to perform these services performing them as a person in business on his own account?" If the answer to that question is "yes", then the contract is a contract for services. If the answer is "no", then the contract is a contract of service. No exhaustive list has been compiled and perhaps no exhaustive list can be compiled of the considerations which are relevant in determining that question, nor can strict rules be laid down as to the relative weight which the various considerations should carry in particular cases. The most that can be said is that control will no doubt always have to be considered, although it can no longer be regarded as the sole determining factor; and that factors which may be of importance are such matters as:

- whether the man performing the services provides his own equipment,
- whether he hires his own helpers,
- what degree of financial risk he takes,
- what degree of responsibility for investment and management he has, and
- whether and how far he has an opportunity of profiting from sound management in the performance of his task.'

Classes of contributions

Class 1 These are payable by employees (primary contributions) and their employers (secondary contributions) and are based on earnings.

Class 1A Payable only by employers in respect of all taxable benefits in kind (cars and fuel only prior to 6 April 2000).

Class 1B Payable only by employers in respect of PAYE Settlement Agreements entered into by them.

Class 2 These are weekly flat rate contributions, payable by the self-employed.

Class 3 These are weekly flat rate contributions, payable on a voluntary basis in order to provide, or make up entitlement to, certain social security benefits.

Class 4 These are payable by the self-employed in respect of their trading or professional income and are based on earnings.

The above case has often been considered subsequently – notably in November 1993 by the Court of Appeal in the case of *Hall* v. *Lorimer*. In this case a vision mixer with around 20 clients and undertaking around 120–150 separate engagements per annum was held to be self-employed. This follows the, perhaps surprising, contention of the Inland Revenue that the taxpayer was an employee.

Further guidance

There have been three cases dealing with musicians, in relatively recent times, which provide further guidance on the question as to whether an individual is employed or self-employed.

- ***Midland Sinfonia Concert Society Ltd* v. *Secretary of State for Social Services*** (1981 ICR 454). A musician, employed to play in an orchestra by separate invitation at irregular intervals and remunerated solely in respect of each occasion upon which he plays, is employed under a contract for services. He is therefore self-employed, not an employed earner, for the purposes of the Social Security Contributions and Benefits Act 1992, and the orchestra which engages him is not liable to pay National Insurance contributions in respect of his earnings.
- ***Addison* v. *London Philharmonic Orchestra Ltd*** (1981 ICR 261). This was an appeal to determine whether certain individuals were employees for the purposes of section 11(1) of the Employment Protection (Consolidation) Act 1978.

  The Employment Appeal Tribunal upheld the decision of an industrial tribunal that an associate player and three additional or extra players of the London Philharmonic Orchestra were not employees under a contract of service, but were essentially freelance musicians carrying on their own business. The facts found by the industrial tribunal showed that, when playing for the orchestra, each appellant remained essentially a freelance musician, pursuing his or her own profession as an instrumentalist, with an individual reputation, and carrying on his or her own business, and they contributed their own skills and interpretative powers to the orchestra's performances as independent contractors.
- ***Winfield* v. *London Philharmonic Orchestra Ltd*** (1979 ICR 726). This case dealt with the question as to whether an individual was an employee within the meaning of section 30 of the Trade Union and Labour Relations Act 1974. The following remarks by the appeal tribunal are of interest in relation to the status of musicians:

  "... making music is an art, and the co-operation required for a performance of Berlioz's *Requiem* is dissimilar to that required between the manufacturer of concrete and the truck driver who takes the concrete where it is needed ... It took the view, as we think it was entitled on the material before it to do, that the company was simply machinery through which the members of the orchestra managed and controlled the orchestra's operation ... In deciding whether you are in the presence of a contract of service or not, you look at the whole of the picture. This picture looks to us, as it looked to the industrial tribunal, like a co-operative of distinguished musicians running themselves with self and mutual discipline, and in no sense like a boss and his musician employees."

Other modern cases have concerned a professional dancer and holiday camp entertainers (all of whom were regarded as employees). In two other cases income from part-time lecturing was held to be from an employment.

Accordingly, if a person is regarded as an employee under the above rules, he or she will be liable to pay contributions even if his employment is casual, part-time or temporary. Furthermore, if a person is an employee and also carries on a trade or profession either solely or in partnership, there will be a liability to more than one class of contributions (subject to certain limits – see below).

Exceptions

There are certain exceptions to the above rules, those most relevant to artists and writers being:

- The employment of a wife by her husband, or vice versa, is disregarded for social security purposes unless it is for the purposes of a trade or profession (e.g. the employment of his wife by an author would not be disregarded and would result in a liability for contributions if her salary reached the minimum levels).
- The employment of certain relatives in a private dwelling house in which both employee and employer reside is disregarded for social security purposes provided the employment is not for the purposes of a trade or business carried on at those premises by the employer. This would cover the employment of a relative (as defined) as a housekeeper in a private residence.
- In general, lecturers, teachers and instructors engaged by an educational establishment to teach on at least four days in three consecutive months are regarded as employees, although this rule does not apply to fees received by persons giving public lectures.

Freelance film workers

There is a list of grades in the film industry in respect of which PAYE need not be deducted and who are regarded as self-employed for tax purposes.

Further information can be obtained from the 2003 edition of the Inland Revenue guidance notes on the application of PAYE to casual and freelance staff in the film industry. In view of the Inland Revenue announcement that the same status will apply for PAYE and National Insurance contributions purposes, no liability for employee's and employer's contributions should arise in the case of any of the grades mentioned above.

However, in the film and television industry this general rule was not always followed in practice. In December 1992, after a long review, the DSS agreed that individuals working behind the camera and who have jobs on the Inland Revenue Schedule D list are self-employed for social security purposes.

There are special rules for, *inter alia*, personnel appearing before the camera, short engagements, payments to limited companies and payments to overseas personalities.

Artistes, performers/non-performers

The status of artistes and performers for tax purposes will depend on the individual circumstances but for social security new regulations which took effect on 17 July 1998 require most actors, musicians or similar performers to be treated as employees for social security purposes, whether or not this status applies under general and/or tax law. It also applies whether or not the individual is supplied through an agency.

Personal service companies

From 6 April 2000, those who have control of their own 'one-man service companies' are subject to special rules. If the work that the owner of the company does for the company's customers would – but for the one-man company – fall to be considered as an employment of that individual (i.e. rather than self-employment), a deemed salary may arise. If it does, then some or all of the income of the company will be treated as salary liable to PAYE and National Insurance contributions. This will be the case whether or not such salary is actually paid by the company. The same situation may arise where the worker owns as little as 5% of a company's share capital.

The calculations required by the Inland Revenue are complicated and have to be done very quickly at the end of each tax year (even if the company's year-end is different). It is essential that affected businesses seek detailed professional advice about these rules which may also, in certain circumstances, apply to partnerships.

Class 1 contributions

As mentioned above, these are related to earnings, the amount payable depending upon whether the employer has applied for his employees to be 'contracted-out' of the State earnings-related pension scheme; such application can be made where the employer's own pension scheme provides a requisite level of benefits for his or her employees and their dependants or, in the case of a money purchase scheme (COMPS) certain minimum safeguards are covered. Employers with employees contributing to 'stakeholder pension plans' continue to pay the full not contracted-out rate. Such employees have their contracting out arrangements handled separately by government authorities.

Contributions are payable by employees and employers on earnings that exceed the earnings threshold. Contributions are normally collected via the PAYE tax deduction machinery, and there are penalties for late submission of returns and for errors therein. From 19 April 1993, interest is charged automatically on unpaid PAYE and social security contributions.

Employees liable to pay

Contributions are payable by any employee who is aged 16 years and over (even though they may still be at school) and who is paid an amount equal to, or exceeding, the earnings threshold. Nationality is irrelevant for contribution purposes and, subject to special rules covering employees not normally resident in Great Britain, Northern Ireland or the Isle of Man, or resident in EEA countries or those with which there are reciprocal agreements, contributions must be paid whether the employee concerned is a British subject or not provided he is gainfully employed in Great Britain.

Employees exempt from liability to pay

Persons over pensionable age (65 for men; 60 – until 2010 – for women) are exempt from liability to pay primary contributions, even if they have not retired. However, the fact that an employee may be exempt from liability does not relieve an employer from liability to pay secondary contributions in respect of that employee.

Employees' (primary) contributions

From 6 April 2003, the rate of employees' contributions on earnings from the earnings threshold to the upper earnings limit is 11% (9.4% for contracted-out employments). Certain married women who made appropriate elections before 12 May 1977 may be entitled to pay a reduced rate of 4.85%. However, they will have no entitlement to benefits in respect of these contributions.

From April 2003, earnings above the upper earnings limit attract an employee contribution liability of 1% – previously, there was no such liability.

Employers' (secondary) contributions

All employers are liable to pay contributions on the gross earnings of employees. As mentioned above, an employer's liability is not reduced as a result of employees being exempted from contributions, or being liable to pay only the reduced rate (4.85%) of contributions.

For earnings paid on or after 6 April 2003 employers are liable at a rate of 12.8% on earnings paid above the earnings threshold (without any upper earnings limit), 9.3% where the employment is contracted out (salary related) or 11.8% (money purchase). In addition, special rebates apply in respect of earnings falling between the lower earnings limit and the earnings threshold. This provides, effectively, a negative rate of contribution in that small band of earnings. It should be noted that the contracted-out rates of 9.3% and 11.8% apply only up to the upper earnings limit. Thereafter, the not contracted-out rate of 12.8% is applicable.

The employer is responsible for the payment of both employees' and employer's contributions, but is entitled to deduct the employees' contributions from the earnings on which they are calculated. Effectively, therefore, the employee suffers a deduction in respect of his or her social security contributions in arriving at his weekly or monthly wage or salary. Special rules apply to company directors and persons employed through agencies.

Rates of Class 1 contributions and earnings limits from 6 April 2004

Earnings per week	*Rates payable on earnings in each band*			
	Not contracted-out		*Contracted-out*	
	Employee	*Employer*	*Employee*	*Employer*
£	%	%	%	%
Below 79.00	–	–	–	–
79.00 – 90.99	–	–	– (*)	– (*)
91.00 – 610.00	11	12.8	9.4	9.3 or 11.8
Over £610.00	1	12.8	1	12.8

* Special rebates deductible in respect of this band of earnings.

Items included in, or excluded from, earnings

Contributions are calculated on the basis of a person's gross earnings from their employment. This will normally be the figure shown on the deduction working sheet, except where the employee pays superannuation contributions and, from 6 April 1987, charitable gifts under payroll giving – these must be added back for the purposes of calculating Class 1 liability.

Earnings include salary, wages, overtime pay, commissions, bonuses, holiday pay, payments made while the employee is sick or absent from work, payments to cover travel between home and office, and payments under the statutory sick pay, statutory maternity pay, statutory paternity pay and statutory adoption pay schemes.

However, certain payments, some of which may be regarded as taxable income for income tax purposes, are ignored for Class 1 purposes. These include:

- certain gratuities paid other than by the employer,
- redundancy payments and some payments in lieu of notice,
- certain payments in kind,
- reimbursement of specific expenses incurred in the carrying out of the employment,
- benefits given on an individual basis for personal reasons (e.g. wedding and birthday presents),
- compensation for loss of office.

IR Booklet CWG 2 (2004 edition) gives a list of items to include in or exclude from earnings for Class 1 contribution purposes. Some such items may, however, be liable to Class 1A (employer only) contributions.

Miscellaneous rules

There are detailed rules covering a person with two or more employments; where a person receives a bonus or commission in addition to a regular wage or salary; and where a person is in receipt of holiday pay. From 6 April 1991 employers' social security contributions arise under Class 1A in respect of the private use of a company car, and of fuel provided for private use therein. From 6 April 2000, this charge was extended to cover most benefits in kind. The rate is now 12.8%. From 6 April 1999, Class 1B contributions are payable by employers using PAYE Settlement Agreements in respect of small and/or irregular expense payments and benefits, etc. This rate is also currently 12.8%.

Class 2 contributions

Class 2 contributions are payable at the weekly rate of £2.05 as from 6 April 2004. Exemptions from Class 2 liability are:

- A man over 65 or a woman over 60.
- A person who has not attained the age of 16.
- A married woman or, in certain cases, a widow who elected prior to 12 May 1977 not to pay Class 2 contributions.
- Persons with small earnings (see below).
- Persons not ordinarily self-employed (see below).

Small earnings

Application for a certificate of exception from Class 2 contributions may be made by any person who can show that his or her net self-employed earnings per his profit and loss account (as opposed to taxable profits):

- for the year of application are expected to be less than a specified limit (£4215 in the 2004/05 tax year); or
- for the year preceding the application were less than the limit specified for that year (£4095 for 2003/04) and there has been no material change of circumstances.

Certificates of exception must be renewed in accordance with the instructions stated thereon. At the Inland Revenue's discretion the certificate may commence up to 13 weeks before the date on which the application is made. Despite a certificate of exception being in force, a person who is self-employed is still entitled to pay Class 2 contributions if they wish, in order to maintain entitlement to social security benefits.

Persons not ordinarily self-employed

Part-time self-employed activities (including as a writer or artist) are disregarded for contribution purposes if the person concerned is not ordinarily employed in such activities and has a full-time job as an employee. There is no definition of 'ordinarily employed' for this purpose but a person who has a regular job and whose earnings from spare-time occupation are not expected to be more than £1300 per annum may fall within this category. Persons qualifying for this relief do not require certificates of exception but may be well advised to apply for one nonetheless.

Method of payment

From April 1993, Class 2 contributions may be paid by monthly direct debit in arrears or, alternatively, by cheque, bank giro, etc following receipt of a quarterly (in arrears) bill.

Overpaid contributions

If, following the payment of Class 2 contributions, it is found that the earnings are below the exception limit (e.g. the relevant accounts are prepared late), the Class 2 contributions that have been overpaid can be reclaimed, provided a claim is made between 6 April and 31 January immediately following the end of the tax year.

Class 3 contributions

Class 3 contributions are payable voluntarily, at the weekly rate of £7.15 per week from 6 April 2004, by persons aged 16 or over with a view to enabling them to qualify for a limited range of benefits if their contribution record is not otherwise sufficient. In general, Class 3 contributions can be paid by employees, the self-employed and the non employed.

Broadly speaking, no more than 52 Class 3 contributions are payable for any one tax year, and contributions cannot be paid in respect of tax years after the one in which the individual concerned reaches the age of 64 (59 for women).

Class 3 contributions may be paid in the same manner as Class 2 (see above) or by annual cheque in arrears.

Class 4 contributions

In addition to Class 2 contributions, self-employed persons are liable to pay Class 4 contributions. These are calculated at the rate of 8% on the amount of profits or gains chargeable to income tax under Schedule D Case I or II which exceed £4745 per annum but which do not exceed £31,720 per annum for 2004/05. Profits above the upper limit of £31,720 attract a Class 4 charge at the rate of 1%.

The income tax profit on which Class 4 contributions are calculated is after deducting capital allowances and losses, but before deducting personal tax allowances or retirement annuity or personal pension or stakeholder pension plan premiums.

Class 4 contributions produce no additional benefits, but were introduced to ensure that self-employed persons as a whole pay a fair share of the cost of pensions and other social security benefits yet without those who make only small profits having to pay excessively high flat rate contributions.

Payment of contributions

In general, contributions are now self-assessed and paid to the Inland Revenue together with the income tax under Schedule D Case I or II, and accordingly the contributions are due and payable at the same time as the income tax liability on the relevant profits. Under self-assessment, interim payments of Class 4 contributions are payable at the same time as interim payments of tax.

Class 4 exemptions

The following persons are exempt from Class 4 contributions:

- Men over 65 and women over 60 at the commencement of the year of assessment (i.e. on 6 April).
- An individual not resident in the United Kingdom for income tax purposes in the year of assessment.
- Persons whose earnings are not 'immediately derived' from carrying on a trade, profession or vocation (e.g. sleeping partners).
- A child under 16 on 6 April of the year of assessment.
- Persons not ordinarily self-employed.

Married persons and partnerships

Under independent taxation of husband and wife from 1990/91 onwards, each spouse is responsible for his or her Class 4 liability.

In partnerships, each partner's liability is calculated separately. If a partner also carries on another trade or profession, the profits of all such businesses are aggregated for the purposes of calculating their Class 4 liability.

When an assessment has become final and conclusive for the purposes of income tax, it is also final and conclusive for the purposes of calculating Class 4 liability.

Maximum contributions

There is a form of limit to the total liability for social security contributions payable by a person who is employed in more than one employment, or is also self-employed or a partner.

Where only not contracted-out Class 1 contributions, or not contracted-out Class 1 and Class 2 contributions, are payable, the maximum contribution payable at the main rates (11%, 9.4% or 4.85% as the case may be) is limited to 53 primary Class 1 contributions at the maximum weekly not contracted-out standard rate. For 2004/05 this 'maximum' will thus be £3025.77 (amounts paid at only 1% are to be excluded in making this comparison).

Further information

Further information can be obtained from the many booklets published by the Inland Revenue, available from local Inland Revenue Enquiry Centres.

National Insurance Contributions Office, Centre for Non-Residents
Newcastle upon Tyne NE98 1ZZ
tel (08459) 154811 (local call rates apply)
Address for enquiries for individuals resident abroad.

However, where contracted-out Class 1 contributions are payable, the maximum primary Class 1 contributions payable for 2004/05 where all employments are contracted out are £2575.48 (again excluding amounts paid at only 1%).

Where Class 4 contributions are payable in addition to Class 1 and/or Class 2 contributions, the Class 4 contributions payable at the full 8% rate are restricted so that they shall not exceed the excess of £2266.65 (i.e. 53 Class 2 contributions plus maximum Class 4 contributions) over the aggregate of the Class 1 and Class 2 contributions paid at the full (i.e. other than 1%) rates.

Transfer to Inland Revenue

The administrative functions of the former Contributions Agency transferred to the Inland Revenue from 1 April 1999. Responsibility for National Insurance contribution policy matters was also transferred from DSS Ministers to the Inland Revenue and Treasury Ministers on the same date. The DSS is now known as the Department for Work and Pensions (DWP).

Peter Arrowsmith FCA is a sole practitioner specialising in National Insurance matters. He is chairman of the Employer Issues Committee of the Institute of Chartered Accountants in England and Wales, and Consulting Editor to *Tolley's National Insurance Contributions 2004/05*.

Social security benefits

There are many leaflets produced by the Department for Work and Pensions. However, due to the nature of the subject social security benefits can be quite difficult to understand. In this article, K.D. Bartlett FCA has summarised some of the more usual benefits that are available under the Social Security Acts.

This article deliberately does not cover every aspect of the legislation but the references given should enable the relevant information to be easily traced. These references are to the leaflets issued by the Department for Work and Pensions.

It is usual for only one periodical benefit to be payable at any one time. If the contribution conditions are satisfied for more than one benefit it is the larger benefit that is payable. Benefit rates shown below were those payable from the week commencing 6 April 2004.

Self-employed persons (Class 2 and Class 4 contributors) are covered for all benefits except earnings-related supplements, unemployment benefit, widow's and invalidity pensions, widowed mother's allowance and industrial injury benefits. Most authors are self employed.

Family benefits

Child benefit (Leaflet CH 1) is payable for all children who are either under 16 or under 19 and receiving full-time education at a recognised educational establishment. The rate is £16.50 for the first or eldest child and £11.05 a week for each subsequent child. It is payable to the person who is responsible for the child but excludes foster parents or people exempt from UK tax. Furthermore, one-parent families receive £17.55 per week for the eldest child.

Those with little money may apply for a maternity loan or grant from the social fund. Those claiming Working Families Tax Credit or Disabled Persons Tax Credit can apply for a Sure Start Maternity Grant of £500 for each baby expected, born, adopted or subject to a parental order. Any savings over £500 are taken into account. This grant will only be paid on the provision of a relevant certificate from a doctor, midwife or health visitor.

A guardian's allowance (Leaflet NI 14) is paid at the rate of £9.70 a week. For each subsequent child the rate of benefit is £11.85 a week to people who have taken orphans into their own family. Usually both of the child's parents must be dead and at least one of them must have satisfied a residence condition.

The allowance can only be paid to the person who is entitled to child benefit for the child (or to that person's spouse). It is not necessary to be the legal guardian. The claim should be made within three months of the date of entitlement.

Disability living allowance

Disability living allowance has replaced attendance allowance for disabled people before they reach the age of 65. It has also replaced mobility allowance.

Those who are disabled after reaching 65 may be able to claim attendance allowance. The attendance allowance board decide whether, and for how long, a person is eligible for this allowance. Attendance allowance is not taxable. The care component is divided into three rates whereas the mobility allowance has two rates. The weekly rate of benefit from 6 April 2004 is as follows:

Care component	
Higher rate (day and night, or terminally ill)	£58.80
Middle rate (day or night)	£39.35
Lower rate (if need some help during day, or over 16 and need help preparing a meal)	£15.55

Mobility component	
Higher rate (unable or virtually unable to walk)	£41.05
Lower rate (can walk but needs help when outside)	£15.55

Benefits for the ill

Incapacity benefit (Leaflet DS 700) replaced sickness benefit and invalidity benefit. The contribution conditions haven't changed but a new medical test has been brought in which includes a comprehensive questionnaire. The rates from 8 April 2004 are:

Long-term incapacity benefit	£74.15
Short-term incapacity benefit	£55.90
Increase of long-term incapacity benefit for age:	
Higher rate	£15.15
Lower rate	£7.80

Carers allowance, formerly invalid care allowance, is a taxable benefit paid to people of working age who cannot take a job because they have to stay at home to look after a severely disabled person. The basic allowance is £44.35 per week, plus an extra £9.70 for the first dependent child and £11.35 for each subsequent child.

Pensions and Widowed Parent's Allowance

The state pension (Leaflets NP 23, NP 35, NP 31) is divided into two parts – the basic pension, presently £79.60 per week for a single person or £127.25 per week for a married couple. Women paying standard rate contributions into the scheme are eligible for the same amount of pension as men but five years earlier, from age 60. The Pensions Act 1995 incorporated the provision for an equal state pension age of 65 for men and women to be phased in over a 10-year period beginning 6 April 2010. If a woman stays at home to bring up her children or to look after a person receiving attendance allowance she can have her basic pension rights protected without paying contributions.

Pension Credit is a new entitlement for people aged 60 or over. It guarantees everyone aged 60 and over an income of at least:

- £105.45 a week if you are single; or
- £160.95 a week if you have a partner.

For the first time, people aged 65 and over will be rewarded for some of their savings and income they have for their retirement. In the past, those who had saved a little money were no better off than those who had not saved at all. Pension Credit will change this by giving new money to those who have saved – up to £15.51 if you are single, or £20.22 if you have a partner.

The person who applies for Pension Credit must be at least 60 but their partner can be under 60. Partner means a spouse or a person with whom one lives as if you were married to them.

Widowed Parent's Allowance

This is a new system of bereavement benefits for men and women introduced in April 2001. Women who were receiving benefits under the previous scheme are unaffected as long as they still qualify under the rules. The Allowance is:

- based on the late husband's or wife's contributions;
- for widows or widowers bringing up children;
- a regular payment.

The main conditions for receiving this benefit are:

- You must be aged over 45 and must have a dependent child or children.
- If you were over the state pension age when you were widowed you may receive Retirement Pension based on the husband's or wife's NI contributions.
- If the spouse died as a result of their job, it is possible to receive bereavement benefits even if they did not pay sufficient NI contributions.
- You cannot receive bereavement benefits if you remarry or if you live with a partner as if you are married to them.
- Bereavement benefits are not affected if you work.

The allowance is £79.60 for those over 55 and varies between £23.88 and £74.03 for those aged between 45 and 54.

There are increases for dependent children. You receive £9.65 for the oldest child who qualifies for child benefit and £11.35 for each child who qualifies.

Bereavement payment and benefits

From 9 April 2001 bereavement benefits are payable to both widows and widowers but the benefits are only paid to those without children. Benefits are based on the NI contributions of the deceased. No benefit is payable if the couple were divorced at the date of death or if either of the survivors remarries or cohabits.

Widows and widowers bereaved on or after 9 April 2001 are entitled to a tax-free bereavement payment of £2000.

The death grant to cover funeral expenses was abolished from 6 April 1987. It has been replaced by a funeral payment from the social fund where the claimant is in receipt of income support, income-based Jobseekers' Allowance, Disabled Persons' Tax Credit, Working Families' Tax Credit or housing benefit. The full cost of a reasonable funeral is paid, reduced by any savings of over £600 held by the claimant.

Child Tax Credits and Working Tax Credit

Child Tax Credits were introduced on 6 April 2003. To obtain them a claim form has to be submitted (Tax Credit Form TC600 is available by either telephoning 0845 300 3900 or applying online – see below). In April 2004 a renewal form was sent out to all claimants. The current deadline for returning that form to the Inland Revenue is 5 July 2004. Missing the deadline may result in a fine of up to £300. For the self employed this may mean estimating the income for the tax year 2003/04 if accounts are not available.

Child Tax Credit has replaced the Children's Tax Credit previously claimed through tax paid. It is paid directly to the person who is mainly responsible for caring for the child or children. A family unit earning up to £58,000 will be entitled to the Tax Credit (£66,000 if the family has a child under one year old). To ascertain which tax credits you could be entitled to, visit the Tax Credits website (www.taxcredits.inlandrevenue.gov.uk).

Child Tax Credits are especially complicated for those on variable income and the self employed. The tax credit for the tax year 2004/05 is initially based on the income earned in the tax year 2002/03. If the income is now lower in 2004/05 than in 2002/03 then potentially you should be receiving more tax credit or even be eligible for it when before you were earning too much. In this situation you should make a protective claim by completing and sending off a Tax Credit Form TC600.

Working Tax Credit

Working Tax Credit is paid to support people in work and is administered by the Inland Revenue. It is not necessary to have paid National Insurance contributions to qualify. Those over 16 who are responsible for a child or young person and work at least 16 hours a week qualify. People without children can claim if:

- they are over 25 and work at least 30 hours a week;
- they are aged 16 or over and work at least 16 hours a week and have a disability that puts them at a disadvantage in obtaining a job;
- a person or their partner are aged 50 or more and work at least 16 hours a week and are returning to work after time spent on obtaining a qualification.

Working Tax Credit is paid as well as any Child Tax Credit you are entitled to. The calculations on how much you receive are complicated but it will depend on how many hours you work and your income or joint income.

If you are employed then you will receive the payment via your employer and if self employed you will be paid direct. If you think you are eligible to receive Working Tax Credit, either telephone 0800-500 222 or visit the tax credits website (www.inlandrevenue.gov.uk/taxcredits).

Disabled Persons Tax Credit

There is a tax credit to assist people with an illness or disability who are in work. It replaced Disability Working Allowance. It is for people who have an illness or a disability which puts them at a disadvantage in getting a job and who:

- work at least 16 hours per week;
- are resident in the UK and are entitled to work here;
- have one of a number of qualifying benefits for disability or were receiving one of them up to 182 days prior to the application;
- have savings of £16,000 or less.

K.D. Bartlett FCA qualified as a Chartered Accountant in 1969 and became a partner in a predecessor firm of Horwath Clark Whitehill in 1972.

Index